PENGUIN BOOKS

DESPERADOS

Elaine Shannon was born in Gainesville, Georgia, and is a graduate of Vanderbilt University. In 1974, she won a Neiman Fellowship in Journalism after covering Watergate for the Nashville *Tennessean*; in 1984, she received the Clarion Award from Women in Communications for a *Newsweek* cover story on the CIA, "America's Secret Warriors"; and in 1985, the New York State Bar Association Award, also for a *Newsweek* cover story, "Rape and the Law." She has reported on the international drug trade for ten years, and has done numerous cover stories on narcotics, espionage, public corruption, and other aspects of the criminal justice system. She is now a correspondent in *Time*'s Washington Bureau and lives with her husband in Washington.

For John Lindsay

O, pardon me, thou bleeding piece of earth,
That I am meek and gentle with these butchers.
      —*Julius Caesar,* act 3, scene 1

Desperados

LATIN DRUG LORDS,
U.S. LAWMEN,
AND THE WAR
AMERICA CAN'T WIN

Elaine Shannon

PENGUIN BOOKS

PENGUIN BOOKS
Published by the Penguin Group
Viking Penguin, a division of Penguin Books USA Inc.,
40 West 23rd Street, New York, New York 10010, U.S.A.
Penguin Books Ltd, 27 Wrights Lane, London W8 5TZ, England
Penguin Books Australia Ltd, Ringwood, Victoria, Australia
Penguin Books Canada Ltd, 2801 John Street,
Markham, Ontario, Canada L3R 1B4
Penguin Books (N.Z.) Ltd, 182–190 Wairau Road,
Auckland 10, New Zealand

Penguin Books Ltd, Registered Offices:
Harmondsworth, Middlesex, England

First published in the United States of America by
Viking Penguin, a division of Penguin Books USA Inc., 1988
This edition with a new epilogue published in Penguin Books, 1989

1 3 5 7 9 10 8 6 4 2

Black and white photo credits: Page 1, top: Jaime Kuykendall; bottom: Reuters/
Bettmann Newsphotos. Page 2, top: DEA; bottom: DEA. Page 3, top: AP/Wide
World Photos; center: Reuters/Bettmann Newsphotos; bottom: AP/Wide World
Photos. Page 4, top left: Reuters/Bettmann Newsphotos; top right: DEA; bottom:
AP/Wide World Photos. Page 5, top left: AP/Wide World Photos; top right:
Reuters/Bettmann Newsphotos; bottom: AP/Wide World Photos. Page 6, top
left: AP/Wide World Photos; top right: AP/Wide World Photos; center left:
Proceso; center right: AP/Wide World Photos; bottom: John Ficara/Woodfin
Camp & Associates, 1985. Page 7, top left: AP/Wide World Photos; top right:
AP/Wide World Photos; center left: AP/Wide World Photos; center right: Reu-
ters/Bettmann Newsphotos; bottom: John Ficara/Woodfin Camp & Associates,
1985. Page 8, DEA.

Color photos courtesy of NBC Photos

LIBRARY OF CONGRESS CATALOGING-IN-PUBLICATION DATA
Shannon, Elaine.
Desperados : Drug Wars: The Camarena Story / Elaine Shannon.
p. cm.
Bibliography: p.
Includes index.
1. Narcotics, Control of—United States—Case studies.
2. Narcotic enforcement agents—United States—Case studies.
3. Narcotics and crime—Case studies. 4. Narcotics, Control of—
Mexico—Case studies. I. Title.
HV5825.S449 1989
363.4'5'0973—dc19 88-31423

Printed in the United States of America · Set in Times Roman

Foreword

In his classic of reportage, *Let Us Now Praise Famous Men*, about a tenant farmer, James Agee wrote, "I know him only so far as I know him; and all of that depends as fully on who I am as on who he is."

In 1968, I was twenty-one, a senior in college and a reporter for *The Tennessean* in Nashville. That was the year marijuana came to town. Pot smoking was not taken lightly at first, because the police had a simple, harsh response. Anybody caught with a joint was busted, strip-searched, and likely to be sentenced to months, even years in jail. Within two years, the criminal-justice system had clogged and broken down. Even in the conservative South, the smell of marijuana wafted through the stadiums during rock concerts.

I arrived in Washington in 1970, about the time Richard Nixon was declaring "war on drugs." The Watergate scandal shoved the drug issue to the back pages, and by the time the dust cleared, Nixonian law-and-order rhetoric was out of favor, marijuana was as common as beer, and cocaine was a staple on the Georgetown party circuit. I saw friends die, or, if they were lucky, just burn out.

Hollywood has stopped playing drug use for laughs, but it probably doesn't matter. A dose of crack-cocaine costs the same as a tank of gasoline, and cocaine peddling is as egalitarian a pastime as cruising. Across the United States, clinics and emergency rooms are packed with overdoses and addicts. Twelve-year-olds are working as runners for eighteen-year-old dealers, who roam the streets with Uzi carbines. Toddlers are dying in the cross fire of gang wars. Police vans are stationed in front of housing projects twenty-four hours a day, and guards are stationed by the vans to keep them from being torched. Colombia is being torn apart by drug-related violence. Panamanians are in revolt against corruption. The power of the drug traffickers has become a national security threat to much of the Western Hemisphere, and now cocaine and marijuana traffickers are extending their networks into Canada, Europe, the Middle East, Australia, and Japan.

Is there a solution? Can a law that is violated regularly by twenty-three million Americans be enforced? The Soviet Union is a police state and cannot contain its growing heroin-abuse problem, imported by Soviet soldiers stationed in Afghanistan. But if the solution is tougher law enforcement, what does that really mean? Execution of drug dealers? Wholesale arrests of drug users? Who will make the arrests? Most big-city police departments have their hands full rounding up dealers. If users could be arrested, where would they be kept? The jails are overloaded with violent felons. And what if the answer is more involvement of the military? How can any military force secure the eighty-eight-thousand-mile perimeter of the United States? If the U.S. military and the American intelligence agencies could not interdict the Ho Chi Minh trail, the supply line to the Vietcong during the Vietnam war, why does anyone think a military solution can be devised to smash trafficking rings that operate in the jungles and mountains of several dozen nations?

Or is the libertarian solution the correct approach? Should we legalize mind-altering substances? Should anyone be able to buy any kind of drug, anytime? Or should the government regulate potency, price, and availability? Should sales to minors be banned? How would the new regulatory system work? If some people were denied access to drugs, and if more powerful substances such as crack, PCP, and heroin remained prohibited, wouldn't the black-market system be perpetuated? Is the answer a government monopoly—a giant government marketing board, like Canada's grain board, that would buy up the entire coca crops of Peru and Bolivia? What would happen when new coca plantations appeared in Brazil, Ecuador, Venezuela, Mexico, Thailand, or Burma?

All these questions deserve a great deal of thought. Undoubtedly, solutions to the drug crisis will be debated in countless books, articles, and symposia in the coming years.

This book does not offer solutions. It is not about what might be, but, rather, what is. It is about the realities of the American government's approach to the dilemmas of drug enforcement, particularly overseas. I hope that when some of the dark corners of the drug underworld are illuminated, citizens will be able to make better-informed judgments about the actions of their leaders. The best ally of the drug traffickers has not been corruption; it has been ignorance. Ignorance cannot be alleviated as long as excessive secrecy is used to mask stupidity, duplicity, venality, and arrogance in the United States government and in those nations it claims as allies.

The story of the international drug trade can be told from many different points of view: from that of the drug user, the dealer, the city cop, the village priest, the Mexican police *comandante,* the Colombian mayor, the Bolivian political reformer, the pilot, the doctor, the teacher, and the social worker. This book is about the politics of drugs, and particularly the tensions and contradictions among the United States' domestic political priorities, its economic and national-security interests, its geopolitical agenda, and its law-enforcement responsibilities. I have focused on how these tensions affect officials in Washington responsible for shaping national policy and agents in the field charged with enforcing the law.

In one sense, this book looks at the drug problem from the vantage point of the DEA. But, as Agee would have pointed out, the perspective, or bias, is mine. Writing is a process of selecting certain facts and incidents that seem to the writer to mean more than others. I have chosen to write about episodes that seem to me to make sense of the tumultuous events of the past two decades. This is not the book that would have been written by DEA administrators Bud Mullen and Jack Lawn or by U.S. Customs Commis-

sioner William von Raab, though they were generous with
their time and unfailingly honest in expressing their observations and opinions, even when honesty required great
courage and political selflessness. Nor do I expect universal
agreement from the many field agents and line prosecutors
who have been kind enough to share their insights with me.

The story that dominates this book is the February 1985
disappearance and murder in Mexico of DEA agent Enrique
Camarena. No event in modern times has been so traumatic
for those involved in drug law enforcement or so revealing
of the strengths and weaknesses of the American drug
policy.

At this writing, no one knows the truth about Kiki Camarena's death. The most reliable information is in the
hands of the DEA and the federal prosecutors who have
spent three years trying to solve the case. I have tried to
give readers information about the facts and theories developed during the course of that investigation so that they
can draw their own conclusions about the evidence.

While researching this book, I interviewed literally
hundreds of political leaders, lawyers, federal agents, policemen, diplomats, and citizens in the United States and in
Mexico and other drug-producing nations. I reviewed large
numbers of documents, both public-record material and internal government cables and memoranda. I read documents filed in Mexican courts, Mexican government press
releases, transcripts of Mexican government press conferences, and articles about the case in the Mexican as well as
the American press.

Throughout the book, I have identified sources as fully
as possible and have tried to avoid the use of unnamed
sources. When certain individuals important to the story
have requested anonymity, I have agreed to withhold their
names. These instances were relatively few. In two cases, I
used pseudonyms because of a sincere belief that the source
would be in physical danger.

One of my aims is to help the reader understand why
American government officials acted as they did. To that
end, I have shared with the reader some information de-

veloped through the use of informants paid by the U.S. government. As in any drug case, informants are often criminals themselves. Some are more reliable than others. At times, informants have made explosive charges of corruption against very high officials in Mexico, the United States, and other nations. In general, I have avoided printing "raw" allegations uncorroborated by other informants or sources. I have made exceptions when U.S. government officials attached enough credibility to the charges to act upon them—for instance, by handing over evidence about an officeholder to the president or attorney general of a foreign nation. In those cases, I thought it was important for the reader to know the information handed over, however controversial, so that he or she could better understand why U.S. government officials chose certain courses of action.

Wherever possible, I tried to corroborate the allegations. In some cases, I interviewed people who made the charges originally and satisfied myself as to whether they could have had direct knowledge of the events in question. In other cases I made an effort to determine how government agents had assessed the credibility of the source. It is the job of U.S. law-enforcement agents to hire numerous informants and evaluate their reliability. Most of the tests are based on common sense: Is there a pattern of accuracy? Is the person emotionally stable? Was he or she in a position to have firsthand knowledge? Does he or she have a motive to lie? I found that in all of the instances reported here in which U.S. government officials acted on informant information, the allegations were backed up by some degree of corroboration, either physical evidence or similar allegations from individuals with independent knowledge.

Many of the government employees who have helped me complete this book have done so at considerable risk to their careers. Their assistance was not motivated by long-standing friendship, ambition, or even shared political and social values. Most were strangers to me when I began my research. I believe these people helped me out of a simple conviction that citizens ought to know the truth about the way their government conducts their business. I might disagree with many of these people on certain issues, but I admire their honesty, compassion, and grace under pressures that are unimaginable for an outsider.

I give special thanks to William Alden, Robert Feldkamp, Cornelius Dougherty, Larry Gallina, and William Deac of the Drug Enforcement Administration and Dennis Murphy, David Hoover, and Ed Kittredge of the U.S. Customs Service.

I received valuable insights, advice, and support from *Time* Washington bureau chief Strobe Talbott; Joseph Harmes; Mary Thornton of *The Washington Post;* Anthony Marro of *Newsday;* Kim Willenson; Ron Ostrow of the *Los Angeles Times;* Jon Standefer and Stryker Meyer of *The San Diego Union;* Terrence Poppa of the *El Paso Herald-Post;* Ann Constable and Ricardo Chavira of *Time;* Joe Contreras, John Barry, Tom DeFrank, and Ann McDaniel of *Newsweek;* John Walcott of *The Wall Street Journal;* Mel Elfin, Mike Ruby, Julia Reed, and Gloria Borger of *U.S. News & World Report;* Peter Kerr of *The New York Times;* Penny Lernoux, Ann Crittenden, Diana Hadley, Drum Hadley, and Juan and Frances Huttanus. Vicki Warren was persistent and adept at researching obscure articles and texts. Dan Morgan, my husband, improved some very rough drafts. Nan Graham, my editor at Viking, was an invaluable help in organizing and clarifying piles of material. Charlotte Sheedy, my agent, was encouraging on dark days. My parents, Kathryne and Edward Shannon, taught me about social justice. John Lindsay, to whom this book is dedicated, is the finest reporter I have ever known.

Contents

Cast of Characters

DEA OVERSEAS POSTS

Johnny Phelps, DEA attaché, Colombia, 1982–85
George Frangullie, DEA attaché, Colombia, 1985–87

Ed Heath, DEA attaché, Mexico, 1983–89

DEA GUADALAJARA

James Kuykendall, resident agent in charge, 1982–85
Tony Ayala, resident agent in charge, 1985–88

Some DEA agents assigned to Guadalajara:
Pete Hernandez
Kiki Camarena (kidnapped February 7, 1985, murdered)
Butch Sears
Roger Knapp
Victor Wallace
Victor Cortez (tortured August 13, 1987, survived)

MEXICO

Gustavo Díaz Ordaz, President, 1964–70
Luis Echeverría Alvarez, President, 1970–76
José López Portillo y Pacheco, President, 1976–80

Miguel de la Madrid Hurtado, President, December 1, 1982–88
Bernardo Sepúlveda Amor, Minister of Foreign Affairs, January 1983–88
Manuel Bartlett Díaz, Minister of the Interior, January 1983–88
General Juan Arévalo Gardoqui, Minister of Defense, January 1983–88
Sergio García Ramírez, Attorney General, January 1983–88

Manuel Ibarra Herrera, director, Mexican Federal Judicial Police (MFJP), 1982–85
Florentino Ventura Gutiérrez, acting director, MFJP, Interpol director, 1985–(suspicious death, September 1988)
Miguel Aldana Ibarra, *primer comandante*, MFJP, Interpol director, 1982–85

José Antonio Zorrilla Pérez, director, Federal Security Directorate (DFS), 1982–85
Armando Pavón Reyes, *primer comandante*, MFJP, in charge of Camarena search (convicted of intending to accept a bribe to let Rafael Caro Quintero leave Guadalajara)

GUADALAJARA DRUG CARTEL

Rafael Caro Quintero, Rafa, El Grenas (marijuana) (arrested)
Ernesto Fonseca Carrillo, Don Neto (marijuana, cocaine) (arrested)
Miguel Angel Félix Gallardo, El Padrino (cocaine) (fugitive)
Juan Ramón Matta Ballesteros (cocaine) (arrested)
Emilio Quintero Payán (marijuana, cocaine) (fugitive)
Juan José Quintero Payán (marijuana, cocaine) (arrested)
Manuel Salcido Uzeta, Cochi Loco (marijuana, cocaine) (fugitive)
José Contreras Subias (marijuana, cocaine) (arrested)

COLOMBIA

Alfonso López Michelsen, President, 1974–78
Julio César Turbay Ayala, President, 1978–82

Belisario Betancur Cuartas, President, 1982–86
Rodrigo Lara Bonilla, Minister of Justice, 1982–84 (assassinated April 30, 1984)
Enrique Parejo González, Minister of Justice, 1984–86 (assassination attempted January 13, 1986, survived)
Virgilio Barco Vargas, President, 1986–
José Manuel Arias Carrizosa, Minister of Justice, 1986–87
Enrique Low Murtra, Minister of Justice, 1987–88
Carlos Mauro Hoyos Jiménez, Attorney General, 1986–88 (assassinated January 25, 1988)
Alfredo Gutiérrez Márquez, Attorney General, January 1988–March 28, 1988

MEDELLÍN DRUG CARTEL

Carlos Lehder Rivas (arrested)
Pablo Escobar Gaviria (fugitive)

Jorge Luis Ochoa Vásquez (fugitive)
Juan David Ochoa Vásquez (fugitive)
Fabio Ochoa Vásquez (fugitive)
Gilberto Rodríquez Orejuela (fugitive)
Gonzalo Rodríquez Gacha (fugitive)

BOLIVIA

General Hugo Banzer Suárez, military ruler, 1971–78 (arrested 1988)
General Luis García Meza, military ruler, 1980–81
General Celso Torrelio Villa, military ruler, 1981–82
General Guido Vildoso Calderón, military ruler, 1982
Dr. Hernán Siles Zuazo, President, 1982–86
Víctor Paz Estenssoro, President, 1986–89

BOLIVIAN MAFIA

Roberto Suárez Gómez (arrested July 1988)

PERU

Fernando Belaúnde Terry, President, 1980–86
Alan García, President, 1986–

PANAMA

Brigadier General Omar Torrijos Herrera, commander in chief, Panamanian National Guard, later Panamanian Defense Forces, 1968–81
General Reubén Darío Paredes, commander in chief, Panamanian Defense Forces, 1981–83
General Manuel Antonio Noriega Morena, commander in chief, Panamanian Defense Forces, 1983–

1
"The *Comandante* Wants to See You"

At two o'clock on the afternoon of Thursday, February 7, 1985, Enrique Camarena of the U.S. Drug Enforcement Administration stashed his badge and his service revolver in his desk drawer and headed for a luncheon date with his wife. As he stepped through the consulate portal into the sunlight, shopkeepers were drawing their blinds and workmen were laying aside their tools for the afternoon siesta. A soft breeze ruffled the skirts of the women passing by. Guadalajara, a slightly grimy pink fleshpot of a city, was carefree and enticing on these warm winter days.

Part of Kiki yearned to stay on. For all the disappointments and the double crosses, there had been good times here. There had been nights fragrant with the smell of lemon trees, when he would sit on the patios of the men who were his eyes and ears in the places he could not go. There would be a bottle of home-brewed mescal and a guitar, and the songs and stories would spill forth. Kiki would nurse his drink and listen. He paid his informants, but loyalty bought with dollars was an ephemeral thing. Kiki had learned that it was wise to make friends of these men, and to win over their sons and their fathers, their mothers and their wives. Friendships were forged in the rituals of family, at weddings, baptisms, funerals, and, after the women withdrew, in the hot glow of mescal, made for centuries from the agave plant, which grew in this region.

The men who lived on the dusty back roads were awed and a bit amused by the American agent with the blood of a Mexican, the deep eyes of an Indian, and the heart of a gringo. Born in Mexicali, raised in California, a high-school football star and an ex-Marine, Kiki was a curious blend of

Latin machismo and Yankee work ethic. When required, he could affect a gregarious, generous air, but that was part of the job. By nature he was serious and rather introverted. Occasionally he stopped working long enough to drink a few beers and shoot a game of pool; but what he really loved was busting dopers. His friends in Guadalajara called him El Gallo Prieto, "the Dark Rooster." It meant a man's man, a fighter, a man who was sure of himself, a man who always won. Nobody else in the Guadalajara DEA office could match Kiki's charisma with informants. He had a way of convincing a man to screw up his courage and venture where he never dreamed he would go. Taut, quick, and powerfully built, at thirty-seven Kiki Camarena looked indestructible.

Now these times were coming to an end. Kiki had asked to be transferred to San Diego. He was leaving in three weeks. This time he had not won. In California he used to hound an outlaw until the man broke. But in Mexico the crooks laughed at him, brushed him off as if he were a scorpion stinging a thick leather boot.

When Kiki Camarena arrived in Guadalajara in 1980, Colombia, not Mexico, was making world headlines with spectacular drug seizures and sensational shoot-outs between the so-called cocaine cowboys. The Mexican border was a forgotten front.

Camarena quickly discovered that his agency's complacency toward Mexico was a serious miscalculation. He found himself pitted against an underworld cartel that was running Guadalajara like an occupation force. A new generation of Mexican drug traffickers had emerged to rival the Colombian drug barons in power, wealth, and brutality. They were as hard and reckless a breed as any in their country's history. Nearly all came from the state of Sinaloa, in the Sierra Madre Occidental, from the highlands where nothing worth anything grew except opium poppies and marijuana. The Sinaloan traffickers had survived clan wars, police sweeps, even a military assault. Every attempt by the government in Mexico City to subdue them had left them fiercer. The only authority the highlanders recognized was what they called La Ley de la Sierra—the law of the mountains, which was the law of the gun.

The Sinaloans had come down from the hills in the late 1970s glutted with the bounty of the smuggler's trade. They traveled around Guadalajara with platoons of guards armed with automatic weapons, and with suitcases full of cash they bought whatever caught their fancy. Slow to bend to civilized ways, they lived like clannish hill people, marrying cousins, entertaining one another with raucous and violent parties, settling scores with impulsive savagery.

The leaders of the Guadalajara cartel were a twenty-nine-year-old named Rafael Caro Quintero, an old *bandido* by the name of Ernesto Fonseca Carrillo, and the saturnine Miguel Angel Félix Gallardo. None of them had better than a second-grade education, yet each had managed to amass hundreds of millions of dollars, much of which was stashed in American banks or invested in Sunbelt real estate.

At the age of thirty-five, Miguel Angel Félix Gallardo dominated wholesale cocaine sales in the lucrative Southern California market. He had perceived the potential of cocaine earlier than his peers and was perfectly positioned to take advantage of his own foresight. Pilots who flew "the trampoline," the overland route from Colombia to Southern California, had to refuel in northern Mexico. Colombian smugglers were hassled or extorted, but not the men who worked for Félix Gallardo. Thanks to his days as a smuggler of heroin refined from Sierra Madre poppies in the little laboratories in Sinaloa, Félix Gallardo had excellent contacts among the police in Baja California and Sonora. He had built a heroin-distribution network in the Southwestern United States that was easily converted to moving cocaine as the market for that commodity grew in the 1970s. By the time Camarena arrived in Guadalajara, Félix Gallardo controlled a multinational business empire that stretched from the Andes to the American Sunbelt. He controlled a bank or two, commanded his own air force and radio network, was building his own cocaine refineries, and was extending his distribution network into Europe.

Rafael Caro Quintero was a natural entrepreneur who

specialized in a different commodity: he transformed Mexican marijuana from common weed to the smoke of connoisseurs. Growers in California and Oregon had pioneered a technique that yielded extraordinarily potent marijuana, called sinsemilla, "without seeds." It was grown by weeding out male plants to keep female plants from flowering, so that resin concentrated in the leaves. Sinsemilla pioneers in the United States worked tiny plots and sold exquisitely manicured clippings for $2,500 a pound, eight times the price of Mexican commercial-grade pot.

Caro Quintero realized that cheap Mexican labor could be used to grow sinsemilla on a grand scale. By 1985, with wit, nerve, and boundless energy, the precocious Rafael had created an efficient integrated industry. He and his partner, Ernesto Fonseca, supervised the cultivation of thousands of acres of irrigated desert using commercial agricultural techniques developed in California's San Joaquin and Imperial valleys. By 1985, he was sending fleets of trucks loaded with sinsemilla to wholesale depots in the United States, on the routes used by shippers of Mexican winter vegetables.

All three men had their claques of sycophants, but it was Rafael Caro Quintero, the youngest and most audacious of the lot, who captured the imagination of the Mexican peasantry. To them, he was David, Robin Hood, Pancho Villa. *Corridos,* heroic ballads laced with populist fervor, were written about him. The richer he became, the more he demeaned the establishment, the more he frustrated the gringo lawmen, the more of a legend he became.

The recent months in Guadalajara had been the tensest that Kiki Camarena and his wife, Mika, had ever known. There had been too many shootings in the street, too many kidnappings, too many bad omens. Mika, who was thirty-four years old, was tiny, pretty, and stoical. She had always been able to live with danger, but now she was beginning to crumble. And Kiki was beginning to burn out.

On September 31, 1984, some men had burst into a restaurant where one of Kiki's Mexican friends, Antonio Vargas,* was eating, and had opened fire with a machine gun. It was a miracle that Antonio survived, but his spinal cord was severed, and he would probably be in a wheelchair for the rest of his life. Antonio was a well-to-do professional whose idealism drew him to Kiki. "The most valuable thing we have is not life," he said. "It's freedom. What use is life if you are a slave?" Vargas called drug abuse slavery and was sickened to see children in his community becoming addicted to drugs, stealing, and selling their bodies. He was even more outraged when he observed high officials kowtow to the Sinaloa gang lords. Vargas used his access to the intricate social and political networks to help Kiki and the other DEA agents document the infiltration of the traffickers into legitimate business in central Mexico. As time passed, he grew bolder and socialized with Rafael Caro Quintero and the other cartel leaders in order to learn about their contacts in the government. He saw Caro Quintero and Fonseca partying at the Federal Security Directorate (DFS) office, making protection deals with Mexican Federal Judicial Police officers, and, on one occasion, attending festivities with one of the highest officials in the land. Vargas reported all that he observed to Kiki and the other agents. After the shooting, he awoke in the hospital to see Kiki sitting by his bedside. He sensed that one of the Americans would be next. "Be careful," he rasped.

Eleven days after Vargas was wounded, the DEA agents received a direct warning. At ten minutes after seven o'clock on the morning of October 10, gunmen unloaded a thirty-round magazine into the side of Roger Knapp's car, tattooing a bull's-eye pattern on the driver's side. A tall, muscular forty-year-old, Knapp had been a drug agent since 1966. That morning, Knapp was still in bed; his wife was in the kitchen, getting their three children ready for school. Carol Knapp had heard the clatter of automatic-weapon fire many times when the family was stationed in Guatemala City; she hit the floor reflexively when she heard the squeal of tires and the metallic pops. If the gunmen had come five minutes

---

* The name Antonio Vargas is a pseudonym.

later, the three children would have been standing where the car was parked, waiting for the school bus.

DEA headquarters ordered Knapp back to Texas. He did not want to go. Meticulous and highly organized, Knapp was running the most complex case in the Guadalajara office, Operation Padrino—*padrino* meant "godfather"—an intelligence-gathering project aimed at Félix Gallardo. Knapp sensed he was on the verge of a breakthrough that might allow agents in the States to seize the ring's next loads. Knapp found the shooting oddly gratifying—a sign that the godfather was losing his cool. But he had his wife and children to consider. The next time might be worse.

The Knapp family's departure was a melancholy event for the tight group of DEA families stationed in Guadalajara. It left just three agents in the Guadalajara office.

James Kuykendall, the eldest of the group, was agent in charge of the Guadalajara resident office. Born in Maverick County, Texas, a federal agent since 1957, Kuykendall had spent a lifetime matching wits with smugglers. With his unruly gray hair, blue-eyed squint, and ornery nature, the forty-eight-year-old Texan resembled a sheriff's deputy, which is what his father had been. He had learned Spanish from his sloe-eyed wife, María Consuela, who came from Matamoros, and from the vaqueros who matched him tequila for tequila in the rickety cantinas on the south side of the Rio Grande. Anglos could barely pronounce "Kirk-endal," his last name, which was Dutch. Mexicans did not try but called him Jaime, which he pronounced explosively, "Hi-*may*," with a hoarse laugh. Kuykendall was the abstract thinker of the group, the talker, the motivator.

Victor Wallace, a big, gentle Mexican American, was patient and constant. Like Kiki and Mika Camarena, Shaggy Wallace had grown up in Calexico, an obscure border town in California's Imperial Valley. When he came of age in 1959, Shaggy joined the Imperial County sheriff's department. Kiki, ten years younger, returned to the valley upon his discharge from the Marines in 1970 and joined the Calexico police force. There was little for a poor boy to do but tend the fields or find a niche on some government payroll, but for Shaggy and Kiki, narcotics work was a commitment that they pursued with righteous fury. Each had lost friends to heroin addiction. Kiki's own brother, Ernesto, had committed a series of petty crimes and had been urged by a judge to submit voluntarily to a drug-rehabilitation program. Together, Kiki and Shaggy formed a little joint task force and spent night after night on the streets looking for heroin dealers. In 1974, when the DEA was recruiting Spanish speakers, both men signed up. Shaggy followed Kiki to Guadalajara in the fall of 1984. By that time, Guadalajara was so dangerous that volunteers for the post were scarce. When Shaggy heard that his old partner needed help, he put in for a transfer. He would have walked through fire for Kiki Camarena.

Kuykendall said that the shooting of Roger Knapp's car was a message to the DEA men to get out of Guadalajara. As far as he was concerned, there was only one way to deal with outlaws who thought they owned the town: give a sign that the DEA men would not be intimidated. But how? Three agents, two secretaries, a modest informant budget, and a few beat-up cars and radios were not much of a threat. The tall weather-beaten Texan took to prowling around the small DEA office at the consulate, grinding the heels of his cowboy boots into the floor, muttering, "Something is going to happen. Next time it's gonna be worse." Mika and Kiki instructed their three sons that they must never answer the door, never leave the walled courtyard in front of the house. Enrique Jr., eleven, Daniel, six, and Erick, four, played in the yard like caged lion cubs. They were very much like their father, full of life, scornful of boundaries. Mika lived in constant fear that they would forget and stray, and she would hear the screech of tires and the metallic *crack-crack-crack* of a machine gun.

Kiki did not talk much, but Mika saw the strain in his face. He was, in the jargon of the day, wired. He never slept. He was always out with informants or with the Federales. It was her lot to wait.

Kiki had told Mika that he did not think the traffickers would actually shoot an American agent. Mika was not so sure, but whatever happened, she knew they had to get back to the States, to some semblance of a normal life. By day, Guadalajara wore a placid face. The city was filled with tourists visiting the Orozco museum, buying the local pottery, taking in the joyous cacophony of the mariachis in the plaza. This was not the Guadalajara the agents and their wives knew. They had seen the city's night side. It was evil and impenetrable, like the countenances of the *brujas*, the witches, who lived in the back streets and sold incantations to vengeful peasants.

Just recently, the drug Mafia had gone on its worst rampage yet. In January 1985, four Mexican police cars had been lured to isolated spots and ambushed. In Los Angeles, the whole police force would have responded by throwing everything they had at the outlaws: barricades, SWAT teams, helicopters, police snipers. In Guadalajara the cops set up roadblocks, searched cars, and took pistols away from petty thieves and frightened merchants, but they left the gang lords alone.

The police measures did not leave the DEA men feeling safer. They could not carry revolvers because of the "depistolization" roadblocks. The local policemen, who detested the American agents, would delight in throwing them in jail for the slightest infraction. The Mexican government had refused to give them diplomatic immunity. As for catching the real outlaws, the roadblocks were a pathetic joke. Anybody who wanted to know where the *narcos* were had only to ask the police.

Nearly every time Camarena and his buddies began reporting on a trafficking ring, they soon ran across the tracks of the Dirección Federal de Seguridad, the Federal Security Directorate. The DFS, as the agency was known, was part of the powerful Interior Ministry. Its mission was the investigation of terrorists, subversives, and communists. DFS officials in Mexico City were valued allies of the U.S. Central Intelligence Agency and the Federal Bureau of Investigation because they shared information gained by wiretapping and shadowing the dozens of Cuban and Soviet agents who used Mexico City as a base of operations. In the provinces, some DFS agents worked as security guards and strong-arms for the narcotics czars. Antonio Vargas said that the chauffeur and bodyguards for Ernesto Fonseca were all DFS agents. Many traffickers and their henchmen carried DFS credentials. They found federal police badges useful for scaring off the lowly uniformed cops who occasionally challenged their right to carry machine guns, drive unlicensed cars, and harass local citizens. Félix Gallardo's personal bodyguards stopped Roger Knapp as he drove past the trafficker's office one day; they flashed Interior Ministry police credentials and questioned him about what he was doing on that particular street.

Camarena's informants said that Rafael Caro Quintero and Ernesto Fonseca often hung out at the Federal Bureau of Social and Political Investigations (IPS), a secretive Interior Ministry agency that, like DFS, was supposed to report on political dissidents. According to a Mexican Federal Judicial Police (MFJP) officer in Guadalajara, IPS Comandante Sergio Espino Verdín collected the body of Ernesto Fonseca's brother from the morgue after he was killed by city policemen after a high-speed car chase.

The cleanest of the police agencies was the Mexican Federal Judicial Police, modeled on the U.S. Federal Bureau of Investigation. Even so, Camarena and his partners often found that when they shared sensitive information with its senior officials, the data leaked back to Félix Gallardo and Caro Quintero. A man who served as an MFJP officer in Guadalajara while Camarena was stationed there confirmed the DEA agents' suspicions. He said that he and certain other MFJP officers supplemented their salaries of about $150 a month by delivering bags of cash to the border for the traffickers, in exchange for which Rafael Caro Quintero or Ernesto Fonseca gave them *regalos,* gifts, of 200,000 or 300,000 pesos at a time. This officer, who attained the rank of *comandante* and was interviewed after he retired, insisted that these were not protection payments, because the traffickers did not need protection. "There weren't any warrants on for the traffickers," he recalled. "The police knew who they were, but you need an arrest warrant. They're never going to have drugs on them. How are you going to prove he's a trafficker? The whole case is in the judge, not the police. That's where a lot of money moves in Mexico, through the judges and the lawyers." The MFJP never tried to build a case on the traffickers, he said. "Why should they?" He said that he and his fellow MFJP officers were aware that DFS officers were moving drugs and guarding the traffickers. "We didn't see," he said, covering his eyes with both hands. "If we did, that would start a war among the factions."

In 1984 and early 1985, Guadalajara had become one of the most hazardous cities in the world for an American agent, but for Camarena, Kuykendall, and Wallace, the worst of it was that their superiors in Mexico City and Washington seemed not to notice. Cables to the embassy or DEA headquarters went unanswered, requests for reinforcements were ignored, calls for diplomatic intervention were dismissed as heavy-handed. The senior DEA officer in Mexico, a Texan by the name of Ed Heath, was a bureaucratic survivor who had not raised alarms at headquarters. Kuykendall and the other men stationed in Guadalajara were sure that bad news stayed bottled up in the American embassy in Mexico City, where the prevailing attitude among many diplomats, and some DEA officials as well, was that corruption and duplicity had to be suffered for the sake of preserving the "special relationship" between the United States and Mexico.

On this particular Thursday in February, Kiki stalked out of the consulate and headed across Calle Libertad to his pickup truck. It was parked in the lot of the Camelot bar, a seedy joint whose proprietor, grateful for the DEA contingent's hefty beer tabs, gave the agents parking privileges.

Camarena must have turned off the truck's burglar alarm with his key and unlocked the door, but he was apparently interrupted before he could get into the cab and grab the two-way radio, which he would have used to alert his partners if he were under attack.

What happened to Kiki Camarena as he stood by his truck would be the subject of inquiry and speculation for years to come. Eventually, Mexican authorities would arrest some suspects and offer this reconstruction of events: five men intercepted Camarena. The leader was José Luis Gallardo Parra, a lieutenant of Ernesto Fonseca, who was called El Güero, Blondie. With him were two Jalisco state policemen and two professional killers. One of the men, Samuel "El Samy" Ramírez Razo, flashed a DFS badge. "Federal Security," he said. "The *comandante* wants to see you." The men grabbed Camarena and shoved him into a beige Volkswagen Atlantic. El Samy threw a jacket over the agent's head, El Güero signaled a direction, and the driver sped away.

Most American government officials came to accept this scenario, but, strangely, DEA agents could never find a single witness who could corroborate the Mexican government's description of the kidnapping or identify the faces of Camarena's assailants. There must have been a number of passers-by on the street at the crucial moment; surely a scuffle among six burly men had not gone unnoticed. Perhaps people in Guadalajara had learned not to ask questions. Or, possibly, as Jaime Kuykendall came to believe, the Mexican government's scenario was not true, and something else happened to Kiki Camarena.

Mika Camarena felt awkward sitting in a restaurant by herself. Kiki had asked her to lunch because they needed some time alone. He had been working late and leaving the house early; they seldom had a moment to talk. She hoped he would come soon. The waiters were beginning to eye her curiously. Or perhaps she was just imagining things. It was hard, these days, not to imagine the worst. After waiting for half an hour or so, Mika called the consulate. The secretary said that Kiki had just left. Mika waited a while longer. Finally she gave up and went home to her sons.

At four o'clock that afternoon, Captain Alfredo Zavala Avelar landed his small plane at Guadalajara International Airport. Zavala, a short, chubby man in his forties, worked as a pilot for the Mexican Ministry of Agriculture. On the side, he worked for the DEA. A retired military pilot, Zavala was cheerful, competent, and eager to please. He had a wife, a houseful of children, and a very small salary. He needed the money the Americans offered, and he worked very hard to earn it. Because he was often at the airport, he was able to monitor the comings and goings of the fleets of planes that belonged to the cartel.

Also, on his trips he would look for marijuana and opium plantations in the central highlands. DEA agents were not allowed to fly over areas where marijuana might be grown. Aerial surveillance by America's agents was forbidden by the Mexican Foreign Ministry. Occasionally Kiki or the other DEA men broke the rule and chartered Zavala's plane for a surreptitious tour.

On this day, Zavala was returning from Durango with an agricultural engineer and two other men. He taxied his plane to the hangar and shut down the engine. The wife of one of his passengers had driven to the airport to meet her husband, and Zavala accepted a ride home. Just as they were about to pull away from the hangar, a brown Ford Galaxie screeched to the side of their car and ordered them to halt. Two men got out and pointed an AR-15 semiautomatic rifle at Zavala. They yanked him out of the car, forced him into the back of the Ford, took the couple's car keys, and sped away. The couple was too frightened to call the police.

Mika woke up with a start. She had put the boys to bed and dozed off. The place beside her in the bed was cold. The clock said it was five-thirty in the morning. Kiki never stayed out all night without telling her where he was going. She stared into the darkness. She wanted to call the other agents, but it was too early. What if he had gone out with the Federales or an informant? Maybe he had tried to reach her while she was at a meeting at the boys' school the previous day. It would not do to seem hysterical. She was an agent's wife. She was expected to be tough. She waited. When the clock read six-thirty, she called Shaggy Wallace.

Mika prayed that Shaggy would not answer. If he did not, that would mean he and Kiki were out on a case together. But Shaggy was home.

"Didn't he meet you for lunch?" Shaggy said groggily.

Mika's heart sank. She knew at that moment that Kiki was missing.

Shaggy tried to ease Mika's fears. Maybe Kiki had gone up to Colima with the Federales. They were out beating the bushes for some thugs who had murdered a *comandante*. It was probably just a communications foul-up. But Shaggy was worried. He knew that Kiki would not disappear this long without telling someone. He had a very bad feeling in the pit of his stomach when he hung up the phone.

Shaggy telephoned Kuykendall. Kiki and Jaime were virtually inseparable. When Shaggy said Kiki had not come home, Kuykendall tensed. He remembered all the times he had said, "Somebody's gonna get hurt."

Now Kuykendall hoped to God he was wrong. He grabbed the telephone and started dialing informants, friends—anyone he could think of. At eight-thirty he called the American embassy in Mexico City.

"I think we've got a man missing," he said.

Jaime jumped into his beat-up government car and floored it all the way to the consulate. When he pulled around the corner onto Calle Libertad, he saw Kiki's powder-blue truck.

And he knew. Kiki loved that dented pickup the way some men loved their horses. He would not have gone off without it. Jaime tried the door. It swung open. Kiki always kept it locked.

Shaggy went to the Camarena house. Mika was composed but now clearly terrified. They sat for a while and stared. There was not much to say. Shaggy drove to the consulate, turned the corner, and saw the abandoned truck. And he knew, too.

In the States, the DEA men would have rounded up twenty or thirty agents, cops, and sheriff's deputies, acquired a batch of warrants, and started kicking doors. Here their hands were tied. They could not enter a home unbidden, or make an arrest, or interrogate anyone. They had to persuade the Mexican Federal Judicial Police to start hitting the houses.

That was not going to be easy. The Federales would

gladly arrest amateur smugglers, gringo kids, or Colombians who had not made the right payoffs. Kiki had tried to change that. He had been hanging around the MFJP office, hoping to cadge a little information or get a little help. Many of the Mexican agents, especially the younger ones, liked him and wanted to do the right thing. They helped on small cases. But when the big names were involved, they became paralyzed. No major trafficker had been jailed for any length of time since 1975—and that one was a transplanted Cuban.

The traffickers owned more houses than anyone had ever counted. Jaime knew that Kiki could be at any one of these places. Or at none of them. The kidnappers could have flown him to Bolivia or Spain by now.

Still, there was a chance that Kiki was somewhere around town, or that someone could be found who knew where he had been taken. Shaggy went to ask the Federales for help while Jaime worked the phone.

The MFJP office was eerily empty. Usually there were ten agents and a dozen or more helpers lolling about the old house that served as the Guadalajara command post. Today there were only two men. Comandante Alberto Arteaga and most of the agents were up in Colima looking for the killer of their comrade. The Americans would have to go to the Jalisco State Judicial Police.

Shaggy's face sagged. The DEA men considered the Jalisco police worse than useless. Some of them moonlighted for the traffickers. Moonlighted, hell, Jaime snarled. There were those among the Judiciales, as they were called, who could often be found at the traffickers' hangouts any time of day. Now the American agents would have to beg them to search for Kiki.

It was no time for pride. Shaggy pleaded his case to an indifferent civil servant. Chief Carlos Aceves Fernández was "unavailable." Shaggy persisted, explaining the situation, asking for other officials, repeating his explanations. He was ignored. Richard Morefield, the American consul general in Guadalajara, telephoned the governor of Jalisco, Enrique Alvarez de Castillo, but he was unavailable.

At about four-thirty in the afternoon, a state official told Kuykendall that he would have to file a formal complaint.

By this time, Kiki had been gone for more than twenty-six hours. Morefield and Kuykendall drove to the state office building. Kuykendall saw Chief Aceves glance their way and vanish, a nice trick for a man of his considerable girth. The state attorney general sent word that he had no time to see them. The two Americans cooled their heels for an hour or so. Finally, they were permitted to give a statement to a junior assistant prosecutor.

Jaime filled out the forms, sweating and cursing to himself. He dared not lose his temper. He would put up with any insult to get the search moving. He went back to the consulate and waited.

Shaggy went to the hospitals and drove past the houses he knew were owned by traffickers. He went back to the MFJP office, hoping that some of the Federales had returned. He found no one.

Mika told her sons that their father was missing. She tried to keep busy, cooking, talking to friends. "We have to be strong," Shaggy told her. "We've got to believe that he is alive." Shaggy and his wife moved into the Camarena house. Mika fought for self-control. Finally, she wept. Shaggy wept with her.

DEA agents began converging on Guadalajara Friday night. There were about thirty men stationed in Mexico City, Monterrey, Hermosillo, Mazatlán, and Mérida, and another twenty agents on temporary duty as advisers to the poppy- and marijuana-eradication program. DEA headquarters dispatched other Spanish-speaking agents from the States. As the American agents arrived, they organized themselves, split up tasks, and tried to map out strategies.

The only DEA agent who did not arrive by airplane was Ed Heath. On Friday evening, Heath boarded the overnight train in Mexico City. He appeared at the consulate between seven and eight o'clock Saturday. Several of Camarena's friends were appalled by Heath's judgment because he was out of reach by telephone for twelve hours in the middle of the crisis. Heath said he had worked late making calls to set the search in motion and had taken the night train be-

cause it would put him in Guadalajara earlier than the
Saturday-morning flights from Mexico City. "It was at my
expense," Heath said later. "I spent the whole damn night
on that lousy train to get there." Four other agents who
worked at the embassy got to Guadalajara quicker: according to one of the men, they found a flight that left Mexico
City about five o'clock Saturday morning and arrived in
Guadalajara at around six. Kuykendall said that Heath's
decision was not impulsive at all, that the DEA attaché had
told him two months earlier that he would arrive on the
train that Saturday morning to attend a Shriners convention.
Kuykendall said Heath had asked Kuykendall's secretary to
make reservations for himself and a few other Shriners.
When Heath walked into the DEA office that Saturday
morning, Kuykendall shot him a look of such fury that some
of the other agents were afraid he would do violence to the
attaché.

The MFJP started moving agents into Guadalajara late
Friday night, and by Saturday morning there were about
eighty Federales. Still, none of them would go door to door.
The Federales complained that they did not have cars, so
the DEA men hit the phones and started renting cars. The
Federales needed radios. The Americans scrounged radios.
More delays ensued and more excuses: every decision had
to be cleared by Primer Comandante Armando Pavón
Reyes, who had been sent from Mexico City to Guadalajara
to lead the search, and he explained that he had to telephone
Mexico City to clear everything important with Manuel
Ibarra Herrera, the head of the MFJP.

Sometime after two o'clock on Saturday, a DEA agent
monitoring the private radio network that belonged to Félix
Gallardo heard the godfather ordering an underling to deliver some cash to the airport. Kuykendall gave Pavón Reyes
a list of the tail numbers of Félix Gallardo's planes. Pavón
Reyes and about thirty men headed for the airport.

Kuykendall signaled to three DEA agents. "Go with
them. Hang on to them. Don't let them out of your sight."

As they pulled up to the airport, the DEA men saw a
Falcon executive jet in the hangar area. It was not one of
Félix Gallardo's planes, but five men with machine guns

were guarding it. Pavón Reyes ordered his men to load their weapons.

The Federales swarmed around the plane, blocking its path. The guards readied their machine guns, and so did the Federales. The air seemed to go thick, like the moment before a thunderstorm. Both sides knew that if one round went off, everyone would start shooting and everyone would die.

After a few tense minutes, the DEA agents saw Pavón Reyes approach the man who appeared to be the leader. He was a swarthy punk with a mop of black curls, a diamond-encrusted bracelet six inches wide, and a blinding mass of gold chains and medallions around his neck. Since none of the Americans had worked in Guadalajara, they did not recognize him, but they were sure that he was a drug trafficker. Pavón Reyes and the punk walked around the side of the aircraft, spoke quietly, shook hands, walked around to the front of the plane, and, to the astonishment of the DEA men, exchanged *abrazos,* embraces. Several of the other MFJP officers spoke to Pavón Reyes and then greeted the punk.

Pavón Reyes said he had to make a telephone call and walked into a nearby hangar, where the Mexican Attorney General's Office maintained a communications center for its drug-eradication aircraft. The punk turned to a guard and ordered, "I want you to call the *comandante* and find out what the hell is going on here." Evidently he meant some police officer other than Pavón Reyes. Just then, Pavón Reyes returned, embraced the punk once more, and motioned to the plane to leave. The pilot started the engines, and the punk climbed into the plane. As the aircraft moved to the runway, the punk waved a champagne bottle, grinned maliciously, took a deep swig, nodding toward Pavón Reyes's men, and then raised his machine gun and shouted, "My children, next time bring better weapons, not little toys."

DEA agent Salvador Leyva left the airport with three of Pavón Reyes's officers. As they drove back to town, one of the Mexican officers told the DEA agent sadly, "Leyva, you know and we know that some of our guys are on the take.

We cannot take some *narcos* to our office and question them because of retaliation against us." "We probably made a mistake," said another officer, "allowing the mafiosi to get too big."[1]

When Leyva looked over a photo spread of the Guadalajara traffickers, he recognized the punk: it had been Rafael Caro Quintero. Later, Ed Heath said that one of the Federales confided in him that the trafficker had promised Pavón Reyes 60 million pesos—about $270,000—to let him leave the airport.

On Saturday morning, Bud Mullen checked with the DEA "war room," which had been set up to coordinate communications with Guadalajara and the border offices. Mullen was astounded to learn that the Federales had not begun a house-to-house search for Camarena and even more upset when he heard that traffickers were being allowed to leave Guadalajara. The DEA administrator, a stiff-necked Scotch-Irish Calvinist from Connecticut, held integrity to be the greatest of virtues and professionalism a close second. He believed in the thin blue line, the fraternity of policemen, the bond that transcended nationalism. Mullen believed that a threat against any officer of the law was a challenge to the system. He had spent most of his career in the Federal Bureau of Investigation, which guarded the system as if it were a priesthood; without the system, the FBI taught, there would be anarchy.

Mullen saw that he would have to go to Mexico. At various international law-enforcement conferences, he had struck up a friendship of sorts with Manuel Ibarra Herrera, the director of the Mexican Federal Judicial Police. Ibarra, a lawyer appointed to the post by President Miguel de la Madrid, was suave and modern, Mullen thought, in his approach to law enforcement. Ed Heath vouched for Ibarra's sincerity. Mullen was sure that if he himself put the case to Ibarra, the Mexican police would turn Guadalajara upside down.

When Mullen landed in Mexico City on Sunday morning, Ibarra was there to greet him. He regretted the delay; his men had been upcountry, away from communication lines.

Now they were in Guadalajara, and they would do their duty. Whatever Mullen wanted, he would have it. Ibarra said he had put his best man on the case, Primer Comandante Armando Pavón Reyes.

Mullen was buoyed by his friendly talk with Ibarra. As they flew to Guadalajara, Mullen's traveling companion, Ray McKinnon, head of DEA's office of foreign operations, tried tactfully to deflate the boss's expectations. In the 1970s, McKinnon had spent several frustrating years tracking Mexico-based traffickers and had received many meaningless pledges of help from Mexican law-enforcement officials.

Mullen's meeting with Mika Camarena was a difficult one. He meant to console her, and she thanked him for his concern, but her eyes flashed with anger. Why was he here? she wondered. Why wasn't he in Mexico City, leaning on Manuel Ibarra? Why wasn't he banging on the desk of President de la Madrid?

Mika was annoyed that Mullen had a dozen Mexican agents guarding him. She did not care that the DEA chief had recently received a threat on his life from the Colombian traffickers. She wanted those Federales out searching for her husband. She thought Mullen looked nervous. Was he afraid, with all these men to guard him? What about Kiki? He had had no bodyguards.

Mika cast a withering glance at Ed Heath, who had accompanied Mullen to the Camarena house. She had never liked Heath. She was once offended by something he had done; she recalled telling Kiki that the attaché was "a disgrace to the Department of Justice." She was incensed that Heath had not called her or sent any message to her after she reported Kiki missing. "Why is he here now?" she said to herself. "I don't think he gives a thought to the people in the field."

Mika turned to Mullen and said evenly, "If Kiki gets back, he's probably going to get angry with me, but I'm going to say something a lot of wives have wanted to say. Washington has not been paying attention to Guadalajara. It isn't that much different from Colombia. All we are to DEA is just numbers."

Why hadn't DEA pressed the Mexican government to

give the agents diplomatic immunity so they could carry guns? she demanded. Why hadn't DEA headquarters sent reinforcements to Guadalajara after the shooting of Antonio Vargas and the destruction of Roger Knapp's car? Kiki had put in for a transfer in November 1984, soon after the Knapp family left. He was notified before Christmas that his transfer to San Diego had been approved, but the reassignment would not take place until March. Mika wanted that transfer badly; because Kiki was on the street and at the MFJP office so much, he was the most visible DEA agent in Guadalajara. But Kiki would not ask for an expedited transfer, and Mika blamed DEA headquarters. When Mika pressed him, Kiki told her he could not bear to leave Jaime and Shaggy to handle the entire caseload. "There's nobody else," he had said plaintively.

Whenever Mika read the American newspapers, all she saw were DEA's concerns about the agents in Colombia. Didn't Mullen know how bad it was in Guadalajara? What had happened to Kiki's reports? Mika asked. They would show that the agents in Guadalajara had been in extreme danger. Why hadn't Mullen acted on these reports?

Mika thought that Mullen looked blank. He had heard of the shooting of Roger Knapp's car, but when she mentioned the Vargas shooting and several other episodes, she saw Mullen turn to Ray McKinnon and say, "I didn't know about that." "How could he *not*?" she thought.

Mika persisted. She was sure that Kiki had written many reports about the state of anarchy in Guadalajara. He had wanted Heath to go to Ambassador John Gavin and persuade him to protest to President de la Madrid. Kiki had told her that he did not think Heath took the warning signs in Guadalajara seriously. Mika thought that Heath cared more about the sensitivities of the Mexican government than the safety of his own agents.

Mullen was obviously uneasy. He had no idea what "reports" Mika was talking about. He never showed his emotions and was uncomfortable around people who did. He had transferred Heath out of Washington headquarters in 1983. As the senior official in charge of all domestic operations, Heath supervised all twenty domestic field divisions and fifty-three resident offices. Mullen's deputy, Jack Lawn, said that paper was not going through Heath's hands; it stopped at his desk.

On the other hand, Mullen considered Heath a brave man, and when he found out that Heath wanted to return to Mexico, where he had served several previous tours of duty, he gave him the position of DEA attaché in Mexico City. The job involved supervising about thirty agents, the largest DEA presence anywhere outside the United States. Mullen was confident that Heath could handle it. He had been told that Heath got on well with Mexico's top police officials and could balance DEA's needs against the agenda of the diplomats with whom he would serve. A DEA attaché could not be single-minded about his mission. He had to adjust to taking orders from American ambassadors. Mullen believed that the president set national policy and it was DEA's job to abide by that policy. "We're just a small cog in the machine," he said. Also, when Mullen arrived at DEA, Mexico City was not a hotspot. Senior DEA executives spoke of the border area as a backwater. Mullen had no reason to think otherwise. He knew that there was corruption in Mexico, but he did not consider the danger to DEA agents worse than in many other parts of the world. The conventional wisdom within the senior ranks of DEA and the State Department was that despite corruption the Mexican government had the traffickers under control.

In his own defense, Heath said he had understood very well what was going on in Guadalajara, but he had not thought, until the Knapp episode, that the traffickers would go after DEA agents. After that, Heath said, it was Camarena who had not taken the danger seriously. As Heath put it to a reporter, "There were orders that were passed on to the field to always run around in pairs, to always be armed, to always account for their movements. In this particular case, it didn't happen. People get lax. . . . I can't supervise the agents' every movement from three hundred miles away." Kuykendall denied that he had ever received such orders. He said Heath could not order the men in the field to carry guns because that would violate Mexican law. Besides, he said, what difference would it have made if Kiki had had his gun? The traffickers invariably traveled in bunches, all armed with AK-47s. How could three men go about in pairs? And what about their wives and children? "Unless you've got a bus, you all can't be together all the time," he said. "Sometimes you have to travel with your family." And, after all, Kiki had not disappeared while haunting the seamy side of town. He had vanished a few yards from the consulate portal at the time of day when the street was busiest.

Mika Camarena did not care about Heath's protestations or Mullen's views on balancing interests. As for things being under control, anyone could see, she thought, that there was no control in Guadalajara. Kiki had not told Mika everything he had learned, but she knew enough to believe that any of the agents, and their wives and children, could have been killed at any time.

Mullen understood very clearly one thing that Mika said. She implored Mullen to pull every string he could. She *knew* the Mexican government could find Kiki if the orders came from high enough. And if the worst had happened, she demanded justice. Her sons must not think that their father had died in vain. She wanted him back, or his body, if that was what it came to, and she wanted his killers found and punished. "Don't let my husband become a number," Mika pleaded.

2
Silver or Lead

Long before the day of Kiki Camarena's abduction, one of the Federales told Kiki and Jaime Kuykendall this story.

It was about the rites of passage for Mexican police officials who assumed high posts in that country, in this case a new *comandante* of the Mexican Federal Judicial Police.

Puffed up with pride, the *comandante* indulged himself in the flattery of his fawning subordinates. Then, one day, he heard the sound of boots stamping into the anteroom. The inner door of his office flew open. There stood the celebrated Rafael Caro Quintero, in tight pants, high-heeled cowboy boots, and an expensive shirt unbuttoned to display a chest glittering with golden chains. Caro Quintero's bodyguards positioned themselves around the room, cradling their submachine guns. The agents in the outer office gaped and fell back.

Caro Quintero sauntered up to the *comandante*'s desk. "Are you with us?" he demanded.

The *comandante* glared at the gaudy young intruder. He had been expecting a visit from the traffickers because he wanted a piece of the action. But he was accustomed to greater deference. This was the rankest of humiliations, the insolence of this punk, dressed like an Acapulco gigolo, slurring his words in the slovenly inflections of the backwoods.

"*¿Qué quieres? O plata, o plomo?*" Caro Quintero hissed. "What do you want? Silver or lead?"

The *comandante*'s face reddened. The younger agents looked at their chief with knowing eyes. His hauteur crumbled, and he nodded. He chose silver. He lived well after that, and his agents did not molest the big traffickers.

At the end of this tale, the Americans looked at each other gloomily. So this, they thought, was how the war on drugs would end, with shrugs and apologies and the quiet rustle of dollar bills.

In Colombia, the *narcotraficantes* were even more arrogant. Having compromised or frightened most provincial policemen and judges, the leaders of the cocaine cartel set their sights on buying the very top of the government. On more than one occasion, they proposed to pay off their homeland's foreign debt if the extradition treaty with the United States were abandoned. They postured as generous benefactors who would save the nation in time of economic distress, much as J. P. Morgan had once bailed out the U.S. Treasury. The offer was slightly less crude than the choice Rafael Caro Quintero had put to the *comandante*, but in substance there was no difference. The traffickers would contribute $14 billion to the Colombian government if they could live on their ranches unmolested. Enrique Parejo, the courageous Colombian justice minister, mocked those offers of silver. He was hunted down in Eastern Europe and shot. By some miracle, he survived three bullet wounds in his head.

By the time Ronald Reagan took office in 1981, the extent of the Latin drug trade and official complicity in it was such that the American president dared not acknowledge it publicly; to do so would insult foreign leaders he valued as trading partners and allies in his struggle against leftist expansionism in the hemisphere.

When obliged to give a speech about crime for domestic political consumption, Reagan confined himself to vagaries that did not inspire but did not sting. Reagan drew more than a few derisive smiles at the Justice Department in 1982, when he made a speech about crime and called the drug traffickers an "invisible empire," as if some dark art enabled them to elude capture.

In fact, the *narcotraficantes* were prominent citizens, well known in their homelands and to American officials. The Colombians sardonically nicknamed them "the magicians" because everyone could see them except the police.[1] Carlos Lehder, a leader of the Colombian cocaine cartel, published a newspaper that he used to attack the United States for everything from drug eradication to imperialism in South America. His countryman Pablo Escobar owned an hacienda so opulent that a Colombian company used it as the setting for a soft-drink commercial. Rafael Caro Quintero had a mansion in Guadalajara the size of a small college. Miguel Angel Félix Gallardo appeared in the society pages of Mexican newspapers blessing the wedding of a provincial governor's son. Roberto Suárez Gómez, the Bolivian cocaine king, lived like a country squire, dispensing favors to peasants who called him Papito, "Little Father." The coca growers of Bolivia and Peru had their own trade associations, which lobbied against acreage restrictions urged by the United States.

Traffickers of every nationality had their meetings and laundered their money in Panama, an international banking haven whose government was controlled by General Manuel Antonio Noriega Morena, the commander in chief of the Panamanian Defense Forces. For years, American diplomats dismissed as "rumor" the mounting evidence that Noriega extracted bribes from drug smugglers, arms dealers, money launderers, and others who wanted to do business in Panama, and the CIA, DEA, and Pentagon maintained a close relationship with the general. But in 1987 and 1988, agents of the DEA, the FBI, and the U.S. Customs Service came up with witnesses who claimed to have firsthand knowledge of Noriega's involvement in corrupt deals. On February 4, 1988, Noriega became the first important foreign leader to be indicted in the United States for drug trafficking. A grand jury in Miami charged Noriega, Pablo Escobar, and fourteen others, including Amet Paredes, the son of General Reubén Darío Paredes, Noriega's predecessor as head of the PDF, with racketeering, narcotics trafficking, and conspiracy. The indictment, based on the testimony of Noriega's former political adviser, José Blandón, and his former pilot, Floyd Carlton Cáceres, alleged that Noriega used his official positions to "provide protection for international criminal narcotics traffickers in-

cluding . . . the Medellín cartel." A second grand jury in
Tampa indicted Noriega and a Panamanian businessman
named Enrique Pretelt for drug trafficking and conspiracy;
the charges were based on the testimony of admitted trafficker Steven Kalish, who told a Congressional committee
that he paid Noriega and his associates $1 million to facilitate
the shipment of two hundred tons of marijuana into the
United States and to launder $100 million through Pana-
manian banks.

Noriega denied the charges and accused the Reagan
administration of manufacturing them in an effort to over-
throw his regime. Noriega's suspicions were not without
foundation. The evidence was real, but it was also true that
Reagan's top officials at the State Department regarded the
indictments as useful tools for forcing Noriega out of office.
Reagan's men seemed motivated less by revulsion at the
allegations of Noriega's drug trafficking than by the conviction that Noriega had lost his political value to the United
States. Panamanians were rioting in the streets to protest
his tyranny. Panama's economy was in crisis. Noriega was
destabilizing a nation vital to American security interests.
Once State Department officials decided Noriega had to go,
they "discovered," as the jaundiced police inspector played
by Claude Rains in *Casablanca* "discovered" gambling at
Rick's place, that Panama was a den of iniquity.

The source of the power of the *narcotraficantes* was not wit
or skill but money, tens of billions of dollars of it, sums that
had been inconceivable a decade earlier. Money bought
guns and sanctuary and, finally, the power to command
provincial and even central governments. No criminal enterprise had ever had the kind of money that was available
to the *narcotraficantes* of Latin America, and there was
plenty more where that came from. Cataracts of dollars
poured out of the United States, whose people seemed to
have an insatiable appetite for cocaine and marijuana.

The sudden popularity of marijuana and cocaine in the
United States was a windfall that changed forever some of
the poorest regions in the Americas. The mountains that
formed the spine of Latin America, the Sierra Madre in

Mexico and the Andes in South America, had the perfect conditions to sustain a large illegal agricultural industry: a hospitable climate, a large labor force, and a weak or indifferent government. There were vast ungoverned and ungovernable regions blessed with fertile soil, rain, long growing seasons, and thousands of subsistence farmers willing to work the fields, the processing sheds, and the makeshift refineries. Coca flourished in the Bolivian and Peruvian Andes; coca paste was converted to white cocaine powder in laboratories in rural Colombia, Bolivia, and Peru. Marijuana abounded in the Sierra Madre, where opium was also grown, and in Colombia's Sierra Nevada and Perija mountains.

Drug trafficking created parallel economies in near-bankrupt countries. By the mid-1980s, coca and marijuana were important cash crops in much of Latin America. Collateral industries—refining, transportation, money laundering—employed hundreds of thousands of people not only in the major producing countries but also in small producers and way stations such as Panama, Guatemala, Honduras, Nicaragua, the Bahamas, Jamaica, Belize, Costa Rica, Haiti, the Dominican Republic, Brazil, Ecuador, Paraguay, Argentina, and Venezuela.

As the American appetite for marijuana and cocaine grew, subsistence farmers clutching handfuls of dollars came into the towns to buy vacuum cleaners for houses with dirt floors, refrigerators, televisions, and videotape decks for homes without electricity, cars they could not drive.

The earnings of the farmers, as grand as they seemed to campesinos who had never owned shoes, were a pittance compared to the profit exacted by the smugglers. Smuggling—the art of the *contrabandista*—was an old and honored profession in much of Latin America. What was different about the drug traffickers who came of age in the 1970s and 1980s was the breathtaking scope of their ambition. Once the purchase of a few kilograms of heroin was a business deal to be celebrated with toasts and pledges of mutual respect and loyalty. In the 1980s, wholesale buyers ordered thousand-pound lots of cocaine and twenty-five tons of marijuana. The business was as brisk and impersonal as arranging a shipment of cattle feed. The illegal drug trade probably equaled the annual international trade in such legal staples as coffee, soybeans, or wheat. Coca brought more revenues to the Andean nations than legal exports.

To the methods of the old *contrabandistas,* the new traffickers added technological improvements in modern aviation, communications, and agronomy, and created intricate multinational enterprises. And they extended the reach of corruption. Their fathers had bribed local police and customs officials. The younger generation, especially the marijuana traders, with their tons of contraband, needed more powerful patrons. They needed assurances that their crops would be ignored by government-sponsored eradication campaigns. They needed access to international air and shipping lanes, telephone lines, radio networks, and international banking services. None of this was possible without the cooperation of policemen, mayors, customs officers, governors, generals, and in some cases cabinet ministers. As their businesses expanded, the traffickers bought off officials at ever higher levels and intimidated potential reformers.

All money, as the capitalist maxim goes, is made in the dark. So it was with the traffickers of cocaine and marijuana. During their formative years, thanks to confusion in the U.S. government and apathy in their homelands, they could build their organizations in obscurity. For years, Latin leaders justified their passivity by blaming the United States for failing to reduce demand for drugs. Many of them changed their minds when their friends were shot and their children began taking drugs. By that time, it was too late. The marijuana- and cocaine-trafficking networks were weeds in a garden gone to ruin, and they had splintered the structures of governments as an unruly vine wrecks an arbor. With silver and lead, men and women from the most isolated corners of the hemisphere countermanded the orders of presidents, evaded government control, perverted criminal-justice systems, undermined efforts to stimulate investments in legitimate agriculture, and sabotaged diplomatic accords.

The traffickers' ability to buy sanctuary defeated the best efforts of committed law-enforcement officers in the United

States. At the time Kiki Camarena was abducted, the American agencies were doing a creditable job by conventional measures. The DEA alone was making nearly fifty arrests *a day,* counting Thanksgiving and Christmas. One of DEA's biggest worries was the security of its evidence vaults, which held a stockpile of cocaine and heroin worth $10 billion on the street. The DEA, the U.S. Customs Service, and the Internal Revenue Service were striking at the financial base of the traffickers as never before, seizing hundreds of millions of dollars in bank accounts, front businesses, and real estate.

Yet by the one measure that counted—the availability of illegal drugs—all that activity was insufficient. Drugs were cheaper, more accessible, and more widely used than ever before in history. Selling drugs was one of the biggest retailing businesses in America. Wholesale and street prices were declining, reflecting a worldwide glut in the production of coca, marijuana, and opium as well. Fleets of interceptor planes and boats manned by the Customs Service and the Coast Guard could stop only a few of the hundreds of thousands of light aircraft and pleasure boats that swarmed toward the southern border, ducking into Mexico, the Bahamas, or Cuba if detected. As William von Raab, Reagan's acerbic commissioner of customs, put it, "We are like the U.S. troops sitting on the Yalu River during the Korean war—well-trained, well-disciplined, well-equipped . . . facing an enemy that has unlimited resources and safe bases."

For a politician with a law-and-order image, Ronald Reagan was strangely disengaged from what had become an unparalleled social and crime problem. He was once described as a "closet tolerant" on some social issues; the description certainly fit his approach to drug-enforcement policy. He made the occasional speech condemning drug trafficking and drug abuse, but his initial budgets proposed to slash funds for drug enforcement and for treatment and prevention programs. Reagan's first budget director, David Stockman, was determined to fulfill Reagan's promise to reduce the size of government and argued that "under the Constitution, criminal law enforcement, drug prosecution, and other such popular causes were state and local responsibilities. . . . Keeping drugs off the nation's streets is an admirable goal. But no matter how many Coast Guard cutters or AWACS type planes we deployed, the stuff still kept coming in, by boat, plane, and even parachutist."[2] The Congress regularly ignored Stockman and expanded the anti-drug budget. After Republican and Democratic hardliners alike disparaged Reagan for lack of leadership on the issue, Attorney General William French Smith prevailed on Reagan to overrule Stockman and declare the Justice Department a "domestic defense" agency and thus exempt from future budget cuts. Still, every year at budget time, Reagan's green-eyeshade people at the Office of Management and Budget sparred energetically with his law-and-order appointees at Justice and Treasury.

In many ways, Reagan's less-than-aggressive stance on the drug issue was good politics. Tens of millions of Americans had come to see marijuana and cocaine use as a relatively harmless form of recreation. Given the national mood in early 1985, a determined presidential crackdown—arresting users on a massive scale, for example—would have been extremely unpopular. Reagan seemed to have learned one lesson from Vietnam. It was not a good idea to be out front in a cause that would fail because the American people did not support it.

Many of Ronald Reagan's backers saw no justification for draconian enforcement of drug laws. Libertarian purists, as well as conservative intellectuals such as William F. Buckley, advocated legalization of marijuana use. Many other conservatives argued that the only proper role for government was to enforce the laws against the production and sale of drugs. Except for cases in which users were clearly a danger to public safety or security, they believed, an individual's decision to use drugs was a personal choice. "I think we ought to weed out air-traffic controllers who are using drugs," as one senior official in the Reagan White House said. "But who cares if the Chicago Bears' secondary is taking it? That's his problem."

At the other end of the political spectrum, well-meaning liberals tended to dismiss trafficking in the "soft" drugs by suggesting that it was a sort of folk craft that benefited the downtrodden peasantry of the less-developed nations. They ignored evidence that the traffickers funded right-wing death squads in Colombia, provided financial support to corrupt officers in the regimes of military strongmen like General Luis García Meza of Bolivia and General Manuel Antonio Noriega of Panama, terrorized priests, tortured and murdered people who worked in development programs that promoted substitution of food crops, and exploited the labor of campesinos everywhere. Idealistic young Americans boycotted grapes and lettuce picked by destitute migrant workers in California and declined asparagus imported from dictator Augusto Pinochet's Chile. When they grew older, they did without diamonds from South Africa. But they bought drugs from merchants who shot children on the streets of Oaxaca, left a Sonora family dead, tongues cut out for talking, assassinated leftist labor leaders in Colombia, and machine-gunned pregnant women in Washington, D.C. Rafael Caro Quintero was a child of the 1960s, too. To look into his face was to see the dark side of the American cultural revolution.

Ever since opium was first imported into the United States in the early nineteenth century, Americans had been profoundly ambivalent about government controls on the use and trade of mood-altering substances.

Morphine was hailed as a "miracle drug" when it was refined from opium in 1805. During the Civil War, in which half a million men were wounded, it was administered routinely to relieve suffering. Morphine addiction was so prevalent among veterans that it was called "the army disease," but it also became a problem among thousands of women who took the drug during childbirth.

The next "wonder drug" was cocaine, which was initially marketed in the 1880s as a local anesthetic. A powerful central-nervous-system stimulant, it was soon being prescribed as a cure for morphine addiction and alcoholism. In the Age of Innocence, Sigmund Freud glorified cocaine use, and patent-medicine makers added the drug, along with morphine and toxic substances such as chloroform and laudanum, to nostrums of all sorts, from nasal sprays to teething syrups for babies.[3]

After the turn of the century, cocaine's addictive potential was becoming evident. Even so, the Congress approached regulation in a gingerly manner. Cocaine and opiates were included as an afterthought, along with other "adulterants," when the federal Pure Food and Drug Act was passed in 1906. The statute, the first to impose federal controls on drugs, was inspired by Upton Sinclair's book *The Jungle*, a powerful exposé of filth in the meat-packing industry.

Despite the Pure Food and Drug Act, psychoactive drugs were still available from doctors and on the black market, and drug abuse worsened with the invention of the hypodermic needle. It was not until 1910 that the medical profession recognized that heroin, a "miracle drug" derived from opium and marketed by the Bayer company in 1889, was even more habit-forming than the drugs it was meant to replace.

Western leaders attempted to join forces to suppress the international trade in opium, which was generally condemned as a vice of Chinese peasants. In 1912, the United States and other Western nations concluded an International Opium Convention, which committed participants to suppress opiates. The British insisted that the treaty extend to cocaine because it was being smuggled into India and China as a substitute for opium. In 1914, to fulfill U.S. obligations under the Opium Convention, the Congress passed the Harrison Narcotics Act, the cornerstone of federal narcotics-control efforts for the next sixty-five years. The first narcotics agents had low-paying, low-status jobs deep in the miscellaneous division of the Treasury Department's Bureau of Internal Revenue. Besides enforcing the Harrison Act, it was the division's ignominious duty to assure the quality of margarine. When Prohibition began in 1919, the narcotics agents became part of the Bureau of Internal Revenue's Prohibition Unit. "Dry" agents were almost universally resented, and except for legendary figures like Elliot Ness and his "Untouchables," they acquired a reputation for corruption, which was shared by the narcotics agents.

Early Supreme Court decisions held that physicians could not legally prescribe addictive drugs for maintenance doses. Narcotics agents arrested thousands of physicians and closed clinics—actions that had the unintended effect of ending research on addiction, driving impoverished addicts to back-alley suppliers, and enhancing the profitability of the black market.

As drug use became associated with certain despised minorities, public attitudes toward drug users took on racist and xenophobic overtones. Mexican itinerant workers—who competed for jobs with Americans—were condemned for dealing in marijuana, Chinese immigrants reviled for smoking and trading in opium. The use of cocaine by blacks aroused intense fears among whites, particularly in the South: cocaine, it was said, made blacks lustful, uninhibited, and impervious to fear and pain. In *The American Disease*, Dr. David F. Musto wrote that some Southern police departments switched from .32-caliber to .38-caliber bullets in the belief that cocaine-crazed blacks could survive gunshots that would fell a normal human.[4]

Reports that two hundred thousand heroin addicts lived in the United States and were widely involved in crime led Congress to pass the Narcotic Drugs Import and Export Act of 1922, aimed at European and Chinese merchants of opium, morphine, heroin, and cocaine.

Articulating the philosophy that would mark American drug-control efforts for the next six decades, Congressman Steven G. Porter, a Republican from Pennsylvania and chairman of the House Committee on Foreign Affairs, insisted that the flow of narcotics had to be controlled *at the source*. In 1924, he led the U.S. delegation to the Second International Opium Convention in Geneva, but walked out when the opium-producing nations, Persia, Turkey, and, in particular, British India, did not agree with Porter's insistence on rigid government controls on production of opium. The convention created international obligations for drug control supervised within the League of Nations, but Porter saw to it that the United States never signed on.

Porter decided that the U.S. government needed an independent agency to foster international control efforts; he

ushered through the Congress a bill that created the Federal
Bureau of Narcotics in 1930. The first FBN commissioner,
Harry J. Anslinger, a formidable character who competed
with the FBI's J. Edgar Hoover for bureaucratic supremacy,
would hold the job for more than thirty years.

In the 1930s and 1940s, the American establishment regarded drug abuse—which by now meant heroin addiction—
as an imminent hazard to society, a cause of predatory crime
and degradation, but a habit confined to the underclass.
"We will use any method we can to 'get' dope smugglers,
dope peddlers, and bootleggers," Henry Morgenthau, Jr.,
President Franklin Roosevelt's secretary of the treasury,
declared in 1934. "We've got to go after them with every
weapon at our command—not in a sissy manner."

Morgenthau's bellicose declaration was widely praised in
the newspapers of the day, which were given to jingoistic
attacks on the opium-producing nations. Typical was the
reaction of the *Atlanta Georgian* in October 1934: "In authorizing a new and relentless drive against narcotics smugglers and racketeers, Secretary Morgenthau is proceeding
in exactly the right way. The Federal Narcotics Bureau [a
part of the Treasury Department] has already made substantial progress in scotching our newest dope menace—
cheap smuggled opium from the Far East." The accompanying cartoon showed Uncle Sam's boot crushing the neck
of a Chinese dragon. The "yellow peril" theme—which had
it that the Asians were using opium as a political weapon—
heightened as Japan marched toward war.

Though some opium and heroin did come through Japan,
the major traffickers were in the Mediterranean area:
Greeks, Slavs, Lebanese, or Corsicans who dealt in heroin
refined from Turkish opium. A secondary source of opiates,
particularly during World War II, was Mexico. Within the
United States, heroin trafficking was a subsidiary business
for racketeers like Louis "Lepke" Buchalter, the Al Capone
mob, and Lucky Luciano, who was convicted of smuggling
Mexican heroin to the United States in 1944. After World
War II, the heroin network became known as the French
Connection; the Mediterranean heroin-refining industry became concentrated in Marseilles and controlled by Corsican

gangsters who supplied Italian-American Mafiosi on the East Coast of the United States.

Marijuana was not proscribed by the Harrison Act. In the mid-1930s, when reports came in from the Southwest that small-town youths were experimenting with the Mexican weed, politicians and community leaders across the region orchestrated a frenzied publicity campaign to outlaw it. FBN chief Harry Anslinger initially opposed the criminalization of marijuana because during Prohibition he had seen judges angered when the government attempted to prosecute citizens for possession of small amounts of liquor. As Musto wrote, "Anslinger realized that similar judicial displeasure might follow if too many marihuana possession cases were taken to federal courts. . . . Naturally this desire to keep within the good graces of the courts caused the FBN to seek control of only the most obviously dangerous drugs—cocaine and opiates. Anslinger 'put sandbags up against the door' whenever anyone suggested that the FBN police barbiturates and amphetamines, for example, because the gray areas meant trouble and perhaps bureaucratic suicide for an enforcement agency with a small budget and staff."[5] Anslinger was overridden by pressure from Southwestern leaders who claimed that the drug caused insanity and depravity in the Mexican barrios and that the habit, unchecked, would infect the white community. Newspapers competed to find lurid crimes perpetrated by marijuana smokers. A wire service circulated a picture of a young man with eyes as round as Ping-Pong balls. The caption read: "THE MOST HEINOUS CRIME OF 1933—Victor Licota, Tampa, Florida, on October 17, 1933, while under the influence of Marihuana, murdered his Mother, Father, Sister and Two Brothers, WITH AN AXE while they were asleep." (Licota had nearly been committed to a mental institution before he began using marijuana, and exhibited symptoms of schizophrenia after the crime.) Hollywood got on the bandwagon with a 1936 film, *Reefer Madness,* depicting the decline of innocents into insanity, rape, addiction, and death, all because of marijuana. In 1937, the Congress approved the Marijuana Tax Act, which placed marijuana in the same proscribed status as heroin.[6]

Cocaine use was revived briefly during the Jazz Age—Gene Krupa's astonishing drumrolls owed something to the stimulant—but for white Americans it remained in the realm of esoterica, used by a relatively small number of upper-class eccentrics, musicians, and movie stars. From the 1940s to the early 1960s, shakers of white powder concocted in mom-and-pop refineries in Bolivia might be found alongside other condiments in waterfront saloons in South American ports, in the casinos of Havana in the years before Castro's revolution, or in Harlem clubs and New Orleans blues joints frequented by blacks. There were adventurous Americans who dabbled in cocaine and marijuana while slumming in Havana or Harlem, but they were rare individuals who ignored the social stigma associated with drug use.

The changes that made the drug trade one of the world's biggest businesses grew out of the complex social and political movements that swept across America in the 1960s and 1970s, when marijuana and cocaine became fashionable, then acceptable, and finally indispensable in some segments of middle-class American culture. Much of the image of drug use as the vice of losers dissolved in the 1960s, when marijuana became known as a "soft" drug and smoking it became "recreational" rather than "abusive."

In 1966, the Federal Bureau of Narcotics estimated that the American black market in heroin was worth $600 million a year to organized crime, an unthinkable figure at the time. By the mid-1980s, tens of billions of dollars—by some estimates more than $100 billion—moved through the underground drug economy each year. Cocaine, which retailed for $80 to $100 a gram in 1986, six times as much as for a gram of gold, probably accounted for well over half the revenues generated by illegal drug sales. Marijuana was the second most lucrative product; synthetic drugs such as PCP—"angel dust"—were third. As a money-maker, heroin dropped to fourth place; U.S. government analysts estimated that the heroin-using population had leveled off at about five hundred thousand people, compared to eighteen million habitual marijuana smokers and six million regular cocaine users.[7]

When millions of middle-class Americans decided to break the law and claimed to have medical opinion on their side, it was inevitable that the politics of fighting drugs would change dramatically. In the 1940s and 1950s, judges had been known to hand down long sentences for possession of a few marijuana cigarettes, but that was when most of the defendants lived in shantytowns.[8] Even those parents who deplored their children's drug habits did not want to see them sent to jail for being caught with a joint.

Richard Nixon and his law-and-order attorney general, John Mitchell, understood the changing social consensus very well. In 1969, they sent a bill to Capitol Hill which drew sharp distinctions between so-called professional traffickers, especially those involved in the heroin trade, and people arrested for possessing small quantities of marijuana. The hundred-page proposal, known as the Comprehensive Drug Abuse Prevention and Control Act of 1970, streamlined and stiffened criminal penalties against wholesale drug dealing but reduced the penalty for simple possession of marijuana to a misdemeanor. Henceforward, youthful first offenders found with small amounts—and in some cases, significant amounts—of marijuana and other "soft" drugs would be shunted to treatment-and-education programs.[9]

The public's lenient attitude toward marijuana use soon extended to marijuana smuggling. Long jail terms for well-connected marijuana smugglers became the exception rather than the rule.[10] Prosecutors routinely declined to try any but the largest smuggling cases. Marijuana had become the Vietnam of law enforcement, a battle the government could neither win nor wholly abandon.

Drug enforcement was a bureaucratic nightmare, fragmented among various federal agencies, demoralized by reports of corruption in the ranks, and exhausted by turf wars. In 1968, President Lyndon Johnson had attempted to consolidate internal narcotics enforcement by combining the old Bureau of Narcotics with several other agencies within a new Bureau of Narcotics and Dangerous Drugs (BNDD). He did not solve the problem of interagency rivalry. Agents of the new bureau fought incessantly with Customs agents; on more than one occasion, undercover men from the rival

agencies drew guns on each other as they attacked the
French Connection trade in New York.[11]

In 1973, Richard Nixon attempted to quell the competitive fires by creating a "superagency," the Drug Enforcement Administration (DEA). The reorganization only internalized rivalries: the new agency was a confederacy of cliques of agents who had started out together in New York, Los Angeles, Miami, the Southwest, Europe, or the Far East. They jostled and schemed like Chinese tongs. Five hundred Customs agents expert in drug investigations had transferred to the DEA. They formed yet another clique, and their transfer did not stop the new agency from fighting with the Customs Service, which had retained authority for enforcing the anti-smuggling statutes. Another faction was composed of sixty CIA veterans, among them Lucien Conein, who figured in the 1963 coup that resulted in the assassination of South Vietnamese President Ngo Dinh Diem.

The agency was born under a dark star. Nixon's first DEA administrator, John Bartels, an affable former federal prosecutor, was bitterly resented by BNDD veterans loyal to their old boss, John Ingersoll. Criticized by nearly every element of the bureaucracy and by some influential members of Congress, Bartels was forced to resign in May 1975. He was replaced by Peter Bensinger, former executive director of the Chicago Crime Commission, an avid bureaucratic infighter and flamboyant publicist who courted journalists and congressmen but treated his subordinates curtly. The field men began joking that the agency's initials stood for "Don't Expect Anything."

The agency's morale sank even lower as narcotics officers realized that in many communities they were not even as highly regarded as sellers of marijuana and cocaine, who were able to bask in the reflected social status of the users. The DEA's targets were no longer "pushers," but "dealers" who served "clients." A particularly ingratiating salesman, who anticipated a customer's needs like a solicitous wine merchant, acquired the honorific title "my dealer," as in "my doctor," "my broker," "my lawyer." He was courted with tips, tickets, and invitations. Narcotics investigators, on the other hand, were not even welcome in neighborhood beer joints; bartenders complained they made the other customers nervous. Many DEA agents would not tell their neighbors what they did for a living, for fear their children would be teased or bullied by their playmates.

In September 1975, a Domestic Council Drug Abuse Task Force chaired by Vice President Nelson Rockefeller produced a "white paper" that would have a far-reaching impact on the bias against enforcing cocaine and marijuana laws. The report dismissed marijuana as a minor problem and stated flatly that "cocaine is not physically addictive."[12] The panel recommended that the DEA and U.S. Customs deemphasize investigations of marijuana and cocaine smugglers and give higher priority to heroin trafficking. That finding was acclaimed by a *Washington Post* editorial as "common sense . . . a welcome departure from the heroics of the past."[13]

If heroin was all the White House wanted to hear about, as far as Bensinger was concerned the DEA's priorities were clear: as an agent in San Diego put it, they were "heroin, heroin, and heroin." The emphasis represented a coup by the DEA's New York clique, which competed for money and people with offices in Miami, California, and Texas, where marijuana smuggling was prevalent and cocaine trafficking was on the rise.

"Bensinger had tunnel vision," said a Mexican-American agent who ran an office near the Mexican border in the 1960s and 1970s. "We had to make our priority heroin and it was nonnegotiable. God forbid that you didn't have your statistics up on heroin. The cocaine connection was evolving into one of the biggest multimillion-dollar violations we've ever seen. Washington's attitude was, We don't want to hear about cocaine." Bensinger's defenders said that he emphasized heroin for the same reason that Anslinger did: the political establishment wanted federal agents to stop the drugs that were the most addictive and toxic, not to attack those that were the most popular. At this time, they said, few members of the medical community expressed concern about the physical hazards of marijuana and cocaine.

———

Relations between the DEA and the White House sank to an all-time low during the tenure of Jimmy Carter. Carter immediately began slashing the drug-enforcement budget and on August 2, 1977, urged the Congress to abolish criminal penalties for the possession of up to an ounce of marijuana. The Georgia moderate did not approve of marijuana smoking but did not condemn those who did. During the 1976 presidential campaign, Rosalynn Carter told AP reporter Lynn Olson that all three of her sons had used marijuana. Jack, the Carters' eldest son, admitted on ABC's *Good Morning America* in 1977 that he was one of fifty-eight young seamen discharged from the Navy for smoking pot. Some of Carter's younger aides smoked pot during his presidential campaign and continued the practice while employed at the White House.[14]

Peter Bourne, a psychiatrist who served as Carter's adviser on drugs, held that "cocaine is probably the most benign of illicit drugs currently in widespread use." In 1974, Bourne wrote:

> At least as strong a case could probably be made of legalizing [cocaine] as for legalizing marijuana. Short acting—about 15 minutes—not physically addicting, and acutely pleasurable, cocaine has found increasing favor at all socioeconomic levels in the last year. Although it is capable of producing psychosis with heavy, repeated use, and chronic inhalers can suffer eventual erosion of the nasal membrane and cartilage, the number of people seeking treatment as a result of cocaine use is for all practical purposes zero. . . . One must ask what possible justification there can be for the obsession which DEA officials have with it, and what criteria they use to determine the priority they give the interdiction of a drug if it is not the degree of harm which it causes the user.[15]

Bourne was forced to resign in July 1978 after it was disclosed that he had written an illegal prescription for Quaaludes, a strong tranquilizer, for his twenty-five-year-old assistant.

In August 1979, the FBI launched a probe into charges that Hamilton Jordan, Carter's most intimate confidant, had used cocaine at Studio 54, a New York disco. The allegations were lodged by two New York disco owners who were attempting to make a plea bargain to avoid being charged with federal criminal tax violations. Justice Department officials did not want to pursue the case. It was almost impossible to charge a person with drug use if he had not been found in actual possession of illegal drugs. Furthermore, even when law-enforcement officers caught a user with drugs, if the defendant was not a significant distributor, he or she would normally be given a sentence of probation and sent to a drug-rehabilitation facility. Attorney General Griffin Bell eventually bent to political pressure and appointed one special prosecutor in the Jordan case and a second special prosecutor to investigate cocaine-possession charges lodged against Carter's appointments secretary, Tim Kraft. Neither investigation resulted in criminal charges.

President Carter himself seemed entirely uninterested in drug-abuse issues. In the fall of 1980, a DEA agent was invited to join a small group of politicians and White House aides who were making small talk with Carter between campaign stops. Carter noticed the large stranger and asked where he worked. "I work for you, sir," the agent said proudly, puffing out his chest. "For me? Where?" Carter asked. "For the DEA," the agent said. Carter stared at him blankly. "DEA," the agent prompted. "Drug Enforcement." Carter's expression changed from puzzlement to boredom. He turned away and began to chat with other guests about politics.

Ronald Reagan asserted at his first press conference in 1981 that he preferred education and prevention to tougher law-and-order measures. "It is my firm belief that the answer to the drug problem comes through winning over the users . . . it's far more effective if you take the customers away than if you try to take the drugs away from those who want to be customers." However, the president did little to further that goal until 1986. His rhetorical forays into the drug war were brief, triggered mostly by election-season polls in 1986 and 1988 that showed that the Democrats were planning to capitalize on his perceived inaction. For most of his presidency, Reagan did not put his personal prestige on the line for what his advisers believed was a lost cause. He left the business of promoting drug education to his wife, Nancy. Mrs. Reagan took the task seriously and became a heroine of the anti-drug movement with her "Just Say No" campaign, but she was not the Great Communicator. From time to time, Vice President George Bush championed the cause of drug interdiction, calling for a "new DEW line" against smugglers in the Caribbean, but he was never able to shake the image of a dilettante who used the issue to shore up his conservative credentials. The political leader who could truly claim to have been in the vanguard of the anti-drug movement was not a conservative at all but a liberal black Democrat, Jesse Jackson. In the mid-1970s, Jackson founded Operation Push, a program to motivate minority youths to break out of the underclass. The cornerstone of Operation Push was abstention from drugs, for Jackson understood that drug abuse was part of the cycle of poverty and dependence that defeated the aspirations of minorities for social and economic justice. Jackson was preaching to youthful audiences about the individual's responsibility for the drug-abuse epidemic for years before George Bush and Nancy Reagan discovered the issue.

On the international front, Ronald Reagan's stated policy of encouraging control of drugs at the source foundered upon the shoals of bureaucratic and diplomatic constraints. The battle against the Latin drug lords was inevitably intertwined with politics and diplomacy. It was of secondary importance, if not a downright threat, to multinational corporations, big banks, and their representatives at the Treasury Department, whose principal interest was sustaining cordial relations with Latin governments that owed U.S. lenders billions of dollars. Reagan himself was obsessed with Soviet and Cuban activism in the Third World. Secretary of State George Shultz and other Reagan foreign-policy advisers gave lower priority to suppressing drugs than to counteracting Cuban and Soviet influence and crushing leftist guerrilla movements in Central and South America. They were especially determined to maintain American influence in two strategically crucial Latin nations, despite evidence that the governments were repressive and riddled with corruption: Panama, home of the strategically vital Panama Canal and base for ten thousand American troops, and Mexico, the United States's third-largest trading partner and its largest source of imported oil.

Reagan could be zealous on the drug issue in one situation—when left-wing guerrillas or Marxist governments were thought to be running a drugs-for-guns trade. When DEA investigations implicated a few Nicaraguan and Cuban officials, Reagan cited these cases as proof of an international communist conspiracy.

But when DEA agents developed evidence of corruption in noncommunist countries willing to cooperate in resisting Cuban and Soviet intervention, Reagan was more than tolerant. "You have to recognize," he told a *Newsweek* interviewer who pressed him on the issue of cooperation with Mexico, "that some of these countries were limited in their means and their ability [and] their personnel in handling a problem as big as this. And it wouldn't do any good to punish them for not being able to do more. It would be up to us to find ways where there could be better cooperation and where we can all be helpful to each other."

Some called it pragmatism; others, hypocrisy. Whatever it was, it left Kiki Camarena and his partners profoundly disillusioned. They believed that the Mexican government did not care and the American government would rather not know about the corruption that advanced the drug trade in Mexico.

As their numbers dwindled and the sense of danger heightened, the agents in Guadalajara felt isolated and betrayed.

"Playing cops-and-robbers won't solve anything," Jaime Kuykendall would say over and over as if reciting a mantra. "It is a *political* problem. It requires a political solution."

The agents yearned to see the embassy, or, better yet, DEA headquarters, or, best of all, Reagan himself come down hard on President de la Madrid. If Mexico wanted loans and free trade, they reasoned, de la Madrid should show his goodwill by calling in the Army, throwing out governors, confiscating airplanes, freezing bank accounts—

by doing whatever it took to make the traffickers outlaws again. Policemen and agents could bust dopers until the end of time, but what good would that do? More would come. It was like sweeping the beach with a broom.

Nothing the little band of agents had said or done had seemed to matter. The American government's line to the public was set in stone: Mexico's campaign against drugs was a "model program." Relations between the DEA and the Mexican police were "excellent." The situation was under control.

U.S. Ambassador John Gavin, a conservative Republican appointed by Ronald Reagan, was vastly more outspoken about Mexico than most of the career diplomats who served in the embassy or in the Department of State's Bureau of Inter-American Affairs; yet in his speeches and interviews, he never hinted at the U.S. government's growing dissatisfaction with Mexico's anti-drug efforts until October 1984, after Roger Knapp's car was shot up. Much later, Gavin said he had thought it would do no good to criticize the Mexican government publicly. Besides, he said, drug trafficking was only one of many issues that diplomats of the two nations had to resolve. Gavin insisted that he had held discreet talks with high Mexican officials as early as 1982 and had warned that if the traffickers were allowed to expand their empires unchecked, Mexico would become another Colombia, terrorized by an underworld cartel with more economic, political, and military power than the central government possessed. DEA attaché Ed Heath agreed: "We have held their feet to the fire many times," he told a reporter in late 1985. "It has never been publicized."

Camarena's partners in Guadalajara said that neither Kiki nor they themselves ever knew that Gavin or Heath was making a strong argument to influential Mexican officials until just before Camarena disappeared: if high-level discussions *had* occurred, they said, they never saw any tangible results.

DFS officers suspected of corruption were not removed. MFJP *comandantes* did not display new fervor. And, as Kuykendall put it, "The traffickers weren't getting the word. They were doing whatever they damn well pleased."

When Kuykendall's forebears settled in Texas, the crooks who preyed on settlers in the frontier were called desperados. They lived life on the run because stealing a horse was a hanging offense. In this beautiful, dreamy, deadly city, the crooks were the hunters. Lawmen were the hunted. Kiki Camarena, Roger Knapp, Shaggy Wallace, Jaime Kuykendall, and all the other agents and policemen on the front lines—they were the desperate ones.

In the lonely twilights of February 1985, as he wondered whether his friend was still alive, Jaime Kuykendall was tormented by the memory of another twilight a few months before. He and Kiki had walked over to the Camelot bar after work to have a beer and kick some ideas around. Roger Knapp had just been pulled back to the States. Jaime swore and schemed. He was furious with headquarters and with Ed Heath, but he wanted to stay on in Guadalajara. He knew it sounded crazy. But, as he explained to mystified outsiders, "If you like to hunt elephants, you like to be where there are elephants. And here, there are elephants *everywhere*."

On that particular evening, as Jaime remembered, Kiki did not talk much. Finally, he looked at the big Texan with his bitter black eyes. "Jaime," he said, "it's time to go. We're way out front. And there's nobody behind us."

3

The Marijuana Border

Jaime Kuykendall remembered a time, years earlier, when he and his partners had truly believed that the United States government was behind them. It was during the twenty-one memorable days in 1969 when President Nixon took the unprecedented step of shutting down the U.S.–Mexican border to stem the tide of marijuana that was pouring in.

Acapulco gold was to the 1960s social revolution what bathtub gin was to the Jazz Age. Marijuana grew luxuriantly in many nations—Jamaica, Panama, Colombia, Morocco, Lebanon, India, Nepal, Thailand—but Mexico was a veritable cornucopia of pot. From the western slopes of the Sierra Madre to the green subtropical basin in Oaxaca, growing conditions were ideal. There were impassable natural barriers along just forty miles of the nineteen-hundred-mile land border between the United States and Mexico. The frontier already supported a thriving industry in the clandestine transportation of illicit commodities. For as long as the U.S. government had had trade restrictions, whatever Americans wanted, Mexican *contrabandistas* had or could get. During Prohibition, Mexico had whiskey. In the late 1920s and early 1930s, when cocaine became briefly fashionable, vials of the stuff arrived in Tijuana and Nuevo Laredo still bearing the trademarks of the French pharmaceutical houses from which they had been stolen.[1] When World War II disrupted the Mediterranean heroin trade, Mexican farmers planted opium. It was only natural that Americans who decided to tune in, turn on, and drop out would go to the Mexican *contrabandistas*.

The marijuana market developed first along Baja California's Pacific coast. Tijuana, the pleasure capital of Baja,

was just sixteen miles south of San Diego, a straight shot
down the broad Pacific Coast Highway that linked San
Diego, Los Angeles, and San Francisco. Beginning in
around 1965, Tijuana's red-light district swarmed with college kids, even high-school kids, looking to score marijuana.
At first they bought just enough for themselves. Before long,
youthful entrepreneurs were all over Baja California, southern Arizona, and South Texas, asking the *contrabandistas*
for hundred-pound lots. In 1964, Customs officials had
seized seven thousand pounds of pot in the United States,
mostly at the Mexican border. By 1968, Customs marijuana
seizures were up to sixty-five thousand pounds and there
was no end in sight. A survey done in 1972 for President
Richard Nixon's National Commission on Marihuana and
Drug Abuse concluded that twenty-four million Americans,
most of whom were between the ages of sixteen and twenty-
five, had used marijuana at least once. "Next to football,"
an overworked Customs official said in 1969, "white-collar
smuggling is becoming the national sport."

The Customs agents stationed along the Rio Grande were
a unique breed. They called themselves "border rats," taking as a badge of honor the disparaging term city-dwelling
Texans used for the gringos who lived in the frontier towns.
They were a far cry from the flashy Easterners who would
be fabled as narcotics detectives in the television dramas of
the 1980s. Ken Miley, a tall, laconic Louisianan, raised Ap-
paloosa horses in his spare time. Terry Bowen, who came
from San Antonio, worked the rodeo circuit on weekends.
Travis Kuykendall, who had the broad, ruddy face and wal-
rus mustache of a circuit-riding judge, trained many a
younger agent in the lore of the frontier. His brother, Jaime
Kuykendall, wiry and restless, might be found hanging
around some tumbledown joint, picking up gossip from the
locals while practicing his sharpshooting by aiming out the
saloon door at beer cans. They were loners and hunters who
lived for the chase. They scorned comfort and mocked ambition. To the border rats, hell on earth was a desk job in
Washington.

The man who embodied the virtues to which the border

rats aspired was Eugene Pugh, the special agent in charge
of the big U.S. Customs office in Laredo. Educated in the
Texas oil fields and the Arizona mines, Gene Pugh had the
coppery, creviced face, the piercing blue eyes, and the modest courage of a Henry Fonda cowboy. "He was what every
young boy wants to be and every old man wishes he had
been," said Travis Kuykendall. When the Kuykendall brothers were growing up in Eagle Pass, they liked to loll about
the main street, hoping for a glimpse of their hero, whom
they called "the Ghost" because he seemed to be everywhere and nowhere all at once.

Pugh had arrested more dope dealers than any of the
young agents had ever met and was proud that he had never
had to kill a man. The code of the West, still honored in
South Texas, held that excessive violence was not a manly
trait. Pugh abhorred the brutality of the Mexican police.
"For six years, I put a hundred twenty-five people in prison
a year, and none of them have come after me," he said. "I
used the Asiatic psychiatry. You don't make a man lose
face. If you treat him courteously and fairly, he will not be
an enemy. But if you abuse him, you'll have an enemy for
the rest of your life." By treating everyone with respect
Pugh developed a long string of sources, from bank tellers
to prostitutes.

"He never bragged on himself," Travis Kuykendall recalled. "He never had to. Years after he retired, I'd be
sitting at a horse race or having a beer in a bar, and somebody'd ease up and say, You know Eugenio Pugh? I used
to work for him."

Pugh understood that undercover work tempted a lawman to fall into the ways of the street. He admonished
younger agents to remember their values even when they
took off their badges. "A dope fiend has to have his dope
and he will do anything to get it," he said. "He cannot tell
you the truth because it's in his nature to lie. But you cannot
tell him one lie, because he will never trust you anymore.
To develop the confidence of the criminal element, you have
to have their respect. They'd like to be like you. They'd
like to be honest and upright. They will know when you're
lying. When you have a man working with you, he has to

respect you and obey you. You have to control him completely. Otherwise, the case will get out of hand, and it will
be an embarrassment because it will not be aboveboard.
You won't be able to differentiate between the criminals
and the officers."

In Gene Pugh's day, there were moral absolutes. The border rats reflected the values of the communities in which
they lived. There were good guys and bad guys, and law-
enforcement officers were the good guys. Their political
views were not questioned, and neither were their tactics.
If an agent yanked a suspect out of a truck, he was not likely
to be pilloried for police brutality. There was no sympathy
for the smugglers, who were social outcasts on both sides
of the border and who dealt mostly in heroin.

Marijuana changed everything. As it changed the children of the middle class, so it changed the border.

The 1960s arrived in South Texas in a Volkswagen van.
Beat-up vehicles with psychedelic decals driven by scraggly-
haired youths showed up at dives known to be favored by
smugglers. They found the way by word of mouth or through
guides in underground publications.[2] In their flowing Indian
cotton shirts and festooned jeans, city kids were hopelessly
conspicuous. A call would go out on the police radio: "Got
a bunch of long-haired hairy legs in Falcon." And the chase
would be on.

At that time, Jaime Kuykendall was stationed in Falcon
Heights, Texas, a hamlet astride one of the busiest smuggling routes in Texas. Falcon Heights, which was really only
a gas station and a saloon, was situated in Starr County, at
a point where the Rio Grande was neither grand nor much
of a river and could be easily traversed by rudimentary raft.
The insouciance of the new breed of college-educated smugglers astonished him, for he and his partners were accustomed to arresting witless wretches. "Kids in their early
twenties would buy cars with cash out of attaché cases,"
Kuykendall said. "They would set up a little company
among themselves and hire secretaries. They'd go into Mexico and make friends, and that would be the beginning of
the operation. We'd catch them with two hundred pounds

of marijuana, which was a lot for those days. Some of them had distribution operations back in their colleges, and they were shipping tons. Some of them got put in jail. Some of them got killed."

Ken Miley, Kuykendall's boss in Falcon Heights, remembered the day his world turned upside down. He had arrested a college student near Falcon Heights. "Long hair, beard down to his navel, sandals, dirty blue jeans, filthy," Miley recalled. "His car was loaded down, several hundred pounds of marijuana. Came time for trial, I didn't know the guy. Clean-shaven, white sidewall haircut, dressed up in a blue blazer, with the father and mother dressed up in business suits. The family was influential. They gave a plea before the court that he'd never do it again, and he got probation. It was the first time in my memory that anybody had gotten a suspended sentence in Brownsville, Texas, for a large load of marijuana."

One of the most remarkable organizations of this period was a group of young San Diegans who called themselves the Coronado Company. They started out as Coronado High School students, paddling small stashes of marijuana from Baja to San Diego on their surfboards in the mid-1960s. Enlisting one of their teachers, they graduated to state-of-the-art radio gear, fleets of trucks and off-loading equipment, and a yacht with a satellite navigational system; by the time the DEA broke up the ring, their operations extended from South America and Mexico to Thailand; they had been in business for nearly twenty years and had accumulated more than $100 million.

The clever young gringos with their bags of cash brought joy to the cantinas of the border towns. "It was like Robin Hood coming," said Miley. "Pancho Villa made them believe in Robin Hood."[3]

The frontier villages had always been ruled by the law of the dollar. It was no accident that northern Mexico was the center of the nation's most conservative, most fervently antisocialist political movements. Poverty was severe everywhere in Mexico, but for the people of the north, the daily struggle to survive was an especially bitter lot. They had only to walk across a bridge to see for themselves the luxuries that even working-class Americans enjoyed. While poor people in southern Mexico and in other Latin nations turned to the political left, the people of the border turned capitalist and cynical.

"All the United States is to Mexico," Jaime Kuykendall would observe, "is a rich, fat whore who *wants* to be plundered."

The border smugglers could smell money the way drilling engineers smelled oil. They comprehended immediately the meaning of the cavalcade of vans and sent word back to their suppliers, who were small farmers down in Sonora and Sinaloa. The farmers expanded their plantings of marijuana. Marijuana fever, heady as a gold rush, spread deep into Mexico, to Durango, Jalisco, Nayarit and Guerrero, then to Veracruz and Oaxaca on the Guatemalan border, then to Quintana Roo and Campeche on the Yucatán peninsula. Farmers sowed marijuana wherever it would grow. They brought their harvest to town on donkeys and sold it to middlemen for about four dollars a kilogram. This was a paltry sum by northern standards, but a peasant could make a thousand dollars a year in this fashion, and for people used to living on less than a dollar a day, that was a fortune. The border smugglers reserved the big profit margins for themselves; they could sell a kilogram block of dried marijuana leaves for seventy-five to one hundred dollars. Border towns like Falcon Heights blossomed. People who had counted themselves lucky to own a few goats and chickens suddenly had new cars and trucks, new houses and television sets. This was economic development that had been promised, but never delivered, by Lyndon Johnson's Great Society.

Where money was to be made, violence followed. Dozens of new trafficking organizations sprang up along the border. The established *contrabandista* families went after these wildcatters with every gun in their considerable arsenals. Jaime Kuykendall remembered sitting in cantinas, listening to the bursts of machine-gun fire in the night.

Just when the border agents felt most embattled, Richard Nixon took office.

Nixon had campaigned against "permissiveness" in the society and had promised to do something about crime.[4] His aides quickly discovered that the federal government had little to say about the enforcement of laws against violent crime, for these were the province of big-city police departments. Nixon did not want to give urban police departments more money because most of the big-city mayors were Democrats. The only federal laws that seemed to touch on street crime were related to drug trafficking. Nixon decided that heroin addiction was largely responsible for street crime and announced he would reduce the supply of heroin in the United States.[5] Yet Nixon's first actions had no connection to heroin and little to do with street crime but, rather, focused on marijuana, whose popularity was packing the jails with college kids.

In June 1969, Deputy Attorney General Richard Kleindienst, a Tucson lawyer with four children and a strong antipathy to pot, went to Mexico City to try to convince the Mexican government to go after the smugglers' sanctuaries. The Mexican officials were cordial but noncommittal. Kleindienst grew visibly annoyed as he realized that the sessions were, in the words of an aide, "just an exercise in hospitality." The communiqué the Mexicans were willing to sign amounted, in Kleindienst's opinion, to the usual platitudes. He concluded that the Mexican government did not have the political will to take on the powerful smuggling families.

Upon his return to Washington, Kleindienst told his boss, Attorney General John Mitchell, "I can tell you how you can get their attention. Just close down the border." Mitchell grunted an assent. And that was how Operation Intercept was born.

Kleindienst did not actually propose to shut the Southwest border. The Customs Service would simply go by the book, exercising its authority to inspect all the traffic coming out of Mexico. Normally, Customs inspectors waved nineteen out of twenty vehicles through the lines. Subjecting every car and truck to a three-minute inspection would clog the lanes, causing fruit and vegetables loaded for American markets to rot and tourists heading to Mexico to change their minds and go elsewhere. The policy would have severe economic repercussions on Mexico's northern states, which were heavily dependent on tourist and trade dollars. The idea was to prod Mexican businessmen interested in normal commercial relations between the two countries to put pressure on the Mexican government to take the anti-drug effort more seriously.

Kleindienst planned the border war with the help of Eugene Rossides, a pugnacious former professional football player–turned–lawyer who, as assistant secretary of the treasury for enforcement, was in charge of Customs. Customs agents were solely responsible for stopping smuggling along the Southern border, while the Bureau of Narcotics and Dangerous Drugs concentrated its personnel in the Northeastern cities to work heroin conspiracy cases.

John Mitchell had little trouble persuading the president of the merits of the plan. Nixon was exasperated with the Mexican government's constant shifting of the blame for the drug problem to U.S. consumers and was not a man to be trifled with. Nixon chose to break the news about Operation Intercept to the Mexican president, Gustavo Díaz Ordaz, in a particularly humiliating manner. On September 8, he met Díaz Ordaz on the border to dedicate Amistad— "Friendship"—Dam, which spanned the Rio Grande near Del Rio, Texas, and Ciudad Acuña, Mexico. Díaz Ordaz must have felt anything but friendship as he was informed that cadres of armed Americans were about to mass along his northern border for the largest peacetime search-and-seizure operation in North American history.

Operation Intercept began on September 21. Tijuana was declared off limits to uniformed U.S. servicemen. Uniformed Customs inspectors scrutinized—"tossed," in the jargon—every vehicle and pedestrian that appeared at border crossings from the Pacific coast to the Gulf of Mexico.

The U.S. Army set up mobile radar units from San Diego to El Paso. Travis Kuykendall went to Animas Valley in New Mexico to run the Customs border air force, which consisted of three small planes rented for the occasion. They were supposed to intercept marijuana-laden aircraft heading north out of Sonora. It was a largely frustrating exercise, since the radar did not see deep enough into Mexico to give the Customs pilots time to scramble.

Jaime Kuykendall, Ken Miley, and hundreds of other Customs agents and Border Patrol officers lay on the north bank of the Rio Grande night after night, forming a human barrier against smugglers sneaking through the brush. Two decades later, the agents who participated in this exercise could recall those nights vividly. They would settle down on the cool dirt of the riverbank and stare out into Mexico, strain to see the shadows move or to discern the sounds of scuffling feet. They pressed themselves into hollows, striving for invisibility, calculating whether they were being approached by armed men or only "burros," peasants paid a few dollars to lug a bale of marijuana or a little heroin. The Customs men shared a horror of shooting one of those sad creatures; the frontier's wanton cruelties would deal with them soon enough.

"It was like waking up every day in a dark room with a rattlesnake," Miley said. "You try to get to the light switch before the rattlesnake gets to you. And the rattlesnake moves every night."

There were magnificent nights when the moon glowed orange as a persimmon and the Milky Way was a streak of hammered silver, and miserable nights when the rain came down in sheets and the agents would shiver and curse under leaky tarpaulins, hoping that the cold tedium would be disrupted by a few moments of acute danger.

Terry Bowen left Falcon Heights for the lonely reaches of Big Bend National Park, where, as the only lawman within sixty miles, he patrolled the canyons on horseback looking for marijuana caravans. One night, he came upon six riders escorting a caravan of forty-four real burros loaded down with four tons of contraband. It looked as if he might be on the verge of making the seizure of his career, but his find was not marijuana at all but wax, a substance prized for furniture polish, which was made from the candelilla plant, native to the Chihuahua desert. Wax making was a government monopoly, so the peasants evaded controls by smuggling the stuff through Big Bend. To the great amusement of his fellow border rats, Bowen seized the caravan and then spent two weeks sleeping in the corral with the livestock, gun at the ready, fending off Mexican Forestales, game wardens, who were trying to rustle the horses, until the confiscated animals could be auctioned off. Thus he assured that the U.S. government would reap the handsome sum of $1.14 for each burro, $20 for each of five horses, and $25 for the party's lone mule.

The agents had few seizures to show for their troubles: all but the dumbest and greediest *contrabandistas* kept to their cantinas, waiting out Nixon's anger as they would wait out a thunderstorm.

Yet for all the disappointments, mistakes, and pressure to produce, the border agents would remember Operation Intercept as their finest moment. Finally, they thought, there was a president who recognized that one big law-and-order problem was festering in no-man's-land. Never before, and never again, did they feel a stronger sense of purpose. "I think we all actually believed that the administration intended to wipe out the narcotics problem," Travis Kuykendall said wistfully. "And we wanted to be part of the effort." "We weren't looking at the big picture," Jaime Kuykendall said. "We thought we were doing a great job by arresting all these bad guys. We thought everybody was on our side. We had a lot of freedom and a lot of authority. We never went to see a John Wayne movie because he never did anything near as exciting as what we were doing, I guarantee you. John Wayne would have been proud of us."

Intercept wreaked more economic havoc than its architects dared hope. On Tijuana's Avenida Presidente López Mateos, sixteen lanes of vehicles inched toward the gateway to Southern California. Mexicans with U.S. work permits were unable to get to their jobs. Mexican tomatoes and peppers spoiled as trucks idled in the sun. Expenditures in Mexico by American visitors dropped by as much as 70 percent.

The mood in Mexico was bellicose. Díaz Ordaz deplored the "wall of suspicion" that had descended between the two nations. The Mexican Confederation of National Chambers of Commerce launched a counterattack called Operation Dignity, which exhorted Mexican citizens not to cross the border. One Mexican newspaper ran a political cartoon portraying U.S. lawmen as Gestapo agents manhandling a Mexican official. U.S. State Department officials responsible for executing U.S. foreign policy toward Mexico privately deplored Nixon's actions. "We support the intentions of our government," an official at the U.S. embassy in Mexico City said. "But, well, we have strong opinions about this. It stinks."

The economic repercussions spread to the American side. Mexican citizens stopped crossing the border to shop. "Our housewives are getting very angry at being searched like criminals," fumed an official in Baja California. "Business isn't bad, it's dead and gone," said an Arizona shopkeeper as he surveyed his empty aisles. Since the administration had refused to admit that the purpose of Operation Intercept was not to seize drugs but to exert economic pressure on Mexico, the failure of the agents to make large seizures inspired derision on both sides of the border.

As the mood in the Southwest soured, the interagency group in charge of Intercept gathered in Richard Kleindienst's paneled office in the Justice Department. Someone suggested that Washington send an emissary, a sort of unofficial ambassador to the border, to travel around, thank the merchants for their noble self-sacrifice, and rally community spirit in the cause of saving America's young.

Gene Rossides offered the services of his assistant, a former FBI agent by the name of G. Gordon Liddy. Kleindienst had never met Gordon Liddy before, but he trusted his friend Rossides and agreed that Liddy should handle the delicate mission.

Kleindienst was mildly surprised when Liddy leaped to his feet, practically saluted, and rushed from the room. The deputy attorney general soon learned that this strange character, with his rigid stance, darting sparrow's eyes, and zealous advocacy of police power, was not exactly the diplomatic type. Liddy had quit the FBI on the grounds that it was soft on crime. The Texas border was a hotbed of Republican conservatism; even so, Liddy managed to offend nearly everyone he met.

"Within thirty hours, I had to send a U.S. marshal to

bring him back," Kleindienst recalled. "Instead of calming
the border down, Liddy was throwing gasoline on it. He
was just the wrong type of personality to be an ameliorative
influence."

After seventeen chaotic days, the Mexican government
had had enough. President Díaz Ordaz sent Deputy Attorney General Franco David Rodríguez to Washington to negotiate an end to the border searches. Kleindienst, Rossides,
and a State Department team spent three days with the
Mexican delegation, "yelling and screaming," as Kleindienst put it. On October 10, the negotiators struck a compromise: Nixon would end Operation Intercept, in exchange
for which Díaz Ordaz would agree to a joint effort called
Operation Cooperation. American agents would be stationed in Mexico with the right to conduct surveillance of
poppy and marijuana fields. The Mexicans would put together a program to attack the marijuana trade.

When Operation Intercept was called off, the marijuana
merchants ended their strategic retreat. Before long, they
were making more money than ever. The Mexican government had no efficient means of eradicating the marijuana
fields: aerial spraying was unknown, so what eradication
occurred was done by hand. Neither the small contingent
of agents from the Bureau of Narcotics and Dangerous
Drugs who were assigned to the American embassy in Mexico City nor the larger force of Customs men stationed along
the Southwest border could keep up with marijuana fever.

"The traffickers got the message for a little while that we
were serious, and they slowed down," Jaime Kuykendall
said long afterward. "But it didn't last. We quit showing
them we were serious, so they figured everything was hunky-
dory. They saw right through us, and they went around
behind us."

As the marijuana trade escalated, Nixon cut his losses and
forgot about it. Nobody on the left and hardly anybody in
the political middle wanted a marijuana war. The country
was being ripped asunder by race wars, age wars, class wars,
and the Vietnam War. In 1972, Nixon faced an extremely
divisive reelection campaign against George McGovern, the

anti-war senator from South Dakota. The Republicans were a minority party and needed the votes of middle-of-the-road Democrats who were put off by McGovern's liberal ideology but feared Nixon's "madman" image.

Nixon toned down law-and-order rhetoric that might be interpreted as anti-youth and anti-black and focused on heroin. The merchants of heroin were easy enemies. Black voters disapproved of heroin as vehemently as whites. Parents of all races and political persuasions shared a common anxiety, that their children would "graduate" to heroin. Nixon knew well how to manipulate that fear. At a State Department narcotics control conference on September 18, 1972, he recast his drug strategy as a "total war" on heroin, a "crusade to save our children."[6]

Nixon could claim some genuine accomplishments in the heroin war. In June 1971, under threat of losing U.S. military and economic assistance, Turkish Prime Minister Nihat Erim agreed to ban all poppy cultivation in his country after the harvesting of the 1972 crop. French authorities were beginning to crack down on the Corsican labs in Marseilles after they discovered that French youths were taking the drug. The BNDD and the Customs Service were making some impressive scores in investigations directed at the French Connection traffickers.

However, the inroads on the heroin trade had little to do with "saving" the children of the middle class from illegal drugs. Few marijuana users were really experimenting with heroin. Those who "graduated" usually moved to amphetamines ("speed"), hypnotics ("downers"), hallucinogens such as peyote and LSD, and cocaine. Such so-called soft drugs were freely available on college campuses across the United States.

In the battle to stop the drugs American young people used, Nixon's "total war" was no more successful than his "limited war" in the jungles of Southeast Asia. Traffickers swarmed across the Mexican border bearing marijuana, hallucinogens, uppers, downers, cocaine—anything affluent young Americans wanted.

Operation Intercept had taught the smugglers a valuable

lesson. "It caused the smugglers to learn to use airplanes," said Ken Miley. "They started hiring pilots. And the loads got bigger."

Operation Intercept taught Washington lessons of another sort. Intercept proved that it was not within an American president's power to sustain even a marginally effective interdiction effort. A permanent Operation Intercept was neither practical nor desirable: even short-term actions carried an economic and political price that most politicians and senior bureaucrats considered unacceptably high. Few American or Mexican citizens understood that the purpose of Operation Intercept was to exert economic pressure on Mexico. Consequently, the absence of large seizures was perceived as failure. White House officials antagonized the press by overselling the project. Even Kleindienst did not urge Nixon to repeat the experiment.

If interdiction was doomed to fail, that left two possibilities for reducing the supply of drugs available in the underground marketplace. The administration could place more emphasis on internal enforcement, ordering more investigations of drug rings and arrests of distributors within the United States. And it could press Mexico and other drug-producing nations to undertake more extensive eradication of illicit crops at the source.

There were obstacles to both approaches. As the border rats had discovered, it was one thing to attack heroin rings aggressively and quite another thing to go after middle-class college students or even professional smugglers who were distributing marijuana. The reluctance of judges to hand out substantial sentences to marijuana smugglers led most U.S. attorney's offices to decline marijuana-smuggling cases as a waste of time. Not that more aggressive prosecution would have mattered: by 1972, the sheer size of the middle-class market for marijuana, hallucinogens, and pills guaranteed that there would be more smugglers than American lawmen could possibly find.

Few politicians and senior officials had the courage to admit that American law enforcement could not control the nation's streets and borders. To the contrary, government officials at all levels fell into the habit of exaggerating successes and pretending progress was being made, while the lawmen on the frontline knew that they were losing ground.

Consequently, officials regularly inflated the importance of major narcotics seizures and hushed up failed operations. In June 1970, for instance, agents of the Bureau of Narcotics and Dangerous Drugs boasted that an East Coast investigation named Operation Eagle had mopped up a gang that was supposedly moving 80 percent of the cocaine in the United States. Five months later, New York police officials claimed *they* had arrested the ringleader of a gang that controlled 90 percent of the cocaine market. As would be evident in coming years, neither arrest had any impact on the cocaine trade. Similarly specious claims were being made about various operations aimed at heroin traffickers.

If enforcement was no more promising than interdiction, what was left? Eradication. For the Nixon administration and much of Congress, "going to the source" was the magic bullet. And that strategy placed severe constraints on candor. Having made a decision to seek the cooperation of foreign governments, American policymakers effectively agreed to keep quiet about the shortcomings of their allies. Corruption was not discussed in large interagency groups, let alone in public. A 1972 federal heroin-smuggling indictment filed against Moisés Torrijos Herrera, the brother of Panamanian strongman General Omar Torrijos Herrera, was sealed. Justice prosecutors kept secret a stack of allegations of corruption lodged by informants against the man who would replace Torrijos, Colonel Manuel Antonio Noriega, then head of G-2, Panamanian military intelligence and the Central Intelligence Agency's closest contact in Panama. In Mexico, Operation Cooperation, the successor to Operation Intercept, produced no perceptible results, but Richard Nixon never again questioned the Mexican government's commitment to his "war on drugs."

Professional lawmen like John Ingersoll, the director of the Bureau of Narcotics and Dangerous Drugs, argued that there was a fourth option: education. They realized that it was deception or self-delusion for anyone to make extravagant claims, that no solution to reduce the supply of drugs would work as long as American middle-class demand for drugs spiraled upward. Since no one in Washington could figure out how to compel, persuade, or teach the 1960s generation anything, the idea sank like a stone.

4
New Treasures of the Sierra Madre

"**A**mapola," the old man sang.

> *My pretty little poppy.*
> *You're like a lovely flower,*
> *So sweet and heavenly.*

Pretty poppy, the red-skirted lady who put silver in the pockets of those mountain men, who kept this shack of a cantina merry, who fed this poor singer—yes, she deserved a love song.

Mexican brown heroin, called Mexican mud, was a last resort for East Coast addicts. But in 1973, that was what it came down to. When the French Connection was broken as a result of the 1972 Turkish opium ban and a series of successful busts by American and French agents, narcotics agents manning wiretaps in New York heard panicky heroin dealers calling all over the country looking for new sources. In September 1973, Nixon declared, "We have turned the corner."[1] Nixon's boast became a great joke among the drug agents. "Yeah, we turned the corner," they would say. "And there was an *army* coming."[2]

The Turkish opium brought the producers and consumers three thousand miles closer together. Heroin smugglers no longer needed a boat or a plane. Any old rusted-out Chevrolet would do. The federal agencies were faced with new players, new routes, new methods—and more of everything. By 1974, the DEA estimated, Mexican traffickers controlled three quarters of the United States heroin market.

"You used to get a hundred kilos coming in on the East Coast docks, packed into a Citroën," mourned a DEA agent in Chicago in 1976. "Now you got maybe nine pounds a whack stuffed into the drive shaft or gas tank of a beat-up car driven across the border by a woman with a bunch of kids."

The peaks of the Sierra Madre Occidental caught the wet gusts from the Pacific Ocean and made the long coastal plain the richest agricultural region in the Republic of Mexico. The area between the ocean and the ridge of the Sierra Madre was the state of Sinaloa, whose capital, Culiacán, was a major hub for the marketing, packing, and shipping of commodities like tomatoes and cucumbers. When the marijuana boom took off, many farmers began raising that commodity as well. Sinaloa's agricultural bounty, legal and illegal, was trucked north on Highway 15, the great north–south artery that stretched from Guadalajara through Culiacán to the Arizona line.

East of the ridge of the Sierra Madre lay the state of Durango. The mountains leveled off to an arid high plateau, which was called "the Land of the Scorpion" because it was the habitat of the rare and lethal white scorpion. Durango was populated mostly by prospectors seeking gold and silver and by employees of big mining companies that exploited the rich deposits of copper, tin, and iron.

For centuries, the people of the highlands in Sinaloa and Durango had reaped little of the wealth that blessed the lowlanders. Neither farmers nor miners, they lived and died in thatched huts miles from paved roads, subsisting on corn and beans and small game, counting themselves fortunate to own a cow and a few chickens. The anti-opium agreement between Washington and Ankara was a curious turn of fate for these people: one of the few plants that grew well on their poor hillsides was the opium poppy.

Poppies had been introduced to the Sierra Madre early in the century by Chinese railroad workers. During World War II, the Mexican government legalized opium production to meet the demand of the U.S. military for morphine.

In the 1950s and 1960s, the *gomeros*—gum makers, as the opium poppy growers were called—made a modest living producing brown heroin for addicts in the barrios of Los

Angeles, Houston, and Phoenix. By the 1970s the opium families were well established. Opium growing was once again condemned by the central government in Mexico City and by the Catholic Church, but such edicts were meaningless in the trackless highlands. "We're dealing with a population," an American intelligence officer assigned to Mexico once observed, "that regards the government as just another natural catastrophe. Morality and concepts of good citizenship simply do not enter into this."

The central government mounted sporadic eradication drives, marching sullen troops into the mountains to swat half-grown poppies with sticks and machetes. Since most of the plots were tiny, well hidden, and two or three days' walk from any road, such expeditions were fruitless.

Many people made fortunes dealing Mexican mud, but one man became a legend: Jaime Herrera Nevares, the leathery patriarch of the huge clan that came from the mountaintop village of Los Herreras, Durango. Jaime Herrera was born in Los Herreras in 1927, one of eight brothers and four sisters. Shortly after World War II, he and his brothers saw the potential for Mexican heroin and founded a refining and distribution network. The first laboratory was in Los Herreras. Jaime Herrera ran it and shipped the finished product to brothers, cousins, and nephews who had moved to Chicago. By the mid-1960s, when the Federal Bureau of Narcotics began keeping records on the family, it dominated the heroin distribution system in Chicago and the Midwest. When the French Connection was broken, the Herreras had a number of laboratories and were poised to supply East Coast dealers with all the heroin they needed.

The Herreras had two advantages over other traffickers: numbers and political power. They had intermarried and produced numerous children and grandchildren, so that by the 1980s the organization was thought to consist of some two thousand blood relations and another three thousand associates. Jaime Herrera Nevares himself married twice, the second time to a cousin named Herrera, and fathered nine children. A son of the second union, Jaime Herrera Herrera, "Jaimillo," seemed destined to succeed his father as the leader of the family. Law-enforcement officers found it extremely difficult to penetrate the organization with informants or undercover agents because family members controlled the whole heroin process, "farm to arm." Older members of the family stayed in the hills, acquired opium gum through a kind of sharecropping system, and ran hundreds of processing centers. Younger family members lived along the pipeline, in Ciudad Juárez, across the Rio Grande from El Paso, or in Chicago. The clan moved heroin north by simple methods, by car and truck, hiding the cargo in spare tires, drive shafts, or hidden compartments in gas tanks. DEA analysts estimated that the Chicago Herreras were grossing $60 million a year by 1978 and had established branches in Denver, Los Angeles, Miami, and Pittsburgh.

Jaime Herrera Nevares assured political protection for the clan's activities by buying off politicians and law-enforcement officials not only in Durango but along the border and probably in Mexico City. From 1966 to 1976, he wore the badge of a Durango State Judicial Police officer.

By investing family profits in legitimate businesses, Herrera became a mainstay of the regional economy. According to DEA records, Herrera Nevares owned at least three houses in Durango and another house in Guadalajara, a ten-thousand-acre cattle ranch and colonial hacienda twenty-five miles northwest of Durango, a truck stop between Mazatlán and Durango, two hotels, a construction company, a disco, a bowling alley, an automobile repair shop, and possibly an aviation company in Durango.

Don Jaime, as the patriarch was called, lived the life of a *padrone,* a country squire. He gave to the poor, befriended the rich, and played the godfather at weddings and baptisms. In the village of Santiago Papasquiaro, where many of the opium farmers lived, the clan built the water system, installed streetlights, and created a town square. Three hospitals reportedly benefited from the clan's philanthropy. It is not enough to say that Jaime Herrera bought off the power structure. He *was* the power structure. As an internal DEA intelligence report put it: "Herreras are and have been chiefs of police at the town and municipal levels, directors of state police, mayors, and police agents in every law-enforcement agency. Those who reportedly respond to the Herreras have been [high officials in the state of Durango]. Jaime Herrera himself is said to encourage bright young men to pursue political careers.''[3]

The Herreras killed opponents when necessary but did not indulge in mindless violence. The family's total control of the heroin-trafficking industry in Durango assured civil calm, for there were no rival gangs to stage bloody turf battles.

Across the Sierra Madre in Sinaloa, where smuggling rings competed ferociously, savage shoot-outs were a daily occurrence. The dominant figure in the Sinaloa underworld was Pedro Aviles Pérez, a gunslinger who burst upon the scene in the late 1960s. Aviles, born in 1940, started out smuggling heroin to Southern California and Arizona, but unlike the Herrera family, he quickly branched out into the "recreational drug" market, moving marijuana in ten-ton loads. Well ahead of his time, Aviles made connections in South America and dealt in multiple kilograms of cocaine.

The Aviles network snaked from Culiacán to Mexicali and Tijuana. Many of the second-generation Sinaloa traffickers who became kingpins in the 1980s learned the business at the feet of Aviles. When he was twelve or thirteen, Rafael Caro Quintero apprenticed himself to Aviles and worked his way up to be the gang's foreman in Chihuahua. Ernesto Fonseca, Aviles's "treasurer," handled the ring's money and investments.

When he was not in Sinaloa, Aviles lived in the town of San Luis Río Colorado, a doleful Sonora village just over the line from Yuma. In 1973, Phil Jordan, a young Mexican American who ran the DEA Phoenix office, persuaded MFJP Comandante Florentino Ventura to raid Aviles's San Luis mansion. The Mexican officers found twenty-five tons of pot, as well as a quantity of heroin and cocaine, but Aviles himself had been tipped off and sped away just before the police arrived. Jordan later heard that Aviles, annoyed at the inconvenience, had put a ten-thousand-dollar bounty on his head. "It should have been twenty thousand," Jordan laughed.

The third great trafficker of this era was Alberto Sicilia Falcón. A flamboyant bisexual Cuban who started out as a street hustler in Miami, Sicilia Falcón had made his way from Miami to Mexico City, where he struck the fancy of a queen of the demimonde who moved with the jet set crowd and introduced pretty girls to men of property. This woman of the world took Alberto under her wing, dressed him up like a playboy, and taught him class. He acquired a horse-breeding ranch and rubbed shoulders with the elite from Acapulco to Madrid.

Sicilia Falcón kept himself in Rolls Royces by pioneering the first major overland cocaine connection from South America through Mexico City, Guadalajara, and Tijuana to Los Angeles. He formed partnerships with some established Mexican marijuana and heroin traffickers such as Pedro Aviles and made contacts in South America for cocaine. He bought off MFJP officers in Guadalajara and Tijuana and moved cocaine and marijuana up the West Coast corridor into Los Angeles.[4]

In late 1973, DEA agents in Los Angeles formed a squad, called a central tactical unit, dedicated to tracing the tentacles of Sicilia Falcón's organization from Mexico through the United States and into Europe. By 1978, the agents had arrested about four hundred people connected with the American distribution network.

Sicilia Falcón was arrested by the MFJP in July 1975. He would be the last major trafficker to be jailed in Mexico for a substantial length of time until 1985. But Sicilia Falcón was not a Mexican. He was a Cuban, a sexual aberrant, and the DEA had harangued the Mexicans relentlessly to bring him in. Once jailed, he continued to run his organization from his cell.

According to DEA agents, one of Sicilia Falcón's enforcers was Manuel Salcido Uzeta, who was called Cochi Loco, "Crazy Pig," on account of his viciousness. After Sicilia Falcón was jailed, Cochi Loco became the drug lord of the coastal city of Mazatlán in Sinaloa and went on to make a name for himself as a member of the Guadalajara cartel. Another Sicilia Falcón associate who would become a leader in the international cocaine trade was a young Honduran

chemist named Juan Ramón Matta Ballesteros, who had
helped the Cuban establish sources of supply in the Andes.
When Sicilia Falcón was arrested, Matta Ballesteros struck
up a partnership with Miguel Angel Félix Gallardo, then a
Culiacán heroin trafficker who aspired to learn the cocaine
trade. With the help of Matta's cocaine connections in Colombia, among them Medellín magnate Pablo Escobar, Félix Gallardo would outdistance even Jaime Herrera Nevares
in terms of wealth and political power.

The small band of DEA agents in Mexico at this time were
the first to sense the Mexican heroin boom. One of these
men was Ed Heath. In late 1973 and early 1974, Heath and
his partners went out into the field to assess the eradication
campaign that was supposed to have followed Nixon's Operation Intercept. They found that poppy cultivation had
spread well beyond the Mexican Golden Triangle, as the
Sinaloa-Durango-Chihuahua highlands were called, to Michoacán, Jalisco, and Guerrero. Once seasonal, opium harvesting was now going on all year long.

The agents concluded that the Mexican Army's eradication drive was worse than useless. Troops were working
under "unbearable conditions" that bred corruption. Sent
into the field without provisions, they were forced to live
off the local farmers, who used small bribes of food and
clothing to buy time to harvest their illicit fields. The first
draft of a DEA study produced in the field around this time
concluded that the eradication campaign was "a vicious
cycle of incompetence, apathy, and corruption." The draft
study was so blunt that DEA officials in Washington had it
rewritten to pacify Mexican government officials who had
seen and objected to the original version. The final report
contained only a vague mention of "certain deficiencies that
require strengthening in future campaigns."[5]

The agents began to press DEA headquarters and the
Mexican Attorney General's Office to institute an aerial
spraying program. Congressman Charles Rangel, who visited Sinaloa in 1975, also advocated broad-scale spraying,
arguing that nothing less could cover the large area under
cultivation. An advantage of spraying, as the agents saw

things, was that it was not so prone to corruption as interdiction and enforcement, which brought policemen face-to-face with rich, well-armed smugglers. Spraying hurt small farmers who had neither influence nor means to suborn or terrorize pilots dispatched from Mexico City.

Mexican Attorney General Pedro Ojeda Paullada resisted the idea on environmental grounds. The newspapers were full of horror stories about the aftereffects of Agent Orange, the defoliant that the U.S. military had sprayed in Vietnam. The American embassy pressed Ojeda Paullada to consider the herbicide 2,4-D, which was already being used by Mexican farmers for other crops. Eventually he agreed.

President Luis Echeverría Alvarez was receptive, a surprising turn of events considering that his foreign policy was stridently leftist and anti-American. Some Americans thought that Echeverría aspired to be secretary-general of the United Nations and did not want to be seen as the leader of the world's foremost heroin-producing country. Other Mexico-watchers thought that Echeverría, who was engaged in a ruthless campaign of repression against political dissidents, acted out of fear that disaffected villagers in the hinterland would use heroin and marijuana to buy arms.

When Echeverría agreed to initiate an aerial spraying program, the U.S. State Department turned on the money pump. Within two and a half years, the Mexican Attorney General's Office would own thirty-nine Bell helicopters, twenty-two small fixed-wing aircraft, and one executive jet—the largest civilian air fleet in Latin America. The buildup, launched in November 1975, required a heavy American presence. Evergreen International Aviation, Inc., an Oregon firm whose pilots, most Vietnam veterans, were known for their skill at maneuvering in dangerous back-country conditions, was hired by the Mexican government to fly the helicopters until Mexican pilots could be trained. Two dozen DEA agents went into the Sierra Madre, most of them pilots who flew DEA spotter planes. They sighted poppy fields, relayed the coordinates back to the helicopter fleet, and verified afterward that the fields had been sprayed. The Mexican government named the eradication cam-

paign Operation Condor. The DEA called its end of the
project Operation Trizo, short for "tri-zone." The Mexicans
and Americans worked well together—not because they
trusted one another, but because each side got exactly what
it wanted. The Mexican government got free favorable publicity. American officials proclaimed Operation Condor/
Trizo "a model program" and took reporters on escorted
tours in an effort to encourage leaders of other nations to
launch similar campaigns.

In 1976, Anthony Marro, then a correspondent for *Newsweek* magazine, described Dr. Alejandro Gertz Manero,
Ojeda's eradication director, dressed to kill, cameramen in
tow, descending upon the field owned by some hapless
peasant:

> Gertz Manero, wearing a brown leather jacket, a purplish-
> red ascot, and sun glasses, and cradling his own M-16,
> stepped onto the field. With an eye toward the cameras
> clicking away, he stood erect in the midst of the swaying
> green field, then reached down and plucked one of the pop-
> pies that was still in blossom. . . . He sniffed it, then raised
> his automatic rifle in one hand and waved with his other to
> motion his men (and the reporters) back to the helicopter.
> . . . "I don't want [the pilots] to tell me how many they
> destroyed," he said. "I just want them to tell me they de-
> stroyed them all."

As its part of the bargain, the Mexican government gave
the DEA freedom of the skies. "We flew every inch of the
country and we knew what they were doing and what was
there," said Jerry Kelly, a DEA pilot who flew verification
flights over the Sinaloa poppy fields. "It didn't matter who
was corrupt. There was no way they could hide what was
going on."

Travis Kuykendall was in charge of DEA operations in
Culiacán in 1974 and 1975. The Mexican press had nicknamed the city "Little Chicago" because of the frequent
disputes among the many gangs that cropped up as the heroin and marijuana businesses grew. At night, Kuykendall
would lie in his hotel room and listen to the machine guns

going off in Colonia Tierra Blanca, the neighborhood where the traffickers lived. They were always squabbling about something, and when they argued, everybody else hit the bricks. There were shoot-outs at weddings and at funerals. Sometimes there were shoot-outs in the hotel where the agents were lodged. On the roadside were little shrines to dead traffickers. The funerals of prominent smugglers were great social events, with bands and mountains of flowers.

When the Mexican authorities finally cracked down, they did so with characteristic brutality aimed mainly at lower-level suspects, while most of the major players were untouched. In 1976, when Culiacán's murder rate hit four a day, officials in Mexico City dispatched two of the brightest stars in the criminal-justice system, Carlos Aguilar Garza of the Attorney General's Office, lionized as the Elliot Ness of Mexico, and Comandante Jaime Alcalá García of the Mexican Federal Judicial Police.

Aguilar Garza and Alcalá carried out their orders to clean up Sinaloa with chilling enthusiasm. "They had control of every movement that went out of Culiacán," said DEA agent Joe González, who worked in Operation Trizo. "They knew everybody: every campesino, every route."

And they knew how to make people talk. Among themselves, the DEA agents routinely referred to the actions of Aguilar Garza and Alcalá as "the atrocities." According to a number of DEA agents attached to Operation Trizo, Aguilar Garza and Alcalá sent soldiers out to round up campesinos who grew opium. Alcalá's Federales would interrogate them for names of their confederates and locations of heroin labs. People who still would not talk went for a ride on the helicopters. The Americans were not supposed to see what happened next, but sometimes they did.

Jerry Kelly, a big Westerner with a ruddy face and easy grin, was often at the Culiacán airport tinkering with his airplane when the Army would bring in campesinos accused of involvement in the opium industry. Ten years later he could describe the scene vividly. "A young kid—they'd take him out to the airport and beat the crap out of him. They'd take them blindfolded [up in the helicopters] and hover about five or ten feet off the ground and shove them out. They [the campesinos] didn't know how high they were and they'd start talking."

In 1977, the College of Attorneys of Culiacán denounced Carlos Aguilar Garza and Jaime Alcalá García for widespread violations of human rights. The attorneys took out newspaper ads and appealed to the United Nations for help. Among the forms of torture they alleged were electric shocks, forcing soft drinks and gasoline up prisoners' noses, forcing their heads into toilet bowls filled with excrement, rape, burning prisoners with cigarettes, gouging eyes. As a result, the attorneys said, some people lost their hearing or suffered kidney damage, legs had to be amputated, women who were pregnant miscarried.

There is no evidence that the Ford or Carter administration ever looked into these allegations. Indeed, the public statements of officials in Washington were nothing short of effusive in praise of the Mexican government.

In 1978, at a Senate subcommittee hearing on the Mexican program, Peter Bourne, director of the White House Office of Drug Abuse Policy under President Jimmy Carter, said: "The ongoing activities of the Mexican and American governments in the field of drug control must rank among the most exemplary forms of international cooperation existing in the world today."

The Carter White House may not have known that the price of the "model program" was a great deal of human suffering. Still, the American government, particularly an administration that made human rights an integral element of its foreign policy, should have been called to account for the consequences of all its policies abroad. Conveniently, American journalists never heard about the dark side of drug work.

Why didn't the DEA agents say something? For one thing, there was the Mansfield amendment, a 1975 law that made it illegal for U.S. agents to be on the scene of an arrest in a foreign country and forbade them to use force, except to preserve their own lives or the lives of others.[6] "We were told, if you could see any action going on, you were too close," said Travis Kuykendall. "Everybody was threatened with disciplinary action if he violated Mansfield." An agent who reported that he had seen a brutal arrest or had witnessed torture during interrogation invited trouble from headquarters. The agents did not expect anyone in a position of power to stand up for them if they admitted violating the Mansfield amendment in order to lodge a complaint about Mexican police brutality.

The agents in Mexico had their own safety to consider. The Mexican government did not want it known that a sizable force of DEA agents was in the Sierra Madre, and it had not granted the agents diplomatic status. Nor had officials at the State Department and DEA demanded that the Mexican government extend to the field agents the same legal protections accorded diplomats and other official representatives. Consequently, the DEA agents assigned to Operation Trizo had to travel on tourist visas. Foreigners were not allowed to possess guns on Mexican soil, so they carried guns under an unwritten "gentlemen's agreement" with Mexico City. If they ran afoul of Mexican authorities, they could be arrested. There was no guarantee they would be treated differently from any other tourist.

The DEA agents said they were certain that the Mexican security police were listening in on their hotel phones. "Every time we'd get in [to a town], if they didn't have an English-speaking person there, they'd bring somebody in," said Kelly. "You knew they knew everything you were doing and what you were saying bad or good about them."

Finally, nobody wanted to be the bearer of bad news. The consensus among the agents who served in Sinaloa was that Washington was interested in just one thing: a successful eradication program. "If you start raising hell about it, they'd just get somebody else," said Kelly. "You're not going to change those people. The relationship at that time was pretty fragile anyway. You got to know that they're all crooked. To handle it puts a lot of pressure on you, because what can you say? It's their country and you've just got to do the best you can."

After Operation Condor, Alcalá was promoted to an MFJP command in Tijuana. Aguilar Garza was named chief federal prosecutor for northern Baja California. In a short

time, both men became conspicuously wealthy. Aguilar
Garza bought an expensive house in San Diego with a swimming pool and an elaborate security system and installed a
retinue of servants and bodyguards. When a *San Diego
Union* reporter named Alex Drehlser began writing about
allegations that Aguilar Garza was involved in drug trafficking, car theft, and other rackets, the prosecutor tried to
buy off the reporter with the gift of a white leather jacket.
In the fall of 1978, after Alcalá had about seventy Tijuana
people rounded up on trafficking charges, four of those arrested asserted that they had been held incommunicado and
tortured. Alcalá's tactics caused a scandal: Baja California
community leaders complained to reporters that they would
not tolerate Sinaloa-style police actions. Alcalá resigned,
moved to Guadalajara, and was assassinated the same year
by some men who burst into his place of business. No one
in the DEA was ever sure why. Aguilar Garza was transferred to the chief prosecutor's job in Nuevo Laredo. He
resigned from the government after a spell and acquired
part ownership of a deluxe hotel. His partner in the enterprise was assassinated, and Aguilar was crippled in a light-
plane crash in 1985. There were allegations in the Mexican
press, which Aguilar denied, that the plane was loaded with
cocaine.

Both governments hailed Operation Condor/Trizo as a
great success. This was true in the sense that the eradication
figures surpassed those of any project that had ever been
attempted anywhere else in the world. At the end of 1977,
the DEA said that twenty-two thousand acres of poppy had
been destroyed, enough to make eight tons of heroin. The
claims of victory were bolstered by some objective evidence:
the purity of Mexican heroin sold at retail in the United
States was at the lowest level in seven years, which suggested
that the traffickers were facing a shortage in supplies and
were cutting the retail product more than usual.

   On the other hand, the fittest of the traffickers not only
survived but prospered. Pedro Aviles, Ernesto Fonseca, Rafael Caro Quintero, Miguel Angel Félix Gallardo, and Manuel Salcido headed for Guadalajara when the troops arrived

in Sinaloa. In a way, Operation Condor/Trizo did them a great service by winnowing out the competition.

In September 1977, the government of President José López Portillo announced its intention to reduce sharply the American government presence in Mexico. Mexicans would handle the eradication program. DEA pilots would no longer fly unescorted through Mexican airspace. In January 1978, Mexican authorities said that the U.S. verification flights would be eliminated entirely.

The advertised reason for Mexico's change of attitude toward the DEA presence had nothing to do with the conduct of the eradication program. Rather, the move was driven by nationalist and anti-American impulses provoked by a bitter dispute with the United States over natural-gas prices. President Jimmy Carter, determined to reduce American dependence on Middle Eastern petroleum producers, was trying to strike a deal with López Portillo for Mexican gas.

Drug cooperation was not specifically linked to the gas negotiations, but when López Portillo said he wanted the DEA out, the State Department and the White House, still hoping to make a gas deal, agreed. There seemed to be nothing to gain, and a great deal to lose, by insisting on continued American intervention in the region. The gas deal stalled, anyway. Thinking solely in terms of his bottom line, Carter dickered, nit-picked, and reneged until Mexican sensibilities were so gravely insulted that the state-owned oil monopoly, Petróleos Mexicanos, burned off the natural-gas surplus rather than sell to the Yanquis at the price Carter wanted to pay. Eventually a gas deal was signed—but at Mexico's price.

DEA agents working in Mexico suspected that the Mexican government had motives beyond nationalism for curtailing their activities. "I think it was corruption. If we were put back on the ground, there was no way we'd be able to tell what was going on out there," said Travis Kuykendall.

Just before they were grounded, DEA agents assigned to Mexico started picking up reports that Mexican pilots were spraying water or were dumping loads of herbicide in the desert. Fearing the eradication program would be thoroughly undermined, Peter Bensinger, the administrator of the DEA, tried to keep his men engaged in the region. Attorney General Griffin Bell was planning to go to Mexico to meet with Mexican Attorney General Oscar Flores Sánchez. Bensinger and Diogenes Galanos, chief of operations for Latin America, tried to explain the stakes to Bell. Bensinger spoke elliptically at first, talking vaguely of assuring the integrity of the project. "Well, Peter, I know why they don't want y'all down there," the attorney general replied agreeably, "because all y'all is, is a bunch of inspectors."

Bensinger tried again, insisting that the DEA had to stay because some Mexican officials were corrupt. Bell looked baffled. "If they're involved," he asked, "why don't you take their names so they can be arrested?"

Galanos could not believe what he was hearing. Take their *names?* Have them *arrested?* Were they going to arrest *themselves?* He started pounding the table. "It's not a matter of a dozen people," he stormed. "It's the whole *system*." Bell listened silently, and when Galanos paused for breath, said in a somber voice, "Oh. I see."

On the way out, Bensinger grasped Galanos's hand and gave it a hearty shake. "You really earned your money today," he said, grinning.

It was all for naught. Bell's meeting was canceled. On March 8, 1978, the DEA pilots flew out of Mexico. From then on, the U.S. government did not verify most eradication reports provided by the Mexican Attorney General's Office. Officials in Washington—at DEA as well as at State and the White House—continued to advertise the Mexican program, now called "the permanent campaign against the narcotics traffic," as a model program. But to the agents in the field, the "permanent campaign" was a joke. "On the eighth of March, 1978," said Travis Kuykendall, "that's when the eradication program turned around and started downhill."

Mexican heroin sales in the United States declined precipitously. By 1979, the DEA said that Mexican heroin was just 30 percent of the U.S. market. Part of the credit was due to the Mexican government's eradication program, but consumer preference probably was more important. American heroin users would invariably choose fine white heroin from Europe and Asia over Mexican brown. In 1978, after a long drought, the so-called Golden Crescent, the opium-growing area that spanned parts of Pakistan, Afghanistan, and Iran, was blessed with favorable poppy-growing conditions and bumper crops.

In the late 1970s the Federales scored two "victories" against the traffickers. But appearances were deceptive. In each case, DEA officials suspected that the police were the tools of the traffickers rather than their masters.

A group of Federales killed Pedro Aviles at a roadblock in Sinaloa on September 9, 1978. DEA agents who followed the trafficker's career believed that he was set up by Ernesto Fonseca or another of his lieutenants. After Aviles died, the gang splintered. Each of Aviles's lieutenants created his own organization and recruited new lieutenants and foot soldiers. Soon there were four or five gangs as powerful as Aviles's had been.

The second victory was equally illusory. On October 10, Jaime Herrera Nevares went to Guadalajara and turned himself in to General Raúl Mendiolea-Cerecero, the head of the Mexican Federal Judicial Police. DEA administrator Peter Bensinger called a press conference in Washington to salute the Federales for arresting the legendary heroin lord. The arrest, Bensinger declared, "reflects the determination of the Mexican government to go after the top level of the heroin traffic." Bensinger believed in saying good things about the Mexican government in public, regardless of the way he really felt, and in this case his statement was disingenuous. An internal DEA memorandum written in 1987 and circulated under the signature of country attaché Ed Heath said that Herrera had turned himself in because of "internecine problems within the Herrera organization." Herrera stayed locked up in the Durango city jail for six months, after which he was released. "His incarceration was based solely on reasons of security," the DEA internal report said, "and not any sudden surge of zeal on the part of the Durango police."

By 1980, the family had established connections in South

America and had diversified into the cocaine business. By the mid-1980s, DEA analysts would estimate that the family's gross income was around $200 million a year.

In June 1985 the Federales arrested Jaime Herrera Herrera—"Jaimillo"—the son and heir of Don Jaime Herrera—on a cocaine-trafficking charge. They also arrested Hugo Quintanilla, the eradication campaign zone commander for the Yucatán, Quintanilla's chief of pilots, and the entire Federales unit in the state of Campeche. Quintanilla confessed to arranging for the Federales to unload one of Jaimillo Herrera's cocaine-laden aircraft at the Campeche airport and also to taking payoffs from old Herrera Nevares, Caro Quintero, and Emilio Quintero Payán in exchange for protecting their opium and marijuana plantings.[7]

The arrests raised hope within the DEA that the de la Madrid government would rein in the Herrera organization. But those expectations were dashed when Jaimillo Herrera's case was transferred from Mexico City to Durango. When he was not immediately released from jail, gunmen noisily assassinated the public security coordinator for Durango, his son, his bodyguard, and a woman friend in downtown Durango as they were leaving a party for the American singer Vicki Carr. The point was not lost on the circuit court judge, who quickly released young Herrera for lack of sufficient evidence.

5
Colombian Gold

Colombia's Caribbean ports had teemed with smugglers ever since the days of the Spanish Main. Smuggling was a primary source of cash for tens of thousands of coastal people, *costeños,* who moved Colombian cattle into Venezuela, coffee and emeralds to the United States, and cigarettes, whiskey, and electrical appliances to South America.

The *costeño* smugglers observed the money being made in the Mexican marijuana boom of the 1960s and early 1970s with more than casual interest. Talented opportunists, they understood instinctively how to beat the Mexicans at the game. They could offer a superior product, more potent and more attractive than Mexican pot, which was sloppily packed with stems and seeds, and could ship it into the eastern seaboard of the United States, where the Mexican networks were weak.

The smugglers commissioned local farmers to plant fields of cannabis in the Sierra Nevada de Santa Marta, a triangle-shaped mountain range just south of the port of Santa Marta. Soon bags of Santa Marta gold, a distinctive mellow-gold marijuana, were showing up in Ivy League colleges and at trendy Manhattan events. Colombian pot was recommended by marijuana aficionados as "the smoke of connoisseurs." It was sold for $400 to $600 a pound wholesale, compared with $300 or so for Mexican commercial grade. The Colombians outpaced their Mexican counterparts in volume as well as quality, loading tons of marijuana on trawlers, called mother ships. As early as 1974, DEA agents in New Orleans were stunned to discover twenty-four tons of marijuana on a single ship.

The most popular loading areas were near the port of

Barranquilla, where the Magdalena River empties into the Atlantic, or along the shore of the Guajira peninsula. The more sophisticated trafficking networks acquired old DC-3s and DC-8s and bulldozed airstrips on desolate stretches in the Guajira. Riohacha, the capital of La Guajira, acquired a sort of Dodge City ambience. Guajiro Indians with guns at their belts shot up flashy new discos. Mercedes sedans bumped along pocked streets. On the back roads, four-wheel-drive vehicles with fancy radios and oversize tires replaced mules. Men born in thatched huts built fortresslike mansions with marble swimming pools and command centers with long-range radios.

The only obstacle to the Colombian traffickers was the competition from Mexico. And that disappeared in 1977, thanks to the Mexican government's use in its eradication program of a herbicide called paraquat. Once again, Ken Miley's bleak assessment was proved true—the drug business would go on and on until the public wanted it to stop. "Agents and police can't change it," Miley said. "It's like trying to stab a piece of mercury with an ice pick. It just goes someplace else."

The U.S. government did not start out to drive the marijuana traffickers from Mexico. DEA and State Department officials tried to prevent resources from being diverted from the anti-opium drive to spray marijuana. Mexican officials went after the marijuana traffickers because they considered marijuana abuse a serious internal problem. The common agricultural herbicide called 2,4-D that was being used on the poppy fields did not work well on marijuana, so the Mexicans substituted the deadly poison paraquat.

The helicopters could never have sprayed enough fields to make a dent in the marijuana supply. The traffickers destroyed the market themselves by harvesting sprayed marijuana and selling it. In early 1977, reports began trickling into Washington that poisoned pot was being sold to American consumers. Under pressure from the Congress and the National Organization for the Reform of Marijuana Laws (NORML), the Carter administration launched a series of inquiries. In February 1978, a subcommittee of the Presi-

dent's Commission on Mental Health estimated that a fifth
of the marijuana confiscated at the Mexican border had been
contaminated with paraquat and recommended that "at the
very least, such spraying should be stopped until the potential health hazards resulting from this poisoning are investigated."[1] A month later, Joseph Califano, the secretary of
health, education, and welfare, announced that a scientific
study had found paraquat to be "a serious risk to marijuana
smokers" that could cause, in the worst case, "irreversible
lung damage."

State Department and DEA officials continued to back
the Mexican program, insisting that their only obligation
was to warn consumers. Anxious not to insult the Mexican
government, Carter himself announced that he "strongly"
supported the marijuana-spraying program.

"In other words," sniped Keith Stroup of NORML, "poisoning marijuana smokers is apparently acceptable, should
the government want to do it. I submit that this is nothing
less than a form of cultural genocide." Junkies had no political clout, but pot smokers did. Stroup made paraquat *the*
symbol of the war between the generations. The majority
of the Congress agreed with him. Senator Charles Percy of
Illinois drafted an amendment to the Foreign Assistance
Act forbidding the use of foreign aid funds for spraying
marijuana with paraquat or any herbicide likely to constitute
a health hazard. The Percy amendment was approved in
September 1978.

Exasperated with the American government's waffling,
the López Portillo government kept the paraquat program
going on its own. The publicity alone was enough to send
American smokers into a panic. Mexican marijuana traffickers could not give the stuff away.

Mexican use of paraquat assured Colombian supremacy in
the marijuana market. By 1978 Colombian gold accounted
for three quarters of the marijuana sold in the United
States.[2] Marijuana cultivation spread deeper inland. New
marijuana strains appeared: Mona, pale as broom straw,
Blue Sky Blond from the Cielo Azul heights, bright green
from the Llanos. Marijuana rivaled coffee as Colombia's

chief export. By 1978, Colombian financial analysts estimated that the traffickers were bringing in $1 billion a year
in "hot money."[3]

At the time when the marijuana networks were gaining
strength, Colombia was in a state of political turmoil; the
nation had not recovered from the period of factional and
class warfare that was called *la violencia*. Nearly three
hundred thousand people had died between 1948 and 1958,
when a truce was declared by the two major political parties,
the Liberals and the Conservatives. They forged a coalition
government, but mainstream politicians could not satisfy the
demands of radical leftists. Through the 1960s and 1970s,
left-wing guerrilla groups inspired by Fidel Castro's Cuban
revolution gained control of large areas of the countryside.
Roving gangs of common criminals pillaged and murdered
at will, unhampered by the legal system, which was in tat-
ters. Alfonso López Michelsen, the president of Colombia
from 1974 to 1978, was bedeviled by debt, student unrest,
labor strikes, rural insurgencies, urban guerrillas, and organized kidnapping and extortion rackets. Drug trafficking
was the least of his problems, or so he thought. For the
most part, the Colombian ruling class was oblivious to the
rapid growth of the drug Mafia.

El Tiempo, the influential morning paper in Bogotá, was
a striking exception. When DEA administrator Peter Bensinger went to Bogotá in July 1978 and suggested that López
Michelsen call in the Army, *El Tiempo* endorsed the proposal in an editorial.[4]

López Michelsen's successor, Julio César Turbay Ayala,
was more alert to the potential dangers of the drug gangs.
In October 1978, Turbay announced that the drug economy
posed "a threat to the national security of the state" and
sent the Army into the Guajira to set up roadblocks, destroy
airstrips, and enforce new air and sea restrictions.[5]

The operation was not a complete failure, but it was not
a success. Too many thousands of people were involved in
the marijuana trade.[6] During the crackdown, *Time* magazine reported, a former assistant attorney general of Colombia, skeptical of reports that twenty-five thousand acres
of marijuana were under cultivation in the Guajira, flew

over the province. He returned to Bogotá badly shaken; he
had discovered that the actual count was closer to two
hundred and fifty thousand acres. Meanwhile, corruption
among the troops was spreading and resulted in the arrests
of a number of Colombian enforcement, military, and
diplomatic personnel. Turbay complained, however, that
"Colombians are not corrupting Americans. You are corrupting us. If you abandon illegal drugs, the traffic will
disappear."

In the immediate post-Vietnam period, American politicians were reluctant to support foreign military actions of
any kind. Insisting that eradication be accomplished with
plowshares instead of swords, the Congress appropriated
$16 million for Turbay's Guajira initiative in 1979 but ap-
pended numerous caveats aimed at preventing conversion
of the money to military or even general police use. Pro-
hibitions on spending for "military" items such as armor for
helicopters and airplanes, communications equipment, and
airborne radar drew howls of protest from DEA and State
Department officers in Colombia. Didn't the Congress understand, they fumed, that eradication *was* an act of war?
"What do they expect us to use, drums?" asked one American official. "We can't spend a farthing on even a crystal.
We can't repair a teletype machine that breaks down in the
middle of a message about confiscations. It's like asking
someone to build a house but telling him he cannot use any
hammers, saws, or nails."[7]

Coldly assessing the vacillation of American politicians,
the conservative National Association of Financial Institutions, a Bogotá-based think tank, began promoting the idea
of legalizing marijuana on the grounds that legalization
would diminish corruption and save the Colombian government $120 million being spent on enforcement. The idea
won the support of the head of the Bogotá stock exchange,
the former head of the anti-narcotics drive, and a number
of prominent businessmen.

In March 1980, Turbay pulled the Army out of the Guajira. Corruption had grown so widespread that soldiers were
said to be loading marijuana on outbound vessels.

While Bogotá and Washington focused on the *costeños* and their marijuana, a far more serious problem was growing in Medellín, the nation's second-largest city. The crime syndicates were building cocaine laboratories.

Set high in the central chain of the Colombian Andes, Medellín was called "the City of Orchids," but there was nothing languid, as the name suggested, about its tough, tenacious people. The city nestled in a narrow valley chosen for its isolation by its founders, Sephardic Jews seeking refuge from the Spanish Inquisition in 1616. Medellín evolved into a trading post for the coffee planters and ranchers who worked the surrounding hills. In the twentieth century cheap hydroelectric power from the mountains made it a manufacturing center and the headquarters of a homegrown Mafia.

Medellín was perfectly situated geographically to become the center for the trade in cocaine. Like the city's legitimate businessmen, the gangsters were organized, hardworking, and highly competitive. Worldlier than most provincial crooks, they used their access to good air connections, communications, and international banks to great advantage. There were money launderers adept at evading government currency controls, black marketeers of all sorts, and kidnapping specialists. The syndicates trained children to be pickpockets and shipped them to New York for the Christmas season. Fledgling assassins were taught the arts of surveillance and ambush.

The cocaine business was late coming to Medellín. In the early 1970s, Cuban traffickers in Miami controlled the relatively minor wholesale cocaine market in the United States. Their customers were mostly other Cuban émigrés. They acquired cocaine from small family refineries in Peru and Bolivia, using Colombian outlaws as their couriers. When native-born Americans started showing up in Miami's Little Havana looking for cocaine, the Medellín syndicates sensed the winds of change. They established their own refining industry, eclipsing the Peruvian and Bolivian suppliers on one end of the trade and the Cuban wholesalers on the other end. They had one great advantage over the Cubans: thanks to Colombian marijuana, the Medellín gangs had access to an extensive network of middle-class distributors through-out the East Coast of the United States. In time, some DEA agents would come to believe that the destruction of the Mexican marijuana industry was directly responsible for the birth of the Colombian cocaine industry.

The pioneers of the Colombian cocaine trade had no way of knowing how successful they would be, but they were willing to take daunting risks. First, they needed assured supplies of coca base: it takes five hundred kilograms of coca leaves to make one kilogram of finished cocaine pow-der. Representatives of the Medellín gangs traveled over perilous dirt roads or flew into ten-thousand-foot-high mountain landing strips to villages in the Peruvian and Bo-livian Andes, forgotten since the reign of the Incas. They commissioned the villagers to plant new stands of coca bushes, which were stripped of leaves four times a year. The villagers reduced the crop to paste by soaking the leaves in kerosene and filtering out the gray residue. The paste was then dissolved in sulfuric acid and potassium perman-ganate, filtered, mixed with ammonium hydroxide, and filtered again. The result was cocaine base. Pilots who worked for the Medellín gangs would collect paste or base periodically.

The final processing was accomplished in laboratories that the gangs built in the forests around Medellín or in the equatorial jungle. "Cooks" mixed the cocaine base with ether and acetone, inducing a chemical reaction that pro-duced a fine white salt that was cocaine hydrochloride. The finished product was packed in plastic bags, loaded into the holds of light airplanes, and flown to staging areas along the north coast.[8]

Miami, just eleven hundred miles from Barranquilla, was the first beachhead of the Colombian invasion. The city had a cosmopolitan ambiénce that disguised the influx of Me-dellín sales representatives, transportation specialists, and money handlers. Few people in the American government and almost no one in the public conceived of cocaine and marijuana traffickers as "organized crime," but the old-line Mafia racketeers who had resettled in Miami began to look tame when the "cocaine cowboys" rolled into town. The Colombians struck at their Cuban rivals and at each other impulsively, in broad daylight. Neighborhoods where the biggest threat to peace had been palmetto bugs were suddenly combat zones.

One afternoon in April 1979, Miami motorists were astonished to see an Audi barreling along an expressway, weaving wildly to evade a Pontiac on its tail, the occupants of the two cars exchanging machine-gun volleys. A few weeks later, a Cuban trafficker named Jesús Hernández was driving through a suburb when a car pulled alongside his red Mustang and a passenger opened up with a machine gun. Hernández slumped dead. His car careened into the parking lot of a shopping mall. Shoppers hit the pavement as high-speed rounds meant for Hernández pierced the glass fronts of the stores.

At around midday on July 11 of that same bloody year, a van painted with the slogan "Happy Time Complete Party Supply" pulled into Dadeland Mall just as a Colombian gangster named Germán Jiménez Pannesso walked into a liquor store. Two men jumped out of the van, followed Jiménez into the store, leveled their MAC-10 submachine guns, and started shooting. When they had shot about eighty-five rounds into the store, Jiménez and his bodyguard were dead, and two passersby had been wounded. The gunmen dashed out of the store, spraying the crowded parking lot with machine-gun fire as they ran, and abandoned their van. The Happy Time van was what the Colombian gangs called a "war wagon." It had reinforced-steel bulletproof plating and gun portholes and was loaded with bulletproof vests and eleven machine guns, all of which had been fired.

"What is particularly frightening," said Captain Marshall Frank, commander of the homicide unit of the Dade County Public Safety Department, "is the rampant and savage nature of these crimes. I would venture to say that the Mafia might well have taken lessons from this more contemporary band of criminals. The Colombian organized-crime groups are more prolific, better armed, and equally, if not better, organized."[9]

The killings went on and on, until the morgues had to

rent extra storage space. A General Accounting Office study called South Florida "a drug disaster area." The DEA began to transfer its Spanish-speaking agents to Miami and South America. The field offices on the Mexican border were reduced in size or closed, a move premised on dwindling seizures of Mexican heroin and marijuana. Even with increased numbers of agents, however, DEA's Miami field office was hard pressed to keep up with the frenetic level of smuggling activity.

Not surprisingly, the first American politicians to perceive the seriousness of the threat from the south were Southerners, in particular Senators Sam Nunn of Georgia and Lawton Chiles of Florida. Nunn, chairman of the Senate Subcommittee on Permanent Investigations, hired as the panel's chief counsel an experienced Miami organized crime strike force prosecutor named Martin Steinberg. At the direction of Nunn and Chiles, Steinberg and his staff put together a set of hearings in 1979 and 1980 that dramatized the Latin drug trade in the same way that televised hearings featuring Joe Valachi brought the gritty reality of the Mafia into American living rooms in the early 1960s. "We are not doing much to defend ourselves against the enemy," Chiles observed. "We have to forget the image of marijuana as a couple of giggling teenagers behind the high-school gymnasium smoking a joint. . . . We are talking about cold-blooded killers and organized crime, an international financial operation which floats billions of dollars from bank to bank around the world."

Dissatisfied with traditional drug-enforcement tactics, Nunn, Chiles, and counsel Steinberg pressed the Treasury Department to bring the Customs Service and the Internal Revenue Service back into the fray in order to track money trails, identify money launderers, and seize assets. They were joined by Democratic Senator Joseph Biden of Delaware, who wrote an influential report to the Senate Foreign Relations and Judiciary committees that concluded: "DEA and the Justice Department generally have achieved, as one Justice official admitted, a 'dismal record' in attacking the financial empires and the merchandising networks of the illegal drug trade. That is a primary reason why major violators can preserve their networks and resources and, in some cases, will continue to operate them from prison."

There was no law against laundering drug money at that time. However, criminal statutes existed that required certain large movements of cash to be reported to the government. Couriers who carried $5,000 or more in cash across the border had to file currency declaration forms with Customs. Banks were supposed to alert the IRS to the names, addresses, and affiliations of people who deposited or withdrew $10,000 or more in cash.

The hitch was, the traffickers knew better than to put their own names on government forms. Their need for financial front men had created a new service industry: money launderers who specialized in high volume, low risk, and maximum secrecy.

Treasury Department officials responded to Congressional pressure by creating an innovative Miami-based financial investigations task force called Operation Greenback. The unit was composed of Customs and IRS agents adept at the use of computers and money flow charts. They found that tracing drug money movements through the launderers' accounts was tedious and often unrewarding. As Customs financial specialist Duane J. Lane liked to say, "The Swiss have a saying. The blood washes off." Lane and his cohorts pored through stacks of paper looking for patterns that fit the profile of a laundering operation. After a money mover was identified, it might take months or years to document a criminal case.

In the late 1970s, the best in the laundering business was a drab little man named Isaac Kattan Kassin. In a town like Miami, where hands glistened with diamonds and sweat and the streets were filled with chrome-sculpted Detroit dragons, Kattan wore nondescript business clothes and drove rented Chevrolet Citations. Nobody who looked at him would realize that he was handling, by Customs agents' estimates, $100 million a year for a dozen large Latin organizations, among them the up-and-coming ring led by the Mexican trafficker Miguel Angel Félix Gallardo and his partner, Juan Ramón Matta Ballesteros.

A Syrian-born Jew whose family had emigrated to Cali, Kattan was a genius at making swift and silent transactions. In a couple of condominiums overlooking Biscayne Bay, he created the nerve center of an international banking network with all the appurtenances of modern finance: Customs and DEA agents who searched the condos found computers, five high-speed money-counting machines with counterfeit bill detectors, a telex terminal for speculating in gold bullion, Krugerrands, deutsche marks, and other currencies.

The business looked complicated, but all laundering schemes operated on the same simple principle: street drug sales were strictly a cash business, but drug producers and traffickers taking in tens of millions of dollars were like officers of legitimate corporations: they needed their money converted into a less bulky form, and they needed to move it quickly, preferably with electronic transfers. Kattan took the duffel bags of five-, ten-, and hundred-dollar bills collected by the street dealers, counted and packaged the bills in his condominium, keeping careful records on his computers, and deposited the cash in any one of dozens of bank accounts he controlled under false names. He would then follow the instructions of the owner of the money. If the trafficker needed to pay a refiner in Medellín, Kattan would telephone or cable his branch in that city to make out a check to the refiner in dollars or pesos. If the trafficker wanted the money wired to a bank in the Cayman Islands or in Switzerland, Kattan would handle the transaction. If he wanted cashier's checks for his investment counselor, Kattan would provide them through one of the Miami bank employees he was paying for special services.

Kattan was accused of bribing a number of bank employees not to file currency transaction reports with the IRS, but many of his transactions were legal. It might have been a long time before he was caught, but he made two stupid mistakes: he opened an account at a vigilant securities firm whose manager blew the whistle to Customs and the IRS when the couriers deposited nearly $12 million over a three-week period, and he was present at a cocaine deal that was being surveilled by DEA agents. Kattan was convicted of possession of cocaine with intent to distribute and sentenced to thirty years in prison. But like everybody else in the drug trade, he was not indispensable. Before long, Greenback investigators were looking at other laundering rings that were moving twice as much as Kattan, and there was no end in sight.

When Ronald Reagan ran against Jimmy Carter in 1980, the phrase "law and order" was returning to favor but in a new context. Parents and teachers had finally begun to understand what serious effects marijuana and cocaine were having on their children. Habitual drug use was no longer just an urban problem. Cocaine was for sale in the Appalachians, in poor fishing villages on the Maine coast, and in Midwest farming towns.

Congressmen advocating stronger enforcement of drug laws had been frustrated by the Carter administration. Carter's law-enforcement appointees—Attorneys General Griffin Bell and Benjamin Civiletti, FBI director William Webster, Justice criminal division chief Philip Heymann, Assistant Treasury Secretary Richard Davis—were intelligent and dedicated individuals who did the best they could with the slim resources they had. But the White House projected no sense of urgency, and there was little coordination at the top levels of government. DEA and Customs agents were at each other's throats again, and Carter's ambassadors and senior foreign-policy makers, by and large, ignored the drug issue.

Federal officers responsible for drug enforcement and interdiction were overjoyed when Reagan took office. They were soon disappointed: Reagan talked a good game, but despite his speeches bemoaning the threat of violent crime, when it came to more money for fighting crime, including drug traffickers, Reagan was as parsimonious as Carter. In fact, in September 1981, David Stockman, head of the White House Office of Management and Budget and a zealot on the subject of reducing the size of the federal government, convinced Reagan to announce a 12 percent cut across the board for all federal agencies except the Defense Department. The law-enforcement agencies, starved for cash during the Carter era, were not exempt and soon showed the

effects of belt tightening. DEA and Customs cars and airplanes were grounded. Money to make undercover buys ran
out. One DEA office held a bake sale to pay for gasoline
so night stakeouts could continue.

In 1981 and 1982, Attorney General William French
Smith succeeded in persuading Reagan to overrule Stockman and hold the law-enforcement budget at current levels.
But money was still tight at the worst possible time, when
drug traffickers were proliferating like fleas on a fat hound.

The absence of presidential leadership left a vacuum
which members of Congress attempted to fill. Senators Sam
Nunn and Lawton Chiles advocated the expanded use of
military assets in the drug war. Nunn attached a rider to a
Defense Department authorization bill to permit the Navy
and the Air Force to forward to the Customs Service and
the Coast Guard information about sightings of suspicious
aircraft or mother ships. The Nunn language amended an
1876 law, called the Posse Comitatus statute, which prohibited the military from carrying out domestic law enforcement.[10] The idea had great appeal on Capitol Hill, where
it was seen as another selling point for Reagan's proposed
military buildup. Air Force and Navy planes flew regular
training missions along the southern coast; Nunn and Chiles
reasoned that they could help spot smugglers in these runs.
As it turned out, Air Force and Navy commanders were
unwilling to divert pilots from normal training routines to
spot light-plane traffic. And military radar, aimed high to
detect enemy bombers, was not well suited to monitor low-
flying light planes.

Congressional drug warriors revived U.S.-funded paraquat programs in 1981 by repealing the Percy ban on spending foreign-aid funds for the herbicide. "If we encourage
foreign governments to crack down, provide them with financial assistance, and yet turn around and prohibit the use
of the most effective eradication tool, it's no wonder there
is skepticism," said Chiles.[11]

Chiles thought the Turbay government could be persuaded to spray Colombian marijuana with paraquat, but
Turbay rejected the proposition out of hand. The Colombians were well aware of the controversy over the health

effects of the powerful chemical, and they noted that the U.S. government was not spraying paraquat on California and Oregon marijuana farms. A State Department official returned from Bogotá and reported that "the Colombians view it [the U.S. position] as industry protectionism." Turbay had strong domestic political reasons for resisting the American arguments. Parts of marijuana country were controlled by the Revolutionary Armed Forces of Colombia (FARC), the armed wing of the Colombian Communist party. An aggressive aerial spraying program might antagonize the campesinos and strengthen the FARC.

In the United States, grass-roots pressure was building for tougher anti-drug measures—and more and more Democratic politicians climbed on the bandwagon. Democratic leaders created a crime task force and named Joe Biden, the senior Democrat on the Judiciary Committee, chairman. Biden's job was to put together a legislative package to modernize and harden the criminal-justice system. It was a sign of the times that every Democrat in the Senate endorsed the bill, though it contained provisions, such as preventive detention, that had once been associated with Richard Nixon's discredited law-and-order campaign.

Biden immediately locked horns with DEA administrator Bensinger. The brash young senator's displeasure was partly a personality clash with Bensinger, but he had substantive complaints. Biden argued that DEA still failed to move effectively to seize assets of the traffickers. With characteristic impatience, he brushed aside the agency's explanations of the legal intricacies of the forfeiture laws and the obstacles presented by offshore bank secrecy. Moreover, Biden charged that none of Reagan's appointees defended law-enforcement budgets, coordinated policy among the agencies, pressed the Pentagon and the CIA to produce useful intelligence on the movements of smugglers, or forced the State Department to raise the priority of narcotics control. The solution, as Biden saw it, was to have a cabinet-level drug czar.[12]

Reagan Justice appointees regarded the drug czar idea as a gimmick but realized that they had to protect their flanks; if they did not regain the initiative, Biden was likely

to hijack the whole criminal justice agenda. The task of
devising an administration strategy fell to Associate Attorney General Rudolph Giuliani, a thirty-seven-year-old from
Brooklyn who was Biden's match in intensity. Giuliani
agreed with many of Biden's criticisms. He did not care for
Bensinger's self-promotional style and considered the DEA
administrator and his top aides disorganized, overly dependent on short-term buy-bust techniques, and lacking in
vision.

Giuliani admired many of the DEA field agents, who
were known for their creativity and street smarts. What the
DEA needed, he decided, were the FBI's organizational
discipline and interest in managing long-running investigations. He considered recommending an outright merger of
the two agencies but rejected the idea in favor of a less
dramatic—and traumatic—halfway measure. In August
1981, Giuliani succeeded in persuading Attorney General
Smith to replace Bensinger with a senior FBI official, Francis
M. Mullen. From then on, the DEA administrator reported
to FBI director William Webster. In effect, the DEA became a wholly owned subsidiary of the FBI. Giuliani hoped
that the move would promote cooperation between the two
agencies.

In fact, other than the arrival of Mullen, his deputy Jack
Lawn, and a few FBI headquarters executives, little changed
except the DEA's morale, which sank. Most narcotics
agents took the reorganization as a vote of no-confidence.
Turf problems were, if anything, exacerbated; the FBI was
granted jurisdiction over the federal narcotics-trafficking
statutes, formerly the sole province of the DEA, which
meant that the FBI could install wiretaps and run undercover cases without informing its "brother" agency. The
institutional personalities did not mesh: the FBI's recruit-
ment policies, which emphasized orderliness and respect for
authority, had produced a homogeneous corps of ambitious,
confident, clean-cut, sometimes naïve agents whose loyalties
to one another and the organization were almost unshakable. DEA agents tended to be rougher, gloomier, more
individualistic, more impulsive, and more willing to question
the decisions of their superiors. They were also more willing

to admit defeat. FBI agents were drilled to succeed. Defeat was part of the daily routine at the DEA. The FBI could single out a few big cases and make them stick, but the DEA was in a war in every town and city in America and in more than forty foreign countries.

The intractable nature of the problem came as a shock to Mullen and Lawn, who had arrived at the DEA sure that the combined forces of the two federal agencies would quickly reduce the trafficking problem to manageable size. After a few months of total immersion, both men admitted that they had been woefully overconfident.

On January 28, 1982, Vice President George Bush, made aware that the cocaine cowboys were becoming an issue for voters in Florida, announced the formation of the South Florida Task Force, a multiagency effort that emphasized interdiction of drug shipments and the arrest and prosecution of smugglers. The task force did not receive any additional funding. Instead, several hundred DEA, Customs, and Bureau of Alcohol, Tobacco, and Firearms (BATF) agents and Coast Guard personnel were sent on temporary assignment to Miami.

Customs and Coast Guard officials were generally pleased with the idea because the project emphasized their mission of interdicting drug traffickers. BATF officials were grateful for the opportunity to have a job that the White House considered top priority. Reagan's Office of Management and Budget had slashed the agency's budget and was considering the idea of abolishing BATF altogether in order to appease the National Rifle Association, which accused BATF of harassing handgun owners. BATF agents redeemed their agency's reputation within the administration by cracking down on the burgeoning black market in machine guns that had so alarmed Reagan-Bush constituents in South Florida's prosperous suburbs.

But DEA officials objected that the task force was no more than a campaign platform for the Republicans and that it solved a political problem in Florida at the expense of neglecting cases in Houston, Los Angeles, and the Northeast. They did not believe the task force concept would advance DEA's mission: to make conspiracy cases against kingpins and to take away their ill-gotten gains. The task force plan called for DEA agents to handle follow-up investigations after Customs or the Coast Guard made a seizure. DEA officials wanted their agents to penetrate the rings at ever higher levels, not to react like firemen to the busts of other agencies.

The Bush plan had a distinctly military slant, which was not surprising, considering that Bush's chief of staff was retired Admiral Dan Murphy, a former commander of the Sixth Fleet and deputy CIA director.

Mullen appreciated Murphy's efforts to persuade the Pentagon to provide military resources and intelligence to the drug war, but he found Murphy insensitive to the civil liberties implications of the idea of sweeping surveillance of pleasure boats and aircrafts. Since the United States knew about every Soviet submarine and every Soviet missile, Murphy kept asking Mullen, Why couldn't the United States detect smugglers? "Well, hell, we can't do that," Mullen snapped to a reporter who raised the issue. "It's impossible. There are hundreds of thousands of boats and planes out there, and you just can't track them all. And I don't think the public would stand for the infringement and the oversight of citizens, to treat Americans as we treat Soviets."

Murphy thought that it *was* possible, technologically and bureaucratically, for the U.S. government to do a bang-up job of tracking surreptitious border crossings by boats and airplanes. He envisioned a military-style command-and-control center where data from Navy and Air Force radar planes, radar balloons, and ground-based radar would be collected, matched with information from DEA, Customs, and CIA human sources, and relayed to law-enforcement officers in time to intercept the smugglers. As it turned out, he could not convince the Pentagon to commit radar planes to devote more than a small number of hours per month to spotting for drug interdiction, and even if there had been twenty-four-hour radar coverage of the coast, neither the Customs nor the Coast Guard had the ability to intercept suspect plans and boats.

Murphy was taken aback by the stiff resistance within

DEA to the concept of a system that might eventually produce real-time intelligence on the movements of suspects. It was an inevitable clash of philosophies, for military men and law-enforcement agents had very different ideas about what constituted "intelligence." DEA agents and many agents in Customs labeled as intelligence the accumulation and analysis of allegations by informants and objective facts such as travel records and business associations that, over time, would create a total picture of a trafficking enterprise. Lawmen used this kind of intelligence to build conspiracy cases meant to send their targets—the insulated leaders of the enterprise—to jail for a very long time and to seize their ill-gotten gains.

Murphy called the law-enforcement definition of intelligence "a Sears Roebuck catalogue." "Recording stuff after the fact like a goddamn history book," he scoffed. Murphy's idea of intelligence was what the military called "tactical intelligence." "Intelligence," said Murphy, "is something you can move out on. What was lacking was the ability to figure out what someone is going to do and when he's going to do it and, with a limited force, get them there at the right time." Law-enforcement officials countered that that approach might lead to the capture of pilots, boat captains, and couriers and the seizure of drugs, but hirelings and commodities were expendable. Interdiction, they said, was expensive and did not get at the ringleaders or their assets.

Friction between Murphy and Mullen became more pronounced as the admiral pressed Mullen to assign more agents to the Bush Task Force. Furthermore, Murphy wanted all federal interdictions in South Florida to be announced by the White House and credited to Bush. As Murphy saw the situation in South Florida, George Bush's task force *deserved* credit for coordinating operations of law-enforcement agencies that, left to themselves, competed as passionately as rival professional football teams. "It was the power and strength of the vice president that made it work," said Murphy. He wanted seizures to be announced by the White House "to show that the United States was doing something about drugs."

Mullen and other DEA officials, and many Customs officials as well, wanted their agencies to announce their own seizures. They complained that Murphy was politicizing the law-enforcement system in order to enhance the images of Ronald Reagan and George Bush. As Murphy badgered Mullen for more bodies—and better statistics—Mullen's hackles rose. The DEA office in Florida was chronically understaffed; the agents on board had no time to handle their own investigations, much less to react to the cases generated by the task force. Mullen's aides met Murphy's demands by "assigning" agents on paper to the task force.

"It was all smoke and mirrors," a top DEA official later said. "Admiral Murphy would call over and say, How many people do you have there today working on the task force? We'd say, How many do you want, we'll have as many as you want. We'd call Pete [Gruden, the head of the DEA Miami office] and say, Pete, the admiral wants more people. He'd say, Okay, tell him I've assigned a hundred people."

Democratic politicians from the East and Southwest, such as Senator Dennis DeConcini of Arizona, protested that the Bush task force was not solving the cocaine cowboys problem but merely displacing it; airplanes and boats of Colombian trafficking rings were showing up in Georgia, North and South Carolina, Louisiana, Texas, Arizona, California, and even New England. The White House and the Justice Department moved to address those complaints.

On October 14, 1982, Reagan himself unveiled with much fanfare another bureaucratic creation, this one Rudy Giuliani's invention. The initiative consisted of a dozen federal task forces, modeled on the organized-crime strike forces established by Attorney General Robert Kennedy, which would pursue conspiracy investigations against major trafficking rings. On the strength of a poll of the ninety-four United States attorneys, all but one of whom (in Salt Lake City) agreed that drug trafficking was the number-one crime problem in his or her district, Giuliani had persuaded the Office of Management and Budget to approve a thousand new agent slots for the law-enforcement agencies and two hundred new prosecutors for Justice. Even so, the White House refused to make a major financial commitment to the program: instead of budgeting additional money, Stock-

man aides quietly transferred funds out of other Justice
Department programs. The budgetary shell game fueled a
new outcry on Capitol Hill; more members of both parties
began to question the sincerity of the White House's rhetoric
on the crime issue. Giuliani's commitment, however, was
never in doubt, and his strategy bridged some gaps in the
federal law-enforcement bureaucracy. The Kennedy strike
forces were doing an outstanding job against the old-line
Mafia families but had neither the manpower, the expertise,
nor the inclination to take on the emerging Latin gangs.
The Giuliani task forces signaled that the top leadership of
the U.S. Justice Department recognized, for the first time,
that Latin cocaine- and marijuana-trafficking groups were
at least as formidable a nationwide organized-crime problem
as the Mafia. Having accomplished that goal, Giuliani abandoned his prestigious desk job in 1983 to return to the field,
as U.S. attorney in Manhattan. There he racked up a series
of convictions of drug traffickers, money launderers, Mafia
lieutenants, and white-collar criminals.

By contrast, George Bush's anti-drug projects were never
taken seriously by many officials in the federal law-
enforcement community, who suspected that they existed
mainly to add a few lines to Bush's political résumé. In
March 1983, the White House launched yet another Bush
initiative, the National Narcotics Border Interdiction System (NNBIS). The system, said a press release, would expand the South Florida Task Force concept to five other
regional centers, in Los Angeles, El Paso, New Orleans,
Chicago, and New York. The announcement explained that
those centers would "monitor suspected smuggling activity
originating outside the national borders and coordinate
agencies' seizure of contraband and arrests of persons involved in illegal drug importation." That, of course, was
exactly what the DEA, the Customs Service, the Coast
Guard, the FBI, and the CIA were doing already, albeit
imperfectly. The White House stressed that NNBIS—which
insiders pronounced "Enbis"—was not supposed to *run* anything. Its staff was to consist of a handful of officers, borrowed mostly from the Coast Guard and Customs, who were
not "operational"—that is, involved in hands-on enforce-

ment work. But if NNBIS personnel were not in charge and not on the street, many field agents asked, what *were* they doing?

Mullen and his aides were deeply suspicious of the new bureaucratic entity. Mullen agreed with Giuliani's concept for the organized-crime–drug-enforcement task forces because he respected the Justice Department official as a serious crime-fighter and thought the task forces filled an unmet need. Also, he got more agent positions out of the deal. But the Bush system was another matter. Murphy said he was reluctant to take on the expanded interdiction project, that it was a further response to pressure from politicians in the Southwest and East who complained that their areas were getting shortchanged. Mullen was not convinced. He viewed NNBIS as purely political empire-building on Murphy's part. Mullen did not doubt that Bush's heart was in the right place—though the vice president did not go to the agencies except for ceremonial occasions or demonstrate interest in the day-to-day problems of agents and prosecutors. But he objected on principle to the idea that law-enforcement activities should be "coordinated" by the White House, especially by the staff of a possible candidate for president, and he felt more lawmen were desperately needed on the streets, not in offices.

Mullen's temper frayed when he found out that Murphy had approached Canadian, Mexican, and Bahamian officials. Murphy said he was only following up on meetings that Bush had had with leaders in those countries, but Mullen believed that Murphy had proposed new intelligence-exchange agreements—agreements already in place through DEA and Customs.

Then DEA executives on the Gulf Coast and in the Northeast told Mullen that some NNBIS personnel were suggesting to local police chiefs and reporters that *they* were in charge of federal drug enforcement for the region and were circulating 800 telephone numbers so that citizens and local cops could report suspicious activity to NNBIS. In a few cases, DEA officials said, NNBIS personnel claimed credit for seizures that were in fact made by federal law-enforcement agencies. Robert Bryden, special agent in charge of the DEA office in New Orleans, told Mullen that the NNBIS public relations blitz was causing confusion among state and local agencies. Bryden said later that his concerns were not a matter of turf protection; rather, he said, he feared that NNBIS announcements would create the impression that a massive new federal program was in place. "Let's be honest with people," Bryden said. "Let's not tell people we're doing something we're not." Mullen agreed with Bryden that these activities violated the agreement he and other senior law-enforcement officials had made with the Bush staff, which was that NNBIS was not supposed to be involved in enforcement work. Murphy conceded that some NNBIS personnel on the Gulf were "eager beavers" and went beyond their mandate.

Mullen and Murphy argued repeatedly over which seizures could be counted as Bush task force seizures and which could not. Mullen had come to DEA troubled by the agency's well-deserved reputation for hype, and he had been trying to restore credibility to the seizure reporting system among other things, he ordered his press officers not to give out astronomical street value figures for seizures. Murphy took the position that "a hit in the South Florida Task Force area was a South Florida Task Force hit" because, he contended, all hits owed something to the coordinating effort of the task force. In January 1984, Bush stopped in Miami on his way back from a bonefishing trip in the Florida Keys and announced that the Bush task force and NNBIS were responsible for the capture of almost five million pounds of marijuana and twenty-eight thousand pounds of cocaine.

That was the last straw as far as Mullen was concerned. *His* figures showed that the South Florida Task Force could claim credit for considerably less: two million pounds of marijuana and eight thousand pounds of cocaine. When he read Bush's announcement in *The Miami Herald,* Mullen hit the ceiling. He told Attorney General Smith that the vice president had been ill served by his staff, that the figures were a fiction and so was most of what NNBIS was advertised to be doing. When Smith asked for a full report, Mullen was more than happy to comply, writing that "the grandiose claims of the National Narcotics Border Interdiction System

are beginning to discredit and devalue the efforts of the
administration's numerous drug-control programs." "If
NNBIS continues unchecked," Mullen's memo warned
darkly, "it will discredit other federal drug programs and
become this administration's Achilles heel for drug law
enforcement."[13]

Mullen's language was so blunt that Smith's aides hid the
memo from the attorney general. Smith found out about it
four months later, when someone leaked it to Joel Brinkley
of *The New York Times*.[14]

Murphy's public reaction was mild: he told the *Times*
that NNBIS personnel should not have announced DEA
and Customs seizures as NNBIS seizures and blamed
"dumb" staff work. But in private, Murphy was seething.
In an interview years later, he called Mullen's accusations
"slanderous" and DEA's figures "ancient—all screwed up."
"I was trying to get a message to the American people that
we were trying to *do* something," Murphy said. He dismissed Mullen's objections as "parochial," a reflection of
DEA's institutional contempt for interdiction. "I don't see
how the United States can do nothing in interdiction," Murphy said. "DEA would just like to screw around in the
jungles of Bolivia and chase the traffickers after they get
into this country."

At the DEA and FBI, bets were taken as to how long it
would be before Mullen was fired. FBI director Webster
told Mullen he would tell the White House that he had
ordered Mullen to write the memo. Mullen was grateful but
the gesture was unnecessary. Ed Meese, then Reagan's
counselor, liked Mullen and made sure his job was safe.

Administration leaders tried to downplay the feud. Smith
told a Senate committee it was all a matter of "growing
pains."[15] But the Bush system was never accepted by the
regular law-enforcement community. In July 1985, two
months after Murphy left the Bush staff, the General Accounting Office said the system's achievements had been
"minimal" and its function "unclear."[16]

As the years passed, confusion persisted over the role
NNBIS played in the drug war. After 1985, NNBIS officials
attempted to carve out a small but useful niche by assuring

that Defense Department resources and intelligence gathered by the CIA reached the proper civilian agencies. Even
after that, however, Bush continued to suggest that NNBIS
had a broader role in drug-interdiction work. In August
1986, the vice president told a press conference that his
NNBIS staff would "coordinate" Operation Alliance, a
Southwest border-interdiction initiative designed and managed by Justice Department, DEA, Border Patrol, and Customs officials. Congressman Glenn English, an Oklahoma
Democrat who monitored interdiction activities closely,
questioned Frank Keating, the assistant secretary of the
treasury for enforcement, about Bush's statement. "I'm a
great admirer of the vice president," Keating replied, "but
I suspect that his eager speechwriter misspoke." Keating
explained that NNBIS had no operational role in the project. "You don't think the vice president knew what he was
talking about?" English asked sarcastically. "The vice president always knows what he's talking about," Keating
replied.[17]

While the American agencies waged bureaucratic battles,
Colombian officials counted themselves lucky to survive.
Asesinos de moto, "motorcycle assassins," who specialized
in ambushing their victims while they were stalled in traffic,
prowled the provinces. In 1980, by one account, seventeen
policemen, four judges, the mayor's chief bodyguard, and
a number of businessmen were assassinated in Medellín
alone. Late in the year, after eleven more judges had received death threats, Medellín's entire bench—one hundred
and eighty judges and magistrates—resigned to protest the
lack of security and returned to work only after President
Turbay promised police protection.

Johnny Phelps, DEA's senior agent in Colombia from
1981 through 1984, was a Texan who had spent most of
his career on the California-Mexico border, in the San
Diego–Tijuana area, and in Kiki Camarena's hometown of
Calexico. It had seemed to him that Mexican authorities
had sufficient control of their country to stop trafficking if
corruption had been contained. By contrast, most of Co

lombia's territory was simply beyond the reach of the central government.

The attitude that trafficking was "the gringo problem" was beginning to fade when Phelps arrived in Bogotá. The Colombian National Police were attempting to improve their ability to deal with the trafficking rings. After years of trying to outmaneuver cynical Mexican *comandantes,* Phelps came to appreciate the openness and courage of the Colombian officers; he was able to form personal and professional alliances with National Police officials on terms that would have been out of the question in Mexico. Mexican police officers acquired their jobs through an unwritten system of patronage and gratuities. Some cooperated selectively with individual DEA agents whom they befriended, but they dared not let those friendships be known. The Colombians were nationalistic but less defensive and self-conscious than the Mexicans. Their National Police had an academy, a paramilitary structure and a tradition of discipline. Corruption was always present among the police, especially local police, but the bribes were small by Mexican standards. Phelps was able to deal constructively with many police officials.

In general, Phelps thought, the major obstacle to law enforcement was not corruption but terror. Even then, when the chips were really down, the Colombian police were ready to fight shoulder-to-shoulder with the Americans. Phelps knew that at first hand. For on February 10, 1982, three years before the Camarena abduction in Mexico, two of his comrades were kidnapped in Colombia.

DEA pilots Kelley McCullough, thirty-nine, and Charlie Martínez, thirty-four, were in the coastal city of Cartagena on an air reconnaissance project when they got a report that a Miami Cuban trafficker by the name of René Benítez might be staying in their hotel. The desk clerk shrugged off their questions, but at half past midnight, the agents were awakened by a loud knock on Martínez's door and a shout—"Police!" Martínez slipped into McCullough's room, which adjoined his, opened the door a slit, yanked it shut, and turned the lock. Four men were outside with pistols drawn.

One of them, Ivan Duarte, slid a National Police identification card under the door. It was real. Duarte had been fired for corruption but had kept his credentials. He demanded to know why the Americans were asking about Benítez. Martínez rang the desk and pleaded with the operator to call the police. She refused. Hotel security guards were drawn by the fracas, but they sided with the gunmen and told the Americans to come out of the room. Finally, the gunmen said they were going to shoot down the door, so Martínez had no choice but to unlock it. The strangers shoved their way into the room. The leader jammed a Beretta .380 against Martínez's head. "I'm René Benítez," he snarled. "This is the only law in Colombia."

The agents were hustled out of the hotel and shoved into a two-door orange Nissan. Martínez was lodged behind the gearshift, between Duarte, who drove, and Benítez. McCullough was in the back with a *pistolero* later identified as Carlos Ruiz. The fourth man, René Benítez's brother Armando, went his own way.

As they headed out of town, Benítez began to grumble. "We're tired of you Americans coming down here messing up our drug business," he said, and to make his point, he fired his pistol into Martínez's hip. After fifteen miles or so, just outside the village of Turbaco, Duarte pulled the car over to the side of the road. Benítez and the other two men got out of the car and began to bicker over whether to kill the Americans in the car or outside.

"Partner, it looks like they're going to kill us," Martínez whispered to McCullough, who could not speak Spanish. Benítez seemed to have made a decision. He ordered the agents out of the car. As the wounded Martínez tried to hoist himself up on the car door, Benítez aimed his gun point-blank at the agent's face. "No, René," Martínez shouted. "No!"

At that instant, McCullough lunged out of the back seat and grabbed for the pistol in Duarte's waistband. It slipped out of his hand. Reflexively, he bolted. A few paces down the road, he heard a shot and Martínez's scream. He dived into the broad ditch that ran alongside the road, regained his balance, and scrambled. He heard Duarte's feet pounding behind him and then the pop of a pistol. The first two bullets missed. The third grazed the back of his knee, and the fourth, his buttock. McCullough fell to the ground. As he struggled to get up, Duarte shot him in the neck. The bullet exited through his armpit.

McCullough lay in the dust for what seemed to him an eternity—later he realized it was about fifteen seconds— waiting for Duarte to finish him off. Finally he shifted his head so that he could see where Duarte had been standing. The Colombian was gone.

McCullough staggered onto the road and headed for the lights of a house. Two men came to the door, with guns in their hands. McCullough mimed a plea for help. The men motioned him to go away. He stumbled back to the highway and started walking, jumping back into the ditch when he thought he saw the orange Nissan. He tried another house, but a woman turned him away.

When he was about to give up hope, McCullough spotted a church steeple a quarter of a mile off the road. He stumbled toward it, banged on the door of the parish house, and awakened the priest. Bloodied and filthy, the Texan looked like a vision from hell, but the *padre* took pity upon him and helped him inside.

The priest, whose name was Guillermo Grisales, fetched a policeman and then drove to the village medical clinic. The doctor wanted to dress the American's wounds and put him to bed, but McCullough refused, saying he had to find his friend Charlie. McCullough thought Martínez was probably dead, but if he was not, there was no time to waste. McCullough was so insistent that the doctor, the priest, and the policeman agreed to help him. The four men piled in the priest's car and drove to the scene of the shooting. The policeman and McCullough walked one way, calling Martínez's name. The doctor and the priest drove the other way.

Suddenly, McCullough heard a whistle and saw Benítez and one of his goons walking toward him. As Benítez leveled his gun at the American, the policeman grabbed Benítez's arm and led him away, motioning to the American to get back to the village. McCullough obeyed.

But as he walked, he began to think things through. He reasoned that Benítez would probably tell the cop that the big gringo was the crook. Benítez's *pistoleros* might go after the priest and the doctor. So when he saw the *padre* driving slowly down the road looking for him, he ducked into the ditch and waited until the priest had passed before he started walking.

Stumbling into Turbaco at four-thirty in the morning, he saw a bus that was bound for Cartagena and climbed aboard. In Cartagena, he found his way to the Bocagrande Hospital. There was a doctor there who spoke a little English; he called the American consul in Barranquilla. The consul said that Charlie Martínez was safe and in the Colombia Naval Hospital at Cartagena. After hearing the good news, McCullough lay back, allowed himself to be treated, and fell asleep.

That Martínez survived was an incredible piece of luck. At the moment when Benítez aimed at his face and pulled the trigger, Martínez shifted quickly and caught the bullet in his shoulder. Benítez put the Beretta to Martínez's forehead and pulled the trigger. The gun did not fire.

Adrenaline pumping, Martínez wrenched away from Benítez and, forgetting the shock of his wounds, ran into the ditch, over the fence, and into the woods. When he heard Duarte's gun going off, he was sure McCullough was dead. He stripped off his white shirt and tumbled under some bushes. After a few moments, he felt stings on his back and chest and realized that he was lying on top of an anthill. He dared not move. He could hear Benítez and the others tramping through the brush; at one point they came within ten yards of him. After he heard the men getting back in the car and driving away, he crawled down a steep embankment, across a creek, up a bank, and found a new hole. It was an arduous process because his hip and shoulder had begun to bleed badly.

Martínez hid in the bushes for what was left of the night. At one point, he heard McCullough calling his name but he thought it was a trick and did not answer. At daybreak, he limped to the highway and tried to flag down a ride. He thought he must have looked like the brigands who terrorized the local people because no one would stop. After forty-five minutes, a young taxi driver picked him up and delivered him to the hospital in Cartagena. Miraculously, neither Martínez nor McCullough had sustained life-threatening wounds and both soon returned to duty.

Kelley McCullough became a sort of legend in the village of Turbaco. Padre Grisales, who had spent the night driving around the countryside searching for McCullough, was overjoyed to learn that the agent was safe. Later, he sent a letter to the U.S. embassy telling how word had spread far and wide of the courage of the pale American:

> How a man, so beaten up and wounded could have endured it . . . What formal preparation you must give your . . . police, or pilots in the United States, is something that astounded me, same with the doctor. . . . How I would like for Kelley's great mother to receive this little letter, for having raised with such feelings her incredible son, whom I could not give all my help that I would have wanted to. [I have been] praying with my town, which is very Christian, several times in Holy Mass for their recuperation, telling them what had happened. . . . They were very moved and astonished by the physical resistance of the young [man] and his moral talents.

The letter was cited when McCullough was presented with the highest commendation of the Justice Department, the Attorney General's Distinguished Service Award. McCullough and Martínez both received the Drug Enforcement Administration award.

After seeing the wounded agents off on a U.S. Air Force Medi-Vac aircraft, Johnny Phelps paid a call upon Director-General Francisco José Naranjo Franco, the head of the National Police. The conversation was quick and to the point. "What do you need?" the director-general said. "F-2," Phelps replied. F-2 was the detective division of the

National Police. "Take whatever you need," the director-
general said.

And that was that. Phelps and his men and an F-2 team
flew all over Colombia looking for René Benítez. The Colombian policemen treated the DEA agents like their own.
"If there was a door to be knocked down, we were standing
beside them," Phelps said. "It was a joint effort from beginning to end."

Finding Benítez took two months of legwork. Since he
was a Cuban and a fugitive from Miami, he was not well
known, even in Medellín. The Colombian policemen fanned
out, asking about hangouts, friends, girlfriends, relatives,
telephones he used. In April the search was narrowed to a
ranch near the Magdalena River. Phelps borrowed a couple
of helicopters from the government and planned a raid to
be carried out by the Colombian policemen. The raiding
party flew to a military base in the river bottom and prepared
to hit the ranch at the break of dawn on April 13.

That day, Phelps rose at three o'clock in the morning
and peered out into a blinding tropical rainstorm. If this
kept up, he would have to postpone the raid. The villagers
would gossip about the helicopters. Benítez would find out
and flee. The Colombians agreed with Phelps. Flying in the
rain was risky, but they hated to see all that work go down
the drain.

At five-thirty, the storm slackened. The men boarded the
helicopters and took off. Jostled by steamy gusts, the choppers clattered low over the river and set down by the ranch
house as the sun rose. The Colombian officers managed to
get through the doors and take aim before the men inside
realized what was happening. Benítez and thirteen others
were arrested. Neither side fired a shot.

DEA agents all through Latin America were mobilized.
One by one, the rest of the gang was run to ground. On
May 20, 1982, DEA agents located Ivan Duarte in Venezuela and prevailed upon local authorities to deport him to
Colombia, where he joined René Benítez in prison. Armando Benítez was arrested in Miami on September 21,
convicted of attempted murder of a DEA agent, and sentenced to life in prison. In April 1983, DEA agents tracked

the fourth man, Carlos Ruiz, to Guatemala. Ruiz was deported to Miami, convicted of manufacturing cocaine, and sentenced to eight years in prison. René Benítez was extradited to the United States in 1986, pleaded guilty to cocaine trafficking, and was sentenced to fifteen years in prison.

Capturing the Benítez gang was a great spiritual victory for the DEA. By their exemplary conduct, the Colombian National Police officials earned the lasting respect of men like Phelps. In terms of the drug trade, however, the arrests had no perceptible impact. The Medellín trafficking rings were growing so fast that the bravest of Colombian police dared not confront them.

The pioneers of the cocaine trade lived hard and died young. They were crude people who had only one way of settling arguments, and the women were as bad as the men.

Miguel Miranda turned a mango grove in suburban Miami into a hedonist's hideaway. Behind the mango trees, he built a long, screened structure that housed a grotto with trees and a waterfall, a pond with goldfish and ducks, a Jacuzzi, and a swimming pool. There was a greenhouse, a kennel for Miguel's Dobermans, and an armory full of machine guns and hand grenades. DEA agents found Miranda's grotto after they shot and killed him when he attempted to run one of them over with his Cadillac. José Antonio Cabrera Sarmiento regarded Miami as a sort of F.A.O. Schwarz for grown-ups. Although he was a fugitive from a murder-one rap in New York, his idea of keeping a low profile was to saunter about Miami wearing a gold Rolex watch with a diamond face and band, loops of gold necklaces, and a medallion of solid gold with his nickname, Pepe, spelled out in diamonds. When he was arrested in Miami in 1981 he was walking around wearing $160,000 worth of gold jewelry and carrying a pocketful of emeralds. He put down $1 million in bail and promptly skipped to Colombia. After being indicted in Miami in 1985 for smuggling eight and a half tons of cocaine, he was extradited from Colombia in 1986, convicted and sentenced to serve thirty years in prison.

Griselda Blanco, a short, stocky former pickpocket and

prostitute, was called La Madrina, "the Godmother." She used a corps of young women couriers to transport cocaine and was wanted for several murders in Colombia. She was caught in Irvine, California, in 1985, convicted of trafficking, and sentenced to thirty-five years in jail.

By 1982, most of the pioneers were being eclipsed by a new generation of traffickers who had come into power in Medellín. The younger traffickers were smoother, more sophisticated, and more enterprising than the cocaine cowboys. In retrospect, it seemed to DEA officials who read the reports from informants, defendants, and undercover penetrations, these groups were attempting to monopolize the production of cocaine. The younger traffickers seemed to have conceived a plan to mass-market cocaine all across America, like so much soap powder, with vertically integrated conglomerates that controlled every step of the commodity business from coca paste production to distribution. There were several dozen major organizations based in the Medellín area, but three young men were destined for international notoriety: Jorge Ochoa, Pablo Escobar, and Carlos Lehder.

The name Ochoa would come to mean to cocaine what the name Duke meant to tobacco and Cargill to grain. The patriarch of the family was Fabio Ochoa Restrepo, a cattle rancher from the Magdalena River town of Puerto Salgar, east of Medellín. In the mid-1970s, Fabio Ochoa moved to the Medellín area and went into drug smuggling.

Fabio's son Jorge Luis Ochoa Vásquez, born in 1949, transformed the family business into a modern corporation. The first the DEA heard about the family was in 1977, when Jorge was linked to sixty pounds of cocaine seized in Miami. The agents determined that the young Colombian was a major source of cocaine up and down the East Coast. Upon being indicted, Jorge fled back to Colombia and managed the business from Medellín, aided by his father and elder brother, Juan David. The youngest Ochoa son, Fabito, remained in Miami and supervised wholesale distribution from a house in Coral Gables.

As the family fortune grew into the tens and then

hundreds of millions, old Fabio, fat and gray-haired, with sunken black eyes, amused himself raising prize bulls, horses, beef and dairy cattle. He owned a ranch on a beautiful stretch of coast between Cartagena and Barranquilla, an estate in the rolling hills south of Medellín, hotels in Cartagena, office buildings in Medellín. Apparently for his own amusement, he ran a Medellín restaurant called La Margarita.

The Caribbean ranch served as the smuggling operation's forward base. It was a showplace, largely self-sufficient, with a milk-processing shop, a bullring, an airport, a huge open-air zoo, its own water system, electrical generators, several swimming pools, comfortable bunkhouses for dozens of ranch hands, and a fleet of motor launches. By day it buzzed with the chatter of farmhands. By night the only sounds were from the coming and going of small planes.

Pablo Escobar Gaviria was born in 1949 to a respectable family in Ríonegro, a mountain village about seventeen miles from Medellín. After graduating from high school, he moved to Medellín and became a thief. By one account, he started by stealing gravestones, shaving off the names, and reselling them. Later, he stole cars.[18]

In 1976, Escobar and five other men were arrested with thirty-nine kilos of cocaine. This was when the police understood that Escobar was no common crook. He was never tried. Two policemen who collared him were assassinated. The records disappeared from the courthouse. According to the Bogotá daily *El Espectador,* nine judges handled the case; each passed it on after receiving threats.[19]

After that, Escobar was on his way to becoming one of Colombia's richest men—perhaps one of the richest men in the world—with a net worth eventually estimated at $2 billion. As he grew rich, he tried to shed his shady past by claiming he was in "tourist development." He acquired land all over Colombia. His special pride was an estate called Hacienda Nápoles in Puerto Triunfo, a pretty Magdalena River town, where a small one-engine airplane, said to be Escobar's first smuggling craft, was mounted over the front gate. *The Miami Herald* reported that Escobar's private zoo boasted four giraffes, two Indian elephants, ten hippopotamuses, and many other exotic animals, a country house that could accommodate a hundred guests, and a swimming pool flanked by a statue of Venus and a mortar emplacement.[20]

Escobar found it useful to become a philanthropist. He launched a program called Medellín without Slums, which was run by a priest. He built a hospital and hundreds of houses for the poor, who called him Don Pablo the Good. According to Alan Riding of *The New York Times,* Bishop Darío Castrillón of Pereira justified the Church's acceptance of his gifts "to prevent it from being invested in brothels, the production of drugs, or any other crime."[21]

In March 1982, Escobar was elected to the Colombian Congress as an alternate representative from Antioquía. The same month, Escobar set a U.S. record. Customs agents at Miami International Airport found thirty-nine hundred pounds of his cocaine—four times the previous record seizure—in a shipment of blue jeans from Medellín.

Escobar's position as a delegate conferred immunity from arrest. In any case, those who knew the source of his wealth did not discuss the matter.

The most flamboyant of the bunch was Carlos Lehder Rivas. Lehder was born in 1947 in Armenia, a coffee town south of Medellín. His father, a German engineer who moved to Colombia toward the end of World War II, and his mother, a Colombian, split up when he was a child. His mother took him to New York, where he acquired a good command of street English, some expensive vices, and a rotten bunch of friends. By the time he was eighteen, maybe earlier, he was stealing cars for a ring operating between Detroit, Canada, and South America. Arrested in Detroit in January 1973, he skipped bail, moved to Florida, and became a courier for a marijuana ring. He was arrested in September of that year in Miami with two hundred pounds of pot. He served nearly two years at Danbury Correctional Institute, where he got a postgraduate education in the American underworld. Upon his release in 1975, he was put on an airplane bound for Bogotá.

As a child, Lehder was bright and inventive. His father once told a *Miami Herald* reporter how Carlos had designed a water pump at age eight. "It was perfect," the old man said wistfully. "It would have worked." As an adult, Carlos turned his talents to trafficking. He learned to fly an airplane and formed a company that specialized in delivering marijuana and cocaine processed by other organizations. By 1978, he was the chief executive officer of a large and very successful multinational conglomerate. That was the year DEA agents in Jacksonville, Florida, picked up his trail.

At first, all the agents had were rumors of hundred-kilogram loads of cocaine going into New York, Los Angeles, Miami, and Palm Beach, at a time when ten kilograms of cocaine was considered a big load. They had no idea who had the kind of cash it took to put together hundred-kilogram loads, but they knew it was not the flash-and-trash Miami dopers, whose idea of opulence was a Rolex watch and a new car.

The Florida agents mounted a project called Operation Caribe. Checking out small airplanes that were making regular runs to the Caribbean, they fixed upon a bunch of bush pilots, soldier-of-fortune types, whose movements fit the profile of the typical transporter of drugs. It took two years of digging, feeding airplane tail numbers into the Customs Service's computerized "lookout system," and poring over ownership records and criminal histories after the trail led to a tiny island called Norman's Cay, a long, narrow outcropping in the Bahamian archipelago. The island had been developed in the 1960s as a resort. There was just one road, with paths running off to villas that dotted the shorefront. The houses were being sold to wealthy Americans and Europeans until a fellow who called himself Joe Leather moved in.

Carlos Lehder—who was in his American phase then and called himself Joe—bought up island properties, turned the yacht club into a disco that blared Beatles music at all hours, and took to flying the German and Colombian flags. He was just twenty-nine, handsome in a kind of baby-faced way, short, and confident as only a man with millions of dollars and a platoon of bodyguards could be. There were girls all over the place for Joe and the wealthy marijuana farmers and cocaine lab owners he entertained. Another frequent guest, according to DEA intelligence reports, was Robert Vesco, the fugitive con man, who was hiding out in the Bahamas. The tycoons, so the story went, whiled away the hours firing machine guns at lizards and coconuts.

With the air of someone who had seen too many James Bond movies, Lehder installed radar and ran aerial surveillance. Packs of attack dogs and machine-gun-toting toughs roamed the island, scaring off innocent yachtsmen who strayed into the area. Lehder frightened the other property owners into selling out, all but a gentle old doctor to whom he had taken a fancy. He built a three-thousand-foot runway, and soon planes flying between Colombia and Florida were landing day and night. These were the cocaine runs that the DEA agents had targeted.

Over time, the agents were able to map Lehder's routes and pick off his pilots and distributors, but they could never get to him. "Lehder sat there in his gorgeous island retreat, a hundred and twenty miles off the coast of Florida, arranging and brokering deals," recalled DEA's Bob O'Leary, who worked in Operation Caribe. "It's like having your neighbor sitting there thumbing his nose and giving you obscene gestures, and you can't do anything about it." Once a couple of DEA agents went to the island posing as tourists. As the Americans were leaving, a van pulled up and a man with a machine gun pointed it at their airplane. The pilot took off like a shot. Even in Nassau, the DEA agents noticed that they were being followed and suspected Lehder of sending his thugs after them.

As a member of parliament, Norman Solomon tried to persuade the government of Lynden Pindling to throw Lehder out of the islands. "All you had to do was be in the area and you could see the planes come and go, and you'd hear them all night long," Solomon complained to NBC correspondent Brian Ross.[22] Solomon pulled up at the Cay in his boat and was ordered off at gunpoint. The police went into the Cay in September 1979 and found a small amount of cocaine but did not find or charge Lehder.[23]

By 1981 DEA agents assigned to Operation Caribe had

enough evidence to support a federal indictment, which was filed against Lehder in Jacksonville. The indictment and the accompanying publicity in the Florida newspapers caused a scandal in Nassau, and the police raided Norman's Cay twice more. The proprietor was long gone.

The agents were convinced that Lehder had been warned by corrupt Bahamian authorities. Because of this case and other allegations of high-level corruption in 1983, the DEA office in Miami planned an undercover sting aimed at Kendal Nottage, Pindling's minister of youth, sports, and cultural affairs, and other high Bahamian officials. U.S. Ambassador Lev Dobriansky blocked the plan out of concern for American-Bahamian relations.[24]

A September 5, 1983, *NBC News* broadcast by Ross disclosed the thwarted sting and quoted a U.S. Justice Department document charging that Prime Minister Lynden Pindling and several cabinet ministers were taking $100,000 a month from Lehder. Pindling, infuriated, called the NBC report part of "a criminally conceived conspiracy against the Bahamas" but convened a royal commission of inquiry to investigate the trafficking problem.[25] The commission concluded that Bahamian officials had taken bribes to allow Lehder and other traffickers to use the islands as a jumping-off point for the States. Several witnesses charged that Prime Minister Pindling was personally involved in corrupt deals. The commission found no credible evidence supporting those charges. An examination of Pindling's bank accounts showed deposits of $3.5 million more than his salary between 1977 and 1983; investigators found that Pindling could not explain $181,000 in deposits, but they reported finding no evidence that Pindling had accepted money from traffickers.

The commission of inquiry agreed with DEA's conclusions that Lehder had enjoyed the protection of the police while on Norman's Cay. Its final report said:

> It is clear that the police and senior government officials were aware of the illegal activities [on Norman's Cay] but their response was adequate. The first police raid was ineffectual while the last two were failures. Moreover, Lehder

was on the Cay after the police were there on a permanent basis. We have concluded, therefore, that there must have been corruption within the police force and that corruption must have reached to a senior level of government.[26]

No senior government officials were successfully prosecuted in response to the commission's recommendations.

Lehder returned to his hometown of Armenia, Colombia, and broke ground for a Bavarian-style resort hotel, which he called the Posada Alemana. Its discotheque featured a statue of John Lennon, nude except for a helmet and a guitar, with a bullet hole through the heart. According to local legend, Lehder seduced local maidens by the score and fathered legions of babies.

Hungry for adoration, he formed a political party, the Movimiento Cívico Latino Nacional (MCLN). His political rallies, which he called "patriotic Saturdays," drew people from all the neighboring villages. With his dark good looks and passionate anti-gringo oratory, Lehder was a striking figure, but many in the crowd were drawn by the thousand-peso notes that were distributed to everyone who attended. His rhetoric was a scramble of fanatic nationalism, anti-communism, and neo-fascism. He seemed to think of himself as a sort of Che Guevara of the right. He loved to rant and rave about North American imperialism and communism. He was fascinated by Adolf Hitler, whom he called "the greatest warrior in history."

He also bought the provincial newspaper, *Quindío Libre*, which he turned into the house organ of the cocaine traffickers. His editorials heaped lavish praise upon Pablo Escobar, his friend and fellow politico.

When Escobar took his seat in the House of Delegates in the fall of 1982, President Belisario Betancur had just been inaugurated. The issue of the day was whether Betancur would enforce the extradition treaty President Turbay had made with the United States. According to the treaty, which had gone into effect on March 4, 1982, Colombia would deliver fugitives from American indictments for certain crimes, including drug trafficking, to the United States

for trial. Like most other Latin American countries and
many European ones, Colombia had refused to extradite
its own citizens. After the treaty went into effect, the U.S.
Justice Department began preparing formal extradition requests for more than a hundred traffickers, including Lehder, Escobar, and Jorge Ochoa.

In the legislative debates over enforcing the treaty, Escobar argued with obviously heartfelt emotion that the
treaty violated Colombia's national sovereignty and its constitution. At times, the press gallery was occupied by the
editor of the *Quindío Libre*. Carlos Lehder was the only
"journalist" who arrived with a complement of bodyguards.

By 1982, DEA agents had become aware that the Medellín
traffickers had formed a cartel. Exactly when was uncertain.
Some investigators traced its founding to November 1981,
when guerrillas of the leftist M-19 (Movimiento 19 de Abril)
kidnapped Fabio Ochoa's daughter Marta, demanding a
ransom to finance their insurgency. The M-19 took its name
from the elections of April 19, 1970, which the group
claimed were stolen from the left.

As Colombian and American reporters pieced the story
together, old Fabio Ochoa called a counsel of war among
his fellow traffickers. Before long, fliers were being distributed all over Medellín announcing the formation of a cooperative venture called Muerte a Secuestradores (MAS),
"Death to Kidnappers," which was dedicated to the "public
and immediate execution of all those persons involved in
kidnapping." A communiqué distributed by MAS said that
kidnappers "will be hanged from the trees in public parks
or shot and marked with the sign of our group . . . retribution
will fall on their comrades in jail and on their closest family
members."[27] Each trafficking family reportedly donated
thousands of dollars and a few *pistoleros* to the effort. In
effect, the traffickers created their own vigilante force, or
death squad, in order to achieve the "justice" that the government was too weak to provide. The *pistoleros* reportedly
killed or kidnapped dozens of M-19 members; Marta Ochoa
was released unharmed in February 1982.

In the ensuing years, the Colombian cocaine cartel and

the guerrilla movements would live in uneasy coexistence.
At times, the guerrilla leaders would denounce the traffickers as corrupt, antisocial capitalists. At other times, reports
would arise that the traffickers were helping to arm the
guerrillas and hiring them as assassins or guards. One thing
was certain: after MAS was created, M-19 did not attempt
violence against the cartel again.

The cartel structure offered the Medellín drug lords a
means to squeeze out strangers, settle differences, and form
a united front against the central government in Bogotá and
the United States. The cartel members began sharing risks;
if a wholesaler in the States ordered, say, six hundred
pounds of cocaine, three groups might contribute two
hundred pounds apiece, so that if the load was seized, each
group's loss would be limited. The loads of cocaine grew
larger. Thousand-pound shipments became the rule rather
than the exception.

The cartel members lent one another skilled employees
such as pilots, chemists, and assassins. They kept out the
small operators, but among themselves they were generous
with their skills. Carlos Lehder organized transportation for
his friends Escobar and Ochoa. An organizational chart
captured from an employee of the cartel showed that Escobar and Jorge Ochoa had drawn up a formal agreement
for sharing vital tasks. Under Escobar's name were "base,"
"laboratories," "transportation," "aircraft," and "U.S.
distribution." Ochoa was responsible for "enforcement,"
which was subdivided into "Muerte a Secuestradores," "Colombian military and police," "hit men," and "guards." He
also provided "bribes and protection," "money," presum-
ably laundering, and arranged protection from "police and
military."[28]

If the cartel leaders had aspired to monopolize the production and wholesaling of cocaine, they had very nearly
succeeded. They had had a sound, fundamental insight: millions of American pot smokers would buy cocaine if the
stuff could be had conveniently and at a reasonable price.
By 1984, they boasted, they controlled 80 percent of the
cocaine manufactured in Colombia. The Medellín cocaine

cartel was the richest and most feared underworld crime cabal on earth.

And U.S.–Colombian relations on the issue were at their weakest in years. President Betancur's sole objective was to negotiate a truce with the leftist guerrilla groups. In 1982, 1983, and the first months of 1984, he all but ignored drug trafficking and opposed the extradition treaty on nationalistic grounds. American officials anxiously waited for signs that Betancur realized that the traffickers were as great a threat to his nation's stability as the guerrillas. They hoped that it would not take some terrible tragedy to move him to take that stand.

6

The Guadalajara Cartel

In the early 1980s, as far as DEA management was concerned, the Mexican border was a post for old-timers and green recruits. DEA headquarters was drowning in fresh crises. Every investigative reporter in the country seemed to be in Miami, writing about the blood lust of the Colombian cocaine cowboys, or in New York, writing about the revival of the Mediterranean heroin connection. Congressional committees were hammering away at the DEA and the other federal agencies to do something—*anything*—about cocaine and heroin trafficking in Florida and the Northeast.

The only "success story" for which U.S. officials could claim credit was Mexico's "permanent campaign" against drug trafficking, which was underwritten by about $10 million a year in State Department funds. Eradication was still very much the gospel in Washington, and Mexico had the only project in the world that involved aerial spotting and spraying of fields of marijuana and opium poppies. The State Department proselytized officials from Colombia to Burma by inviting them to Mexico to watch the spray helicopters in action.

Kiki Camarena used to regale his partners with a story that one of his informants told about the spray helicopters. As the story went, a blue-and-white chopper from the Mexican Attorney General's Office had shown up at the marijuana plantation where the informant worked.

Informant: "The helicopter comes. *Ch-ch-ch-ch-ch-ch.*" (With his hand he mimicked a helicopter landing.)

Kiki: "Then what happened?"

Informant: "The field manager comes out and talks to

the pilot." (He mimed the manager dealing out bills from a fat bankroll.) "*Ch-ch-ch-ch-ch-ch.*"

Kiki: "What happened then?"

Informant: "The helicopter goes away." (His hand took flight.) "*Ch-ch-ch-ch-ch-ch-ch-ch.*"

For Camarena and the other agents stationed in Guadalajara, the pattern had become all too familiar. They would hear about a field of marijuana or opium and tell their superiors in the U.S. embassy in Mexico City. The embassy would pass the word to the Mexican Attorney General's Office, which controlled the eradication air fleet given to Mexico by the U.S. State Department. After a time, the Attorney General's Office would say that the pilots had reported that they had seen nothing.

"Or they'd say they'd sprayed, and we'd send an informant up there and he'd bring back a sprig of marijuana that was perfectly healthy," said Butch Sears, one of Camarena's partners. "If we showed it to them, they would say, You are wrong, or your informant is wrong."

Like many DEA agents assigned to Mexico, Camarena and Sears believed that corrupt officials in the Attorney General's Office were sabotaging the aerial spraying program, pocketing the State Department's money, and taking payoffs from the traffickers. The State Department officers responsible for disbursing U.S. funds regarded those charges as ill-informed and cynical. The agents countered that the State Department officers *had* to say the program was successful to keep the money coming. If they admitted defeat, Congress might reduce the budget for the program or even abolish it.

Once Sears went to the embassy and got into a shouting match with some State Department officers about whether some marijuana fields had been eradicated. The diplomats were taking the side of the Mexican government. Finally Sears yanked a stem of marijuana out of his jacket.

"If you can find paraquat on this," he roared, "I'll eat the son of a bitch at high noon."

In 1980, Mexican officials made the grandiose claim that they had "virtually wiped out" the marijuana and heroin trade.[1] State Department and DEA officials knew this was not true but were not inclined to set the record straight. In an era when drug traffickers were rampaging all through Latin America, the Mexican program was, as a senior State Department official said, "part of our litany, something we could point to, and the numbers verified it."

In fact, the numbers were shaky. The staff of the U.S. embassy's Narcotics Assistance Unit (NAU), which was the embassy branch of the State Department's Bureau of International Narcotics Matters, was supposed to monitor the eradication, but its staff was too small and too disorganized to keep up with its own paperwork, much less to go into the countryside to check that fields of poppies and marijuana were actually being sprayed with herbicide. Unable to observe eradication activities regularly themselves, and unwilling to turn the job over to the DEA, NAU officers simply passed along the Mexican government's figures.

But all along the Southwest border, DEA and Customs agents were seeing signs that the Mexican trade was reviving. They knew that those statistics official Washington found so reassuring were only snapshots of the past. A drought had hit the Sierra Madres in the late 1970s. Along with the eradication program, the arid weather had hurt the marijuana and poppy farmers badly. But now the drought was over, and in the fall of 1980, DEA offices along the border predicted that the next year would bring bumper crops of both opium and marijuana.

Sure enough, one day in 1981, pilot Jerry Kelly, stationed in the DEA office in San Diego, got a hushed telephone call from an informant who had helped him when he was in Sinaloa for Operation Condor/Trizo in the 1970s. The man said that the marijuana and opium fields were coming back and that the police were covering for the growers. The informant offered to guide Kelly to the new plantations. Kelly asked for permission to fly a DEA plane down to Sinaloa. His boss said no. Kelly tried another angle. He would take a fishing trip, fly his own plane, go on his own time. If he happened to see some illegal fields on his vacation, well, so could any other camper. His boss still said no, headquarters would never accept such a plan. The 1978 agreement that forbade DEA aircraft from entering Mexican airspace was still in force. It was not worth the international incident that would be caused if he crashed.

At about the same time, Phil Jordan, the agent in charge of the DEA Phoenix office, saw that a new generation of Mexican traffickers was on the move. When DEA headquarters paid no attention to his warnings, he helped *The Arizona Republic*, a Phoenix daily newspaper, compile a series of stories on the emerging kingpins, among them Miguel Angel Félix Gallardo, Manuel Salcido Uzeta (Cochi Loco), and José Contreras Subias. Jordan was severely disciplined by his superiors for going public. "I'm not going to shy away from a reporter to protect a dope peddler," he said unrepentantly. "These traffickers were insulated in Mexico. These were the sources of supply that were furnishing the heroin and the cocaine and the marijuana to Arizona. A lot of it was public record. I was not divulging anything that would embarrass DEA or the United States government." But he was. Like the State Department, DEA headquarters toed the official line, which was very close to Mexico's official line, which was that "the Mexican traffickers are out of business."

When the change began, Kiki Camarena was in Fresno, California, spending night after night in the barrio hangouts, negotiating with drug wholesalers whose pilots flew into the isolated airstrips of the San Joaquin Valley.

The brawny young agent was a natural in the theater of the street. He would slip effortlessly into a Puerto Rican accent or toss off Mexican gutter slang—whatever the role demanded. As a teenager, he had dreamed of becoming an FBI agent. He lost interest after a few years as a narcotics agent. The business of tracking embezzlers and con men through piles of receipts paled beside the raw street dramas in which he played nightly.

Narcotics agents, the good ones, tended to become obsessed by their cases. Kiki Camarena was a driven man even by those standards. When he was off duty, his mind strayed back to his job. He would go for an after-hours drink with a bunch of guys from the office, but when they tried to talk football, or girls, he would bend the conversation back to whatever conspiracy they were trying to unravel.

Camarena and his buddies made dozens of busts, but no matter how many arrests they chalked up, there was never a shortage of dope. Obviously, the local creeps they had been hauling in were expendable. Where was all this junk coming from? Who were the suppliers? Who gave the orders? Who managed the money? Where was the money? Where did the chain begin, and where did it end? How could it be broken? Who *wasn't* expendable? The solution, wherever it was, was not here in Fresno. The San Joaquin Valley was just a way station between the border and the big markets in Los Angeles and San Francisco.

One day early in 1980, Kiki Camarena got a call from Pete Hernandez. The gregarious little Texan was Camarena's *compadre*, the godfather of his sons, the closest friend he had made in the DEA. Now Hernandez was in the Guadalajara office and wanted Kiki to join him.

Hernandez made a convincing case. This was Kiki's chance to escape the sweltering monotony of the central California farmlands. Taking a foreign assignment would be good for Kiki's career. DEA never ordered agents abroad; they volunteered, and the agents willing to go received extra points in their personnel files. Besides, Hernandez said, Guadalajara was good for a man with a family. There was an American school for the boys. A government salary would pay for a nice house and a maid. The weather was always like spring.

As for work, there was plenty of it. Pete had been up in the Sierra Madre. There were new marijuana and poppy fields. Guadalajara had become the rest and recreation spot for the traffickers from Sinaloa and Durango. They were all over Guadalajara, buying bars and hotels, spreading money around the police forces, acquiring fleets of airplanes. There was going to be a lot of action.

That sounded good to Camarena. He was ready for action. He knew that the city had a savage side. Some months before, one of his friends from Mexicali, a *comandante* of the Federales named Rafael Davila, had been transferred to Guadalajara. Davila had refused to play the traffickers' game and was cut down by a machine gun in front of a downtown discotheque. The way he died was worse than vicious; it was arrogant. The open execution meant that gunmen expected to get away with it, and they did. However, to Camarena, the allure of Guadalajara was precisely what made the place dangerous. He loved living on the edge. If the big boys were in Guadalajara, that was where he wanted to be.

Mika Camarena, who was pregnant with her third son, welcomed the move for her own reasons. She knew there would be risks, but for a narcotics agent, no city was safe. She took some comfort in the fact that it was illegal for American agents to work undercover in Mexico. Kiki would have nights and weekends at home. Mika thought the family would be drawn closer together. She did not have the heart to complain about Kiki's frequent absences, having seen her husband's face light up when a case was about to break. At home, he would sit in the living room or at the dinner table and chuckle to himself. Mika would look up, bewildered. It was always something having to do with a case. She knew that she would always have to share him with the DEA.

Camarena's transfer came through in June 1980. His buddies in the DEA office in Fresno outfitted him with a sombrero and a "Mexican emergency ration kit"—a six-pack of beer and a dead chicken. He shared a last few rounds with the guys and headed south.

Jaime Kuykendall arrived in Guadalajara some twenty months later, in February 1982. After tours in Quito and Houston, he had been appointed Guadalajara's new "RAC"—DEA jargon for resident agent in charge. The office was supposed to have seven or eight agents. Kuykendall found himself confronted with two very angry young men. Pete Hernandez and Kiki Camarena were working furiously, literally and figuratively. They were double-timing it, trying to keep up with the frenetic movements of the traffickers. Kiki was so wound up that during a dispute over an assignment, he had punched a previous supervisor in the jaw. He should have been disciplined, but the other man had not reported him.

It was not the physical burden of the workload that upset
the young agents; it was headquarters' insistence on stats.
DEA headquarters made a religion of arrest-and-seizure
stats. Kiki and Pete were perfectly capable of delivering
what headquarters wanted. They could go up into the mountains, contact some peon, arrange a buy of a couple of keys
of heroin, then have the Federales arrest the guy and all his
friends. Rolling up enough arrests to collect medals was no
challenge.

But to what end? The agents believed such exercises were
fool's errands. They wanted to devote their time to long-
range projects, gathering intelligence on the major traffickers. From the sheer volume of contraband that informants
said was being moved, Pete and Kiki figured that the leaders
of the rings must enjoy the protection of a large number of
officials; the Federales were never willing to take on the
real traffickers. But the agents did not know the traffickers
well enough. Tracking their movements was like watching
a shadow puppet show. The ringleaders were extremely well
insulated. It would take months to figure out exactly what
they were doing, where their money was, who was working
for them, whom they were paying off. The agents could not
set up arrests of dozens of little guys and have time left to
trace the big boys.

The new generation of traffickers who occupied Guadalajara were the transplanted Sierra Madre highlanders
who had learned the trade as disciples of Pedro Aviles, the
late great drug lord of Sinaloa, and Alberto Sicilia Falcón,
the imprisoned Cuban cocaine king. They shuttled between
Sinaloa and Guadalajara. Guadalajara offered international
communications and banking facilities and was a more luxurious place to live than Culiacán, Sinaloa's bleak capital.
Their business ventures were amazingly sophisticated, for
they themselves were unlettered and barely civilized. Their
pleasures were food and Tequila and girls and, most of all,
guns; their idea of a good weekend was to go out to somebody's ranch, get drunk, and haul out the machine guns to
make the horses dance. But they had come to understand
that feuding with one another as their fathers had done
would only weaken them. So, like the cocaine traffickers of

Medellín in Colombia, they had formed a sort of cartel for the resolution of grievances and the pursuit of common goals, such as the suborning of government officials.

Three men seemed to dominate the Guadalajara cartel: Ernesto Fonseca Carrillo, Rafael Caro Quintero, and Miguel Angel Félix Gallardo. Below them were perhaps a dozen lesser warlords, including Manuel Salcido Uzeta (Cochi Loco), Javier Barba Hernández, and Juan José Esparragoza Moreno, who was called El Azul because his skin was so dark he looked blue.

Ernesto Fonseca, born in 1931, was the eldest of the cartel leaders. He was nicknamed Don Neto, which translates into English something like "Sir Goodprice." "So that evil old man is showing up again," Kuykendall thought. He had encountered Fonseca in 1973 in Ecuador. Well ahead of his time, Fonseca had been smuggling cocaine and had been caught by the Ecuàdoran Army with thirty kilograms.

By 1982, Fonseca was thought to be shipping bigger loads of cocaine to Tijuana, San Diego, and Los Angeles. Informants said that he was financing the cultivation and distribution of marijuana and heroin as well, sometimes in league with the Félix Gallardo organization, more often in partnership with Caro Quintero.

Fonseca had gone through several wives and numerous mistresses and had fathered many children. He looked like a hill country *bandido*, but the DEA agents took him very seriously. People said that in addition to his own trade, he provided enforcement services for the other gangs.

Rafael Caro Quintero dressed like a Mexican version of a rhinestone cowboy. The Caro and Quintero clans, who were from miserable mountain towns in the Sierra Madre uplands north and south of Culiacán, had been in smuggling for generations. Rafael's uncles, Emilio and Juan José Quintero Payán, were well-known marijuana and heroin traffickers, as was another uncle, Chapo Caro, and cousin, Francisco Javier Caro Payán. Baby-faced Rafael, born in the village of Lenoria, Sinaloa, in 1952, looked as if he was going to be even more important. He had been Pedro Aviles's foreman in Chihuahua. When Aviles was killed, Rafa, as he was known, began acquiring marijuana and opium plantations on his own.

Miguel Angel Félix Gallardo, slim and quiet, masked his lower-class origins behind a slick veneer. He was, by all accounts, a pitiless killer, but he could put on a tailored suit and look the part of a fast-track entrepreneur, which, in fact, he was. He was born in the Culiacán area in 1946. In the 1970s, he had worn the badge of the Sinaloa State Police and had been a bodyguard for Leopoldo Sánchez Celis, the governor of Sinaloa until 1980. By the 1980s, he reportedly hobnobbed as a social equal with the prominent families of Sinaloa, not only the Sánchez Celis family but the family of the succeeding Sinaloa governor, Antonio Toledo Corro. Eventually the DEA agents concluded that it was Félix Gallardo who had "brokered" the introductions of Caro Quintero, Fonseca, and other cartel members to powerful politicians and police officials in Guadalajara and the state of Jalisco and also set up protection arrangements with key federal officials.

There was something else that made Félix Gallardo of special concern to the DEA. In his activities, they began to detect, for the first time, an ominous new development that was certain to have great implications for American and Mexican government efforts to contain the traffickers.

Félix Gallardo was specializing in moving cocaine on a scale that had been accomplished only by Colombia's Medellín cartel. It appeared, in fact, that he had the potential to restructure the entire Mexican drug-trafficking industry so that it became a pipeline for South American cocaine. Cocaine was far more lucrative than marijuana and heroin combined, and because it arrived in Mexico in refined form, it was far less vulnerable to detection than marijuana and opium poppies, which, when growing, could be spotted from the air. The DEA agents realized that if the Mexican traffickers shifted from marijuana and heroin to cocaine, they would be virtually unstoppable. Eradication efforts would not touch them, and neither would conventional air surveillance. Mexico was dotted with thousands of isolated airstrips, where cocaine pilots flying out of South America could land unnoticed. The U.S. government's ability to conduct radar surveillance of airplanes crossing the long land border was no better than it had been during Operation Intercept in 1969—that is, it was almost nonexistent.

The DEA agents knew very little about Félix Gallardo's current operations, although the agency had been aware of him since 1975, when DEA agents found out he had formed a partnership with Juan Ramón Matta Ballesteros, the cocaine chemist who had been the South American connection for Alberto Sicilia Falcón. In early February 1977, Johnny Phelps, then stationed in the San Diego DEA office, got word that three hundred kilograms of cocaine had arrived in Culiacán from Colombia and that a private plane carrying half that load was heading for Tijuana. In those days, a load of that size had never been seen west of the Rockies. At five o'clock in the morning of the appointed day, Phelps rousted out a bunch of Federales and talked them into going to the Tijuana airport. When the plane landed, Phelps and the Federales watched another team of Federales meet the plane, stand guard as a pile of suitcases was loaded onto a truck, and form a motorcade to escort the cargo to a stash house. The Federales with Phelps raided the stash house, found 141 kilograms of cocaine, and became heroes for setting a record. The *comandante* of the Federales and the agents who stood guard over the airplane were fired. The man Phelps wanted most, the man who was supposed to have imported the cocaine from Colombia to Culiacán, was Félix Gallardo. He had had the sense to stay down in Sinaloa, where American agents had no influence to force his arrest. By 1979, Félix Gallardo was listed in DEA files as a middleman specializing in transportation, suspected of running outsize loads of cocaine into Arizona and Los Angeles.

In 1982, the Félix Gallardo cocaine organization was the focus of an intelligence project managed by Butch Sears, who had transferred to Guadalajara at about the time that Kuykendall arrived. The project, which became known as Operation Padrino, Operation Godfather, confounded Sears by its complexity; his early attempts at flow charts looked like spiderwebs. Eventually DEA intelligence analysts would conclude that Félix Gallardo was not only Mex-

ico's biggest cocaine dealer but also one of the biggest
traffickers in the Western hemisphere. His organization
grew to the point where he was shipping a ton and a half
to two tons of cocaine *a month,* which made him as powerful
as the Medellín kingpins.

Listening to Hernandez and Camarena, Kuykendall realized that the Guadalajara scene was worse than he had
imagined. He was impressed with the work that the young
agents were doing and understood their frustrations. An
iconoclast himself—he was not from Maverick County for
nothing—he had an affinity for men who did not take the
path of least resistance. He was one of the DEA's most
vociferous advocates of methodical intelligence gathering,
as opposed to superficial buy-busts. He realized that the
DEA, as an institution, knew very little about the way the
cartel leaders operated. Astonishingly, although more DEA
agents were based in Mexico than in any other foreign nation, not one of the new generation of kingpins had been
indicted in the United States. If Caro Quintero or Félix
Gallardo had shown up at DEA headquarters, there was
nothing the American agents could have done but buy them
a drink.

Kuykendall told the younger men he wanted them to find
out everything they could about the cartel leaders and their
silent partners in the political and economic establishment.
He expected that they would draw some heat from headquarters, but the hell with headquarters. He, Kuykendall,
would take the heat. "We're doing our job, and we're doing
a lot more than they think we are," he said. "We've got to
find out what the big boys are doing. I'm willing to forgo
the statistics as long as we see the big picture and eventually
get some of these big boys."

Kuykendall's consulate quarters took on the appearance
of a country sheriff's office. There were rusty spurs on his
desk, and usually his big boots were alongside them. He
was an immensely engaging man who enjoyed telling tall
tales in beer joints, a pastime that caused some of the North-
ern-born DEA agents to dismiss him as a good old boy. But

the cowboy façade masked a passionate seriousness about the theory and practice of law enforcement. When it came to evidence, Kuykendall was an exacting taskmaster. He never accepted obvious or easy solutions. He examined an informant's story from ten different angles and then ten more, looking for signs of duplicity and self-interest. He was insatiably curious about who the traffickers were and how their organizations were structured. He had a populist's love of common people and disdain for institutions, including his own. He agreed with the DEA's critics in Congress and at the Justice Department, who charged that the agency was more interested in seizing loads of drugs than in developing long-term strategies to strike at the hearts of the trafficking organizations. "Most DEA agents are content to make a bust," Kuykendall said. "They don't look past the arrest. They got the dope in one hand and the crook in the other, and that's all they care about."

Kuykendall prodded the younger agents to care about every detail, no matter how trivial it seemed at the time. He passed on Gene Pugh's lessons about the care and feeding of sources. "An informant," he said, "has to like you." You had to be his friend, go to his son's baptism, his daughter's wedding, take little presents to his mother, drink with him, sing with him.

Camarena and Hernandez were deeply influenced by Kuykendall. They threw themselves into their projects, fanning out, developing dozens of contacts, concentrating on Rafael Caro Quintero, Ernesto Fonseca, and other traffickers who were in the marijuana business. Camarena possessed charisma with informants that no one else could match. He was quieter than Hernandez, who could sing and tell stories all night, but there was something about his aggressive, direct manner that inspired confidence. People would follow him anywhere. Kuykendall recognized Kiki's animal magnetism and coached him on how to use his talents more effectively.

In May 1982, one of Camarena's informants came in with an outlandish tale. The man said that there were 220 acres of marijuana growing in the state of San Luis Potosí, about two hundred miles northeast of Guadalajara. The agents were skeptical. The plantation the man described would have been ambitious anywhere. This place was in the middle of the vast central Mexican desert. Nothing grew there but cactus.

The man insisted that such a thing *was* there. The plants were irrigated by underground wells. The marijuana stalks were already five feet high. The plantation belonged to Rafael Caro Quintero, Ernesto Fonseca, and Juan Esparragoza Moreno, who was known as El Azul.

The agents realized that the charges, if proven, would thoroughly discredit the Mexican eradication campaign. The Attorney General's Office, which was in charge of eradication, divided the country into zones. The airplanes provided by the U.S. government were supposed to fly over the zones at regular intervals. While it was difficult to spot a marijuana field on the forested western slopes of the Sierra Madre or in the jungles of Veracruz and Oaxaca, a field of any size in the desert would stand out like green neon. If the Caro Quintero–Fonseca–Esparragoza group had planted a third of a square mile in the desert of San Luis, this was a brazen and provocative act. And if the Mexican government personnel responsible for the zone failed to find it, the agents reasoned that meant one of two things: that they knew about it and were not telling, or that they did not know about it because they were not running reconnaissance missions contemplated in the agreement with the United States. In the first case, it was likely they were taking bribes. In the second case, they were taking U.S. money and aircraft under false pretenses. Either way, it was a slap in Uncle Sam's face.

And it meant that somebody was making big, big money. The marijuana patches in the Sierra Madre were only modestly profitable because of relatively high transportation and handling costs. Marijuana could not be cut, as heroin and cocaine were, to increase the take. The only way to become rich in marijuana was to cultivate and ship the commodity on a massive scale, as the Colombian traffickers were doing. That was hard to accomplish in the rugged backcountry of the Sierra Madre; but if Mexico's flat, arid central highlands could be converted to agribusiness with intensive irrigation and tons of fertilizer, just as California's central valleys had been, the profit potential was enormous.

The easiest way to find out what was going on would have been to fly over the place, but the DEA agents needed official escorts to do that, and they were not ready to tell the Federales what they knew. Kiki planted more informants inside the ring. According to Camarena's case files, those informants reported that a *comandante* of the Federales was protecting the plantation and had delivered arms there. They said that an Army lieutenant had been given a new Ford pickup truck by Esparragoza's assistant. Camarena and his partners became convinced the story was true. "The more we learned, the more awestruck we were with what was going on," Kuykendall said later.

Kuykendall tried to impress State Department officials in Mexico City with the significance of the desert plantation. In August 1982, he went to an embassy staff meeting and described the evidence Camarena was developing. He proposed extreme measures: shut down the border, as Richard Nixon had done in 1969 with Operation Intercept.

The diplomats shrugged off Kuykendall's exhortations: jawboning Mexican officials, they said, was counterproductive. Closing the border would be an act of economic war that would stir up anti-American resentment; a nationalistic reaction would undermine U.S. influence on narcotics and a range of issues. DEA attaché Dave Burnett noted that Camarena did not even know for sure that the plantation was out there.

It was a Catch-22 situation: Camarena had no proof because he could not fly over the area. He could not fly over the area because he did not have proof. The Mexican Attorney General's Office would not fly a DEA agent over the area without an explicit request from the embassy. The embassy was loath to press the issue without harder evidence.

Camarena went back to work. He secured a photograph of the area and enough detail to persuade the embassy that the plantations existed. In early September 1982, Camarena's evidence was presented to the Mexican Attorney General's Office. It was so compelling that Mexican officials ordered a search-and-destroy mission.

Seven helicopters took off early on a bright September morning, bearing a team of Army personnel and agents of the Mexican Federal Judicial Police. Camarena and Kuykendall were aboard. Even with all that they had heard, the DEA agents were shocked when the choppers dropped through the cloud cover and the emerald marijuana plantation came into sight.

Years later, Kuykendall could remember every detail: "When we were about twenty miles away, we began to see the dark-green spot. The clouds cleared from around us, and the closer we got, the more incredible it became. When we landed, we stood out in the middle of that damn thing and just looked at each other. It was overwhelming. If nothing else, the two of us knew at that moment that the magnitude of the problem was enormous. Because it was in the middle of the desert. You couldn't miss it. There wasn't anything green for miles. It was under a regular airline route. It was three miles from the major north–south railroad route, seven miles from a paved road. There was a little village nearby that was obviously being supported by these people living on the farm. The government could not have helped but know it was there. And after all, *we* found out. We had to do it covertly. You would think that the Mexicans, with a hell of a lot better control over their country than we had, who were able to ask questions under their own law, could find out."

The raid set a record, netting four thousand tons of high-grade sinsemilla marijuana. The plantation had been cultivated with the latest agricultural techniques: three deep wells irrigated the fields, and there were twenty tons of chemical fertilizer in the shed. The raiding party found barracks with beds for a hundred people and fresh food in the kitchen, but there was not a living soul within miles. According to Camarena's informants, an MFJP officer aware of the planned action had sent word just before the raid, giving the traffickers time to flee.

The Public Ministry in San Luis Potosí gave Camarena

evasive answers when he tried to obtain records concerning the ownership of the property. Camarena gave the Federales the information he had obtained from informants about the reputed owner, Antonio Pérez Parga, but Pérez was not arrested.

As Camarena and Kuykendall stood in the plots in the desert, amid robust marijuana stalks seven and eight feet high, they were more than ever convinced that, as Kuykendall put it, "fighting official corruption is going to solve the problem, not playing cops and robbers." In the minds of the DEA men, the question of corruption had been answered: they concluded that some MFJP officials in San Luis Potosí and Jalisco states had to be involved, as well as elements of the Army and possibly other government officials.

But they were up against the bureaucracy of their own State Department and of their superiors as well. Senior DEA officials in the embassy doubted that the discovery was all that significant. "They said it was a shot in the dark," Kuykendall said. "They said it was unique, that there weren't going to be any more cases like this. We said that it was *everywhere*."

Some weeks later, word of a second large plantation belonging to Caro Quintero, this one in the state of Sonora, reached Camarena. Kuykendall alerted the DEA office in Mexico City, which persuaded MFJP headquarters and the Army to send in a raiding party. Roger Knapp, who had recently joined the DEA group, went up to Culiacán to join the Federales on the raid.

The fields were exactly where the informant said, out in the open, 170 acres of marijuana. Knapp and the Federales went to Ciudad Obregón and spent the night, intending to begin the sweep at dawn. They rose at six o'clock in the morning, to find the MFJP *comandante* from Culiacán waiting for them. This *comandante,* said to be a close friend of Esparragoza, had been deliberately excluded from the raid. Evidently, he had heard about it during the night because he had driven over the mountains to Sonora to meet the raiding party. The *comandante* insisted on a delay. After waiting all day, Knapp decided the situation was hopeless and headed back to Guadalajara. Later the informant told him that the Federales had seized some of the marijuana but had allowed other fields to be harvested that day.

DEA agents based in northern Mexico were also hearing about Caro Quintero's desert plantations, and they encountered similar difficulties when they tried to have them raided. According to a DEA affidavit filed in federal court in San Diego in 1987, a DEA informant reported that in 1982 a Mexican Federal Judicial Police *comandante* in Hermosillo, Sonora, "was paid to provide protection of marijuana fields in Sonora financed by Rafael Caro Quintero and others." The informant located several fields for the DEA agents, who reported them to the Mexican government. Also that year, the affidavit said, the MFJP *comandante* from Hermosillo "attempted to intercede on Rafael Caro Quintero's behalf" when Rural Police in Linares, Nuevo León, found a large marijuana plantation. The *comandante* of the Linares Rural Police told DEA agents that he had rebuffed the MFJP *comandante*'s pleas and had destroyed the plantation.

In his year-end report to his superiors, Kuykendall wrote: "There is no longer any question but what things are bad. Now, the only question is, what are we going do about it?"

Kuykendall had very definite ideas about how to proceed. He argued that if narcotics traffickers were operating openly and on a grand scale, it was because the government, at a high level, had given them license to maneuver. A government that permitted flagrant criminality was either negligent or corrupt, but in either case, that government had to be convinced, or forced, to take drastic action. And that kind of convincing had to be done by the president of the United States, the senior officials of his administration, and the Congress.

"What the hell can twenty-five agents do in Mexico that two thousand agents can't do in the States?" Kuykendall scoffed. "We shouldn't be making busts abroad. A DEA agent should be overseas to gather intelligence and make enough cases to make the point, to tell the U.S. government what is going on, so that the government can take the appropriate political action."

To further that plan, in early 1983 Kuykendall went to

a San Antonio meeting of DEA officials from Washington and the border armed with a stack of blown-up photographs showing Camarena in the San Luis fields, almost hidden by the robust foliage. Kuykendall put the pictures on the wall and sat in a corner. When asked what the pictures showed, he said, "Corruption." They did not cause as much of a stir as he had hoped; he left believing that no one was interested.

Kuykendall tried again, writing in a report to the DEA office in the embassy, dated February 3, 1983: "Guadalajara continues to be the home of many major drug traffickers involved in the traffic of every drug of abuse. . . . Corruption within the law-enforcement community continues to be the major obstacle to effective investigative activity."

After a normal day's work, Kuykendall, Camarena, Hernandez, Sears, and Knapp would repair to the veranda of the Camelot bar, where they would watch the last rays of the sun as it set behind the U.S. consulate across Calle Libertad, discuss the meaning of snippets of fact, compare hunches, and talk philosophy.

At dusk, when Guadalajara smelled of rain and cooking, the veranda was a good vantage point from which to contemplate the vanity of American power, as personified by the drab concrete consulate, and the decline of the West, embodied in the Camelot's peeling caramel stucco, decrepit plumbing, and encroaching vines. The U.S. mission cut a dour and slightly comic figure among the carefree pastels of its neighbors. It looked like a minor civil servant delivering a summons at a garden party.

The DEA men would order a bucket of Estrellitas, icy, fist-sized bottles of Estrella-brand beer, and try to make some sense of the morass in which they found themselves. For one thing, they bitterly resented the fact that they did not have diplomatic immunity. The Mexican government granted the agents in Mexico City diplomatic status but refused to extend similar privileges to the agents in the resident offices. There remained from the 1920s an unwritten agreement between the DEA and the senior officials of the central government that DEA agents could carry their personal handguns, but when they did, they were in violation of Mexican law and therefore at the mercy of local officials.

Butch Sears had nearly been killed for lack of diplomatic credentials. He had gone up to the Zacatecas prison to see a guy he hoped to recruit as an informant. The jailkeepers did not understand what Butch wanted, and they seemed to believe that if he was really an American official, he would have a black passport, the universally recognized sign of diplomatic credentials. They locked Sears in the prison yard. He spotted some men that he had caused to be arrested and knew that if the men came after him, the guards would not interfere. Fortunately for Sears, the men went about their business, evidently assuming that no gringo would be in the Zacatecas jail. After about nine hours, the prison officials released Sears without explanation. Sears was really outraged when he found out that, unlike the DEA agents, forty Americans assigned to the U.S.–Mexican Screwworm Eradication Program, which studied the problem of parasites in the cattle of Texas and northern Mexico, had black passports.

A more fundamental dilemma was that the agents were constantly in the position of dealing with officials whom they did not trust. The very fabric of the Mexican system was knit together with patronage and, in some cases, an almost feudal arrangement that required junior officials to send their mentors tribute derived from "taxes" extorted from illegal enterprises. Mexico did not have the popular mechanisms that forced anti-corruption drives in the United States—newspaper crusades, partisan political campaigns, citizens' commissions. DEA agents habitually gathered information on their own, as best they could, and went to the Mexican Federal Judicial Police at the last possible moment. There were some courageous *comandantes* who would make arrests if they were approached correctly and if the trafficker in question had not made payoffs to officers more senior. But other *comandantes* would betray every DEA move to the crooks. When he worked in Calexico, Camarena made friends of some of the Federales in Mexicali. He tried the same tactics in Guadalajara, spending a lot of time at the MFJP office, talking, cajoling, charming, trying to pick up

bits of useful information. For a while, he thought he had
a friend or two. But then he found out that these men were
doing errands for the traffickers. Eventually, he and his
partners concluded that the MFJP was so leaky that they
dared not share sensitive information with even those Mexican police officers who seemed willing to help. The DEA
agents could never be sure that the men they considered
their allies were not playing a double game.

The DEA agents agonized constantly over how to give
the Federales enough information to form the basis for an
arrest and yet protect sources from being identified and
tortured or murdered. Even carefully laid schemes occasionally ended in tragedy. One time, Camarena and his
partners arranged for an informant to go to the Guadalajara
International Airport to buy some drugs from a midlevel
trafficker named Rogelio Guzmán. They asked the MFJP
comandante, Nicolás Flores Almazán, to meet them at the
airport, figuring that once he saw the buy, he would have
no choice but to order Guzmán locked up. Guzmán did not
show. Neither did the informant. The agents checked the
hospitals and morgues, to no avail. Finally, they gave the
informant's name to Flores in the hope that one of his men
might be able to locate him. A few days later, Camarena
found the name of the informant in an obituary notice that
said he had been killed by a gunshot. Sears went to the
morgue and identified the corpse. A hand was gone, ripped
from the man's body. The DEA agents speculated that
somewhere along the way, someone with access to the information they had given Flores had tipped the trafficker.
In time they were told by another informant that one of the
Federales was responsible for the leak that caused the man's
torture and death.

Neither DEA headquarters nor the U.S. Attorney's offices
along the border displayed any interest in pressing for indictments of Caro Quintero, Félix Gallardo, and the other
kingpins. Federal prosecutors were reluctant to devote time
and energy to developing conspiracy indictments against
foreigners who seldom came to the States; many DEA field
offices tended to concentrate on smugglers and distributors

who worked on the U.S. side of the line, where evidence was more readily obtainable. The only one of the cartel who had been indicted by this time was Ernesto Fonseca, and that case had been made by Customs agents in San Diego. Indeed, DEA headquarters had blocked the Customs investigation for weeks because of a turf struggle.

The investigation had begun in December 1982, when Customs agents working a money-laundering case were tipped to a group of Mexicans who were smuggling large amounts of cash from San Diego to Tijuana.[2] The trail led to a house in Rancho Santa Fe, an exclusive suburb high on a bluff overlooking the Pacific. The house was occupied by Ernesto Fonseca and some relatives of Rafael Caro Quintero. They were using a paging service and beepers to supervise the delivery of tons of marijuana, heroin, and cocaine to Los Angeles and to move millions of dollars back to Mexico.

The Customs agents asked the U.S. Attorney's Office to apply for a court order to wiretap the phone in the house. The DEA field office went along, but middle managers in DEA headquarters objected on grounds that Customs agents were supposed to stick to anti-smuggling investigations and had no jurisdiction to man a tap based upon the domestic narcotics trafficking laws. (Customs was working the case under the Bank Secrecy Act, which covered money-laundering violations, but since that statute was not on the list of violations that could justify a legal wiretap, Customs asked for a tap under the narcotics trafficking statutes.) When the turf dispute got to Jack Lawn, he saw that the important thing was to get the tap going, so he offered a compromise: he would deputize—"cross-designate" in the jargon—certain Customs agents so they could work the Fonseca wiretap. However, on January 28, 1983, just as the Customs agents were about to install the wiretap, Fonseca skipped town. The Customs men arrived at the house to find clothes in the closet and food on the table, as if Fonseca had been tipped, but they could never prove that the trafficker acted on more than his own keen instincts for survival.

———

By the middle of 1983, Kiki Camarena was convinced that Caro Quintero was establishing great sinsemilla plantations all over the central highlands. He wanted to get up in the air himself, on his terms. Maneuvering informants into position took weeks or months and was dangerous for them and tedious for him. He was fed up with what he had to do to get the MFJP to raid a place. Having to persuade the U.S. embassy was even more humiliating. Camarena, Knapp, and Kuykendall sometimes sneaked rides with pilot Alfredo Zavala Avelar, but what they saw was no good as evidence, since they could not admit where they had been.

Camarena went into his office and banged out a plan on his battered typewriter. He proposed that the Guadalajara office charter a plane, hire a pilot, and run its own air reconnaissance missions, without Mexican government pilots. It was a radical idea and Camarena knew it. He called his plan Operation Milagro, "Operation Miracle," because, as he told Kuykendall with a thin smile, it would be a miracle if anybody approved it.

Kuykendall approved it, and over the next months, in meetings among DEA supervisory personnel in Mexico City, he promoted the idea of DEA monitoring. He insisted that the State Department was understating the marijuana production estimates to accommodate Mexican government sensitivities.

Kuykendall always returned from these meetings in a state of rage, saying that the meetings had degenerated into shouting matches and that he had been told he was too dramatic.

No doubt about it, Kuykendall was dramatic. With his unruly shock of gray hair, his glittering blue eyes, and his apocalyptic prognostications, he looked something like an Old Testament prophet after a bad day with the Almighty. Younger agents admired his audacity, but in the DEA hierarchy and among the diplomats, he was getting a reputation as a loose cannon. He responded that his doubters were willfully deluding themselves, because facing the truth would require the American government to take political action that would disturb the tenuous peace between the two governments.

"There were hundreds of tons of marijuana being produced in Mexico in 1982 and 1983, and DEA didn't recognize that," he said. "It should have been obvious that trouble was coming to Mexico, because by then there were plenty of intelligence reports that indicated that the problem in Mexico was much larger than had been reported. All through 1983, our reports were indicating more, and more, and more."

The tension between Mexico City and the Guadalajara office worsened after Ed Heath was named DEA attaché in Mexico City in mid-1983. As DEA attaché in Colombia, Johnny Phelps regularly called or cabled Mullen or Lawn in Washington, and Mullen could recite every subtle threat against DEA's presence in Colombia. The same was true of Ray McKinnon, the attaché in Bangkok, another dangerous DEA post, where DEA objectives frequently collided with State and CIA priorities that emphasized Thailand's role as the United States' staunchest ally in Southeast Asia. But Heath steered clear of Mullen and Lawn. If he had problems with State and the CIA, they never knew about them: he did not send messages that grabbed their attention, as Phelps and McKinnon did. Heath made friends of officials in the Mexican Attorney General's Office and MFJP headquarters, particularly MFJP director Manuel Ibarra. His slow, solicitous approach to his prickly counterparts gratified Ambassador John Gavin and many U.S. embassy political officers but ensured clashes with Kuykendall and other field men. Diplomacy was the art of compromise. Kuykendall and many other field agents viewed compromise as a slippery slope. "Ed Heath," Kuykendall fumed, "has the worst case of client-itis I've ever seen."

The antagonisms were more than a matter of personality and style. The Guadalajara-based agents thought that Heath was overly trusting and told his contacts in the MFJP too much too soon. The agents said that in the summer of 1983, after they had spent several months working on identifying the members of Caro Quintero's network, Heath told Kuykendall to send him the names and addresses of all Caro Quintero's people in Guadalajara. One agent recalled that Heath said he would arrange for a "clean" task force of

Jaime Kuykendall (LEFT), Kiki Camarena (RIGHT), and a Mexican helicopter pilot prepare to accompany Mexican police on a raid. The DEA agents locate the marijuana fields and the Federales destroy them—sometimes.

Zamora, Mexico, March 6, 1985—The bodies of Kiki Camarena and Alfredo Zavala Avelar were found on a roadside in Michoacán. Kiki's friends called him "El Gallo Prieto," the dark rooster, the one who always wins.

San Diego, March 8, 1985—Enrique Camarena Jr., Mika Camarena, and Shaggy Wallace meet the U.S. Air Force plane bearing Kiki Camarena's body. "The war on drugs," said Jaime Kuykendall, "began on February 7, 1985. Nobody did anything until Kiki Camarena was gone."

San Diego, March 8, 1985—Kiki Camarena's casket is carried from the U.S. Air Force plane by an honor guard of U.S. Marines. The honor Mika wanted for Kiki was high-level U.S. attention to the war that killed him.

Mazatlán, Mexico, February 13, 1988—Ronald Reagan said that the Mexican president, Miguel de la Madrid, was doing all he could to stop drugs; de la Madrid said the American president was not doing enough. Kiki would have agreed with the Mexican president and argued adamantly with his own.

LEFT TO RIGHT: U.S. Attorney General Edwin Meese, U.S. Associate Attorney General Steve Trott, and Mexican Attorney General Sergio García Ramírez attend an October 1986 "drug summit" in Puerto Vallarta, Mexico. Meese said the Mexican officials were cooperating, but they withheld crucial evidence in the Camarena murder case.

Washington, D.C., September 14, 1986—President and Mrs. Reagan in their White House living room, moments before a joint televised appeal to "just say no" to drugs. Their commitment, some said, was long on words, short on cash, and driven by polls.

ABOVE: Northern Colombia is dotted with airstrips built by traffickers, who load drug shipments with little or no interference.

UPPER LEFT: The world's largest cocaine-refining complex, in Tranquilandia, Colombia, was set afire by Colombian security forces in March 1984. A U.S. satellite located 44 buildings, 6 airstrips, 9 laboratories, 10 tons of cocaine and cocaine base, and 10,800 drums of chemicals and aircraft fuel.

LEFT: Weeks after weapons and cocaine were seized in the 1984 Tranquilandia raid, Colombian Justice Minister Rodrigo Lara Bonilla was assassinated by gunmen linked to the Medellín cartel, which owned this cocaine-processing plant.

LEFT: San José del Llano, Mexico, September 27, 1977—A Mexican government eradication helicopter lands in an opium poppy field in the Sierra Madre mountains. The U.S. government gave Mexico the largest civilian airfleet in Latin America to mount an aerial spray campaign, Operation Condor, to kill the illicit crop.

RIGHT: When Mexican police dragged their heels in the search for Kiki Camarena, U.S. Customs Commissioner Willy von Raab ordered full inspections of all vehicles at the border, causing traffic to grind to a halt. DEA agents believed this act of economic warfare led to the discovery of Camarena's body.

March 29, 1988—Willy von Raab, U.S. commissioner of customs, waits to testify before the House Select Committee on Narcotics Abuse and Control. He said of Mexico, "Until I'm shown that an individual is not corrupt, the level of corruption is so great my presumption is that he *is* corrupt."

LEFT: General Manuel Antonio Noriega helped the CIA, Castro, the Contras, the Sandinistas, the DEA, and, said his associates, the cocaine kingpins of Medellín.

RIGHT: Five weeks after his arrest on November 21, 1987, Jorge Ochoa of the Medellín cocaine dynasty walked out of a Bogotá prison. Colombian Attorney General Carlos Mauro Hoyos Jiménez investigated his release—and was assassinated.

LEFT: Mexican journalists called Miguel Angel Félix Gallardo *narcopolítico* because of his extensive political connections; DEA called him "El Padrino," the godfather. He ruled a cocaine-trafficking empire that stretched from Peru to California to Europe.

RIGHT: Ernesto Fonseca, a.k.a. "Don Neto," Sir Goodprice, said that when he found out that his partner, Rafael Caro Quintero, had allowed Kiki Camarena to die, he slapped him and said, "Idiot! You made the baby, now you live with it."

Bud Mullen, DEA administrator until March 1, 1985, broke the American government's long silence on corruption in Mexico. "People here say, Well, there's a different mentality in Mexico and we should accept it," he said. "I just don't agree. It is not acceptable."

LEFT: Carlos Lehder, the wildest member of the Medellín cartel, was the first to be convicted in the United States.

RIGHT: Medellín cartel kingpin Pablo Escobar became one of the world's richest men in the cocaine trade, won a congressional seat, and is known as "Don Pablo the good" for his gifts to the poor.

LEFT: Rafael Caro Quintero, an illiterate entrepreneur, made the desert green with thousands of acres of sinsemilla marijuana and became one of the world's major drug dealers.

RIGHT: Juan Ramón Matta Ballesteros, multimillionaire alleged partner in Miguel Antel Félix Gallardo's organization, claimed he was the victim of a smear campaign after being seized by Honduran officers and forced to fly to the United States in April 1988.

Jack Lawn became acting administrator of the DEA in the middle of the Camarena crisis. The White House wanted him to plug anti-Mexico leaks. He refused, saying, "If I can't speak out when one of my men is in trouble, I won't be able to look myself in the mirror."

San Diego, March 8, 1985—Mika Camarena leans against Jack Lawn as Kiki Camarena's casket is carried from a U.S. Air Force plane. Just weeks before he disappeared, in despair over lack of U.S. attention to the drug trade and to corruption in Mexico, Kiki asked, "Does somebody have to die?"

MFJP agents from Mexico City to come to Guadalajara and hit the houses. Kuykendall did not like the idea but had no choice; it was a direct order. The Federales arrived and checked into the Motel de las Américas, which belonged to Miguel Angel Félix Gallardo. By the time they started searching the houses, in desultory fashion, everyone they were supposed to find was gone. Camarena and his partners spent months trying to find new addresses and telephone numbers for the gang members.

In May 1983, Pete Hernandez asked for a transfer back to Texas. He told his partners he wanted to put somebody in jail who would stay in jail. He was tired of seeing the dopers pay their way out and fed up with being laughed at by the Federales. He was accustomed to being pushed around by lawyers and snubbed by diplomats, but he said he could not stand being slighted by the embassy and the DEA hierarchy.

A few months later, Butch Sears heard there was an opening in Bolivia and he applied for the job. He said he figured that Bolivia might be corrupt and backward, but the embassy officers and the DEA agents seemed to be on the same side.

One reason Sears was frustrated was that no one at the embassy had pressed his case with the Mexican government for access to bank records that might have shed some light on the inner workings of the cocaine-trafficking organization of Miguel Angel Félix Gallardo. Camarena, Hernandez, and Knapp had been able to run informants into the Caro Quintero operation with relative ease, but that was because marijuana trafficking required thousands of farmers, overseers, engineers, truck drivers, and guards. Sears had had no luck penetrating the Félix Gallardo ring. Trafficking in finished cocaine was capital intensive but not labor intensive. A man like Félix Gallardo needed only a small core of trusted lieutenants, but he had to be able to move millions of dollars into numerous countries to pay for cocaine, airplanes, trucks, and bribes. Sears figured that the best way to break into the tight cocaine cabal was by analyzing its financial transactions.

In early 1982, Sears came to suspect that Félix Gallardo

had acquired an interest in a Guadalajara bank in order to launder his money. He asked the Mexican government for the trafficker's bank records and was refused outright. Later in the year, DEA agents in Lima came across a cashier's check from the Bank of America in San Diego. Jerry Kelly and some other DEA agents in San Diego had the Bank of America records subpoenaed. They were astonished to find that the Félix Gallardo organization had moved $20 million through one Bank of America account in a single month. At that rate, the agents figured, the ring could be grossing $200 million a year, or even more, considering that big narcotics operations scattered their holdings among many banks.

As the agents pieced together the scheme, proceeds from cocaine sales on the West Coast were being collected and trucked to Guadalajara, deposited in Félix Gallardo's bank there, and wired back to the Bank of America in San Diego. Félix Gallardo's money handler, Tomás Valles Corral, would withdraw the money in the form of cashier's checks in denominations of $40,000 or $50,000 and send them to South America to pay the cocaine producers.[3]

The canceled checks were the first solid clues the DEA had to Félix Gallardo's sources of cocaine. Some checks had been cashed in obscure jungle towns in Colombia, some in the wilds of the Peruvian Andes, some on the Peru–Bolivia border. Four checks worth $200,000 turned up in Switzerland, in the possession of Roberto Suárez, Jr., of the famous Bolivian cocaine family. Sears and Kelly took copies of the canceled checks to Mexico City to show them to bank regulators and Mexican Customs officials. Once more, they asked for access to Mexican bank records, which they thought would disclose Félix Gallardo's associates and investments. Once more, they were rejected. Sears hoped someone in the embassy would make an issue of the case at high-level meetings. That might not work, but Sears would have been happy with any sign that Operation Padrino mattered to somebody besides himself and his partners. When there was no action from the embassy, Sears took that as a sign of another sort.

Sears's mood improved briefly when an informant slipped

him the radio frequencies that Félix Gallardo's communications network used to orchestrate the movements of planes and trucks. DEA-Guadalajara asked the CIA station in Mexico City to help set up a system to monitor the radio traffic. But no response came, so the agents bought some equipment from a Radio Shack outlet in the States and patched together their own monitoring system. Sears said that was the last straw and packed off for Bolivia.

Roger Knapp replaced Sears as case agent for Operation Padrino. Just before Easter in 1984, Knapp got a tip that a big load of cocaine was coming into Guadalajara. Félix Gallardo was supposed to meet it himself. MFJP headquarters in Mexico City agreed to send in a "clean" team of agents. Exhilarated, Knapp waited for the Federales to catch the godfather red-handed. But the delivery never materialized, and Félix Gallardo did not show.

There were several possible explanations. One was that DEA's intelligence had been faulty. The other was that there had been a security breach or, worse, a deliberate leak on the part of the Mexican officials who knew of the planned bust. There were a good many officials who were aware of the operation, including Miguel Aldana Ibarra, the leader of Operation Pacífico, the MFJP's campaign against drug trafficking.

The son of a general, Aldana had worked his way up through the ranks of the DFS and in the last years of the López Portillo regime was a senior commander of the DFS.

Miguel de la Madrid, who ran for the presidency in 1982 promising a "moral renovation campaign," tapped Manuel Ibarra Herrera, a Mexico City lawyer, to run the MFJP, with orders to transform the agency into a respected professional force. Ibarra chose his kinsman Aldana, who had a reputation for toughness and professionalism, for the best job in the MFJP, *primer comandante* in charge of the Mexico City office of Interpol. The Interpol job was prestigious because it gave its holder entrée to multilateral law-enforcement convocations and access to sensitive information developed by foreign police agencies, including forthcoming operations against international traffickers in drugs and arms. Ibarra also gave Aldana command of Operation

Pacífico, a high-profile job that would keep his picture on the front pages of the Mexican newspapers. Whenever the Federales made a major bust, the barrel-chested Aldana would show up in camouflage fatigues, carrying an AK-47, to take charge and pose for newspaper photographers.

The raids Aldana led netted many small fish but never any kingpins. As time passed, the same questions kept arising: Had someone in Aldana's Operation Pacífico tipped off the key traffickers? Were security procedures sloppy? Or had DEA's intelligence been wrong?

The congressmen and journalists in Washington who followed the progress of the traffickers in Latin America never heard from the Reagan administration about Félix Gallardo's expanding cocaine empire or about the giant marijuana plantations Caro Quintero and Fonseca were financing. On June 22, 1983, Dominick DiCarlo, the assistant secretary of state for the Bureau of International Narcotics Matters (INM), testified before the House Select Committee on Narcotics Abuse and Control about the status of illicit drug cultivation in various nations. DiCarlo's testimony painted Mexico's marijuana- and opium-eradication program in rosy terms. The Mexican program was so successful, DiCarlo said, that the growers had countered by planting fields that were "smaller, more isolated and more difficult to detect." He told the committee that the marijuana fields averaged one fourteenth of a hectare, or less than eight hundred square yards.[4] There was nothing small and difficult to detect about marijuana fields Camarena and his partners were finding in the desert, but DiCarlo did not mention these large, open plantations at all.

The position of the State Department's Narcotics Assistance Unit (NAU) in Mexico City was that the desert fields were aberrations. The NAU's priority was opium. NAU officers were devoting nearly all their time to studying poppy growing in the Sierra Madre. In that region, poppy fields and marijuana plantings were relatively small due to the steep terrain and the risk of air surveillance.

Even so, INM's reports to the Congress were less than straightforward. DiCarlo's aides conceded much later that they had known in 1983 that the Mexican anti-drug campaign was eroding under their feet. They had a tendency, as one official would later acknowledge, "to pull punches and say yes, the program is in place, it's working."

Jon Thomas, who joined DiCarlo's staff in 1982, saw immediately that the Narcotics Assistance Unit in Mexico City was in trouble. It was chronically understaffed; ambitious foreign service officers would not take NAU jobs. "In the Carter administration, being involved in narcotics in the Department of State was like running a VD clinic on an Army base," said Thomas. "You had to have one, but nobody talked about it in company." The manager of the Mexico City Narcotics Assistance Unit had allowed a mass of paperwork to build up and could not account for hundreds of thousands of U.S. government dollars that were supposed to have gone into maintenance of the eradication air fleet, which was literally falling apart. Thomas shook up the Mexico office and set about recruiting fresh staffers.

In 1983, the INM acquired a type of spray aircraft called the Turbothrush, a fast, fixed-wing crop duster that could spray fields more efficiently than helicopters. At that point, Thomas and other members of his bureau were still convinced that inefficiency, rather than corruption, was the major obstacle to be overcome in Mexico. But when the Thrush was sent into the Sierra Madre for a demonstration, its American test pilot noted, with considerable dismay, that opium poppies and marijuana were growing all over the place, far more extensively than the Mexican government had acknowledged. When the Mexican government denied the pilot's report, Thomas saw that the American government would have to have some kind of independent verification of the eradication figures the Mexican government was churning out.

Even so, Thomas did not suspect that the desert plantations that the Guadalajara group had discovered were significant. The Thrush tests were conducted in the western Sierra Madre, hundreds of miles from the area where Camarena and his partners had located the big fields. "I didn't think in late 1982 to early 1983," Thomas said later, "that within two years we'd have large-scale marijuana production because it would've been impossible to do that without detection. Or so we thought." In retrospect, Thomas realized that the agents in Guadalajara "were on to something that wasn't fully recognized. For whatever reason, the information being developed didn't cause the DEA to ring the alarm bells."

In August 1983, Chairman Charles Rangel and eight other members of the House Select Committee on Narcotics Abuse and Control and the House Judiciary Committee went to Mexico City on a fact-finding mission. Kuykendall asked to speak to the congressmen about the desert fields. The American embassy refused permission. The congressmen were kept busy attending scheduled briefings at the embassy and the Mexican Attorney General's Office. The committee's trip report suggested that the warm Mexican reception had had the desired effect. It said that DEA and MFJP officials had not been on speaking terms during the last eighteen months of the López Portillo regime but that all was forgiven:

> With the start-up of the de la Madrid administration eight months ago . . . DEA is highly enthusiastic that its renewed cooperation with the Federal Judicial Police will lead to substantial narcotic arrests, seizures, and prosecutions on both sides of the border in the traffic affecting the United States. . . . The Mexican government . . . has built the world's finest aerial crop-eradication program. Its size, professionalism, competence, performance, and experience make it the world leader in this technique. . . . As always, Mexico has been our "Good Neighbor."[5]

Some members of Rangel's delegation were more skeptical than the report reflected. Rangel later said that the embassy briefing was so vacuous that he felt insulted and walked out. Gavin agreed with him and demanded yet another shake-up of the NAU staff. Congressman William J. Hughes, a New Jersey Democrat and former prosecutor who was chairman of the House Judiciary Subcommittee on Crime, took a hard look at Ed Heath's list of joint investigations with the MFJP and sensed that something was wrong. DEA stationed more agents in Mexico than in any other foreign country, but Hughes thought the list was too short to justify that substantial DEA presence. He had just been to South America and observed that DEA offices with three or four agents were working more cases than thirty agents in Mexico were handling. When Hughes asked about cooperation with the Federales, DEA officials told him there were problems, as with any foreign government, but not serious ones. Hughes was not satisfied, but he could not come up with any hard evidence to refute this claim. When Hughes returned to Washington, he went straight to Mullen's office to express his misgivings about the situation. In 1985, when he found out about the extent of corruption among the Federales, he complained to Jack Lawn that he had been "grossly misled." If he and his colleagues had known how bad things were, he said, the delegation might have raised the issue with de la Madrid's aides, and that might have prevented the situation from getting out of hand. Lawn agreed with Hughes on both counts. Yes, he had been misinformed. Yes, a Congressional scolding might have helped. Lawn had had a similar experience. He had gone to Mexico in 1982 and had made further inquiries in 1983 and, he ruefully recalled, "Everybody said everything is wonderful."

A few weeks after the Rangel delegation left Mexico, the DEA agents in Guadalajara heard of yet another big desert plantation, two hundred acres of sinsemilla in Zacatecas. They alerted the Federales, who went in and claimed to have destroyed the plantation. Later, two informants told the DEA agents that the marijuana had actually been harvested and stacked by soldiers in the Mexican Army.

By January 1984, marijuana seizures along the Southwest border had increased fivefold over 1980 and would undoubtedly have been greater if more DEA and Customs personnel had been on the border. This was another strong warning that the Mexican government's claims of victory over the marijuana growers were exaggerated. Still, DEA headquarters took no notice. One reason was bureaucratic inertia: no single person in headquarters saw the reports from Mexico and the border. Reports from Lima or La Paz went to just one place, the cocaine desk. Reports from Bogotá were rated top priority. They went straight to the front office and were closely read by Mullen, Lawn, and all their top aides. The fact that every imaginable variety of illegal substance came from or passed through Mexico had the perverse effect of guaranteeing that no one at headquarters would see the whole picture. Reports from Mexico were scattered among the cocaine desk, the marijuana desk, the dangerous drugs desk, the heroin desk, and various subsections in the intelligence division. Since no senior official was directly accountable for anticipating problems in Mexico or for coordinating activities on the border and in Mexico, middle managers at headquarters did not make a vigorous effort to put together a comprehensive assessment of the trafficking scene in Mexico, nor did they suggest to Mullen or Lawn that the conventional wisdom—that the Mexican program was working well enough—was dated.

Headquarters' indifference was a black joke among the border rats. Ken Miley, who was now the agent in charge of DEA's McAllen, Texas, resident office, was fond of describing the mindset in Washington by scrawling a rough map of the United States on a scrap of paper. The map had four dots on it, which Miley would spear with a sharp pencil as he talked.

"All people at headquarters know about," he would say, piercing the first dot, Washington, "is New York"—blackening the second dot—"because they came from there, Miami"—circling the third dot—"because people from New York go there on vacation, and Los Angeles"—spiking the fourth dot—"because that's where they make all the movies and television shows they watch."

"All the rest," Miley would drawl, shading the whole scrap, "is Indian country."

Bud Mullen bristled when he heard, years later, of these murmurings of dissension. If the agents on the border felt strongly that a problem was being neglected, he said, they should have spoken up. He had attended many meetings of the SACS, the special agents in charge, at which concerns might have been raised. The flaw in that argument was that east of San Diego none of the agents in charge of the border offices were SACS. They were RACS, resident agents in charge of small offices, and they rarely attended senior management conferences. Most were former Customs agents with few close friends at headquarters, where former BNDD officials from the Northeast still dominated the hierarchy. Many of the agents in the Southwest and Mexico had other problems communicating with headquarters. They were wonderful raconteurs but reluctant writers who had neither the time, the inclination, nor the skill to dash off brilliant, provocative intelligence analyses that might have commanded the notice of Washington policymakers.

The border rats tried, in tentative ways, to have more impact on the decision-making process. In January 1984, Travis Kuykendall, the resident agent in charge of the DEA office in Tucson, convened a meeting of border RACS from Texas, New Mexico, Arizona, and Mexico. He invited headquarters to send a representative. "We said, hey, this stuff is swamping us," Kuykendall said. "DEA headquarters was so concentrated on South America, this other thing slipped out of hand." The border agents hoped to convince Washington that a substantial increase in people and money for the region was essential to head off a new Mexican drug explosion. There was no response. A couple of months later, the Tucson office made its biggest haul in years, two tractor-trailer loads of marijuana, thirty-nine thousand pounds in all.

The most important case of Kiki Camarena's career took shape in early 1984. An informant reported that the Guadalajara traffickers had formed a syndicate to finance thousands of acres of sinsemilla marijuana plantations in Zacatecas, Durango, and Chihuahua. The list was a Who's Who of the Mexican narcotics industry: Rafael Caro Quintero, Ernesto Fonseca, Juan Esparragoza, and twenty-one other men.

Camarena tapped his sources to find out more about the syndicate. In violation of the agreement between the United States and Mexico that banned air surveillance by American agents, Camarena paid Captain Alfredo Zavala Avelar, the former Mexican military pilot, to fly Kuykendall and himself to Zacatecas to see the marijuana fields, which were exactly where Camarena had heard they would be. Back at the consulate, Camarena and Kuykendall wrote a blizzard of cables about their find. Agronomists had been hired, modern farm machinery trucked in. According to Camarena's case notes, his informants said that DFS *comandante* Felipe Aparicio Núñez and MFJP *comandante* Galo Gutiérrez were not merely taking money to look the other way but had invested in the marijuana farming venture. One informant claimed to have seen the DFS *comandante* take 50 million pesos from a bagman for Rafael Caro Quintero. The informant told Camarena that the MFJP *comandante* told him "he welcomed traffickers to plant in the Zacatecas area and he would provide protection and introduce them to the DFS *comandante* and the military in order to make arrangements with them for protection." When Camarena and Knapp talked to MFJP *comandante* Gutiérrez about his relationship with the traffickers, he made no bones about it: "They come and make you an offer," the *comandante* said, as Knapp recalled. "We'll make you wealthy or make you dead. So you'd rather be wealthy than dead."

In late May, Heath's deputy, Walter White, told Camarena and Kuykendall the Federales knew of the Zacatecas plantations and were planning to raid them. Kuykendall concluded from the conversation that Heath had informed MFJP headquarters over his objections and those of Camarena, who said that it was not time to hit the fields because the marijuana hadn't grown big enough. Camarena exploded at Kuykendall for being unable to talk Heath into delaying the raid. "What's the sense in my working if he's going to do that?" he stormed, as Kuykendall recalled.

The Federales, led by Primer Comandante Miguel Aldana Ibarra, moved in on the plantations shortly thereafter. The seizure amounted to 150 acres of marijuana fields, 20 tons of manicured marijuana, about 200 liters of hashish oil, and enough marijuana seed to plant 6,500 acres of marijuana. According to Mexican newspapers, Aldana announced that his forces had arrested 177 people. What the stories did not say was that, as usual, the major suspects were nowhere to be found.

The raid made headlines in the Mexican papers, but Camarena was crestfallen. Twenty tons of marijuana was nothing, compared with what he had believed was there, based on the informant's accounts and his own observations from the air and on the ground. "It should have been a lot more," Kuykendall agreed. "There probably were hundreds of acres, but they held us off for a few days before we actually went in. It was my opinion that the delay was so they could either harvest or plow under the fields."

The disappointment the agents felt was reflected in Kuykendall's May 30 report on the raid:

> RAC Kuykendall believes the operation went well despite the low number of plantations located, and he achieved what he set out to do: demonstrate to the government the widespread marijuana cultivation in the state of Zacatecas, the greatly improved agricultural techniques now employed, and the extensive official corruption which has allowed it to occur. The several eradication zone coordinators present during the operation, originally gleeful over lack of plantation findings, now have little to say in view of the MFJP findings during this long weekend. There truly is evidence of extensive marijuana cultivation and no doubt remains as to malfeasance on the part of GOM [government of Mexico] officials in that area. The MFJP investigation is now winding down, when, if U.S. federal agents were in charge, it should be picking up momentum. The MFJP has done a commendable job. But its investigative interests are considerably different from ours. . . . Prior to kicking off the operation, the prior suspects were clearly alerted, since they had left for other parts and it was apparent that the Mexican Army in Zacatecas had made a concerted effort to destroy *plantios* [farms] during the several days preceding MFJP arrival in the area.

There was something else that troubled the American agents. The Caro Quintero gang now knew who Kiki Camarena was and what he looked like. Having broken one rule against flying over the plantations alone, Camarena had

broken another, against working undercover. Fed up with
having his intelligence reports questioned, he had decided
to make his own observations. According to Kuykendall,
Camarena went undercover to the Zacatecas plantation,
looked around, and had an informant introduce him to Caro
Quintero's overseer, Manuel Chávez. Chávez saw Camarena with the Federales when they arrested him. The overseer was freed a short time later. Kuykendall and
Camarena assumed that Chávez told Caro Quintero about
Camarena's role in the case.[6]

The frustrations of the Zacatecas investigation only caused
Camarena to work harder. He made new sources among
the merchants and farmers who sold things to the traffickers.
He ran an informant into the MFJP office in an effort to
find out who was tipping the traffickers. He and his partners
worked the banks, the airport, the hotels, the bars. In mid-
summer, 1984, they developed intelligence that Caro Quintero and his syndicate were establishing other large
plantations in the desert states of Chihuahua, Sonora, and
Baja California.

   Caro Quintero's style was not cramped in the least by
the unwelcome attentions of the DEA. He acquired dozens
of ranches and villas all over northern and central Mexico.
He bought twenty-five acres in an affluent suburb of Guadalajara with $4 million in cash that he produced from the
trunk of his car. He built a seventeen-foot-high cement wall
around the perimeter and broke ground for a palatial residence. As this ostentatious mansion went up, everyone in
Guadalajara could see that Rafael Caro Quintero was no
outlaw. Outlaws had hideouts. Rafael lived where he
pleased.

"War without Quarter"

For nine months in 1983 and 1984 Rodrigo Lara Bonilla, the Colombian minister of justice, was Latin America's most forceful voice against drug trafficking. The thirty-eight-year-old crusader survived two assassination attempts but sensed that his luck had run out. On April 30, 1984, he paid a somber courtesy call upon his friend U.S. Ambassador Lewis Tambs. Lara Bonilla was leaving in a few days to become Colombia's ambassador to Czechoslovakia. He thought—at least he hoped—that the drug cartel could not reach behind the Iron Curtain.

That evening, Lara Bonilla headed home in a chauffeur-driven Mercedes tailed by four armed bodyguards in a jeep. As the motorcade cruised through a residential neighborhood, a car pulled out and blocked the way. Two young men riding a motorcycle broke through the bodyguards and unloaded their submachine guns into the Mercedes. Lara Bonilla was killed instantly. One of the assassins was killed in the cross fire. The other quickly confessed that he and his companion had been paid $20,000 by the leaders of the Colombian cocaine cartel.

At two-thirty the next morning, President Belisario Betancur went on television to announce a state of siege, which suspended individual rights and gave the military broad civil law-enforcement powers. "We are unleashing a war without quarter against the crooks who sow terror in cities, towns, and the countryside," Betancur declared.

Then, at Lara Bonilla's graveside, Betancur announced that he would enforce the extradition treaty with the United States signed by his predecessor, the hawkish César Turbay. This must have been a wrenching decision for Betancur, who had entered office with deep reservations about the treaty. He had hoped for a time when Colombian drug traffickers would be tried and sentenced in Colombia. As he stood beside his young aide's mangled body, he abandoned that dream. "Stop, enemies of humanity," he said, voice trembling, as he gazed into the throng of mourners. "Colombia will hand over criminals . . . wanted in other countries so that they may be punished as an example."

One of the first extradition orders was for Carlos Lehder, a leader of the Medellín cocaine cartel. Security forces fanned out into the countryside. Hundreds of small-time hoodlums were rounded up, but Lehder and his fellow kingpins, Jorge Ochoa and Pablo Escobar, had vanished.

A pacifist populist with a visionary streak, Belisario Betancur had campaigned on a promise to bring the disenfranchised and disaffected into the political process. He was the first real peace candidate in years and a most unorthodox standard-bearer for the Conservative party, which was associated with the old-money aristocracy. One of twenty children of an impoverished mule driver from central Colombia, Betancur had worked his way though college and law school, sleeping on park benches when he could not pay for shelter. At his inauguration in August 1982, he had declared, "I am extending my hand to the rebels in arms so that they may join in the full exercise of their rights." A flock of white pigeons had been released to flutter above the heads of the crowd.

Betancur freed political prisoners, offered an amnesty to dissidents, and began negotiating a cease-fire with the guerrilla groups who held much of the countryside. Drug enforcement was not high on his agenda. Betancur's economic reform package included an "immediate, wide, and generous amnesty" on undeclared income. The measure was meant to bring capital back into the country and to expand employment, but it had the effect of allowing the traffickers to launder and invest *dineros calientes*, drug money.

Rodrigo Lara Bonilla, a young lawyer from the Liberal party who was appointed justice minister in August 1983, grasped the implications of the expanding cocaine empire earlier than most of his countrymen. He was determined to make Betancur see that the traffickers as well as the guerrillas jeopardized Colombia's national security.

"I am a dangerous minister for those who act outside the law," Lara Bonilla declared. "I only hope they don't catch me by surprise."

Lara Bonilla created a scandal by accusing the drug cartel of using drug money to buy hidden interests in six of the country's top professional soccer teams. The justice minister told reporters that two well-known traffickers, Gonzalo and Justo Pastor Rodríguez Gacha, were main stockholders in Bogotá's Millionarios team. He added that Hernán Botero Moreno, of a prominent Medellín family, indicted for money laundering in a Customs investigation in Miami, owned part of Medellín's Atlético Nacional and that brothers Gilberto and Miguel Rodríguez Orejuela of Cali controlled that city's América team as well as discos, restaurants, airplanes, and radio stations.[1]

This was like telling Americans that the Mafia owned the Washington Redskins, the Dallas Cowboys, and the Chicago Bears. Badgered by Lara Bonilla, the Colombian Institute of Youth and Sport—Colombia's version of the National Football League—launched an investigation.

As Lara Bonilla railed against *dineros calientes*, Carlos Lehder and Pablo Escobar retorted, accurately, that both major political parties had accepted $1 million from cartel members for the 1982 elections, during which Escobar been elected to Congress. The traffickers produced documents showing that Lara Bonilla himself had taken $12,000 in *caliente* money. Confronted with this evidence, Lara Bonilla admitted taking the money but said he was unaware of its source. The attack on his integrity only made the young minister more strident. He revoked airplane licenses traced to suspected drug dealers and campaigned for enforcement of the extradition treaty. Carlos Lehder attacked him vociferously, using his newspaper, *Quindío Libre,* to brand the minister a *vende-patria*, a traitor, who collaborated with the "imperialist" forces of the Reagan administration.

Lara Bonilla's most intriguing assertion, and the most difficult to support, was that the Medellín traffickers were funding paramilitary death squads. This was certainly true in late 1981, when the Medellín cartel had openly created the organization called Muerte a Secuestradores (MAS), "Death to Kidnappers." The vigilante group's original mission was to find Marta Ochoa, the daughter of Medellín cartel leader Fabio Ochoa, who had been kidnapped by the leftist terrorist group M-19. Numbering between a thousand and fifteen hundred people, the M-19 gained international recognition in 1980, when it captured the Dominican embassy and held U.S. Ambassador Diego Asencio and eighteen other diplomats hostage for two months. The siege ended peacefully when the Colombian government agreed to allow the guerrillas to fly to Havana. In 1981, presented with evidence that the Castro government had been training M-19 guerrillas and infiltrating them back into Colombia, President Turbay suspended relations with Cuba. "It was a kind of Pearl Harbor for us," he said.[2]

After Marta Ochoa's rescue, assassination squads using the MAS name were implicated in the deaths of dozens of journalists, labor leaders, human rights activists, lawyers, professors, and other citizens with real or purported connections to the left. Human rights activists charged that the death squads were driven by radical rightist elements within the Colombian military who wanted to undermine Betancur's cease-fire so that they would be free to wage war on the guerrillas. Betancur took the charges of military involvement seriously. If Army leaders were using terror to provoke the guerrillas to retaliation, his negotiations for a cease-fire would never work. Betancur asked the attorney general, Carlos Jiménez Gómez, to look into the operations of the MAS squads. In early 1983, Jiménez Gómez reported that he had identified fifty-nine active-duty military personnel on MAS squads. Military leaders responded that the charges were an insult to the Army's honor, refused to allow Army personnel to be tried in civilian courts, and promised that every soldier would contribute a day's pay to defend his colleagues accused of death squad activity.[3]

Jiménez Gómez could not prove that the Medellín traffickers continued to back MAS death squads. He concluded that MAS was not a single entity but "a state of mind," a *nom de guerre* used by a number of cliques and gangs. Lara Bonilla charged that the traffickers were still supporting the death squads, but he did not offer incontrovertible proof. Certainly there was circumstantial evidence that the right and the traffickers were sometimes allied—notably Carlos Lehder's sponsorship of "patriotic Saturdays," at which he gave fanatical speeches praising Adolf Hitler, and the allegations that he offered paramilitary training for young men who joined his National Latin Movement. Another interesting, though inconclusive, scrap of evidence was the organizational chart DEA agents found on a lower-level member of the Medellín cartel. Disclosed in November 1984 at hearings of President Reagan's Commission on Organized Crime, the chart listed "Muerte a Secuestradores" along with "police and military" among the functions of the enforcement arm of the Ochoa family.[4] The commission's final report did not explore the Medellín-MAS connection further, but DEA officials who helped the commission prepare the report said they believed that the traffickers were involved in some death squad activity after 1981.

For Colombian military leaders and the conservative Bogotá elite, the question of an alliance between the cartel and the extreme right was overshadowed by fear that the leftist guerrillas would make a pact with the traffickers and use drug profits to buy arms, either on their own or in concert with Cuba and Nicaragua.

This fear was not only shared but encouraged and exploited by conservatives in the Reagan administration. For several years, the right wing in the United States had been predicting that leftist terrorists and cocaine traffickers would merge into a diabolical conspiracy of "narcoterrorism." This faction held that Cuba and Nicaragua, with the sanction of the Soviet Union, would facilitate the drug trade in order to defile American youth and acquire hard currency for the export of Marxist revolution.

What appeared to be the first direct evidence that Cuban officials were involved in the drugs-for-guns trade came on November 7, 1981, when the Colombian Navy sank a ship named *Karina*, which was loaded with a hundred tons of arms that were believed destined for M-19.[5] Ten days later, Colombian forces seized a second ship, the *Monarca,* after it had delivered its loads of weapons.

Both weapons-laden vessels were traced to a Colombian trafficker named Jaime Guillot Lara. Guillot Lara was arrested in Mexico for using false identity papers. A CIA officer who interviewed Guillot Lara in jail reported that the trafficker admitted making a deal with high Cuban officials to use Cuba as a safe haven for his marijuana-smuggling boats. In exchange, he said, he had agreed to deliver weapons to M-19.[6]

The American and Colombian governments both tried to have Guillot Lara extradited, but the Mexican government released him. In November 1982, a federal grand jury in Miami issued a drug-smuggling conspiracy indictment naming Fernando Ravelo Renedo, the former Cuban ambassador to Colombia, Vice Admiral Aldo Santamaría, head of the Cuban Navy, and two officials of the Cuban Communist party. The Cuban officials and Guillot Lara were never tried.

Moderates in the State Department, the CIA, and the DEA did not doubt that some Cuban officials had seized the chance to arm the M-19 guerrillas and that they had raked off some drug money on the side, but they did not believe the case showed the Castro government had undertaken drug running as a matter of state policy. The ideological right wing of the administration, Congress, and certain archconservative interest groups studied the Guillot Lara case with endless fascination, sure that it proved an international conspiracy of the extreme left and the drug cartels.

The question of complicity between the guerrillas and the traffickers arose anew in early 1984, when the Colombian National Police discovered a massive laboratory complex in the equatorial jungle.

The investigation began to unfold on March 8, when Johnny Phelps, the DEA attaché in Bogotá, received word from Washington that ether shipments were going into the equatorial jungle about three hundred and fifty miles southeast of Bogotá. The information was produced by an innovative DEA project called Operation Chemcon. The project followed unusually large orders of chemicals used in cocaine and heroin refining by checking the documentation, querying informants, and, in promising cases, by tagging barrels of chemicals with beepers that sent signals to a U.S. Defense Department satellite.

Phelps alerted Colonel Jaime Ramírez Gómez, the head of the elite Special Anti-Narcotics Unit (SANU) of the Colombian National Police. Ramírez planned a raid on the location pinpointed by the satellite data. At five o'clock in the morning of March 10, Ramírez and about sixty men flew to a remote jungle settlement called Tranquilandia. As the choppers landed, snipers opened fire. After an extended firefight the police arrested about forty laboratory workers. A second firefight erupted about two hundred and fifty yards inside the complex. The policemen reported that they had been fired upon by about a hundred snipers wearing fatigues.

Documents found in the buildings at Tranquilandia suggested that the complex was a cooperative venture used by senior members of the Medellín cartel. There were references to Pablo Escobar, Carlos Lehder, old Fabio Ochoa and his son Jorge, and Gonzalo Rodríguez Gacha. One ledger showed that several hundred kilograms of cocaine base had been supplied by the Bolivian godfather, Roberto Suárez Gómez.

Within a seventy-mile radius were five other large laboratory complexes. By March 16, Ramírez's men had seized seven aircraft, forty-four buildings, six airstrips, and nine laboratories. The cocaine seizure set a world record: there were ten tons of cocaine and cocaine base. The policemen also found 10,800 fifty-five-gallon drums of ether, other refining chemicals, and aircraft fuel.

DEA officials in Washington regarded the discovery of the complex as a major setback for the Medellín traffickers. "If this doesn't cause cocaine to become scarce and the price to go up," worried Gary Liming, chief of intelligence at DEA headquarters, "then we've got a real problem in this country." When cocaine remained plentiful and the price actually dropped, Liming and his colleagues at headquarters realized the truly awesome scope of the cocaine business.

The Tranquilandia raid had a political impact far beyond the magnitude of the seizure itself. The Colombian police reported that they believed the snipers who fired at them were members of the Fuerzas Armadas Revolucionarias de Colombia (FARC), the Revolutionary Armed Forces of Colombia, the armed wing of the Colombian Communist party.

In the next weeks, Colombian forces who scoured the area for more laboratories found additional signs that guerrillas had some sort of relationship with the laboratory operators. On April 4, a DEA pilot flying over the region spotted what looked like a lab complex. When the Colombian police moved into the place, La Loma, they found a cocaine refinery and, half a mile away, a camp that appeared to have been used by FARC guerrillas. There was an airstrip, a uniform shop where military-type garb was being made, a firing range, an obstacle course, and a soccer field. On May 6, 1984, the police went into another large jungle lab complex called El Refugio. They found three hundred empty ether barrels, an arsenal of weapons, and an FARC uniform.

Only five months later, in October 1984, the Colombian police learned that the La Loma refinery was being rebuilt and raided it again. They reported that they had again engaged in a firefight with guerrillas and that they had found an FARC dialectic handbook and a diary that indicated that FARC guerrillas were involved in cocaine processing.[7]

For the Reagan right, all this was proof that the narcoterrorism marriage had been consummated. Lewis Tambs, the U.S. ambassador to Colombia, went so far as to suggest that the labs were somehow linked to Cuba. After the raid on Tranquilandia, Tambs flew to Washington and offered a background briefing to a few American reporters. He emphasized the presence of guerrillas. The reporters received copies of a cable written by Tambs's embassy staff which said that trafficking "appears to have been sanctioned by the FARC's seventh conference." According to press accounts of the session, the cable cited an informant's statement that one FARC faction was receiving more than $3 million a month from the traffickers.[8] The cable went on to say: "We doubt that Cuba has given up this lucrative business which not only provides a source of capital but also provides the means to subvert, corrupt, and undermine the American public and other democratic countries. It would not be surprising, then, if the FARC . . . deals directly through the Communist party with Cuba in this venture."[9]

Colombian Defense Minister Gustavo Matamoros D'Acosta also accused Cuba of involvement. According to printed reports, Matamoros said, "Everyone knows that the planes leave Colombia with cocaine and that they return with weapons from Cuba."

U.S. law-enforcement agencies were far more cautious in their statements on the Cuban government's possible role in the guns-for-drugs trade. DEA and Customs agents had picked up some reports that smuggler planes and boats loaded with drugs were ducking into Cuban territory, but the quantities involved were not large and there was no hard evidence that the landings were sanctioned by the most senior officials of the Castro government.

As for the Colombian guerrillas, there existed numerous credible reports that some FARC fronts "taxed" the traffickers who wanted to run laboratories in their territory. Beyond this, DEA analysts were not convinced that the guerrillas were engaging in cocaine refining on a significant scale or that they were using trafficking as their primary source of money for weapons, and their CIA counterparts agreed. DEA analysts discounted entirely the report circulated by the embassy that the FARC was collecting $3 million a month from the traffickers. The insurgents were still kidnapping people for ransom, a tedious, dangerous business that would not have been necessary with millions of dollars in income. To DEA officials, it appeared that sometimes the guerrillas and the traffickers fought one another and at other times they cooperated opportunistically in acquiring arms or driving government forces out of an area.

Intrigued by the Tranquilandia raid and the related seizures, CIA director William Casey ordered his analysts to examine the "narcoterrorism" question in depth. Casey's

fascination with the links between drug traffickers and leftists went back to 1981, when he learned that the twenty-
thousand-member army of the Burmese Communist party
controlled the north of Burma and therefore most of the
opium grown in the Golden Triangle. This opium was actually refined along the Thai-Burma border by members of
an anticommunist insurgency, the fifteen-hundred-member
Shan United Army, and by remnants of Chiang Kai-shek's
Nationalist Chinese Army based in northern Thailand, but
it was the Burmese communist connection that had held
Casey's interest. He ordered the CIA station in Bangkok
to persuade the Thai military to move aggressively against
the Golden Triangle traffickers. The Thais complied by running secret bombing missions against the Shan Army's refineries across the border in Burma—which had not given
permission for bombing in its territory. The missions, a
strange replay of CIA-sponsored cross-border actions in
Laos and Cambodia during the Vietnam War, violated Burma's sovereignty and did not achieve their objective. Thanks
to the thick forest cover, neither the Shan nor the Burmese
communists suffered more than temporary inconvenience
from the air strikes.

In the case of Latin America, the CIA analysis came
back with much less evidence of a narcoterrorism merger
than Casey had expected. So he scrapped the study and
ordered a second one. This effort produced a mild white
paper that asserted, in the words of one official, that the
terrorists and traffickers "fed at the same trough." That is,
these groups coexisted in rural areas in a number of countries, exploited the state of anarchy in these areas, and sometimes shared facilities such as landing strips.

Though the evidence of a merger between the guerrillas
and the traffickers was tenuous, the Tranquilandia seizure
was enough to arouse members of the Bogotá power structure who had not bothered about the traffickers before.
Ambassador Tambs and other U.S. officials hammered on
the narcoterrorism connection in meeting after meeting with
Colombian officials.

"Slowly this national security specter began to be raised,"

said Jon Thomas of State's Bureau of International Narcotics Matters. "We said to the Colombians, You're threatening your own existence. We tried to create the image that narcotics trafficking, left to run out of control, would eventually create rival power bases that would come back against the government. The national security issue kicks in, and you get a new set of players—the president, the vice president, the defense minister." Another issue that helped mobilize the Colombian elite was that cocaine addiction was becoming prevalent among the youth of Colombia's educated class. In the late 1970s, in an effort to end their dependence upon Bolivian and Peruvian coca growers, Colombian cocaine traffickers had planted their own coca in the lowlands of the Llanos, the plains region of Colombia. The plantings yielded coca low in the alkaloid that made cocaine, so the traffickers dumped the inferior coca base, called *basuco*, on the domestic market in small, cheap packages. *Basuco* became the rage among students and trendy young city dwellers. *Basuco* was something like the cocaine base Americans called "crack." Both were inexpensive and addictive. Because it was smoked, the stimulant made its way to the user's brain in a matter of seconds, inducing an intense high and an equally strong craving for more. Since gasoline was sometimes used in processing *basuco*, it was laced with lead and other impurities that caused permanent nerve and lung damage. In September 1983, Colombian officials recognized drug abuse as "one of the principal health problems of the country." The Ministry of Health estimated that more than six hundred thousand Colombians under the age of eighteen regularly smoked *basuco*.[10] *Basuco* abuse caused the formation of a Colombian political constituency in favor of strong law enforcement without requiring its adherents to take positions that were overtly pro-American.

And that was good news for American policymakers. "We suddenly had a combination of issues that created a new political commitment to drug enforcement," said Jon Thomas of the State Department. "As the political commitment in a country grows, the demand for outside financial assistance goes down."

For the Medellín cartel, the Tranquilandia raid was a moment of truth of another sort. The ease with which the police had picked off the labs forced the traffickers to take account of their vulnerability to air reconnaissance. They decided to move their base of operations.

In early April 1984, Pablo Escobar and Jorge Ochoa summoned Barry Seal, the American pilot who managed their shipping operations, to a meeting at Las Lomas, the Ochoa family estate near Medellín. Seal would later testify that they told him that they were going to relocate in Nicaragua, where they had bribed some officials for permission to build an airstrip, a hangar, and a laboratory.[11]

"We are not communists. We don't particularly enjoy the same philosophy that they do," one of the traffickers said, as Seal recalled. "But they serve our means and we serve theirs."[12] Nicaragua was one place the Americans could not go, or so the traffickers reckoned. What they did not know was that this three-hundred-pound Louisiana good old boy was a DEA plant.

The doubling of Adler Berriman Seal was the most successful penetration of the Colombian cocaine trade the DEA had ever maneuvered. He was already *there,* in the inner council. He was one of the few Americans the cartel considered invaluable. He could fly anything with wings, he was a superb organizer, and he was immensely resourceful under pressure. Exuberant and infectiously confident, Barry Seal seemed to enjoy adventure as much as making money, probably more.

As a young man, Barry Seal had done a stint in the Army Special Forces and then had taken a job as a flight engineer for Trans World Airlines. He scaled the airline's career ladder in record time, piloting a Boeing 747 by the time he was twenty-six. But Seal was bored and went looking for excitement. In 1972, he contracted to fly a load of plastic explosives to Mexico for a man who said he belonged to an anti-Castro group planning a new invasion of Cuba. The only problem for Seal was, the man was an informant and this was a U.S. Customs sting. The case against Seal was thrown out of court, but he lost his job with TWA. He became an airplane broker, knocking around Latin America, buying and selling planes.

In 1977, Seal went into the smuggling business and became a subcontractor specializing in moving contraband for Latin trafficking organizations that were long on cash and cocaine and short on planes and pilots. After he became established, he stopped flying loads himself. He hired other pilots to do that. He was a genius at creating complex schemes to evade conventional radar and interdiction measures. As he described the technique to the President's Commission on Organized Crime, his pilot would take off at night someplace in Louisiana. Near the Gulf Coast, he would slow down and drop to five hundred feet so that anyone watching FAA radar would think he was a helicopter shuttling to the Gulf oil rigs. Well out in the Gulf, he would climb to seventy-five hundred feet and head south over the Yucatán and across southern Mexico. He would enter Colombian airspace around dawn, during a predesignated "window" of time that the ring had bought from Colombian officials. Landing at a strip somewhere in northern Colombia, he would load up and head back, flying low and slow among the oil rigs as before, and sink to two hundred feet at a prearranged drop zone, where a ground crew would be waiting. The copilot would toss out the cocaine, packed in duffel bags.

In 1981, Jorge Ochoa contracted with Seal to handle the family's cocaine runs. Seal charged $3,000 to $5,000 a kilogram and grossed as much as $1.5 million a trip, but Ochoa and the other kingpins deemed his organizational skills worth the price.

Although DEA agents in Louisiana and Florida had their suspicions about Seal's line of work, he eluded them by running his business from a pay phone and keeping his name off documents. In the spring of 1983, his luck ran low. DEA agents in Miami linked him to a load of Quaaludes, leading to his indictment in Miami. A short time later, he was indicted on a cocaine charge in Fort Lauderdale, and he was also under investigation in Louisiana. Seal was an arrogant sort who thought he could wiggle out of most kinds of trouble, but when he was convicted in Miami and sentenced to ten years in prison, he thought about his wife and his five children and all those millions of dollars he would not be able to spend, so he decided to make a deal.

Seal was such a consummate liar that he had a hard time convincing the federal government to bargain with him. He approached a DEA agent in Miami, who thought his claims of working for the Medellín cartel sounded like the product of a desperate imagination. Then he tried to talk to Stanford Bardwell, the U.S. attorney in Baton Rouge, but Bardwell would not give him an appointment.

In March 1984, while out of jail on an appeal bond, Seal flew his Lear jet to Washington and telephoned Vice President George Bush's office. Baffled Bush aides called DEA headquarters. Before long, Seal was spilling his tale to agents Ken Kennedy and Frank White. Kennedy called a young DEA supervisor in Miami named Bob Joura. He said he was with a character who was dropping the names of Jorge Ochoa and Pablo Escobar and claiming they wanted him to fly three thousand kilograms of cocaine into Louisiana. Seal said he was willing to let the DEA in on the whole thing in exchange for help with his legal problems. It was hard to believe—nobody had ever shipped that much coke in a single load—but did Joura want to talk to him? "I'll talk to anybody," Joura said.

When Seal showed up in Miami, Joura understood Kennedy's misgivings. Seal looked like a fat loudmouth. But Joura was impressed by the fact that he did not drink, smoke, or do drugs of any kind and would not allow his pilots to indulge—he said it broke the concentration. Joura also noted that Seal was meticulous about his job and had a phenomenal memory for such details as telephone numbers. The agent decided that if Seal was really in with the heads of the cartel, he was worth a deal. Joura and his group signed him on as an informant. Seal was so eager to head off a long prison term that he provided his own airplanes and paid his own expenses.

On April 6, 1984, Seal flew to Medellín to plan the giant shipment. Upon his return, Seal told his DEA contacts that Escobar and Ochoa were moving their base of operations to Nicaragua. Seal was supposed to pick up the three thousand kilos at the Ochoa ranch south of Medellín, refuel at a military base outside Managua, and fly into Louisiana. Seal said he did not like the idea of flying into Nicaragua, but Ochoa had told him not to worry, that he had made the right payoffs to people in the Sandinista government.

While Seal was back in Miami, arranging the logistics, Rodrigo Lara Bonilla was assassinated. Jorge Ochoa and Pablo Escobar fled to Panama. Seal met Ochoa there and concluded the plans for the shipment.

On May 28, Seal flew his Lockheed Lodestar to the Ochoa ranch. Typically, Carlos Lehder was the only one of the bunch who had dared to stay in Colombia. With his usual flair, Lehder rode up on a white horse and supervised as a crew packed the load into the cargo hold. By this time the shipment had been reduced to fifteen hundred kilograms, but Seal thought it was too much for the old Lodestar, especially on the muddy strip that passed for a runway. When Seal balked, Lehder aimed his automatic weapon in the pilot's direction and said, "Get out of here."

Seal got. Or at least he tried, but the Lodestar went into a skid and crashed. The Ochoas sent in another plane, a Titan twin-engine that could hold about seven hundred and fifty kilograms of coke. On June 3, Seal packed it up and flew from Medellín into Nicaragua. He landed, as instructed, at the Los Brasiles airfield, a few miles north of Managua. He later reported that he had been met by some military personnel who were being ordered around by a Nicaraguan named Federico Vaughan. Seal refueled, waited till dark, donned his night-vision goggles, and took off.

Flying without lights, Seal headed along the coast of Lake Managua. As he passed over Sandino International Airport, he heard the sound of gunfire from the antiaircraft emplacement. The plane took a round in the left engine and shuddered out of control. Seal could not return to Los Brasiles, which was closed for the night, so he put out a mayday and landed at Sandino International. The soldiers arrested him, commandeered the plane, and locked him and his crewmen in Somoza's bunker.

The next morning, Seal was allowed to contact Federico Vaughan. Seal was not sure what Vaughan did, but he seemed to have clout. Seal said that Vaughan posted guards around the Titan, which was parked in the military section of Sandino International, and took him to a mansion in Managua where Pablo Escobar was staying. Seal said that Escobar and Vaughan ordered soldiers to unload the cocaine and stash it in the mansion until Seal could return with a new plane.

Back in Miami, Seal bought a big old Fairchild C-123-K of Vietnam war vintage, painted with camouflage colors, and christened it the *Fat Lady*.

When CIA officers in Miami found out that Seal was planning on flying into a Sandinista military base, they pleaded with the DEA agents to let them talk to him. They asked if Seal could work a camera. He said he could, so they asked him to shoot a few pictures of the air base as he was landing. "Are you crazy?" he roared. There were going to be a lot of guys with guns who would not take kindly to having their pictures snapped by an American of any sort. The CIA men suggested that Seal shove the camera under the instrument board. They could put some Velcro there to hold it.

Seal rolled his eyes at the DEA agents. The CIA technicians went back to the drawing board and came up with a new proposal. They would hide a couple of automatic cameras in the plane, one in the nose, the other in the bulkhead, pointing backward toward the cargo door. Seal agreed to the plan. But after the cameras were installed, he realized this was no James Bond job. The remote-control shutter looked like a cigarette lighter with a five-foot antenna. As Seal clicked it, the motorized cameras whined loudly. Seal groaned but said he could drown out the noise if he kept the plane's power supply running.

But how was he to hide the antenna? The CIA people suggested that Seal cut a hole in his pocket and run the antenna down his leg. He did so and pointed out that there were about four inches of antenna protruding from his cuff. The DEA agents threw up their hands in exasperation, grabbed some rubber bands, and secured the antenna to Seal's calf.

On June 24, Seal headed for Nicaragua and landed at

the Los Brasiles airport. The camera in the nose failed. The camera in the rear worked and snapped pictures of Federico Vaughan and Pablo Escobar loading duffel bags of cocaine onto the aircraft with the help of some soldiers. Seal said that another cartel member, Gonzalo Rodríguez Gacha, was off camera. A U.S. intelligence satellite trained on the area took high-resolution photographs of the *Fat Lady* on the ground.

Once he left the Nicaraguan airport on the night of June 26, Seal was free of the traffickers and in complete control of the cocaine. Escobar and Ochoa trusted him so completely that they did not send one of their own men along to watch him. His job was to fly the cocaine to South Florida and have it packed in a Winnebago motor home that he had bought with an advance from the traffickers. He was supposed to leave the Winnebago in the parking lot of a shopping center in Miami. A distributor who worked for the cartel had a set of keys to the motor home and would pick it up.

Returning to the United States with the cocaine, Seal guided the *Fat Lady* into Homestead Air Force Base, the tactical air base south of Miami where the U.S. Customs air wing was hangared. Bob Joura and his partners from the DEA Miami office were waiting with the Winnebago. The DEA agents loaded the cocaine and drove the motor home to the shopping center on June 28. When the distributor picked it up, the DEA agents followed and rammed their car into the Winnebago's side, faking a crash that snarled traffic on Biscayne Boulevard for blocks. The Miami police arrived on cue and "discovered" that the Winnebago was packed floor to ceiling with cocaine. The Colombians never suspected a thing. In fact, the Ochoas told Seal he was so valuable they wanted him to stop flying cocaine into the States. Others could take that risk. His next mission was to set up an air shuttle to move coca paste from Peru to the lab in Nicaragua.

Seal was elated. He made fantastic plans, talking of luring Escobar, Ochoa, and maybe even Lehder onto the *Fat Lady*. Next thing he knew, he said, they would be looking at Homestead and a platoon of U.S. marshals. The agents dared not hope for such a prize, although they knew it would be the coup of the decade if Seal could pull it off. They were content to have someone on their side who enjoyed the trust of the cartel leaders.

Unfortunately, a National Security Council staff member by the name of Oliver North, a lieutenant colonel in the Marine Corps who was detailed to the White House, was involved in a deliberate decision to blow the Seal penetration. If the cartel had decided to set up a laboratory just about anywhere else in the world—Panama, Guatemala, Brazil, Texas—no one outside the DEA would have paid any attention, but the White House and the CIA cared tremendously about everything that happened in Nicaragua. Noncommunicative about its own sources and methods, the CIA seemed to be gossipy when it came to those of other agencies. Within a few days of Seal's return from Managua, DEA agents heard that CIA officials had sent the president enlargements of the pictures from the *Fat Lady*. It was just at this moment when the administration was under tremendous pressure to justify its support for the Nicaraguan opposition forces known as the *contrarevolucionarios,* or Contras.

The administration's "secret war" against the Sandinista government—which was no secret to anyone who had read a newspaper in the past three years—was the cause nearest and dearest to Ronald Reagan's heart. The president regarded Nicaragua as what one aide called a "double Cuba." He was obsessed with the notion that the Marxist Sandinistas would transform postrevolutionary Nicaragua into a forward base for the Soviet Union. Reagan compared the Contras to the Founding Fathers and declared, "I am a Contra, too." "Central America," Reagan said in a televised address on May 9, 1984, "has become the stage for a bold attempt by the Soviet Union, Cuba, and Nicaragua to install communism by force throughout the hemisphere."

Congressional leaders were uneasy about the expanding covert war but went along with it until early April 1984, when *The Wall Street Journal* reported that the CIA had supervised the mining of Nicaragua's harbors. Members of both parties were incensed. House Majority Leader Tip O'Neill called the Contras "marauders, murderers, and rapists." Senate Intelligence Committee chairman Senator Barry Goldwater, who had been unaware of the mining, was beside himself with rage and released a letter he had sent CIA director William Casey that announced, among other things, "I am pissed off."

House Intelligence Committee chairman Edward Boland, a Democrat from Massachusetts, renewed his efforts to cut off U.S. funding for the Contras. The Boland amendment, which proposed a ban on CIA assistance to the Contras, was favored by a majority of House members, but lacked sufficient votes in the Republican-controlled Senate. However, the administration's mendacity over the mining gave Boland the edge he needed in the Senate. The secret mining scandal gravely endangered Reagan's request for $21 million in emergency aid for the Contras, who would run out of money in early May.

Two pivotal events occurred on June 25, while Barry Seal was in Managua. The first happened in public: the Senate rejected Reagan's "urgent" request for the $21 million Contra aid package.

The second event was a closely held secret. The Contras were flat broke, and Reagan and his top advisers were casting frantically about for an alternate source of funds. On June 25, in a meeting of the National Security Planning Group, CIA director Casey urged Reagan to seek assistance from other nations. Secretary of State George Shultz worried that such an act might constitute an "impeachable offense," so the president made no decision at that meeting, according to those present. But earlier that day, North, who was the National Security Council's liaison with the CIA for the Contra cause, had arranged for millions of dollars in Saudi Arabian government money to be deposited to an offshore bank account in the name of Adolfo Calero, the leader of the Contras. North's boss, NSC adviser Robert "Bud" McFarlane, had met with Saudi ambassador Prince Bandar Bin Sultan some weeks earlier and had elicited a pledge of $1 million a month to sustain the Contras through the end of 1984.[13]

North, McFarlane, and other White House aides knew that the Saudi money was only a stopgap and were anxious to turn the tide in Congress before votes on Reagan's request for $28 million to support the Contras during the fiscal year to begin on October 1, 1984. Under these circumstances, supporters of the Contras within the administration found the Seal penetration too tempting to be kept secret.

The first leak came from General Paul Gorman, commander of the U.S. Southern Command in Panama from 1983 to 1985. Gorman was a combative anticommunist who referred to Nicaragua as "a Marxist garrison state" and favored an aggressive U.S. military posture in the region. On June 29, the feisty general attended an American Chamber of Commerce luncheon in El Salvador and blurted out the accusation that the Sandinista government was engaged in the cocaine trade. A short dispatch quoting Gorman was published in *The New York Times* on July 1.

Gorman's statement gave no specifics, but it hit the Justice Department and the DEA like a ton of bricks. Seal was planning another trip to Managua. Ochoa and Escobar wanted him to bring them $1.5 million in cash, which their distributor in Miami had collected; Seal told DEA agents that the traffickers intended to bribe Sandinista officials with the greenbacks. At the traffickers' request, Seal packed the *Fat Lady* with twenty thousand pounds of equipment for the cocaine lab they were building and with piles of recreational equipment—inflatable boats, skis, scuba tanks— they could not get in Nicaragua. DEA officials were most interested in the traffickers' order for radio equipment: Ochoa and Escobar wanted Seal to set up a high-frequency communications system between Managua, Medellín, and their coca paste suppliers in the Andes. DEA officials hoped Seal could find a way to install devices that would allow DEA to monitor the cartel's radio traffic.

Now that Gorman had shot off his mouth, Justice officials contended that Seal's cover was blown. The prosecutors in Miami thought they had a good case against the cartel and did not want to risk losing the key witness. Associate Attorney General Lowell Jensen agreed with the prosecutors. But the DEA agents in Miami wanted to keep the case running. They had never been able to infiltrate the cartel's inner circle, and there was a lot more they wanted to know about its activities.

The decision went to Jack Lawn, the deputy administrator of the DEA. As was his habit, Lawn, who had not been out of the field long himself, sided with the agents. He said this was not some bureaucrat's choice to make. It was Seal's life; let Seal decide—Seal and the agents controlling him.

Seal wanted to go. He was proud of what he had done. He had the zeal of a fresh convert. Also it was a legal way of having more adventures. The field agents agreed. They said that Gorman had not given away Seal's cover. Besides, the field men said, Seal could talk his way out of anything.

Seal took off from Miami at two o'clock in the morning on Saturday, July 7. Lawn told Ron Caffrey, who ran the cocaine desk at DEA headquarters, to call him at home without fail the minute Seal got back into the States. Saturday was a long day for Lawn, and Sunday was longer. Finally, on Sunday afternoon, Caffrey telephoned Lawn's house. "Hey, boss, ya heard the bad news?" Caffrey chortled. "Oh, crap," Lawn started. But Caffrey was laughing. Just kidding, he said. "He's back." Lawn sighed. He was never quite prepared for Caffrey's gallows humor.

On July 17, *The Washington Times* ran a front-page story by Edmond Jacoby outlining the Seal mission to Nicaragua in vivid detail. Some details of the story were off, but the disclosure that a DEA-backed pilot had infiltrated the Medellín cartel was all too accurate.

That finished the investigation. The "Nicaragua connection" made front-page headlines all across the country. The prosecutors in Miami went to the federal grand jury with Seal's evidence. On July 27, the grand jury indicted Carlos Lehder, Pablo Escobar, Jorge Ochoa, and Gonzalo Rodríguez Gacha. Federico Vaughan, the Nicaraguan who had rescued Seal from the military jail, was also indicted. The court papers described Vaughan as an aide to Borge, the interior minister, an identification that had been supplied by the CIA.

Bob Joura and his partners in the DEA's Miami office felt betrayed. It was bad enough that the story had destroyed a very promising investigation into the biggest names in Colombian crime. Worse, the leaker had dealt cavalierly with Seal's life. It was sheer luck that Seal had not been in Colombia or Nicaragua when the story hit the papers.

Mullen and Lawn began an informal leak investigation. They were sure they would find that the leak had come from the White House—most probably from North. They remembered that in early July, as Seal was preparing to fly to Nicaragua for the second time, Ron Caffrey went to the White House to brief a small group of presidential aides on the case. When Caffrey walked in, North was passing around the photographs of Escobar and Vaughan taken by Seal's hidden cameras. Caffrey knew that DEA had not provided those pictures to the White House; he figured they came from the CIA. He was introduced to Duane "Dewey" Clarridge, chief of the Latin American division of the CIA directorate of operations, who was deeply involved in managing the Contra war. A White House political aide, whose name Caffrey could not later recall, was also present.

The political aide seemed enthusiastic about the cartel case, but Caffrey thought North was distracted and bored with everything he had to say, except when Ron Caffrey mentioned something about bribing Nicaraguan officials. Caffrey stressed that he was not ready to conclude that Escobar and Ochoa had bought off senior members of the Sandinista government. As he described the briefing later, he told the White House officials, "It could've been some local military commander. We've got to go on the facts and not what we think. Just because the Sandinista interests are inimical to ours, that doesn't change the complexion of the case. We want to find the lab, capture a couple of these guys, find out a little bit more—we want to play with it a little bit."

When the White House aides heard that Seal was going back to Managua to deliver $1.5 million in cocaine profits to Ochoa and Escobar, North perked up. As Caffrey recalled, North suggested that Seal divert the plane and give the cash to the Contras instead.

"That would fuck up our case!" Ron sputtered. Ochoa

and Escobar would catch on to Seal's ruse in a minute. The White House political aide agreed with DEA that the case should go forward. Caffrey found that ironic. "I figured a guy with a military background or in an intelligence agency would be more akin to the kinds of things that we do, and that a political guy wouldn't give a damn as long as he could get a vote passed in the House or get a headline in the newspaper," he said later.

After the leak of the Seal penetration, North telephoned Ron Caffrey, who blasted him with a litany of Brooklynese curses. As Caffrey recalled the conversation, North did not deny that he was responsible for the leak: "We understood it was okay to release all this stuff," North said. The DEA official said that it was *not* okay. Seal could have been killed, and besides, didn't the White House care about stopping the Medellín cartel? "All these guys give a shit about," he thought, "is the Contra thing, trying to get the funding passed through the Congress by blaming [the Sandinistas] for being dope traffickers. Our agenda was making the best case we could make, and if it turned out the Sandinistas are involved in the dope traffic, okay. I don't see why we couldn't have had compatible interests, but we had to find out first."

Since the DEA investigation did not produce truly sensational material on the senior figures in the Sandinista government, somebody else in the administration embellished upon the case before it was leaked. *The Washington Times* story had said that the Seal penetration had implicated Tomás Borge, the interior minister and a member of the clique that ruled Nicaragua, and Humberto Ortega, the defense minister and brother of President Daniel Ortega. In fact, Seal had never discussed Borge and Ortega with DEA agents to whom he reported. He had met just one person who he thought was an influential Nicaraguan. That was Federico Vaughan, and Seal did not know exactly how he was connected to the power structure. It was the CIA that advised DEA that Vaughan was an aide to Borge, the interior minister, but where the story was embellished to include Borge and Humberto Ortega would remain a mystery.

The attempt to link Borge and Ortega to the case when there was no hard proof was an amateurish ploy that quickly backfired.

Far from persuading the Congress to support the Contras, the leak of the Seal story aroused suspicions that the whole case was trumped up. When Seal returned from Managua, Joura and his partners had joshed that the CIA camera was a good idea after all, or else somebody would accuse the DEA of staging the whole crazy scheme on a back lot in Hollywood. Now it was no joke. Some people even doubted that Barry Seal had gone to Nicaragua. Other lawmakers were willing to accept the fact that some officials in Nicaragua were corrupt, but that did not override their more profound misgivings about the Contras.

On August 2, the House debated the administration's $28 million Contra aid bill. The congressmen voted three to one in favor of the Boland amendment to end aid to the Contras. Five days later, hoping to hold the pro-Contra line in the Senate, Senator Paula Hawkins, the archconservative Republican from Florida, called a press conference and displayed blown-up copies of the photographs of Vaughan and Escobar taken by Seal's hidden cameras.

On September 14, 1984, Secretary of State George Shultz made his first speech on the subject of drug trafficking to the Miami Chamber of Commerce. The theme that dominated the speech was not drugs but politics—specifically East-West politics and the threat of "narcoterrorism," as practiced, Shultz asserted, by the Cubans and Nicaraguans:

> The complicity of communist governments in the drug trade is cause for grave concern among the nations of the free world. It is part of a larger pattern of international lawlessness by communist nations that, as we have seen, also includes support for international terrorism, and other forms of organized violence against legitimate governments. . . . We know that, with their failing economies, Cuba and Nicaragua need hard cash to buy essential goods. . . . It is not hard to imagine that smuggling massive amounts of drugs into Western nations may serve their broader goal of attempting to weaken the fabric of Western democratic society.

Despite the best efforts of Shultz and his allies on Capitol Hill, the Senate rejected the Contra aid package. The Contras were off Uncle Sam's payroll effective October 1, 1984.

The Seal case joined the Guillot Lara case and the Tranquilandia raid in the administration's litany of propaganda against Nicaragua and Cuba. In March 1985, the State Department published a booklet entitled *The Soviet-Cuban Connection in Central America and the Caribbean*, which used the Seal photographs under the heading "Castro: Subversive Catalyst."

Oliver North incorporated the pictures into the slide show and lecture he developed to induce rich conservatives to contribute funds for the Contras while the ban on aid was in effect. In March 1986, William O'Boyle, a New York investor sympathetic to the Contras, was ushered into a conference room in the Old Executive Office Building, where North proceeded to frighten the wealthy Manhattanite with dire intimations of dark Soviet designs on the hemisphere. On one side of the room were pictures of a Nicaraguan airport that, O'Boyle understood, "was intended . . . to recover the Russian Backfire bombers after they made a nuclear attack on the United States." On the other side were the Seal photographs. After the pitch, O'Boyle hastily agreed to contribute $130,000 to the Contra cause.[14]

On March 16, 1986, Reagan displayed one of the Seal pictures during a television broadcast intended to rally public support for a $100 million appropriation for the Contra war. "Every American parent," Reagan said, "will be outraged to learn that top Nicaraguan government officials are deeply involved in drug trafficking. There is no crime to which the Sandinistas will not stoop. This is an outlaw regime."

The president's statement put DEA officials in an awkward position. The agency had nothing more substantive on the Sandinistas than had been passed along by Seal, and those data did not implicate "top Nicaraguan government officials." Reporters who called the DEA public affairs office after Reagan's speech were read a brief statement, which said: "DEA receives sporadic allegations concerning drug trafficking by Nicaraguan nationals. One DEA investigation resulted in the indictment of the Nicaraguan aide to the minister of the interior; no evidence was developed to implicate the minister of the interior or other Nicaraguan officials." The statement earned the DEA an unwelcome headline in *The New York Times:* "Drug Agency Rebuts Reagan Charge." DEA's stock sank at the White House. *The Washington Times* attacked Lawn's senior spokesman, a respected former journalist, Robert Feldkamp, for failing to support the president.

By the time Reagan showed off Barry Seal's pictures, the man who had taken them was dead.

After North and his cohorts blew the cartel case, Seal went to the Turks and Caicos Islands, a tiny British colony in the Caribbean, and developed information that top officials were allowing traffickers to land on the islands in exchange for large cash payments. Seal's work led to the drug-trafficking convictions of Chief Minister Norman Saunders and Commerce Minister Stafford Missick.

Then came Seal's own day of reckoning, when he had to face the trafficking charges that had been lodged against him. The judge in the Fort Lauderdale case reduced his sentence to time served and five years' probation. Seal's lawyers made a plea bargain with federal prosecutors in Louisiana in which he would plead guilty to two felony charges and submit to a sentence no worse than the one in Florida. The deal infuriated U.S. District Judge Frank J. Polozola of Baton Rouge, who called it "coddling." "People like you, Mr. Seal, . . . ought to be in a federal penitentiary . . . working at hard labor," Polozola said.

In return for taking pictures of the Nicaragua airfield, Seal asked CIA officials in Miami to give him a letter which he could use at his sentencing hearing. He wanted the agency to confirm that he had done an unspecified service for the U.S. government and had been truthful and cooperative in all his dealings with the CIA. DEA agents who witnessed the conversation said the CIA men readily agreed. Their words meant nothing. Much later, Seal's attorney told the DEA agents that when he tried to reach the intelligence officer who had made the promise, the CIA replied that no one by that name worked for the agency. The man had given Seal and DEA a phony name.

The DEA agents who had worked with Seal in Florida vouched for his conduct during their supervision, hoping the judge would order him to a distant military base or rehabilitation center. Polozola sentenced Seal to spend six months living in a Salvation Army halfway house in Baton Rouge and warned that if Seal or his bodyguards carried guns, he would take that as a violation of probation. "I'd love for this plea agreement to be broken," he growled.

Seal's friends in the DEA were worried. An informant in Texas had sent word that a contract had been placed on Seal's life. Seal had refused to go into the witness protection program. Seal had spent ninety days in the program, weeks at a time in isolation in a windowless room, weeks more in a special section of a federal prison in New York where he had been unable to see his wife and children. He said he would take his chances on the outside.

It was a gamble and he lost it.

Seal made the fatal mistake of moving about Baton Rouge with complete predictability. Beginning January 24, 1986, he left the Salvation Army at eight-thirty every morning to go to his job as an aviation consultant, returned at six o'clock in the evening, and was always in his white Cadillac Fleetwood, usually alone. On February 19, two men walked up to Seal's car and began firing a submachine gun. Seal died instantly. Within three days, the FBI had tracked down the suspected shooters and four other men, all Colombians. DEA agents believed that they worked for the Medellín cartel—not for the Nicaraguans. Three Colombians were convicted of the murder in Lake Charles, Louisiana, and sentenced to life imprisonment without parole. The fourth Colombian was not tried with the others because a witness against him failed to cooperate. He was held in Miami on federal gun charges.

Barry Seal was buried in Baton Rouge with a Snickers bar, a telephone pager, and a roll of quarters for that great pay phone in the sky. Despite the service that Seal had rendered to the Reagan White House, neither the president nor any other senior official mentioned the assassination in public statements. The DEA agents who had befriended Seal received orders from a supervisor not to attend his funeral. They never knew the reason.

Oliver North had no qualms about using Seal's death to dramatize himself and to serve his political ends. In May 1986, North told the FBI that his dog had been poisoned, his car had been vandalized, he had been followed, and a fake bomb had been left in his mailbox. According to several FBI memos made public in 1988, North claimed he was the target of "active measures" instigated by the Sandinista government. Congressional investigators concluded he was actually trying to manipulate the FBI into investigating certain anti-Contra activists and journalists who were asking questions about his role in the covert Contra war. When the FBI did not do what he wanted, North passed on a more alarming threat. An FBI agent reported that on June 3, 1986, North approached him and "expressed further concern that he may be targeted for elimination by organized crime due to his alleged involvement in drug running in view of the murder on February 17, 1986 [sic] of a Drug Enforcement Administration (DEA) agent Steele [sic], on the date prior to Steele's testifying against the Sandinista drug involvement." FBI officials found no evidence that North was actually harassed by anyone, discounted North's claim about the drug Mafia, and closed the case.

In the fall of 1986, North's Central American schemes began to unravel. In a bizarre turn of events, Seal's old plane, the *Fat Lady*, played a prominent role in North's undoing. In mid-1984, as the Boland prohibition was about to take effect, North had created an off-the-books covert operation, called "the Enterprise," to take the place of the CIA pipeline. North would later testify that, at the suggestion of CIA director Casey, he recruited retired U.S. Air Force Major General Richard V. Secord to direct this private arms-running network, which would buy supplies for the Contras with the Saudi money and any other funds North could lay his hands on. If DEA had been willing to contribute the cartel's money to the Contra cause, that, too, would undoubtedly have gone through the Enterprise.

In August 1985, North had found another source of funds. President Reagan had agreed to sell arms to Iran in a futile effort to buy Iran's help in freeing American hostages kidnapped in Beirut. North was the NSC action officer for those clandestine arms sales. He used the Enterprise to move the arms to Iran and, by the estimate of a joint Congressional committee that investigated the affair, diverted at least $3.8 million of the Iran arms sales profits to the Contras.

The Enterprise used the Saudi contribution and the Iran arms profits to buy several planes, including two old C-123 aircraft. One was the *Fat Lady*, which Seal had sold before he was sentenced. On October 5, 1986, the *Fat Lady* left Ilopango air base in El Salvador loaded with rifles, ammunition, grenade launchers, uniforms, and medicine for the Contras. Nicaraguan forces shot the plane down. Three American crewmen paid by the Secord-North Enterprise were killed. Sandinista troops captured the fourth man, Eugene Hasenfus, who declared that he was on a mission for the U.S. government. The Reagan administration denied any connection with the flight, but documents aboard the plane linked it to Southern Air Transport, a former CIA proprietary in Miami which serviced the aircraft for the Enterprise. Reporters in El Salvador obtained telephone records from the house where the *Fat Lady*'s crew had lived; one number rang at the White House, at a telephone North had used. Another number traced to Secord. On March 16, 1988, North, Secord, former NSC adviser John Poindexter, and Secord's business partner, Albert Hakim, were indicted for fraud, conspiracy, and theft of government property for diverting Iran arms profits to the Contras and for arming the Contras in violation of the Congressional ban.

When Ronald Reagan went on television to brand the Nicaraguan government an "outlaw regime," he did not tell the whole story. If he had, alongside Barry Seal's snapshots of Pablo Escobar in Nicaragua would have been pictures of Escobar, the Ochoas, and Seal hatching the plot in the luxury of a Panama City hotel suite. The display might have included pictures of the Panamanian banks where the car-

tel's profits were laundered. Reagan's rogues gallery need
not have stopped with Nicaraguan leaders. The American
president would have been equally justified in condemning
General Manuel Antonio Noriega, the de facto dictator of
Panama since 1983, for allowing Escobar, Gonzalo Rodríguez Gacha, and all three Ochoa brothers to hide in Panama
after the Lara Bonilla assassination. Indeed, it was difficult
to argue that they were "hiding," as they had taken several
suites in the plush César Park Marriott with their wives,
children, and servants.

With his pitted face, hard eyes, and reputation for cun-
ning and cruelty, Noriega inspired fear throughout Panama
and revulsion within the U.S. government. "I don't know
anyone who has ever dealt with General Noriega in an official capacity for the United States government who would
not have preferred to be dealing with somebody else,"
SOUTHCOM Commander Gorman testified in 1988. "It
was quite evident that very little was going on of a commercial nature in Panama from which he did not, in some
sense, directly profit. [He] was certainly venal, was involved
in a lot of very, very shady kinds of undertakings."

Gorman said that he never saw a report "that pinned
him specifically to a criminal act or undertaking of the sort
that one could adduce in a court."[15]

But the suspicions of American officials were aroused
because Noriega lived in a manner that could not possibly
have been supported on his soldier's salary: he had several
houses in Panama, a flat in Paris, a place in the French Alps,
fleets of cars and airplanes, and, always, a bevy of lovely
young women in attendance. Ever since the early 1970s,
when Noriega was a colonel in charge of G-2, military intelligence, American law-enforcement agencies had collected numerous allegations from informants that Noriega
was taking protection money from drug traffickers and other
racketeers. In 1972, officials at the Bureau of Narcotics and
Dangerous Drugs considered Noriega a major hindrance to
their efforts to shut down Panama as a staging area for
shipments of heroin from Europe and cocaine from South
America. One hotheaded BNDD agent wrote a memo proposing that Noriega be subjected to "total and complete

immobilization," a euphemism for assassination. Then-
BNDD chief John Ingersoll rejected that suggestion out of
hand, but he took the allegations of corruption seriously.
In the summer of 1972, at the direction of Nixon's domestic
council chief, John Ehrlichman, Ingersoll went on a secret
mission to confront General Omar Torrijos Herrera, Panama's military leader, with what the United States knew
about drugs and corruption in his ranks. As Ingersoll recounted the meeting, Torrijos was merely angry when the
American envoy said that the general's brother, Moisés,
had been charged in a sealed indictment in New York on
May 16, 1972, for smuggling 155 pounds of heroin into the
United States the previous year. "I'll talk to him," Torrijos
growled, as Ingersoll recalled. (Moisés Torrijos was never
tried in the United States.) When Ingersoll raised the second
point, the Nixon administration's belief that G-2 chief Noriega was facilitating the drug trade, Torrijos's expression
changed from vexation to fear. "It was almost as if he were
afraid to do anything about what I was telling him," Ingersoll
said. "Everybody was afraid of him," William Jorden, U.S.
ambassador to Panama from 1974 to 1978, observed some
years later. "He had dossiers on everybody in government."

In the late 1970s, when it was clear that Noriega was too
powerful to be forced out, DEA officials switched their strategy and cultivated him. "Sometimes the philosophy of this
agency is, a pact with the devil is better than no pact at all,"
said DEA spokesman Robert Feldkamp. By the mid-1980s,
DEA agents based in Panama were defending Noriega as a
staunch ally in the war on drugs and insisting that his wealth
was "clean rake-off money," from prostitution, gambling,
and various businesses, as opposed to "dirty rake-offs" from
drug traffickers. Noriega repaid these blandishments by arresting and deporting to the United States some mid-level
traffickers, by seizing a number of shipments of drugs and
refining chemicals, and by allowing DEA to operate undercover in his country.

Panama's main value to the traffickers was as a money-
laundering center. With about a hundred thirty banks holding assets in excess of $30 billion, Panama provided the
traffickers, like other international commodity traders, with

instant access to banking and investment networks all over
the world. On a few occasions, Panamanian authorities took
punitive action against suspected money launderers. In
March 1985, Panama's National Banking Commission
seized First Interamericas Bank on grounds that it was being
used for money laundering. Until late 1984, DEA officials
said, the bank had been owned by reputed cocaine kingpin
Gilberto Rodríguez Orejuela, who transferred control to
another Colombian businessman.[16] In early 1987, after intense pressure from the United States, Panamanian officials
froze a number of accounts that DEA said belonged to the
Medellín cartel. For the most part, however, DEA and Customs agents were unable to break through the wall of bank
secrecy.

The State Department, the intelligence agencies, and
U.S. military leaders had made pacts of their own with
Noriega. Because the government of Cuba conducted many
of its commercial transactions in Panama, the CIA, National
Security Agency, and Defense Intelligence Agency used the
small but strategically located nation as a listening post on
Cuba, Nicaragua, and other Latin nations. The CIA ce-
mented a relationship with Noriega early in his career as a
military intelligence officer. U.S. officials believed that Noriega played both sides of the street, courting Fidel Castro
and passing information he had gleaned from his U.S. contacts to Cuba and leftist leaders in Nicaragua and El Salvador. As former Ambassador Jorden said, "We all felt that
he was abusing his power and swinging deals outside the
military intelligence area." In spite of Noriega's relations
with the Cubans, or perhaps because of them, the CIA
continued to regard him as a useful source and conduit.

The U.S. Department of Defense took the position that
American national security required a strong alliance with
the Panamanian leadership, which, for all practical purposes, was the Panamanian Defense Forces. The Panama
Canal, vital to American military and commercial interests,
would revert to Panamanian government control in 1999.
The Pentagon had a particular interest in staying on good
terms with the PDF, whose officers could make life exceed-

ingly unpleasant for the ten thousand American servicemen
and -women stationed at SOUTHCOM.

The American relationship with General Torrijos was
complicated by Torrijos's intense nationalism, but Torrijos
was a man of vision, who, associates said, discouraged his
subordinates from the most rapacious forms of corruption.
After Torrijos died in a mysterious plane crash in 1981,
reports of PDF involvement in extortion, racketeering, and
protection of drug traffickers proliferated. In 1983, Noriega
became commander in chief of the Panamanian Defense
Forces and moved rapidly to extend PDF control over most
functions of the government, from traffic through air- and
seaports, to immigration and customs. Panama was called
a democracy but Noriega ran the country with an iron hand.

Although Noriega boasted of his friendship with DEA,
he held no fear for the leaders of the Medellín cartel. They
were so confident that Noriega would not deport them after
the Lara Bonilla assassination that they made their presence
in Panama City known to the Betancur government with
one of the most arrogant and bizarre offers in the annals of
organized crime.

On May 6, 1984, according to Colombian government
officials, former Colombian President Alfonso López Michelsen was staying at the César Park Marriott as a guest of
the Noriega regime, to observe the Panamanian presidential
elections. López Michelsen received a call from Escobar
and Ochoa, who announced that they had something "very
important" to tell him. López Michelsen invited them to
drop by his suite. As López Michelsen told the story later,
the traffickers claimed that they had not been involved in
the justice minister's death. All they wanted was to go home.
They said that if Betancur gave them amnesty, they would
dismantle their cocaine empires.

Colombian Attorney General Carlos Jiménez Gómez
went to Panama shortly thereafter and listened to the
Ochoa-Escobar "peace proposal." Jiménez said he asked
the traffickers to put their plan in writing so he could present
it to the president. In this remarkable document, which was
leaked to the Colombian papers, the traffickers asked Pres-

ident Betancur "to consider our reincorporation in the near future into Colombian society so that we can fully enjoy it as good people, as citizens. It is Colombia, the fatherland, that we want for our children, and the fatherland that we deeply love." The cartel claimed to represent 80 percent of Colombia's cocaine industry and to have a combined income of $2 billion annually. They offered to give up their laboratories, their clandestine airstrips, and their air fleets, to help in the substitution of food crops, to work with the government to stop *basuco* smoking, and to rehabilitate Colombian addicts. They would repatriate their vast wealth and invest in Colombia. In essence, their strategy was to defuse the outrage of the Colombian elite, which, for the first time, was demanding reform. In return, they wanted immunity in the Colombian courts and a guarantee that they would not be extradited to the United States.

The traffickers miscalculated. When the Bogotá daily *El Tiempo* broke the story of the peace proposal in July 1984, there were calls for Jiménez's resignation. Church leaders warned the government not to negotiate with the cartel. Journalists and political leaders were aghast.

"To call on drug traffickers to teach us how to stop drug traffic is like inviting bank robbers to a symposium on bank security," said Congressman Ernesto Samper Pizano, Liberal party leader in Bogotá. "Today," said Congressman José Fernando Botero Ochoa, "it could be the narcotics traffickers, tomorrow a gang of kidnappers . . . the day after, a gang of smugglers, and who knows who else attempting to defy the law."[17] Betancur denied that he had seriously bargained with the traffickers. "There hasn't been and there won't be any negotiations between the government and the authors of the memo," he said.

Why didn't the Reagan administration ask Noriega to deport Escobar and Jorge Ochoa to Miami or Bogotá? When members of the House Foreign Affairs Committee raised that point at a hearing in 1986, DEA headquarters submitted a statement asserting that officials of the Panamanian Defense Forces "were not aware of the visit nor of the meeting until after the Attorney General [of Colombia] departed." By that time, the DEA statement said, the cartel leaders had dispersed.[18]

What DEA headquarters did not say was that DEA agents in Miami had known that the cartel leaders were in Panama since early May. Their informant, Barry Seal, was meeting with the Ochoas in Panama City and reporting back to them. As Seal would eventually testify, Jorge Ochoa summoned him to Panama soon after the Lara Bonilla assassination. Seal said he found the Ochoa family in tears, anxious for the patriarch, old Fabio, who had stayed behind and had been briefly detained by the Colombian police, and fearful that no one would feed the animals in their zoo. He said he planned the details of the Nicaragua shipment in the Ochoa suite at the César Park Marriott.[19] The agents in Miami said they reported Seal's observations to DEA headquarters but no one acted on the information, probably because officials in Washington still doubted Seal's veracity.

Suppose DEA had put Noriega to the test. Would he have expelled Escobar and Ochoa? Some American officials doubted it. "Occasionally the Panamanians swing some poor slob out, in effect give him away to make us feel they're cooperating, but it's nobody close to Noriega," grumbled U.S. Commissioner of Customs William von Raab. "It's just a kind of sacrifice bunt they perform to make us happy."

Von Raab's skepticism seemed confirmed when in February 1988 José I. Blandón, formerly Noriega's top political intelligence adviser, broke with the general and testified against him before a federal grand jury in Miami and the Senate Subcommittee on Terrorism, Narcotics, and International Communications. Blandón said that Noriega knew very well that the cartel leaders and their retinues, seventy-five to one hundred Colombians in all, were in Panama. In fact, Blandón said, Noriega assigned members of the PDF to act as bodyguards for the Colombians and exacted between $4 million and $7 million from them in exchange for official protection. "Noriega has turned Panama into a gigantic machine for all sorts of criminal activities and enterprises," Blandón said. "The relationship between drug trafficking and the political life of Panama began in 1982 and culminated in 1984 when they [the cartel] came to control the political life of Panama totally." He estimated that Noriega accumulated between $200 million and $1 billion from trafficking in drugs, arms, phony visas, and other contraband.

U.S. officials often cited as evidence of Noriega's cooperation on drug enforcement a raid that occurred on May 29, 1984. On that day, while Noriega was traveling in Europe, officers of the PDF busted a cocaine laboratory that was under construction in Darién Province, Panama, near the Colombian border. Twenty-three Colombians were arrested, and a short time later, the PDF arrested one of Noriega's top aides, Lieutenant Colonel Julián Melo, for helping set up the laboratory. According to *The Miami Herald*, Noriega piously announced he dismissed Melo because he was "weak, morally, and fell victim to the consequences." Melo was not prosecuted.[20]

Blandón's version of the Darién laboratory bust was considerably different. Blandón testified that Pablo Escobar and several other Medellín traffickers paid Melo $5 million in protection money, $2 million of which went to Noriega. After the lab was raided, Blandón said, he received an urgent call from Noriega, who was in London. As Blandón told the story, Noriega believed that Escobar was going to have him assassinated for allowing the raid. Blandón said that Noriega told him to go to Havana to beseech Fidel Castro to mediate the issue; Noriega himself arrived in Havana on June 27, 1984, and, according to Blandón, met with Castro and a representative of the Medellín cartel. Blandón said that Castro worked out a deal so that Noriega could save his neck by giving back the $5 million and the lab machinery and releasing the Colombians. To support his story, Blandón gave the Senate Foreign Relations Committee and the FBI photographs of himself, Castro, and Noriega which he said were taken during the meeting over the Darién lab.[21]

A second witness before the Senate subcommittee corroborated some important aspects of Blandón's testimony. Floyd Carlton Cáceres, a Panamanian pilot and admitted trafficker, testified that he had been Noriega's intermediary in a 1982 negotiation in which Escobar and his cohorts agreed to pay Noriega $100,000 for each shipment of cocaine dispatched through Panama. Carlton said that in May 1984, after the Lara Bonilla murder, Escobar, the Ochoas, and other cartel leaders in Panama City told him that they were paying Noriega $4 million to $5 million for protection. Carlton said that Noriega approved the raid on the cartel's new lab in Darién because other PDF officers had found out about the laboratory and had told the Americans, so Noriega "felt pressured and had to act." "He would deal with God and with the devil at the same time," said Carlton. " 'I will deal with you today. Tomorrow I will sell you.' "[22] The evidence presented by Carlton, Blandón, and others who claimed to know of Noriega's transactions with traffickers served as the basis for Noriega's indictment in Miami and Tampa in February 1988.

The Medellín traffickers regarded bustling Panama City as a nice place to visit, but they did not want to live there. They yearned to return to their ranches, but by the fall of 1984, it was clear to them that Betancur did not intend to abandon his pledge to extradite them to the United States. The Colombian legal system was processing the first batch of U.S. extradition requests. Furthermore, for the first time, the Colombian courts began to develop serious criminal cases against the kingpins. In October, Bogotá superior court judge Tulio Manuel Castro Gil issued indictments in the murder of Lara Bonilla. Pablo Escobar was charged as the "intellectual author" of the justice minister's assassination. Castro Gil summoned Gonzalo Rodríguez Gacha, Lehder, and the Ochoas for questioning.[23]

The traffickers attempted to intimidate Enrique Parejo González, a lawyer and Liberal party activist who had replaced Lara Bonilla as justice minister, but Parejo proved as stubbornly courageous as his predecessor. He resisted every attempt to accommodate the cartel, declaring, "The drug traffickers have destabilized the very basis of our morals because they corrupt everything. They invade everything. Not the least, they buy officials." One day, Parejo received a tape-recorded cassette of his voice, made by the

traffickers from a wiretap. On another occasion, a stranger
approached some visitors to his house and asked them to
tell Parejo that he was going to die.

On November 14, 1984, Betancur authorized the extradition of six people, among them Hernán Botero Moreno,
the Medellín hotelier and soccer team owner wanted
for laundering $55 million through a bank in the Miami
area.

The next day, police in Madrid arrested Jorge Ochoa and
Gilberto Rodríguez Orejuela on a warrant from the United
States. It was the arrest that DEA agents wished had been
made six months earlier at the Marriott Hotel in Panama.
But it was better late than never. DEA agents had tracked
the pair to Spain, where they had acquired an estate in the
Madrid suburbs and a ten-thousand-acre ranch near the Portuguese border. The agents believed they planned to set up
a laboratory complex at the ranch to serve the European
cocaine market.

Spanish authorities agreed to hold Ochoa and Rodríguez
while the United States applied for their extradition. Before
long, Spain's embassy in Bogotá received threats.

Bud Mullen ordered the DEA agents posted in Medellín
and Cali to retreat to Bogotá after the Colombian National
Police came up with evidence that they were under surveillance and their telephones were tapped. The cartel had
also eavesdropped on top Colombian officials evidentally
with the help of someone in the telephone company. On
November 26, a car containing several sticks of dynamite
exploded on the street in front of the U.S. embassy in Bogotá. Tall steel gates prevented the blast from damaging the
embassy, but a Colombian woman was killed and four other
Colombians were injured.

In December, State Department officials ordered Lewis
Tambs back to Washington because of a threat on his life.
Edwin Corr, the U.S. ambassador to Bolivia, withdrew to
Washington in December after the DEA learned that the
traffickers had infiltrated his security guard.

On January 5, 1985, Colombian National Police hustled
Hernán Botero Moreno, Ricardo Pavón Jatter, his brother
Said Pavón Jatter, and Marcos Cadavid onto a plane bound

for Miami. They were the first four traffickers to be extradited under the treaty with the United States. All four were convicted.[24]

Within days, informants reported that the Medellín traffickers intended to retaliate against Americans. The hit list put American embassy officials first, wives and children of embassy officers next, then American businessmen and journalists. Children of American embassy personnel were dispatched to the States. Embassy personnel traveled to and from work in armored vehicles. In Washington, the State Department warned travelers not to go to Colombia. A number of multinational companies pulled their employees out of the country.

A report reached Washington that the cartel had placed a $350,000 price on the head of Bud Mullen. Informants warned that the cartel was gunning for several other DEA officials, including Johnny Phelps, who had recently moved to headquarters to run the DEA cocaine desk. In Miami, extra guard details were assigned to all federal judges, U.S. Attorney Stanley Marcus, the federal courthouse, and the DEA field office.

Betancur, Parejo, and other top Colombian officials traveled about Bogotá under tight security, but everyone knew that a determined gunman could get past any security detail. "They are perfectly capable of carrying out their threats," Parejo said in an interview in January 1985. He smiled calmly as he gazed about his austere office in a fortified sector. "This is a war to the death in which they win or we win. We are not going to change by even one millimeter our policy against the drug traffic."

Betancur vowed to continue the extraditions, despite an outpouring of threats against himself and his children. "The drug traffickers' actions have provoked such justifiable repudiation in Colombian society and condemnation by the entire world," he said, "that the government could not leave our society unprotected, whatever may be the risks to government officials, among them the president himself." By the end of his term, Betancur would send sixteen prisoners to the United States.

In January 1985, a few days after the Colombian National
Police had pounded through the Colombian-Brazilian frontier in yet another futile search for him, Carlos Lehder coolly
summoned a Spanish television crew to his jungle sanctuary.
It amused him to treat Betancur's "war without quarter" as
a great game of hide-and-seek. In the television footage, he
looked none the worse for the wear of life on the run.
Surrounded by guards with automatic weapons, gold chains
cascading down his chest, Lehder bared his glittering white
teeth and declared that he was devoting his millions to the
destabilization of the Colombian government.

"I am here to dialogue with . . . M-19," he announced.
"Ours is a revolutionary fight against the United States and
the oligarchic monarchy. The bonanza is a revolutionary
means to fight against the oligarchy and imperialists—and
to stop extradition . . . Lara Bonilla, Tambs, and Betancur
united to conspire against the interests of this country. Lara
Bonilla was executed by the people."

It was a wild and confused jumble of leftist and rightist
rhetoric. One minute Lehder boasted that he intended to
arm the urban guerrillas, the next minute he was singing
the praises of Adolf Hitler.[25] "Cocaine is the Latin American atomic bomb," he sneered. "This stimulant that [North
Americans] need is fueling the Latin American revolution.
They need it to function and their dollars give sustenance
to the Latin revolution. We will fight against the imperialists
who try to corrupt us. We will fight to get the dollars to
liberate ourselves."

At DEA headquarters, Bud Mullen and Jack Lawn
watched the tape intently. Were these the ravings of a coked-
up egomaniac? Or was Lehder really planning to bless the
terrorists with his billions?[26]

Ever skeptical of the narcoterrorism theory, Lawn looked
into Lehder's claim that he was joining forces with M-19.
Lawn could find no evidence that Lehder really did so, and
Colombian military officials told him that they believed that
Lehder was stoned on cocaine and rambling. They did not
think the luxury-loving Carlos was meant for the ascetic life
of a revolutionary.

Mullen agreed. Narcoterrorism was not the problem. "I

don't see a Communist conspiracy," he said. "It's not left wing or right wing. It's just money. I do believe there are ulterior motives on the part of some countries, that they see this as hurting the United States, as undermining our government and our society. But they don't have to *do* anything, that's the beauty of it. We're doing it to ourselves."

The pragmatic assessment of the DEA officials was not acceptable to Reagan's more ideological advisers. Reagan's men were absolutely convinced that M-19, the drug cartel, the Cubans, and the Sandinistas were all in bed together, and they did not let facts, or the absence of them, stand in their way. In late 1985, Reagan's advisers attempted to twist a tragic internal conflict in Colombia into a propaganda victory for the administration's cause in Central America.

On November 6, 1985, M-19 guerrillas managed to slip into the Palace of Justice in downtown Bogotá and to capture the jurists and employees inside. The next day, the military, acting under orders from President Betancur, stormed the building. Nearly a hundred people were killed in the cross fire, including eleven Supreme Court justices and all but one guerrilla. In the fires that broke out, the judicial archives were destroyed. In the political heat of the moment, some Betancur ministers charged that the Medellín drug cartel put the M-19 guerrillas up to the act of terror in order to get rid of official records of their activities. "There is an alliance between the guerrillas and the drug traffickers," Justice Minister Enrique Parejo González said. "The Supreme Court judges had been threatened by drug traffickers regarding the extradition treaty. . . . It could be a coincidence but I don't think so. I think it's possible drug traffickers financed the guerrillas [in the takeover]."[27]

Parejo's assertion was greeted with more than a little skepticism in Bogotá. The Betancur government, which was being widely condemned for bungling the military raid and killing the hostages, seemed all too eager to taint the guerrillas. Also, eyewitnesses said that army shelling, not the guerrillas, started the fires that destroyed the court records. Betancur's advisers soon backed off the charge that the Medellín Mafia played a part in launching the siege.

It was at this point that members of the Reagan administration began offering a startling theory of their own about the incident: the real culprits, they suggested, were the Nicaraguan Sandinistas. And if the Sandinistas were in league with the Medellín drug cartel, the Palace of Justice affair had been an act of narcoterrorism.

At best, the theory hung on some very flimsy threads. First was the suggestion, no more than speculation at that point, that the drug traffickers were behind the incident. Second, when soldiers picked their way through the burned-out wreckage they found two Belgian-made automatic rifles that were traced to a 1979 Venezuelan arms shipment to the Sandinistas when they were waging a guerrilla war against dictator Anastasio Somoza. Also, a few Uzi submachine guns that had been used by Somoza's guards were found in the rubble.[28]

At a meeting of top intelligence and law-enforcement officials, Jack Lawn argued that the presence of a few Nicaraguan weapons did not mean that the Sandinistas had put the guerrillas up to taking over the Colombian court. Lawn pointed out that a number of weapons found in the Palace of Justice had been made in the United States. Did that mean, he asked, that the Reagan administration was also behind the M-19?

CIA professionals agreed with Lawn, but higher-level Reagan administration officials persisted in putting out the word that Nicaragua and the traffickers aided the M-19. On November 20, then Deputy National Security Adviser John M. Poindexter told a meeting of the National Drug Enforcement Policy Board, according to its minutes, that the NSC intended to produce a directive on Cuban and Nicaraguan drug trafficking and "those aspects of international drug trafficking that could undermine democratic institutions around the world." On December 2, at a meeting of the Organization of American States in Cartagena, Colombia, U.S. Secretary of State George Shultz asserted publicly that a connection existed between the M-19 guerrillas and the Nicaraguan government. Shultz did not go into detail, but according to an Associated Press dispatch, "diplomatic sources" said that Shultz's claim was based on the discovery of the Nicaraguan weapons in the wrecked Palace of Justice.[29]

Reagan reiterated this claim on December 15, declaring in his weekly radio broadcast that "Nicaragua's connection with the recent terrorist attack against Colombia's Supreme Court is now clear." In a January 1986 interview with *Notícias de México*, a Mexico City paper, Reagan went still further:

> The hand of the Soviet Union and its Cuban surrogate can be found behind terrorist movements such as the M-19 in Colombia. . . . It is behind the Nicaraguan government's subversion of its democratic neighbors. And the link between the governments of such Soviet allies as Cuba and Nicaragua and international narcotics trafficking and terrorism is becoming increasingly clear. These twin evils—narcotics trafficking and terrorism—represent the most insidious and dangerous threats to the hemisphere today.

In April 1986, Reagan signed a National Security Decision Directive (NSDD) that resulted from the Poindexter study on drug trafficking in Nicaragua and Cuba. Vice President Bush disclosed portions of the NSDD two months later, on June 7. The Reagan directive, entitled "Narcotics and National Security," cast the war on drugs as a counterinsurgency struggle; it declared that "some insurgent and terrorist groups cooperate closely with drug traffickers and use this as a major source of funds." The administration evidently intended to use the document as a philosophical basis for insisting that the U.S. military and the intelligence community play a bigger role in countering drug trafficking. In disclosing the NSDD, Bush told a Houston press conference, "The demonstrable role drug trafficking played in the [Supreme Court] massacre is anything but an isolated event."

Ten days after Bush made this statement, a special investigative tribunal of magistrates appointed by the surviving members of the Supreme Court announced its conclusions: the guerrillas had attacked the Palace of Justice to further their own interests, not at the instigation of the

traffickers or of Nicaragua. Colombian Attorney General
Carlos Jiménez, who conducted a separate inquiry for the
Colombian Chamber of Representatives, criticized Betancur for choosing a purely military solution but concluded
that M-19 acted on its own. Both panels concluded that the
fires that destroyed the extradition files might have been
accidental.[30]

The findings of the Colombian panels were largely ignored in the United States. The claim the traffickers and
the Nicaraguans were to blame for the Supreme Court massacre became a factoid, a claim that many people accepted
unskeptically. It made its way into various articles and books
about terrorism. The administration continued to exploit it.
On March 9, 1988, Elliott Abrams told the House Foreign
Affairs Committee, "In Colombia . . . the combination of
guerrillas and drug traffickers is obvious and direct. And
the best example is the attack on the Supreme Court . . .
where the guerrillas went into the Supreme Court building,
the M-19, but the targets were justices and files that had to
do with extradition, so there was a direct link there. I think
we also see something of a direct link in Cuba. . . . They've
got plenty of resources, military resources, and they control
their airspace extremely carefully, so the use of that airspace
[by traffickers] is suggestive of some kind of cooperation
between the Castro regime and traffickers."

In an interview in December 1988, German Caño, a top
official of the Department of Administrative Security
(DAS), Colombia's version of the FBI, said that information
had recently come to the government's attention which supported the theory that the traffickers had financed M-19's
assault on the Palace of Justice. Caño said that informants
within M-19 had told DAS that some guerrilla leaders had
accepted a large sum of money from the traffickers and had
agreed to intimidate the Supreme Court. The informants
claimed to be members of a faction of M-19 which had
disapproved of the assault on the court. A number of Colombian and American officials found this information
plausible. However, DAS was unable to come up with
documents or other hard evidence corroborating the payment. Furthermore, as Caño acknowledged, it was possible

that the story was disinformation, told by surviving members of M-19 in order to distinguish themselves from their dead comrades or ingratiate themselves with the government.

Whatever the truth was, it was not in the files of either the Colombian or the U.S. government. To be sure, in 1988 and 1989, evidence mounted that some units of the FARC guerrillas had gone into the cocaine refining business. In December 1988, Jamaican authorities seized a shipload of Portuguese weapons worth $8 million which was apparently bound for the FARC. How could the guerrillas have amassed that kind of money *without* selling cocaine? However, as *Semana* magazine noted, the guerrillas appeared to a "third cartel," processing and selling a modest amount of cocaine in direct competition with the Medellín and Cali cartels.

As troubling as this development was, Colombian officials were more concerned by the menace from the right. Paramilitary death squads backed by Medellín kingpins Pablo Escobar and Gonzalo Rodriguez Gacha stepped up their activity in late 1988 and early 1989. Many of their targets were guerrillas, but others were human rights workers and civilians. On January 18, 1989, Colombia was traumatized once more when a death squad linked to Rodriguez Gacha murdered two judges and thirteen other members of a government commission which was looking into narco-paramilitary activity in the provinces.

8
"Does Somebody Have to Die?"

Kiki Camarena had developed all the qualities that made a fine agent: tenacity, creativity, passion. For all his outward machismo and occasional infractions of the rules, he remained something of an innocent, which was a virtue in a law-enforcement agency. A cynical officer was a dangerous man, corruptible, lazy, and undependable in a fight. Camarena knew that the United States was inundated with drugs, yet he believed—he *had* to believe—that an individual could make a difference. In any other circumstance, he would have been one of his agency's brightest stars.

In Guadalajara, he had no chance to shine. Nobody in authority seemed to know what he was doing. When he disappeared, DEA officials in Mexico City and Washington did not give reporters an accurate account of the cases on which Camarena had been working.

DEA agents were not judged on what they were but on what they did. Those posted abroad were measured by how many important arrests and seizures they convinced the host police force to make and how much narcotics intelligence they produced. For Camarena and his partners, the possibility of significant arrests was foreclosed entirely. Every time they were hot on the trail of one of the kingpins, they bumped up against a Mexican police badge.

They concentrated, instead, on gleaning intelligence, but, even so, in the eyes of headquarters officials their performance did not match that of agents in other foreign posts. Corruption checkmated them in this endeavor as well. In most countries, DEA agents could find helpful police narcotics squad commanders who would assign junior officers to do legwork such as staking out suspects and pulling business and telephone records. In return, the DEA agents shared information about international movements of the local traffickers. The system made everybody happy. The local commander could impress his superiors with his sophisticated knowledge of the global narcotics trend. The DEA agents could send headquarters on-the-scene intelligence reports rich in detail and color. DEA agents in Mexico could not rely on that sort of symbiosis. They tried to cultivate some of the younger Federales, but it was always with the thought in mind that, after all the drinking and bantering, one of these men might sell the names of their informants to the traffickers for a few hundred dollars.

It was a struggle just to stay even, but the agents would not have minded the hard work and the added dimension of unpredictability, had it not been for the fact that nobody outside their immediate circle seemed to notice.

"As long as you get the recognition from your peers within your organization, that's all anybody asks for, really," Kuykendall reflected some years later. "You want somebody to believe what you're saying. You want somebody to listen to your suggestions. Can they change things? It doesn't matter so much that they can't, as long as they try. That matters more than anything in the world, not that they accomplish change but that they really *try*. And that they know *we* are trying."

They were accustomed to feeling expendable, but it was truly painful to realize that they were invisible. For Camarena, the sense that he was being ignored and distrusted by his own government was a crushing blow. Born in Mexico, he took immense pride in having earned American citizenship and having served two years as a Marine. He and his partners had celebrated the inauguration of Ronald Reagan, confident that Reagan would act decisively to counter the menace of Latin American drug trafficking. When Reagan did not challenge de la Madrid on the drug issue, the agents surmised that the foreign-policy and intelligence communities had prevailed in order to preserve the status quo, not only for reasons of state but on narrow grounds of bureaucratic clientism, as well.

For all DEA agents in Mexico and on the border, the most maddening feature of the American government's political agenda in Mexico was its insistence on maintaining productive relations with the Dirección Federal de Seguridad (DFS), the Federal Security Directorate. This shadowy arm of the Interior Ministry, widely feared by Mexican citizens, was known as the "political police" because it was responsible for suppressing dissidents and identifying terrorists and "subversives."

Most DEA agents who worked in Mexico and on the border considered the DFS the private army of the drug traffickers. They called the DFS badge "a license to traffic." Corrupt Federales might take money from the traffickers to look the other way, but so many DFS agents worked actively for the traffickers as enforcers and security men that the DEA agents felt it was not worth the risk to find the few men and women in the organization who might be trusted. DFS credentials conferred the legal authority to carry a machine gun, to install wiretaps, and to interrogate troublemakers, all of which made a card-carrying DFS agent extremely useful to the trafficking networks. DEA and Customs agents on the border picked up numerous informant reports that some DFS agents rode security for the traffickers' marijuana-laden truck convoys, used the Mexican police radio system to check border crossings for signs of American police surveillance, and ferried contraband across the Rio Grande by boat.

In California's Imperial Valley, for instance, DEA agents received information that cocaine was being smuggled in cartons of frozen shrimp packed in Baja California for export to the United States. DEA started tracking all the loads of shrimp that came across the line. One shipment was suspect because it did not go to its destination in Los Angeles but was diverted to a cold-storage warehouse near the border. When the agents arrived, the warehouse manager said that a bunch of men who identified themselves as DFS agents had shown up at the warehouse late one night and had insisted on taking certain cartons of shrimp, about six hundred pounds in all. The DEA agents did not find any cocaine in the remaining shrimp, but they staked out the warehouse. A few days later, some men came to the warehouse, packed the rest of the shrimp in a truck, and drove it back to Baja California. The DEA agents, who followed the truck to the border, guessed that the shrimp cartons were going to be recycled to smuggle more cocaine, but they were never able to identify the suspected smugglers or determine whether they were, in fact, DFS agents.

Nearly all the major traffickers carried DFS credentials, which they had been given or sold by bona fide DFS agents— although, because many DFS agents bought their jobs, it was hard to distinguish between genuine Mexican government employees and *pistoleros* with bought badges. One night Kiki's talkative buddy, Pete Hernandez, encountered Jaime Herrera Nevares, the Durango heroin king, at a cantina in Guadalajara. Curious to know more about the legendary outlaw Don Jaime, Hernandez pretended to be a corrupt Mexican cop and ordered rounds of drinks. Herrera reached into his pocket and pulled out a DFS badge. "I'm one of yours," he said, winking.

This was truer than Don Jaime knew. To Hernandez's intense irritation, the DFS *was* treated like a member of the family by the DEA's bureaucratic "brothers," the Central Intelligence Agency and the Federal Bureau of Investigation.

DFS officials worked closely with the Mexico City station of the U.S. Central Intelligence Agency and the attaché of the Federal Bureau of Investigation. The DFS passed along photographs and wiretapped conversations of suspected intelligence officers and provocateurs stationed in the large Soviet and Cuban missions in Mexico City. This information was of crucial importance to U.S. counterintelligence specialists at the CIA and FBI. KGB officers usually arranged to meet Americans they had compromised in Mexico City. The DFS also helped the CIA track Central American leftists who passed through the Mexican capital. Finally, the DFS provided security details for the U.S. ambassador and other American dignitaries.

Formed after World War II, the DFS started out as Mexico's answer to the CIA and the counterintelligence division of the FBI. This internal security police force developed an unsavory reputation during civil unrest in the early 1970s, when DFS agents were accused of resorting to torture, assassination, and disappearances to crush urban guerrilla groups. In 1977, a secret police unit called the Brigada Blanca, the White Brigade, thought to be an offshoot of the DFS and extreme elements of the military, formed death squads to eliminate the violent left. Popular outcry forced López Portillo to dismantle the White Brigade in 1980. But in López Portillo's last years and through the first two years of the de la Madrid administration, the DFS expanded, by one estimate, from eight hundred to two thousand positions.[1]

Alan Riding, the New York Times correspondent in Mexico City for many years, wrote in his authoritative 1985 book about Mexico, Distant Neighbors, "Even now, the occasional release of someone who has 'disappeared' for several weeks or months serves to confirm the continued use of the old tactics by the Security Directorate. (In 1983 and 1984, there were several brief incidents of 'kidnappings' of political activists, including three journalists, two Chilean exiles, and a human rights worker. In each case, the government denied responsibility.) And the interrogation of suspected terrorists still routinely includes beatings and torture."[2]

The extent to which the U.S. government was willing to tolerate criminal activity by DFS officials in exchange for help in collecting intelligence was graphically demonstrated in the early 1980s, when an FBI undercover penetration of a Mexican car theft ring operating in Southern California led to the top of the DFS.

The case, called Operation Cargo, began in November 1980, when some California highway patrolmen arrested two Mexican car thieves. One suspect became an FBI informant; he said that he belonged to an organization that was stealing thousands of Jaguars, Jeeps, Porsches, and other luxury cars on order, right down to the color and upholstery style, for VIPs in Mexico City.

The California Highway Patrol called in the FBI. "I was told, You can't do anything about it, it's all political," said Norman Zigrossi, then the special agent in charge of the FBI field office in San Diego. "I couldn't believe that." Under Zigrossi's guidance, a young FBI agent named Bobby

Montoya penetrated the ring, posing as the cousin of the informant. The FBI provided the ring with an apartment in Chula Vista and a "cool car"—a Volkswagen van—both of which were wired for sound and contained hidden cameras. Montoya was able to present enough evidence to support the indictments of thirteen DFS officials for allegedly controlling the ring, among them Estéban Guzmán, the highest-ranking career officer in the agency, and another *comandante* named Javier García Morales, the son of Javier García Paniagua, president of Mexico's ruling Institutional Revolutionary party.[3]

The informant told the investigators about an even higher official: he said that in November 1979 he had accompanied DFS agent Cipriano Rodríguez to the home of Miguel Nazar Haro, DFS director since 1977, and had seen Rodríguez give Nazar Haro a stolen yellow Dodge van. The informant said he also saw a gold Porsche and a blue Ford van at Nazar Haro's house, both of which proved to have been stolen from the Los Angeles area.

The FBI agents did not have enough evidence to justify the indictment of the DFS director, but they came to believe that some senior DFS officials in Mexico City were deeply involved in running the stolen car network. Numerous cars stolen from the United States were parked in the lot at DFS headquarters in Mexico City. When an FBI agent tried to take pictures of the cars, DFS agents confiscated his camera.

In July 1981, the car thieves became suspicious of the informant and his "cousin" Bobby Montoya after the informant wrecked a jeep loaded with automatic weapons on instructions from the FBI agents, who did not want the weapons delivered to buyers in Mexico. Soon afterward, FBI agents heard through the bugs that DFS employee Enrique Castillo, a reputed hit man, had been sent up from Mexico in order to kill the informant and Montoya.[4] FBI agents and California highway patrolmen raided the gang's San Diego hideout, arrested fifteen people, and found, among other things, the private phone number of DFS chief Nazar Haro.

Two gang members arrested in the July raid agreed to cooperate with the prosecution. These new witnesses corroborated and expanded upon the informant's allegations against Nazar Haro, claiming that he was personally protecting the operation.

Douglas Schwartz, the assistant U.S. attorney handling the case, wanted to seek Nazar Haro's indictment for conspiracy. Gordon McGinley, FBI legal attaché assigned to the U.S. embassy in Mexico City, spoke to Nazar Haro and, according to an FBI affidavit, elicited admissions that Nazar Haro had met the leader of the car theft ring at DFS headquarters in Mexico City and had accepted one of the vehicles. But as Schwartz began putting together an indictment of the DFS leader, McGinley sent a flurry of cables to San Diego and Washington protesting the proposed indictment on grounds that Nazar Haro was "an essential repeat essential contact for CIA station Mexico City." In one cable, dated August 17, 1981, he wrote: "CIA station and [FBI] legat [legal attaché] believe that our mutual interests and as a consequence the security of the United States, as it relates to terrorism, intelligence, and counterintelligence in Mexico, would suffer a disastrous blow if Nazar were forced to resign."

The case caused a bitter debate within the FBI. Zigrossi, of the San Diego FBI field office, and his allies in the FBI's criminal division wanted an indictment badly, but the FBI counterintelligence division resisted, siding with McGinley and the CIA station in Mexico City. Prosecutor Schwartz and his boss, U.S. Attorney William Kennedy, joined Zigrossi in pressing for the indictment. Lowell Jensen, then assistant attorney general in charge of the Justice Department criminal division in Washington, and his aides were sympathetic, but they came under intense pressure from the intelligence community and the State Department.

Nazar Haro resigned in January 1982, after the investigation leaked to the Mexican press. Even then, Jensen and his aides would not allow prosecutor Schwartz to present an indictment to the grand jury. One reason was that an indictment would be a symbolic gesture that would serve no good end and do great harm to Mexican-American relations. No one believed that the retired Mexican official would dare enter the United States.

U.S. Attorney Kennedy wrote letters urging Jensen to approve the indictment, arguing that the Mexican government had made no effort to recompense the thousands of Americans victimized by the ring. Montoya's partners at the FBI estimated that over a period of years the ring had stolen four thousand cars, worth more than $30 million. On March 26, 1982, in a story in *The San Diego Union,* reporter Jon Standefer wrote that Kennedy had confirmed to him that the CIA was blocking the indictment because of Nazar Haro's "indispensability as a source of intelligence in Mexico and Central America." "I realize this must be factored in, but I'm concerned about the victims—car owners or the insurance companies—that have paid off claims," Kennedy added, according to Standefer's story.[5] Although Kennedy did not give away any truly secret sources and methods—it was general knowledge the CIA maintained liaison with the heads of other intelligence services—Attorney General William French Smith recommended that the president fire Kennedy. Kennedy refused to quit, was fired, and issued a statement calling the *Union* story "an accurate confirmation. There is nothing more to add or apologize for." Kennedy became a hero in San Diego and was appointed to a local judgeship.

Confident that the case was over, Nazar Haro flew to Los Angeles and called a press conference on April 21 at the office of his attorney, Marvin Mitchelson. He filed an $11 million defamation lawsuit against *Time* magazine for linking him to the car theft ring. Schwartz wanted to charge Nazar Haro on the spot. Justice Department officials in Washington refused to approve that action but finally allowed Schwartz to subpoena the fifty-seven-year-old Mexican to appear before a grand jury in San Diego.

After hearing two days of testimony, the grand jury indicted Nazar Haro on a string of car-theft and conspiracy charges. Nazar Haro was arrested late in the afternoon of Friday, April 23, and spent twenty-seven hours in jail. Schwartz had proposed to set the former official's bail at $1 million, the same amount set for the other men who had been arrested, but Justice Department officials in Washington ordered him not to request bail greater than $200,000.

On Saturday night, a lawyer dispatched from somewhere in Mexico bailed Nazar Haro out with $200,000 in cash. Nazar Haro fled across the border and was listed as a fugitive, along with most of the other indicted DFS officials, including ex-*comandantes* Estéban Guzmán, Javier García Morales, Ramón Peseros, and Guillermo Lira. Ex-*comandante* Jaime Alcalá was later reported to have died. Gilberto Peraza Mayén, the head of the car theft ring, was convicted, served time, and, after his release, was reported to have been shot to death in Baja California in December 1987.

Nazar Haro's successor as head of the DFS was José Antonio Zorrilla Pérez. The intelligence relationship between the DFS and the CIA and FBI continued. Gavin justified it on grounds that "the collection of information can't stop." "Sometimes we go down into the gutters, practically, to get information," Gavin said. "That doesn't mean we should condone every sort of activity."

The American ambassador took the same position voiced by the CIA officers, that there were two factions of the DFS, a "good" group in Mexico City and a "bad" group in the provinces. "You can't say that the entire agency is corrupt," Gavin said. "We feel that there are some people there who are straight and who are trying to do the right thing for their country, and they gain and we gain from the liaison that we've established." As a sign of his confidence, Gavin used DFS agents as his personal bodyguards.

Most DEA agents thought Gavin's view was generous. They argued that there were corrupt senior DFS officers in Mexico City who had a vested interest in allowing the provincial officers to work the rackets; those officers shared in the take when a DFS agent in the provinces was forced to pay his local *comandante* so much each month and the *comandante* had to send money back to a corrupt superior in Mexico City. The amount of money generated by drug trafficking and other rackets explained why some DFS jobs went for exorbitant prices. Two informants approached a DEA agent in El Paso and said they had been offered DFS agent positions for $30,000 each. The DEA agent was tempted—

"What better way to get information than from the inside," he said—but DEA could not afford the fee.

In 1984, Camarena and Kuykendall found out that a certain DFS officer had been assigned to provide security for Michael Reagan, President Reagan's son, who was vacationing in the Pacific resort of Puerto Vallarta. Camarena and Kuykendall called the U.S. Secret Service to warn that this particular DFS officer would not be an ideal security guard because he was known to be a close friend of Manuel Salcido Uzeta (Cochi Loco), the most sadistic of the Guadalajara-based traffickers.

The DFS zone commanders who controlled the border with the United States were equally outrageous. Daniel Acuña Figueroa, who was in charge of the lucrative Tijuana-Mexicali corridor, built a fabulous Chinese pagoda–style mansion and swimming pool amid the slums of downtown Mexicali. When Acuña was an MFJP *comandante* in Tijuana, some DEA agents asked him to arrest a suspected drug trafficker who was also a leather goods manufacturer. The next day, the DEA men went back to the Federales office. Everyone had on leather jackets, even the secretaries. Acuña, who had the finest leather jacket of all, said he could not arrest the manufacturer because of a legal technicality.

In 1986, the U.S. Attorney's Office in Brownsville filed a civil action seeking to seize two houses in McAllen, Texas, owned by Rafael Chao López, the DFS zone commander for the North Mexico region bordering on South Texas's Rio Grande Valley, one of the busiest smuggling corridors in the United States. In an affidavit filed in U.S. federal court, prosecutors alleged that Chao had acquired the properties, which were valued at more than $300,000, with the proceeds of drug trafficking. According to the *El Paso Herald-Post,* DFS zone commander Rafael Aguilar Guajardo, who lived in Ciudad Juárez and led the DFS in the states of Chihuahua and Durango until 1985, was arrested for possession of drugs and illegal arms by the Mexican Federal Judicial Police in September 1986, but a judge in Ciudad Juárez dismissed the charges, citing insufficient evidence. At the same time, Aguilar came under investigation by the DEA. In 1988, the U.S. Attorney's Office in El Paso would file a civil suit seeking forfeiture of Aguilar's property in El Paso—a condominium, two houses, and a Porsche—which was reportedly worth more than $1 million.[6]

After he had been in Mexico for a while, the habitually blunt Kuykendall told a senior CIA officer that he was fed up with the way the agency protected the DFS. "Protect!" the CIA man exploded. The agency was not responsible for what went on in the boondocks, did not approve of drug trafficking, and besides, DEA had no proof of the DFS's collusion with the traffickers. All right, then, Kuykendall shot back, maybe his choice of words was wrong. How about "defend"?

At embassy staff meetings, whenever the DEA men criticized the DFS, CIA officers would affect bored glances and talk about the national security threat of regiments of Cuban and Soviet agents. "They don't give a damn," Kuykendall said later. "They turn their heads the other way. They see their task as much more important than ours."[7]

Kuykendall and the other DEA agents in Mexico tried to document allegations that many DFS officers were working for the traffickers, but without the power to subpoena records and install wiretaps they were generally unsuccessful. In 1986, American agents recruited an informant who claimed that he had been on the inside of the DFS from 1973 to 1981. Gabriel (a pseudonym) was a rare individual, a college-educated man, a Hollywood jet-setter and sinsemilla marijuana purveyor who said he had worked as a contract agent, financial adviser, and arms dealer for Nazar Haro and his senior officers. Gabriel told a story that startled even veteran agents, but they came to believe that he was credible because he was able to telephone old contacts among the police and the traffickers; while the agents listened, he and his friends discussed the deals they had done together. In 1988, he agreed to an interview.

Gabriel said that in the mid-1970s, when the Sinaloa gangs were warring with one another and with the MFJP and DEA, DFS *comandantes* Estéban Guzmán and Daniel

Acuña went to the Sinaloa drug warlords—Ernesto Fonseca, Miguel Angel Félix Gallardo, the Caros, and the Quinteros—and advised them to end the violence and build a base of operations in the United States. As Gabriel told the story, the DFS officials convinced the Sinaloa traffickers to relocate in Guadalajara. He said that the DFS created a veritable narcoindustrial complex; DFS officers held off the MFJP, introduced the traffickers to people of influence in Guadalajara, found them houses, and assigned them DFS bodyguards. The traffickers provided muscle and blood, he said, and DFS leaders contributed brains, coordination, insulation from other government agencies, and firepower, in the form of thousands of smuggled automatic weapons. "They gave the traffickers computers," he said. "They gave them protection. They organized them."

Gabriel claimed to have attended strategy sessions held by top DFS officials in Mexico City as they plotted multinational drug deals. He said he saw DFS officers berate Ernesto Fonseca for becoming addicted to cocaine and running his business sloppily. "I watched the cocaine business replace the oil business as the main source of loose capital in Mexico," he said. He explained that the DFS hired advisers like himself to help the families establish networks in the Hispanic communities of East Los Angeles, Chicago, and Texas and to invest hundreds of millions of dollars in Sunbelt real estate. In exchange, Gabriel said, DFS took a quarter of the drug profits.

According to Gabriel, one DFS-sponsored smuggling operation in the late 1970s was called "La Pipa." He said that the DFS acquired about six hundred tanker trucks, ostensibly for transporting natural gas, and dispatched them north packed with marijuana, three to five tons at a time. He said DFS agents paid key Mexican officials and some U.S. Immigration and Customs inspectors $50,000 a load to let the trucks pass. "They ran ten to twelve trucks a day into Phoenix and Los Angeles," he said. "They had the whole border wired."

Because of his background as an expert grower of fine sinsemilla marijuana for the California market, Gabriel said, one of his jobs was to help the DFS resell drugs that had

been seized by the MFJP in conjunction with the DEA. "I
went to the Ministerios Públicos [Mexico's equivalent of
U.S. Attorney's Offices] to evaluate the quality of drugs
that had been seized," he says. "I established a price and
made an offer based on that to the officials at the Ministerio.
It came out to a small percentage of actual net. DFS would
send down Mafia drivers with stash trucks. Several late-
model Chrysler New Yorkers would arrive, with four
DFS officers with machine guns in each one. The DFS officers would bodyguard the shipment to a warehouse someplace around Guadalajara. A few DFS agents would stay
around the warehouse, just to make sure the *pistoleros* did
their job."

Gabriel claimed to have direct knowledge that the DFS
operated an assassination squad and a division that handled
offshore money-laundering for high officials throughout the
government. DFS officials in Mexico City, he said, kept
dossiers on top PRI politicians and their families.

Some of Gabriel's charges were corroborated by several
former Mexican officials who were fired by the Mexican
government and recruited as informants by U.S. Customs
and DEA agents. One former MFJP *comandante* told
American agents that MFJP officers in trafficking strongholds were told by their superiors in Mexico City to provide
protection for certain traffickers. According to agents who
debriefed this official, the MFJP provincial officers were
allowed to make money by extorting lesser traffickers and
gangsters but were not permitted to shake down the cartel
leaders who had made arrangements with corrupt DFS and
Mexican military officials. Gabriel recalled a time when an
MFJP *comandante* broke the rules by demanding large fees
from several Guadalajara cartel leaders; he said a DFS assassination squad was dispatched, and the MFJP *comandante* died in a hail of machine-gun fire.

Another U.S. government "client" whose value was hotly
disputed by the DEA agents was the Mexican attorney
general's eradication program, which was monitored by the
State Department's narcotics assistance unit (NAU). The
DEA Guadalajara office filed report after report about the

expansion of Caro Quintero's marijuana empire. If Caro Quintero was sinking millions of dollars in large, visible desert plantations, Kuykendall insisted, the conclusion was inescapable: the marijuana kingpin must have obtained guarantees of protection, not only from the Federales, who were responsible for arrests of traffickers, but from officials in the Attorney General's Office.[8]

The administration's public pronouncements toward Mexico's anti-drug programs remained effusive. In July 1984, Assistant Secretary of State Dominick DiCarlo assured the House Select Committee on Narcotics Abuse and Control that "current relations between the Drug Enforcement Administration and the MFJP are excellent. DEA informs us that cooperation with MFJP has considerably improved during the past year and that consequently the number of significant bilateral investigations has increased."[9] DiCarlo acknowledged to the committee that marijuana and opium production was rising but minimized the significance of the trend, blaming evasive action by resourceful traffickers—"selection of sites which are remote, frequently smaller and more difficult to detect" and "improved weather."[10] Gary Liming, head of the intelligence division at DEA headquarters, echoed State's position in an interview with *The New York Times:* Mexican traffickers, said Liming, had been "changing the size of their plots, moving to smaller, widely dispersed fields . . . camouflaging the plants by growing them in between other crops."[11]

In private, in fact, attitudes at the American embassy in Mexico City were becoming somewhat more pessimistic. Senior DEA and State narcotics assistance officials were coming around to the view that the Mexican government's eradication program was no longer defensible. The primary reason for the change of heart was not the DEA-Guadalajara reports but rather accelerating marijuana and heroin seizures along the border. Mexican marijuana and brown heroin were available all over the Southwest, and prices were low. That undeniable fact rendered implausible the Mexican government's claims of massive eradication. The Mexican Attorney General's Office flight logs for the spray helicopters showed that the choppers were flying just

25 percent of the time. The aircraft had not been maintained
properly over the years and a number of choppers were
grounded. The spare parts inventory was scattered and full
of obsolete or useless parts.[12] Informants who worked for
a number of DEA field offices in Mexico were reporting
that herbicide was being watered down or dumped in the
desert.

Ed Heath began promoting the idea that the eradication
program required DEA intervention. State Department officials in Washington also concluded that drastic measures
were in order. Ambassador Gavin, who had been preoccupied by the Mexican debt crisis and by trying to cool
Mexico's relationship with Nicaragua, had not agitated for
radical change in Mexico's anti-drug campaign. Once he
found out that the eradication program was in trouble, he
wanted action, and he wanted it *now*. "Herbicide was being
watered, people were being informed of raids," Gavin said
later. "It just got to the point where it was not tolerable
and where we had to make stronger representations. As far
as being forceful, I certainly did my job."

Gavin realized that before the embassy could challenge
the Mexican government on the eradication program, DEA
and State had to agree upon a course of action. The interagency arguments were familiar to the point of monotony:
DEA agents said that State officers doled out cash with naïve
generosity and did not hold the host government accountable for the expenditure of American taxpayers' money.
State officers countered that the agents were jealous of State
and numb to the sensitivities of their hosts. What DEA
agents saw as corruption, State officers interpreted as Third
World inefficiency. Gavin told his deputy chief of mission,
Morris Busby, to arbitrate between the warring bureaucrats.
Eventually the consensus was reached that the embassy
would ask the Mexican government to let DEA agent-
observers fly over fields of poppies or marijuana that were
supposed to have been sprayed so that they could verify
eradication claims. Ed Heath named the project Operation
Vanguard.

On the surface, the Vanguard plan resembled Kiki Camarena's Operation Milagro. But Camarena advocated that

DEA pilots fly spotter planes. As Heath presented Operation Vanguard, Mexican pilots and Mexican planes would do the flying. DEA agents would go along as passengers but would not have control of the flight plans. When Camarena heard about the Mexican pilots, according to Kuykendall, he wanted nothing to do with the project.

Even with that concession to Mexican sensitivities, the embassy could not get the plan past Jesús Antonio Sam López, who, as the chief deputy attorney general in charge of eradication and narcotics control, had produced the allegedly inflated eradication figures. Finally, Gavin appealed to Attorney General Sergio García Ramírez, a genteel law professor who was brought into government to advance de la Madrid's "moral renovation" campaign. In October 1984, García Ramírez agreed to the terms of Operation Vanguard. As a bow to the Americans, he took the project away from Sam López and gave it to an official untainted by charges of corruption in the program: José María Ortega Padilla, a lawyer who served as the department's inspector general.

The acrimonious debates within the embassy and the months of negotiation with the Mexican government were kept secret from the Congress, the press, and even from DEA's top officials, Bud Mullen and Jack Lawn. "As little as we could see that the Mexicans were doing, [going public] would even damage that," said a DEA agent attached to the U.S. embassy in this period.[13]

In October, twenty DEA agents were sent to Mexico on temporary detail to fly on the verification aircraft. According to the DEA agent in charge of the project, Ortega Padilla kept them waiting for weeks, explaining that the air fleet was not ready. Finally, the American agent blew up, threatening, "When I go back and the ambassador asks me what's going on now in the program, I'll say it sucks, We've made our commitment. You haven't."

The airplanes were produced around November 1. The DEA agents who were taken aloft confirmed the worst suspicions of the agents in Guadalajara: there was more marijuana and opium growing out there than anyone had imagined.

In the autumn of 1984, gang warfare broke out on the streets of Guadalajara. Rival traffickers ambushed each other and the police on the avenues and at the cafés. Jaime Kuykendall felt as if he were back in Laredo in 1969, when the marijuana industry took off and every punk on either side of the Rio Grande had to show off his store-bought sidearms. Guadalajara in 1984 had the same feral smell. The air carried the same night sounds: the blare of the mariachi bands, the clatter of machine-gun fire. To the American agents, the pattern of events said, clearly as a full-page advertisement, that the Mexican government had abandoned any pretense of control. The *narcos* used to suppress their passions until they were past the city limits. There were a lot of nameless corpses out in the ravines. But that was when the governor of the state of Jalisco was Flavio Romero Velasco, a tough old bird who had reportedly put out the word that if the *narcotraficantes* wanted to do business in his territory, they had better keep the streets clean. In 1984, Romero Velasco was replaced by a less forceful man, Enrique Alvarez de Castillo. The traffickers became so blatant that they dueled in front of the governor's mansion. However, to assign blame to the governor would be simplistic. There was no pressure from any significant Mexican constituency to run the traffickers back to the mountains.

The DEA agents shared a sense of foreboding. Kuykendall described it as that feeling you got when you walked into a strange bar, and nobody said a word, but you knew you'd better get out of there.

Shaggy Wallace, who replaced Butch Sears, arrived at the Guadalajara office in September 1984. When he reported for duty, Jaime and Kiki sat him down and told him never to relax. This was not like home, not like the worst barrios Shaggy had ever worked. In the States, the dopers knew that if they shot a cop, they'd bring down the heat. There was no heat in Guadalajara.

On September 31, Antonio Vargas was shot. Then, on October 10, Roger Knapp's parked car was machine-gunned. Knapp was sure that the shooting had been ordered by Félix Gallardo. It was the same car that Knapp had driven past Félix Gallardo's office some months earlier. At that

time, he had been pulled off the road and questioned by
Félix Gallardo's bodyguards, who had flashed police credentials from the Interior Ministry, the parent agency of
the DFS.

Early in the year, Félix Gallardo had demonstrated that
he knew about Knapp's investigation of his ring, Operation
Padrino, Operation Godfather, and that he did not like it.
On March 28, a former *comandante* of the Federales had
called upon Camarena with a message from the godfather.
The message was that the DEA agents would be wise to lay
off Félix Gallardo, who was an honest businessman. They
would do better to pursue Rafael Caro Quintero.

But the DEA only intensified the investigation, not only
in Mexico but across the Southwest. In June 1984, the DEA
Guadalajara office received a tip that led their fellow agents
in Los Angeles to a motel room in Anaheim. Inside were
two money-counting machines and $4 million in bills that
bore traces of coke. Scraps of paper found in the room led
to bank accounts in San Ysidro, Laredo, and El Paso, all
controlled by Tomás Valles Corral, Félix Gallardo's money
man. All told, DEA and IRS agents were able to tie up $13
million of money linked to the Padrino organization.[14] They
had no illusions about what they had accomplished. "What
we have here is pocket change," said agent Scott Adams of
the DEA El Paso office.

In August, sheriff's deputies in Gila County, Arizona,
seized sixteen hundred pounds of cocaine traced to the Félix
Gallardo ring. That much cocaine would have brought $30
million or more in the Los Angeles wholesale market. The
DEA deserved no credit: a retired state policeman and his
wife were out cutting wood, saw the airplane land, got suspicious, and called the law.

Nevertheless, Félix Gallardo seemed to blame the DEA.
Roger Knapp heard that the word was out that the gringos
were in big trouble and so was anyone seen with them.

When his car was shot up, Knapp assumed that Félix
Gallardo had cleared the "warning" in advance with high-
level federal police officials. For one thing, uniformed police
had arrived almost instantly. Normally, they might take half
an hour to answer a call for help. Comandante Flores of

the MFJP and a DFS agent also showed up. Knapp figured they were checking to make sure nobody had been hurt.

After the police left, Knapp called Mexico City and reported the incident to Walter White, Heath's deputy. White called back a short time later and said that headquarters wanted Knapp to get back to the States, pronto.

"Wait a minute, Walter, they obviously didn't want to hurt anybody this time around," Knapp pleaded. "I'd really like to leave in an orderly way."

Knapp did not want to leave at all. He had put a great deal of work into investigating the Félix Gallardo organization. It was finally starting to pay off. He had the feeling that a breakthrough was imminent. White had another talk with headquarters and secured a stay. But the next day, Knapp heard that the Los Angeles DEA office had seized 372 pounds of cocaine that appeared to belong to the Félix Gallardo ring. The seizure took place just a few hours after the shooting of Knapp's car.

"Time to go," Knapp told his wife. He had had nothing to do with the seizure, but Félix Gallardo's goons would not know that.

And then there were three. Jaime, Kiki, and Shaggy.

John Gavin called upon Attorney General Sergio García Ramírez and Interior Minister Manuel Bartlett Díaz. His message, he would later recall, was that should something else happen to a DEA agent, "we would consider it an extremely serious matter with very deep and very long-lasting repercussions."

Kuykendall hoped that Gavin would raise a loud public protest. "If you don't create a stink," he said, "the Mexicans aren't gonna do a damn thing." He was incensed at DEA for quietly pulling Knapp out. As far as he was concerned, this was terrorism and his agency was giving the terrorists what they wanted.

"In the United States, you *do* something, you retaliate," he said. "In Houston, if a gang threatens a police officer, does the city of Houston move the cop? Do they send him to Detroit? Hell, no. They move the threat. They deal with the gang, right there on their turf. DEA, they transfer you.

It may not be your problem any longer, but it's the next guy's problem. And it's probably worse for *him*, because the trafficker is more confident. The office has no continuity, no institutional memory, no cumulative experience. It takes an agent a while to learn a place, to figure out who's who, to get the kind of sense of play that is essential to the production of good intelligence analysis. By achieving the transfers of the Roger Knapps, the trafficker has just accomplished his objective, and he hasn't had to shoot it out."

"Something's going to happen," Kuykendall told Shaggy. He said it over and over again.

Kiki agreed. He said something worse was going to happen. Shaggy Wallace figured he would stick it out as long as Jaime and Kiki did. "You can't run away from it," he said. "If you're afraid to confront it, you might as well get on an airplane and go home."

On November 6, Kuykendall wrote a memo to Heath that reflected the agents' preoccupation with the state of anarchy that prevailed in Guadalajara:

> The violence previously reported has increased drastically without any serious consequences for the traffickers. The local government is apparently completely compromised, and unwilling to cope with a deteriorating situation. On some occasions local police officers have been killed in shoot-outs with traffickers and still no action has been taken. The traffickers commonly travel the streets and highways armed with automatic weapons and usually carrying credentials from DFS or some other federal law-enforcement agency.

A series of chance events confirmed what the DEA Guadalajara office had been reporting about both Caro Quintero and Félix Gallardo but that also left the agents feeling acutely vulnerable to reprisals by the traffickers.

Around November 1, reports trickled into the DEA office in Mexico City that there was a large marijuana cultivation and processing complex out in the Chihuahua desert. Thousands of people were said to be working in the fields and the packing sheds. Tips had come to two or three DEA resident offices from campesinos who had left the complex. Heath gave this information to the Mexican Attorney General's Office. After some days, the response came back that the information was inaccurate. There was nothing out in the desert.

Heath and his deputies badgered the Attorney General's Office and MFJP headquarters. Finally, the Mexican officials agreed to put together a raiding party. On the night of November 6, officials of the MFJP, the Attorney General's Office, and the Army met with a group of DEA agents and planned the assault: they would move teams of soldiers and MFJP agents into the Chihuahua desert early the next day. Comandante Aldana would lead the assault force.

The raiders headed into the Chihuahua desert at dawn. Nearing the village of Búfalo, Chihuahua, the Mexican and American lawmen in the choppers saw irrigated fields, barracks, and drying sheds that were thirty to fifty feet wide, three hundred to four hundred feet long. It took the raiders two days to reconnoiter the area. They found two other such sites, near the Chihuahuan villages of Julimes and Chilicote. The dimensions of the project were astounding: the Mexican government seized and destroyed between five thousand and ten thousand tons of high-grade sinsemilla marijuana. There were five cultivation sites and twenty-five to thirty drying sheds, most bigger than football fields.

The seizure set a new world record. No one had ever seen that much marijuana in one place. The fields were irrigated with water pumped from deep wells, well fertilized, and managed with the latest high-tech intensive agricultural techniques. There was much more marijuana at the place than could have been grown in the fields, leading the agents to conclude that the Chihuahua complex was a storage and processing center for marijuana grown all over Mexico.

The agents were told by a number of informants that the complex belonged to a syndicate put together by Rafael Caro Quintero. Caro Quintero later confirmed that he owned the complex and complained that he had sunk $20 million into it. DEA officials estimated that, had the marijuana been sold on the street, it would have brought more than $2.5 billion.

About seven thousand frightened campesinos were found at the three sites. They had been recruited from southern Mexico and offered the grand sum of 2,500 pesos a day, then about $6, to work the fields. Some of the peons said that at about one o'clock in the morning, about five hours before the government forces landed, the overseers got word that troops were moving in. The laborers told DEA agents on the scene that they had been awakened with the words "You're free to go. We got problems." They could not go far. They had no transportation and very few provisions. By the time the troops found the last of them, some had wandered off into the desert and had been without food and water for nearly three days. A few of the overseers did not escape. Five men carrying DFS credentials were among those arrested, according to DEA agents.

A DEA agent who spoke fluent Spanish talked with some of the peons about a helicopter flown by the assault force. The chopper had the distinctive blue-and-white markings of the Attorney General's Office's eradication fleet. "The peasants said they were surprised that we conducted the raid because they had been assured it was a government project," the agent said. "They said they used to see the same helicopters that we used to hit the place. They said they saw them hovering here all the time. Sometimes they'd land. Bring people down here, take people away. They were very noticeable, blue and white."

State Department officials were skeptical of this claim. But there was no question about the betrayal of the raid itself. That meant there was at least one double agent at the senior levels of the Mexican government. The strategy session in Mexico City had concluded late in the evening of November 6. If the workers were aroused at one o'clock on November 7, that meant the traffickers were warned within an hour or two after the meeting concluded. Many people had been at the meeting: Army officers, the top leadership in the Attorney General's Office, a number of MFJP *comandantes*. Also troubling, according to a Congressional report, was the fact that the fuel trucks that were supposed to refuel the helicopters were sent to the wrong location; the raid had nearly been canceled because of this "mistake."[15]

"The bust of the century," *Time* magazine called it. The size of the Chihuahua complex knocked the U.S. government's statistics into a cocked hat: in 1983, U.S. analysts had concluded that twelve thousand to fifteen thousand metric tons of marijuana were being consumed in the United States. Here, in a single location, was at least a third of that amount.

DEA headquarters, the State Department, and the embassy now accepted what Camarena and his partners had been saying since 1982 about the phenomenon of desert plantations. The photographs taken at Chihuahua had finally shattered the conventional wisdom. Chihuahua made a difference because there were pictures, because there was international publicity, because of the human drama of those wretched laborers abandoned in the desert. The pictures proved what DEA-Guadalajara had been reporting, that it was intimidation and bribery, not stealth, that gave the traffickers their edge, and that the real danger was not from those tiny, clandestine plantings high in the mountains, as State and DEA headquarters had believed, but giant, technically advanced open field plantations which could not exist without official protection in Mexico City.

Jon Thomas, who had recently replaced Dominick DiCarlo as assistant secretary of state for international narcotics matters, went to Chihuahua himself, stood there in the fields, and said to himself, "How could this happen?" The answer, Thomas knew, was that Caro Quintero and the others must have had assurance from some significant authority that they could put all that money into the huge complex without fear of its being destroyed. "Chihuahua brought home, more than any other issue, that we were really not in control," Thomas acknowledged.

Gavin was deeply troubled, but no less concerned, he insisted, was Attorney General García Ramírez. Gavin believed that García Ramírez was making a sincere effort to master the sixteen-hundred-employee federal criminal-justice bureaucracy and that he anguished over his inability to find the bad apples. "There were so many meetings when we had to discuss whether operations were being jeopardized by leaks," Gavin said later. "That's a way of life."

Public pronouncements by the U.S. embassy and by officials at DEA and State praised the Mexican authorities fulsomely and credited them—falsely—with discovering the Chihuahua complex. One statement prepared by embassy officers and released to the press said:

That bust is a real credit to the Mexican authorities who coordinated it. It is a statement to the drug syndicates that Mexico is serious about interdiction and there will be no easy transiting of drugs destined for the U.S. through Mexican territory.

Another statement distributed by the embassy was even more extravagant:

The Mexican Attorney General's Office [have] stepped up their efforts and have publicly gone on record as staunch supporters of the "war on drugs." The recent dramatic sweep actions of the MAGO [Mexican Attorney General's Office] throughout Mexico have clearly indicated Mexico's intention to wipe out heroin poppies and marijuana at their roots. . . . Since 1974, as the result of their commendable efforts . . . over twenty-four thousand metric tons of marijuana have been destroyed in the field . . . a record of which the government of Mexico can be deservedly proud.

Years later, the informant Gabriel and other informants for DEA and U.S. Customs would charge that the Chihuahua complex had been organized by officers of the DFS and the Mexican military. "Rafa [Rafael Caro Quintero] couldn't have done it without DFS," Gabriel said in an interview. "He couldn't have kept track of the money. He can't count that high."

The DEA Guadalajara office did not contribute to the American embassy actions that led to the Chihuahua bust. Indeed, Kuykendall and Camarena were angry that the DEA and the State Department had not comprehended until this moment the extent to which the eradication program had been subverted. The fact that DEA headquarters was surprised by the discovery of the Chihuahua plantations was a symptom of a massive intelligence failure. State Department officials said that either DEA's intelligence or its intelligence analysis was bad. Kuykendall countered that the raw intelligence was there, if DEA's analysts had bothered to look at it. All the men who had been stationed in Guadalajara echoed this complaint: why had they spent night after night working the streets and roaming the villages of the back country if their intelligence reports were going to be discounted or disregarded by headquarters and the embassy? "If they don't believe the people in the field," said Kuykendall, "they ought to get them out."

Within the DEA hierarchy, Ed Heath's office reaped the rewards for instigating the Chihuahua raids. This was as it should be, but Kuykendall was distressed that Camarena had not been similarly honored for his earlier discovery of Caro Quintero's plantations in the desert states. Kuykendall had nominated Kiki for an award in March 1984, but months had passed and the award had not come through.

If there was a price to be paid for the Chihuahua busts, however, Kuykendall figured that the Guadalajara DEA office would bear the brunt of it, simply because Caro Quintero knew the agents there were responsible for his earlier losses in Zacatecas, San Luis Potosí, and Sonora.

Kuykendall put in another request for diplomatic passports and for reinforcements. He wanted four men, at least. Two men came. On November 14, the newcomers drove out to the airport and noticed that Félix Gallardo's hangar was open. This seemed a good opportunity to document the tail numbers of his airplanes. They shot a few pictures, then glanced around. Miguel Angel Félix Gallardo was staring at them through the window of their car. He was clearly not amused. The agents headed for the terminal, pronto, followed by *pistoleros*. The Federales had to go over and escort them out of the terminal. The agents left Guadalajara the next day. They were brave men, but they did not like being in a place where the traffickers were so obviously in charge.

Within days, Félix Gallardo's cocaine operation suffered more losses at the hands of U.S. lawmen.

On November 17, lawmen in California seized $3.7 million in cash that was traced to the Félix Gallardo ring.

On November 26, a deputy sheriff in Mohave County, Arizona, happened on a small plane parked on a deserted landing strip and looked inside. The cargo hold was loaded with seven hundred boxes wrapped for Christmas in red, white, and green foil. In the boxes were about fifteen hundred pounds of cocaine. The plane was traced to a member of Félix Gallardo's group.

The discovery of the cocaine went almost unnoticed by the American press, but Kuykendall, Camarena, and Wallace hunkered down. With this seizure and the August bust, the godfather had lost thirty-two hundred pounds of cocaine, for which he had probably paid $10 million up front. The DEA men guessed that he would send another warning, shoot up another car, or maybe blast the consulate.

Pete Hernandez, Camarena's compadre, pleaded with Kiki to come back to the States. They would arrest dopers together, just like old times. Kiki wrestled with his feelings for his work, his wife, his sons, for DEA. On one hand, he would be able to put people in jail again. Diogenes Galanos, the special agent in charge of DEA–San Diego, admired Kiki's skill and dedication to his work and was eager to sign him up. All the young agents loved working for Dodge Galanos, a big, friendly bear of a man who had once worked the Texas border with Kuykendall, Ken Miley, and the other border rats. The thought of working in San Diego cheered Kiki immeasurably. "We're gonna go up to San Diego and kick some *ass!*" he told a friend. He considered that he would have time for his family again. He bought an old Ford Mustang and talked about fixing it up. Mika loved the change in him. He had never allowed himself the luxury of a hobby. She sensed that a new side of him was about to break through.

On the other hand, Kiki wanted to stay after Caro Quintero, and he felt that leaving would let Jaime and Shaggy down. But what about backup? Before they gave you a badge and a gun, they told you that when you were going into something that could turn into trouble, you were supposed to have a partner—better yet, a half dozen people—waiting around the corner or in a car or in the next room. The office knew where you were. You had radios. That was backup. It was not because you were scared; it was because your team was prudent and professional. Kiki knew that Shaggy and Jaime were behind him, and he was behind them, but who else did they have? The agents in the States were aware of the extreme danger in Guadalajara. Three agents had recently declined the post.

But DEA headquarters seemed to be unaware of how dangerous Guadalajara was becoming. Bud Mullen and Jack Lawn had made a point of bucking up agent morale by visiting various hazardous-duty posts. Mullen had gone to Bogotá at the height of the threats against Americans, and Jack Lawn had popped up everywhere from Chiang Mai in northern Thailand to Lima. Neither man had ever made an appearance in Guadalajara or mentioned it in his frequent speeches and testimony on the Latin American trafficking situation.

Ever since the November 26 bombing at the U.S. embassy in Bogotá, DEA headquarters had seemed totally preoccupied with the situation in Colombia. Reading newspaper articles about DEA headquarters' fears for DEA agents in Colombia, Kuykendall kept thinking, But what about Mexico? The only headlines about Mexico were those that praised the Federales for "discovering" the Chihuahua plantations.

One evening in late November, Kuykendall and Camarena were over at the Camelot having a few Estrellitas, pondering the future. The embassy kept saying things were fine. Nothing was fine. The traffickers were shooting at Mexican policemen with impunity. Anybody who wanted to go after a DEA agent could do so. Camarena told Kuykendall that he was putting in for a transfer to San Diego. Kuykendall did not want Camarena to leave, but he understood his restlessness. Kuykendall sent a letter to DEA headquarters recommending Camarena's transfer to San Diego. As for himself, Kuykendall thought he would stay a while longer. Despite all the frustrations, he loved stalking the kingpins at close range, and he felt that sooner or later the American government would realize that the Mexican traffickers were a bigger threat than even the Colombians.

Mika was relieved when Kiki told her of his plans, but she was also alarmed, especially when he said that he did not think DEA could move him right then; it might take a couple of months. "What are we going to do?" she asked. How bad was it? What did he know? Did he think there was immediate danger? Should she take the boys to California and wait for him? Kiki said he didn't think the traffickers would actually shoot Americans. He wanted to leave because he was discouraged, but he did not sense imminent danger.

"Then I'm staying," Mika said.

Mika did not share Kiki's confidence that Americans were not targets. On December 2, four Americans—Dennis and Rose Carlson from California, Ben and Patricia Mascarenas from Nevada—disappeared. They were Jehovah's Witnesses and had been proselytizing in a residential neighborhood. Consulate officials presumed they were dead. Some people thought that they had stumbled onto a stash house—that the Sinaloans, not known for their intellectual acuity, went after anyone foolish enough to identify himself as a "witness." Others said that they had been kidnapped because of their religious views. The incident seemed to have little to do with the DEA, but it made Mika that much more anxious to go home. She kept after Kiki about the transfer. He told her that DEA headquarters had not done the paperwork. In fact, he was trying to wrap up some loose ends on his investigations and had not asked for an expedited transfer. As bad as things were, he just could not bring himself to pack it in. Dissembling with Mika, he kept buying time, hoping to make a breakthrough somewhere.

Just before Christmas, Kiki was presented with a last chance to settle the score with Primer Comandante Miguel Aldana Ibarra, whose much ballyhooed Operation Pacífico campaign against the drug traffickers was, in the opinion of the DEA agents, all hot air and leaks. A man of Camarena's acquaintance came to him one day and said that he was going to see President de la Madrid on business. The man said that he was outraged at Aldana's sanctimonious posturing and lack of substantive achievement. Camarena agreed and seized the opportunity to ask the man to show the Mexican president a statement to a prosecutor signed by a Colombian arrested at the Mexico City airport in September 1984. The statement alleged that Aldana had been protecting a cocaine-smuggling ring. According to the Mexico City magazine *Contenido*, the Colombian recanted the statement, contending that he had been tortured by the

DFS, and Aldana also denied the charges, saying the accusations were invented by his enemies within the DFS.[16]

Aldana left the MFJP for unstated "personal reasons" in early January. It was never clear to the DEA agents whether de la Madrid had gotten the information Camarena had sent or, if he had, whether he had acted on it. Officials at the Mexican embassy in Washington suggested another reason for Aldana's quiet departure: they said Aldana was one of a number of senior Mexican police officials blamed for failing to solve the assassination of Manuel Buendía, an influential columnist for the Mexico City daily *Excelsior*. Buendía, who inveighed against government corruption, drug trafficking, right-wing violence, and the CIA's presence in Mexico, was gunned down in Mexico City's fashionable Zona Rosa on May 30, 1984. According to an article by Dan Williams, Mexico City bureau chief of the *Los Angeles Times,* Mexican journalists campaigning for justice in the case blamed the DFS, whose agents were the first on the scene when Buendía died and who reportedly cleaned out his office files.[17]

That Camarena attempted to back-channel material about Aldana to de la Madrid was a measure of his desperation. He had no proof that the cocaine-trafficking charges against Aldana were true, and nothing ever came of them. To his friends, the episode signified that he had given up hoping that senior embassy officials would demand the removal of police officials who were not doing the job, for whatever reason. By sending information about Aldana directly to de la Madrid, Camarena violated embassy reporting procedures. Undoubtedly, he would have been disciplined by the DEA, had his action been discovered.

Aldana's name would come up again when DEA agents retrieved Kiki's work diary after his murder. There was a notation that referred to Aldana. DEA agents said the notes were of an interview that Camarena had conducted with a Mexican informant in Guadalajara several days before the agent disappeared.

In January 1985, two investigators from the staff of the House Foreign Affairs Committee came to Mexico. Sensing that problems were being glossed over, Marian Chambers and Richard Peña declined to travel with a member of State's Narcotics Assistance Unit and insisted on a DEA escort. The agent assigned to them happened to be a close friend of Camarena and took them to Guadalajara.

Kuykendall and Camarena were overjoyed. Finally they had an opportunity to make their case to people with access to real power. They went to the investigators' hotel prepared to make an impassioned plea for political action.

They said that DEA's situation was hopeless. Corruption was everywhere. Every avenue for redress was gone. Pressure had to come from the highest levels of the American government, from the Congress, from the White House. The Congressional staffers promised to do what they could in Congress but said it would take time. They kept their word: the report they filed was tougher on the Mexican government than any official study that had been done in years. But because of printing schedules, it would not be published until February 22, 1985.

The Congressional staffers urged Camarena and Kuykendall to go public with what they knew. The agents ought to go to the press, Chambers and Peña said. They had credibility. Why didn't they tell a reporter or two what the embassy would not? Kuykendall and Camarena recoiled as from a snake. They did *not* talk to reporters. They were *not* whistleblowers. They believed in the system. This could be handled within the American government. But Washington had to do something dramatic. As the agents saw it, the only thing the Mexican government understood was raw force. If Reagan closed the border as Nixon had done, that would do it. That would get de la Madrid's attention.

The Congressional aides were sympathetic, but they said they could not imagine that the American government would do such a thing. There were too many other interests. To close the border would affront powerful economic interests, and the State Department would scream. No, it would *never* happen.

"What's gonna have to happen?" Camarena said miserably. "Does somebody have to die before anything is done? Is somebody going to have to get killed?"

9

The Search for
Kiki Camarena

"**D**on't let my husband become a number." These were Mika Camarena's words and Bud Mullen was both haunted and stung by them. So she thought that Kiki was going to be written off.

It was February 10. Kiki had been gone for seventy hours. Mullen found Guadalajara's Sunday-night lethargy stifling. After leaving the Camarena household, he told his driver to take him to the office of Comandante Armando Pavón Reyes, the MFJP official sent from Mexico City to lead the search.

No stone unturned, not a moment to lose, a matter of great importance to the president of the United States—the DEA administrator was not a demonstrative man, but he conjured up every exhortation he could think of to encourage the Mexican officer to action. The handsome young *comandante* stared at him with a blank, courteous smile.

The next day, Pavón Reyes's men started hitting the traffickers' houses. They were deserted. Rigid with anger, Mullen telephoned his deputy in Washington, Jack Lawn. He had banged on every desk between Mexico City and Guadalajara. Still, the Federales were barely going through the motions. Lawn relayed the news to Attorney General William French Smith. A stubborn, stiff New Englander, Smith looked a bloodless sort, but he had a temper. Smith drafted a cable to the attorney general of Mexico: "I am deeply distressed by the kidnapping . . . and by the reaction of your government in not moving as swiftly as possible."

The cable set off alarm bells—but not where Smith intended. When the State Department got a copy, political officers insisted that a toned-down version be sent. Smith had anticipated as much and had already sent an unexpurgated copy to Ambassador Jorge Espinosa de los Reyes.

The DEA agents in Guadalajara were making a little headway, thanks to a few Mexican citizens. From a man who had been at the airport, the agents got a description of the kidnappers of Alfred Zavala. A man who had been standing on Calle Libertad during Kiki's kidnapping had seen four men dragging someone who looked like Kiki into a light-colored Volkswagen. He had not reported it immediately because he had thought it was a police action. He could not identify the men. A Mexican businessman who contacted the DEA office at the consulate was afraid. Some men had come to his office the day before and had warned him not to tell what he had seen: a black Gran Marquis, followed by a small white Volkswagen, driving by his office at three-forty-five on the afternoon of February 7, the day of the kidnapping. There were three people in the back seat of the Gran Marquis. Two of them had been striking the man in the middle with what looked like pipes. But that was all. The DEA agents picked up other bits and pieces here and there, but they could find no one who had seen or heard of Kiki since February 7.

Early on the morning of Tuesday, February 12, Mullen flew from Guadalajara to Mexico City to confront Manuel Ibarra Herrera, the director of the Federales. "Every time your men hit a place, it's empty," he snapped. Ibarra offered more apologies, more explanations, but Mullen was now convinced that Ibarra was feeding him a line.

Next, Mullen confronted the U.S. embassy. Even at this late date, embassy spokesmen were faithful to the fiction that the American agents and the Mexican police were on the same side. The day before, Ambassador John Gavin had issued a statement through a spokesman, announcing that Camarena was missing and declaring that neither the United States nor Mexico would be "intimidated by Mafia thugs."[1]

Gavin had kept the announcement of the kidnapping nonaccusatory in the hope of securing the cooperation of the Federales. Mullen thought it would take stronger words—public words—to make Mexican authorities take the kidnapping seriously. He said the Federales were completely intimidated by the Mafia—or worse. Manuel Ibarra had admitted as much. He had told Mullen that the search had begun slowly because his young officers were afraid of the traffickers. This had astounded Mullen almost more than anything he had heard in Mexico. He could not imagine the leader of any police agency, particularly one that the Mexican government considered its elite, *admitting* that he could not secure the streets because his men were afraid. Mullen was shocked at the way officials in Mexico City openly dismissed what Mullen regarded as an act of terrorism. A high Mexican official had told a reporter from *The New York Times* that the only unusual thing about the case so far was that Kiki had been kidnapped. "They usually just kill them," he said.

After talking with Mullen, Gavin decided it was time to turn up the heat. He called a press conference and, with Mullen at his side, sketched a picture of organized crime engulfing Mexico. By new DEA estimates, he said, Mexico was the second-biggest producer of heroin and marijuana imported into the United States and the transit point for at least a third of the South American cocaine destined for the U.S. market. Guadalajara, the jewel of the heartland, was inhabited by eighteen major gangs and was fast becoming one of the world's most important drug-trafficking centers.

The press conference set Mexico City on its ear. *Proceso,* a respected Mexico City newsmagazine, said that Gavin and Mullen had revealed more information about Mexico's drug trade in one press conference than the Mexican government had disclosed in years. "On the narcotics traffic in Mexico, Gavin demonstrates he is better informed than the Attorney General's Office," *Proceso* editors wrote.

In the eyes of the Mexican government, Gavin's press conference was one more example of interference in internal Mexican matters, an intrusion upon Mexico's sovereignty. The scene at the U.S. embassy represented everything the ruling class of central Mexico detested about the United States: the towering, disdainful ambassador, speaking Spanish with the accent of the reactionary North, the icy-eyed

American lawman at his side. From the Mexican perspective, they were arrogant Yanquis with an inflated sense of moral superiority.

Reporters flooded the Mexican Justice Ministry with questions about cocaine trafficking, corruption, and gun running. The Attorney General's Office responded with categorical denials. A written response to questions submitted by the *Newsweek* Mexico City bureau declared: "In Mexico, South American traffickers do not exist. In Mexico, there does not exist a guns-for-drugs trade. In no . . . state in the republic are military officers or politicians taking *mordida* [bribes] from the traffickers."

Jesús Antonio Sam López, chief of the attorney general's narcotics control directorate, told *The Washington Post:* "In Mexico there is no force stronger than the state, and there is no zone where the state will permit drug traffickers to exercise control."

Jaime Kuykendall was in despair. The Gavin-Mullen press conference had aroused a certain amount of nationalistic acrimony, but it was not helping Kiki at all. The Federales were searching houses in a sluggish and sullen fashion. They had not made a single arrest.

Mullen thought DEA's end of the search was being sloppily managed. He had lost his temper at Ed Heath and had ordered him to stay in Guadalajara until Camarena was found. Kuykendall could not imagine why Mullen thought that would improve the situation. Kuykendall was still smarting over the fact that Heath had not flown to Guadalajara but had taken the overnight train. Heath defended his decision as proper but Kuykendall thought Heath's sense of urgency just did not seem to be aroused.

Mullen was stunned when Heath came up with a tip from one of the Federales that Rafael Caro Quintero had promised Comandante Pavón Reyes 60 million pesos to let him fly out of Guadalajara on February 9, two days after Camarena was kidnapped. The tipster said the money had been delivered by Rogelio Muñoz Ríos, a former MFJP and DFS agent who allegedly served as Caro Quintero's bodyguard and bagman. Mullen was ready to believe the worst of Pavón

Reyes. Mullen thought that the man who had passed this information along to Heath was an honest Mexican agent who was trying to help the Americans. Kuykendall thought it was a mistake to take the tip at face value. Maybe Pavón Reyes was being set up. Pavón Reyes was a novice, dull-witted, unsure of himself. Kuykendall observed that every time someone from DEA had asked Pavón Reyes to do something, he insisted on telephoning Manuel Ibarra in Mexico City. Kuykendall was sure that if Ibarra had wanted to see Kiki's kidnappers caught, he would never have put someone as inexperienced as Pavón Reyes in charge.

As Kuykendall saw it, the case cried out for wily old Florentino Ventura, who had been a *primer comandante* of the MFJP in charge of Interpol until Ibarra had kicked him out and given the job to his cousin Miguel Aldana Ibarra. Ventura was a fearsome character, with eyes like slits and the grim visage of an Aztec warrior. He had arrested many traffickers back in the 1970s. In the opinion of the DEA men who knew Ventura, neither the Guadalajara traffickers nor Ibarra would have dared to try to push him around.

Kuykendall had not been surprised to see that Ibarra and Pavón Reyes had shrugged off Bud Mullen's solemn lectures. Hard words and cold looks might work in Washington, but they did not bother the Federales. Kuykendall wondered if Mullen, with his perfect suit and tidy New England values, could ever understand what it was like to work this territory.

Kuykendall drove to a local hotel, mustered up his nerve, and knocked on the door to one of the rooms. A man answered.

"I'm James Kuykendall. I'm with the DEA," the agent said.

The man motioned him inside.

"I'm not supposed to be here."

"Yes, I know," the man said.

Jaime Kuykendall had confronted a lot of hazards in his day, but this was the first time he had ever come face-to-face with a reporter.

Kuykendall scorned reporters. He considered them meddlesome, sensation-seeking voyeurs. Liberals. Probably they smoked pot. He distrusted reporters almost as much as he distrusted lawyers, and he disliked lawyers more than anyone in the world, except maybe dopers. Now he figured that the only way to find Kiki was to generate so much publicity that the Mexican government would have to produce him. He thought that if he could keep the story alive, maybe he could keep Kiki alive. It was a forlorn hope, but it was all he had.

Kuykendall gave the reporters and television producers the addresses of the kingpin's houses and hangouts. He told them about Miguel Angel Félix Gallardo's hotels and Ernesto Fonseca's Japanese restaurant, and about the Canadian girl who had been beheaded by some coked-up locals. He told them where to find the mansion Rafael Caro Quintero was building. These meetings accomplished what Kuykendall wanted. The television crews and many of the print reporters stayed on in Guadalajara for days. The Camarena story moved to the front pages and the prime slots on the nightly news.

The journalists impressed Kuykendall with their boldness. Unable to get past the gates of Caro Quintero's fortresslike estate, a network crew borrowed a hydraulic lift, a cherry picker, from the local electric company and shot pictures over the high walls. This was not something a DEA agent would do. It was a good way to get shot. The Federales began assigning men to stake out the hotels where the journalists were staying. Several journalists found that their rooms had been searched. They suspected that someone was listening in on their phones. But they stayed on. Kuykendall began to revise his opinion of journalists. They were unkempt and under foot, but even the women, he said dourly, had more guts than some of the desk jockeys at DEA headquarters.

After Gavin's press conference, Mullen asked for the embassy's secure telephone and called Jack Lawn, as he always did when there was trouble. It was odd that they had become good friends, because they were opposites in so many ways. A problem-solver who thought in abstract terms, Mullen, fifty, had risen through the FBI bureaucracy with lightning speed and had become one of FBI director

William Webster's closest confidants. Mullen prided himself
on his managerial abilities. He was impatient with the fail-
ings of lesser mortals and had an aura of Presbyterian pro-
bity that had once reduced an errant subordinate to tears.
Mullen made decisions, stuck by them, and spent his leisure
hours playing combative tennis.

Lawn, forty-nine, had a master's degree in English literature and read books, including books with a decidedly
liberal slant. Born in Brooklyn, an Irish Catholic with a
strong streak of populist idealism, Lawn was ill at ease in
the corridors of power. He loved the field as he had loved
the Marine Corps, in which he had risen to the rank of
captain.

Lawn was not as decisive as Mullen, nor did he have
Mullen's competitive edge, but he was more intuitive. He
was affected by human pain as Mullen seldom was, afflicted
by moments of self-doubt that Mullen never suffered. Mullen looked ahead, anticipating the eventual rewards and
pitfalls of each course of action. Lawn lived in the here and
now, focusing on the job at hand and the welfare of his
men. He was skeptical, irreverent, and inventive, and he
could live with intractable problems that Mullen found maddening. Mullen and Lawn both confronted trouble head-
on. Mullen set his jaw and glowered. Lawn defused stress
with a grin and a black joke. A few weeks earlier, when the
DEA had picked up word that the Ochoa family of Colombia had put out an assassination contract on Mullen, the
DEA administrator had obstinately insisted on maintaining
his jogging schedule. Lawn, who jogged with him, had a T-
shirt printed up with a large horizontal arrow and the message: "I'm not Bud Mullen. He is."

When Mullen called from the embassy, Lawn, for once,
could not manage a smile. Lawn thought that Kiki did not
have long to live. So did Mullen. They did not need to say
much. Both could read the signs. Each had dealt with more
murders, kidnappings, assassinations, and terrorist actions
than he liked to think about, and there were distinctive
characteristics to every sort of crime.

The signs in this situation were the marks of a hopeless

case. There were no notes, no ransom demands, no calls. That meant that the kidnappers did not want to bargain. This was not a simple revenge killing, or they would have mowed Kiki down on the street. Probably they wanted information. Even if they got it, they could not set him free. He would know too much about who they were and what they wanted. The fact that the kidnappers acted in broad daylight meant that they thought they could get away with it. They might be right.

And it might not be over. A DEA agent in El Paso who was working on some cases involving the Guadalajara cartel had found the brakes on his car cut twice. A caller told him he was going to die in three days. A prosecutor in El Paso was receiving anonymous threats.

It seemed to Mullen that the Mexican government was more interested in protecting its image than in fighting corruption. He thought that if the Mexican officials cared so much about their image, perhaps shame would rouse them, as appeals to honor had not. Mullen asked Lawn to call a reporter from *Newsweek* who was working on a cover story about the DEA. He had a few things to say when he returned to Washington the next night. Mullen had very little practice in dealing with journalists, and most of the encounters he had ended badly, but now he knew it was up to him to keep the spotlight on Mexico.

On the morning of February 14, Mullen told Attorney General William French Smith that his message to the Mexican attorney general had not mattered. Mullen thought that it would take an order from President de la Madrid to get the Federales moving. Smith called the White House, meaning to talk to the president. He got as far as Donald Regan, the chief of staff, who did not think it necessary to bring Reagan into the fray. The next day, Smith tried again. He talked to Regan and then to Robert McFarlane, the president's national security adviser. McFarlane hesitated because, in the words of an aide, "the view is the Mexicans are doing really all they can and working with us." Finally, late on Friday afternoon, Smith worked out a compromise. Reagan would send a discreet note to de la Madrid, expressing his own concern about the matter and thanking the Mexican president for his personal interest.

Mullen began giving interviews. When the *Newsweek* reporter arrived, the DEA administrator was waiting in his office, his face grim, his facts carefully assembled.

"The audacity of this act is just astounding," he began.

Mullen recounted the agonizingly slow response of the Federales and the anguish of Camarena's wife.

"I think it's out of control." Mullen glared at the paneled wall of his office. "I've been saying that Mexico has a model program," he snapped. "Why *have* I been saying that? Well, I'm not going to say it anymore."

What Mullen saw in Mexico stunned him. He had thought that things were going reasonably well. Obviously, they were not. There was marijuana all over the place, in great irrigated fields, waving in the wind like Iowa corn. There were opium poppies everywhere. And cocaine. Three years ago, cocaine was almost unheard of in Mexico. Now tons of the stuff was coming through the mountain passes south of Phoenix and Los Angeles.

Mullen felt betrayed by Manuel Ibarra. When he had set off for Mexico, Mullen had told his associates that he was sure his friendship with Ibarra would make all the difference. Ibarra was attractive, educated, and polite, and he had said all the right things. Now that Mullen reflected on Ibarra's graceful attentions, he detected a patronizing edge. Was it possible that Ibarra had been playing a game with him?

Then there was the spectacle of Comandante Armando Pavón Reyes, the leader of the search, nodding and smiling, promising immediate action. If Ed Heath's informant was right, the only thing Pavón Reyes was in a hurry about was a delivery from Caro Quintero's bagman, Rogelio Muñoz.

Mullen and Lawn received a cable from the DEA agents in Guadalajara which they regarded as the final proof of the Federales' treachery. At Miguel Angel Félix Gallardo's place, one of the searchers had come across a snapshot. A DEA agent had snatched it before the Federales realized how damaging it was. It was a photograph of a grinning

Kiki Camarena with several of the Federales. It had been taken at the MFJP office in Guadalajara, probably after one of the marijuana raids. Had one of Kiki's friends in the Federales betrayed him to Félix Gallardo? It looked that way. With any luck, the picture might lead to the kidnappers. Ultimately, Mullen would have to accept that there was not going to be any luck in this case.

Late on the afternoon of Friday, February 15, Mullen was sitting in his office with Jack Lawn, wondering if there were any strings left to pull. The telephone rang. It was Willy von Raab, the U.S. commissioner of customs, calling to complain about some inexcusably bureaucratic intransigence on the part of the DEA agent in charge of the Miami field office. "That guy is really a jerk," von Raab began with his usual tact.

Mullen smiled despite himself. He was fond of von Raab, who was no bureaucrat. The forty-three-year-old New Yorker, short and as pink of cheek as the day he left Yale, had the face of a choirboy but the mentality of Dirty Harry. A Manhattan lawyer active in conservative Republican political circles, von Raab had never been involved in law enforcement before, but once installed at Customs, he pursued his mission with a commitment that was absolute. State Department hands, whom von Raab regularly derided as soft on drugs and corruption, thought he made Attila the Hun look like a moderate.

Mullen listened to von Raab's grievance for a few moments and then changed the subject. "Listen, Willy, we could use some help," Mullen said. "Could you take a look at the border for us?" It was a long shot, but Mullen thought that if Customs agents could question some of the people who showed up at the checkpoints, maybe somebody would know something.

"I'll do better than that," von Raab said. "I'll question *everybody*."

Mullen had not said much, but von Raab could sense the strain in his friend's voice. Von Raab remembered, with intense displeasure, the lecture on sovereignty he had once received from Bernardo Sepúlveda Amor, the Mexican for-

eign minister, when he had proposed to run Customs surveillance airplanes along the south side of the border. Well,
he thought, the United States could play the sovereignty
game. All he had to do was go by the book.

Von Raab summoned Gene Mach, the assistant commissioner in charge of inspection and control. "I want you
to crack down on the Southwest border," von Raab said.
"I want inspections on everything that comes across.

"Are you kidding?" Mach gasped.

No, he was not kidding. "I want you to pitch in," von
Raab said. Mach cabled the inspection force: at six o'clock
in the afternoon, Eastern Standard Time, Operation Camarena was to go into action.[2]

Soon after he gave the order, von Raab drove to his
cabin in Virginia for a weekend with his wife and did not
watch the nightly news. If he had, he would have seen footage of thousands of motorists raging and cursing all along
the Southwest border. Once again, as in 1969, Customs
inspectors began searching everything that rolled, walked,
or flew out of Mexico. This was exactly what Camarena and
Kuykendall had hoped to see: a new Operation Intercept,
such as Richard Nixon had ordered.

Outraged Mexican politicians charged that this was the
work of Ronald Reagan or at least Secretary of State George
Shultz, perhaps punishing Mexico for refusing to support
the Contra war. They were wrong. George Shultz had not
even known about the border action and had exploded in
anger when he heard about it.

The first von Raab learned of the trouble he had caused
was when his telephone rang at seven o'clock the next morning. It was his public-affairs officer, Dennis Murphy, who
cheerfully announced, "All hell is breaking loose."

The telephone rang again. It was Bud Mullen, who
sounded optimistic for the first time in the long week. "It's
great," Mullen bubbled. "Willy, you can't believe it. The
Mexicans are starting to respond to us."

But they weren't. Appearances of activity came to nothing.
And on the night of Saturday, February 16, Manuel Ibarra

personally intervened to allow another member of the Guadalajara cartel to leave Mexico.

Two days before, in a house in the exclusive Colonia de Valle section of Mexico City, DEA agents had located Juan Matta Ballesteros, the Honduran who was Miguel Angel Félix Gallardo's cocaine connection. Matta was traced with the help of a telephone intercept, on which Matta could be heard complaining to an associate that he did not know what the fuss was all about. "I paid my taxes," he whined.

According to an internal DEA report, DEA agent Walter White, Ed Heath's deputy at the U.S. embassy, "passed [the address] directly" to MFJP director Ibarra.

Nothing happened. On Saturday, the agents went to Gavin, who called Attorney General Sergio García Ramírez. The attorney general told Gavin he would have the apartment raided immediately.

Getting it done was not so easy. According to Mullen, García Ramírez could not find Ibarra. Finally, on Saturday evening, he reached Ibarra's deputy, who ordered a raiding party. Just before the Federales were to move in, Ibarra materialized and stalled the raid. Moments later, DEA agents staking out the apartment saw four people leave the house, get into a car, and speed away. The Federales went into the apartment on Sunday morning. They found a woman who said, yes, Juan Matta had been there—he had left the night before.

Gavin told a reporter for *Newsweek* magazine that he understood Ibarra had not allowed the Federales to enter the apartment because he thought Matta was being protected by DFS officers and feared an embarrassing shootout between the two federal police agencies; he said Ibarra had decided it would be better to arrest Matta at the airport. David Westrate, DEA's chief of operations, later told the House Foreign Affairs Committee much the same story: "There was a discussion about the tactics to be used in arresting Matta Ballesteros," Westrate testified. "Mr. Ibarra, at the time, stated that his intention was to arrest him at the airport and there was a judgment call on his part as to when would be the best time to do it. . . . We are talking here a period of maybe a day and a half."[3]

Mullen was not mollified. "I think that is shocking," he said when he heard Ibarra's purported rationale. "If we said the FBI wouldn't conduct a raid because DEA agents were protecting an individual, there would be a scandal unmatched in our nation's history."

Ibarra would not return Mullen's calls, so the DEA chief never heard a direct account of Ibarra's reason for stalling the raid. Nor would Ibarra respond to calls from reporters. Mullen was convinced that somehow, by means of bribes or threats, Matta had gotten to Ibarra. What other explanation was there? And if the traffickers could get to the head of the Mexican Federal Judicial Police, who would stand up to them?

Mullen had a few allies in Washington. Besides von Raab, there was Jon Thomas, the assistant secretary of state for international narcotics matters. Of all the State Department officials with whom DEA dealt, Mullen had always gotten along best with the pragmatic Thomas. Without being asked, on February 14, Thomas had thrown his weight behind the Camarena case. It was time for the State Department's annual report to Congress on source countries for drugs, and the report Thomas released did not mince words about Mexico. Thomas blamed the expansion of drug trafficking in Mexico on official corruption, pure and simple. "Protection schemes are well known and widely used and have developed into well-established institutions which wield economic as well as political power," the document said. "It would appear that drug traffickers have attained at least the potential to become a potent political entity in Mexican affairs."

The report made the headlines Thomas expected. In 1984, State's position on Mexico had been bland. That year's report had blamed factors beyond de la Madrid's control— the economic crisis and good weather—for the rise in opium and marijuana production. Thomas used the 1985 "report card" to send a sharp message to de la Madrid. The annual document represented the official position of the U.S. government on the performance of the nations that produced illegal drugs. A low mark would adversely affect a nation's prestige in international circles. "For a State Department report it was very bold," Thomas said with satisfaction. "The lines were drawn."

In Mexico City, John Gavin had been heaping fuel upon the fire that Mullen and von Raab had started. He told American correspondents that he intended to recommend that the State Department issue a travel advisory for Mexico. Tourism was Mexico's second most important net source of foreign exchange, after petroleum. The mere mention of a travel advisory in the press would cost the country millions. Gavin and his aides encouraged public speculation about a possible advisory; even if they failed to convince State to issue a formal advisory, the publicity would work almost as well. Sure enough, dozens of tour groups canceled excursions to Mexican resorts.

On the evening of February 20, State Department officials recalled Gavin to Washington for "consultations." Gavin defended von Raab's decision to close the border, insisting that nothing else would have gotten the Mexican government's attention. Mullen hoped that the State Department would hang tough. "It's the only two-by-four we've got," he said.

But the border operation was being sustained at serious political cost to the administration. The large American banks were putting pressure on the Treasury Department because they were holding about $25 billion in Mexican debt and were anxious to see Mexico rebound from its economic slump. Recovery required a massive infusion of investment capital, which would not materialize if the United States exacerbated Mexico's already shaky economic situation. The Sunbelt business community was dead set against the border action, which amounted to a trade sanction. Mexico was the United States's third-largest market, and most of the goods sold to Mexico came from the Southwestern states.

Besieged by protests from Southwestern merchants, the Congressional Border Caucus lodged furious protests with the White House. Texas Senator Lloyd Bentsen called the inspections "pure harassment" and "bureaucratic interference" with the border economy. "We are hurting ourselves as much as we are hurting Mexico," he said. The Texas Senate voted unanimously to condemn the federal government's car-by-car searches.

On Thursday, February 21, Mexican ambassador Jorge Espinosa de los Reyes delivered a diplomatic note to Kenneth Dam, the deputy secretary of state, protesting the border inspections as "inconsistent with the spirit of friendship and understanding that both governments have resolved to develop." The next afternoon, when the Customs searches continued, President de la Madrid telephoned President Reagan.

The two presidents spoke for about fifteen minutes through interpreters. Who had the better of this brief conversation would remain a matter of conjecture. Each man authorized his aides to give reporters a version that served his own interests. De la Madrid's aides said that the Mexican president told Reagan that the Customs action "did not constitute the most appropriate means for combating drug trafficking." By the Mexican government version, de la Madrid reminded Reagan that several members of the Mexican police had died recently, "reflecting the efforts that the Mexican police are taking and the reaction of the drug traffickers against the energy with which they are being combated."

The White House version had Reagan replying that while he appreciated the inconvenience of the border crackdown, "he was deeply concerned about the safety of Americans in Mexico." White House aides said that Reagan did not specifically raise complaints about the complicity of Mexican officials, nor did he protest the slowness of the search for Camarena.

Reagan's spokesman, Larry Speakes, told reporters that the White House view was that, while Mexico was cooperating with U.S. officials, "we would like to have more cooperation, and the only tangible evidence of cooperation would be some progress in solving the case and releasing the agent."

But by the end of the day, the White House had concluded that it was time to call a halt to the operation. Gavin went along with the decision. "I think we made the point," he said. Von Raab was out of the country and had no chance to argue. Mullen disliked the decision but did not fight it. Al DeAngelus, the deputy chief of Customs, called off the border searches, effective the next morning.

Upon his return to the States, von Raab was summoned to the office of Treasury Secretary James Baker. Baker and his deputy, Richard Darman, began to grill him. Who had cleared his border action? Anyone at Treasury? What about the State Department? Von Raab said he had told his immediate superior, John Walker, the assistant secretary of the treasury for enforcement, and John Gavin, who had agreed. No, he did not call main State. "They've tried to stop us at every turn," he said truculently.

"Next time, tell *me*," Baker scolded. "Any time you want to call me, you know my number, you know Dick's number."

"Yeah, the next time you want to declare war or are planning an invasion, let us know," Darman said. But he smiled, and Baker started laughing. Von Raab relaxed. He had gotten away with it. Once. He knew that there would not be a next time.

Mexican government officials professed to be mystified by the American government's reaction to the kidnapping. An assistant to de la Madrid told an American reporter, "How can the United States make such a scandal over one of its agents' abduction? You should not find it surprising that anybody fighting drug trafficking is abducted or killed."

Like Kuykendall, Mullen and Lawn saw that they had only one weapon left. They told the agents in the border offices to brief local reporters on whatever they had on file about trafficking and corruption in Mexico. Mullen scheduled a series of interviews with reporters. He told the agents in Mexico City to produce a list of every allegation of corruption that had been lodged against a Mexican official. The sheer bulk of the data came as a revelation. He was shocked to find that the Mexican police had not arrested a major trafficker in eight years.

As the stories multiplied, in *The San Diego Union,* the

El Paso Herald-Post, The Arizona Republic, White House officials began to tire of Mullen's outspokenness. "People here see that the Mexicans haven't done things very well," said one presidential aide. "But we don't think running around telling everyone how the Mexicans have screwed up gets you the cooperation you need from them. A lot of this comes from frustrated and irritated law-enforcement officials close to the scene. It's all accurate, but it's not very helpful."

On the afternoon of Friday, February 22, Mullen's telephone rang. He spoke briefly, hung up, and turned to Jack Lawn with a grimace. "That was Bud McFarlane," he said. "He knows I'm going on the Brinkley show Sunday. He wants me to say something nice about Mexico. I can't think of anything nice to say."

Mullen arrived at the Brinkley studio meaning to make headlines, and he did. For the first time in public, he described how the Federales had allowed Rafael Caro Quintero to escape. "He had as protection members of the DFS," Mullen said. "So you had police protecting and another element of the police letting this individual go for whom there is a warrant outstanding. . . . Because of the slowness in getting into the investigative activity, all of these people are gone, some as far as Europe," he added indignantly. "It seems to me they were given adequate time to depart the area."

This was the first time an American official charged on the record that something worse than inefficiency was afoot. In so many words, Mullen was accusing the Mexican police of obstructing justice.

The next day, *Newsweek* disclosed how Manuel Ibarra had allowed cocaine trafficker Juan Matta Ballesteros to escape. The same day, Mullen told Mary Thornton of *The Washington Post* that the Mexican government's entire anti-drug campaign had been phony. "They were happy to have us come in and make a big headline once in a while," he said. "But when it finally started to hurt, when they thought we were getting dangerously close [to the traffickers], they backed off."

Mullen knew that he was getting a reputation as a maverick around Washington, but he did not care. Months before, he had made plans to retire on March 1, eleven weeks after his fiftieth birthday. Lawn, who would be taking over the DEA under a new attorney general, Edwin Meese III, was more vulnerable. The Camarena affair might sink Lawn's chances of nomination for the DEA post. Lawn said it didn't matter. "If I can't speak out when one of my men is in trouble," he said, "I won't be able to look myself in the mirror."

Mullen and Lawn sent Ken Miley, who was in charge of the agency's McAllen, Texas, office, to organize the American investigative activities in Guadalajara. Miley kept a cool head in a crisis, had the rank to give orders to every other DEA agent in Mexico, spoke fluent Spanish, and would never be assigned to Mexico himself, which meant that he did not have to be diplomatic in dealing with MFJP *comandantes*. The Federales put Miley's legendary patience to the test. "We'd say, Let's go. And they would say, It's almost lunch." Miley sighed. "We'd say, Let's go after lunch. They would say, Let's do it tomorrow. And the crooks would be gone."

At one point, the DEA agents thought that Kiki might have been taken to the ranch that belonged to Emilio Quintero, Caro Quintero's uncle. It was a forbidding place, with guard posts and a radio communications center, but when the DEA agents persuaded the Federales to raid the place, they found only a few terrified servants and Emilio's pet lions. A team of DEA agents located a cocaine laboratory, which they believed belonged to Miguel Angel Félix Gallardo. They followed the Federales into the place and saw that beans were still boiling on the stove. Again, it looked as if whoever was planning to eat them had been warned of the raid, just in time.

The Federales in Guadalajara managed to detain exactly one witness: Marciano Belaztejoitia, Caro Quintero's pilot, who had returned to the city. According to Mexican authorities, Belaztejoitia admitted that on February 9 he had flown the trafficker from Guadalajara to Caborca, Sonora, where Caro Quintero had extensive property. After interrogating Belaztejoitia briefly, the Federales released him.

While Mullen and Lawn met reporters and went to meetings at Justice and State, the second and third tier of headquarters officials assembled in DEA's fifth-floor "war room," a windowless chamber with wall-to-wall maps and charts. They read the cables coming in from the agents in Guadalajara and the border offices, forwarded investigative leads, and coordinated movements of teams of agents.

Johnny Phelps, who had recently moved from Bogotá to headquarters, seemed to be almost obsessed. The tall Texan was always in the war room, Sunday mornings, Friday nights, quietly reading cables, jotting down notes, sending messages out to the field.

For the first few days, Phelps was hoping that Kiki would be found alive. He was remembering how it had been in Colombia—how Kelley McCullough and Charlie Martínez had survived being kidnapped and shot. He thought about how the Colombian police had stood shoulder-to-shoulder with him and his men until they had rounded up the kidnappers. As the days passed, that memory became very painful. Once it had been that way in Mexico. When Phelps had worked the Mexican border, there had been corruption, but it had been surmountable. Some of the *comandantes* had been his friends, or at least they had shared his kick-ass spirit. Had Mexico been lost to neglect? Phelps thought so.

Like Phelps, nearly all the men who haunted the war room had recently transferred in from the field. Washington was full of people worn smooth by ill winds, and the previous group of DEA executives had been no exception. Nobody had to tell them to keep their mouths shut. But this new crowd had all their rough edges intact. Every time they sensed that State or the White House was pushing Mullen and Lawn to ease up, they pushed the other way, egging them on to keep the story on the front pages.

"Suddenly, we had this influx of people who knew what it was really like in the field and wanted to tell it like it was," observed Robert Feldkamp, DEA's chief public affairs officer, who had been at headquarters since the Ford administration. "They dug in their heels to make sure they were not being political. They acted like big gruff cops, but you could tell how much they cared about each other. I don't think I had ever had such a good look at the soul of this agency."

On the afternoon of February 25, Angel Villa Barrón, commander of the Mexican Federal Judicial Police office in Tijuana, called a press conference to announce that his men had arrested the "mastermind" of the Camarena kidnapping. Tomás Morlet Borquez and two other men were paraded before the cameras. According to Mexican and American press accounts, Morlet was a twenty-two-year veteran of the DFS. He said he had served as the head of security for the late Shah of Iran when the Pahlavi family had encamped in Cuernavaca, and he had guarded the former American secretary of state, Henry Kissinger, on Kissinger's visits to Mexico. The two other men also carried DFS credentials. All three denied complicity in the Camarena case. The Mexico newspapers called them "sacrificial lambs."

Some evidence suggested that this was true. But DEA agents thought Morlet knew *something*. Terry Bowen, the DEA agent in charge in Calexico, California, knew an MFJP *comandante* who was a good lawman and asked him to have the Federales detain Morlet for questioning. DEA wanted to talk to Morlet about a strange episode that had occurred at one of the border crossings. A young Mexican woman whose car was being searched said angrily to a U.S. Customs inspector, "What are you looking for? Everyone knows the agent is dead." The inspector asked her how she knew, and she said that her father, Tomás Morlet, had been in Guadalajara at the time of the kidnapping and had told her what he had heard.

Still, there was something very odd about the way the Federales behaved toward Morlet. They stopped him on the afternoon of Saturday, February 23, on the highway between Tijuana and Tecate in Baja California. "I thought you were going to stop me in Tijuana," Morlet complained.

The Federales apologized and said they were only carrying out orders. Morlet said he hoped that was true, or they would be in a lot of trouble.

Morlet did not know that one of the men in the police car was a DEA agent who spoke Spanish. The American agent sent a cable to DEA headquarters about the conversation. When reporters called DEA headquarters to ask about the arrest, Jack Lawn told them flatly, "That was a sham."

Soon after the press conference, the Federales quietly released Morlet and his men for lack of evidence, and the DEA was never able to talk to him. Nearly two years later, Bowen got word that Morlet was dead, assassinated by a gunman in a dark car as he was coming out of a bar in Matamoros.

10
The Bodies at
the Bravo Ranch

On Thursday, February 28, Comandante Armando Pavón Reyes of the MFJP showed Jaime Kuykendall and another DEA agent, Tony Ayala, an anonymous note, which said that Camarena was being held at the Rancho El Mareño, near a village called La Angostura, about seventy miles away in the neighboring state of Michoacán. The ranch belonged to Manuel Bravo Cervantes, a former Michoacán state congressman. The writer said that he or she had seen Camarena at the Bravo ranch. If the DEA agent was not alive, the letter said, his body would be in Bravo's orchard.

Kuykendall did not think the note was particularly significant. In recent days, the worldwide publicity about the kidnapping had attracted a flurry of anonymous letters and calls, all spurious. Kuykendall had never heard of Manuel Bravo and did not think he was connected with the Guadalajara drug cartel. But he asked to make a copy of the letter so that DEA could study it more closely. Pavón Reyes snatched it away.

For reasons that Kuykendall could not understand, the young *comandante* was extremely agitated and said that he intended to send a team of MFJP agents to Michoacán early Saturday morning. Kuykendall thought this was strange. Up to now, Pavón Reyes had been exceedingly slow to make decisions—and why chase this particular tip, when there were many others? Kuykendall and Ayala asked Pavón Reyes to take some DEA agents with him. He agreed but said they must be at his office promptly at eight o'clock on Saturday morning.

Ayala and a team of Americans showed up at the MFJP office at the appointed hour only to find that the raiding party, led by Comandante Alfonso Velázquez Hernández, had left two hours before. Ayala jumped in his car and drove to Michoacán. By the time he pulled up in front of the small stucco ranch house, it was over. Manuel Bravo and his wife were both dead. The woman appeared to have been shot in the back. Two sons, Hugo and Manuel, were lying dead in the yard. The third son, Rigoberto, had been shot, possibly in his bed. One MFJP agent had been killed with an automatic weapon.

As the Federales told the story to the DEA agents and reporters, they had arrived at the house at seven-fifteen in the morning. They said that when they ordered the family to surrender, automatic-weapon fire had erupted from the house, killing the MFJP agent. The Federales said that the firefight had lasted for a good half hour. They said they had shot the men, and when they went through the door, Señora Bravo, lying wounded on the floor, had fired a handgun at them, so they had killed her, too. In the midst of the battle, they said, the wives of two of the sons had shown up at the ranch with a carload of ammunition. The Federales said they were holding the two young women for questioning.

Camarena was not in the house, and the DEA agents were unable to persuade the Federales to look in the orchard, where the letter said his body might be found. The Federales insisted on burying their dead comrade before they made a search.

The more the DEA agents looked into the incident, the uglier it got. After the raid, the Federales told reporters they had seized a veritable armory of weapons from the Bravos. The Federales would not let the DEA agents examine the weapons. After much haggling, the Federales agreed to provide a list of serial numbers, but when the DEA agents tried to run the numbers through the gun-tracing system of the U.S. Bureau of Alcohol, Tobacco, and Firearms, the computer rejected every number. The Federales had not even given the DEA the correct number of digits. The DEA agents doubted that the Bravos had really used automatic weapons, as the Federales claimed. And if they had not, it meant that the dead MFJP agent might have been killed by one of his own men.

Then there was the question of the anonymous note. The writer claimed that Camarena had been kidnapped by mistake. That made no sense. If Camarena's kidnapping had been a blunder, why had Alfredo Zavala been kidnapped? Two mistakes, two hours apart? No, the DEA agents concluded, those acts were not coincidental. And if the note was real, why did Pavón Reyes refuse to give the Americans a copy?

The widows of Manuel Bravo's sons were quickly released—an odd event if they had really been delivering ammunition, as the Federales claimed. The young women accused the Federales of murdering their husbands and in-laws in cold blood. A boy from the neighboring ranch told a CBS News crew that the Federales had fired the first shots. Governor Cuauhtémoc Cárdenas of Michoacán, the son of former Mexican President Lázaro Cárdenas, sent an angry protest to Mexico City. "They were victimized," Cárdenas's spokesman, Octavio Ortiz, said. If the Bravo family had been arrested alive, he told *The Washington Post*, "they might also have been released like the others were."[1] Such an outcry arose over the incident, which had become known as the massacre at the Rancho El Mareño, that Attorney General Sergio García Ramírez ordered an investigation of the conduct of the MFJP officers involved.

As Kuykendall pieced the story together, two of Manuel Bravo's sons, Hugo and Manuel Bravo Segura, had lived in Zamora, two blocks apart. The third son, Rigoberto, was handicapped and lived with his parents at the ranch. Señora Bravo's brother, Wenceslado Segura, lived about fifteen hundred feet from the ranch. Celia Bravo, the widow of Hugo, told Kuykendall that at about seven-fifteen in the morning of March 2, Uncle Wenceslado called her husband, frantically shouting on the telephone that he could hear shooting at the ranch house. Hugo fetched his brother Manuel and had headed out to the ranch, which was about twenty-two miles from Zamora.

Celia Bravo and Manuel's wife, Eleuteria, were terrified,

for each had a young son staying at the ranch. They went to the office of the Michoacán state attorney general to get help. The officials there were sympathetic and assigned six Michoacán state policemen to drive them to the ranch. When they arrived there, at about nine o'clock, there were a lot of cars around the house, and Celia heard gunfire. Some armed men slipped up behind them, identified themselves as Federales, and ordered the Michoacán state police officers to lay down their guns. Surprised and outmatched, the Michoacán policemen complied. The Federales blindfolded the women, slapped them around, and shoved them into a shed.

Celia had caught a glimpse of a body in the front yard which she thought might be her husband, but she was not sure. Then she heard someone say, "Give it to him," and a gunshot. Sometime later, she heard a man say, "He was really tough. He died without giving away anything." During the afternoon, she said, men came in, hit them, and asked where Enrique Camarena was, but she did not know what they were talking about.

But late in the afternoon, the Federales released the women, who discovered their sons badly frightened but physically unharmed. Celia's son Hugo told her that he and his cousin Manuel had been sleeping in Rigoberto's room when they heard loud noises that sounded like someone trying to get into the house. Rigoberto shouted to his father that thieves were breaking in. Then armed men burst into the bedroom and took the boys out of the house. Little Hugo said that he heard his grandfather refuse to surrender and shout for someone to get the police. After that, he said, all he heard was shooting and screaming.

On Tuesday, March 5, Comandante Pavón Reyes allowed the DEA agents to take a crew of laborers to the ranch to dig up the orchard. The agents and their crew went over every inch of the ranch and found nothing. Late in the afternoon, they gave up and returned to Guadalajara.

Sometime after six o'clock, a young villager named Antonio Navarro Rodríguez was walking down the road behind the ranch and was overcome by a gust of fetid air. In a clearing a few yards from the road, he spotted two big plastic bags, like fertilizer sacks. One bag was open. A pair of rotting human legs jutted out.

Navarro ran into the village of La Angostura and fetched Salvador Sandoval Alvarez, the police chief. By the time Sandoval returned with Navarro, a crowd of villagers was standing at the clearing. Sandoval ordered them to back away, and he inspected the bags. Inside were two cadavers, black with decay. Sandoval headed into the nearest city, Zamora, to report the discovery of the bodies to the Michoacán state police. The police took the bodies to the Red Cross Hospital in Zamora. MFJP Comandante Pavón Reyes was notified and flew from Guadalajara to Zamora that night, but he did not alert DEA.

At seven o'clock the next morning, Mexican television stations in Guadalajara and Mexico City announced that the bodies of DEA agent Enrique Camarena and Captain Alfredo Zavala had been discovered. A few minutes before the seven o'clock broadcast, Mike O'Connor, a CBS-TV producer covering the story in Guadalajara, received a call from a Jalisco state official whom he had been cultivating; the man said the bodies had been located. O'Connor and his crew were on their way to Zamora well before DEA found out what was going on. It was not until seven-forty-five that the Federales called the DEA office, and even then they would not explain anything until Ed Heath presented himself at the MFJP office. By that time, it was about nine o'clock.

The delay and the leaks to the press were insults, but there was nothing the DEA men could do about it. One of Pavón Reyes's assistants explained that the bodies had been found and said that a helicopter would transport the American agents to Zamora. The helicopter flight was delayed for an hour while the Federales waited for Manuel Ibarra's secretary, Alberto Carrasco, to arrive from Mexico City. Carrasco appeared at nine-fifty, videotape recorder and still camera in hand. Heath and agents Joe González and Bobby Castillo quietly followed the Federales aboard the chopper, which arrived at Zamora at about ten-fifteen in the morning. They were driven to the Red Cross Hospital and allowed to look at the bodies.

The American agents could not identify either corpse. The faces were gone, rotted away. The bodies were almost skeletons, just bones stuck together with a thin layer of shrunken flesh that looked like dried, burned leather. The doctors estimated that they had been dead twenty to twenty-five days.

According to Heath's report on the autopsy, cadaver number one, as the Red Cross doctors labeled it, was that of a muscular Hispanic male in his thirties, with black hair and dark brown eyes. Three ribs on the left side were broken. The right arm was broken and showed numerous lesions. The doctors thought that a foreign object, possibly a stick, had been forced into the rectum. The left side of the skull was caved in, probably from a blow with a blunt instrument. The body was clothed in Jockey shorts, the hands and feet tightly bound.

Cadaver number two was an adult male in his forties, heavyset, with black hair and brown eyes. The doctors did not comment on lesions or bruises but said the rectum had been violated. The jaw was gaping and the hands had broken free of their bonds. The doctors were of the opinion that the man had been buried alive and had suffocated.

The doctors thought the bodies had been buried, dug up, and dumped on the roadside. The DEA agents who observed the autopsy agreed. For one thing, the soil on the bodies was black, and the soil at the Bravo ranch was lighter in color. Heath reported to headquarters that the whole thing looked like a plot by someone to have the authorities "find" the bodies and frame the Bravos, who were conveniently dead.

DEA agents who went to the place where the bodies were found did not turn up any useful evidence such as tire tracks or footprints because the Federales had not preserved the scene. During the sixteen and a half hours between the moment when Antonio Navarro spotted the bodies and the arrival of the DEA agents in Zamora, many people had trod across the field. The agents asked for the sacks in which the bodies had been found, hoping to lift some fingerprints, but the Federales claimed they had been lost.

Jack Lawn was in the administrator's office when he heard the news. The agents thought these might be the bodies of Camarena and Zavala, but they could not be sure. There had been a string of false alarms; at least five decomposed cadavers had turned up during the month since the search began, each discovery sparking a brief flurry of activity until the body was found to be older, younger, bigger, smaller than Camarena's. Lawn called the Armed Forces Institute of Pathology at Walter Reed Hospital in Washington and secured the help of a Navy pathologist who had experience in identifying the decomposed bodies of servicemen killed in Vietnam. Kuykendall telephoned from Guadalajara. He said the Mexican authorities might not allow another autopsy.

Lawn saw that the next few days would be a diplomatic mine field. He had to get permission for the autopsy, and if the body was Kiki's he would have to get the body returned to the United States. That was not a sure thing. De la Madrid was under severe political pressure not to give another inch to the Americans. The Federales could hold the body for months, even years, as evidence in a homicide case.

A call came from the Mexican Attorney General's Office. Lawn hoped it was the permission he needed. It was not. It was not even a call of condolence. It concerned public relations. An assistant to Attorney General García Ramírez was on the line; he understood that Lawn was scheduled to go on ABC-TV's *Nightline* that night. Did he intend to criticize Mexico?

Lawn gritted his teeth. At this moment, he needed every bit of the discipline drilled into him by the Marines and the FBI. "These guys really fry my ass," he muttered to a friend, but toward the Mexican officials he maintained a rigorous civility. Lawn said no, he was not going on *Nightline*. A short time later, permission came through for the autopsy.

On Thursday morning, Dr. Jerry Douglas Spencer, a Navy Medical Corps captain specializing in forensic pathology, flew to Guadalajara with two forensic specialists from the FBI laboratory. Late that afternoon, using dental records and fingerprints, the team determined that the younger man was indeed Enrique Camarena, and the elder, Alfredo Zavala. The pathologist found that Camarena had suffered extensive injuries to the head, bruises around the face and head, multiple skull and jaw fractures, and rib fractures. The cause of death, he said, was probably a puncture wound on the left side of Camarena's skull caused by a blunt instrument like a tire iron or crowbar that had been driven into the skull. Spencer believed that the two men had probably died on February 8, the day after they were abducted.

The Mexican government agreed to release Camarena's remains to the American government. Lawn arranged for a U.S. Air Force transport. Then he called a press conference.

Lawn spoke slowly and in a flat tone, but his eyes glittered with pain and rage. He described the condition of the body and alluded to his doubts about the Bravo ranch raid. Then he responded to Mexican government charges that the United States had overreacted to the loss of a single officer, when Mexico had lost more than three hundred men over the previous few years.

"We've lost a number of agents over the years," Lawn said. "Certainly, this is the price. [But] an agent losing his life in an investigation is very different from what transpired in Guadalajara. Here we have an act of terrorism in which an individual is abducted, not while working an investigation but while going to lunch with his wife. There is a period of inactivity, of inertia on the part of the Mexican government, which is the most critical time in any kidnapping, the initial seventy-two-hour period. We cannot categorize the disappearance of Special Agent Camarena with the lives lost by personnel of the Drug Enforcement Administration or by law enforcement in general, including the substantial numbers of Mexican officers who have been lost in this battle. Every nation fighting the battle expects to sustain losses. We are willing to accept our losses. What we will not accept is terrorism. And this has only strengthened our resolve."

When Camarena's body was found, Bud Mullen was at home, packing to move back to Connecticut. For the first time in twenty-three years, Mullen felt like a free man, answerable to no one. On March 7, he gave one last interview, to *Newsweek* magazine. The interview became known as "Mullen's explosion." He said all the things that he had repressed while there was hope that Kiki might be found alive:

> People talk of sending the FBI down, or sending in more DEA agents, but there's only one government in the world that can clean up Mexico, and that's the Mexican government and the Mexican Federal Judicial Police, and they've got to do it. We can go on forever making a seizure here and there, but until the Mexicans themselves root out corruption, I don't think we'll ever stop the flow of drugs from Mexico. Everybody seems to know it's there and it's happening, but nobody wants to talk about it publicly. I think it's time to ignore the sensibilities of some individuals and face the fact that we have a problem down there. People here say, well, there's a different mentality down there and we should accept it. This is the way it is. I just don't agree. It is not acceptable. Not when it's affecting our country the way it is—and their country. I think it's just a blight on Mexico that this could happen. People disappear and that's it. They don't even have an investigation. I just can't believe that people still go down there.

On March 9, the streets of Calexico were jammed with mourners walking to Our Lady of Guadalupe. Kiki had married Mika in the dusty little chapel fifteen years before. Now the bells tolled for a memorial Mass.

In the congregation, Ambassador Gavin and other dignitaries mingled with the people of the barrio. A small box containing Camarena's cremated remains was brought up the center aisle and placed on a small table in front of the altar. An honor guard of four Marines marched slowly to the altar. The bishop of Mexicali and the auxiliary bishop of San Diego joined the priest of Our Lady of Guadalupe in praying for Enrique Camarena's soul.

After the Mass, Jack Lawn presented the flag that had covered the coffin to Dora Camarena, Kiki's mother. It was the second flag she had accepted in this way. The first had draped the casket of Kiki's older brother, Eduardo, who had died in Vietnam. The tiny old woman held the flag high over her head toward the statue of Christ above the altar and then broke down weeping.

Until this moment, Mika Camarena had held her emotions tightly in check. Tears began to course down her cheeks. Fighting back tears himself, Lawn put his arm around her. She allowed herself to slump against his shoulder. Then she composed herself and carried on.

Mika kept the last ceremony to herself. She slipped away from the crowd of mourners who milled about Dora Camarena's house, evaded the throng of reporters, and drove to the strip of asphalt that served as Calexico's airport. The one-engine plane that belonged to the DEA-Calexico office was warming up. She climbed aboard.

The pilot guided the small craft over the treetops and slipped along the border, heading toward the bare grayish-brown peak that Mormon settlers had named Mount Signal. The pioneers had used this stone as their guide into California as they drove their wagon trains west across the desert from Yuma. Now it straddled the border and loomed over the badlands outside Mexicali and Calexico.

Mika scattered Kiki's ashes on the mountain's face. She did not want Kiki's body to lie under the dust of Calexico. Like the rock, he belonged to the histories of two frontiers. She gave him back to the wind that carved the sand dunes and to the cobalt sky that arched over both nations.

11

Cover-up

Dead men can tell you a lot if you know what to ask.

After he returned to Washington, Jack Lawn asked the Navy pathologist, Dr. Jerry Spencer, to come in for a chat. Lawn wanted to know everything Spencer had observed, no matter how trivial. Perhaps there was something that had not been in the brief autopsy report, some detail that might shed more light on how and when Camarena and Zavala had been killed.

From the autopsy report, it was clear that Kiki had been tortured. There was not a bullet in him, just a lot of broken bones and that terrible puncture wound that looked as if a tire tool had been jammed into his brain.

What Lawn did not know—what the DEA had to find out—was *why*. What were the killers after? Whatever it was, did they get it? Or would they go after someone else? The marks on the bodies would not say why, but they might show how and when and where, which might lead to who. Which might get Lawn back to why.

The pathologist said there *was* something he had left out. There had been no insect bites on the bodies. If the corpses had been exposed for any length of time, even overnight, there would have been insect bites or rat bites.

This—and the specks of black dirt, which did not match the pale dust around the Bravo ranch—told Lawn that the bodies had been buried quickly, exhumed just as quickly, and dumped on the roadside a few hours, no more, before they were found. It meant to Lawn that the Bravos could not have put those bodies there, because all the men in the family had been dead for three days when the bodies showed up.

There were a couple of innocent explanations for this bizarre turn of events. One was that the Federales had gone to the ranch believing that they were heading into a nest of copkillers, panicked, and shot it out with the Bravos. But that did not explain how the bodies got to the road behind the ranch three days later. It was possible that on Tuesday, when the Federales and the DEA agents returned to dig up the Bravos, Camarena's murderers took advantage of the commotion and dumped the bodies where they would be found. Someone could have been trying to embarrass the Federales or frame the Bravos.

But there were simply too many questions and inconsistencies for Lawn to accept those scenarios. If the Federales sincerely believed that Camarena, or his body, might be found at the ranch, why hadn't they searched the place once the Bravos were dead? Why had Comandante Pavón Reyes refused to let the DEA copy the note so it could be subjected to forensic examination? Why had the leader of the raid, Comandante Alfonso Velázquez Hernández, avoided taking DEA agents along? Why did the Federales give the DEA nonexistent serial numbers for the guns they claimed to have found at the ranch? Why had they released the wives of the Bravo sons if, as the Federales claimed, the women were delivering ammunition, a very serious crime in Mexico? When the Michoacán police arrived to help, why had the Federales held them off at gunpoint? When the campesino found the bodies, why had the Federales waited thirteen hours before making the initial call to DEA?

All those questions raised in Lawn's mind a third possibility: that with the pressure mounting on the Mexican government from the American side, someone in authority had attempted to placate the DEA by giving them a plausible group of murderers—the Bravos—and by producing the victims. As Lawn's aide, Charlie Hill, put it, the message was "Okay, you got the bodies, you got the suspects. Next case." Probably, Lawn said, the guy who was supposed to deliver the bodies to the ranch was late and panicked when he saw the DEA agents in the orchard, so he dumped his cargo on the roadside behind the ranch.

Lawn thought back to March 6. Mexican television had flashed the first bulletin that the bodies had been found at seven o'clock in the morning. The source of the report appeared to be someone in the Mexican government.

Then there was the strange arrival from Mexico City of Manuel Ibarra's secretary, Alberto Carrasco, loaded down with photographic equipment to make a pictorial record of the "discovery." What sort of discovery did Ibarra expect? DEA agents Heath, González, and Castillo did not look at the corpses until shortly after ten-thirty that morning, three and a half hours after the first news bulletin. When they did see the bodies, they could not make positive identifications. The Navy pathologist did not give his conclusions until late the next afternoon—nearly two days after the bodies were found.

And it was not as if these were the only bodies the police might come upon. Besides Camarena, four male Americans in their twenties or thirties had disappeared from Guadalajara recently: Ben Mascarenas and Dennis Carlson, the Jehovah's Witnesses, on December 2, John Walker and Alberto Radelat on January 30. No one knew how many Mexican men had disappeared recently. In fact, four or five corpses had been found in the first few days of the searches. How could Ibarra, in Mexico City, be so confident that two faceless corpses dumped on a dusty roadside sixty-five miles from Guadalajara would turn out to be the remains of Kiki Camarena and Alfredo Zavala?

Looking back at the information that DEA had, it seemed clear to Lawn that some officials of the Federales were clearly involved in allowing the escape of Rafael Caro Quintero and Juan Matta Ballesteros and in the obvious attempt to frame the Bravo family.[1] Also, no one at the MFJP had ever explained how the snapshot of Camarena taken at the MFJP office had gotten to Miguel Angel Félix Gallardo's house.

For Lawn, the pathologist's report made a pattern of all the strands of fact and conjecture. Suddenly he knew—he could not prove, but he *knew*—that a massive cover-up was under way, a conspiracy that was not confined to provincial policemen but reached to Comandante Pavón Reyes, who received the "note" leading to the Bravo ranch and to Comandante Alfonso Velázquez Hernández, who had led the raid on the Bravo ranch. Lawn suspected the cover-up might go even higher. He was profoundly disturbed by MFJP director Manuel Ibarra's conduct, which he found obstructive and unprofessional. Did anyone really think the Americans were dumb enough to fall for a scheme this transparent? Lawn concluded that very powerful interests had to be at work. If someone in the Federales had engineered this clumsy "discovery," Lawn wondered what awful secrets he was trying to protect.

And what if Kiki's tormentors had not gotten what they wanted? Who was the next target? Informants were coming in with all sorts of stories about plots against the Americans and their sources in Mexico. Lawn had hundreds of people to worry about: thirty DEA agents permanently assigned to Mexico, most with wives and children, dozens more agents and families stationed along the border, multitudes of paid informants, many of them husbands and fathers, like Alfredo Zavala.

Nothing was more important to Lawn at this moment than finding out who had killed Kiki Camarena and who in the Mexican government had helped either to plan the crime or to cover it up. Whoever had done it would probably kill again.

There were faint trails in every direction, but wherever they led were stone walls. Even those Federales who might have helped under ordinary circumstances were not likely to break ranks now. Anyone who cooperated with the Americans was suspect. Attorney General García Ramírez had even asked Gavin to stop saying that the American government mourned Camarena's murdered pilot, Alfredo Zavala. Gavin was puzzled and finally assumed that the Mexican government did not consider Zavala a victim but rather a traitor. Lawn knew that whoever helped him and his men risked his own life. He wondered how many more would die before this nightmare ended.

Around March 10 or 11, Comandante Pavón Reyes left Guadalajara abruptly. Officials in the Attorney General's

Office would not tell the DEA agents where he was. Some
DEA agents asked reporters what *they* knew about Pavón
Reyes.

Pavón Reyes's absence began to make sense when the
Americans found out that Primer Comandante Florentino
Ventura had arrived in Guadalajara. His presence was not
explained to the DEA agents, but soon after he showed up,
things started to happen. On March 12, Ventura and the
Federales rounded up thirteen people, including seven
Jalisco state judicial policemen and six former Jalisco po-
licemen. The most important was Comandante Gabriel
González González, head of detectives for the Jalisco State
Judicial Police force. González González was in charge of
the homicide squad that handled the Camarena and Zavala
cases for the state of Jalisco.

DEA agents were encouraged by the arrests but appalled
when they learned that by the next evening Gabriel González González was dead. A statement released by Francisco
Fonseca, the spokesman for Mexican Attorney General
García Ramírez, said that González González had died of
"acute pancreatic hemorrhaging" while in MFJP custody.
Evidently anticipating questions about torture, the statement said that an autopsy showed no evidence of external
wounds on the body, but this pronouncement did not allay
widespread suspicion that González González had been
beaten to death.

Two other Jalisco policemen who had been detained,
Group Chief Víctor Manuel López Razón and homicide
detective Gerardo Torres Lepe, had confessed to kidnapping Camarena, according to Fonseca. The government
spokesman said a third Jalisco policeman, Group Chief Benjamín Locheo Salazar, had confessed to collaborating in the
abduction, and other Jalisco officers were accused of the
abduction of pilot Zavala. Fonseca said the Jalisco state
officers were "all very strongly involved with the drug
traffickers, receiving money in exchange for protection and
tip-offs about police activities." He distributed a statement
describing González González as a "cocaine addict" and
"intimate friend" of "the known drug traffickers" Rafael
Caro Quintero, Miguel Angel Félix Gallardo, Manuel Sal-

cido Uzeta, Juan José Esparragoza Moreno, Ernesto Fonseca Carrillo, and Javier Barba Hernández.

According to reports in Mexican and U.S. newspapers, Locheo Salazar admitted that the cartel paid him 600,000 pesos a month to warn them of roadblocks and let the traffickers know when their runners and bodyguards were arrested. Homicide detective Torres Lepe, who confessed to having helped kidnap Camarena, said two of his division chiefs drove their police cars as escorts for a major shipment of marijuana a few weeks before Camarena was kidnapped. Torres Lepe's statement to the court also said Commanders Gabriel González González and Víctor Manuel López Razón escorted Caro Quintero to his private jet at Guadalajara International Airport. López Razón's "confession" said that Fonseca had given him a special radio to use in relaying tips to the drug dealers. According to press accounts, the statements said that at least thirteen Jalisco state policemen were among the seven guests at a two-day celebration of the wedding of one of Ernesto Fonseca's brothers.[2]

The statements made for lurid reading. Ultimately, though, Ventura's actions disappointed his old friends at the DEA. He did not attempt to answer questions about the possible complicity of MFJP officers in the escape of Caro Quintero and in the Bravo ranch massacre. The de la Madrid administration made it clear that these arrests were supposed to close the case. "This is not a Mexico City problem," Fonseca told American reporters. "This is a problem of the city of Guadalajara."[3]

In Mexico City, Ambassador Gavin praised the arrests, saying that they "underscored the commitment of President de la Madrid and his cabinet to a campaign for moral renovation." But Gavin would not be satisfied with the arrests of a few Jalisco cops. "Unfortunately, there will also be some other elements, supposedly defending the law and wearing badges, that will be brought in," he told reporters pointedly. "At least this is what we understand from Mexican authorities. They themselves are fully aware, and assured us that they are aware, that they have a housecleaning process here."

Signaling his own doubts about the thoroughness of the

investigation, Attorney General Ed Meese issued a statement in Washington allowing that he was "moderately encouraged." Lawn had nothing good to say about the arrests. "To say that it's confined to Jalisco state police—that's a lot of b.s.," he said, shrugging.

The Federales would not tell the DEA very much about why they had arrested the Jalisco policemen, but two weeks later, Ed Heath was able to obtain a copy of Ventura's report. According to this document, the Jalisco policemen had confessed that Caro Quintero and Félix Gallardo ordered the kidnapping of Camarena and Zavala because Caro Quintero blamed Camarena for having cost him the $20 million which he had invested in the Chihuahua marijuana-processing complex. If this was so, it was a tragic mistake: Kiki Camarena had not worked on the Chihuahua case. But it might not be so. All the policemen who were detained recanted their confessions when they were brought into court. They claimed they had been tortured, and the reporters who were present in the courtroom believed that was possible: the reporters saw that all the men had bruised noses and a few showed black-and-blue ribs and backsides. One man dropped his trousers and offered to show reporters his bruised testicles.

Lawn knew that persuading his own government to use leverage on the Mexican government would be the most daunting task he faced. In Washington, unanimity was as rare as humility. In foreign-policy discussions, whenever the subject of drug trafficking came up, so did the phrase "other issues." Every faction of the American government had its own policy toward Mexico.

When Camarena's body was found, George Shultz exploded, "Our level of tolerance has been exceeded by these events." With his next breath, however, he made clear that he was prepared to tolerate more bad behavior before he would endorse punitive measures against the Mexican government, such as trade sanctions or a travel advisory. "I don't think it is a good idea to play around with those kinds of sanctions," he said. White House aides described Nancy Reagan as "devastated" and staff chief Don Regan as seeth-

ing, but agreed with Shultz on the matter of economic retaliation. "We've got a lot at stake besides drugs," said a
White House aide. "It's really a tough diplomatic situation."
Gavin also took pains to reassure the Mexican government
that the Camarena case would not disrupt economic relations between the two nations. "We cannot allow recent
events—as tragic and as difficult as they have been to many
of our citizens—to impinge on our overall cooperative efforts and on our good bilateral relations," Gavin told
reporters.[4]

On March 11, Shultz's ire was roused anew by Mexican
Foreign Secretary Bernardo Sepúlveda Amor, who arrived
in Washington for a round of meetings. On March 11, Sepúlveda emerged from a two-and-a-half-hour session with
Shultz, smiled, and told reporters that he and Shultz had
agreed that "this issue is typically just a police matter and
unfortunately it has been elevated to the level of major
foreign policy." "The impression I have from the conversations today," he added airily, "is that this is behind us."[5]

Shultz's aides were incensed. Jon Thomas told reporters
that, in fact, Shultz had lectured Sepúlveda sternly. "Sepúlveda was embarrassed," Thomas said in an interview.
"No doubt was left in the Mexican government that this was
a very important foreign-policy issue."

Sepúlveda's remarks had an incendiary effect upon John
Gavin. "As I pointed out to him, to the president of Mexico,
and to other people, this was a very important matter to us,
a matter we took seriously, to which we gave great, great
weight, and we continue to," Gavin said between gritted
teeth.

Paula Hawkins, the conservative Republican senator
from Florida, let fly with a blast of invective. "We got nothing from the Mexicans this time around. *Nothing*," she raged
at a hearing. "Now that the pressure is off Mexico, now that
Enrique Camarena's twisted, broken body has been found,
dug up from its grave and deposited at the side of the road
. . . what will we do? Are we going to back up and say,
'Hit us again'?" Hawkins and like-minded members of Congress began to talk of blocking Mexico's access to loans from
the International Monetary Fund.

In fact, the Treasury Department was negotiating a new bail-out package of loans for Mexico, and the State Department was planning to increase Mexico's share of State's narcotics aid budget. Jon Thomas knew he was going to face a lot of heat from Hawkins and other politicians for giving Mexico *more* money for drug control, in view of the evidence that Mexican officials had pocketed much of the appropriations of the last three or four years. However, Thomas felt trapped in a Catch-22 situation.

"You've got a worsening narcotics problem, and production and smuggling from Mexico," he said. "You've got a worsening performance record, and the first inclination of somebody is to say, Well, we're going to start cutting their funds, that'll get their attention. Well, Mexico was in absolute hock and their people were coming to us and saying, Look, we don't have the money to run these eradication operations and we need three more aircraft. To cut back and start grounding the fleet made absolutely no sense whatsoever. I'm afraid that the way out of the Mexican problem is not to cut the programs you've got, you've got to make the programs work."

Called to the House Foreign Affairs Committee on March 19, Thomas faced a barrage of questions about why State intended to continue aid to Mexico and other nonperformers, particularly Bolivia. "I would not hesitate to recommend to the secretary of state that we cut off assistance if I were convinced it would further our narcotics objectives," he said. "But . . . there is not . . . a single source country where our narcotics objectives in our opinion would be enhanced by suspending assistance. We could cause increased instability leading to very unwelcome developments. We could further depress already precarious economies. But would we inflict any pain on the traffickers?"[6]

Some members of Congress were incredulous when they heard that Lawn supported Thomas on the aid issue. Called before the Senate Subcommittee on Security and Terrorism, Lawn said he felt that "when this is over, we will be able to work with Mexico again."

"I wonder how you can even ask a DEA agent to go down there," Patrick Leahy, the Democratic senator from

Vermont, told Lawn. "It looks like Mexico said, Okay, you can come on down, but if you guys ever start accomplishing anything, we will kill you. . . . We will just do whatever we want if it works within our own corrupt system, and the hell with what that might do to the people in the United States."

Lawn had decided to go along with State and the White House. It was tempting to think about pulling out of Mexico, but he could not bring himself to do it. How could DEA pursue Camarena's killers without keeping people inside Mexico? The agency also needed intelligence about drug shipments bound for the United States. Working with a system in which there was corruption yielded more information than isolation. Finally, Lawn thought the eradication program could be saved. Lawn agreed with Thomas, who argued that eradication in Mexico *had* to work. If it did not, what was the point in pressing the issue in other countries? Mexico alone could produce all the heroin, marijuana, and pills American consumers would buy and probably could grow coca if the Andean crops were destroyed. And if the Mexican anti-drug program did work, that would relieve the DEA and the Customs Service of an enormous workload. Lawn did not want it on his record or his conscience that he had been the one to give up on Mexico.

Lawn's decision did not sit well with many of the field agents, or with some headquarters officials recently promoted from the field. These men saw their mission in straightforward terms: find out about the people who were breaking the law and stop them. They had no use for the oblique maneuvering that went on in the higher reaches of government. Compromise was not part of their vocabulary. At a senior DEA staff meeting, as the merits of reaching an accommodation with the Mexican government were discussed, one official mourned, "We're sounding like State Department people, talking about 'weighing interests.' We're *law enforcement*. We're supposed to *find the truth!*"

But it was one thing to find the truth in an American city, where a recalcitrant mayor or a crooked police chief could be whipped into line by a well-aimed contempt-of-court citation. In a place like Mexico, where DEA agents were guests, and not welcome ones, lawmen had to learn the subtleties of diplomacy, mixing charm and intimidation—the steel fist in the silk glove, as envoys put it. The trouble was that silk was in short supply at DEA, and steel was scarcer yet. The decisions that counted—whether to help Mexico refinance its debt, whether to take away trade concessions—were made at the White House, State, Treasury, and on Capitol Hill. Being a realist, Lawn knew that the administration was not going to cut off aid or squeeze loans, as ultraconservatives like Paula Hawkins urged. Lawn had no illusions about his own influence, and he saw no profit in becoming known as the leader of a rebel agency. The prudent course, he decided, was to build a coalition with Meese, Thomas, and Gavin—and with von Raab if he would go along, though it was doubtful, for von Raab was a firebrand. Lawn pinned most of his hopes on Meese. Meese was a hardliner on law-enforcement issues and seemed genuinely interested in DEA. He liked Lawn and made sure that the president nominated him to replace Mullen, despite the complaints of State and White House aides that DEA was overstepping its bounds by putting out information about corruption in Mexico. Mexican officials knew that Meese was very close to Ronald Reagan. Possibly, Lawn thought, Meese could prevail where others had failed. Camarena was dead, but Lawn still wanted his killers, and he wanted to curb the flood of drugs coming in from Mexico.

On March 22, at Meese's invitation, Attorney General García Ramírez flew to Washington for a "law-enforcement summit." Lawn laid out the American government's agenda. First, he wanted a dozen joint task forces—teams of MFJP and DEA agents—to search for Caro Quintero, Fonseca, Félix Gallardo, "Cochi Loco," and the other Guadalajara kingpins who had scattered after the kidnapping. He wanted to revive Operation Vanguard, the verification program. He wanted access to the men already in custody and the physical evidence from the place where Camarena's body had been found. And he wanted to see corrupt officials prosecuted. At the top of his list was Comandante Armando Pavón Reyes.

The meeting went remarkably smoothly. García Ramírez

promised to deliver everything Lawn asked. Meese and Lawn were impressed with the Mexican attorney general. He seemed sincerely committed to reform. García Ramírez gave the DEA chief reason to hope that the Camarena investigation was on track at last.

Lawn never imagined that the Mexican police would bring Camarena's killers to justice without a struggle. He had been around too long to believe in easy victories. Every time he felt buoyed by some momentary breakthrough, he would remember how hard it was to make the system work. Most of his illusions had been kicked out of him when he had handled what FBI director William Webster had called the most difficult FBI investigation of his tenure: the search for the assassins of U.S. District Judge John Wood of San Antonio. Lawn and his team had cracked the conspiracy, but it had taken every weapon in the FBI's arsenal, and more man-hours than any case since the assassination of President John F. Kennedy. And when it was over, the jury acquitted the accused murderer.

In many ways, that case had presented more of a mystery than the Camarena case. John Wood had been killed by a single rifle shot fired by a sniper on the morning of May 29, 1979, as he had left home for the San Antonio courthouse. It was the first murder of a U.S. federal judge since frontier days, and to the judges, prosecutors, and agents who made up the federal criminal-justice system, it was an attack on the system itself. Attorney General Griffin Bell and Webster, both former federal judges, had made the case the FBI's top priority.

There were no eyewitnesses and no murder weapon. The list of felons who had a motive to kill "Maximum John" Wood was a mile long. The FBI focused immediately on Jamiel "Jimmy" Chagra, a vicious El Paso trafficker and professional gambler. On the day he was killed, Wood was scheduled to preside over Chagra's upcoming trial for drug conspiracy and probably would have sent him away for the rest of his life. Chagra owned huge, gaudy houses in El Paso and Las Vegas, paid his gambling debts with footlockers full of cash, lavished a sultan's ransom in rubies and emeralds upon his wife, Elizabeth, and had snagged a walk-on part in Robert Redford's film *The Electric Horseman*. The smart money said that Jimmy would do anything but time. Six months before Wood's assassination, Assistant U.S. Attorney James W. Kerr, who had been putting together the government's trafficking case against Chagra, was ambushed while driving near his home in San Antonio. Twenty-one bullets pierced Kerr's car; he escaped death by ducking beneath the dashboard.

There was not a shred of hard evidence that Chagra was indeed behind the assassination of Wood or the attempt on Kerr's life. So confident was the Chagra family that in August 1980 Joseph Chagra, Jimmy's brother and lawyer, told reporters, "Wood wasn't murdered. He started committing suicide years ago. A million people hated Judge Wood. When you step on people every day of your life, something's going to happen. He was not a fair judge."[7]

Ten months after the murder, Webster sent Lawn to San Antonio. Whatever he needed, he could have it, the FBI director said. Just find Wood's killer. By this time, Chagra was in the federal prison in Leavenworth, Kansas, serving thirty years without the possibility of parole. Judge William Steele Sessions, who had presided over Chagra's trafficking trial in Wood's stead, had given Chagra the maximum sentence after his conviction for running what prosecutors called one of the largest and most powerful drug rings in the Southwest.

Lawn called an FBI agent named Walter Witschardt, who handled Leavenworth, Kansas. "What's your office of preference?" Lawn said. "Find me a snitch and you've got it." Witschardt sought out Jerry Ray James, a bank robber who was the unofficial mayor of Leavenworth. James had never actually killed anyone, but he cultivated the legend that he was the meanest man in the yard. As Witschardt had suspected, Chagra had latched on to James and had boasted, according to James, that he was the one who had put the contract out on Judge Wood. James had no love for Chagra and was ready to inform on him—for a price. Lawn pulled the case files on Jerry Ray James and discovered his little secret. Since James had never committed a crime of violence, Lawn could offer him a deal. James told the FBI that Chagra claimed he had paid a Dixie Mafia hit man named Charles Harrelson $250,000 to get Wood.[8]

Lawn's team bugged cells, pay phones, even the phone in the prison chapel. The bugs in the visitation room picked up Chagra and his brother Joe plotting to break him out of jail and sell a shipment of drugs. On April 15, 1982, thirty-four and a half months after Wood was shot, a grand jury indicted Jimmy Chagra and Charles Harrelson for the murder of Wood. Joe Chagra, who acted as his brother's lawyer, and Jimmy's wife, Elizabeth, were indicted for conspiracy to murder Wood. Jimmy, Joe, and Elizabeth Chagra, Harrelson, and Harrelson's wife, Jo Ann, were indicted for conspiracy to impede the investigation. Harrelson was convicted of murder and murder conspiracy and would be sentenced to two consecutive life terms plus five years for obstruction of justice. Elizabeth Chagra, who, according to testimony, delivered the $250,000 to Harrelson's daughter, was convicted of conspiracy to commit murder and sentenced to thirty years in prison; her conviction was eventually overturned.[9] Jo Ann Harrelson was convicted of perjury and sentenced to twenty-five years in prison.

Joe Chagra pleaded guilty to murder conspiracy in exchange for a ten-year sentence. He refused to testify against his brother. Jimmy Chagra insisted on a jury trial, and his gamble paid off. The government put on nearly ninety witnesses, including Jerry Ray James, who said that Chagra had confided his guilt to him. Prosecutors played hours of tapes, including a conversation between Jimmy and Joe Chagra in the prison visitation room; in it, Joe Chagra could be heard to whisper, "They know that you [hired Harrelson] and he killed Wood." "Of course they know," replied Jimmy Chagra.[10]

Jimmy Chagra's lawyer, Oscar Goodman of Las Vegas, put up a fifteen-minute defense: he attacked James's credibility by calling to the stand a man whom James said Chagra boasted of having had killed. Goodman contended that everything Chagra had said in prison was a lie designed to enhance his image among the other inmates.[11] The jury was not allowed to hear that Joe Chagra had confessed to conspiring with his brother to murder conspiracy.

On February 7, 1983, the jury convicted Jimmy Chagra of conspiracy to obstruct justice and of marijuana trafficking but acquitted him of the murder charge. Judge Sessions sentenced Chagra to fifteen years in prison on the lesser charges.

When the verdict was announced, Lawn tried to be philosophical. "If you believe in the system, you believe in the system," he told reporters. But he confided to a friend, "I wanted to throw up."

Sessions's toughness and tenacity during the long rounds of prosecutions attracted the attention of Ed Meese, then counselor to President Reagan. In 1987, when William Webster was made CIA director, Meese chose Sessions to become the new director of the FBI.

The case advanced Lawn's career as well, but he learned never to underestimate the capricious nature of the criminal justice system. It was a lesson that played on his mind when he contemplated the Camarena case. If a sleazy and not particularly clever fellow like Jimmy Chagra had managed to defeat the mighty American justice machinery, roaring full throttle toward a single objective, how could Lawn possibly hope to see justice done in the case of the murder of Kiki Camarena?

Corruption in the Mexican law-enforcement system was the worst obstacle, but not the only one. The methods used by the Mexican police were antiquated at best, violations of basic human rights at worse.

Wiretaps were illegal in Mexico. Police agencies often installed them anyway, but the evidence they produced was inadmissible in courts of law. Mexico did not have a conspiracy law, so Mexican prosecutors did not work up the ladder, making deals with lower-level felons to get to insulated kingpins.

Instead of plea-bargaining, Mexican journalists and human rights activists charged, the Mexican police often resorted to torture to extract confessions.[12] Besides being immoral, in the opinion of Lawn and every DEA agent who served in Mexico, torture was worse than useless. A couple of days in a Mexican police station, and a man would sign just about anything, whether he had committed the crime or not. American lawmen were trained to ask questions that did not telegraph what they already knew. Details could be checked against established evidence to judge a suspect's veracity. Mexican interrogators were prone to ask leading questions, such as: "Were you at the house of Rafael Caro Quintero on the night of February 7? Did you see . . ." "And did you then go to . . ." If a person had been tortured, the answers were invariably *"Sí, Comandante."*

Or he would end up like the Jalisco chief of detectives, Gabriel González González, hemorrhaging to death in a stinking cell. Why González González had not "confessed" was an intriguing question. Surely he knew he was going to be blamed for Camarena's death anyway. Some of the American investigators thought perhaps he had things to say that the Federales did not want anyone else to hear. Or maybe he was just unlucky.

12

The Hunt for Caro Quintero

In late March, DEA agents assigned to the U.S. embassy in Costa Rica got word that Pablo Escobar had just bought a villa outside San José for $500,000 in cash. Everyone in the DEA knew who Pablo Escobar was—one of the two or three richest and most notorious cocaine traffickers in the world.

Don Clements, the DEA attaché in San José, persuaded the Costa Rican police to install a wiretap. Bad news. There were no Colombians on the premises and no one who sounded or acted like the imperious billionaire Escobar. There was only a bunch of foulmouthed Mexican thugs.

It sounded disappointing, but the information might be worth something. The Mexicans were spreading a lot of money around. They might be *pistoleros* for any of the thirty or forty Mexican drug warlords who had scattered out of Guadalajara. Costa Rica was a famous haven for fugitives from many nations. Known for its gentle people, wonderful climate, and pacifist politics (it was a democracy that had abolished its army in 1949), the country was just eight degrees north of the equator but was saved from becoming tropical jungle by the altitude, eleven hundred meters above sea level. The cool nights and gentle days made perfect conditions for growing coffee. Or for doing nothing.

A long holiday was approaching, Semana Santa, the seven days before Easter that shut down governments throughout Latin America. When DEA-Mexico did not express any interest in the villa, Clements decided this would be a fine time to go to sea. With his clipped black beard and mustache, arched eyebrows and tautly muscled torso, the fifty-year-old DEA attaché looked like a seaman and was, in fact, an old Navy man. Clements planned an outing, a photo reconnaissance mission to observe smuggling boats off Costa Rica's Pacific coast. The weather was superb; and this probably would be Clements's last excursion. He was moving to San Diego in a few weeks.

Clements, his deputy, Sandalio González, and their assistant, a former Costa Rican policeman named Victor Mullins, left San José at about four-thirty in the morning of Wednesday, April 3, and headed for the seacoast town of Puntarenas.

As they were boarding their boat, the telephone at the marina rang. It was DEA headquarters. Clements looked at his watch. It was nearly six-thirty. Low tide was at six-forty-nine. He had to be out of the harbor in fifteen minutes.

"Tell them to go to hell," Clements said to the dockhand. "I'll call them later."

No, the caller insisted, Clements had to come to the telephone. It appeared that some of the fugitives from Mexico *were* in Costa Rica. Clements had to get back to the embassy and get on the secure line. Also, there was some cable traffic he needed to see. Clements doubted it was that important, but he had no choice. He gathered his men and steamed back to San José.

Clements called headquarters. The news was that seventeen-year-old Sara Cristina Cosío Martínez was in San José. Rafael Caro Quintero was undoubtedly with her.

Caro Quintero had kidnapped Sara Cosío the previous December. The charges filed against him for masterminding the Chihuahua marijuana complex had not cramped his style, nor had the fact that he was already married. Smitten by her wild black eyes and ripening figure, he had taken her to Sonora. The Cosío family hushed up Sara's disappearance to preserve her reputation. Her father had been minister of education for the State of Jalisco; her uncle was once head of the Institutional Revolutionary party (PRI) in Mexico City. It would not do to have people say that the girl's honor had been tainted by a relationship, however unwilling, with the Sinaloan. Caro Quintero relented and returned Sara to her parents on Christmas Day, but on March 8, while hiding out from the search for Camarena's killers, Caro Quintero had ordered his henchmen to grab Sara again and bring her to him. The story got to the Mexican newspapers. The Cosío family began cooperating with the Federales. From helpful MFJP agents, the DEA was able to learn about the information the family had passed on.

Clements called Ed Heath in Mexico City. Heath suggested that Clements check with the Mexican embassy in San José. The family thought that Sara might contact someone there about her passport. If she showed up, Clements could have her tailed.

Before Clements could make the call, a cable landed on his desk. It was sketchy, just a phone number and the notation that Sara Cosío had called Mexico from this number. Working through his contacts at the telephone company and the police, Mullins ran a trace. The trail ended not far from San José, at a coffee plantation called La Quinta. It was not the house the agents had been tipped about, but it was in the same neighborhood. Two Mexicans named Jesús Félix Gutiérrez and Inés Calderón Quintero had paid $800,000 cash for it.

González and Mullins borrowed a plane and took aerial photographs. It was a magnificent place, a walled compound with a main house, a Jacuzzi, a pool, a guest house, and a cabana. Flowers of all kinds trembled in the soft breeze; endless varieties of butterflies and birds twinkled in the treetops.

The DEA men made inquiries around the neighborhood and in the city. The local people said, yes, there was a young man at the plantation who resembled the man the Americans called Rafael Caro Quintero, but the description— black hair, brown eyes, five feet ten inches tall, thirty-two years old—could apply to any number of people. More encouraging, people reported seeing a girl who fit the description of Sara Cosío. It was impossible not to notice her. The people in the neighborhood had also noticed that the newcomers had flashy clothes and fancy cars. Combined with the information about the telephone call, the DEA men figured they had enough to justify a search.

The ambassador, Francis McNeil, had just been reassigned, so Clements alerted George Jones, the chargé d'affaires. Jones asked everyone in the embassy to pitch in. Jones's order gave Clements control of the communications system and the embassy aircraft. CIA officers called their contacts in the government.

The task at hand was to convince the Costa Rican police to raid the plantation. That was not going to be easy. The Costa Rican government was legalistic in the extreme and did not take such matters casually. Furthermore, the entire government was on holiday for Semana Santa.

Clements located Benjamín Piza, the minister of public security, at his holiday place in Puntarenas. Piza was the Americans' best hope; he was a bright, urbane businessman drafted by President Luis Alberto Monge for the job of modernizing the justice system.

Piza listened for a few moments. His questions were short and to the point. Did Clements believe this man was Caro Quintero? Well, then, what did he need? Clements said that there would probably be twelve or thirteen bodyguards with machine guns. Colonel Luis Barrantes Aguilar, the commander of the police, had about fifteen men available, but they were not equipped for the kind of firefight that might break out. Clements thought the assault required the anti-terrorist team of the Departamento Inteligencia Seguridad (DIS). This highly secret commando unit had been trained in the United States and was meant to be deployed only in the most extraordinary circumstances. Most Costa Ricans did not know the unit existed.

Piza agreed to use the anti-terrorist team. Rafael Caro Quintero was no terrorist, but from the sound of him, he qualified as a national emergency. The DIS team would deployed.

Clements was impressed by Piza's political courage. "He made his decision and authorized it totally on my word and nothing else," the agent said later. "I can't think of any American in a comparable position, a mayor, a governor, our attorney general, who would ever turn American forces over to a foreign agent to direct like that, for any reason whatever. If it went wrong, it would be his head. And the retaliation would have been awful. The country would have gone bad if anything had gone wrong."

A police surveillance team was assigned to watch the house. Clements shut himself up with Colonel Barrantes Aguilar and Major Miguel Torres Sanabria, the head of the DIS anti-terrorist unit. From photographs, they made diagrams of the area. The plan they came up with was a classic SWAT team assault. They hoped it would translate to San José. The Costa Rican troops were brave men who had performed well in exercises, but most were young and had not seen battle. The commanders thought it best to over-prepare and hope for the best.

Clements briefed George Jones on the worst-case scenario. The Mexican traffickers were known for their reck-lessness. Clements thought that there would be shooting and possibly a serious incident. He explained that he had to be there, armed, and so did González and Mullins. Jones knew the Mansfield amendment as well as Clements did. It said DEA agents abroad must not be present at arrests. Clements told Jones that he would have to push the line. He understood the political risks, but he could not ask Costa Rican policemen to risk their lives and say, "Call us when it's over." "I'll do what I can to comply with all the regulations," Clements said, "but I am not going to let this go. Whatever circumstance, we are going to take him." "Do what you have to do, but do it right," Jones told Clements.

Clements marveled at the chargé's sangfroid. Jones was well aware that there might be shooting. What if it went wrong? What if innocent people or Costa Rican officers were killed? What if Sara Cosío were killed in the gunfight? "All of this would come down on two people before me," Clements realized. "George Jones and Minister Piza."

As for himself, Clements said later, "I knew what every DEA agent in the world expected of me. They expected me to go and get that son of a bitch, so even if I'd gotten in trouble with the State Department, I bet I could have stomped all over the man and Jack Lawn wasn't going to let me go down the tubes. I'd have got a disciplinary transfer to heaven—San Diego. I had everything to gain. I knew I would be the guy that took Rafael Caro Quintero. I didn't want to be the guy that *didn't* get him, but I knew if he was there, that wasn't going to happen."

At a quarter to one on April 4, the plan was ready. It was time to find a judge to issue a search warrant. Given the holiday, that was not going to be easy. The police commanders located Judge Jorge Meza. Meza was sorry, but it was against the law for him to sign a warrant in the dark of the night. It would have to wait until sunrise.

Around four o'clock the commandos began to filter into the plantation. They slid around the walls, positioned themselves within striking distance of the heavy doors, and hunkered down, waiting for the sun.

González and Mullins were pacing like bloodhounds, avid to get to the front. So was Clements, but to stay in technical compliance with the Mansfield amendment, the Americans parked their car a two- or three-minute drive from the plantation. They would use a radio to communicate with the commandos. Waiting in the rear was an ordeal.

"Look, we know what we want to do, but we've got a good team, these guys are good," Clements told his partners. "They're going to do it good, and we're going to go in a step behind. And we're going to make sure they do it right, but George has opened the door for us and we're not going to slam it in his face."

The car radio crackled. The commando leader reported that one of the peasants guarding the compound had stepped on one of the commandos. "We had to take him out," the commando said.

"Aw, shit," Clements muttered. He hoped the man was a Mexican. What he did not need was a dead Costa Rican civilian. But at this point, he thought, we'll just keep going, don't stop. There was no time to talk about it.

The man was, as Clements feared, a Costa Rican. However, he was not dead. One of the commandos whipped a garotte around his neck, shoved a gag in his mouth, and released the pressure on his windpipe, all in a matter of seconds. The poor fellow went limp with fright.

He was blindfolded, his hands cuffed behind his back, and thrown in a truck. A couple of commandos bent over him. Would he keep quiet? He nodded his head, so they removed the gag. Who lives in the house? How many Mexicans? *"Cinco,"* he gasped. *"Quatro hombres y una mujer."*

Four men and a woman. The commandos smiled. Only four men? This would not be as much of a problem as they had thought. They left their prisoner trembling and returned to the house.

Just before dawn Colonel Barrantes went to the judge's house, roused him, and drove him to the Santamarta Airport, which was just up the road from the plantation. As the first rays of the sun splashed across the hills, the judge signed the warrant. Barrantes radioed Clements in the DEA car. It was done.

González punched the button on the radio and signaled the commandos. *"Vámanos."* "Let's go." It was just after six o'clock.

The next sound was the thunder of explosives and the crash of wood as the commandos blew the doors on the compound. Gambling that everyone was sleeping in the main house, they crashed inside and fired volleys of warning shots. In less than two minutes, five men—one more than the guard had said—were blindfolded and on their bellies on the floor, their hands cuffed behind their backs. The girl was cowering in her bed. The commandos had kicked the Mexicans' guns out of their reach.

"We're in!" the commando leader radioed. The DEA agents started their car, roared the several hundred yards to the house, and sprinted the last few yards.

Hearts pounding from the run, eyes straining after more than twenty-four hours without sleep, the Americans stalked from room to room trying to determine how many people were down. Clements was desperately trying to make sure these were the right people.

Everyone was coiled like a steel spring. It had been perhaps three or four minutes from the time the team entered, and the place was under control. But it was superficial control. The commandos had not been in all the nooks and crannies—the attic, the basement if there was one. There could have been twenty more *pistoleros* in the house. The Costa Rican commanders were shouting orders, and everyone was peppering the downed men with questions.

The men on the floor all claimed to be named José or Juan or Miguel. The one in the room with the girl had the most creative name. Marcos Antonio Ríos Valenzuela, his passport said. Mark Anthony.

The Mexicans had turned the place into a dump. There were Scotch bottles everywhere, and the kitchen was littered with spoiling food. There were closets full of clothes, and new cars in the driveway. There was $40,000 in cash lying around, $150,000 in checks, and a veritable arsenal of weapons. One Colt .45-caliber pistol had a gold handle inset with diamonds. The monogram "R-1" (Rafael number one) was spelled out in rubies. Another Colt .45 bore the stamp of the DFS. An automatic weapon had the insignia of the Nicaraguan National Guard on the stock.

Clements raced about the mansion, scrutinizing the captives, trying to figure out if any of them matched the hazy snapshots that had been sent from Mexico City. Ten or twelve minutes into the search, Clements became despondent. He knew they had done everything right, but the man they were after did not seem to be there. He turned to Victor Mullins and said, "I think the son of a bitch got away."

A moment later, his radio crackled. He heard Sandy González yell, "That's him!" Clements raced toward the master bedroom.

The picture González had of Rafael Caro Quintero did not look like the man who lay prostrate on the floor. This guy had no mustache, he had gray in his hair, and his eyes were swollen. If he was really only thirty-two, he had lived a hard life.

Sara Cosío looked exactly like her pictures, voluptuous. Her mane of hair streamed about her shoulders; she had creamy skin; her eyes were clear. She sat very still, like a frightened deer.

Sandy González approached her. "*¿Cara mía, quién es?*" he said gently. "My dear one, who is that?"

"Caro Quintero," she said, so softly that González asked again, "*¿Quién?*"

"Rafael Caro Quintero," she said, louder.

"*Puta,*" the man on the floor said, and spat. "Whore." González knew he had him.

Just then, Clements burst into the bedroom. González

told him Sara's story. Even then, the older man was not totally convinced. He wanted the punk on the floor to admit it himself.

"What is your name? That's not your name, what is your name?" Clements roared. "Marcos Antonio Ríos Valenzuela," the bound man repeated stubbornly. A commando yanked his head up and put the picture sent from Mexico beside his head. Clements looked at the picture and back at the shirtless prisoner, wriggling helplessly in his designer jeans. "Yes, it's him," he said finally. "Add a mustache and it's him." The police agents stood Caro Quintero up, photographed him, and then marched him outside.

One of the commandos motioned to Clements and whispered, "Do you want to kill him here or over there?"

Clements contemplated the possibility of blowing Caro Quintero off the face of the earth. "The goddamn Mexican government will let the son of a bitch go," he muttered to himself.

But then he put such thoughts away. "Because it's wrong," he said later. "If you're a soldier—and I have been—no problem. Your job is to waste the enemy. Take him out. No soldier in the United States is ever told to take prisoners unless it's for television purposes. I've been in combat and they don't tell you to go out and see how many prisoners you can take. They tell you to go out and take out the enemy. Waste him. Kill him. Whether it's distasteful morally or whatever, that's your damn job. But a policeman's job is to use all the force necessary to effect the arrest. You are not the judge. You are not the jury. It is your job to bring him before the judge and the jury. If you live with that for twenty-some-odd years, as I have, you can't turn it off."

"We're not going to kill him," Clements told the commando. "We're going to take him and put him in prison, and I want to give him to Mexico."

It had been a perfect operation. No one had been killed, no one injured. Only one shot had been fired by the Mexicans. The commandos had performed beyond the most optimistic expectations.

Clements only hoped his luck would hold. Caro Quintero could not be extradited to the States. The DEA had never bothered to build a criminal case against him, since he did not travel to the United States to ply his trade. Clements wished his colleagues had been more foresightful. Mexico, on the other hand, had a strong case for his extradition, because there was an outstanding warrant for him as the mastermind of the Chihuahua marijuana complex.

Clements focused on getting Caro Quintero moved to Mexico before he summoned his *pistoleros* and busted himself out of jail. The Costa Rican extradition process was lengthy and risky. The local jails were flimsy affairs. On two occasions, Clements had almost completed the paperwork for the extradition of two traffickers when they escaped. Those guys were petty crooks compared with Rafael Caro Quintero, who could have fifty men in San José in a matter of days. The jail would never withstand an assault from a force of that size.

Also, although corruption was not as big a problem in Costa Rica as it was in Mexico, it was certainly possible that Caro Quintero could bribe some prison guards. Possible, hell, Clements thought, Caro Quintero had enough money to pay the national debt. And there was always the chance that Rafael would simply hire a smart lawyer to tie his case up in the Costa Rican courts. The longer he stalled, the more men he could infiltrate into San José and the more officials he could suborn. Rafael was being guarded by the commando unit, but that would not last.

No, Clements decided, he could not wait for an extradition order. Caro Quintero would have to be deported. There was only one problem. Costa Rica had stopped deporting criminals a few years back, when a judicial opinion handed down in a civil suit brought by a fugitive from the FBI ruled the practice illegal.

Clements knew from painful personal experience the legal problems he was facing. When he first arrived in Costa Rica, Clements had gotten in trouble for attempting to arrange a deportation without making use of the extradition process. He had done this on a number of occasions in Mexico: he would make friends with an immigration officer,

point out a crook, explain that he was an illegal alien, and
the Mexican would usually say, Sure, take him, and the next
thing the guy knew, he was looking at sunny San Diego. In
Costa Rica, Clements made more formal arrangements with
senior police officials to deport a fugitive but did not go
through the court system, which infuriated nationalists and
very nearly caused him to be declared persona non grata.
He was rescued by Ambassador McNeil, who persuaded
Costa Rican authorities that Clements did not know any
better and the suspect was a truly awful character. He started
calling Benjamín Piza. In the next twenty-four hours, he
would call Piza perhaps thirty times. At first, Piza said he
saw no way he could do it legally. Clements agreed but
pressed him: "We've got to do it. Will you take a chance
this time?" Would Piza violate the law this once? He would
not. He reminded Clements that he was the protector of
the public security.

"Well, speaking of public security, you know this guy's
a real threat to the country."

"Why?"

"Well, I think there'll be a rescue attempt."

"Well, if he's a threat," Piza said deliberately, "his presence is a threat to the public security of my country. Then
I can deport him on that ground by my authority. All I need
is the acquiescence of the president."

National security. Every nation made exceptions to ordinary legal process for national security threats. Clements
thought Piza was brilliant. Now, if the president would
agree, everything would be in order. Clements rang off and
waited for what seemed like an eternity. The telephone
rang. Piza was on the line. President Monge had agreed.
"I'm going to deport him to Mexico if they want to take
him," Piza said.

Clements called the DEA office in Mexico City. How
fast could the Federales send a team?

MFJP Comandante Florentino Ventura showed up the
next day with two Mexican government airplanes and a
group of Federales armed to the teeth. By Friday afternoon,
Rafael Caro Quintero was in a secure prison in Mexico City.

The Costa Rican police threw in a bonus. A few hours

after Caro Quintero was captured, three more Mexicans showed up at his villa and were detained by the narcotics officers searching the place. They were Juan Carlos Campero Villanueva, a young woman named Violeta Estrada, and a man who was wanted by the Federales as badly as the DEA wanted Rafael Caro Quintero. He was José Contreras Subias, who had made a reputation as the meanest man on the border.

In the late 1970s, Contreras Subias took residence in Tucson, where he proceeded to terrorize the community. (A picture of José from this period depicted him posing in a Nogales brothel, an automatic pistol stuck in his belt, like a modern-day Pancho Villa.) DEA agents in Arizona classified Contreras Subias as one of the biggest cocaine and marijuana smugglers on the Arizona–Sonora line, but they could not manage to keep him locked up.

In November 1984, Contreras Subias was in the headlines again, this time for a particularly heinous attack upon two young Federales. The story DEA agents in San Diego pieced together went like this: Some MFJP agents from Tijuana were in Baja California looking for a warehouse of contraband consumer goods, when they stumbled onto nine tons of marijuana. They reported the finding to their *comandante*. What they did not know was that the warehouse belonged to Contreras Subias. Contreras Subias flew into a rage and lured two of the agents to the warehouse. When they showed up, the doper opened up on them with a machine gun. He threw them both in a car and had it driven down into Baja California, doused with gasoline, and torched.

One of the MFJP agents was dead. His partner, though badly wounded, was able to crawl away from the blazing vehicle. Some Mexican soldiers garrisoned nearby spotted the flames, rescued the wounded Federale, and began a sweep of the area. Within a few days, the Army had found more than one hundred tons of marijuana and had arrested fifty people. It was the biggest seizure ever recorded in Baja California del Norte. José Contreras Subias vanished.

On the flight from San José to Mexico City, Contreras Subias glowered at Ventura's men as if memorizing their faces. "Eyes that kill," one of the men said, shuddering as he recalled the tense flight.

When the plane landed, Contreras Subias was packed off to the federal prison in Tijuana. Sara Cosío was delivered into the arms of her frantic parents.

Weeping for his lost love, whom he had forgiven for betraying him, Rafael Caro Quintero was taken away to the Reclusorio del Norte, a federal prison in the slums of Mexico City.

José Rojo Coronado, a flamboyant Mexico City attorney who had represented a number of leftist guerrillas and students, announced he wanted to defend the imprisoned trafficker on grounds that he had been deported illegally.

"They have violated the Constitution in this case," Rojo announced. "The Constitution," he added cynically, "is like a señorita who is violated daily but according to her father she is still a virgin."

The motto of the Reclusorio del Norte penitentiary is *"La justicia no es castigo."* "Justice is not punishment." Prison officials passed out matchbooks thus inscribed. This was supposed to mean that prisoners would not be tortured. In practice, it meant that inmates were treated according to their ability to pay. The poorest inmates made do with gruel, but those with means had meals and strong drink brought in. Visits with wives and girlfriends were permitted. Suites could be had, and many other luxuries.

After some days in this setting, inmate Rafael Caro Quintero felt himself up to granting an interview to a group of journalists. Actually it was more like an audience. Rafael played the baffled country boy, speaking of his love for the campesinos, "a pure and noble people, as I am."

"I am sure of myself," he said. "I feel content with the time I have lived and that I am living still. I have no enemies. There is no one who wants to kill me. My heart is for all the world."

Did he himself use drugs? "No! None!" he said. "The only thing that I can say to young people is to withdraw from drugs."

Then he lapsed into sentimental musings.

"I have one weakness," he said. "Women and gold. I love all women, because I was born of a woman. The narcotics trade pleases me. And it pleases me to help the poor people, because I suffered much as a kid. . . . I have already retired from business, and my life, I cannot speak of it because I have suffered much."[1]

Caro Quintero was able to buy many things that made prison life tolerable—a videotape player, good food, Scotch. In late summer, a DEA informant passed word that Caro Quintero had thrown a lavishly catered party, complete with mariachi band.

The young trafficker's fame spread throughout Mexico. Plays were written about Caro Quintero and movie companies filmed his life story. DEA agents were the villains. Cantinas resounded with *corridos,* ballads, honoring Caro Quintero as Robin Hood, David defying Goliath. He had become a symbol of the courageous, clever Mexican defying the Colossus of the North. A typical *corrido,* this one by Los Invasores de Nuevo León, commemorated his capture.

> *Born in Sinaloa*
> *The kind that are not born every day*
> *And that don't give up.*
> *For killing a policeman. . . .*
> *Today he is found arraigned*
> *They say they want to judge him,*
> *The Americans over there in their lairs.*
> *They take him to make our souls sweat.*

Don Clements got several reproachful calls from other agents, who said such things as "I can't believe you didn't kill that son of a bitch. Knowing you, I can't believe you."

Months later, sitting at his small desk in a windowless room in DEA's squat office on the wrong side of San Diego, Clements pondered the choice he had made.

See I'm the one they figured would do it. There are probably DEA agents right now who are cussing me every day for not wasting him. They're probably calling me a coward, a wimp, a sissy, or whatever. I don't worry about that because they weren't there. And had they been there, they probably

would have done exactly the same as I did, because they are
police officers, they are not murderers. You see, it would
have still been murder. Am I capable of it? Yes. Absolutely.
But I have a wife, I have a son. Again, I had a commitment
to the chargé d'affaires, George Jones. I had a commitment
to Benjamín Piza. I never forgot that commitment. I couldn't
forget that commitment. I knew that had I blown him away,
I'd be a hero right now. As it is, I'm just a guy doing a job,
but had I blown him away, I'd be a hero. Even though there
would have been people saying, Oh, we lost the intelligence,
we lost that and we lost this, they'd still say goddamn, he
took him out.

13

Confessions

On the day Caro Quintero was brought to court to be charged, the clerk took four hours to read his "confession." Mexican authorities said that Caro Quintero had admitted to financing the huge Chihuahua marijuana complex, bribing hundreds of officials, including local, state, and federal policemen, DFS officers, Customs officers, members of the attorney general's drug eradication group, and Army officers; supposedly, he had given two hundred new Fords to law-enforcement officials throughout Mexico.

The most senior officer implicated by the statements made available to reporters was Primer Comandante Jorge Armando Pavón Reyes of the Mexican Federal Judicial Police. Caro Quintero allegedly admitted paying Pavón 60,000 pesos to let his jet leave the Guadalajara airport on February 9, two days after Kiki Camarena was abducted.

When he appeared in court to be charged, Caro Quintero denied that he had done the things recorded in the "confession." "They kicked it out of me," he said. "The signature is mine, but the things it says are false."[1] Motioning to the reporters from the glass cage in which he was displayed like a captive bobcat, the trafficker unbuttoned his shirt and displayed scars on his shoulders, back, and arms, which he said were caused by police beatings. Although his face was haggard, the wounds looked old.

The one thing to which Caro Quintero had not "confessed" was the murder of Kiki Camarena. But another "confession," from the eldest of the Guadalajara cartel, blamed the agent's murder on Caro Quintero and no other.

This statement came from Caro Quintero's old friend and partner Ernesto Fonseca.

On April 7, 1985, the Army had stumbled upon Ernesto Fonseca in the Pacific beach resort of Puerto Vallarta. His capture was a fluke. During holidays like Semana Santa, the Easter week celebration, extra police details, called preventive police, patrolled the tourist zone in Puerto Vallarta to discourage muggers and pickpockets. According to DEA agents, on the Monday after Easter, when some louts got into a barroom brawl in the village, the preventive police were summoned. They chased the debauched rustics to a villa. Seeing gun barrels emerge from the windows of the house, the cops beat a strategic retreat and called in soldiers from a nearby Army post. The soldiers stormed the place and captured two dozen men, along with an array of weaponry from machine guns to grenade launchers. It was a foul and bleary-eyed lot, which, for all its artillery, had not managed to kill a single raider. To their surprise, the soldiers discovered that they had Ernesto Fonseca himself. A fortune in gold and baubles was strewn about the place. Fonseca, like Caro Quintero, had a .45 caliber semiautomatic pistol plated with gold and studded with diamonds.

Ernesto Fonseca's "confession" said that Caro Quintero thought Camarena was responsible for the loss of the Chihuahua plantations and had suggested having Camarena interrogated in order to get the names of his informants. According to Fonseca's "confession," Fonseca had agreed but had admonished his young partner not to hurt the American, only to scare him.

The rest of the confession went like this: Fonseca saw the agent sitting on a bed, his arms bound behind him, at Caro Quintero's house on the afternoon of February 7, the day of the abduction. Too drunk to speak to the agent, Fonseca had wandered off and fallen asleep. The next day, he returned to find the agent dying. Fonseca flew into a rage and bellowed, "You are a pig. You don't have a brain. . . . Camarena is an agent of the United States. Idiot!" He slapped Caro Quintero's face and stomped off, snarling,

"You made the baby. Now you live with it."[2] Fonseca's confession said that he did not see Camarena killed but that he later heard that the agent had been buried in the Bosques de Primavera, a woodland preserve twelve miles northwest of Guadalajara.

Appearing in court, Fonseca, like Caro Quintero, charged that he had been beaten and subjected to the torture the police call *la tehuacán*, in which carbonated mineral water (like the popular Tehuacán brand), laced with the juice of chili peppers, was forced up the victim's nose while his mouth was gagged shut. If he had indeed endured this ordeal, Fonseca had not lost his sense of humor. He winked at the reporters and clowned with a pair of dark glasses when the flashbulbs of the photographers went off. As he left the hearing room, according to one account, the old *bandido* made a V with his fingers and exclaimed, *"Amor y paz."* "Love and peace."[3]

From the DEA's point of view, the most useful "confession" came from Samuel Ramírez Razo, a forty-nine-year-old former DFS officer who was one of Fonseca's top *pistoleros*. Mexican officials said that Ramírez Razo, nicknamed "El Samy," had admitted to kidnapping Kiki Camarena. His "confession" told this story:

On the morning of February 7, Ernesto Fonseca ordered El Samy to go with José Luis Gallardo Parra ("El Güero") and to pick up Kiki Camarena at the American consulate. Gallardo Parra drove the car, a late-model beige Volkswagen Atlantic. The others in the car were two Jalisco state police officers, Gerardo Torres Lepe and Víctor Manuel López Razón, and a *pistolero* for Caro Quintero nicknamed "El Chino."

Gallardo Parra parked the car across from the consulate and waited. When Camarena came out of the consulate at about ten minutes after two, the men piled out of the Volkswagen and approached him. "Federal Security," El Samy said, flashing a DFS credential. "The *comandante* wants to see you." Camarena said okay but he would have to tell his office. El Güero pulled a gun; Camarena yielded, walked to the Atlantic, and got into the back seat. El Samy took off his jacket, pulled it over Camarena's head, and drove away.

The *pistoleros* delivered the agent to a house where Caro Quintero waited. At that point, Caro Quintero's men took control of the American. After a while, Ramírez saw Ernesto Fonseca arrive with a Guadalajara lawyer-turned-gangster named Javier Barba Hernández. Fonseca and Barba Hernández spoke briefly with Caro Quintero. Shortly afterward, Fonseca and Barba Hernández left. El Samy went with them and knew nothing more about how Camarena was actually killed.

All the "confessions" were self-serving, but the consensus of the DEA agents was that there were grains of truth in them. The problem was sorting out fact from fiction. The stories were full of gaps and contradictions; the interrogators had clearly been uninterested in getting the whole story. There was nothing about how or exactly when Kiki had been killed. Who had interrogated him? Who killed him? Who buried him? Who unburied him? Who threw his body on the roadside? Who wrote the note that led the Federales to the Bravo ranch? None of these questions were asked or answered. There was no attempt to explain how the Bravo ranch massacre unfolded. There were no indications that questions had been asked about the pilot Alfredo Zavala. Most significant, where was Miguel Angel Félix Gallardo during all these events? None of the suspects mentioned his presence. The Americans found it impossible to believe that the *padrino* had nothing to do with the murder. Félix Gallardo had as strong a motive as Caro Quintero to interrogate the agent. And why had Camarena's photograph been found at Félix Gallardo's house?

The portions of the "confessions" that touched on high-level corruption might be read as an indictment of de la Madrid's "moral renovation" campaign. But on closer reading, the damage to the central power structure of Mexico was limited. No cabinet ministers were named, nor were the highest-ranking officials of the MFJP and the Mexican Attorney General's Office tainted. The agency most heavily damaged by the fallout from the "confessions" was the DFS, but this had to be read in the context of Mexico City's bureaucratic antagonisms: the MFJP and the DFS were the bitterest of enemies. In Guadalajara, Federales and DFS agents thought nothing of settling quarrels by shooting at each other on the street.

Most DEA agents were willing to accept the MFJP thesis that Rafael Caro Quintero and Ernesto Fonseca were major players in the murder. Jaime Kuykendall did not even accept that much of the story. He believed that the "confessions" might be largely fictional, designed to convince the Americans that the crime was the impulsive act of traffickers. He believed that the crime was organized with care and was carried out by government officials, most probably in the DFS, possibly also in the MFJP, who were worried about Camarena's knowledge of drug-related corruption. Kuykendall thought it possible that Caro Quintero and Fonseca were being hung out to dry because they were the usual suspects. Kuykendall had no proof, but he said, "If it had been the traffickers, we would have known about it. We had *very* good informants."

On the other hand, he could not explain why the police forces would have kidnapped a DEA agent for interrogation. The MFJP already had access to a great deal of the information DEA agents developed. As Ed Heath himself said, "If [federal police officials] here in Mexico City wanted to know what DEA had in mind, they would have come to the embassy." DFS officers in the central command had more subtle ways of gathering intelligence as well, through liaison with the embassy and by means of wiretaps.

Heath believed that the missing elements of the confessions meant that the police were protecting politicians and legitimate businessmen who had been taking money from the traffickers. "Who had more to lose if the DEA continued its investigations?" he said. "The traffickers are able to live with their losses. Other people would lose their reputations, their status in the community. . . . What they wanted to find out was what DEA knew. I think we're looking at a group of people who had been hidden behind the skirts of the traffickers."

Heath's theory did not explain one thing: why would

people in the power structure believe that they had anything
to lose because of the American government's actions? To
be sure, the drug cartel had lost a great deal of money
because of the DEA, but the U.S. embassy had not been
threatening to go public with what the DEA knew about
the traffickers' connections in the political and business
communities.

The Mexican newspapers could not get enough of the story.
As usual, most of the credit for the crackdown went to
Mexican authorities. "Mexican police in the last five days
have achieved what seemed impossible," a newscaster for
the government television station said.

Ambassador John Gavin told reporters that he was glad
to see that the allegations of corruption were finally being
taken seriously by the Mexican press. "It's amusing, if not
ironic," Gavin said archly, "to note that sources in some of
the same local media and papers which were attacking us
are now saying that, indeed, we knew what we were talking
about."

The reaction of the Mexican government was far short
of the Watergate-style investigation that Americans had
grown to expect. If two Mafia chieftains had confessed to
bribing the head of the CIA and hundreds of intelligence
officers and federal agents, special prosecutors would have
been appointed, informants enlisted, wiretaps installed,
bank accounts audited, records subpoenaed, Congressional
inquiries launched. Mexican officials had no intention of
putting their own institutions through that kind of agony.

Allowed to sit in on a few interrogations, Heath saw that
when a suspect began to talk about officials who had taken
bribes, the interrogators did not write down his statements.
"When they're writing a report, allegations regarding corruption and payoffs don't go in there," he said. "I report
the allegations separately, and I tell them those are my rules.
I say, What are you going to do about this statement? He
made a statement under oath that he was paying someone
ten thousand pesos a month. They say, Well, we're going
to take care of it the Mexican way."

Manuel Bartlett Díaz, the minister of the interior, shook

up the DFS, firing more than four hundred DFS officers and about twenty *comandantes*, including the powerful zone commanders who presided over the Mexican–American border: Daniel Acuña Figueroa of Mexicali, Rafael Aguilar Guajardo of Ciudad Juárez, and Rafael Chao López of Monterrey. Bartlett reorganized the DFS and its brother agency, the Bureau of Political and Social Investigations, into a new Directorate of National Security.[4]

Firing was the worst punishment most disgraced officers faced. The only Mexican police officer who was actually arrested at this time was MFJP Comandante Armando Pavón Reyes, whose behavior at the Guadalajara airport had received international publicity.

One high official who left the government under mysterious circumstances was José Antonio Zorrilla Pérez, who had been director of the DFS at the time of the Camarena kidnapping. According to reports in the Mexican and U.S. press, Zorrilla left the DFS on February 28, 1985, and announced as a candidate for the Chamber of Deputies from the state of Hidalgo. Soon after Caro Quintero was returned to Mexico, Jack Lawn received a call from Ed Heath, who reported that Zorrilla was among the officials whom Caro Quintero had confessed to paying off. But when Caro Quintero's "confession" was read at his arraignment, Zorrilla's name was not mentioned.

On May 25, according to a report in the *Los Angeles Times*, Zorrilla abruptly resigned as a candidate and left the country on an Iberia Airlines flight headed for Madrid.[5] John Gavin asked the CIA to trace Zorrilla's movements and was told that Zorrilla did not get off in Spain. "Apparently," the ambassador fumed, "he was *assisted* in eluding us."

The first story suggesting that Zorrilla had been linked to the traffickers appeared in the June 3, 1985, edition of *Proceso* magazine. In an article by Fernando Ortega Pizarro, headlined "According to the DEA, Zorrilla Is the Key to Unraveling the Narcotics Trade in Mexico," an unnamed DEA official was quoted as saying that Zorrilla's signature was on the DFS credentials carried by Rafael Caro Quintero and other traffickers and that the DFS chief had shared in the profits of the drug trade. The *Proceso* article caused a furor in Mexico City, for no charges had been or would be lodged against the former DFS chief.

The article caused great chagrin within the U.S. embassy as well, because neither DEA nor the intelligence agencies could back them up with hard evidence. Gavin issued a statement denying that anyone in the embassy had given an interview to *Proceso* and asserting that DEA "had no proof that Zorrilla was involved in the drug trade." *Proceso* then revealed that the source of the story was Ed Heath. Heath incurred Gavin's wrath by admitting, belatedly, that he had indeed talked to the Mexican reporter. "It was not our finest hour," said a flustered Gavin aide. Gavin decreed no one in DEA in Mexico should talk to any reporter again without his express consent.

Was the substance of the article true? Mexican government officials flatly denied that the DFS credentials to which the article referred existed. "It is a myth," Deputy Attorney General José Maria Ortega Padilla said. "We have searched for these credentials, and we don't have them in our files." DEA agents who were present when Caro Quintero was arrested in Costa Rica said that they did not see any DFS credentials among his possessions. Ed Heath stuck to his story: he said he had seen Rafael Caro Quintero's DFS credentials and they bore Zorrilla's signature. He had not made a copy or photograph. He suggested that Ortega Padilla could not find the credentials because they had been destroyed soon after Caro Quintero was jailed because they were "an embarrassment" to the Mexican government. Heath acknowledged, however, that he did not know whether Zorrilla had personally issued the credentials to Caro Quintero. He conceded that the signature could have been made by a machine. The point was, he said, "obviously this man could answer a lot of questions, had they taken the time out to talk to him."

"A lot of things get into the political fiber of this country," Heath observed. "They say, for what purpose but to satisfy the curiosity of the United States? They can't quite understand what all this means to us. They got the body, they've got the confessions. They don't understand conspiracy investigations in the United States which involve individuals three, four times removed. We always want to know who's really behind this. They may have an interest in it, but they have so many things to worry about. They're up to their eyeballs in alligators."

The U.S. officials who were still frustrated with the Mexicans' handling of the Camarena murder investigation had one small opening for pursuing their grievances: an American grand jury. The murder of Kiki Camarena was a violation of the U.S. laws against kidnapping, killing, or attempting to kill American officials anywhere in the world. DEA and Justice officials decided to take the case to a federal grand jury in Washington. To coordinate the gathering and analysis of evidence, Jack Lawn set up a task force within DEA headquarters. Agents assigned to the team would perform like homicide detectives, sorting through the masses of data gathered by Kuykendall, Wallace, Miley, and other agents who had been in Guadalajara during the time Camarena was missing. There were piles of cables from the DEA agents in the border offices, South America and Europe, where Félix Gallardo and his partner, Matta, had cocaine connections, and more reports and cables from the FBI and Customs.

Lawn's choice for chief of the task force was Bill Coonce. "Don't worry about politics or diplomacy," Lawn told Coonce. "Just get the facts."

If Lawn wanted someone who worshiped facts, he had his man. A garrulous, edgy Arizonian, Coonce was a meticulous shoe-leather detective who would do battle at the slightest hint of politics. Coonce was known for his writing skills, his incisive analysis, and his fierce integrity, no matter how influential his target. When Lawn looked for someone who was not afraid of offending big shots, everyone recommended Coonce. His jokes offended his own superiors regularly.

To fill out the task force, Coonce tapped Matty Maher and Bill Mockler. Maher, a former professional baseball player whose flattop, basset eyes, and ribald humor disguised a piercing intellect, would pound through steel to get what he wanted. Mockler was a street-wise New Yorker with a phenomenal memory. Two DEA intelligence analysts, two FBI agents, and some FBI laboratory technicians completed the team.

They called the project Operation Leyenda. They took the name from a cable that described a meeting of the traffickers in December 1984. According to an informant, one crook said to another, "What is happening with *el leyenda?*" The translator thought that because *ley* means "law," *leyenda* meant "lawman." Coonce and his buddies spoke only gutter Spanish and thought the conversation referred to Camarena. Actually, *leyenda* means "legend." Evidently the traffickers had been talking about somebody who considered himself a great outlaw. When Coonce found out what the title really meant, he kept the name. "Operation Legend" fit the black humor of their situation.

Shortly after five o'clock on the afternoon of Friday, April 12, two months after Camarena had been killed, Coonce flew to Guadalajara with four FBI evidence specialists. They planned to take soil samples from the Bravo ranch and the Bosques de Primavera. At the airport, DEA agent Ralph Arroyo met them with terrible news. The day before, the Federales had found the house where Camarena was probably tortured. They had managed to keep the DEA agents away until they swept the place clean.

Arroyo explained that the house, at 881 Calle Lope de Vega, had not been on the list of known residences of Caro Quintero. The trafficker had acquired it very recently, through a couple of businessmen who handled his investments. The Federales must have found out about it from some of the men in jail. Arroyo said that late the previous night, two female "chemists" had arrived from Mexico City and had gone to the house with MFJP Comandante Silviano Brusolo. The next morning, Arroyo and Kuykendall had picked up hints that something was going on, but could not reach Brusolo. At around two-thirty in the afternoon, DEA agents in Mexico City came through with the address. Kuykendall and Wallace dashed to the house. Arroyo went to the MFJP office. There he saw the chemists with a plastic bag that appeared to contain cloth or clothing of some sort, papers, and cord—evidently material that had been gathered at the house. Arroyo heard the women ask Brusolo for money or tickets so they could return to Mexico City. Brusolo had made some effort to be cooperative, asking the women to stay to talk to the FBI lab technicians, but the women refused, saying they had instructions to return to Mexico City immediately.

Arroyo took Coonce and the FBI men to the Calle Lope de Vega address. It was a walled modern villa with six bedrooms, a guest house, a tennis court, a swimming pool, and two patios. The rooms were freshly carpeted and painted, and all the furniture, including the pictures on the wall, were sparklingly new. Behind the house, next to the tennis court, the agents saw a 1985 beige Volkswagen Atlantic without plates. It matched the description of the car seen by one eyewitness to the kidnapping.

The walls had been washed, the floors picked clean, but the FBI agents worked until nine o'clock that night, taking fiber samples of the carpets, soil samples, dusting for fingerprints, making photographs. They returned the next morning. At that time, FBI agent Ron Rawalt noticed a glint of light metal underneath a drain vent grating near the tennis court. He pulled up the drain and found a Jalisco state license plate, broken in two.

As FBI fingerprint specialist Carl Collins lifted a partial print from the tag, the Federales called Comandante Brusolo, who arrived within minutes. Brusolo was not so cooperative now. He took the plate away and put it in the trunk of the Volkswagen. One of the DEA agents overheard Brusolo order his subordinates to pay more attention to what the Americans were doing and to keep their eyes on them at all times.

The American agents asked the Federales to run a trace on the Volkswagen and the tag through the motor vehicle registry. The Mexicans reported back that the Volkswagen had been purchased by a "Martín Sauzeda." The tag in the drain also traced back to a "Martín Sauzeda," but there was no one by that name at the address "Sauzeda" had given. The name was clearly phony.

If the eyewitness to Camarena's abduction was right, the tag found in the drain did not belong on the Volkswagen. The witness remembered that the tag on the Volkswagen had two letters, then a "B," then the numerals 117. The tag in the drain was JEM 786. That was very close to the tag the second witness thought he had seen on a black Gran Marquis in which two men were beating a third man with pipes.

Two weeks earlier, DEA agents had found just such a black Gran Marquis hidden behind a concrete-block wall in a house owned by a man whose daughter was the common-law wife of César Fonseca, a nephew of Ernesto Fonseca. The man had said that the car had been hidden there on instructions from Ernesto Fonseca. The Gran Marquis was traced to a Ford dealership owned by Rafael Caro Quintero. Through this dealership, Caro Quintero had obtained the hundreds of cars that he had given to police officials, friends, and relatives. This particular Gran Marquis had a police siren.

An FBI forensic team lifted a number of fingerprints from the Gran Marquis. They found dried human blood in the right rear floormat and recovered hairs from the front and back seats.

Coonce had a lot of questions about the Gran Marquis. For some reason, the Federales did not want to talk about it. During the questioning of El Samy Ramírez, the interrogators did not ask about the Gran Marquis, only about the beige Volkswagen. Coonce theorized that the Gran Marquis had been driven by a prominent policeman, or maybe a trafficker who liked to pose as a policeman.

The swimming pool at the villa was murky and full of junk. The DEA agents told the Federales they wanted to have the pool drained so that the FBI evidence team could look for things that might have been discarded. Assuming that this would take a few days to arrange, they left the villa and went out to the Bosques de Primavera and the Bravo ranch to collect soil samples. When they returned to the house, they found that the Federales had drained, cleaned, and refilled the pool. The Mexican agents assured them that nothing of interest had been found. FBI technician Carl

Collins went to work anyway, crawling about the edge of the pool, retrieving cigarette butts and bits of cord and taking dirt samples.

Back in Washington, the FBI evidence specialists determined that two hairs found in the beige Volkswagen Atlantic matched Camarena's hair. One hair looked as if it had been yanked out. Two more hairs matching Camarena's were found in the guest house of the Lope de Vega villa. A Kleenex tissue in the trunk of the Volkswagen Atlantic had blood on it. The FBI lab subsequently determined that carpet fibers taken from the guest house's living room and dining room matched fibers taken from Zavala's clothes.[6]

But the FBI lab also found hairs in the black Gran Marquis that matched Kiki Camarena's. The citizen who claimed to have seen a man being beaten with a pipe in the back seat of a black Gran Marquis thought he had seen the car pass by his place of business at about three-forty-five in the afternoon. That story did not square with the account of El Samy Ramírez, who said the kidnappers had taken Camarena straight to Caro Quintero's house. The witness's place was on the other side of town from the Lope de Vega house, but it was near the Bosques de Primavera, where Fonseca and Ramírez said they thought Camarena had been buried. Finally, the witness said he had seen dealership stickers on the Gran Marquis. His description of the stickers matched precisely those on the beige Volkswagen Atlantic but not on the black Gran Marquis.

The witness could have been completely wrong. But then why would he say that some men had threatened his life if he talked? Why would he have come forward, facing such a risk? Obviously, he had picked up some details that seemed real. Mulling over these riddles, Coonce and Maher concluded that the witness might have confused his days and scrambled his facts. He might have seen this incident the day *after* the kidnapping. And he might have seen someone being beaten *next* to the Gran Marquis instead of inside it. The business about the dealership stickers could be explained by the theory that the witness had seen a convoy of cars, both the Volkswagen and the Gran Marquis, and was confused about which car had which plates and stickers. Suppose the investigators accepted El Samy's story that Kiki was taken directly to the Lope de Vega house in the Volkswagen Atlantic. If Kiki died the next afternoon, as the pathologist thought, he could have been transported to the burial site past the witness's shop in the Gran Marquis.

The answer to the confusion about the license plates seemed obvious. The minute the DEA agents had those tag numbers, they had given them to the Federales, and the word went out on the police radio to stop any car with similar tags. It was logical that the traffickers would have gotten rid of the plates.

Whatever the truth was, it was not in the trash that had been left for the Americans to find. They had to get someone in the inner circle of the Guadalajara cartel to talk and to talk directly to the DEA and the grand jury. Besides Caro Quintero and Fonseca, the list included Miguel Angel Félix Gallardo and his partner in the cocaine business, the Honduran cocaine chemist Juan Matta Ballesteros; Caro Quintero's fellow marijuana traffickers Manuel Salcido Uzeta, a.k.a. Cochi Loco, of Mazatlán, and René Verdugo, of Mexicali; and Francisco "Paco" Tejeda Jaramillo, who, according to DEA informants, was possibly a DFS agent and was one of Caro Quintero's top enforcers and money couriers.

DEA agents in Europe and South America were working hard to find Matta Ballesteros. Unlike Caro Quintero, Matta had been formally charged with federal trafficking offenses in the United States, and a warrant had been issued for his arrest. If the DEA could locate him anyplace but his native land, Honduras, there was a good chance of getting him extradited to the United States.

Matta had been reported in Spain, but there were signs he might be heading to Colombia. Soon after Matta vanished from Mexico City, his wife had been sighted getting off a plane at Bogotá International Airport. She had been met by a former Colombian government official. DEA agents in Colombia began tracking her, hoping that she would be joined by her husband. They were confident that Colombian National Police would arrest Matta if they could find him.

On April 29, the DEA agents traced Matta to a house in the resort city of Cartagena. When the Colombian police raided the place, according to the DEA, the Honduran coolly offered them the equivalent of $435,000 to leave him in peace. The Colombian officers shoved aside his money and took him off to jail. Within hours, the U.S. Justice Department presented the Betancur government with a diplomatic note requesting Matta's extradition.

Although the Colombian authorities were glad to make the arrest, they were not willing to take the political risk of deporting Matta to the United States without going through the formal extradition process. They jailed him in La Picota prison in Bogotá to await the decision of the Colombian courts.

DEA's next target was Paco Tejeda, allegedly Caro Quintero's top *pistolero*. DEA informants in Texas and California said that Tejeda, thirty-three, had been at the Lope de Vega house at the time Camarena was supposed to have been there. Tejeda hung out in Tijuana, where the DEA agents had an extensive network of sources. Agents in San Diego put out the word in the informant network that whoever delivered Paco would be well rewarded.

14

The Secrets of Primavera Park

On June 19, 1985, the Federales in Guadalajara told the DEA that they had discovered the bones of two gringos in an isolated section of the Bosques de Primavera, outside Guadalajara.

Dental records sent from the United States would soon confirm what almost everyone, including the families, believed. The bones were the remains of the two young Americans who had disappeared in Guadalajara on January 30, exactly eight days before Kiki Camarena was kidnapped. One was John Walker, thirty-six, a disabled Vietnam veteran who had been living in Guadalajara working on a novel, and the other was Alberto Radelat, thirty-two, a dental student from Fort Worth.

Through a twist of fate, the grieving families of the two missing men owed the discovery of their bodies to DEA agents who were searching for the truth about the murder of Kiki Camarena and Alfredo Zavala. The American agents had not succeeded in their own mission, but one mystery had unlocked another.

In early June, DEA agents in San Diego had received a tip that Paco Tejeda, reputed to be Caro Quintero's best enforcer, was holed up in a house in Tijuana. At DEA's request, the MFJP sent a *comandante* from Mexico City to Tijuana to bring Tejeda back. On the morning of June 6, the *comandante* and his men burst into Tejeda's Tijuana hideout and yanked him from a woman's embrace. Tejeda was carrying DFS credentials. He claimed he was no longer a security policeman, but according to DEA agents who worked with the Federales on the case, the DFS *comandante* in Tijuana showed up at the MFJP Tijuana office and demanded to know why one of his agents was being held. The Federales rebuffed the DFS officer and took Tejeda to Mexico City. The next day, his interrogation began.

DEA attaché Ed Heath and another American agent, Bobby Castillo, were allowed to sit in on the initial session. Tejeda did not want to talk, so the Federales summoned El Samy Ramírez, the Fonseca *pistolero* who had admitted kidnapping Camarena and taking him to Caro Quintero's house on Calle Lope de Vega. Questioned again, Ramírez said that he and the other members of the kidnap team delivered Camarena into the hands of Caro Quintero and four of his *pistoleros,* one of whom he knew only as "Paco." When Tejeda was brought into the interrogation room, Ramírez said, "That's him, that's Paco." Ramírez added that he had been told that Paco and another Caro Quintero thug called "El Chavo," "the Kid," had stood guard over Camarena while he was in the house.

At first, Tejeda denied being involved in Camarena's murder. After a couple of days in the hands of the Federales, he still denied killing the agent, but he was considerably more talkative about what he had seen at the house on Lope de Vega. He suggested that Camarena had been murdered by the Félix Gallardo gang. He claimed to have seen Camarena being beaten and kicked by three of Félix Gallardo's men, "Cuco," "El Chango," and "La Calaca," and by El Chavo and a fellow named Carlos Martínez, who worked for Caro Quintero. Tejeda said that he saw Miguel Angel Félix Gallardo himself come to the house that evening. Later in the night, he said, he saw Cuco and El Chango again striking the DEA agent while he was being interrogated.

Tejeda said that the next day, he was summoned from his bedroom by El Chango. He said he followed El Chango into the bedroom and saw Camarena semiconscious, blindfolded and bound, dressed in undershorts. He said the agent was mumbling in Spanish, asking not to be killed, saying that he had a family. Tejeda said that he and El Chango dragged the agent out of the house and shoved him into the trunk of a light-blue Dodge Dart. Tejeda said the last he saw of the American agent was when Félix Gallardo's *pis-*

toleros El Chango, Cuco, and another guy, called "Flaco," got into the car and drove away.

Tejeda said that he and fourteen other men accompanied Caro Quintero to the airport the next day, which was Saturday, February 9. From there, he said, he flew with Caro Quintero to Caborca, Sonora.

To the disappointment of the DEA agents, Paco could not or would not say where the bodies of Camarena and Zavala had been buried. However, on June 19, the Federales announced that Tejeda had led them to a place in the Bosques de Primavera where he and his partners had buried two other innocent people he claimed Caro Quintero had killed.

Until Camarena was kidnapped, the U.S. consulate in Guadalajara had kept quiet about the disappearances of John Walker and Alberto Radelat. Even after that, the American mission gave the impression that the disappearance of the two American civilians was not worth rocking the boat about. Some U.S. officials in Mexico added to the anguish of the missing men's families by suggesting to reporters that the young men had been looking for dope, asking too many questions, hanging out in seedy places.

Paco Tejeda, who claimed to have been present when they died, told a very different story. He said the two just happened to be in the wrong place at the wrong time.

While serving in the Marines in Vietnam, John Walker had stepped on a mine and shattered his leg, a mishap which entitled him to veteran's disability pay of $450 a month. He took his wife, Eve, and their two daughters to Guadalajara, where this modest amount would stretch further while he tried to finish his book about the antics of a football team.

In the fall of 1984, Eve Walker returned home to Roseville, Minnesota, to enroll the girls in school. Walker stayed on and invited a friend, Alberto Radelat, to stay at his apartment. Radelat had been studying at the medical school in Monterrey; he was planning to take over the dental practice of his father, Dr. Felipe Radelat, a Cuban American who lived in Fort Worth. Alberto was taking a break before his last year.

On January 29, Alberto telephoned his parents to say that he would be home in two days, but when the plane arrived, Alberto was not on it. The Radelats hoped that Alberto had changed his mind and headed for the beach. They heard nothing from him, and after ten days, when they read of the death of Camarena, they flew to Guadalajara. John Walker's landlady said that she had seen neither Radelat nor Walker since the night of January 30, when they went out to celebrate Radelat's last evening in Guadalajara.

Trips to hospitals, clinics, and morgues yielded nothing. The Radelats stayed on in Guadalajara, asking questions, pushing the consulate, hounding the police. Tracking back from the place where Walker's car was found, Dr. Radelat located a cabdriver who cruised the area. He said he had seen the Americans go into La Langosta.

La Langosta, The Lobster, served the best seafood in the city. Located near a tourist zone on a main thoroughfare, it had a high thatched roof in the style of Mazatlán, the charming beach resort on Sinaloa's Pacific coast. Most customers did not realize that La Langosta was a hangout for Sinaloa marijuana trafficker "Cochi Loco," whose real name was Manuel Salcido. Caro Quintero and Fonseca were also seen there on occasion.

As Paco Tejeda was later to confess, Radelat and Walker had come into La Langosta while Caro Quintero was throwing a party. When the trafficker saw the gringos, he was sure they were DEA. They were the right age, and they spoke good Spanish with American accents. Caro Quintero's men fell upon the strangers like a pack of jackals. They used fists, ice picks, knives, and finally guns. When the strangers stopped moving, Tejeda and the others wrapped the bodies in tablecloths, drove out to the Bosques de Primavera, and dumped them in shallow graves.

When Felipe Radelat went to the restaurant, the waiter who came to his table had a gun in his belt. Radelat thought better of asking questions. This was a job for the police—but how to make the police act?

According to Radelat, one consular official told him that once a person disappeared in Mexico, there was no hope.

Radelat remembered vividly that the officer said, "You can do whatever you want, but I don't think you're going to get any results."

Felipe Radelat's slight stature, neat gray hair, and gentle countenance concealed courage and resourcefulness. He was convinced that his son's disappearance was somehow linked to that of the American agent. He asked to see Jaime Kuykendall. Consular officials told Radelat that Kuykendall was too busy but, in fact, Kuykendall did not get the message. Radelat asked to see U.S. Consul General Richard Morefield but was told that Morefield was also too busy.

Radelat tried his luck with the attorney general of Jalisco, Jaime Alberto Ramírez Gil. Would his people interview the employees of the restaurant? Nothing happened. At the Rotary Club of Guadalajara, he found help. One of his fellow Rotarians was the head of a local television station and agreed to broadcast a picture of Alberto Radelat. No one responded.

The Radelats sensed that they were being followed. Ana Radelat, Alberto's mother, was terrified but stayed on. As the days passed, the Radelats began to despair. They flew to Mexico City and sought appointments with officials of the federal Attorney General's Office and at MFJP headquarters. They elicited vague promises of assistance, but nothing seemed to change. Finally, they found an American embassy officer who took them seriously and got them in to see U.S. Ambassador John Gavin.

Radelat found Gavin to be a man of compassion. The American ambassador elevated the case to the level of a political issue, putting out the word to reporters that the U.S. State Department would warn Americans away from Mexico if nothing was done to find Walker, Radelat, and four Jehovah's Witnesses, Dennis and Rose Carlson, from California, and Ben and Patricia Mascarenas, from Nevada, who had disappeared in Guadalajara on December 2, 1984. The threat of a travel advisory was, as always, the one card that seemed to get results in Mexico.

According to reports in U.S. and Mexican newspapers, in mid-April the Mexican police announced that they had interviewed employees at La Langosta and that the manager and a waiter had confirmed that the two Americans had walked into the restaurant as a private party hosted by Rafael Caro Quintero was getting under way. According to the Mexican government account, the employees said Caro Quintero's men beat and kicked the two Americans in the main dining room, then dragged them into a storage room, where Caro Quintero and eight of his men stabbed them with knives and ice picks for more than half an hour; the restaurant's night watchman claimed to have found a large pool of blood in the storage room.[1]

The Radelats were not satisfied. They wanted their son's body, and they wanted the people responsible for killing him charged. At Gavin's request, Consul Morefield saw the family. Morefield empathized. His own son had been murdered by robbers in a McDonald's restaurant in Washington. Morefield himself had been one of the American diplomats held hostage for 444 days in Iran in 1979 and 1980. Morefield took Radelat to see Governor Enrique Alvarez del Castillo. Radelat complained that the police interviews with the people at the restaurant were inadequate. He had been doing his own detective work and had a tip. Someone named Paco was among the killers. Ask around about Paco.

As Radelat recalled the scene, the governor flushed with anger. Morefield prodded him, pointing out that the Congressional foreign relations committees were drafting the yearly foreign aid bill; under consideration was an amendment mandating a tourist travel advisory for Mexico. The state was heavily dependent on tourists who visited Guadalajara and Puerto Vallarta. The bill was due out of committee in thirty days.

"Listen, Governor, I think this problem could be easily solved," Morefield said. "You are very anxious that the U.S. should not pass the bill with a travel advisory. I think that it would be wise of you to solve the problem of these families and solve the problem of Guadalajara."

"You are giving me thirty days!" the governor snapped.

"No, I'm not, I'm giving you an alternative," Morefield replied evenly. "It's up to you."

Throughout this painful experience, Felipe Radelat's conviction grew that the two young men had been mistaken for DEA agents or informants. Alberto Radelat and John Walker had spent a lot of time at Uncle Sam's, an expatriate hangout frequented by Americans. Walker received regular U.S. government checks and cashed them at a local bank.

The Jalisco attorney general refused to see Radelat again. So did the governor. Though Morefield was generous with his time, Radelat understood that he could not force the Mexican government to do much more.

When Caro Quintero was arrested in Costa Rica on April 4, Radelat saw one more chance to find the truth. If the Mexican police interrogated the gang members about his son, surely one of them would know what had happened. Felipe and Ana Radelat and Eve Walker met in Washington and contacted Representative Jim Wright and Senator Lloyd Bentsen of Texas. The legislators made an appointment for the family members at the State Department. There, officials assured them that everything possible was being done.

Radelat did not think that was true. Despondent, he and the two women trudged to the Fourteenth Street headquarters of the DEA, where they saw Ray McKinnon, head of DEA's foreign operations. Finally, they felt they had found someone who did more than offer condolences. "I can't promise anything," McKinnon said. "But I won't let it drop. We have our sources. I'll do my best to find out what happened." Leaving the DEA building, Radelat thought that, whatever happened, he would not forget McKinnon's kindness. "He gave me hope I didn't have when I got to Washington," he said later.

McKinnon kept his word. He called Matty Maher at Operation Leyenda and passed along Radelat's plea that the MFJP ask Caro Quintero and his men about the Walker-Radelat case. McKinnon felt for the families, and he was also struck by the pattern: two men disappear, one obviously Anglo, one Hispanic, both seen frequently in gringo hangouts; eight days later, two more men disappear, one an American agent, one a Mexican who worked for him. Like Dr. Radelat, McKinnon thought the dopers might have mistaken Walker and Radelat for agents or informants. Perhaps when the American consulate did not kick up a fuss, the traffickers thought they could do it again. Jack Lawn agreed.

The American government's failure to make an outcry, he said, might well have precipitated the attacks on Camarena and Zavala.

Maher made sure that the question of Walker and Radelat was raised with the Federales. Less than two weeks later, the Mexican authorities announced that Paco Tejeda had confessed to seeing the Americans killed and had led the Federales to the bodies.

The Radelats and Mrs. Walker were summoned to a fly-infested morgue to identify the bodies. Eve Walker told Jerry Seper of *The Washington Times* that a Jalisco state policeman had shown her a skeleton assembled on a slab and asked, "What's the matter, Mrs. Walker? Isn't that your husband?" She heard the policeman laughing.[2]

Satisfying as Tejeda's explanation sounded, Jaime Kuykendall was not convinced that the La Langosta story was true. Kuykendall did not like to accept anything the Federales said until he had corroborated it five different ways and exhausted all other possibilities. He found it suspicious that the Federales had excluded the DEA when they took Tejeda to the Bosques de Primavera to dig for the bodies. All the Americans knew about what Tejeda said on this score was what the Federales had told them. Kuykendall was afraid the Americans had fallen into a trap again, giving the police enough leading information to guarantee a quick "solution." "The Mexicans tell us what we want to hear," Kuykendall said. "We tell them it happened in La Langosta. They go in, beat the shit out of the waiter, and he says, Sure, it happened just that way."

Bill Coonce and his Operation Leyenda team were not inclined to dismiss the entire story the Federales told. They believed that whatever else happened that January night, Walker and Radelat's bodies had been buried in the park. The DEA and FBI agents found the site to which Tejeda supposedly had led the Federales. A stench rose from the soft black earth as the agents took soil samples. Some days later, the FBI lab reported that the soil, black loam, high in volcanic material, was chemically identical to the dirt on Camarena's remains. This suggested that the bodies of Camarena and Zavala had also been buried in the same part of Primavera park before they were removed to Michoacán. In an effort to locate the exact spot, the DEA flew in a dog team trained to find cadavers. Ed Heath, Jaime Kuykendall, and the dog team searched the northern section of the park for a day, looking for likely graves. The dogs did not alert and were sent back to the States.

Despite the lack of incontrovertible proof, the pattern suggested that Walker and Radelat were indeed murdered by the same people who killed Camarena and Zavala. One of Caro Quintero's gang said that a black Gran Marquis was in the convoy that took the bodies of Walker and Radelat to the park. This statement was corroborated months later, when the Federales arrested another of Caro Quintero's *pistoleros*, a man by the name of José Luis González Ontiveros, and DEA agents in Mexico City were allowed sit in on part of the interrogation. González Ontiveros claimed not to know anything about Camarena. But, according to the DEA agents, he said he did know about Walker and Radelat. González Ontiveros said he had been standing guard outside La Langosta when the two young Americans came in. He said he had helped drag them to the back room, where Rafael Caro Quintero, Ernesto Fonseca, Samy Ramírez Razo, and José Luis Gallardo Parra were waiting. He said the others killed Walker and Radelat and brought them out wrapped in tablecloths. González Ontiveros said that three cars had gone out to Primavera park that night. Javier Barba Hernández was driving a black Gran Marquis. His passengers were Caro Quintero and Fonseca.

Bill Coonce and Matty Maher thought this might be the same car in which two of Kiki's hairs had been found, the same car that had been hidden by the nephews of Ernesto Fonseca, the same car that might have been part of the convoy that took the bodies of Camarena and Zavala to their burial places.

Eventually Coonce and Maher came up with a theory that explained why they could not find the spot in Bosques de Primavera where Camarena and Zavala had been buried: the DEA agent and the pilot had been buried right on top of Walker and Radelat. As the theory went, when the American government kept the heat on the Mexican government, someone who knew where all the bodies were buried decided to let the remains of Camarena and Zavala be "found." Whoever made this decision did not want all four bodies found jumbled in a mass grave because it would look as if the traffickers and their friends in the police had formed death squads and had declared war on Americans. And in that case, the story would not fade away; the press would go wild. It was not in the interest of the traffickers to allow the discovery of a common grave; the heat would only get worse. Nor was it in the interest of the Mexican government. Publicity of that sort was more damaging than a State Department tourist advisory. The American political establishment might respond by enacting harsh sanctions against Mexico. This theory raised another question: Why had the Bravo family been framed? Why weren't the cadavers simply dumped on the street someplace in Guadalajara? The answer, the DEA agents thought, was that someone wanted badly to satisfy the Americans' quest for suspects—and, as the cliché went, dead men tell no tales.

After Paco Tejeda was captured, the Federales interrogated El Samy Ramírez again to compare the stories of the two men. The Mexican authorities seemed to be eager to produce a story that would get the Americans off their backs. But the interrogations of Ramírez and Tejeda only excited the curiosity of the DEA agents. These interrogations, some of which Heath and Castillo witnessed, became known around DEA as "the door guard story." Each of the *pistoleros* claimed to have been minor players, mere door guards, who did not actually see Camarena killed.

Ramírez claimed that a few hours after he had delivered Camarena to the house on Calle Lope de Vega, he learned that Camarena was being beaten; he rushed into the bedroom and saw the agent, blindfolded and dressed only in his shorts, with his hands tied behind his back and his feet tied together. Five men—Carlos Martínez, "El Chavo," "El Chango," "Cuco," and "La Calaca"—were standing over him, beating him with their feet and fists. Paco Tejeda was watching. Ramírez insisted that he had intervened to stop the beating and that he helped Camarena to the bed. After that, he said, Félix Gallardo showed up at the house, went into a room with Caro Quintero, and shut the door.

Ramírez said that when he left that night, he saw a blind-folded man with his hands bound, sitting on the floor in a service area. Ramírez asked a guard who the man was. *"Un soplón. Un dedo,"* the guard said. "A snitch, a finger." The next evening, at about seven o'clock, Ramírez said, he returned to the house with Fonseca and Barba Hernández and saw Tejeda and "El Chavo" helping a man out of the house. He did not recognize this man, who was blindfolded and fully clothed, with his hands and legs untied. He said the man was shoved in the trunk of a late-model beige car, not the Volkswagen but another one. "Chelín" told him the man in the trunk was Camarena. Fonseca told Ramírez they should leave because the man was already dead. Ramírez said that he later heard that the DEA agent had been buried somewhere in the Bosques de Primavera. This description was so completely at odds with every other element of Ramírez's story that the DEA agents concluded that the victim he described was Alfredo Zavala, not Camarena. For reasons that the DEA agents could not understand, the Federales customarily did not ask suspects any questions about what had happened to Zavala.

Ramírez added one important new name to the conspiracy: Sergio Espino Verdín, the former Guadalajara *comandante* of the federal intelligence service known as Investigaciones Politicales y Sociales, or Political and Social Investigations (IPS). Like the DFS, this agency was part of the Interior Ministry and was supposed to keep tabs on political dissidents and other enemies of the state. Ramírez said that Espino had arrived at the house with Fonseca and Javier Barba Hernández, the lawyer and reputed executioner for the Caro Quintero–Fonseca organization. At one point during these interrogations, Caro Quintero and Fonseca were brought into the room so that they could see that Ramírez and Tejeda had been talking. Confronted with them, Caro Quintero finally admitted having been in the house on Lope de Vega when Camarena was there. Still, he insisted that he had not known what was going on; he

had not even known that Camarena and Zavala were there.
He said the whole thing was the idea of Félix Gallardo.

The American agents were ready to believe that Félix
Gallardo was involved in the murder, but, as Caro Quintero
undoubtedly knew, it did not matter what he said about the
Godfather. The Federales said they had not a clue where
Félix Gallardo was. The DEA agents did. They had heard
he was back in Sinaloa, where the best-intentioned of the
MFJP *comandantes* would not venture to arrest him.

15

The Camarena
Tapes

When the first big break came in the Camarena case, it was not because of some brilliant piece of detective work; nor was it a result of the extra degree of diligence in DEA offices around the world. It was the work of the CIA.

After Camarena disappeared, officials in DEA headquarters received a few calls from Langley. Were DFS officials who worked closely with the agency involved? Were "our" *comandantes* being arrested? Were they talking? And could the agency be of assistance? Even CIA officers who had sparred with DEA agents in Mexico over the relationship between the CIA and the DFS now offered to help.

Most DEA agents wrote off the CIA offers as obligatory courtesy calls with more than a touch of self-interest. But the intelligence agency came through.

On the morning of April 17, Bill Coonce and Jaime Kuykendall flew from Guadalajara to Mexico City to brief Jack Lawn, who was due in Mexico that morning to meet Attorney General Sergio García Ramírez and MFJP director Manuel Ibarra Herrera. Coonce and Kuykendall arrived first and went to the DEA office at the embassy. As they were chatting, Walter White, Ed Heath's deputy, mentioned that a memorandum had come in from the CIA station. It recounted an informant's tale so bizarre that Heath had hesitated to pass it along. It said that Camarena's captors had tape-recorded his interrogation; the agency's source claimed to have heard the tape.

Kuykendall squinted at the slip of paper. There on the page was a nickname that Kiki had used for one of his informants. No one but Kiki and Jaime had ever known that nickname. He looked at White and Coonce with blazing eyes. "This is *real*," he said. "They've *got* it."

Kuykendall charged upstairs to see the intelligence officers. After a few minutes of conversation, Kuykendall was satisfied. "Your information is good," he told them, and went back downstairs to tell Coonce. Coonce began to pace back and forth, talking to himself as much as to Kuykendall. This was *it*, the opening he had been hoping for. Voice analysis might reveal the identities of Kiki's killers. Certainly, a tape would shed some light on the motives of the people who did this. For weeks, Coonce and his partners had been saying, "All we need is a little luck." Here it was, almost within their grasp. But how to get the tape? The Mexicans, Coonce muttered, wouldn't tell him if his pants were on fire.

When Lawn appeared in the embassy, Coonce pulled him out into a corridor and whispered the news. There was a tape of Kiki's last hours, Kuykendall was sure of it. The agents did not know whether the Mexican police had it, but there was a good chance they did. Lawn hurried to Gavin's office. He said he *had* to have that tape. He would fight for it however he could.

"Don't ask," Gavin said with a cold smile. "Demand."

To ask, the diplomat said, or to display the slightest hint of uncertainty would give the Mexican officials an opening to say the tape did not exist or to destroy it. Gavin said he would play "good cop" and offer to mediate a compromise. Lawn would play "bad cop."

It was clear from their faces that García Ramírez and Ibarra had not expected DEA to learn of the tape. Initially, they refused to concede that it existed, but Lawn was stubborn. "I demand it," he repeated, like a litany. When the Mexican officials tried to change the subject, Gavin would shepherd the conversation back to the tape. "Now, Jack, what did you say you needed?"

Finally, García Ramírez acknowledged that there was a tape of Camarena. He said the municipal police had found it in the villa in Puerto Vallarta where Ernesto Fonseca had been captured.

Lawn asked for the tape. Ibarra said no, it was too sensitive, and besides, it was not in Mexico City. Ibarra said that it was being held by Florentino Ventura, the *primer comandante* in charge of the Camarena investigation. The exchange grew hotter until García Ramírez offered a compromise. That evening, Ventura would bring the tape to the attorney general's offices. Lawn could listen to the tape, and then the U.S. Justice Department could make a formal request for a copy.

As Lawn walked away from the attorney general's office, Garcia Ramírez's deputy, José María Ortega Padilla, approached him to say that the deal was off. He was sorry, but the attorney general was mistaken. The tape would not be available after all. "That's insubordination!" Lawn exploded, wheeling around. "I'm going to tell the attorney general about this right now!" Ortega Padilla caught up with him before he got to García Ramírez's door. All right, he could hear the tape, but he could not have a copy, and he could not disclose its existence.

Late in the afternoon, in a room in the attorney general's building, Lawn listened intently and took down a precise record of what he heard, hoping agents who had served in Mexico would pick up nuances he missed. The tape did not contain the noise of a beating, but the agent's strained voice said it all. Those and his plea, "Don't hurt my family." Amid the babble of voices, Lawn heard one main interrogator. His voice was low and patient. He asked questions, again and again, in a practiced, professional manner. Is he giving up names? Lawn asked Heath. Heath said, "No, none." Lawn didn't believe him. It was macho to pretend a DEA agent would never break, but this wasn't the movies. "I have to know," Lawn snapped. Lives were at stake. "Yes," Heath said, "There were names." This man, it seemed to Lawn, had conducted interrogations before. His probing showed that he was familiar with details of DEA's activities in Mexico. He touched on the Chihuahua raids, Kiki's knowledge of Ernesto Fonseca, Rafael Caro Quintero, Miguel Angel Félix Gallardo, and Juan José Esparragoza, and the roles of Jaime Kuykendall, Roger Knapp, and Shaggy Wallace. He asked where Antonio Vargas, now wounded and helpless, was hospitalized.

At several points, Kiki called the interrogator *"comandante."* This fit in with the description of the kidnapping given by El Samy Ramírez, Caro Quintero's *pistolero*. El Samy had claimed that he had approached Camarena with the words "The *comandante* wants to see you." Was the interrogator a police commander? Or was Kiki using the term as an honorific? This was a question that Lawn would turn over in his mind many times, but he would bet a year's pay that the man had been trained in police interrogation techniques. He was too methodical to be an amateur.

Then Lawn was permitted to hear a second tape. This cassette recorded the DEA's radio traffic in Guadalajara on the morning of March 2, when the Federales raided the Bravo ranch. The tape itself was mostly static, but to Lawn this was a highly significant piece of evidence. Someone had wanted an exact record of the interrogation of the agent. That same person, or perhaps a confederate, taped DEA's reactions during a crucial moment in a cover-up—a cover-up perpetrated, Lawn was convinced, by elements of the Mexican Federal Judicial Police. It appeared that someone with police experience was among Camarena's murderers. Did this man have ties to DFS or some other sort of internal security agency? To the Federales? Or to the Jalisco police? Whatever the case, Lawn judged that some members of the various Mexican police forces were, for once, working together. There was nothing like a common foe to unite adversaries. Lawn realized that he had no real allies in Mexico, with the possible exception of the attorney general himself, and it was obvious that the orders of García Ramírez were often disobeyed. Now Lawn understood what the agents meant when they complained about working in Mexico. It was not the danger that burned them out. It was the frustration of never knowing the truth. Even if you found the truth, how could you tell? The place was all shifting sand, with no place to plant your feet and nothing to lean on. Everybody Lawn met seemed to be trying to manipulate him and everybody else, for reasons he could not imagine.

That evening Manuel Ibarra invited Lawn to dinner. With

an engaging flourish, he described a delightful country restaurant about twenty-five miles outside Mexico City. Twenty-five miles? Lawn snarled that he did not trust Ibarra twenty feet away. "I'm afraid just sitting across the table from you," Lawn snapped.

Later, when Lawn related the anecdote to Heath, the attaché was mortified. "I hope you didn't tell him that," Heath pleaded. Heath still defended Ibarra as a friend of DEA.

"I don't trust the son of a bitch, and that's what I told him," Lawn said.

Lawn returned to Washington shaken but also exhilarated. He had done it: bluffed the Mexican authorities into admitting that tapes existed. Now, he was sure, the DEA would get copies. But when he arrived at his office, he found he was in trouble. Gavin had sent a cable to the State Department describing explicitly how Lawn had pressured the Mexican officials into letting him hear the Camarena tape. Someone had brought the cable to George Shultz's attention. The hot-tempered secretary of state guarded his turf, and what he supposed was his turf, like a mother tigress. When he found out what Lawn had done, he telephoned Ed Meese and loudly vented his spleen. He said that Jack Lawn had been out of line and that he would have to send his people to Mexico to mend fences.

Meese summoned Lawn. Lawn was nervous, but the attorney general was smiling serenely. After hearing what Shultz had said, Lawn explained that he had not *said* anything that could be considered insulting. As far as he was concerned, he had simply been persistent and professional. He had to listen to that tape that day and make a record of the contents. The names of other DEA agents were on it. They might be targets. Maybe the Mexicans would hand the tape over, but if they did not, his job was to protect the lives of his men.

"Next time, tell me first," Meese said. "Don't worry about Shultz." Lawn was grateful. He did not know Meese well, but he was beginning to appreciate the attorney general's guileless manner and his unswerving loyalty. When

FBI director William Webster heard about what Lawn had done, he was not so understanding, scolding that Lawn had overstepped the bounds. Lawn was sorry Webster did not agree with him, but he believed he had done the right thing. So what if he got hell for it? The worst thing they could do, he told his friends, was bust him back to the field. It would not be so bad to be a real brick agent again, away from all the politics and personalities.[1]

John Gavin was also in trouble with George Shultz. Two or three weeks after Lawn returned from Mexico, Gavin got a telephone call from Robert Tuttle, the personnel director at the White House. Tuttle told the ambassador to get his affairs in order; he was about to be relieved.

A freewheeling California conservative, Gavin had never been accepted by the Washington establishment. His low regard for Mexican officialdom was obvious. He had nearly been declared persona non grata by President López Portillo for remarking that Mexico's stability was threatened by the debt crisis.[2] Undaunted, he had carried on a running battle with de la Madrid's left-leaning foreign minister, Bernardo Sepúlveda Amor. When Sepúlveda had complained about Gavin's condemnation of official corruption in Mexico, Gavin had remarked, shrugging, "Bernardo, if the shoe fits, wear it." The American ambassador was less than diplomatic with the Mexican press, which he called "the bought press."

Worst of all, from the point of view of the career foreign service officials who populated the State Department, Gavin had been among twenty-two non-career American ambassadors who signed a letter endorsing Senator Jesse Helms for reelection in 1984. It was unheard-of for ambassadors to get involved in domestic political issues and even more shocking when the beneficiary of their activism was a politician who advocated causes far to the right of the administration's position. Helms had supported Argentina in the 1982 battle over the Falkland Islands, backed right-wing politician Roberto D'Aubuisson against moderate President José Napoleón Duarte in El Salvador, and praised Augusto Pinochet, the repressive president of Chile. In early 1985,

State's foreign service officers persuaded Shultz to remove all "political" ambassadors appointed during Ronald Reagan's first term. That meant Gavin and also Lewis Tambs, who had been pulled out of Colombia but was hoping to be posted to Costa Rica.

Lawn hoped Meese would intervene. The DEA administrator stayed away from politics and did not know what Gavin thought about most issues, but he was convinced that the Mexican government would interpret Gavin's removal as a signal that the United States was backing down on the requests for evidence in the Camarena case. Meese was not particularly helpful. He wrote a letter to the White House on Gavin's behalf but did not press the case.

Willy von Raab, who had become a close friend of Gavin, understood better than Lawn which buttons to push. He called another member of the conservative network, Senator Paula Hawkins. Hawkins braced Reagan at a Republican party function. What did he mean, trying to fire Gavin? Did he know what that would do to the war on drugs? Reagan was startled. His old friend Jack Gavin? Of course he was not going to fire him. On August 22, Gavin and his wife, Constance Towers, attended a Republican dinner in Beverly Hills at which Reagan was to speak. Before he launched into his prepared speech, Reagan picked Gavin out of the crowd. "Jack has been doing a superlative job out there," Reagan said with a twinkle in his eye. "I think he's one of the best ambassadors this country has ever had, and we're enormously pleased that he's going to stay on in his post and continue his great work." Gavin was delighted. He knew that Reagan's message was not meant for a Los Angeles audience. The president seemed to be aiming about three thousand miles to the east—toward Foggy Bottom. "A little sprinkling of holy water doesn't hurt, but that was a deluge," he chuckled. Afterward, Shultz called Gavin and asked him to stay on in Mexico City.

In June, Coonce flew to Mexico City once more to pursue the tapes. He could get no further than Ortega Padilla, who brushed him off. It might be possible to give the Americans versions of the tapes, the Mexican official said, but with

Camarena's responses deleted. He would take the matter under consideration.

Coonce was appalled, but he held his tongue. Lawn had promised to have Meese raise the matter of the tapes at the next meeting of the attorneys general in August. Surely, Coonce thought, the Mexican attorney general would not reject a direct request from Meese.

In the meantime, Coonce and his partners went to work to identify the *"comandante"* Lawn had heard interrogating Camarena. After rereading the interviews of informants and the accounts of the interrogations of the *pistoleros* El Samy Ramírez and Paco Tejeda, Coonce focused on Sergio Espino Verdín, the former commander of the Mexican federal bureau of Political and Social Investigations (IPS). It was Espino who, according to Ramírez, had arrived at the house on Lope de Vega with Fonseca and Javier Barba Hernández shortly after the kidnappers delivered Camarena. While it was unwise to rely on the statement of a prisoner such as El Samy, Coonce also had reports from informants—some of them gathered by Camarena himself—that supported the idea that Espino had often done the cartel's dirty work.

In Camarena's files was a memo dated April 12, 1984, which noted that "Ernesto Fonseca Carrillo befriended Comandante FNU [first name unknown] Espino from the Bureau of Political and Social Investigations." Kuykendall told Coonce that Camarena and he were intrigued by Espino for several reasons. During the López Portillo administration, the Bureau of Political and Social Investigations had been a small Interior Ministry agency that had reported on political dissent in the provinces. After de la Madrid assumed office, the agency expanded dramatically.

Sergio Espino Verdín had secured the job of IPS *comandante* for the state of Jalisco and began to enlarge his empire by hiring numerous police agents and flunkies. Camarena persuaded some of his informants to take jobs at the IPS office. Through this penetration, Camarena was told that Caro Quintero and Fonseca were paying the rent for the IPS office and had bought the radio equipment and cars. In return, Espino had given the traffickers Interior Ministry credentials and was performing other services.

Few citizens in Guadalajara had known anything about this shadowy police agency until a balmy night in November 1984, when "El Doc" Fonseca, Ernesto Fonseca's younger brother, got drunk and started shooting up a Chinese restaurant. As Kuykendall and Camarena pieced the story together, when the uniformed police arrived, sirens bawling, El Doc and his wife, the sister of Rafael Caro Quintero's wife, María Elenes, leaped into a black custom-armored Gran Marquis with another couple and sped away, firing out of the vents at their pursuers. Even after the cops shot out the tires, El Doc kept going, running on the rims until he had jumped a curb and ripped out the car's suspension. When the four young Sinaloans opened the car doors, the police cut them down with machine-gun fire. The Guadalajara papers reported, and an MFJP officer confirmed, that credentials from the Bureau of Political and Social Investigations were found on young Fonseca's body. His mangled corpse and the corpse of María Elenes Caro's sister were later collected from the morgue by Comandante Espino. This public display of fealty to the traffickers caused a scandal in Guadalajara. Soon afterward, Espino left the IPS job.

Coonce passed word to the field that Espino was a prime suspect in Camarena's death. In late June 1985, an informant reported that Espino was at his mother's house in Durango. The DEA embassy office passed this information on to MFJP headquarters. Some days later, MFJP officials sent word to the embassy that a team of Federales had been to Durango but had been unable to locate Espino.

The DEA agents talked to the informant again. He said that the Federales had gone to Durango, all right, but Espino boasted that he had paid "the right people" so that the Federales would not arrest him. The informant said that the Federales hung around in front of Espino's mother's house for a few days but did not bother Espino as he came and went. The informant's story rang true when a DEA agent obtained independent evidence that on August 19 Espino went to a judge in Durango and obtained an *amparo,* a court order instructing the Mexican government not to stop, detain, question, or interfere with Espino.

On August 13, Meese met García Ramírez in Mexico City
to discuss progress in the Camarena case. The Mexican attorney general seemed anxious to show that the de la Madrid
moral-renovation campaign was back on track. Just before
Meese arrived in Mexico City, García Ramírez dismissed
Manuel Ibarra Herrera, by abolishing the post of director
of the MFJP in what was billed as an economy measure.
He dismissed about three hundred employees of the Attorney General's Office and reorganized the MFJP and the
eradication program. García Ramírez named Primer Comandante Florentino Ventura, Aldana's successor as Interpol director, "acting" director of the MFJP and gave Deputy
Attorney General Ortega Padilla charge of both the Camarena investigation and the anti-drug campaign.

García Ramírez promised Meese that the tapes would
soon handed over. Once Meese left Mexico City, Ortega
Padilla let Ed Heath listen to four cassettes but would not
allow him to take the tapes to the U.S. embassy. It was the
first time DEA heard of the existence of two additional
tapes—Lawn had seen only two tapes.

One of the new cassettes continued the interrogation of
Camarena. The other raised major new questions about the
extent of the conspiracy. It recorded the interrogation of a
small-time drug trafficker named Anthony Brito and his wife
or girlfriend. Coonce's team ran a quick background check
on Brito. It turned out that he had been working as an
informant for the FBI in Texas. He was a Cuban Marielito
whose real name was Antonio Vásquez Casada. He had
moved to the Southwest border a few years back and had
started to work for Rafael Caro Quintero, running marijuana out of Zacatecas and Chihuahua. After being caught
smuggling in Texas, Vásquez had agreed to become an FBI
informant. The FBI got the charges dismissed and had the
Cuban's name changed. In his incarnation as Tony Brito,
he had agreed to inform on the movement of drugs, guns,
and money across the border.

After Camarena was kidnapped, FBI agents in Texas who
thought Brito might know something useful had summoned
him to a meeting with DEA agents in El Paso. Brito had

shown up around March 6. The agents had taken the usual precautions, booking a room in a local motel for the clandestine talk. After the meeting, Brito had headed back ~~across the border.~~ Neither his FBI contacts nor the DEA had seen him since that time.

When he heard about the tape of Brito's torture, Coonce figured that Brito had been followed into El Paso, seen going into the motel, followed back into Ciudad Juárez, and waylaid there. It made sense that if Caro Quintero's men were looking for DEA informants, they would have pinpointed Brito. He had known about some of the big plantations Camarena had discovered. His loyalties would have been suspect, since he was not "family." If it was true, as the Mexican officials said, that this tape was found with the Camarena tapes and the Bravo ranch tape, the same people had to be involved in all these incidents.

Late in August came the most stunning news of all. Once again, the CIA was responsible for the breakthrough. One day, an agency employee arrived at DEA headquarters in Washington with a transcript of another interrogation. The transcript appeared to be from the interrogation of Kiki Camarena, but it matched neither the first tape cassette Lawn had heard nor the second tape Heath had heard.

Reading this document, the DEA agents could understand why it had been suppressed. The interrogator asked his subject what he knew about "Arévalo Gardoqui." There was a notation that the questioner apparently referred to Mexico's minister of defense, General Juan Arévalo Gardoqui.

Over the years, DEA agents had picked up unflattering rumors about Arévalo Gardoqui, but Mexico was a gossipy place, and there were rumors about nearly everyone in power. Arévalo Gardoqui was responsible for a major part of Mexico's anti-drug campaign: some twenty-five thousand Mexican troops under his command were assigned to manual eradication of poppies and marijuana. According to a DEA affidavit filed in Tucson in May 1988, a former Mexican military officer had told DEA agents in Sonora that

Rafael Caro Quintero and his partners had paid Arévalo
Gardoqui $10 million to protect the Chihuahua complex;
he said they had videotaped the transaction.

From time to time, DEA and Customs agents in Mexico
and on the border heard allegations from their informants
that Arévalo Gardoqui associated with traffickers or permitted them to operate freely in certain areas, but none of
the American agents was able to come up with hard evidence
supporting the charges. Whatever uncertainties American
officials held about the Mexican defense minister were rarely
voiced in public. In February 1987, Representative Larry
Smith, chairman of the House task force on international
narcotics control, raised the question in an oblique way
when Secretary of State George Shultz appeared before the
House Foreign Affairs Committee for a routine authorization hearing. Smith had been told that Arévalo Gardoqui
was about to be given an award by the U.S. Defense Department; he checked into the general's background and
was disturbed by the nature of some of the allegations, even
though they were unproven. Smith asked Shultz, "Do you
believe it is in the best interest of the United States to
provide official U.S. government awards or compensations
to high-ranking foreign government officials whom we have
reason to believe are involved in facilitating the narcotics
trade? . . . Quite possibly this will be happening shortly,
and a lot of us are awfully concerned about it, and I will
talk to you privately." "We appreciate any information you
have," Shultz replied, "because we certainly want to reward
our friends and punish our enemies in this regard and not
the other way around."[3] Sources close to Smith said afterward that the congressman was referring to Arévalo Gardoqui and that the award was never made.

DEA agents in the Southwest had heard many allegations
that Juan Arévalo Lamadrid, Juanito, the general's son, was
involved with organized crime. These dated from the time
when he had served as a federal prosecutor in Baja California. None of these stories had been proven. At one point
in 1985, Ambassador Gavin found the list of allegations
against Juanito so compelling that he presented them to
President de la Madrid in a private meeting. At that time,

according to Mexican officials, the defense minister's son was a senior official in the Interior Ministry. Gavin said in an interview that he told de la Madrid that the United States did not have sufficient evidence to make a criminal case against the defense minister's son, but that officials in DEA and the intelligence agencies took the position that "if he walks like a duck and talks like a duck, he's probably a duck." Gavin explained that he was concerned that the traffickers might try to use the son to get to the father, who was crucial to the success of the eradication campaign.

The DEA agents who read the transcript obtained through intelligence sources did not know why an interrogator would have asked Camarena about Arévalo Gardoqui. Camarena had not been actively investigating the defense minister, and the transcript did not contain any information that suggested that the defense minister had had anything to do with the kidnapping of Camarena. However, there were many voices on the tapes and many questions about all sorts of people, from traffickers to informants to DEA agents. On one of the tapes, the interrogator even suggested that Camarena was corrupt. He asked Camarena, who is paying you? and Camarena said, "No one."

A second line of questioning in the transcript introduced an equally interesting name. The interrogator asked what his subject knew about Miguel Aldana Ibarra, the former *primer comandante* of the MFJP and chief of Interpol. Ever since he had found Aldana's name in Kiki's last work diary, Coonce had tried to figure out where Aldana fit into the story. Why had Aldana left the Federales on the heels of his greatest triumph, the Chihuahua seizure, which was being hailed as "the bust of the century"? Aldana's role as leader of the Chihuahua raid was of interest to the Leyenda team because that bust seemed to have been a catalytic event for Rafael Caro Quintero and his associates. DEA agents estimated that the raid had cost Caro Quintero hundreds of millions of dollars; they developed information that he had formed an investment syndicate and had convinced other traffickers to sink millions of dollars into the Chihuahua operation as well. Eventually, DEA officials would file an affidavit in a U.S. court estimating that the raid had cost the Caro Quintero organization $2.5 billion to $5 billion in lost street sales of the five-thousand- to ten-thousand-ton stockpile of sinsemilla marijuana found at the complex.[4]

Coonce knew that Camarena had started gathering information about Aldana. Looking over Camarena's records, Coonce found that five days before he died, Camarena had seen an informant who had talked about Aldana.

After Camarena's death, a number of DEA agents on the border received allegations from various informants asserting that Aldana had been protecting large marijuana-growing operations in northern Mexico. Coonce was particularly interested in a report of a DEA agent whose informant claimed that Caro Quintero had savagely upbraided Aldana for permitting the Chihuahua raids. According to the DEA agent's report of the informant's statement, Caro Quintero had warned Aldana, If you don't take care of the problem, we will.

Most of the allegations that DEA received about Miguel Aldana Ibarra would remain closely held within DEA files, but in 1988, Terrence Poppa, a reporter for the *El Paso Herald-Post,* published secret federal grand jury testimony of an admitted drug trafficker and cocaine user named Carlos de Herrera, who worked as a paid informant for DEA in 1985 and 1986. Miguel Aldana was not charged in connection with this case; de Herrera had only hearsay knowledge about Aldana. According to the transcript of that testimony, de Herrera said that in 1985 and 1986 he was the "collector" for a large Ciudad Juárez drug ring, whose boss, Gilberto Ontiveros, raised and sold marijuana in his own right and invested in Caro Quintero's Chihuahua marijuana complex. When a grand juror asked de Herrera if the ring had official protection, he replied, "Protection money was paid through Policía Judicial Federal, through Aldama. Aldama was the godfather of the protection. Aldama is in Mexico City." From the context of de Herrera's testimony and from his interviews with other admitted associates of the ring, Poppa inferred that the man de Herrera referred to as "Aldama" was Miguel Aldana Ibarra.

According to the transcript of the grand jury testimony, given October 7, 1986, de Herrera went on to say this:

In Mexico, there's two different kinds of mafias. . . . One of them does not exist any more over the Camarena incident. . . . The two most strong mafias in Mexico at that time was DFS, which is Seguridad Federal, and Policía Judicial Federal. . . . The commander from the DFS [in Juárez], Rafael Aguilar, had Gilberto Ontiveros working under him, Rafael Caro Quintero and Don Neto [Ernesto Fonseca]. . . . DFS had a ranch specially built just to grow marijuana, and it was called the Búfalo. The people in charge was Rafael Caro Quintero, money investments was Gilberto Ontiveros, Rafael Caro Quintero himself, Rafael Aguilar, and Don Neto. This was one of the most organized plantations ever seen in the history of the dope scene. . . . It was supposed to be one of the most sophisticated, highly secretive plantations for the DFS. . . . The people that seized this place was Policía Judicial Federal. When they seized this place, most of the confidents [guards] there had badges from the DFS. Most of them were signed by [DFS zone commander] Rafael Aguilar. . . . That's when things started changing. That's when Gilberto changed from DFS, after that bust, to Aldama, to PJF [MFJP]. . . . The only one to carry the money to Aldama, his name was Carlos Magaña. . . . Twelve dollars a pound [went to the police]. Anything extra, extra favors would be subsidized in a Rolls Royce or a Corvette or—

Q. It would be taken to Mexico City and given to one of the officials there in Mexico City?

A. Right.[5]

Another informant, Gabriel,[*] a contract agent for the DFS from 1973 to 1981, contended that when Aldana was at DFS headquarters during the López Portillo administration, he "was in charge of protection for DFS" and maintained close ties with Caro Quintero and Fonseca. Gabriel said in an interview in 1988 that he had recently been asked to "place"—invest—about $100 million for Aldana and other DFS officials. On the basis of the informant's statement, U.S. Customs officials launched a money-laundering investigation.

Bill Coonce knew he could not resolve his own suspicions about Aldana or any other Mexican official until he found Kiki's interrogator. Coonce sensed that locating that

_____

* The name Gabriel is a pseudonym.

particular suspect would be the hardest job of all. "The
Mexicans are absolutely scared to death about that *comandante,*" he said.

Shortly before Labor Day, García Ramírez fulfilled his
promise to Ed Meese. The four tapes that Ed Heath had
heard were delivered to the DEA office in the U.S. embassy
in Mexico City. The tapes were dispatched to the FBI laboratory, where they were enhanced so that the speakers
could be heard more clearly. The background noises were
filtered out and analyzed.

For the first time, DEA agents in Operation Leyenda
were able to hear the tapes for themselves and to play and
replay them. The voice on the first tape, the tape Lawn had
heard, was strong. The voice on the second was that of a
dying man. There were no screams, but Kiki's voice was
feeble. From time to time he groaned and shifted himself,
as if he were trying to find a less painful position.

Both Camarena tapes seemed to have segments missing.
There were breaks in the middle of conversations, as if the
recorder had been turned on and off. Questions and answers
did not fit, as if large chunks had been excised. The tapes
that arrived at the embassy did not seem to be original
recordings but duplicates—or, perhaps, excerpts. Could
someone have doctored the tapes? There were any number
of possibilities. The traffickers themselves could have tin-
kered with the tapes, or someone in the government could
have done so. The Mexican government had repeatedly
given the DEA several different accounts of which government officials had handled the tapes. The DEA agents did
not believe they had the straight story, but they surmised
that at least four and possibly six government entities had
them somewhere along the way. One version of the story,
conveyed by Deputy Attorney General Ortega Padilla to
U.S. Assistant Attorney General Steve Trott, was that the
tapes were found by the Puerto Vallarta municipal police,
who gave them to the governor of Jalisco, Enrique Alvarez
de Castillo, who gave them to Attorney General García
Ramírez, who gave them to the MFJP. If the story of the
discovery of the tapes was true, if the Army had helped

capture Ernesto Fonseca, and if he had been found at a
DFS safe house in Puerto Vallarta with DFS agents working
as his *pistoleros*, that raised the possibility that military officials or DFS agents might also have handled the tapes.

The DEA agents thought that there should have been
many more tapes. If El Samy Ramírez and Paco Tejeda
were right, Kiki had been killed after nightfall on February
8, which meant that the traffickers had held him at the house
for about thirty hours. If the interrogators had gone to the
trouble of making a record, why hadn't they been more
thorough?

The provenance of the Brito tape was equally mysterious.
The FBI lab determined that the voice of the interrogator
who questioned Brito and his girl was not the same as the
voice of Camarena's interrogator. Yet there were similari-
ties: the second inquisitor also appeared to have had police
training and had also been interested in what his victims
knew about police officials. Among other things, he had
asked Brito what he knew about Rafael Aguilar Guajardo,
who had been DFS zone commander in Chihuahua and
Durango until the mass firings of DFS officers after Caro
Quintero's capture.

What Coonce and his partners could not fathom was why
Mexican officials maintained that the tapes had been found
together.

To the DEA agents, the ramifications of that story were
devastating to the Mexican government. Here, supposedly
rescued from a single hiding place, was evidence of nine
murders that had occurred in three different states: the murders of Camarena and Zavala in Jalisco, of Brito and his
girl in Chihuahua, and of the five members of the Bravo
family in Michoacán. If you counted John Walker and Alberto Radelat, eleven murders were at issue. That suggested
a sustained, systematic conspiracy, involving not only the
Guadajalara cartel but also officials or former officials of
several different Mexican government agencies. By averring
that the tapes were found together, Mexican officials raised
all sorts of questions. Why *did* the perpetrators of these
crimes act as if they could get away with murder, time after

time after time, in any place they chose? The answers might be very messy. So why did the Mexican government invite trouble by suggesting that tapes of all these different events had been discovered in a single collection? Ortega Padilla insisted that he knew only what he was told by the Jalisco state authorities: the tapes were found together, in Ernesto Fonseca's Puerto Vallarta hideout. If the tapes were altered, he said, that was done before they entered the custody of the federal attorney general.

The DEA agents had no reason to believe that Ortega Padilla and his colleagues would make up an account that would cause them to be bombarded with questions. But they found it highly implausible that a primitive fellow like Ernesto Fonseca, running for his life, would have been carrying with him the most incriminating pieces of evidence that existed. Fonseca and Caro Quintero had "confessed" to serious crimes, but not to Camarena's murder or to anything else that would get them a long prison sentence, and then they had recanted. The DEA agents wondered whether the traffickers were taking the rap for some members of the power structure. Was the deal a few months in the slammer and out? A jailbreak or a quiet dismissal and a fast flight to retirement in some sleazy resort?

The Mexican government's line seemed to be that the murders of Camarena and Zavala were the impetuous acts of some illiterate dope peddlers. Yet the tapes showed that there had been a great degree of advance planning and considerable sophistication. Experienced interrogators had been engaged and electronic equipment employed in the Camarena and Zavala cases and also in the case of Brito and his girl. The victims had probably been under surveillance for some time before they were kidnapped. These were not opportunistic acts.

There were other instances of premeditation. For example, in the case of the five Bravo family members killed on March 2, the Federales had shown the DEA an "anonymous letter" about the Bravos on February 28, two days before the raid. On September 10, García Ramírez tried to put the Bravo massacre scandal to rest by announcing that Alfonso Velázquez Hernández, the *comandante* who led the raid on the Bravo ranch, had been arrested for homicide, along with seven other policemen. The attorney general did not explain who wrote the note that caused Velázquez and his men to go to the Bravo ranch in the first place. The DEA's questions on the issue of the Bravo ranch were met with stony silence.

That the murders had been conducted systematically suggested a system. Or *the* system. Did it stop with corrupt policemen? Or did it go into the political leadership of the ruling Institutional Revolutionary party? That the PRI would seem to sacrifice the head of the MFJP and the former head of the DFS was significant. More interesting was the fact that even after Ibarra, Zorrilla, and numerous other officials departed, the Mexican government still stonewalled. At this moment de la Madrid was desperate to refinance his national debt. Why was he risking Washington's anger by continuing to withhold information vital to the resolution of the case?

Jaime Kuykendall thought that the Mexican government was covering up darker secrets than even he suspected. "They *cannot* admit the truth," he said. "They *have* to cover it up because the government's involved. It's the only thing that makes sense. They're covering up something they can't afford to let out." But what was this truth that was so terrible it could not be disclosed? He did not know.

He suspected someone in the DFS knew the answers. The footprints of the DFS seemed to be everywhere. What if DFS agents, not Fonseca, made the tapes? What if DFS agents had taken Camarena?

But some of the Federales were also implicated. Comandante Pavón Reyes, who let Caro Quintero leave the airport and who gave the order to raid the Bravo ranch, had been arrested on April 15 and was being prosecuted for bribery. But Kuykendall had obtained records of long-distance calls made from the telephone that Pavón Reyes had used when he allowed Caro Quintero to fly out of Guadalajara International Airport two days after Kiki's abduction. The records showed that one call went to a telephone within the Attorney General's Office building in Mexico

City. According to senior DEA officials in Washington, agents in Mexico City determined that the telephone on the receiving end was a private line that rang in the office of MFJP director Manuel Ibarra. The DEA agents did not know who might have had access to that particular telephone at the time when Pavón Reyes appeared to have placed a call to Mexico City. Most everyone else in the DEA accepted the story that Pavón Reyes had taken a bribe from Caro Quintero. Kuykendall did not know if he had or not, but he was not so sure Pavón Reyes had made the ultimate decisions in the case. The story about the bribe, which an MFJP agent from Mexico City had told Ed Heath, seemed to Kuykendall to be a little too neat. It was easy to paint Pavón Reyes as a villain. Kuykendall suspected that the young *comandante*, who was rather stupid, had not acted alone.

Kuykendall had planned on pursuing these lines of questioning and many others. But then he was told he was being transferred back to Laredo and should be ready to report for duty in Texas in October. Jack Lawn intended to replace him with Tony Ayala, who was not so emotionally involved in the case. All the things Kuykendall had asked for were coming true. Lawn had expanded the DEA office in Guadalajara to about a dozen positions. Ed Meese had twisted George Shultz's arm until he had approved diplomatic passports for DEA agents in the provinces. The award Kuykendall had recommended for Kiki in March 1984 finally came through. DEA presented it to his widow. "It took a man's life and worldwide publicity," Kuykendall said bleakly. "Talk about closing the barn door after the horse is gone."

What made this an especially bitter passage for Kuykendall was the fact that Lawn did not intend to replace Ed Heath. Lawn was angry with Heath for not keeping him better informed about problems in Mexico and for alienating many of the field agents, but he thought he could improve things by sending Heath an aggressive deputy with orders to keep headquarters alerted to trouble signs. Lawn insisted that desk officers at headquarters watch Mexico more closely. He himself read every cable that came out of Mexico. Lawn had thought about moving Heath but was swayed by something John Gavin had said to him. "Well, Jack, I tell you one thing, he's got that palaver. He gets along with the Federales, he gets along with the A.G.'s Office. He does a good job in keeping things from getting stirred up." Kuykendall, on the other hand, had kept things stirred up. His relentless curiosity, cantankerous individualism, and uncompromising attitude toward his job had drawn younger agents to him, but for many of the people who worked in the American mission in Mexico, these were not virtues. Looking back, the tall Texan regretted not stirring things up more.

Kuykendall's mood turned volcanic. By day, he worked the telephone, pausing frequently to curse the DEA in general and Ed Heath in particular. He stalked the streets at night, searching for what? Oblivion, his friends thought. If he cared that he lived or died, it didn't show. Kuykendall rattled about the back streets of Guadalajara alone, bashing his battered old mule of a sedan over clay and cobbles, staying out till all hours with the men of the villages. "I eat to stay alive," he snapped when a visiting agent tried to buy him a decent meal.

His friends said that he should accept his fate, that he was not doing Kiki any good, that he was too angry to work. He agreed that he was angry. He fed that anger, stoked it until it was white-hot. He did not know whether he could solve the case, but he did not trust anybody else to do it, not even Coonce and Maher. Somebody had to keep the heat on, and that meant keeping it on the American government as well as on the Mexicans. Other agents had their own careers to think of. Kuykendall figured his was over. He was convinced that if he left Guadalajara, the case would be washed out with another handful of forced confessions, a show trial, and a sheaf of congratulatory press releases from the American embassy. If that happened, everything Kiki had fought for would die with him.

Kuykendall took to wearing his gun again, not because he thought it would help him survive an ambush—"What good would this little popshooter do against a bunch of AK-47s?" he said with a crooked smile—but so anybody who came after him would not have the chance to beat him to death. He would make them shoot him.

On a silvery twilight in September, a few weeks before he was due to leave Guadalajara, Kuykendall drove to the edge of the city to see some people who had been friends to him and Kiki. He sat in the courtyard, smelling the lemon trees, sipping the host's brandy. The men of the neighborhood drifted in to sing and drink and tell bawdy stories.

A heavyset man with sad eyes and a broad white smile appeared with his guitar. In a rich baritone he sang a song he had written for Kiki Camarena.

> *Your mission was to fight those you had in your book.*
> *It didn't matter to you to die.*
> *You were not afraid of them.*
> *You knew the danger. You didn't worry about anybody.*
> *Your chief, with great respect keeps you in his heart.*
> *We called you the* gallo prieto, *the dark rooster.*
> *You never ran away.*
> *Adiós, Kiki Camarena.*
> *Your friends say to you,*
> *Let the dark Virgin pardon your assassins.*

The singer turned to Kuykendall and said that the Lady of Guadalupe might forgive, but he would not.

Jaime Kuykendall would never forgive. At times he sat on the veranda of the Camelot bar, watching the sky fade, and thought of the comradeship he and Kiki and the others had shared here, tossing down Estrellitas, happily scheming against Caro Quintero and all the rest. He stared across Calle Libertad at the consulate. He was the last of the old bunch. Shaggy Wallace was gone. He hadn't wanted to leave, but somebody picked up word that El Azul, Juan Esparragoza, was gunning for him. Roger Knapp, Pete Hernandez, and Butch Sears were long gone. In a few weeks, he would be back where he had started, in Laredo.

"I need somebody to give me back some faith," he said. "I have lost faith."

16
"We Don't Want a *Solution!*"

By October 1985, the DEA investigation of Kiki Camarena's murder was just about stymied. The tapes were the only solid evidence of the murder that the Mexican government had given the DEA investigators.

Most of the other agreements Ed Meese had negotiated with Attorney General Sergio García Ramírez had been ignored. At their March 1985 meeting, Meese had given his counterpart a list of suspects that DEA wanted questioned, but nearly all of them were still at large. Meese and García Ramírez had agreed to create ten DEA–MFJP task forces to go after the Guadalajara-based kingpins and their *pistoleros*. The task forces had never materialized. García's aides would not even tell the DEA whether warrants had been issued for the arrests of the suspects.

In June, Bill Coonce had given Deputy Attorney General José María Ortega Padilla a routine list of investigative requirements for Operation Leyenda, DEA's Camarena homicide investigation. The Leyenda team wanted its own interviews with Caro Quintero, Fonseca, and the *pistoleros* arrested with them. The DEA agents wanted to study the evidence taken from the house on Calle Lope de Vega and the clothing and bindings from the bodies. Also, they needed fingerprints and hair samples from everyone in custody. FBI print specialists had lifted one hundred fifty latent prints from the car, the license plate, and the house on Lope de Vega. These unknown prints had to be compared with the prints of those in jail. In exchange, Coonce had offered to give Mexican prosecutors the FBI lab's findings concerning the prints and other physical evidence.

Ortega Padilla had bristled, saying that the Mexican gov-

ernment did not need American help and had sufficient
evidence to prosecute those in custody. This burst of nationalistic fervor caught Coonce unprepared. Matching fingerprints from a crime scene to the prints of suspects was
standard police procedure all over the civilized world. What
reason could there be to hold back—unless the prints of the
people in custody did not match the prints found at the
scene? Aside from the "confessions," which raised more
questions than they answered, the Mexican government had
produced no independent evidence that the men in jail had
actually murdered Kiki Camarena. It occurred to Coonce,
and to Matty Maher, his partner, as it had occurred to Jaime
Kuykendall, that the Mexican government might prosecute
the wrong men.

Stewing in his dingy office at DEA headquarters, Coonce
banged out a letter to Ortega Padilla, listing the various
promises that he felt had been broken. "Is there an active
investigation being conducted in Mexico relative to the kidnapping and murder of DEA agent Enrique Camarena Salazar?" Coonce wrote sarcastically. "If so, who is in charge
and what investigative course of actions are currently being
pursued?"

It was a rude letter, but Jack Lawn liked it. He put his
own signature on it and handed it to Ortega Padilla when
the Mexican official showed up in Washington at the end of
October. Ortega Padilla tried to smooth things over by
promising Lawn the physical evidence Coonce had requested. But when Ortega Padilla returned to Mexico City,
he told Ed Heath a different story. He said that all but small
samples of the ropes and sheets had been destroyed months
before, on orders from a Jalisco state judge. Lawn was
shocked when he read the cable from Mexico City. He had
never heard of a judge ordering the destruction of evidence.
He could not imagine a system that not only permitted but
ordered evidence destroyed *before* a trial.

DEA agents in Guadalajara confirmed that a judge had
indeed issued such a bizarre order. But according to those
agents, the date on the order was March 8, three days after
the bodies were discovered. It referred to the material found
on the bodies. The judge's order could not possibly have

meant the material found at the house on Calle Lope de Vega. The Federales did not find the house until April 11, or so they said. The next day, DEA agent Ralph Arroyo had seen Mexican evidence technicians at the MFJP office in Guadalajara with bags of sheets, cords, and other things that they said came from the house. They had been on their way to catch a flight for Mexico City. At his meeting with Ortega Padilla in June, Coonce understood the Mexican official to say that the evidence was in his personal possession in Mexico City.

At a meeting in December 1985, Lawn confronted Ortega Padilla about the missing evidence. As Lawn recalled the discussion, the Mexican official acknowledged the destruction of the sheets and other evidence but maintained that he had done it because of "putrefaction." Later, DEA learned the attorney general's office had retained samples of the cloths and cords; agents obtained these samples by slipping some cash to a Mexican with access to the evidence vault. The Mexican government gave DEA some sets of fingerprints of the men in custody in Mexico, but, according to DEA, most of the prints were smeared so badly they were useless.[1]

On October 25, 1985, José Contreras Subias, one of the few kingpins who had been arrested, bought his way out of the Tijuana jail. Contreras Subias had been detained with Caro Quintero in Costa Rica, deported, and locked up in Tijuana to face charges of murdering an MFJP agent in Baja California. Mexican authorities announced that two jail guards had admitted that they had driven Contreras Subias to San Diego. Mayor René Treviño Arredondo, a reformer who had worked hard to dispel Tijuana's reputation as "sin city," fired the jail warden and ordered the guards arrested. A judge in Tijuana indicted the warden, his secretary, the two guards, and three municipal policemen for bribery, helping in an escape, and interference with the judicial process.[2]

The escape of Contreras Subias was a humiliation for the de la Madrid administration. Even the staunchly pro-government newspaper *Excelsior* editorialized that Mexico's war on drugs was being poorly managed by the central government: "It is distressing for Mexico that only the intervention of foreign interests in the combat against narcotics traffickers has made possible the discovery of the large interests related with this activity."

A few weeks later, DEA agents in Guadalajara discovered that José Luis Gallardo Parra was staying at his uncle's house in Guadalajara. According to El Samy Ramírez, when Caro Quintero's thugs had grabbed Camarena, Gallardo Parra had driven the kidnap car. Tony Ayala, who had replaced Jaime Kuykendall as the resident agent in charge of the Guadalajara office, persuaded a team of Federales to go to the house. Moments before they arrived, DEA men staking out the house saw Gallardo Parra dash out the door, leap into a car, back out, and peel away.

Several other men on the DEA's list of suspects were back in Guadalajara. Javier Barba Hernández, the lawyer who was said to be an executioner for Caro Quintero, Fonseca, and Félix Gallardo, had been in the city, always with an entourage of bodyguards. On two occasions, DEA agents found and interviewed Rogelio Muñoz Ríos, the former DFS officer who stood accused of delivering 60 million pesos to MFJP Comandante Armando Pavón Reyes for helping Caro Quintero flee Guadalajara after Camarena's death.

As the DEA agents persisted, they began to hear warnings that traffickers were looking for them and might retaliate. One source reported that Mexican policemen had put up a roadblock between Mazatlán, Sinaloa, and Durango and were looking for DEA agents. An American tourist told consular officials in Mazatlán that some men had stopped his bus at a roadblock between Mazatlán and Culiacán and had said they were looking for DEA agents.

Just before Christmas, Bill Coonce was promoted to a senior headquarters job, and his friend Carlo Boccia, a gravel-voiced Bronx native, took over as chief of Operation Leyenda. Boccio had the qualities Jack Lawn valued: he was skeptical, irreverent, and willing to listen to anybody. "You gotta kiss a lot of frogs before you get a prince," he liked to say. Lawn considered it a virtue that Boccio had never worked in Mexico or the Southwest. The DEA chief wanted a man who did not bear old grudges against the Mexicans and warned Boccio to form his own opinions. The investigation was a killer. It possessed men and burned them out. At times Lawn, too, felt overwhelmed with fury.

Lawn was particularly disturbed by evidence Matty Maher had developed which suggested that the cover-up extended into the ranks of Mexican Army officers.

In early December, an undercover DEA agent had lured a Costa Rican pilot named Werner Lotz into Panama by pretending to contract for an airplane to fly cocaine. The agent had prearranged for the Panamanian Defense Forces to arrest the pilot and put him on an airplane bound for Miami. DEA agents took him into custody at Miami International Airport.

Charged with cocaine trafficking, Lotz began to bargain and to talk about an experience he had had in Mexico. Maher flew to Miami to debrief him. According to an affidavit subsequently filed in federal court in Los Angeles, Lotz told DEA agents that in early March, shortly after Camarena's body had been discovered, he had received a cryptic telephone call from a Mexican man named Inés Calderón Quintero, a cousin of Rafael Caro Quintero. Lotz said Calderón told him there was a man in Mexico who had many political enemies and needed to get to Costa Rica. Lotz took the job.

According to the affidavit, Lotz told the following story. He landed at the airport in Mazatlán on March 16 and met a man named Albino Bazán Padilla, who gave him some expense money. The next morning, the pilot claimed, a Mexican Army colonel gave him a package of documents for "El Señor," the person he was to fly to Costa Rica. The colonel told him to fly to another airstrip about thirty miles north, near the town of Escuniapa. Lotz said this private airstrip was guarded by fifteen to twenty heavily armed officers. When he landed, he met Inés Calderón Quintero. Standing beside him was a curly-headed young man with hard eyes. Lotz said he handed the documents to the man. "Yes, from the colonel," the man said, and boarded the

plane, along with two girls and three men. The man was
Rafael Caro Quintero. One of the girls was Sara Cosío
Martínez. The other was her friend Violeta Estrada. He
identified photographs of the three other men: they were
José Contreras Subias, Juan Carlos Campero Villanueva,
and Miguel Juárez Medina. Upon arriving in Costa Rica,
Lotz said, he accompanied Caro Quintero to the coffee plantation named La Quinta. There, a man named Jesús Félix
Gutiérrez greeted them. After several days, Lotz said, he
met Caro Quintero once more, and the trafficker was edgy,
complaining that he was being followed. Lotz asked why he
was so nervous. Caro Quintero replied that he was being
sought for the Camarena murder and he intended to hide
in Costa Rica until "his people" in Mexico had taken care
of things.

At first, the DEA agents had some problems with Lotz's
credibility. They said that Lotz attempted to conceal previous dealings he had had with Caro Quintero. At first, Lotz
pretended that he had never met Caro Quintero before the
flight from Mazatlán, but DEA developed an informant
within Caro Quintero's family who said that in 1983 Lotz
had flown a load of cocaine for Caro Quintero to a private
Sinaloa airstrip that was owned by former Sinaloa governor
Antonio Toledo Corro. After Lotz made a deal to plead
guilty to a drug-trafficking charge with a relatively modest
six-year sentence, the agents said, he talked more freely,
and they came to believe his version of events.

Early in 1986, Lawn, Boccia, Coonce, and Maher spent
several hours with Ortega Padilla and acting MFJP director
Florentino Ventura asking for help in establishing basic facts
about the traffickers' movements around the time of the
kidnapping.

When Ortega Padilla promised to provide a solution to
the case, Maher went off like a rocket. "We don't want a
solution!" he bellowed. "We don't want to have someone
to *blame*. What we want is the *truth,* and when the truth
comes out, if the truth does come out and we're to blame,
we'll accept it. This country is *consumed* with truth. We're
not interested in the solution to the case. We want the facts,

and we hope that your investigation will give us the facts that we need to come to the truth in this case. This case will never be settled until we know the truth."

"I don't want you to think that America has a monopoly on the truth," Ortega Padilla snapped, as the agents recalled.

What about the Bravo ranch? Maher said. What better evidence that the Federales wanted to create a "solution"? "It doesn't work," he said, "because we know that the bodies weren't buried there. The soil that was found both on the bags and on the bodies and on the wrappings and everything is geologically incompatible with that area."

By the end of the session, the Americans had not gained a single concession. Boccia prided himself on his objectivity, but he came to the same conclusion that Coonce and Maher had reached before: that Mexican officials would make all sorts of promises but did not mean to give the DEA any useful evidence.

The impasse in Mexico and the capture of Werner Lotz changed the DEA's strategy. Instead of badgering the Federales to round up suspects, Boccia and his partners decided that the DEA should make its own collars. That would be more difficult, for it meant luring suspects across the border or to Panama, where the Panamanian police were generally willing to deport criminal suspects to the United States. But they saw no other way to produce witnesses for the federal grand jury that had been empaneled in Washington.

"Once they're in Mexican custody, they're going to confess to whatever has to be confessed to fit into a prearranged scenario," Boccia said. "Certainly we don't have the same methods available to us. But one thing we will get is the truth. We will not hear what we want to hear."

Well before Boccia joined the team, Bill Coonce had been thinking along the same lines. Whenever he had sent a list of suspects to Mexico City, he intentionally left off one name: René Martín Verdugo Urquídez. Verdugo, thirty-four, was a wealthy businessman who was reputed to be a

marijuana trafficker and friend of Caro Quintero. He lived
in Mexicali, just across the border from Calexico.

The agents had a witness who said that Verdugo was
there when Camarena was being tortured. DEA agents in
Guadalajara reviewed records at the Guadalajara Hyatt Hotel which, they reported, showed that Verdugo had checked
in on February 7, the day Kiki Camarena was abducted,
and checked out on February 9.

Until recently, Verdugo had had a green card allowing
him to work in the States and to enter and leave anytime
he wanted. He treated San Diego as his second home, so
DEA agents thought they would have a chance to arrest
him in California. The hitch was, little was known about
him, and he had never been charged in the United States.
Dave Gauthier, a San Diego–based agent attached to Operation Leyenda, had a lucky break. He called upon a former pot distributor named Victor Vidal. Vidal had agreed
to testify against a number of other traffickers in exchange
for leniency in his own case. Vidal said sure, he knew René,
and claimed to have bought a ton of pot from him. Vidal
gave Gauthier enough evidence to justify filing a complaint
against Verdugo and issuing an arrest warrant. Then Gauthier and partners began to track Verdugo's movements.

Born to a respectable Mexicali family, Verdugo turned
out to be a talented young entrepreneur with a string of
businesses, from real estate to tourism in Baja California.
He would eventually be charged with commanding one of
the biggest and most technologically advanced marijuana-
smuggling operations in the Southwestern United States.
Unlike the Colombian marijuana traffickers, who dispatched twenty tons of pot on mother ships, Mexican pot
smugglers sent their commodity north by truck in numerous
small loads, forcing their drivers to gut it out at the Customs
checkpoints. The indictment based on the investigation by
Gauthier and his partners, Joe González and Tom Kelly,
and Customs agent Joe Martínez, traced Verdugo's rise in
the trafficking business: it alleged that Verdugo went into
partnership with a bunch of hotshot gringo pilots and
learned the lesson that Silicon Valley had taught the Rust-
belt—technology and organization beat muscle and blood

every time. Verdugo allegedly finessed the Customs problem by organizing an airlift that used the best equipment: state-of-the-art navigational equipment, night-flying goggles, portable landing-strip illumination and marking systems, radio communication systems, portable aircraft-refueling equipment, satellite dishes. According to the indictment, his planes were outfitted to handle as much as a thousand pounds of marijuana at a time, and he had recently acquired a Sikorsky helicopter that could land almost anywhere and carry as much as two tons of marijuana.

The DEA agents pursued their investigation based on the suspicion that Verdugo had worked his way up into one of the top executive spots in the Caro Quintero organization. Creative, well-spoken, good-looking, Verdugo was, by the standards of the Sinaloans, a man of the world. The agents surmised that an ambitious hick like Caro Quintero, who had recently forced himself to learn to drink Scotch, probably liked the idea of having Verdugo around. In corporate terms, the agents sized up Verdugo as senior vice-president in charge of transportation and wholesaling for California.

The DEA agents were sure that they would get Verdugo in late 1985, when his wife, Teresa, was in a San Diego hospital where she had given birth to their first son. They staked out the hospital for days, but Verdugo never visited. They realized then that Verdugo knew they were on his trail.

Matty Maher called his old friend Don Ferrarone, a former DEA agent who was then at the U.S. Marshals Service. The marshals specialized in fugitive cases and had no qualms about reaching across borders to get wanted men. Ferrarone agreed to help and, with the aid of Tony Pérez, a fellow marshal with great Baja sources put together a plan to snatch Verdugo. Ferrarone made a deal with a Mexicali-based Baja California state police supervisor with the improbable name of Mohammed Ali Hoy Casas. Hoy Casas agreed to have his subordinates find Verdugo and deliver him to the border. Stanley Morris, the head of the Marshals Service, gave the plan a green light. So did the Justice Department attorneys handling the Washington grand jury. Members of the Leyenda team deliberately kept the plan from Ed Heath, who,

they feared, would feel obliged to inform the Mexican Attorney General's Office.

Perez, Ferrarone, and their partners located Verdugo in
San Felipe, a parched Baja California fishing village. Verdugo had built a hideaway for himself and his wife on a
magnificent bluff overlooking the Gulf of California. Grand
stone steps, mock Mayan temple, descended to the water.

On the night of January 24, 1986, Hoy Casas and five of
his men moved into San Felipe. According to Verdugo's
lawyer, Howard Frank, one car skidded into Verdugo's path
as he drove down the street. Two other cars pulled up. Six
men jumped out and surrounded Verdugo's car, guns
drawn. Frank said they yanked him out of his car, handcuffed and blindfolded him, and threw him into the back of
one of the cars. After a spine-shaking rampage across fields
and back roads, the car screeched to a halt outside Mexicali
at the flimsy fence that marked the U.S.-Mexican border.
The men hauled Verdugo out of the car and shoved him
through a hole in the fence, into the arms of a group of
U.S. Border Patrol officers. They were paid $32,000 by the
U.S. government for performing this service.

The Border Patrol took Verdugo into Calexico and
handed him over to Ferrarone, who booked him on a fugitive warrant and delivered him to San Diego, where Matty
Maher and Dave Gauthier were waiting. The DEA agents
said they had Verdugo stripped naked, photographed, and
weighed so that he could not claim he was tortured or
starved. They took fingerprints and samples of his hair to
be matched to the prints and hairs the FBI had found in the
house on Lope de Vega.

Verdugo was arraigned, whisked to Washington, D.C.,
and brought before the grand jury hearing evidence in the
Camarena case. According to DEA officials, Verdugo declined to testify or to cooperate in any way in the investigation.

Verdugo was indicted in San Diego on drug-trafficking
charges. Gauthier and his partners went to work gathering
more evidence. As the investigation progressed, the federal
grand jury in San Diego issued new indictments charging
that Verdugo had violated the continuing criminal enterprise

or "kingpin" statute, which was the toughest drug-trafficking law on the books. The kingpin statute carried a minimum of ten years without the possibility of parole and a maximum of life imprisonment. Since Verdugo was not a hard-boiled guy—he was young and vigorous, with a beautiful wife and a new son—the agents hoped that the prospect of decades in prison would loosen his tongue.[3]

The Leyenda team had wanted Verdugo as a witness, but the FBI lab results elevated his status: he became prime suspect in the Camarena murder. The lab made a positive match between Verdugo's hair and hairs found in the Lope de Vega house. The lab findings and other evidence of Verdugo's presence in Guadalajara at the time Camarena was kidnapped led the agents to believe he was involved in the murder conspiracy. If that proved to be the case, Verdugo's cooperation was DEA's best bet for finding the rest of the truth.

But Verdugo's arrest would cost the DEA dearly, for it had antagonized Steve Trott, the assistant attorney general in charge of the Justice Department's criminal division.

Trott was a formidable adversary. A Harvard graduate, Rhodes scholar, and successful U.S. attorney in Los Angeles, the tall, exuberant Californian was ambitious and an eager bureaucratic infighter. He retained the prosecutor's single-minded drive to win, was extraordinarily forceful in his arguments, and naturally dominated any policy debate in which he participated. When the subject of Mexico arose, Trott's oratory took on an especially fervent tone. Of all the officials in Washington who played a part in the making of U.S. policy toward Mexico on the drug issue, Trott seemed to be the only one who truly sympathized with Mexican officials. State Department officials maintained an air of civility in their discussions with Mexican officials, but theirs were professional smiles. With rare exceptions, they did not pretend to like the people they dealt with. Trott appeared to have struck up a genuine friendship with Mexican Deputy Attorney General Ortega Padilla. The Justice Department official had spent several years of his youth living in Mexico, spoke Spanish fluently, and seemed convinced that he could convert his strong personal affinity for the place and its people into political action.

Trott assured reporters and skeptical Congressional committees that Ortega Padilla and his boss, Attorney General García Ramírez, were doing their best to cooperate with the U.S. government. "We're in this for the long haul with Mexico, not for one case or two cases or five minutes or six months," he said in one interview. "We want to set up a regularized system involving the exchange of information that'll be long-term and useful. And the only way you can set something like that up is with goodwill and cooperation on both sides of the equation. You can't bludgeon somebody into something like that. It requires respect and trust."

From the start of Operation Leyenda, Trott had not seen eye to eye with the DEA agents, who thought the Justice Department official had been beguiled by the Mexican officials' words—and by his own.

Consequently, when the opportunity to have Verdugo captured presented itself, the agents assumed Trott would disapprove and did not tell him. They were right. He was furious and complained bitterly to DEA and Marshals Service officials that they had run roughshod over Mexican territorial rights.

Afterward, according to DEA officials, Trott did not act on a number of requests from Boccia for letters of judicial assistance, also called letters rogatory, which were demands for evidence, the equivalent in international law of subpoenas. In an interview in July 1986, Trott denied that he refused to grant DEA's requests for letters rogatory. "That's a complete mischaracterization of what's going on," he said. Trott contended that the U.S. government was in fact receiving evidence from the Mexican government "for any purpose that we need it. Is there a free flow, is there as much as we would like? I'm not sure yet, but we've made some recent requests and are waiting to see what happens."

However, Trott acknowledged that he did not want to go through the letters rogatory process, in which a U.S. court order would be presented by the U.S. State Department to the Mexican Foreign Ministry, which would present it to a Mexican court, because it was "an eighteenth-century way of doing things." "We're working on an informal basis," Trott said. "The secret here is a long-term relationship where we create a flow of information back and forth. The Mutual Legal Assistance Treaty is the modern way and you either do it informally or with a Mutual Legal Assistance Treaty, and that's what we're aiming for." Trott began campaigning for such a treaty with the Mexican government. The treaty negotiations turned out to be more protracted than he had anticipated: he optimistically alerted Congressional committees and reporters several times in 1986 and 1987 that the treaty was on the verge of being signed, but Attorney General García Ramírez delayed the signing until December 9, 1987, and it did not take effect at that time because, as is the case with all treaties, the legislative bodies of both nations would have to ratify it.

Boccia did not object to Trott's quest for a new treaty, but since it might not materialize before the U.S. statute of limitations expired on the crimes Operation Leyenda was investigating, Boccia wanted to use letters rogatory, which he had often used with French and Italian authorities. Denied that option, his only recourse was to send the Mexican Attorney General's Office "officios," written requests for information that did not carry the force of a letter rogatory but did not require Trott's approval.[4]

The differences between DEA and Justice over letters rogatory were resolved in September 1986, when Trott was promoted from assistant attorney general to associate attorney general, the number-three job in the Department of Justice. William F. Weld succeeded Trott as chief of the Justice criminal division. Corruption investigations were Weld's passion: as U.S. attorney for the district of Massachusetts, the forty-year-old prosecutor had distinguished himself by filing corruption charges against 111 public officials and convicting all but three. Once installed in the Justice Department, Weld approved a letter rogatory for evidence in investigations related to the Camarena murder. After Weld's arrival, Boccia returned to DEA headquarters from a meeting at Justice shaking his head in wonder. "I went in with my chain mail on and my white steed, ready to do battle," he told a friend, "and it was a cocoa and ladyfingers operation."

Ultimately, though, the letter rogatory process proved no more effective than Trott's gentle persuasion or Boccia's officios. According to Justice and DEA officials, the letters rogatory went unanswered and so did nearly all the officios.

In one instance, there was a partial response. The Mexican Attorney General's Office sent DEA a photostatic copy of the anonymous note that had led the Federales to the Bravo ranch, behind which the bodies of Camarena and Zavala were found. The DEA had asked for the original copy, so that it could be tested for fingerprints, or at least a photograph, so that the FBI laboratory could run some handwriting analyses. The photostatic copy was no good for either purpose. In fact, the response of the Mexican Attorney General's Office raised more questions than it answered. Along with the copy of the note, the DEA received a copy of the envelope in which it had allegedly been mailed. The postmark, from Los Angeles, was dated two days *before* the date on the note that Comandante Pavón Reyes had shown Jaime Kuykendall and Tony Ayala before the Bravo ranch raid. On the photostatic copy that Operation Leyenda received, according to DEA agents who saw it, the date on the note was marked through and an earlier date was scratched in that corresponded to the date on the postmark.

U.S. District Judge Lawrence Irving of San Diego ordered Verdugo held without bail, but the accused trafficker turned out to be more of a stoic than the DEA agents had anticipated. When he still had not talked after five months, Boccia went to Mexico City to appeal directly to Ortega Padilla for help in prosecuting Verdugo for marijuana trafficking. A few days after Verdugo was arrested, Terry Bowen, the agent in charge of the Calexico office, had talked a friendly MFJP *comandante*, Enrique Salazar Ramos, into obtaining the permission of MFJP chief Florentino Ventura to search Verdugo's houses in Mexicali and San Felipe. The *coman-*

dante had kept the seized guns, money, and cars but had given Bowen what he wanted: a stack of documents and address books which Bowen believed related to Verdugo's alleged business. Boccia wanted Salazar Ramos to testify in Irving's court that the Federales had legally seized those records.

As Boccia recalled the meeting in Mexico City, Ortega Padilla refused to authorize the MFJP *comandante* to testify in San Diego, on grounds that Verdugo had been kidnapped and the *comandante*'s testimony would amount to a conspiracy with the DEA to violate the rights of Mexican citizens. Boccia badgered Ortega Padilla until embassy officers signaled him to back off. Boccia later heard that Ortega Padilla had sent word to DEA headquarters that Carlo Boccia should not be sent back to Mexico City. Boccia found that vastly amusing. "I hope the son of a bitch lights a candle to the Lady of Guadalupe for my demise," he said, grinning.

As it turned out, the Mexican government's refusal to allow the *comandante* to testify was not DEA's only legal problem in the Verdugo case. In February 1987, Judge Irving ruled that the documents the MFJP had seized from Verdugo's houses in Baja California were inadmissible in a U.S. court on grounds that the search was unconstitutional because it had been requested by the DEA and should have been authorized by a search warrant from a U.S. court.[5] The Ninth Circuit Court of Appeals agreed with Irving. Prosecutors took the question to the U.S. Supreme Court, which pushed Verdugo's trial into the latter part of 1989.

During pre-trial litigation in the Verdugo case, a curious thing happened. Verdugo's lawyers in San Diego had filed a discovery motion seeking the tapes of the Camarena interrogation and the FBI laboratory's analyses of the voices and background noises. Assistant U.S. Attorney Warren Reese opposed the motion on grounds that the material was irrelevant to the marijuana-trafficking case against Verdugo. The written analysis was part of the evidence in the separate grand jury proceeding devoted to the Camarena murder. Judge Irving denied the defense request.

The FBI had not identified the voices on the tape but the analysis would be valuable to anyone interested in precisely what the American government knew and did not know about those who had tortured Camarena. It might have been coincidence, but a few days after Verdugo's motion was denied, Ortega Padilla asked Ed Heath for substantially the same material—the tapes and the FBI analysis—that Verdugo's motion had covered. As Heath relayed the request to Boccia, Ortega Padilla said he wanted the material for a Mexican government inquiry. Boccia refused to release it.

Ortega Padilla appealed to Trott, and Trott asked Lawn to honor the request on grounds that Ortega Padilla was a "friend" of the United States. Lawn stalled, saying he saw no reason to share the lab findings when there was no reciprocal action on the part of the Mexican government. Also, he had serious reservations about the security of the Mexican Attorney General's Office. The DEA office in Mexico City had recently asked Ortega Padilla personally to have the Federales check out several telephone numbers that DEA agents in Mexico had linked to traffickers. According to reports that DEA-Mexico sent to DEA headquarters, all the numbers went dead within a day. There was one more number the DEA did not give Ortega Padilla—and it stayed active. When asked about this incident and other leaks, Ortega Padilla said, "I take measures daily trying to put in jail those who are disloyal. I cannot suspect everyone." "There's corruption on both sides of the border," he added. "If we exchange information, there's the possibility of getting the traffickers, and those who are corrupt will show themselves. If we don't work together, we'll never get anywhere."

Ortega Padilla asked Lawn to reconsider his request for the tapes. Lawn said he did not understand why the Mexican government needed new copies of the tapes. As Lawn recalled the conversation, Ortega Padilla replied that the old copies had been lost in the earthquake. Lawn asked why the tapes were not kept in an evidence vault; he was told that they were kept in a safe that had flown open. Eventually, Lawn agreed to give Ortega Padilla duplicates of three tapes, the two Camarena tapes and the Brito tape, but not the FBI analysis. Boccia and Coonce had to obey Lawn, but they could not resist a parting shot. They labeled the three tapes "two" through "four," signaling that they believed that the Mexican Attorney General's Office had withheld at least one more cassette: the tape on which the interrogator had asked Camarena what he knew about the minister of defense, General José Arévalo Gardoqui, and Miguel Aldana Ibarra, the former *primer comandante* of the MFJP.

17
Conflicts of
Interest

A year after Camarena's murder, the Reagan administration had all but abandoned the battle against Mexican corruption. Attorney General Ed Meese no longer played an adversarial role in his talks with Mexican Attorney General Sergio García Ramírez. Meeting García Ramírez in Cancún, Mexico, in April 1986, Meese did not even raise the issue of the Camarena case. Instead, both attorneys general spoke warmly—and vaguely—of their mutual commitment to "the spirit of Cancún," which, a joint communiqué declared, would lead to "enhanced security for our citizens, a safer border, and a hemisphere free of drug trafficking and indeed of drug use."

The rapprochement was something that senior officials at the State Department had urged for months, but the man who brought Meese around was Assistant Attorney General Steve Trott, who pronounced himself confident of the Mexican government's resolve to win the drug war. "They've opened their doors, opened their books," Trott said a few weeks before the conference. "They've done everything we asked them to do. I'm *convinced* the program they've got going will work."

Despite his disappointment with the stalemate in the Camarena case, Jack Lawn went along with the conciliatory tone set by Meese and Trott. For one thing, he had no choice. Meese was his boss, and Lawn respected Meese's right to set policy. Also, Lawn was a pragmatic man, and at this point he was willing to try just about anything. Since belligerence had failed, he supposed that the amicable approach Trott advocated was worth a shot—though Trott's capacity for optimism in the face of unremitting adversity never ceased to amaze him.

The reports from DEA agents in Mexico and on the border were uniformly dismal. What many U.S. officials overlooked in their haste to applaud Mexico's imprisonment of Rafael Caro Quintero and Ernesto Fonseca was that nothing had changed. "Ford Motor Company doesn't stop supplying cars just because one plant goes on strike," said Ken Miley, who was back at DEA's McAllen, Texas, office. In December 1985, Miley's agents had seized $33 million in cash and assets from the branch of the Caro Quintero family led by Emilio and Juan José Quintero Payán, Rafael Caro Quintero's uncles. The Quintero brothers were indicted by a federal grand jury in Houston, which charged them with perpetrating an elaborate money-laundering scheme that involved some forty banks in Texas, California, New York, and the Cayman Islands. The confiscated assets represented only a fraction of the family holdings, and the brothers remained free to direct the family trafficking business from ranches and front businesses in northern Mexico. In 1984 and again in 1987, a cousin, Francisco Javier Caro Payán, was charged with drug trafficking and money laundering in connection with the family's marijuana-trafficking operations in Baja California. Eventually, DEA would assess the value of his ring's real-estate holdings in the United States at more than $50 million.[1]

Even Caro Quintero and Fonseca could not be counted out of the game. It appeared to DEA agents in Mexico that they were running their organizations from the luxurious accommodations they had arranged for themselves and their men in the Reclusorio del Norte in Mexico City. In January 1986, according to Mexican newspapers, Caro Quintero accused prison officials of robbing him of $700,000 in cash which he kept in his cell, along with a video system and a pair of handmade cowboy boots.

Cocaine trafficking through Mexico to the Southwest doubled and redoubled.[2] DEA's intelligence analysts believed that the Félix Gallardo group, still the biggest cocaine enterprise in Mexico, might be moving as much as four tons of cocaine a month into the United States. Other Mexican

traffickers had taken up the cocaine trade; in times of increased vigilance by U.S. lawmen, cocaine was easier to
hide than marijuana and more lucrative than either marijuana or heroin.

By all available evidence, the level of corruption was
unprecedented. One reason was the new influx of wealth
generated by the cocaine trade. The other factor was the
plummeting value of the peso. The September 1985 earthquake that struck Mexico City had accelerated the flight of
currency and assets out of the country, further depressed
the value of the already battered peso, and rendered drugs
an even more precious all-purpose currency because they
could readily be converted into dollars—dollars that were
worth more than ever before. Mexican police officers were
more desperate than they ever had been to obtain Yanqui
money in the face of their own country's slide into debt and
ruin. In the past, when twenty-four pesos bought a dollar,
policemen who extorted protection money did not soil their
hands with actual work. After the quake, as the peso
plunged past the six hundred mark, U.S. lawmen saw numerous signs that senior police officials, including *comandantes*, were performing sweaty physical labor for the drug
rings, standing security at stash houses, driving marijuana
convoys to the border, loading and unloading cocaine from
the smugglers' airplanes.[3]

As far as U.S. officials were concerned, the eradication
program existed mostly on paper. In the fall of 1985, just
as the Sierra Madre opium harvest was about to begin,
Hurricane Waldo crashed across Mexico's west coast, ren-
dering useless the entire eradication fleet based in Culiacán,
Sinaloa. Just one field of opium poppies was reported
sprayed in Durango between June and December 1985.[4] In
February 1986, three more spray helicopters crashed in the
Sierra Madre. What was left of the air fleet was falling apart
for lack of maintenance.

At the time of the Cancún meeting, Operation Vanguard,
the eradication monitoring program that Gavin and García
Ramírez had established nineteen months before, was
barely sputtering along. Twenty DEA agents were in Mexico
to man the verification flights, but they were grounded most

of the time. Mexican officials gave many reasons for the delays: the earthquake, damage to the telephone system, bad weather, and, always, broken aircraft. The State Department had sent money to Mexico to pay the pilots, but a DEA official who looked into the matter discovered that "the money went into the Mexican government—but it didn't come out for a long time. So the pilots refused to fly."

On the occasions when they were allowed to fly, DEA verification teams saw marijuana and opium thriving in the highlands. "We looked down at the field they sprayed," said one DEA agent, "and then we looked up, and the whole mountain was terraced with opium poppies." Often, DEA verification teams could not even find the fields that were reported sprayed because Mexican eradication pilots were not required to give them the geographical coordinates.[5] Further confirmation that the eradication program was not working was the appearance on the U.S. market of a new type of Sierra Madre heroin called "black tar." The gummy resin was sold on the street in purities ranging to 85 percent, yet the price was cheap, $3,000 to $5,000 an ounce, compared with $5,000 to $10,000 in 1984, all of which suggested that the Sierra Madre opium poppy farmers—the *gomeros*—were harvesting bumper crops.

Neither Lawn nor his senior staff members at DEA alluded in public to their distress over the Mexican eradication program. Just as Mexico's staggering debt held American banks hostage, so its potential as an outlaw haven kept the American law-enforcement community engaged. The DEA hierarchy had decided that, as one top DEA manager put it, "the Mexicans are manipulating our operation. The human reaction is to walk away. It's very frustrating when you remain, to be screwed around. On the other hand, if you pull out, you've got nothing. Their system has won."

The only open criticism of Mexico came from two of Washington's most doctrinaire conservatives—Senator Jesse Helms and William von Raab, the U.S. commissioner of customs.

———————

It was ironic that the right wing should take the lead in accusing Mexico of corruption, oppression, and election fraud. These were positions usually associated with American liberals. Many conservatives, including Ronald Reagan himself, considered Mexico a bulwark against communism. For this reason Reagan had sought a special relationship with President Miguel de la Madrid. Moderates of both parties were in agreement with Maryland Republican Senator Charles Mathias when he said that in contrast to other Latin nations, "the Mexicans have been able to keep peace in their own society and to respect a measure of civil liberty for their people."

On the other hand, those on the far right of the American political spectrum called Mexico a one-party state of the left, a totalitarian system that maintained cordial relations with Fidel Castro. The Helms wing of the Republican party pointed out, accurately, that Mexico had not had a genuinely democratic election since the Institutional Revolutionary party took power in 1921. Even Mexico's staunchest defenders in the United States acknowledged that it was not communists that the PRI feared but northern Mexico's conservative pro-business, pro–United States National Action party, whose organizers and poll workers made credible charges they were threatened, jailed, and beaten, and that vote fraud marred every major election of the 1980s. For Helms and like-minded ideologues, deepening corruption and increasing violence along the American-Mexican frontier raised the specter of civil war between conservatives in the north and leftists in the south and the ascendancy, at least in southern Mexico, of a Nicaragua-style pro-Soviet regime.

Von Raab, fervently anti-Soviet and a good friend of Helms, had not participated in the debate over the stability of Mexico. He was, as he liked to say, a "linear person." His commander in chief had told him to wage war on drugs, and that was what he intended to do. He had courted his Mexican counterparts with gifts of aircraft and surveillance equipment and when they failed to use them against traffickers, he had said nothing in public about it. It was not until February 15, 1985, when he ordered thorough Customs inspections of all vehicles leaving Mexico, that Mexican politicians recognized von Raab as an adversary, and even when von Raab issued the order that snarled border traffic from the Pacific Ocean to the Gulf of Mexico, he ~~said~~ nothing critical of the Mexican government.

But as von Raab watched the Mexican police stonewall Jack Lawn in the Camarena case, and as the smuggling "threat assessments" filed by von Raab's own offices in the Southwest grew more alarming, the Customs commissioner became increasingly frustrated. In early 1986, a sequence of events occurred that hardened von Raab's resolve to take a public stand against official corruption in Mexico.

At nine-thirty on the night of February 21, 1986, Customs Patrol Officer Glenn Miles was driving down a back road in the southernmost stretch of Arizona's Papago Indian Reservation when he saw three hikers who looked to be backpacking marijuana. Miles, a forty-four-year-old Papago, radioed his partners for backup and set out after the figures scuffling through the bush.

When the two other Customs officers arrived, they found Miles's empty truck hidden behind some scrub. They saw a light in the dust, off to the other side of the road. It was Miles's flashlight. Next to it was his body.

Miles's partners picked up the killers' tracks. The trail led to a break in the flimsy barbed-wire fence that marked the border and south toward a ranch a hundred yards inside Mexico. The ranch was a well-known staging area for drug and alien smugglers. As far as Miles's partners could determine, the men who had killed Miles were Mexicans who had hiked out of the ranch on a smuggling run for some Colombian gangsters who had moved into the area.

For Miles's partners, the awful thing was that they could see the ranch, photograph it, fly close enough to make the dust whirl, but as far as the law was concerned, it might as well have been in Burma. The Mexican police passed along a little information but could not seem to find any traffickers anywhere.

Von Raab invited the Papago tribal elders to Washington. He was moved by this meeting as by few other events since he had taken office. The old men told him of their

fears for their children. In the old days, a boy could camp
out on the range with nothing but the moon and stars to
see him. Now there was no peace. One who stumbled into
a bunch of strangers might be shot for pure mischief. The
young people were falling into bad ways, buying marijuana
and beer and even heroin, hiring on as burros for the gangs.
There were no jobs. Many of the young men committed
suicide. This was why Glenn Miles had worked for the Customs Service. He had been a reformed alcoholic himself.
Arresting the traffickers was his way of helping younger
tribesmen.

Drastic measures took shape in von Raab's mind. "We're
hiring five people to replace Miles," he announced. "If they
come at us again, we'll hire more. We'll react with more
and more force." He offered a $100,000 reward for infor-
mation leading to the capture of the killers.

The murder of Miles had not been premeditated, as the
Camarena killing had been, but for von Raab it was a moment of truth. He realized that as long as sanctuaries like
this ranch existed, nothing could prevent wanton murderers
from violating the border. The shooting also confirmed what
von Raab had feared, that as the Customs–Coast Guard
interdiction net had tightened around South Florida, Colombian traffickers would move to the land border and form
alliances with established Mexican smuggling networks.

There were two things von Raab felt he had to have in
order to be able to do his job. One was access to Mexican
airspace. Customs agents had mapped nearly 500 airstrips
and 132 stash houses within a hundred miles north or south
of the land border. The pilots who made nightly runs with
marijuana and cocaine flew in low and made touch-and-go
landings or did not land at all but dropped their cargo by
parachute. The only chance Customs had to make a seizure
was to be there at the instant of the drop. That required
advance warning. There was no way a Customs interceptor
aircraft could scramble fast enough to rendezvous with an
intruder whose penetration of U.S. airspace lasted but fifteen or twenty minutes.

"We're like a guy standing by a fence waiting for base-

balls to come over," von Raab said. "It's not easy to catch
them when they're thirty feet in the air and moving." He
reasoned that Customs radar-surveillance planes patrolling
east to west a hundred miles inside Mexico could detect
smuggling aircraft heading north in time to scramble Customs interceptors.

Von Raab had made a number of overtures to Mexican
Customs to conduct joint air-surveillance projects, appeal-
ing to the government's interest in controlling the flow of
arms to dissident groups and also in collecting duty on *fa-
yuca*—black-market electronic equipment, appliances, and
other consumer goods. In 1983, he ordered his agents to
send intelligence on southbound flights to Mexican Customs,
but no drug intelligence came north. To make matters
worse, von Raab found out that some Mexican officials were
using the U.S. data to extort smugglers. Von Raab's cooperation was severely criticized by the newspapers in Texas
when Mexican authorities shot down a plane piloted by a
Texan, so he ended the project.

Then von Raab gave Mexican Customs an old Navy
Grumman S2-D tracker airplane refitted with forward-
looking infrared radar that could spot aircraft at night and
through clouds. The plane crashed a few months after the
Mexican pilots began using it. Mexican Customs officials
blamed sabotage, but U.S. Customs officials who examined
the wreckage discovered that the Mexicans allowed it to run
out of gas.

The other thing von Raab considered essential was for
the Mexican government to clean out the safe havens on
the south side of the border. He was convinced that the
border sanctuaries flourished because Mexican officialdom
was bought off from the top down. Corruption, he said, was
why the killers of Kiki Camarena and Glenn Miles and every
other crook who had enough brains to pay off the cops got
away.

Indeed, just as von Raab was pondering the problem, a
report arrived from the Naco, Arizona, Customs office. It
seemed that a uniformed Mexican customs officer had tried
to cross into the States with a hundred and fifty pounds of
marijuana in his trunk. The Mexican officer hit the U.S.

Customs inspector who confronted him and ran south, leaving the marijuana, the car, and his uniform jacket. Von Raab sent a letter of complaint to the director of Aduanas, the Mexican customs service. The only answer he got was a request to return the jacket.

That was the last straw for von Raab. This was not some informant report. Here was hard evidence that Mexican lawmen were smuggling, and officials in Mexico City felt free to thumb their noses at him. Ever since Treasury Secretary Baker had chastised him about closing the border, von Raab had kept his mouth shut. What good had it done? He could see no evidence of meaningful cooperation, and as far as he was concerned, it was sheer self-delusion to believe that anything was going to change.

Von Raab set his aides to devising ways to strengthen the interdiction net on the U.S. side. They came up with Operation Blue Fire, similar to a federal-local interdiction project in Florida called Operation Blue Lightning. The plan was a way of harnessing all the law-enforcement resources in the area toward the common goal of interdicting smugglers. Customs would create a radio network linking all Customs units, police departments, and sheriff's offices along the border. Ordinarily, local officers went their own way and did not communicate with one another or with Customs. By distributing radios tuned to a common frequency, Customs could make it possible for local officers from the Gulf coast to the Pacific to talk to one another and to receive signals from a Customs command center, which would coordinate tips from informants, radar sightings, and other data.

Von Raab thought he could justify Blue Fire to Meese's National Drug Policy Board on grounds that he was simply improving interdiction capabilities in the region. But he also knew that publicity about the border buildup would put pressure on the Mexican government to do something about corruption.

Von Raab decided to skip Meese's "law-enforcement summit" in Cancún. He thought that all that meeting and smiling and communiqué writing compromised everyone involved and set the process back. The Mexican officials were rewarded with good publicity, which von Raab said they did not deserve, and the Americans fooled themselves into believing that they had accomplished something.

Like Mullen, von Raab had observed that the only thing that seemed to move the Mexican government to take action against corrupt officials was bad publicity. Indeed, terrible publicity. And he did not plan to wait for the press to catch on to the significance of Operation Blue Fire. He intended to take the offensive.

Von Raab tested his new approach at a March 18 hearing of the House Select Committee on Narcotics Abuse and Control. "We must sound the alarm that our border is being violated at will," von Raab declared.

> Our southern border is fast becoming what South Florida was like six years ago. The corruption and ineptitude of law enforcement in Mexico . . . is a serious national security concern. If law enforcement can be so easily bought by drug smugglers, it can be just as easily bought by terrorists. If a small planeload of terrorists flew across our border from Mexico and bombed San Diego or Tucson, there would be a great hue and cry. But planeloads of drug "terrorists" fly across our border every day . . . drop their load of cocaine bombs, and they fly back into the safe haven of Mexico. I personally do not see the difference between a drug smuggler and a terrorist. Cocaine is wreaking as much havoc in our country as any terrorist bomb ever could. Corruption in Mexican law enforcement is commonplace, and corruption is the food of these terrorists.[6]

The congressmen, accustomed to hearing administration spokesmen drone through lifeless and uninformative statements, sat up and took notice—and began to pepper von Raab with questions. The hearing, though sparsely attended, made a few headlines. Von Raab made an even bigger splash after he gave a series of interviews to correspondents from *The Washington Post, Newsweek* magazine, and *The New York Times*. The interviews had been scheduled so that von Raab could explain his new border-interdiction project, but he also went out of his way to assert

that he did not intend to join Meese and the Mexican officials
at Cancún. The first of the articles, entitled " 'Crisis Zone'
on the Border," appeared on April 14 in *Newsweek*. The
item quoted von Raab as saying, "I believe I can be more
productive trying to improve our defenses than going down
there to sit and basically talk." [7]

A Justice Department official called Meese in Cancún
and read the *Newsweek* item. Meese was thunderstruck. It
was bad enough that the customs commissioner had declined
to attend. But to suggest in public that he was boycotting
the meeting, to disparage the session as "talk": Meese and
his aides saw this as the worst sort of posturing. Deputy
Attorney General Lowell Jensen, who had accompanied
Meese to Mexico, telephoned von Raab, who could hear
Meese raging in the background. Von Raab replied blandly
that he wished Meese well, but as for himself, he had better
things to do with his time, like expand the Customs presence
on the border.

Meese prevailed on Frank Keating, the assistant secretary of the treasury for enforcement, to prevent von Raab
from carrying out his project unilaterally. However, Meese
liked the idea of building up the Southwest border-
interdiction net. It would appeal to influential interest
groups in the Sunbelt. It was one of the few of von Raab's
ideas that Southwestern businessmen would not consider a
loss. Intensified law enforcement in the Southwest would
not pose the political drawbacks of tightening inspections
at the ports of entry and losing lucrative trade. To the contrary, an expanded law-enforcement presence in the Southwest would reassure citizens, make the streets safer, and
would bring into the states new federal contracts that would
create new jobs.

Keating, von Raab's immediate boss, told von Raab to
stop contacting state and local officials and to stay away
from the press. The National Drug Policy Board, which
Meese chaired, would create a broader and more elaborate
Southwest border plan involving all the federal agencies.

"The Drug Policy Board," von Raab thought, rolling his
eyes. His simple, practical idea was doomed to travel the
infinity loop of bureaucratic consultation: how many trees

would die to make policy papers? But he got the picture. He had moved too far out front again. He was being included out.

Von Raab often talked out his frustrations with Jesse Helms, who was fascinated by the younger man's tales of greed and treachery. Von Raab knew very little about Mexico and was interested only in stopping drugs. But for Helms, who had constructed an entire foreign policy around the opinions of conservative economists and political theoreticians, these anecdotes proved what he had been preaching, that the Mexican Institutional Revolutionary party's brand of left-wing authoritarianism would cause Mexico's social order to break down. And when it did, Helms contended, refugees would flood across the border, the American banking system would totter, and Marxist elements within and without Mexico would grab for power.

Helms was exasperated by the Reagan administration's benign neglect of the nation to the south. He thought the American government should exert more pressure upon the Institutional Revolutionary party to democratize the political process and move to a free-market economic system. In 1982, Helms had opposed a Reagan-sponsored package of loans to rescue Mexico from its financial crisis because President López Portillo's response had been to nationalize the banks. Helms had charged that nationalization only invited corruption, as evidenced by the recent corruption scandal within Petróleos Méxicanos, the government-owned oil industry. "Mexico needs to send signals which assure the world that a bloated, mismanaged, and corrupt image is being restrained, and redirected, to more responsible and market-oriented mechanisms," Helms had said.

At the time, the North Carolina senator had been ignored by the administration and nearly all of his colleagues. But as the corruption scandal sparked by Kiki Camarena's murder unfolded, Helms sensed he could find allies among Washington's mainstream political establishment. The members of the Congressional law-and-order coalition, including Democratic House members such as Charles Rangel of New York and Larry Smith of Florida, and Democratic

Senators Joe Biden of Delaware and Dennis DeConcini of Arizona, were grumbling about the administration's past lack of candor on the sorry state of Mexican drug enforcement. Such other influential lawmakers as Republican Senator Phil Gramm of Texas were vexed by the Mexican government's failure to denationalize key industries and to lower barriers to foreign investors. (IBM, the giant computer manufacturer, had had to fight for permission to build a plant and create thousands of jobs in Mexico.) De la Madrid was seeking Treasury Secretary James Baker's help in arranging a new bailout package for $6 billion, and Baker's most optimistic aides could offer no guarantee that this "emergency" would be the last.

Helms did not believe in bargaining behind closed doors for incremental changes in policy. A onetime broadcast commentator, he liked to marshal public support for dramatic change by staging spectacular events. On the morning of May 13, 1986, Helms set off on the most inflammatory incursion into Mexican affairs since Black Jack Pershing charged into Chihuahua looking for Pancho Villa.

The subject of the hearings of the Subcommittee on Western Hemisphere Affairs was blandly given as "the situation in Mexico," but the topics due to be covered—corruption, drug trafficking, electoral fraud, human rights violations, economic mismanagement, and political stability—were the most divisive issues on the bilateral agenda. Sensing good copy, reporters had packed the cavernous Foreign Relations chamber; what seats were left had been taken by Mexican diplomats sensing trouble. Mexican Ambassador Jorge Espinosa de los Reyes had approached Senator Charles Mathias to try to head off public hearings. This ill-advised contact served only to inspire Helms to wrap himself in the flag of the First Amendment.

"There have been strong attempts to thwart these hearings," Helms announced as he gaveled the first session to order. "It has been charged that these hearings are inappropriate and somehow interfere with Mexico's sovereignty. . . . Obviously the people in Mexico and in this country don't know me very well."

The first bombshell was the State Department's testimony, a scathing critique of Mexico's failure to curb corruption and allow truly democratic elections. Assistant Secretary of State Elliott Abrams, a favorite of Secretary George Shultz, had made a deliberate decision to use this hearing to send a tough message to the Mexican ruling elite. This was no favor to Helms, with whom Abrams frequently sparred. Abrams, a combative young conservative, was genuinely worried about Mexico's stability in the face of ravening corruption and de la Madrid's economic dithering. He also knew that to gloss over the symptoms of impending trouble would further undermine the State Department's credibility. Consequently, he appeared before Helms prepared to deliver the harshest assessment of Mexico's political system ever to issue from the Reagan State Department. Seven months before, Abrams's deputy, James Michel, had assured a House subcommittee that Mexico's anti-drug program was "one of the world's most successful" and would soon be "revitalized." "Police forces have been reorganized to reduce corruption, and efforts are under way to restore the effectiveness of the eradication program," Michel had said confidently. "We have engaged in discussions with the government of Mexico and it has taken positive steps, which are encouraging. I think we will see more effective cooperation on the narcotics front."[8]

Abrams's tone was considerably gloomier. "Perhaps the most debilitating and frustrating [problems between the U.S. and Mexico] are those created by narcotics and corruption. . . . We have told the Mexicans in no uncertain terms that we are deeply troubled by the widespread drug-related corruption . . . [and] about the influence the traffickers are beginning to exert within Mexican society." Abrams went on to say that the Mexican government's resistance to adopting free-market economic policies might prevent de la Madrid from securing new loans. Most surprising of all was Abrams's blunt assertion that the administration believed that the PRI had been rigging elections. In the past, Shultz and his aides had steadfastly refused to answer reporters' questions about allegations of election fraud. Abrams broke the unwritten rule, asserting that charges of fraud "have raised serious questions about the quality of Mexican democracy" and could "trigger a widespread loss of confidence [which could] lead to a general crisis in governance."

DEA's presentation was not meek by the standards of the past. David Westrate, chief of operations for the agency, testified that trafficking groups traveled around Mexico "very overtly, in large numbers, with protection by police officers and constant contact with the official police establishment," and the police officers exhibited "no concern at all" when DEA agents saw them with traffickers.

But Willy von Raab upstaged all the other witnesses. When Helms, playing straight man, asked about the extent of corruption among the Mexican police, von Raab lashed out with a theatrical flair. "My response would just be one word, massive," he said. "It's just all the way up and down the ladder. There are large payments being made at very high levels of the police—and by the police I include all sworn officers in the Mexican law-enforcement establishment." "Until I'm shown that an individual is not corrupt," von Raab added provocatively, "the level of corruption and the degree of corruption is so great my presumption is that he is corrupt."

Helms asked von Raab about reports that he said Miguel Angel Félix Gallardo was being sheltered by the governor of Sonora. Helms later said he had meant the governor of Sinaloa, Antonio Toledo Corro, not the governor of Sonora. DEA and Customs had a number of informant reports which said that Toledo Corro had been playing host to Félix Gallardo. Some of these reports had been shown to Helms. Von Raab did not catch Helms's mistake but grabbed his briefing book, flipped to the section on Sonora, and read it off. "The only information I have on the governor of Sonora," he recited, "is that he is alleged to own four ranches located near Alamosa in Sonora, on which all four ranches is grown marijuana and opium poppies. We believe these ranches are currently or occasionally guarded by the Federal Judicial Police and the Mexican Army."

That allegation set off a scramble among the Mexican reporters. Sonora, the northern Mexican state that bordered on Arizona, was an increasingly important marijuana-growing area. Rafael Caro Quintero owned extensive property there. In October 1986, Gilberto Ocaña García, the brother of the former governor, Samuel Ocaña García, would be arrested by the Federales and accused of owning and operating several marijuana farms in southern Sonora, according to Mexican officials.[9]

But at the time von Raab spoke, the governor of Sonora was Rodolfo Félix Valdés, a reform candidate hand-picked by Miguel de la Madrid, who was making a highly publicized effort to clean up corruption in the state. Von Raab did not accuse Félix Valdés of being personally corrupt and would later attempt to clarify his testimony by adding that the lands to which he referred belonged to the governor's office and passed from governor to governor. However, Mexican politicians and reporters and many American politicians as well thought von Raab *had* made an unjustified attack on Félix Valdés.

Word of the hearing hit Mexico City like another earthquake. Within hours, the Mexican Foreign Relations Secretariat issued a statement calling the allegations "slander" and expressing "repudiation of the series of declarations of an interventionist nature . . . that attempts to violate Mexican sovereignty and interests." Ambassador Espinosa de los Reyes delivered a note of protest to the State Department condemning the hearing for "falsifying the facts and provoking a distortion of the reality in my country." "It is contemptible," he said, "that a member of the Senate would organize months in advance a hearing . . . for the sole purpose of hurling absurd accusations against Mexico and spreading disinformation about our country." Espinosa told reporters the statements came from a "dogmatic and extremist political faction" in the U.S. government.

Excelsior ran three stories on the front page under the headline "Mexico: Interventionism and Slanders in the U.S. Senate." The newspaper's Washington correspondent, José Manuel Nava, wrote that the Helms hearings represented an "unusual change in U.S. foreign policy toward its southern neighbor, with whom Washington traditionally has tried to solve its differences at a distance from the press and

publicity." Another Mexico City newspaper, *El Nacional*,
headlined its account "U.S., the Leading Promoter of Drug
Trafficking." The Mexican newspaper *La Jornada* ran a cartoon strip that featured Jesse Helms wearing a sombrero
and smoking a marijuana cigarette. "With you, Sen. Jesse
Go to Helms, U.S. expert on Mexico," the caption said.

President de la Madrid himself appeared on a Washington television show, *John McLaughlin's One on One*, to
counter von Raab. "I think Mr. von Raab acted very friv-
olously in making the remarks that he did," de la Madrid
said on the broadcast, which was aired on WRC-TV June
22. "He slandered a governor who is well known in Mexico
for being exceptionally honest. Thus, since he lied about
the good conduct of a governor, I would doubt the veracity
of everything else that he said. In my opinion, Mr. von Raab
is an official who does very little to further Mexican–United
States friendship."

Elliott Abrams's audacious remarks on electoral fraud inspired speculation in Washington and Mexico City that the
Helms hearing was the first volley in a frontal assault on the
PRI, something like the administration's recent campaign
to force Philippines dictator Ferdinand Marcos out of office.
State Department officials denied that a plan was afoot to
unsettle the Mexican government. "We wanted to get the
mule's attention," said a senior State official who insisted
on speaking without attribution. "There was a general feeling that the situation in Mexico is not good. We thought,
What do you do about it? And one thing you do is talk
about it. There will now be a cooling-off period. We are not
planning to keep it up. There is no campaign here, just a
decision to apply a little candor."

Abrams had not cleared his testimony with Ronald Reagan or even White House chief of staff Donald Regan. "It
was not a command decision," a White House official said.
That official stressed, however, that the tone of the statements was not unauthorized or inconsistent with Reagan
policy. "There's a feeling around here," one White House
official said, "that Mexico is so incredibly corrupt that if it
continues on this path, it could have serious instability in

the 1990s. We've winked at Mexican corruption for so long, but it could turn around and bite us." On May 14, State Department spokesman Charles Redman told reporters that the Helms hearing "was a candid, public, balanced review of our concern over narcotics-related corruption and other issues."

But von Raab was in trouble. His zeal had led him to talk before he thought. State spokesman Redman told reporters pointedly that "it is not our position that all Mexican law-enforcement officials are corrupt." Sources close to Elliott Abrams said that Abrams was annoyed with von Raab for his remarks about the governor of Sonora and Edmundo de la Madrid, a cousin of the president of Mexico.[10] John Gavin was livid. Félix Valdés happened to be a personal friend of Gavin and of Gavin's mother, who was from Sonora. Gavin personally apologized to the Sonora governor and issued a statement to the Mexican press asserting that "there is no information in our possession that gives any sustenance in any form to the allegations."

The day after the hearing, Jesse Helms went to the White House and told Ronald Reagan and Don Regan that "if anything happened to Willy von Raab as a result of his coming before a Congressional committee and telling the truth, then there would be a wide schism between [the White House] and the rough element in the Senate like Jesse Helms and a few others." Helms was able to elicit assurances that von Raab would not be fired. But the allegations against Félix Valdés were denied, even by the Sonora governor's opponents. Von Raab's reputation suffered accordingly. "We've got a good case against Mexican corruption," a White House aide told reporters. "A screwup like this gives the Mexicans room to wiggle out of it."

No one in Washington was angrier at von Raab than Ed Meese. From Meese's point of view, not only had von Raab besmirched an innocent person, but his sweeping condemnations of Mexican officialdom—particularly his "presumption" that Mexican police officials were corrupt until shown otherwise—had shattered the fragile peace between the Mexican and American law-enforcement establishments.

Coming so soon after Meese's friendly Cancún talks, the caustic statements made by von Raab might lead the Mexican government to believe that the Reagan administration was divided, confused, and did not have a coherent policy toward Mexico. As well, Meese feared that extreme nationalists within the PRI would seize the chance to unseat Attorney General García Ramírez, who was regarded in some circles as overly responsive to the Yanquis.

Late on the afternoon of May 22, Meese called García Ramírez to try to smooth things over. He had been out of the country when all this was going on, and he hoped that the spirit of cooperation that had been fostered at Cancún still lived.[11] The next day, Meese had his press office issue a statement repudiating the "views" expressed at the Helms hearing.

Meese had never been known to use a stiletto when a sledgehammer was at hand. The effect of his sweeping statement was to disavow not only von Raab's statements but the testimony of the State Department, the DEA, the Border Patrol, and everything said by the members of the Senate Foreign Relations Committee as well. "I don't know what Meese is referring to," State Department spokesman Redman said frostily.

Meese escalated the war of words by appearing on ABC's Sunday news show *This Week with David Brinkley* to announce that, far from the impression created by the Helms hearings, "There's not one country . . . in the free world that isn't cooperating with the United States in some way in trying to eradicate the drug crops and go against the drug traffickers."

"One of the things that particularly disturbed me about the reckless charges that were made by *some* people in Congress and by one of the *unfortunate* people in the Customs Service," Meese said, "was that they implied that the whole government of Mexico was in league with drug traffickers and that simply isn't so. The present President de la Madrid has personally assured President Reagan of his efforts against drug trafficking. I can tell you from personal knowledge that the attorney general of Mexico is absolutely determined to root out both drug trafficking and also the corruption it spawns."

ABC news correspondent Sam Donaldson shot Meese a quizzical look. Was Meese saying there was no corruption in Mexican law enforcement? "Oh, there's tremendous corruption, and the attorney general of Mexico and the leaders of the country are trying to root it out," Meese replied. ". . . You've had more heads of the police agencies in Mexico fired, you've had more of them arrested and jailed in the last two or three years than we've had in the last ten or twelve years, and this idea that somehow the present administration is doing less than was done ten years ago is just absolute foolishness."

"Why did you feel that it was necessary," Donaldson asked, "to undercut the State Department by calling personally?"

"I didn't undercut the State Department at all," Meese insisted. "As a matter of fact, my views are shared directly by George Shultz and by all the other cabinet heads that are knowledgeable about this matter."

This was hot copy. Reagan's appointees often took potshots at each other privately but not on national television. All over Washington, switchboards lit up with calls from reporters. Official corruption in Mexico was a front-page story—thanks to Jesse Helms and Willy von Raab, but thanks also to Ed Meese. Meese's attack on von Raab antagonized a number of influential conservatives on Capitol Hill, who deluged Customs with offers to speak out in von Raab's favor.

The White House issued a "clarification." The code words signaling reconciliation were all there: "frank and productive" meetings between the two countries, the assertion that the Mexican government was "committed" to the drug fight and that there would be efforts to "improve U.S.–Mexican cooperation." The statement asserted that the Mexican government was prepared to prosecute "any persons involved in drug trafficking or corruption, regardless of their position in the government or society."

Since the White House statement was being read as a

slap at von Raab, Treasury Secretary James Baker issued a
clarification of the clarification: "The White House statement was not in any way intended to be a repudiation of
. . . von Raab. It is a simple restatement of our drug enforcement policy with respect to Mexico."

Baker's statement only added to the confusion. Von
Raab realized to his dismay that instead of shaping the issue,
he had made himself the issue. But he refused to back off.
"My feeling about law enforcement is that you must be true
to certain basic philosophies of life," he said. "And two of
them are candor and honesty. I do not believe in the approach of not giving accurate answers to a direct question,
particularly when it's being asked by the Senate of the
United States."

Over at the DEA, Jack Lawn's telephone rang. It was a
State Department official with whom he had had a long and
rather testy professional relationship. The man offered his
congratulations. Dave Westrate's demeanor before the
Helms committee had been commendable, the fellow said:
balanced, reasonable, positive on the eradication program.
It was truly an indication, he said, of the close working
relationship between DEA and the State Department.

"Oh Jesus, don't tell me that," Lawn groaned. "If I'm
working closely with the State Department, I'm not doing
something right."

But, in fact, Lawn had joined Meese in moving to a
course more conciliatory than the line taken by the Abrams
faction in the State Department. He justified his new re-
straint by saying that it would not make life easier for DEA
agents in Mexico to keep the Mexican Attorney General's
Office in a permanent uproar. Although the Federales were
not setting any records for diligence, there was still a good
deal of intelligence to be had. Lawn believed that DEA's
mission of gathering intelligence abroad had to be pursued
no matter how hostile the environment. He regarded the
expanding number of Colombians in Mexico as an urgent
problem and additional justification for maintaining a large
DEA presence. He was a pragmatic man and believed that
the end justified tolerating a certain amount of bad behavior

on the part of his foreign counterparts. "There are provocations in every country where we have people," he said.

But those who worked with Lawn daily sensed that he was torn. "He's so honest he hurts himself sometimes," Bob Feldkamp, Lawn's spokesman, said. "He's not afraid to speak out. He really bristles when it's suggested to him, Watch what you say. He's not political in that sense. But he's very supportive of Reagan."

Lawn had his own bureaucratic battles to wage. At the time, a number of top FBI executives were trying to persuade Meese to merge the DEA into the FBI. Although he was a career FBI man, Lawn adamantly opposed the idea. As a matter of principle, he did not believe there should be one federal law-enforcement superagency. He thought that consolidation of the two agencies would stifle competing opinions within the law-enforcement community. Also, he agreed with DEA careerists that the FBI had avoided narcotics enforcement for so long that it had very little institutional experience in working the streets. If Lawn opposed Meese's policy on Mexico, as von Raab had, he would risk his fight to preserve DEA's independence. When a DEA headquarters desk chief questioned Lawn's stance on Mexico, Lawn replied, "You don't understand, there are bigger issues at stake here." At the time, the DEA man did not comprehend what Lawn meant. It was not until April 1987, when Meese announced that he did not intend to merge the FBI and DEA, that the man saw Lawn's relieved grin and realized what he had been talking about.

As well, there was a part of Lawn that believed, because he wanted to believe, that things were getting better. Most of his subordinates were gloomier. They thought the "spirit of Cancún" was a fantasy on Meese's part, and although they were inclined to distrust any Customs commissioner, they grudgingly admired von Raab's directness and wished that Lawn had taken a similar stand. One senior DEA executive in the field wrote von Raab a fan letter.

At a meeting of the DEA senior staff, Bill Coonce found himself in the unaccustomed position of defending von Raab. "For Chrissake, he's right," he said, as one participant recalled. "I'm glad somebody has the balls to say it.

If it's a political reality that we can't do anything about drug trafficking, then why in the hell are we going through the exercise of meeting those cutthroats every four months and stroking them?"

Even when Ed Heath reported that the Mexican Attorney General's Office was threatening to throw DEA out of the country and scrap the eradication program, some mid-level officials actually hoped that Heath was right. They reasoned that the DEA would be freed of the obligation to say that the Mexican police were cooperating at times when they were not.

American politicians who represented constituencies more concerned about domestic crime than foreign affairs began to rally, if not to Helms's defense, at least to his general point of view on Mexico.[12]

Dennis DeConcini summoned Lawn to his office. Lawn said that things were not all that bleak, that, in fact, the eradication program was going much better. "Stop bullshitting me," DeConcini snapped.

"I don't have to take that from anybody, Senator," Lawn said, stalking out.

"We were told that things weren't great, but [nobody said that it] was as bad as it turns out that it was," complained Larry Smith, head of the House Foreign Affairs Committee's task force on international narcotics control. "Now, every time I ask a question about how did it get so bad, everybody shrugs their shoulders and nobody really knows. I think that the administration has to be honest with the American people, no matter what it means in terms of statements about other countries. The American people are entitled to that."[13]

Testifying before Smith's panel, Westrate of DEA steadfastly refused to be drawn into any position that could be construed as critical of Mexico. His insistence that progress was being made on the Camarena case earned him a lecture from Congressman Benjamin Gilman of New York, who served on Foreign Affairs and was also the ranking Republican on the House Select Committee on Narcotics Abuse and Control.

"Mr. Westrate," Gilman said, "it seems to a number of us that the bottom line in this case is that our own agent and the DEA contract pilot were killed with the complicity of some of the enforcement officials in Mexico and that those officials have attempted to either stonewall, cover up, or delay or prevent the trial in this case, and that even our own government has been less than enthusiastic about pursuing the eventual trial of this case, and I'm puzzled, too, that our Customs Service has apparently been taking a stronger stand on this issue than our own DEA."[14]

Smith concluded that Westrate was only obeying orders from Meese and Trott, who had declined to testify. "I've found the Attorney General's Office to be arrogant and evasive," Smith said after the hearing. "I personally am convinced that the Justice Department is against the best interests of the United States in terms of stopping drugs. I think that those decisions have also affected the ability of the DEA to do their work, and the morale of the DEA agents, and I just don't think that the Justice Department is committed to pushing the Mexicans on a resolution to the Camarena case. What has a DEA agent who puts his life on the line got to look forward to? The United States government is not going to back him up. I find that intolerable."

At the White House, Ed Meese had earned the sobriquet "No Problems Ed" because of his refusal to acknowledge errors, lapses, or dissension. Like the president, Meese was not a detail man. The attorney general had a habit of glossing over, misstating, or forgetting discordant facts. He decreed that the Mexican eradication program was working; he ignored bad news. He treated dissenters as turncoats or denied they existed. When he was asked by a reporter if he was upset about criticism of his stand on Mexico, he replied cheerily, "I haven't heard any criticism. All I've heard is criticism of the other side and praise for my standing up. Who's criticizing?"

Except for Lawn, DEA officials had nothing good to say about Meese. They did not think the attorney general was a bad man, but they thought he was a weak man. Meese was anxious to preside over a successful war on drugs at a time when most agents found themselves gripped by the Vietnam syndrome. They were winning case after case, battle after battle—everything but the war. To any agent who had ever worked in Mexico, Meese's faith in meetings with Mexican officials was unfathomable. He called the publicity surrounding von Raab's outburst a "tragedy," trivializing the real tragedies that unfolded daily because of the drug trade. He persisted in prophesying that the eradication program and the Camarena murder investigation would soon produce results. But hope born in Mexico City and Washington could not survive the cruel extremes of drug country.

Meese's stand on Mexico was symptomatic of a more fundamental conflict between the way he approached his job and the credo of the professional investigators and lawyers who worked in the Justice Department. The career people spoke reverentially of "the search for truth"; they protested vigorously at the slightest hint of an effort to shade decisions for reasons of politics or foreign policy. That Ed Meese had spent more years of his life in politics than in a courtroom was painfully obvious when he arrived at the Justice Department. Full of ideological boosterism, he staked out positions as he would erect a circus tent, banners flying, hammers banging. The search for truth took second place to the search for policy.

Ironically, Meese's first major speech as attorney general, to the Washington Press Club, urged journalists to cooperate in the administration's "mobilization of public opinion" against drug use. "I would like to suggest that there are no neutrals in the war on crime," he had said. "The message must get through, and that's where you and I can work together." He had urged the reporters to "press hard on this story and connect the occasional cocaine user . . . with the governments that support this trade." At the time, Meese's suggestion brought a sharp rebuke from Spencer Claw, editor of *Columbia Journalism Review*, who said, "It's not up to him to tell reporters to help the government push a particular point of view. . . . That's exactly the role that's allotted to the press in socialist countries. The function of the press in socialist countries is to educate people and persuade them about the truth as the government sees it."[15]

When he spoke to the press club, Meese did not name "governments" whose support for the drug trade should be exposed, but because the speech came in March 1985, amid the furor over the Camarena murder, many in his audience assumed that he was referring to Mexico. But by the time of the Helms hearing, the position that Meese had taken at the press club seemed to have been discarded. As more and more reporters began to inquire into reports of official corruption in Mexico, Justice officials sent word to the DEA that agents were expected to keep their complaints about Mexico to themselves. Meese's foreign policy was simple: "People who are cooperating don't badmouth each other," he told an interviewer. The DEA snapped shut. DEA executives declined most calls from reporters and Congressional staffers. "The word is out," one harassed DEA official said, "that Mexico will be exonerated and Lord help the son of a bitch who goes against them and the Department of Justice."

However, Jesse Helms and Willy von Raab had started something that Ed Meese could not stop. Lawn and his senior staff obeyed the attorney general. Abrams turned his attention to other issues. Even von Raab held his tongue for a while. But Meese would not be able to persuade the press or the Congress that he had turned things around in Mexico. There were still plenty of agents in the field who wanted to keep the heat on the Mexican government and solve the Camarena case.

American television networks sent crews along the border to describe the trafficking scene. The July 1986 gubernatorial elections in Chihuahua received more coverage in the American press than any Mexican election in years. Almost without exception, the election coverage in the American press cast the Institutional Revolutionary party in a harsh light. The PRI candidate, Fernando Baeza, formerly a top official in the Mexican Attorney General's Office, won the election, but PAN leaders cried foul. *The New York Times* headlined the event "Mexicans Count Votes amid Accusations of Fraud." In the July 21, 1986, issue of *Newsweek*, Joe Contreras, *Newsweek* Mexico City bureau chief, wrote: "The smart money said that the Chihuahua elections would have to look clean. Mexico's ruling Institutional Revolutionary party (PRI) couldn't risk the bad publicity of a rigged contest. But when election day arrived last week, it came with the usual trimmings: stuffed ballot boxes and hot disputes among poll watchers. PRI leaders said the voting had been fair and claimed a landslide victory. But Carlos Anaya, whose nonpartisan Committee for the Democratic Struggle (COLUDE) monitored the election, called it 'a complete and total fraud.' "

The New York Times and *The Wall Street Journal* sent teams of reporters to Mexico. An October 25, 1986, story by *Times* Mexico correspondent William Stockton bore the headline "Bribes Are Called a Way of Life for the Mexicans." A November 19, 1986, story by *Journal* reporter John Fialka was even harsher: "Death of U.S. Agent in Mexico Drug Case Uncovers Grid of Graft—Police at All Levels Profited from Trade in Marijuana, '85 Murder Shows." The *San Diego Union, El Paso Herald-Post, Arizona Republic, Dallas Times Herald, Miami Herald,* and *Los Angeles Times* ran story after story about drug trafficking, corruption, electoral fraud, poverty, and worsening economic conditions in Mexico. The U.S. Treasury Department made a concerted effort to shore up the business community's confidence in the de la Madrid government. At a June 12 hearing called by Helms, David C. Mulford, an assistant secretary of the treasury, heaped praise upon de la Madrid's economic program: "Through determination and perseverance, Mexico became a model adjuster in the post-1982 period as it eliminated its current account deficit even in the face of sharply reduced economic output."

But the peso continued to tumble, more and more middle-class Mexicans moved their money to U.S. banks, many multinational companies declined to invest in Mexico, and large American lending institutions grew increasingly skittish about their outstanding loans to that nation. Some U.S. officials who had not given much thought to Mexico's stability before worried that the Mexican government was losing its grip—and that Helms's apocalyptic predictions might very well come to pass.

18
Nightmare in Sinaloa

In June 1986, Jack Lawn pulled his agents out of Sinaloa. It was a step he hated to take. DEA offices were seldom closed, and then only when a post was in imminent danger of armed attack or, very rarely, to make a political point about the absence of cooperation. Despite the danger and the constant tensions between the DEA and officials in Mexico City, Lawn kept the office in Guadalajara open. The DEA had to find out what had happened to Kiki Camarena, and there were still a lot of possible witnesses and suspects in Guadalajara. Also, the agency had a job to do, the same job Camarena had been doing—collecting intelligence about the movements of the traffickers. Guadalajara was one of the best places to do it.

The other prime vantage point was the state of Sinaloa. Native sons like Miguel Angel Félix Gallardo who had forsaken the Sierra Madre highlands for the graceful mansions of Guadalajara were returning. Guadalajara was the traffickers' playground, but Sinaloa was their fortress. They paid some officers of the police as a matter of course, but their roots went deep into the political and economic structure of the state.

It was Félix Gallardo's acquaintance with some powerful figures in the state that inspired the Mexican press to nickname the cocaine trafficker "*narcopolítico*." In mid-1985, *Proceso* magazine published a picture of Félix Gallardo and his wife, María Elvira, with Leopoldo Sánchez Celis, who had served as governor of Sinaloa from 1974 to 1980. According to *Proceso*, the picture was taken in May 1983 and showed the Félixes performing as the godparents of the wedding of Rodolfo Sánchez Duarte, the former governor's son. The magazine published a second photograph, which it said was taken in January 1985, showing Félix Gallardo opening a car dealership in Culiacán; his partner in the venture, *Proceso* said, was Rodolfo Sánchez Duarte. After the photographs appeared, *Proceso* carried a second article about Sánchez Celis: the article said his lawyer, Ignacio Moreno Talgle, denied that the former governor had had any improper dealings and said that his family's social connections with Félix Gallardo dated from the time when the trafficker had served as a Sinaloa state policeman and member of the governor's bodyguard. Attorney General García Ramírez said that no charges had been leveled at the former governor which merited investigation.

From 1980 to 1985, Sinaloa Governor Augusto Toledo Corro ran the state like an old-fashioned *cacique*, a provincial warlord. During the search for Kiki Camarena's killers, numerous DEA informants reported that Félix Gallardo was hiding out at Toledo's house in Mazatlán. This allegation was first published by *The Washington Post* on February 22, 1986.[1] Questioned on Mexican television, Toledo denied the charge and retorted that the traffickers must have been visiting the home of his neighbor, Elayne Urban, the American consul in Mazatlán.

Jack Lawn and other DEA officials told Mexican officials that their informants said that Félix Gallardo had appeared at weddings and other social events in Culiacán, the state capital. Some of this information came from the Mexican press: in March 1986 *Proceso* reported that on the previous December 21 Félix Gallardo had been in Culiacán to preside over a coming-out party for his fifteen-year-old niece. But Mexican officials contended that DEA had no specific evidence, only rumors and gossip. If the Federales were not able to locate Félix Gallardo in time to capture him, they said, it was because Sinaloa was a big state, and the trafficker had innumerable hideouts.

The DEA Sinaloa office was in the U.S. consulate in Mazatlán. Mazatlán, Mexico's largest Pacific port, was crowded with American tourists and visiting seamen, which made it safer for American agents than the inland city of Culiacán, 125 miles to the north. The only thing tourist

guidebooks said about Culiacán was to avoid it. In the highlands, many people still regarded outlaws as Robin Hood
figures. In the middle of Culiacán stood a shrine to a man
named Jesús Malverde, who had been hanged in 1909. *Proceso* called him *"el narcosantón,"* "the narco-saint," and
wrote that he was "idolized by narcotics traffickers, thieves,
smugglers, judicial police, and politicians." In the 1970s,
Mexicans had called Culiacán "Little Chicago" because of
the shoot-outs between rival gangs. In 1985 and 1986, as
the traffickers returned, laden with automatic weapons, terror pervaded the community. The traffickers shot women
and children, businessmen, politicians, journalists, and anyone else who asked too many questions. By mid-1986, Culiacán's murder rate had soared to five a day, worse than
during the darkest days of the 1970s drug explosion. People
were afraid to sit by their windows for fear of being hit by
stray bullets. Many of the traffickers still had the backwoods
habit of stealing teenage girls from the poor barrios for
"brides." One Mexican Army officer told an American reporter that each year perhaps five hundred girls were being
kidnapped and raped in Culiacán.

Corruption in the police force was of legendary proportions. Officers made perhaps a hundred dollars a month,
not enough to pay for the expensive boots and cowboy gear
in which they dressed. The policemen, heavily armed with
Uzi and AK-47 machine guns, bunkered in a heavily fortified
concrete blockhouse and engaged in shoot-outs with small
traffickers, but when it came to the kingpins, they walked
away. In July 1986, after a prominent journalist from a
nearby city was killed, the editors of the Culiacán daily
Noroeste issued an impassioned plea for an end to the may-
hem. "Far from combating the delinquency, gangsterism,
and drug trafficking," the editorial said, "the police forces
and their superiors close their eyes and leave Sinaloa to
become a state without law."

Mazatlán was outwardly more peaceful than Culiacán,
but there was no question about who was in control of the
city. When Rafael Caro Quintero fled Guadalajara two days
after the Camarena kidnapping, he went first to Caborca,
Sonora, where he had ranches and relatives. But according

to the Costa Rican pilot Werner Lotz, when the manhunt continued, Caro Quintero headed for Sinaloa. If Lotz, who was cooperating with DEA, could be believed, Caro Quintero had made his escape to Costa Rica from an airstrip between Mazatlán and Culiacán—and that flight was arranged with the help of a Mexican Army officer.[2]

It was the job of the two DEA men who worked at the DEA-Mazatlán post to find out more about the possible involvement of some members of the Mexican Army in Caro Quintero's flight. The American agents were also trying to track down Félix Gallardo and other Guadalajara cartel members who had returned to Sinaloa and the neighboring state of Durango. In early summer of 1986, they observed that they were being followed. Some *pistoleros* tried to bribe the consulate's security guards for information about their movements.

Then one of their informants was murdered in such a brutal and ostentatious fashion that they felt sure the act was a warning.

At six o'clock on the morning of June 22, 1986, the body of Martín Aguirre Orozco floated into the shallow water on the Mazatlán beach known as Playa Escondida. The body was a mess. Local officials ruled the death an accidental drowning and said that the cuts and bruises had been caused by the waves' pounding the body against the rocks.

But there were no rocks where Aguirre's corpse was found. Playa Escondida was the only stretch of pure sand in Mazatlán. And Aguirre was a paid informant for the DEA. DEA agents who went to the morgue saw lacerations on the wrists, cheek, and nose, all of which suggested that Aguirre had been bound and gagged—and none of which had been mentioned in the coroner's report. Nor did the report mention the ice-pick wounds on Aguirre's legs and the fact that the body had been found in a bathing suit several sizes too large. Aguirre's DEA contacts knew it was unlikely that he would have been out in the deep water and caught unawares by a riptide. Martín Aguirre could not swim.

Informants were killed from time to time, because they

were found out or because they were making drug deals on the side and had double-crossed somebody. But the death of Martín Aguirre, coming seventeen months after the murders of Kiki Camarena and Alfredo Zavala, sent shock waves through DEA. It raised alarms that history was about to repeat itself, that the drug lords were once again on the offensive, rolling up the networks of informants and preparing to attack DEA agents themselves.

The skinny, scraggly-haired informant could have been murdered by any number of people in the Sinaloa underworld, but Carlo Boccia and Bill Coonce saw an uncanny resemblance to events that had taken place in Guadalajara in the months prior to the Camarena murder. Before kidnapping Camarena, the traffickers had shot one of Kiki's friends, menaced Roger Knapp, and murdered two American tourists, John Walker and Alberto Radelat, whom they had evidently taken for DEA agents or informants. The body of Aguirre showed ice-pick marks and signs of a particularly cruel torture called "bone tickling," in which the point of the pick was shoved in so that it scraped the bone, where there were many nerves. It was not certain that Walker and Radelat had been tortured, but the Federales said they had been stabbed to death with ice picks and knives.

Most significantly, Walker, Radelat, and Aguirre had all been killed within the domain of a particularly sadistic pal of Caro Quintero named Manuel Salcido Uzeta, who was commonly known as Cochi Loco, Crazy Pig. Walker and Radelat supposedly died in La Langosta, the Mazatlán-style restaurant in Guadalajara where Salcido and the other traffickers sometimes presided over long tables groaning with heaps of shrimp, bottles of scotch and tequila, and piles of cocaine. Salcido's main base of operations was in Mazatlán, where he owned property valued by one local businessman at about $35 million.

Salcido had fled Guadalajara like the other traffickers but had gone no farther than Mazatlán. According to DEA agents and Mazatlán residents, he felt sufficiently secure to drive about town openly with a couple of dozen Sinaloa state judicial policemen as bodyguards. Local people said that he ran his busy marijuana wholesaling business from a modern office building. On Saturday night, his *pistoleros*, distinguished by expensive cowboy outfits and AK-47s, could be seen prowling the local nightspots, which resounded with a *corrido* written in praise of Cochi Loco.

> They say this man is very bad
> *Señores*, I don't believe it,
> Because he is legendary and valiant,
> Because of this they are scared of him,
> But at the bottom of his soul,
> He is a sincere friend.

Born October 21, 1947, in a poor hamlet in the foothills of the Sierras, Manuel Salcido, tall, fair, and blue-eyed, moved to Mazatlán as a youth and worked as a waiter. DEA agents said that he rose rapidly in the underworld, eliminating rivals with rapacious zest. According to DEA files, at the time when Miguel Angel Félix Gallardo was branching out into South America, California, and Europe, and Rafael Caro Quintero was pioneering a marijuana empire in Sonora, Zacatecas, San Luis, and Chihuahua, Salcido stayed close to home, consolidating his control over marijuana, cocaine, and heroin trafficking in the southern half of Sinaloa. By the mid-1980s, he owned a half-dozen tourist hotels, three movie houses, restaurants, cantinas, small shopping complexes, a water slide, an office building, and a disco.

For many Mazaltecos, Salcido's interest in the city was not entirely unwelcome. "The traffickers are the only ones investing money in Mexico," one businessman told a reporter in mid-1986. "The rest take their dollars out. They are building roads, drainage, restaurants, and hotels, which creates jobs." "If your property costs a hundred million pesos," said another, "Salcido will pay one hundred and ten million. It will be a fast deal, dollars or pesos." However, there were those who feared the intrusion of this crude *arriviste*. "If Salcido only owns ten percent of your business," said one man who wished to run an honest establishment, "he *owns* the business."

Jack Lawn had repeatedly asked Attorney General García Ramírez to have Salcido arrested for questioning in the Camarena murder case. Soon after Camarena's disappearance, a DEA informant had claimed that Salcido had been threatening to kill American agents in Guadalajara because DEA "had fucked too much with him and his people." This might have been an idle boast, or something that the informant had invented, but Lawn considered it sufficient basis for further inquiry.

Also, Salcido was a DEA target in his own right. Since the arrests of his friends Caro Quintero and Fonseca, Salcido had emerged as one of the most important and feared drug kingpins in Mexico. Martín Aguirre's mission had been to penetrate the Mazatlán underworld and eventually to get close to Crazy Pig himself. He died before he fulfilled that assignment.

After Aguirre's death, Jack Lawn asked Deputy Attorney General Ortega Padilla for extra security for the DEA post. According to DEA officials, Ortega Padilla replied that the central government could not guarantee their safety as long as they remained in the state of Sinaloa.

Pulling the agents out was a tough decision for Lawn. Their withdrawal would signal a victory for the Sinaloans. On the other hand, the traffickers knew already that they were winning. Whether the Federales were paid off or afraid, it was a fact that a Sinaloa warlord had occupied a big chunk of the Pacific coast without shedding any of his own men's blood, and the Mexican government's only response was to advise Americans to get out of town. Were "signals" worth the risk of sending another man to his death? Lawn thought not. He ordered the men to temporary quarters in Mexico City.

Several weeks after they left, Joe Harmes, a *Newsweek* correspondent, went to the city to write a story about the Aguirre case. Harmes met a man who claimed to be the local representative of the Interior Ministry. He introduced the American to two other men who claimed to be Interior Ministry officials; later, a local reporter told Harmes they were lieutenants of Salcido. Whatever they were, they knew who Martín Aguirre was. "*Ay*, goddamn, that bastard?"

one of the thugs sneered. "He drowned. Go ask the coroner. Maybe he did have a lot of marks on his body. I don't know if he was stabbed, but he drowned." After this, the Mexican reporter warned the American correspondent that Salcido "would know whatever he had said by the next morning." "They'll pay a call on you," he warned, gesturing toward Salcido's *pistoleros*. The next day, as Harmes and his wife were driving from Mazatlán to Culiacán, three men in a baby-blue van with a red police dome light pulled onto the highway, chased them at top speed for some minutes, and then wheeled off the road, vanishing as quickly as they had appeared.

The Aguirre story was every DEA agent's nightmare come true. When it happened, DEA officials had reason to fear that Mexican officials were trying to break through American government security and get at DEA's sources and methods inside Mexico.

In May, just after the Helms hearings, a warning had come from another informant that Florentino Ventura, the head of the MFJP, had issued orders to his commanders to identify DEA informants. While the tip might be braggadocio on the informant's part or a plot by dissidents within the MFJP to discredit Ventura, DEA agents dared not discount the story. A number of DEA officials respected Ventura as a professional officer, but they recognized that his loyalties belonged to his system, not theirs.

Meese made the situation even tougher by promising Attorney General García Ramírez to share evidence of corruption. García Ramírez had demanded the material when Meese had telephoned him to try to repair the political damage caused by the Helms hearings. Meese thought García's request reasonable in view of his pledge to attack official corruption, so he agreed.

A reasonable request it might have seemed, but Jack Lawn found it impossible to satisfy. García Ramírez asked for access to informants and details of allegations lodged against any Mexican official. Lawn said that handing over informants was out of the question. Beyond that, he knew that DEA could not accommodate requests for detailed intelligence reports. Usually no more than three or four people were part of a particular drug transaction; it did not take a master detective to figure out who was the informer. The traffickers did not require proof beyond a reasonable doubt to order a suspected snitch's execution.

Lawn told his subordinates that DEA would produce a report for the Mexican attorney general—but not the sort of exhaustive white paper the American government issued when it was trying to prove something. "Our role is not to furnish intelligence to the Mexican Federal Judicial Police," he said. "It's to look for a few honest cops that we can work with." It was not DEA's job, he added, to clean up the Mexican government. If the Mexican attorney general wanted to do that, Lawn said, his detectives could do what American investigators did whenever an American official was accused of corruption: check his bank accounts, trace his travels, talk to everyone who worked with him, run an informant at him, install a wiretap—no magic, just a lot of shoe leather. If the Mexicans were serious about stamping out corruption, they would have to provide their own shoe leather. Lawn did not want to take the chance that DEA's information could be used to protect suspects, to extort them, or to help corrupt cops nail informants.

The task of writing the report fell to Carlo Boccia. Drafting a document specific enough to satisfy Meese but vague enough to protect DEA sources and methods was an unrewarding job. Boccia did not care if the Mexican government found the report persuasive or even adequate. All he wanted to do was contain damage. U.S. Customs agents were equally edgy and deleted a number of passages referring to their investigations of official collusion in smuggling and money laundering. Not surprisingly, the finished product was watery, with passages beginning vaguely, "It has been said that . . ." and with allegations that had long been discounted by American investigators. Ann Wrobleski, the acting assistant secretary of state for international narcotics matters, complained to Lawn that the report was a piece of junk; it did not tell the Mexicans anything useful. "I know it's awful," Lawn said, "and I know that's not going to satisfy them, but we didn't open the can of worms, so the best we can do is to try to whet their appetite a little bit."

Despite the precautions, DEA and Customs officials worried that the Mexican police would find ways to use the report or other contacts in the American government to triangulate on their sources. When Martín Aguirre was killed, their anxieties heightened. Aguirre's death was probably only a coincidence—he had not been working for DEA very long and had not produced evidence deemed important enough to go into the report given to García Ramírez. But it was an ugly coincidence, and it reminded DEA agents of the vulnerability of the people who worked for them.

For a man who constantly professed his admiration of police work, Ed Meese was oddly oblivious to the commotion his attempt to accommodate the Mexican attorney general set off at DEA and Customs. So eager was Meese to emphasize that the Mexican government was "fully cooperative" on drug enforcement that in July 1986 he made a stunning assertion to an interviewer: "We're giving them [Mexican officials] full information, including the names of informants." When the interviewer said that Meese must be mistaken, Meese's aides insisted that the statement was true and Meese did not object to having it printed.

Meese's remark astonished DEA officials. As far as anyone could tell, no names of active informants had been passed to Mexico, but this was an extraordinarily insensitive statement for the manager of a law-enforcement organization to make in any case. The names of sources of information were the most closely held secrets that law-enforcement and intelligence agencies possessed, not only in the United States but in most other nations. Agents recruited informants by offering assurances of complete anonymity, guaranteeing that their identities would not be revealed to other nations, other law-enforcement agencies, or to most other investigators in the same agency. Even on secret U.S. government reports, informants were identified only by number.

Aware they were operating in a political minefield, agents working in Mexico and on the border took extra precautions

to keep the identities of informants secret not only from
Mexican officials but from their superiors in the American
government. When U.S. embassy officials asked DEA and
Customs agents to list their sources in the embassy's informant registry, they refused. Agents deliberately kept embassy political officers and Justice Department officials from
hearing about sensitive cases until after the papers were filed
in court. Lawn was a bit surprised when a number of agents
on the Southwest border pleaded with him not to tell Ed
Heath about their investigations, for fear Heath would tell
his friends in the Mexican Attorney General's Office and
the MFJP. A few agents even kept secrets from Lawn.

The closing of the DEA-Sinaloa office was just one of many
obstacles Mexico-based DEA agents faced as they attempted to collect useful information about trafficking and
to resolve the Camarena case.

To fill the intelligence gap, Lawn authorized a new kind
of project, called Operation Columbus, which involved
long-term penetrations of the gangs, using informants dispatched into Mexico from the border offices. The project
was the idea of Don Ferrarone, who had returned to the
DEA after his stint at the U.S. Marshals Service, where he
had devised the Verdugo snatch. In the past, DEA field
offices along the border had operated independently, communicating erratically with headquarters, offices in Mexico,
and one another. Ferrarone and his boss, heroin desk chief
Michael Tobin, proposed Operation Columbus as a way of
coordinating and focusing intelligence on the border and in
the cities where the Mexican rings' distribution networks
were based—Chicago, Los Angeles, and Phoenix. Ferrarone and Tobin recognized the isolation that Camarena and
his partners had felt and did not want it to happen again.
They saw Columbus as a way of assuring that agents in
remote outposts would have a voice at DEA headquarters.

Operation Columbus led to a number of major cocaine
seizures, but progress was not measured in old-fashioned
terms of pounds and arrests. The new strategy was to find
out everything possible about the organizations and their
support networks—which officials they had bribed, where

they were getting their supplies, how their routes were organized—and to file charges against corrupt Mexican and American officials.

Operation Columbus would score many successes, but none brought DEA closer to finding out what had happened to Kiki Camarena. The central suspects in the murder of Camarena remained out of reach.

On May 29, 1986, there came what looked like a breakthrough. The Federales arrested Sergio Espino Verdín in Durango. Espino had given the Federales the slip three times before, but DEA agents in Guadalajara located him one more time and persuaded the Federales to detain him. The former IPS *comandante* from Guadalajara remained DEA's primary suspect as the "*comandante*," the interrogator who could be heard on the tapes of the Camarena interrogation. DEA agents Bobby Castillo and Victor Cortez were allowed to sit in while the Federales interrogated Espino. According to a State Department report summarizing that interrogation, Espino acknowledged that he had been present at the house where Camarena was interrogated and admitted involvement in drug-trafficking operations. The Mexican Attorney General's Office charged him with murder, kidnapping, and drug trafficking and sent him to prison in Mexico City.[3]

Carlo Boccia asked to run a voice print on Espino. That required a tape in which Espino repeated phrases identical to those the interrogator had used. The phrases had to be repeated several times, because voice patterns changed under stress. Months later, the Mexican Attorney General's Office sent a tape of Espino's voice to the DEA. But whoever in the Mexican government had made the recording had not followed the instructions. There were not enough voice samples, called "exemplars," to permit the FBI lab to do a proper analysis. When Boccia asked to have the test redone, the reply came that Espino's lawyer had obtained a protective order that prevented Mexican authorities from making a new tape. Bobby Castillo listened to the tape recordings of the Camarena torture and told Operation Leyenda agents that he could identify Espino's voice as the *comandante* on the tape. But Castillo and his partners were unable to arrange to see Espino again in order to conduct further interviews for the grand jury proceedings in the States.

The two men the Leyenda team most desperately wanted to talk to were Miguel Angel Félix Gallardo and Javier Barba Hernández. Félix Gallardo was at the top of the list because DEA believed he knew more about high-level corruption than any other trafficker in Mexico. If he had not been involved in Camarena's murder, the agents thought, he probably knew who was, and whether influential government officials had condoned the murder or the cover-up. Barba was important because he had brains. As a lawyer, he had strong ties with the Jalisco political and police establishment. He was also known as an executioner for Félix Gallardo and Fonseca. Boccia thought Barba might be one of the men whose voices could be heard on the tapes.

"If and when they do get captured," Carlo Boccia said gloomily, "they'll be delivered on a slab."

His prediction was at least half right. On November 17, 1986, Federales in Mazatlán gunned down Barba. They claimed not to know who he was—as DEA agents reconstructed the story, the Federales said they had attempted to arrest three strangers, gotten into a gunfight, and been forced to kill all three. Boccia observed that the Mexican Army had managed to take Ernesto Fonseca and twenty-three *pistoleros* without killing any of them. Also, Barba died suspiciously soon after his name appeared at the top of a list of suspects that Boccia had sent to Mexico City.

Boccia asked for fingerprints and samples of Barba's hair to compare with hairs and prints the FBI forensic team had found in the house on Calle Lope de Vega in Guadalajara. The Attorney General's Office replied, according to agents in Operation Leyenda, that it was too late because the body had already been cremated. Since cremation was unusual in Mexico, DEA dispatched an informant to check out the story. The informant reported that the body had been buried, not cremated, and reposed in a certain graveyard.

DEA agents in Mexico and Europe picked up reports that Miguel Angel Félix Gallardo was traveling in Spain and

Switzerland, setting up a cocaine-distribution network. His partner, Juan Matta Ballesteros, had made his way back to his homeland, Honduras, which did not extradite its own citizens. On March 19, 1986, Matta had walked out of a prison hospital in La Picota, Colombia, by spreading $2 million among eighteen guards. Colombian President Virgilio Barco angrily ordered an investigation of the prison warden and guards, but Matta was well away.[4] Once back in Honduras, Matta ingratiated himself with the local people, buying football uniforms and desks for the school, and set up shop. By late 1987, Honduras was a major transshipment center for cocaine, and Matta was living like a king in a fabulous villa in Tegucigalpa. DEA had to open a new office in Honduras to handle the new volume of cocaine shipments. Some Honduran Army officers sought DEA's help in keeping Matta and other traffickers from corrupting their men.

By the fall of 1986, two U.S. grand juries, one in Los Angeles and one in San Diego, were hearing evidence in the Camarena homicide.

"What we've done here," said Boccia, "and what we're continuing to do in the United States—I can say with some degree of pride, but also it's a damn shame—we've done it totally by ourselves. And if there comes a time that anyone is indicted for kidnapping-murder, it's going to be totally due to the work done on this side of the border. And that's a sad state of affairs."

DEA agents stepped up their efforts to capture in the States peripheral figures in the Guadalajara cartel—distributors, money launderers, enforcers—who might know something about Camarena's murder.

For a while, they thought they had a strong suspect in a DFS officer named Carlos Mario Martínez Herrera, whom they located in Chula Vista, California, and booked as a material witness. They had a tip from an informant that Martínez had been at the house on Lope de Vega the day Camarena was taken there. When Martínez denied that he had ever been in Guadalajara, the San Diego grand jury indicted him for perjury. At the trial, Mike Malone, an FBI forensics expert, testified Martínez's hair matched hair the FBI forensic team had found in the house. Martínez was convicted of perjury just before Christmas of 1986. After serving a sentence of one year, he was released and deported to Mexico; he had never admitted knowing anything about the murder.

The next target was Jesús Félix Gutiérrez, a.k.a. "Cachas," the proprietor of an East Los Angeles seafood import business and a reputed marijuana distributor and money launderer for Caro Quintero. As a DEA affidavit filed in federal court in Los Angeles would disclose, agents in Costa Rica and California found that Félix Gutiérrez owned the Costa Rican coffee plantation where Rafael Caro Quintero was captured on April 4, 1985; the investigation showed that Félix Gutiérrez had bought the place for $800,000 cash in January 1985. According to court documents, pilot Werner Lotz said that he saw Félix Gutiérrez with Caro Quintero at the villa in Costa Rica.[5]

DEA agents in Los Angeles and San Diego looked for Félix Gutiérrez for more than a year, tracing him from Los Angeles to Chile to Argentina to Brazil to Colombia to Mexico and Agents Mary Cooper and Lisa Binsack found him in Los Angeles on Christmas Eve, 1986, on his way to visit his children. The Los Angeles grand jury indicted him for conspiring with Caro Quintero and six others to distribute drugs. In June 1987, he pleaded guilty to drug-trafficking charges, but even when he was sentenced to fifteen years in prison, he would not talk about Caro Quintero.

In March 1987, the Federales, at DEA's urging, arrested José Galardo Parra, the Fonseca *pistolero* known as El Güero, who allegedly led the kidnap team that snatched Camarena from the steps of the U.S. consulate. DEA's efforts to interview him were thwarted when his lawyer secured a court order protecting him from having to answer questions.

The same month, the Mexican Army went into Sinaloa after Manuel Salcido. Several of his relatives were killed, but once again, Cochi Loco got away.

19
The Andean Coca Wars

In the summer of 1986, the U.S. Army staged a sensational airborne assault on the Bolivian cocaine industry.

On July 18, U.S. Army Blackhawk helicopters bearing fourteen-man squads of Bolivian security policemen and DEA advisers glided into the trackless El Beni rain forest and descended upon cocaine laboratories hidden under the jungle canopy. Over the next four months, Bolivian forces dismantled twenty-two cocaine laboratories with a production capacity of fifteen tons of cocaine a year—a quarter of the United States' estimated annual cocaine consumption.

Operation Blast Furnace, as the unprecedented joint exercise was called, appeared to be a quick, decisive victory for Bolivia's fledgling reform government and for the Reagan administration's war on drugs. U.S. Ambassador Edward M. Rowell told reporters that the operation had a "dramatic impact" on the coca economy. In the short run, this was true. With the onset of the raids, every trafficker in El Beni skipped the country, and Colombian coca paste buyers stayed away. With no buyers in sight, the coca leaf market collapsed. A pound of coca leaves that cost forty cents to produce and normally sold for a dollar and a half went for ten cents on the pound. Panicked coca farmers appeared at U.S. Agency for International Development stations asking for seeds for citrus, cacao, rice, and beans.

Over the longer run, though, the results were mixed. Blast Furnace was a testament to the durability of the cocaine trade. After the Blackhawks left Bolivia on November 15, 1986, the coca trade returned to business as usual. The traffickers soon replaced the destroyed labs, and Colombian refinery operators, who had avoided Bolivia during the

heavily publicized blitz, resumed their purchases of Bolivian
coca. Coca leaf prices shot back up to a dollar or more a
pound.

Only one person, a teenage boy, was arrested during the
raids. The absence of traffickers at the lab sites was blamed
on the large, visible American presence—it had been impossible to disguise the arrival in Santa Cruz, Bolivia, of
three U.S. Air Force transports, six Blackhawks, one
hundred sixty American soldiers, and perhaps two dozen
DEA agents. In fact, the element of surprise had already
been lost. The traffickers had departed well before the
American transports arrived, leading U.S. officials to suspect that corrupt government officials had leaked the plans
to the traffickers.

The availability and price of cocaine sold in the United
States did not change because the Bolivian cocaine-refining
industry was a new and relatively minor part of the world
production picture. Most of South America's refineries were
in Colombia and produced more cocaine than American
consumers could use in a year. Indeed, the lab strikes actually benefited the Colombian trafficking establishment,
whose near-monopoly on the refining and wholesaling of
finished cocaine had been threatened by Bolivian inter-
lopers.

The most important achievement of Operation Blast Furnace was as a symbol: it showed that the Bolivian government could take on the cocaine traffickers and survive
politically. When there was no coup attempt, when people
did not riot on the streets of La Paz, U.S. State Department
officials believed that President Víctor Paz Estenssoro, a
seventy-eight-year-old political idealist who had come to
power the previous year, was emboldened to take the next
step, to attempt a ban on the cultivation of coca for export.

However, it was highly unlikely that a ban could actually
be enforced. President Paz could attack the relatively small
number of traffickers and refiners because those aspects of
the drug business were not traditional in Bolivia. But even
to the most idealistic of Bolivians, coca growing was difficult
to condemn, and eradication without compensation to the
farmers was unthinkable. The coca industry was woven into

the social fabric of the country and could not be disrupted without unraveling the nation's economic and political structures. Coca provided sustenance for three hundred thousand campesinos. The only other industry that contributed significantly to exports was tin mining, and because of depressed world tin prices, mining was in a state of collapse. Bolivian economists estimated that the nation would earn $400 million in hard currency from legitimate exports in 1986, while coca exports would return an estimated $600 million.

As Fernando Illanes, Bolivia's ambassador to the United States in 1986, put it, in order to eradicate substantial amounts of coca, "you would have to go in with armed forces and start killing people—relatively innocent people."[1]

The coca bush, which resembles the tea plant, has been cultivated for centuries in the fertile eastern foothills of the Bolivian Andes. This area, called the Yungas, extends laterally across the La Paz Department, which borders on Peru, and into the Cochabamba Department, which forms the geographical center of the country. Yungas coca has sweet, tender leaves favored by peasants who chew them to stave off hunger, fatigue, and cold. Yungas coca is valued by cocaine traffickers because it contains a very high level of the alkaloid that is refined to make cocaine hydrochloride, the white salt known to cocaine users. But the rugged, dry region has never produced sufficient coca to meet the demands of the laboratories. In around 1960, when the modern cocaine-refining industry was in its infancy, campesinos began planting new stands of coca in the semitropical flatlands of the Chaparé province, a part of the Cochabamba Department. Though the Chaparé coca is not acceptable for chewing, it is adequate for making coca paste for the refining industry. Because of greater rainfall and ease of cultivation, the Chaparé soon outstripped the Yungas in volume of coca produced.

By 1986, the U.S. State Department estimated that nearly one hundred thousand acres of coca were being cultivated in Bolivia; after allowing for legal internal consumption of coca leaves, Bolivia's crop could have produced as much as forty-six metric tons of finished cocaine. State Department eradication advisers in the embassy in La Paz considered main State's estimate too low by half. In 1987, according to the U.S. General Accounting Office, the U.S. embassy's Narcotics Assistance Unit believed that coca production in Bolivia was closer to two hundred fifty thousand acres.[2]

The Bolivian refining and trafficking organizations were allied in a cartel known as the Santa Cruz Mafia, named for the city of Santa Cruz, the center of Bolivia's illicit drug trade. Bolivians called the Mafia leaders "the untouchables" because of their influence with the government. The most important of the organizations was headed by Roberto Suárez Gómez. Born in 1932 to one of Bolivia's oldest and most aristocratic families, Suárez shamed his relatives, respectable cattle ranchers, by establishing laboratories in the Beni Department, a lowland area east of Cochabamba that was part pampas and part jungle. Suárez lived in a pampas cattle town called Santa Ana de Yacuma, where he was known as "Papito," "Daddy," benefactor of the poor. He had ranches all over the departments of Cochabamba, Santa Cruz, and the Beni, and, it was said, as many mistresses as ranches.

In 1980, as Bolivia was about to hold a democratic election after sixteen years of military rule, General Luis García Meza staged a coup, the one hundred eighty-ninth coup in Bolivia's one hundred fifty-four years of independence. *The Miami Herald* called it "the cocaine coup," and *Newsweek* magazine termed the regime a "narcokleptocracy": it was widely reported in the American and Bolivian press that García's grab for power was financed by the Santa Cruz Mafia.[3] The civilian presidential candidates in 1980 were Víctor Paz Estensorro and Hernán Siles Zuazo, both heroes of the 1952 popular revolution against an earlier military dictatorship. These men were dedicated reformers antagonistic to interests of the big-time cocaine and coca-paste dealers. An internal DEA memorandum dating from this period said:

It is believed that an important force behind the coup was the desire of certain leaders to protect their interest in the cocaine traffic from the supposedly reformist civilian government. The current information on Bolivia alleges that the coup was financed by the [Santa Cruz] Mafia. Shortly after the coup, a well-known trafficker and leader of a right-wing paramilitary group in Santa Cruz announced at a meeting that the Mafia was prepared to supply all the money that is needed by the new military government for a period of several months. . . . An alleged contributor to the new government and a representative member of the Mafia has been successful in arranging the appointment of two of his relatives to lucrative government positions after the coup.

In short order, García Meza and his colonels made Bolivia the pariah of the world. In June 1981, *Newsweek* magazine correspondent Larry Rohter reported that Klaus Barbie, the former Gestapo commander of occupied France, lived in Cochabamba under the alias Klaus Altmann; the article said that Bolivian exiles charged that Barbie advised Bolivian security forces under both García Meza and his predecessor, military dictator General Hugo Banzer Suárez. *Newsweek* reported that the Banzer and García regimes employed gangs of Nazis who trained right-wing hit squads, smuggled cocaine, and gathered in the evening to sing Nazi battle songs and watch World War II documentaries.[4] According to a 1982 article by correspondent Edward Schumacher of *The New York Times*, Barbie was a frequent visitor to the Bolivian military command, had a bodyguard supplied by the Interior Ministry, and was reportedly on good terms with two of the last three military presidents, including García Meza.[5]

A U.S. indictment would later charge that García Meza's interior minister, Colonel Luis Arce Gómez, ordered the formation of paramilitary enforcement groups, called the Servicio Especial de Seguridad (SES), which would seize cocaine from traffickers who were not paying for protection and deliver it to traffickers who were. The indictment charged that Arce Gómez's appointees and special representatives would sell and distribute cocaine which had been previously seized and stored in Bolivian bank vaults. One of the traffickers who profited from the arrangement, the indictment said, was Roberto Suárez.

Because of the junta's alleged relationship with Suárez and other cocaine traffickers and its rampant violations of human rights, President Jimmy Carter cut off all economic and military assistance to Bolivia in 1980. The next year, responding to international censure, García Meza launched a crackdown against the cocaine traffickers but, according to a report by Warren Hoge of *The New York Times*, a Suárez associate claimed that Suárez promised General García Meza $50 million to end the Santa Cruz operation. Hoge reported that the crackdown ended "abruptly."[6]

The Reagan State Department kept up the pressure on the García Meza regime. A State Department report published in a House committee report in July 1981 asserted that "there has been consistent and persuasive reporting linking the García Meza regime directly with the cocaine traffic. In fact, it has been suggested that the only financial buttress of that regime has been trafficking payoffs in return for governmental noninterference."[7]

On April 26, 1983, a federal grand jury in Miami indicted former Interior Minister Arce Gómez and six other Bolivian officials for conspiring with Suárez and nine other traffickers to export cocaine to the United States.[8] None of the officials was ever tried.

By the time the indictments came through, the military was out of power. García Meza was deposed in September 1981 by a group of colonels called "the Black Eagles," headed by General Celso Torrelio Villa. Torrelio was replaced in July 1982 by General Guido Vildoso Calderón. In September 1982, in the midst of an economic crisis and a general strike by workers who demanded democracy, the Black Eagles allowed the Congress to elect a civilian president: Hernán Siles Zuazo, who had served as president from 1956 to 1960, was sworn in on October 10, 1982.

The Reagan administration resumed foreign-aid payments to Bolivia, in exchange for which Siles promised to rein in the illegal coca trade. The Bolivian president was unable to make good on that pledge. Siles was preoccupied by ruinous inflation, constant strikes, the impending collapse

of the mining industry, which accounted for nearly 60 percent of legitimate exports, and shortages of food and fuel.
His shaky coalition of centrist, leftist, and communist factions could not govern the country. Corruption in the security forces remained rampant, production of coca soared,
and Roberto Suárez was as brazen as ever. According to
The Miami Herald, in June 1983, when Interior Minister
Mario Roncal Atenzana sent troops into the Beni looking
for Suárez, Suárez insouciantly took out newspaper ads accusing Roncal of complicity in the cocaine trade. Roncal
denied the charges but could not lay hands on the elusive
and well-insulated cocaine king.[9]

Suárez's son, Roberto Suárez Levy, born in 1956, had
become a pilot and, DEA officials said, was being groomed
to carry on the family business. In 1982, Suárez Jr. was
arrested in Switzerland and extradited to Miami. According
to internal DEA files, at that time an informant told DEA
that Suárez had hired eight mercenaries to kidnap two federal judges in Miami; security around the U.S. Courthouse
was increased. Young Suárez was acquitted and returned to
Bolivia, but his father was not assuaged. In 1983, DEA
agents were pulled out of Bolivia for a short while because
of informant reports that Suárez Sr. had placed contracts
on their lives. In around 1985, Robert Suárez Sr. was forced
into retirement by his nephew, Jorge Roca Suárez, who took
over the family business.

In 1985, Víctor Paz Estenssoro was elected to succeed Siles,
who ended his days in office virtually paralyzed by warring
political factions. Paz introduced a program of economic
reform that reduced his country's 23,000 percent inflation
rate to 20 or 30 percent. By early 1986, he was ready to
fulfill his campaign promise to go after the traffickers. He
was facing a U.S. Congressional deadline that mandated a
reduction in U.S. foreign aid unless Bolivia launched an
eradication campaign.[10] Beyond the motivation of continuing U.S. aid, Paz, a founder of the National Revolutionary
Movement and president of Bolivia from 1952 to 1956,
spoke of creating a new Bolivia, respected and legitimately
prosperous. He believed that, as the 1980 coup had shown,

Suárez and the other cocaine lords were enemies of democracy.

Paz's advisers were dubious about his intention to go after the traffickers. "Running the economic side," Planning Minister Gonzalo Sánchez de Lozada said, "I said to Dr. Paz, when we're fighting bare-handed with a tiger, we don't take on an alligator."[11] But Paz persisted. "If we do not address this problem decisively—to eliminate it—the day could come when the economic power they wield could result in their governing the country, including via democratic means," he told *Newsweek* magazine.[12] "Election campaigns cost more and more every day, and the economic influence of the cocaine Mafia could lead to unexpected results in terms of who runs the country."

The trouble was, Paz had no means to execute a crackdown on his own. In the last days of the Siles government, the Bolivian police anti-narcotics unit, "the Leopards," had grown from a force of two hundred men to a force of seven hundred men, but they remained the worst-equipped police unit in Latin America. Their few helicopters were falling apart, their weapons and communications equipment were primitive; they could not even afford ammunition. A number of their officers were believed to be on the traffickers' payrolls.

Most important, they did not have the hearts and minds of the common people. An acre of coca was worth as much as $3,000. The Paz government was offering perhaps a third of that amount in aid for those who would substitute food crops.[13] In January 1986, two hundred forty-five Leopards who had moved into the Chaparé region to find and destroy illegal coca paste- and base-making operations were besieged by seventeen thousand protesting farmers. The five-day siege ended when Paz agreed to meet with the farmers himself to hear their grievances. Paz's advisers came up with a plan to wean the farmers off coca but judged it would cost $300 million over three years, of which Bolivia could pay but $60 million. Hoping to convince the United States and European nations to pay the rest, Paz agreed to commit the Leopards to an action proposed by the DEA to raid fifty or so cocaine laboratories in the Beni Department, many of which belonged to the Suárez family.[14] In April 1986, Paz's aides asked DEA to provide heavy-duty military helicopters for the exercise.

When Ed Meese presented Paz's request to the cabinet, George Bush offered to help enlist the Pentagon. Bush's role in twisting arms at the Pentagon reflected the conventional wisdom within the Reagan White House and among some circles in Congress that the drug trade would yield to technology and military action.

Pentagon officials resisted Bush's entreaties at first, remembering the beating they had taken fighting a counter-insurgency war in Vietnam. "We couldn't interdict the Ho Chi Minh trail," one Air Force official said, referring to the thousands of peasants who had lugged supplies from North Vietnam to the Vietcong guerrillas. "Right now, coming up from the south, we have a Ho Chi Minh trail four thousand miles wide." Said another senior military official: "You have to reckon that the most important figures in that trade are going to be very sophisticated, very well equipped, very well protected physically and politically. It's the marginal operators who will get zapped—unless the United States can somehow turn the tide in the producer countries themselves." Defense Secretary Caspar Weinberger's aides also feared that the Congress would use the military budget as a deep pocket. As one of these men put it, "People want to use the military not so much to solve a problem as to solve it without spending money." But under the cajoling of Bush and his staff, Pentagon officials relented.[15]

Paz, his advisers, and DEA officers had envisioned a quiet surgical action, using perhaps four helicopters and about twenty U.S. Army pilots and crew members—"like an Israeli operation," said Planning Minister Sánchez de Lozada.[16] Once the Pentagon became involved, its requirements drove the operation. Military officials insisted on layer upon layer of redundancy and assigned dozens of mechanics, cooks, medics, communications experts, and other support personnel to the task force. American transports landed in Santa Cruz on July 14 and made the La Paz papers the following morning. The Beni raids were launched three days later.

On the first foray, the raiders found a large lab in the

process of being dismantled. Peasants said they had seen the traffickers packing up even before the story made the papers, confirming what American officials had feared, that Suárez and the other traffickers would find out about the operation from their own sources within the Bolivian government. DEA agents later determined that in the days preceding the raid there had been a massive exodus of traffickers and airplanes to Panama City.

The operation continued at no small political risk to President Paz. The noisy arrival of American troops and hordes of American journalists triggered protests from nationalistic and leftist opposition groups in Bolivia. Juan Lechín Oquendo, boss of Bolivia's leftist labor movement, attacked Paz as a "servant" of American interests. Julio Rocha, head of the main farmers' federation in the Chaparé, accused Paz of allowing the Americans to violate Bolivia's sovereignty. Peasants demonstrated in front of the U.S. embassy chanting "Long live coca!"

But the Paz government survived the attacks, and after the Blackhawks returned to the United States, the Bolivian president vowed to keep up the pressure. The State Department gave the Leopards six Vietnam-vintage Huey helicopters, and the Defense Department's Southern Command sent fourteen U.S. Army Green Berets to the Chaparé as trainers and advisers to the Leopards. However, mechanical breakdowns and Bolivia's inability to obtain insurance for the pilots and crews kept the Hueys grounded until August 1987, nine months after they arrived.

The efforts of DEA agents and U.S. military advisers to persuade the Leopards to sustain the pressure on the traffickers were hampered by chronic lassitude, failure of leadership, and corruption. In late 1986, a Bolivian congressional committee investigation took testimony from Leopards officers that their colleagues took bribes to allow small airplanes to land at clandestine airstrips in the Chaparé and load coca paste or base. According to press accounts and U.S. State Department officials, a number of Leopards officers, including the leader of the crucial Chaparé command, were relieved of their jobs for suspected graft. The scandal extended up to Interior Minister Fernando Barthelemy, who resigned in early 1987 after being accused of receiving pay-offs to protect the operators of a large cocaine lab acciden-tally discovered by a Bolivian scientific team in September 1986. A Bolivian congressional subcommittee asserted that Barthelemy delayed a military raid by one day and the co-caine traffickers escaped.[17]

Paz and his aides were well aware that the solution to the coca problem was not bullets but long-term social and economic change. They were grievously disappointed by the Reagan administration's refusal to underwrite their $300 million economic development plan. Soon after Operation Blast Furnace began, Washington turned down flat a Bo-livian request for a $100 million development loan. In early 1987, the Paz government and the State Department agreed on a more modest plan: the United States would provide $68 million if the Bolivian government promised to eradicate all coca grown for export within three years. The United Nations Fund for Drug-Abuse Control agreed to contribute $22 million over the next five years.

Soon after the agreement was reached, thirty thousand farmers in the Chaparé demonstrated against Paz's plan: since Chaparé coca was grown entirely for export—for re-fining to cocaine—the Bolivia–U.S. agreement would out-law their whole crop. The protests ended in the summer of 1987, when Paz negotiated a settlement with farm and labor leaders. The new agreement specified that reduction of coca cultivation would be voluntary for twelve months, that farm-ers would receive aid in making the transition to growing legal crops, and that aerial spraying of herbicides would be not used against coca.

Many eradication targets had been set over the years, and none had been met. What incentive did farmers have to abandon coca, a crop that yielded about five times more profit than food crops, could be reduced to paste or base which did not spoil, and did not have to be transported to market? The market—representatives of refiners—came to the villages in airplanes to buy the commodity.

A United Nations development project in the Yungas region was showing some promise, but the Yungas growers, who produced coca mostly for domestic leaf chewing, were peaceful and somewhat amenable to change. The more numerous Chaparé growers were well organized, militantly opposed to eradication, frequently violent, and wealthy enough to make payoffs to the police.

To make matters worse, in 1987 the Paz government closed most state-owned tin mines and threw twenty-three thousand miners out of work. Thousands of them and their families went to the Chaparé to seek jobs in the coca industry. The coca growers did not welcome them: Alberto Vargas, executive director of the area's biggest coca farmers federation, told *Washington Post* correspondent Tyler Bridges: "We don't want them growing coca because that would increase supply and cause prices to drop."[18] But the miners were desperate and many did end up in coca country.

In all of 1986 and most of 1987, the Bolivian government eradicated less than five hundred acres of coca.

If Bolivia was ever to meet its long-term eradication goal, and no one seriously believed it would, there would still be Peru. Three hundred thousand acres of coca, possibly more, grew on the eastern slopes of the Peruvian Andes. The most concentrated growing area was the valley of the Upper Huallaga River in the departments of San Martín and Huánuco, northeast of Lima. The center of the coca paste trade was Tingo María, Huánuco, a tough mountain town full of guns and new money.

The Peruvian coca growers benefited from the benign neglect of the weak oligarchy that had ruled Peru during the late 1970s and early 1980s. Things began to change in July 1985, when Alan García, a charismatic thirty-six-year-old leftist, took office. The idealistic García was stridently anti-American on nearly every subject but the drug trade. He had appealed to popular yearnings for legal and social justice by promising to fight corruption and brutality in the police and military. As one Latin expert put it, "One of the few things that García can offer that does not cost money is moralization." Immediately after his inauguration, García cashiered fifteen hundred policemen and military officers accused of corruption.

García pronounced the presence of cocaine traffickers in

the Andes a threat to Peru's internal security. Like Bolivia, Peru had not been a refining state, but in 1984, after President Betancur of Colombia launched his crackdown on the cocaine trade, refiners based in the Amazon jungle along Colombia's southwestern border had fled into Peru and had set up shop.

García was intensely concerned about the Sendero Luminoso (Shining Path) terrorists, a Maoist insurgency born in the southern Andes which specialized in bombing government installations, railroads, and power lines. The Senderos had expanded their control into the central Andes, pushing the Peruvian Army steadily back. Sometimes the Senderos warred with the drug traffickers and sometimes they appeared to be acting in concert. Whatever the political implications of these contacts, the fact was, the presence of well-armed cocaine-trafficking gangs and experienced terrorists made it all but impossible for the Army to secure the region.

In August 1985, in an unusual joint operation with the Colombian government, García sent Peruvian troops into the Amazon jungle to hit the traffickers' border sanctuaries. At the same time, Colombian forces moved into their side of the frontier, squeezing the traffickers in a pincer movement. Operation Condor, as the Peruvian foray was called, was a military success, but it also demonstrated that the Peruvian cocaine-refining industry was far more advanced than had been imagined. In vine-choked huts perched on pilings astride snaky inlets, soldiers found centrifuges, diesel generators, water pumps, hydraulic presses, drying facilities, and underground warehouses for storage. The largest processing lab was capable of refining five hundred pounds of cocaine a week. The traffickers had used barges to bring in bulldozers to make landing strips, as well as elaborate communications systems, trucks, boats, and video systems for the entertainment of the workers. At one laboratory complex there was a paved, all-weather airfield two thousand feet long and one hundred feet wide, longer and better maintained than most legal airports in the Amazon. Another complex had six dormitories, each capable of housing one hundred persons.

Peruvian troops destroyed the laboratories, but once the troops left, the traffickers rebuilt them. García launched another, more elaborate phase of Operation Condor in August 1986. Peruvian Air Force jet fighters bombed and strafed airstrips while troop-filled helicopters seized drugs and equipment and destroyed laboratories. By the end of 1986, Operation Condor troops had seized one hundred sixty-five airstrips, thirty-six laboratories, seventy aircraft, and thirty tons of coca paste and base.

Like his Bolivian counterparts, García faced overwhelming popular resistance when he tried to eradicate coca. The growers were a powerful, organized grass-roots political force in the Andean highlands. The traffickers were well armed and savage. In July 1986, they murdered six eradication workers in the Upper Huallaga valley, forcing the government to halt the project temporarily. By the fall of 1987, the Peruvian Army had been pushed out of the Upper Huallaga and García government officials were in Washington seeking State Department aid to enable them to retake the region.

The ultimate test of military strikes and eradication programs in the growing and refining countries is the effect on cocaine prices in the United States. Because of chronic overproduction of coca in South America, prices dropped steadily. In 1982, when the Bush task force was created in South Florida, a kilogram of cocaine could be purchased on the Miami wholesale market for $47,000 to $60,000. For most of 1986, the same kilogram of cocaine wholesaled for $25,000 to $28,000. Toward the end of the year, DEA undercover agents in Miami were able to buy cocaine for as little as $14,000. By the spring of 1987, the asking price in Miami was down to $12,000 a kilogram. According to an indictment filed in San Diego in January 1988, the alleged leaders of a newly formed Bolivian cartel called "the corporation" offered undercover agents from the DEA and Customs five tons of cocaine at $5,500 a kilogram. Coca was so cheap in Bolivia that the Bolivian traffickers were able to sell high-quality finished cocaine at half the price the Colombians were charging.

20
Drug War
Fall

The 1986 political season would go down in history as "Drug War Fall." For a variety of reasons, some rational, some opportunistic, some sheer blind panic, the press and the political establishment abruptly proclaimed the nation's drug problem a four-alarm emergency—and the hottest issue of the midterm election campaign.

As any beat cop or schoolteacher could attest, the "emergency" had been around for twenty years and was likely to linger for at least another decade. Yet in the spring and summer of 1986, a series of events occurred that triggered a political stampede.

The press sounded the first alarms by "discovering" something that medical researchers had confirmed a full century earlier: cocaine was addictive. In the 1970s and early 1980s, affluent coke users—and their sympathetic friends and relatives—had been able to deny the depredations of habitual use by glossing over the side effects or by seeking help at discreet private treatment centers.

But then cocaine became so cheap that nearly everybody could afford it and so potent that compulsive users became obvious dangers to themselves and to others. As the South American coca glut depressed cocaine prices, street dealers competed by selling higher-quality merchandise. In late 1986, the purity of street cocaine was approaching 65 percent, compared with 35 percent in 1983.

In 1982 or 1983, "crack," a Caribbean invention distributed by nomadic Jamaican gangs, was introduced in the ghettos of Los Angeles and Miami. By 1986, it had spread to the slums of New York, Detroit, Houston, and a few other major cities. "Crack," or "rock," was cocaine free-base, so called because boiling cocaine hydrochloride powder with baking soda "freed" the cocaine base; the pebblelike residue of the boiling process was smoked in a pipe. Since smoking was the most direct route to the brain, crack hit the nervous system like a jackhammer, inducing instant euphoria, followed by profound depression. Full-fledged addiction might develop in six to ten weeks.

Crack opened up vast new markets for cocaine because it was priced within reach of the very young and the very poor. A hundred-milligram dose of crack could be had for $10, compared with $80 to $100 for a gram of cocaine. Many dealers preferred to sell crack, although the profit margin per dose was less than for cocaine powder, because the pool of potential customers was larger than for cocaine and the profits on repeat sales were astronomical. A study conducted by pharmacologists at the University of California at Los Angeles showed that the average cocaine addict snorted two grams of 50 percent pure cocaine powder each week, spending $200, while an average cocaine-base addict consumed ten and a half grams of 95 percent pure crack or freebase, at a cost of a $1,000.[1]

Crack abuse created enormous problems for city police departments as addicts turned to theft to satisfy their habits. In contrast to the limp, withdrawn heroin addicts that the cops used to encounter, cocaine addicts thought they were supermen; they gave a new meaning to the cliché "crime spree." By the middle of 1986, half the drug cases handled by the U.S. Attorney's Office in Manhattan involved crack. A study conducted by the National Institute of Justice found that of four hundred people charged with crimes in Manhattan in September and October 1986, more than 80 percent tested positive for cocaine, compared with 42 percent in 1984. The study showed that between 59 percent and 92 percent of persons charged with robbery in Manhattan in 1986 tested positive for cocaine; in the same period, more than 70 percent of those charged with burglary were high on cocaine.[2]

In early 1986, crack abuse did not rank as a nationwide problem. Alcohol, marijuana, and cocaine powder remained the intoxicants of choice in most communities. But because the crack craze hit Los Angeles and New York early and hard, it claimed more than its share of national publicity.

In May 1986, *The New York Times* published an alarming account of crack abuse and teenage crime. That inspired a June 16, 1986, cover story in *Newsweek*, entitled "An Inferno of Craving, Dealing and Despair." Reading the first draft of the story, *Newsweek* editor in chief Richard Smith thought he spotted a national trend in the making and declared his own war on drugs. In a striking turnabout for a magazine whose readers were predominantly affluent, liberal baby-boomers, Smith published a letter to readers, headlined "The Plague Among Us," which blamed drug use for every sort of social and economic ill, even the loss to the Japanese of America's competitive edge. He pledged to cover the "drug crisis" "as aggressively . . . as we did the struggle for civil rights, the war in Vietnam, and the fall of the Nixon presidency."

By tragic coincidence, on June 18, Len Bias, a twenty-two-year-old University of Maryland basketball star and top draft choice of the National Basketball Association, died of a cocaine overdose while celebrating his signing with the world champion Boston Celtics. Eight days later, Cleveland Browns defensive back Don Rogers, twenty-three, died of a cocaine overdose at his bachelor party. Neither athlete had been using crack, but, rather, cocaine powder taken through the nose. Both were in superb physical condition.

The athletes' deaths underscored what medical research had established long before: that cocaine in any form places great stress on the human body. A cocaine high—"a fire in the brain," as *Time* magazine once put it—sounds considerably less romantic when described in clinical terms. Cocaine appears to act on the brain's reward system by stimulating the release of dopamine, a neurotransmitter associated with pleasure. As an unwanted side effect it activates the central nervous system's "flight-or-fight" mechanism. The heart rate and respiration become more rapid, blood pressure rises, and the chances of heart attack, cerebral hemorrhage, or convulsions heighten. Because the nervous system builds up a tolerance to the pleasure-inducing effects of the drug, the user has to take more and more cocaine to feel the old euphoria. At the same time, the cardiovascular system and the brain become sensitized to the drug. After a while, what the user thinks is a recreational dose may turn out to be toxic because of the "kindling effect" of repeated sensitization.

In the 1970s, physicians did not regard cocaine as "addictive" because abstinence did not cause the physical withdrawal symptoms associated with heroin. In the mid-1980s, the medical community was redefining "addiction" to include the implacable craving induced by cocaine. Doctors had also come to realize that cocaine dependency was complicated and resistant to cure. "There are actually several consequences to cocaine abuse that have to be neutralized," observed Dr. Roger Brown, director of Neurosciences Research at the National Institute on Drug Abuse (NIDA). "First is the immediate toxicity, which is usually why the abuser shows up in the emergency room in the first place. But after that . . . are the biochemical readjustments which the body has made in response to cocaine, the euphoria and the anguish and depression. All of these need attention in order to prevent relapse."[3]

From time to time, a number of publications had printed thorough, dispassionate articles on the forgotten perils of cocaine. One was James Lieber's "Coping with Cocaine" in the January 1986 issue of *Atlantic Monthly*. But they did not shake the popular presumption that cocaine killed only people who engaged in protracted binges of drug abuse. The deaths of Len Bias and Don Rogers carried the message that it could happen to anyone, that taking cocaine was like playing Russian roulette.

Suddenly, newspapers, television shows, and magazines from *People* to *Sports Illustrated* to *Good Housekeeping* were packed with horror stories about cocaine abuse. It seemed that everyone wanted to "confess" an addiction: movie stars, teenagers, physicians, housewives, stockbrokers, and football players eagerly related intimate details of cocaine-ravaged lives. The CBS News contribution, *Forty-eight Hours on Crack Street*, earned the highest Nielsen rating of any documentary in the past five years. *Life* magazine's issue of October 1986 showed a young man puffing on a crack pipe. The headline read " 'I AM A COKE ADDICT'—What Happens When Nice Guys Get Hooked."

Time magazine's September 15, 1986, issue attempted to moderate the discussion, noting that cocaine abuse killed a fraction of the people who died in car wrecks; alcohol exacted a higher social cost than illegal drugs. But the message was contradicted by the magazine's cover, a death's-head with a blazing yellow caption, "Drugs—The Enemy Within." It was quite a change from the Christmas catalogue look of a 1981 *Time* cover that showed a martini glass filled with sparkling white powder.

The sudden journalistic interest in drug abuse was hardly altruistic. Drug stories sold. But they sold because "drug crisis" coverage struck a nerve in American society. The landscape was littered with burned-out cases. The 1960s people no longer laughed at the slogan "acid, amnesty, and abortion" when they saw brothers, sisters, and friends with wasted minds or when they found out that their own fourteen-year-olds were turning on and tuning out. Cocaine-overdose deaths were still unusual, and marijuana fatalities virtually unknown, but the side effects of habitual "recreational" use were exacting an increasing if intangible toll on the quality of life for tens of millions of American families. A *New York Times*/CBS poll listed drug abuse as "the nation's leading overall concern." A Gallup poll conducted for the National Education Association and released in late August 1986 found that parents considered drugs in school the nation's number-one educational problem. By wide margins, adults approved of expelling students caught using drugs and thought teachers should be allowed to search lockers for drugs.

By some measures, marijuana appeared to be falling out of favor. Even high-school kids were starting to talk about the "amotivational syndrome"—the glassy-eyed stare—of habitual users, and some researchers were writing that marijuana caused long-term brain damage. A National Institute on Drug Abuse survey conducted in 1985 suggested that marijuana consumption was declining slightly, especially among Americans twenty-five years of age and younger. However, there were still a lot of Americans using marijuana: NIDA pollsters estimated that 18 million people, a tenth of the American population, had smoked pot within a month of their survey. (A separate survey of high-school seniors, conducted annually by the University of Michigan, supported the NIDA survey's finding: the Michigan study showed that marijuana use had been declining among seniors ever since 1979, when 37 percent of those polled said they had used marijuana within the preceding month. By 1986, that group was down to 23 percent, and by 1987, to 21 percent. The Michigan survey was controversial because it did not poll dropouts and absentees, the youths most likely to be on drugs.)

The good news about marijuana, such as it was, was offset by bad news about cocaine. NIDA analysts projected that 5.8 million Americans had used cocaine at least once in the month preceding the survey, compared with 4.2 million in 1982. Cocaine use among under-twenty-five-year-olds appeared to be leveling off, but "older" Americans appeared to be using more cocaine and using it in more dangerous ways, by smoking it as crack, by snorting more potent cocaine powder, or by injecting it intravenously, risking exposure to Acquired Immune Deficiency Syndrome.

The NIDA survey in 1985 projected that 870,000 Americans were using cocaine once a week or more. If that was so, the threat to public health and safety was comparable to the heroin "epidemic" of the early 1970s, which was thought to have involved 700,000 addicts. Some health experts predicted a cocaine "implosion," a severe bout of deaths and emergencies within the cocaine-using population. Already, the casualties were showing up in jails, emergency rooms, clinics, and, in small but rapidly increasing numbers, in morgues.

People across the country began to demand governmental solutions. This posed a dilemma for official Washington, which had entertained countless ideas over the years but none resembling a solution. Leaders of both parties saw that, like it or not, drug abuse was going to be *the* issue of the fall campaigns, and they dared not leave the field to the opposition. Lurching into action, partisan tacticians rummaged through ideological closets and emerged with a variety of shopworn notions, which they shamelessly repackaged.

Republican pollster Richard Wirthlin was one of the first to sense the grass-roots anti-drug sentiment and to urge the White House to do something about it. In the spring of 1986, Wirthlin wrote a memo to White House chief of staff Donald Regan, advising him to consider the drug issue as the next major presidential initiative after tax reform, which would be law by Labor Day. Wirthlin had detected in polling and focus groups a new intensity of concern about drug use—not only as an external threat, as a cause of crime and automobile accidents, but as an intrusion into the family, the workplace, and the community.

As Wirthlin saw it, the drug issue had the right elements for Ronald Reagan. It was something he could genuinely care about. There was less ambivalence about drugs among the American voters, less talk of legalization or decriminalization of drugs than in the past. People wanted real change and were prepared to support drastic action to get it. "The key to this president's popularity is that he's viewed as being able to change things for the better," Wirthlin told a reporter. "And that, in turn, is part of what makes him successful at it. Americans will tend to support a president if they consider him a major agent of change." Reagan signed off on the proposal in late May, and Don Regan set to work rounding up elements of a package from the various bureaucracies. White House aides decided that the thrust of Reagan's initiative would be "demand reduction": in layman's terms, convincing young people not to start and drug users to stop.

Prevention through education was hardly a new idea. Soon after Richard Nixon launched his war on drugs, on December 3, 1969, John E. Ingersoll, director of the Bureau of Narcotics and Dangerous Drugs, warned a White House governors conference, "To talk only in terms of eliminating the illicit drug supply is, in my judgment, a shortsighted approach. What we need is a concomitant long-range program that will eliminate the demand. We must restore and emphasize some established and tested values—family cohesiveness and intrafamily communication."

Ingersoll's message had been lost in the tumult of the times. The governors could not keep their own kids away from pot, much less restore family values in a time of war between the generations. It had been easier to create drug task forces and fund eradication programs overseas than to turn the tide of social change at home.

In the early 1980s, the only public officials who were talking about demand reduction were the frontline law-enforcement officials, paradoxically the beneficiaries of expanding drug-enforcement budgets. The new wave of law-and-order conservatism that swept through both political parties was of little comfort to men and women in the trenches, who knew only too well that there were more dealers and smugglers than law-enforcement agencies could possibly hope to catch. The State Department estimated that enough coca was being grown in Latin America in 1986 to produce as much as 377 metric tons of cocaine. That was five times the amount of cocaine Americans consumed in 1985, by NIDA's estimates.[4] There were literally millions of poor people willing to risk their lives growing and smuggling cocaine and marijuana, a fact that rendered traditional deterrents to crime such as long sentences and preventive detention as futile as bullets against ants.

The reality was that anti-smuggling laws acted very much like a trade embargo. As history had often shown, trade embargos did not work. "Supply-side" efforts to stop the drug trade could lock up some bad people and discourage marginal operators, but they did not stop trade. When President Carter refused to sell grain to the Soviet Union after the USSR's invasion of Afghanistan, the Soviets simply turned to Argentina, which was angry with the United States for supporting Great Britain against Argentina in the Falklands war. When President Reagan tried to prevent Iran from buying weapons for its war against Iraq, Iran got arms from international arms dealers and, eventually, from Reagan himself. Drug users would always get drugs, one way or another. Members of the law-enforcement community

knew that and could only hope that American children
would learn, one day, to reject mind-altering chemicals.

"When we point a finger," Jack Lawn often said, "we
should point in the mirror." One of Lawn's first acts as DEA
administrator was an education project to help high-school
coaches counsel their players. A coach by the name of Frank
Parks from Spingarn high school in a tough part of Southeast
Washington had come to him desperate for straightforward
medical information to give his charges. Many of the boys,
Parks said, spent more time with him than with their fathers,
if they had fathers, and he did not want to lose them to the
street. Lawn, who had coached basketball in Brooklyn while
studying for his master's degree, knew just how Parks felt
and was appalled that this man had had nowhere to turn
but a law-enforcement agency. Lawn helped Parks set up a
program of peer counseling that became a model for coaches
across the country. Then the DEA administrator scraped
together a little money to distribute literature and films and
prevailed upon Olympic stars and professional ballplayers
to appear at schools to talk to students. The small program
impressed a number of other government officials; Colonel
Ralph Milstead, director of the Arizona Department of Public Safety, told the House Narcotics Committee in early 1986
that the DEA coaches' program was about the only useful
thing he had seen come out of Washington. He bluntly
advised the politicians to stop appropriating money for cops
and jails and to spend it in schools instead. "It is not a
matter of a few holes in the dike that can be plugged by
additional manpower," Milstead said. "The dike is gone.
We will hear people say, Well, the problem is Mexico; the
problem is Bolivia; the problem is Afghanistan; it is Colombia. The problem is in the hearts and minds of our citizens who desire this flight from reality, this escape."
Milstead scoffed at law-enforcement solutions as being like
"killing a snake, tail first." "We ought to start at the head,"
he concluded, "and the head, of course, is demand."[5]

From the first days of the Reagan White House, drug
education had been left to Nancy Reagan, whose advisers
had introduced her to the issue as a means of dispelling her
clotheshorse image. To her credit, she took it seriously and

stuck with it, appearing at school after school, tears welling in her eyes as she urged young people to "just say no." Her commitment was genuine, and her mother-to-mother talks with other first ladies were probably as effective as anything the State Department had accomplished in the way of diplomacy against drugs. Mrs. Reagan used plain talk with which parents could identify. "We must create an atmosphere of intolerance for drug use in this country," she told her audiences.

Yet when it had come to spending money, the Reagan administration had favored "supply-side" interdiction and enforcement efforts. Federal funds for drug treatment and prevention programs had decreased 40 percent between 1980 and 1986, from $333 million to $235 million, according to an analysis by the National Association of State Alcohol and Drug Abuse Directors.

In the spring of 1986, as White House political strategists realized that Ronald Reagan had to join his wife in urging measures that discouraged the use of drugs, the plan they devised was vintage Reagan: long on inspirational words, low on cost. The Great Communicator would use the bully pulpit of the presidency to urge more volunteerism: schools should suspend users and pushers, communities should launch drug-education programs, private industry should institute preemployment screening for drug use. Reagan delivered his anti-drug message on August 4. "To rely totally on government is to fall prey to an illusion," he said. The only federal measure he proposed was controversial but cheap: drug testing of government employees with "sensitive jobs." To set an example, Reagan took a urine test himself.

A *New York Times* editorial quickly dismissed the Reagan message as "fuzzy" and advised the president he had to offer more than a "verbal assault."

Reagan's initiative was a broad target for the Democrats, who had not lost their enthusiasm for Great Society–style spending programs. A week after Len Bias died, Congressman Charles Rangel introduced a billion-dollar anti-drug legislative package to fund new education programs and state and local law-enforcement projects to go after street dealers. "Even though the administration claims to have declared 'war on drugs,' " said Rangel, "the only evidence I find of this war are the casualties." In the 1960s, the term "law and order" had been a code for anti-youth, anti-black police actions. In 1986, it was politically acceptable for Rangel, a Harlem Democrat, to inveigh against drug abuse and for Jesse Jackson, a liberal black candidate for president, to deliver a sermon on law and order, calling drug dealers "terrorists and death messengers . . . the hound of hell for this generation."

In early summer, pollster William Hamilton produced a nationwide survey that caught the attention of Congressional Democratic leaders. Hamilton found that voters consistently listed domestic issues such as drugs, health care, and education as more urgent than development of the Strategic Defense Initiative ("Star Wars") program or funding for the Nicaraguan rebels. In other words, Hamilton found, people liked Reagan but did not share his priorities. The poll asked voters whether they would favor increased government funding for "more and better law enforcement to stop drug smuggling or to build a new, advanced missile system to stop enemy attacks." Two thirds of the respondents favored the drug option. The conclusion, as one Democratic staffer put it, was: "We have to point out that Reagan doesn't have a real policy to fight drugs."

The Democrats attempted to portray Reagan's August message as eleventh-hour opportunism. "Congress has been taking the initiative on this issue for years," said House Majority Leader Jim Wright. "The president's budgets have asked for curtailments. Congressional budgets restored all those monies. This isn't all of a sudden for us." The Democrats intended to fund new programs that would make the previous efforts look parsimonious. Democratic Congressional campaign chairman Tony Coelho of California told a reporter, "Whatever it costs, we will do it. . . . We intend to bust the budget on this."

Congressional Republicans who had spent years badgering the White House to pay attention to the drug issue were annoyed by the way the Reagan White House came on, as one GOP staffer said, "like a locomotive." Further, when it came to relations with other nations, House Republicans were inclined toward von Raab–style confrontation rather than the friendly approach favored by Meese.

Capitol Hill went from the doldrums to hyperactivity as members of both parties sprinted for the hopper, proposing bills banning crack pipes, regulating private air traffic, imposing special penalties on dealing drugs near schoolyards. The docket became so crowded that House Speaker Tip O'Neill designated a task force to come up with a bipartisan omnibus bill combining the proposals of all twenty-two committees.

After Labor Day, the Congress went into a frenzy. No one wanted to be tarred as soft on crime. "It's mob mentality in there," said Brian J. Donnelly, a Democrat from Massachusetts, as he walked off the House floor. Republicans and Democrats scratched and clawed one another to offer yet more draconian amendments. On September 11, by a vote of 392 to 16, the House approved a bill that was breathtaking in its scope, authorizing $6 billion over three years for both "supply-side" interdiction and enforcement measures and "demand-side" education and treatment programs.

Among the dozens of amendments were provisions to make money laundering an explicit crime, to outlaw the manufacture of "designer drugs," and to impose a ten-year mandatory minimum sentence on first-time offenders if they were ranked as "major traffickers" and a twenty-year minimum sentence on anyone convicted of a drug offense from which death or serious bodily injury resulted.

One audacious provision gave the military sweeping authority to make searches, seizures, and arrests, not only on the high seas but, in a case of hot pursuit, within the borders of the United States. Even more extreme was an amendment authored by Congressmen Duncan Hunter, a Republican from California, and Tommy Robinson, a Democrat from Arkansas, which directed the president to deploy military forces along the entire southern border of the United States within thirty days and to "substantially halt" the influx of narcotics from anywhere in the world within forty-five days.

Flabbergasted Pentagon officials calculated that to provide continuous radar coverage of the southern border would require ninety Boeing AWACS airplanes, fifty-eight more than the entire U.S. AWACS fleet, or eighty-eight Navy E-2C "mini-AWACS," eight hundred helicopters, ten divisions of the U.S. Army, and eighty new military bases. Noting that the provision would provide a windfall of new business for military contractors, Senator Sam Nunn of Georgia sniped, "We might call this the Boeing amendment before it is over."[6]

The House ignored the objections of civil libertarians in accepting an amendment by Representative George Gekas, a Republican from Pennsylvania, to impose the death penalty on persons who knowingly caused the death of another while engaging in a continuing criminal enterprise. The legislators also voted to permit evidence obtained in illegal searches to be used in criminal trials.

Liberal opponents of the bill charged that the House was acting out of panic. "I fear this bill is the legislative equivalent of crack," said Massachusetts Democrat Barney Frank. "It yields a short-term high but does long-term damage to the system, and it's expensive to boot."[7] But House leaders said they were simply taking advantage of their constituents' sudden interest in the issue. "One of the unfortunate by-products of the television age is the short attention span of the American public," observed House Majority Leader Wright. "We walk along, fat, dumb, and happy, until a crisis grabs us by the throat. Once it is off the front burner of nightly television coverage, we go back to sleep."[8]

Professional law-enforcement officials found the rush to legislate unsettling. "It's hysteria," Jack Lawn remarked, shuddering. "But the nice thing is, after the election, it'll be over." When the Congress ordered a long list of bureaus and agencies, from the Federal Communications Commission to the U.S. Forest Service, to take up arms in the drug war, DEA officials dreaded a repetition of the bureaucratic fragmentation and rivalry that had existed in the 1960s. Tom Cash, a DEA headquarters executive and veteran of the bad old days, whipped up a "citizen's self-arrest form." "I want to give all American citizens Title Twenty-one narcotic investigative jurisdiction," Cash announced with mock solemnity. "They can arrest each other. They can arrest themselves. There's a place for you to put your fingerprints and everything. Mail 'em in. Save $500 million. We abandon DEA right away."

The fall's political campaigns were almost too wild to parody, though cartoonist Gary Trudeau tried, devoting several episodes of *Doonesbury* to the question of whether patrician congresswoman Lacey Davenport would agree to her sleazy opponent's demand that she take a urine test. Real politicians engaged in "jar wars"; and heaven help the pol who admitted that he had once smoked pot.

Not to be outdone on the rhetoric front, White House speechwriters set to work on a statement to be delivered by President and Mrs. Reagan and televised on September 14. The advance public-relations campaign was grandiose, culminating in a press release that asserted, "When the chapter on how America won the war on drugs is written, the Reagans' speech is sure to be viewed as a turning point."

The live broadcast featured President and Mrs. Reagan sitting on a couch in the living quarters of the White House. Holding hands, the Reagans took turns evoking the old-fashioned values—love of family, community service, patriotism. "There is no moral middle ground," Mrs. Reagan said. "Indifference is not an option. . . . To young people watching or listening, I have a very special personal message for you. There's a big, wonderful world out there for you. It belongs to you. It's exciting, stimulating, rewarding. Don't cheat yourselves out of this promise. Our country needs you. But it needs you to be clear-eyed and clear-minded. Say yes to your life. And when it comes to drugs and alcohol, just say no."

"My generation will remember how Americans swung into action when we were attacked in World War II," Reagan said. "Now we're in another war for our freedom, and it's time for all of us to pull together again. . . . What they [the Americans killed in World War II] did for us means that we owe as a simple act of civic stewardship to use our freedom wisely for the common good. Please remember this when your courage is tested: you are Americans. You are the product of the freest society mankind has ever known. No one—ever—has the right to destroy your dreams and shatter your life."

Afterward, the White House sent to the Hill a bill called the Drug-Free America Act of 1986. The price tag was a modest $900 million in the first year.

On September 25, Senate Majority Leader Robert Dole and Minority Leader Robert C. Byrd devised a "consensus" bill incorporating much of the Reagan proposal and the less inflammatory provisions of the House legislation. The Dole-Byrd bill omitted the death penalty for narcotics felons and House provisions requiring the military to secure the border from smugglers. Even so, Senate moderates complained that they were being bulldozed. Senator Daniel J. Evans, a Republican from Washington, pleaded with his fellows not to join "a sanctimonious election stampede." "If we vote for legislation to win an election and trample the Constitution in the process," Evans said, "we have not served the country very well." Evans's was a voice of reason, but few politicians seemed to believe that reason won elections. The Senate adopted the measure five days after it was introduced.

When the bill came back to the House, House members attempted to reinstate the death-penalty language but relented when a group of senators threatened to filibuster the bill. On October 17, both bodies passed a compromise measure authorizing $1.7 billion in spending in fiscal 1987. The Anti–Drug Abuse Act of 1986, as the final version was called, consumed fifty-six pages of the *Congressional Record* and touched on every conceivable aspect of substance abuse, from marijuana eradication in the national forests to alcoholism on Indian reservations. Ronald Reagan signed the bill on October 27, declaring, "Drug use is too costly for us not to do everything in our power, not just to fight it, but to subdue it and conquer it."

Ninety days after he signed the omnibus drug bill, President Reagan sent his fiscal 1988 budget proposal to Capitol Hill with an anti-drug agenda that was nearly $1 billion lighter than the spending that was taking place in 1987 under the drug bill's expanded programs. The 1988 Reagan budget proposed to kill Congressman Rangel's $225-million-a-year grant program for state and local law-enforcement agencies. It contained no new money for drug-treatment programs, which had received $175 million in 1987, and proposed to slash spending for drug education from $200 million in 1987 to $100 million in 1988. The Reagan budget contemplated cuts of another $500 million for Customs and Defense Department interdiction, $75 million for drug-abuse research, and $20 million for foreign aid to drug-producing nations.

Although Reagan had never endorsed the big spending portions of the bill, community leaders perceived his low-budget approach as a retreat. Ignoring Reagan, legislators restored education and treatment programs to their 1987 levels and budgeted $75 million for the law-enforcement grant program.

Nonetheless, Reagan took credit for escalating the "war." In 1988, as the elections loomed, President Reagan declared, with characteristic ebullience, "I believe the tide of battle has turned and we're beginning to win the crusade for a drug-free America." Nobody believed that but Reagan. "If we are winning the war on drugs," said Sterling Johnson, special narcotics prosecutor in New York, "every American just better pray each night we don't lose."

The 1988 political season set Washington off on another drug war spending spree. Just before Election Day, Congress passed yet another omnibus drug bill authorizing $2 billion over the next few years for anti-drug programs. One controversial but popular provision was a death penalty for traffickers involved in murder. Senator Joseph Biden's pet project, the creation of a cabinet-level "drug czar," finally became reality.

The uproar over the Camarena case and the escalation of cocaine trafficking in the Southwest ensured that Congress would authorize a major buildup of drug interdiction resources along the U.S.–Mexico border.

The installation of new radar systems on the border to detect "low-and-slow" aircraft penetrating U.S. airspace from Mexico was an idea that Democratic governors Mark White of Texas and Tony Anaya of New Mexico began promoting in the early 1980s. They argued that the states should not have to pick up the tab for dealing with the havoc wreaked by traffickers, particularly the new influx of Colombians settling in northern Mexico and in Texas and California. Besides, they argued, this was a national security problem. Some of those smuggling planes could be loaded with explosives and Middle Eastern radicals. Existing radar installations, even the powerful North American Air Defense Command (NORAD), picked up nothing that flew in lower than ten thousand feet. Over Big Bend Park, there was no radar coverage below fourteen thousand feet. National security policy held that "low-and-slow" coverage was unnecessary because an enemy plane could not drop an atomic bomb from lower than ten thousand feet, but that was Cold War thinking, and did not foresee the world of the cruise missile and the car bomb.

Senator Dennis DeConcini and Representative Glenn English drafted a bill in early 1986 to harden the "soft underbelly" of U.S. air defenses. The bill contained about $300 million for the Defense Department and Customs Service budgets for radar balloons and military surveillance aircraft to be deployed along the Southwestern border.[9] The English-DeConcini plan, which became part of the omnibus drug bill, was expensive but popular. Drug-war hawks envisioned a radar net as impenetrable as the airspace over Eastern Europe. Congressional moderates agreed that the United States should police its own frontier before criticizing poor Mexico for failing to interdict smugglers. There was also a bit of pork barreling going on. The first balloon radar platform would be anchored in DeConcini's turf in southern Arizona. The main command, control, communications, and intelligence center would go into English's hometown, Oklahoma City, a mere seven hundred miles from the border.

DEA officials opposed the plan on grounds that spending on interdiction equipment such as airplanes and radar would prove futile. "We could have the whole country surrounded," Lawn said, "and people who want to get drugs are going to get drugs, even if they have to manufacture them themselves." Also, it rankled DEA officials that the

omnibus bill contained $60 million in additional funds for
their own agency, a fifth of what the Congress contemplated
spending on interdiction. The additional funding for DEA
was enough to hire five hundred new agents, which would
swell the organization's workforce to nearly twenty-nine
hundred agents. That was nearly a thousand more agents
than when Ronald Reagan took office, but the expansion
looked meager compared with the hundreds of thousands
of drug traffickers in the world.

Willy von Raab did not intend to spurn Congressional largesse, which pushed the Customs Service budget past the $1
billion mark, but he was aware that all that expensive hard-
ware would raise expectations that could not possibly be fulfilled. Like any other executive, he would rather have good
tools than none, but he continued to advocate political pressure on Mexico, insisting that if the de la Madrid government
was unwilling to clean out the border sanctuaries and patrol
its own airspace, the U.S. government's ability to interdict
smugglers at the land border would remain severely limited.
As von Raab cautioned a Congressional committee, "We
can use the balloon to count the number of planes coming
over. So we know a plane is coming. It drops a load by parachute and flies back into Mexico. What good does it do us?
We're not going to shoot him down. As long as they have a
safe haven across the border, all of the detection equipment
isn't going to do any good. The first thing we have to address
is the issue of—call it corruption, call it better cooperation,
depending on how you want to characterize it."[10]

At first, the Reagan White House opposed the English-
DeConcini plan as too extravagant. But in the summer, as
the bill was clearing the final hurdles in the Congressional
appropriations process, Treasury and Justice officials were
hard at work drafting an administration interdiction plan
for the Southwest border which they called Operation Alliance. Operation Alliance was based on von Raab's Operation Blue Fire idea which he had conceived back in April.
Meese appropriated the idea, and put Steve Trott, Assistant
Treasury Secretary Frank Keating, and the staff of the National Drug Policy Board to work on creating a flashy new
interdiction project. The finished plan included every agency

with a presence in the Southwest, from the FBI to the Border Patrol. In late July 1986, seeing that the English-DeConcini bill was going to pass anyway, Meese's aides brazenly co-opted it and added it to the Operation Alliance press release as if it were their invention.

Several other elements of Operation Alliance were lifted from Congressional initiatives. For instance, in early 1987, the Office of Management and Budget proposed to reduce the Customs staff by fifteen hundred employees. The Senate Appropriations Committee restored those positions and added another three hundred. The Senate bill was well on its way to passage when the Operation Alliance plan was being drafted. So, in the Operation Alliance press release, Meese's staff simply listed the three hundred positions as an administration idea.

Operation Alliance was a standing joke among DEA and Customs Service personnel, who recognized a public-relations gimmick when they saw one and called it "Operation Dalliance." The unwieldy organizational structure and overlapping jurisdictions guaranteed that officers of the various agencies involved would spend as much time fighting over turf and equipment as enforcing the law. Most law-enforcement professionals doubted that Operation Alliance would accomplish anything that the various agencies would not have done on their own. They believed that the administration's motive in pushing the plan was mainly defensive— to prevent Congressional Democrats from taking full credit for defending the Southwest border from drug traffickers, gun runners, and terrorists.

Brushing aside the skepticism, Meese planned an elaborate unveiling ceremony for mid-August. Nearly every federal law-enforcement official would be there, except for von Raab, who was pointedly excluded. Vice President Bush would share the spotlight with Meese. Though Bush had had little or nothing to do with planning the initiative, some pro-Bush Treasury officials hoped the visibility might enhance Bush's image as a tough guy and improve his chances of getting the 1988 Republican presidential nomination.

21

The Torture
of Victor Cortez

The last thing President Miguel de la Madrid needed in August 1986 was another police corruption scandal.

The Mexican government would soon be unable to service its foreign debt unless it could get $12 billion in new financing. Jittery American banks, which were owed about a quarter of Mexico's $97 billion foreign debt, were refusing to make new loans until the International Monetary Fund and World Bank committed substantial sums to the bailout.

Drug-war hard-liners in Congress were raising a potential obstacle: they were drafting the provisions of the omnibus drug bill that would compel American members of international financial organizations to oppose new lending until de la Madrid moved aggressively against drug trafficking.

Reagan's advisers, hoping to raise the confidence of U.S. banks and avoid a disastrous default, turned to public relations. They arranged for the Mexican president to make a "working visit" to Washington during the second week of August. The purpose of the meeting, as Reagan aides freely acknowledged, was not work at all. It was an elaborate photo opportunity, a way to show that Ronald Reagan was completely at ease with de la Madrid's economic plans and unworried by talk of Mexico's political instability.

"It's discouraging to think that the president is only going to have a big public-relations love-in with Mr. de la Madrid, when there's an opportunity to really do some good," grumbled Senator DeConcini of Arizona. "They're making a huge mistake to soft-pedal election fraud, corruption, and the narcotics problem."

On August 13, as planned, Reagan emerged from lunch with de la Madrid and held a press conference in which he heaped praise upon the Mexican president and his ministers for their "courageous, determined effort to face up to their nation's fundamental economic problems and to turn a difficult situation around." Reagan pronounced the United States "ready to lend a hand when and where it can make a difference," urged the private banks to "move quickly" on the new loan package, and, as a token of his goodwill, disclosed that he was lifting a six-year-old embargo on the importation of Mexican tuna, imposed by President Jimmy Carter during a long-simmering dispute over territorial fishing rights. Reporters peppered White House spokesmen with questions about whether Reagan had pressed de la Madrid on the drug issue. At an afternoon briefing, a Reagan aide told reporters that as far as Reagan was concerned, "President de la Madrid made very strong and forceful his commitment to acting against the production and trafficking of drugs in Mexico. And we could not be more impressed by and happy with the strong position that he took on these issues."

At the very moment when these words were being spoken, DEA agent Victor Cortez was being tortured by Mexican police in Guadalajara.

A thirty-four-year-old from Brownsville, Texas, Cortez had been in Guadalajara a few months and was still getting acquainted with the city. On the morning of August 13, Cortez set out with Antonio Garate Bustamente, a former Jalisco state policeman who had turned to drug trafficking and then to informing. They took Garate's car and drove around town looking at some restaurants and houses frequented by traffickers. At about two o'clock, Cortez called the U.S. consulate from a bowling alley and asked his partners to pick him up.

Cortez and Garate were sitting in the car, waiting for the other DEA agents, when another car darted out of the traffic and pulled alongside. Three men in street clothes got out, identified themselves as Jalisco state policemen, and motioned them out of the car. The cops saw that Garate's car was illegally registered and found a semiautomatic rifle and a nine-millimeter machine gun in the trunk. Knowing that possession of an automatic weapon was a serious offense and wanting to protect Garate, Cortez said that he was a DEA agent and the guns were his. The cops said both men were under arrest.

Cortez had left his diplomatic passport and other credentials at the consulate. As he was trying to talk the cops out of taking him to jail, two other DEA agents arrived. They saw Cortez with the strangers but did not hear what he was saying and assumed he was setting up a drug deal. They kept on walking into the bowling alley. Cortez asked the Mexican policemen to go after his partners so that they could identify him, but the cops refused. Three more police cars screeched to a halt. Finding themselves staring at eight heavily armed men, Cortez and Garate had no choice but to submit.

At the Jalisco police station, the cops put Garate in a cell. They took Cortez into an interrogation room, stripped him, tied him down, and began to pound his stomach. Cortez contracted his abdominal muscles to ward off the blows. That worked for a few minutes because he was a weight lifter with muscles thick as cordwood, but eventually the pounding fists wore him down. The cops held electric cattle prods to his shins and forced fizzy mineral water laced with hot chili pepper oil up his nose. All the while, they demanded the names and home addresses of the agent's partners and details of DEA investigations in Guadalajara. They were particularly interested in how the American agents had found out about several recent shipments of cocaine, which the Federales had seized on the insistence of the American consulate.

The cops told Cortez he would soon be a dead man. Did he remember what had happened to Kiki Camarena? As soon as it was dark, they said, it would happen to him. Cortez was sure they meant it.

The ordeal went on for four hours. Sometime after seven o'clock in the evening, the cops ordered Cortez to get dressed. He figured this was it—the ride out of town, a shot in the head if he was lucky. Left alone briefly, he found a newspaper, tore out the letters *p* and *d*, and hid them in a matchbook. He stuck the matchbook back in his pocket, hoping that if his partners found his body, they would guess that he had been taken by the Jalisco police.

Cortez walked unsteadily down the corridor, his legs aching from the electric shocks. He saw an open door and thought about running, but then he thought that the policemen only wanted an excuse to shoot him in the back. As he pondered whether to break for the door, he saw a wonderful sight. Standing at the front desk was his boss, Tony Ayala, filling out the papers for his release. Ayala saw Cortez, and a look of immense relief passed over his face. He knew by the way the agent was walking that he was in pain, but Ayala did not say anything. He just wanted to get Cortez out of there. Later he would tell the battered agent just how lucky he was. He owed his life to two courageous Mexican citizens.

The two DEA agents who had gone into the bowling alley waited for about fifteen minutes, went outside, and saw that Garate's car was gone. They went back to the consulate and told Ayala what had happened. Ayala told the agents to assume that Cortez was missing. He gave out assignments and got on the telephone himself—to the embassy, to State officials, to the MFJP. When no one turned up word of Cortez, his partners began to fear the worst.

Around six o'clock, the Mexican husband of an American woman who worked at the U.S. consulate arrived to take her home. She apologized for keeping him waiting, saying that a DEA agent had disappeared after failing to show up for a meeting at a bowling alley and everyone was frantic. The man said that he had seen a confrontation of some sort on the street outside that bowling alley. Perhaps, he said, it had involved Cortez.

Some DEA agents went back to the bowling alley and found a sidewalk vendor who had seen Cortez and Garate being taken away. The vendor had written down several numbers from the plate of one of the cars. The agents could tell from the sequence of the numbers that the license belonged to an unmarked state police car.

Ayala called the Jalisco state police headquarters and

asked for the director. He was told the director was on vacation. Ayala said it was an emergency; could he speak to his deputy? The switchboard operator told him that someone would call back. Twenty long minutes later, a functionary returned Ayala's call. Ayala asked if the police had Cortez. "We'll check," the caller said. Twenty more minutes passed. An officer called. Yes, Cortez was there. He was being detained on a weapons charge. By this time, it was seven-thirty in the evening. Ayala sped to the police station and started filling out release forms. Cortez staggered down twenty minutes later.

Cortez would not leave the station without Garate. It took some negotiating, but around nine o'clock, the police agreed to let Garate go. He had not been beaten and was only frightened.

They drove to the consulate, where Ayala had color photos taken of the bruises on Cortez's shins caused by the cattle prods and the contusions on his shoulder from the beating. Then they went to the hospital for X-rays. Cortez needed a neck brace, but he was fortunate: no bones were broken, no organs ruptured.

Ayala and Cortez left the hospital at about one o'clock in the morning. To their horror, they spotted a Jalisco state police car on their tail, but this time they were not alone. Two Federales who were friends of Cortez had joined them and would hold off the Jalisco cops if need be. Ayala thought it best to avoid a confrontation and wheeled hard around a corner, skidding through side streets until he lost the cops.

Half an hour later, Cortez was home. His pregnant wife was sleeping, unaware of all that had happened. His two sons were in their beds. His dinner was on the table. Ayala had not told Estele Cortez that her husband was missing until he was sure Cortez was all right.

Cortez asked the two Federales to stay at the house for the rest of the night. Late the next afternoon, Cortez and his wife packed up what they could carry, dressed the boys, and boarded a flight bound for Los Angeles. By early Friday morning, they were in Tucson, at the home of Cortez's parents. Later on Friday, DEA agents arranged a visa for Garate and got him on a flight into the States.

Jack Lawn got word that Cortez was missing a few minutes after de la Madrid left the White House. Lawn was told a few hours later that Cortez had been located, but he did not find out that Cortez had been tortured by Mexican police until six o'clock the next morning. The agents in Guadalajara did not think that the attack on Cortez was a premeditated attempt to derail de la Madrid's meeting with Reagan. It looked as if a few of the Jalisco cops had simply taken advantage of Cortez's vulnerability.

Lawn went over to the Justice Department and broke the news to the attorney general. For Ed Meese, this was all very inopportune. Mexican Attorney General Sergio García Ramírez had come to Washington with de la Madrid and was due at the Justice Department at ten o'clock. At four o'clock that afternoon, Meese planned to announce Operation Alliance. He hoped that García Ramírez would join him on the podium and make the interdiction effort a demonstration of bilateral cooperation—in "the spirit of Cancún," as Meese liked to say. How could García Ramírez participate if he was beset by American reporters who wanted to talk about police brutality? How could Meese make good news about Operation Alliance when the press went for the bad news coming out of Mexico? Lawn told Meese that he would not raise the Cortez matter at the press conference. Meese could stick to his agenda. Lawn would tell the press about Cortez the next day.

García Ramírez appeared shocked when Lawn told him what had happened in Guadalajara. He promised to do whatever he could—which Lawn took to mean that he would investigate and take action against the policemen involved. But he declined to join Meese in participating in Operation Alliance. He intended to leave Washington with de la Madrid immediately after lunch.

Throughout the morning of August 14, word of the assault on Cortez spread rapidly through the clannish DEA and then to reporters who covered drug stories. As the press began calling with questions, Justice Department officials told the DEA's chief public affairs officer, Robert Feldkamp, to keep the lid on the Cortez matter until after the Meese press conference.

The fact was, a story of this magnitude could not be contained. Feldkamp knew that and answered reporters' calls candidly. So did DEA's other spokesmen and most of the agents in the Southwestern field offices. By the time the press conference was starting, a bulletin with sketchy facts had moved over the AP wire.

Meese did not prepare himself for the inevitable questions. At the first mention of the case, his face clouded and he grew sullen and unresponsive. He said he did not know the name of the agent or the name of the police force or any other details. He said that it was true that a DEA agent had been "detained and allegedly mistreated in Guadalajara," but he contended that Mexico was cooperating with U.S. requests for an investigation and had "pledged prosecution of the people involved if there is wrongdoing found."

"Why do you say 'allegedly' mistreated?" a reporter asked. "Haven't you asked him whether he was beaten, or don't you believe him?" "As *you* know," Meese said sourly, "*you* always like us to be fair and to say 'allegedly' until someone's been proven guilty in a court of law."

Lawn twisted uncomfortably in his seat and said little. Afterward, DEA chief of operations Dave Westrate pulled him aside. "We've *got* to do something," he said. "The agents are calling." Lawn vacillated. Loyalty to Meese pulled him one way; loyalty to the agents pulled him the other.

Democratic hard-liners saw the assault on Cortez as proof that the Mexican government was not serious about curbing police corruption. "I think it stinks," Larry Smith exploded. "What do you say when you're not sure whether the bad guys or the police are worse threats to your agents. If the Mexican government can't guarantee the safety of our people, we ought to pull them out."

"I know what has happened to Meese," scoffed De-

Concini. "It's easy to have it happen. You visit with the attorney general. You visit with their foreign minister. You have big banquets. They show you some charts and maps and you think, by God, they're really doing something. Wow, this is terrific. In fact, they're covering it up. And we're covering up."

Overnight, Meese apparently was made aware that he needed to appear more indignant, for he asserted on the *Today* show the next morning, "There is no question that our agent was badly treated, and we are not going to stand for this kind of conduct."

Even then, Meese doggedly defended the de la Madrid administration. "I think it is important to recognize that this was done by some state policemen in Jalisco and it does not represent either the approach or the commitments that we have received from the president of Mexico and the attorney general there," he said. He dismissed the assault on Cortez and the murder of Kiki Camarena as "isolated incidents," "exceptions to . . . a day-to-day working relationship that our people have had" with Mexican police officials.

Later in the day, presidential press secretary Larry Speakes read a statement deploring the actions of the Mexican police but expressing confidence that de la Madrid would do the right thing. "It is particularly unfortunate," the presidential spokesman said, "that this incident occurred during the very successful visit to Washington of Mexican President de la Madrid, whose government has been working closely with us to address the danger of narcotics between our two countries."

Meese and the White House were in for a shock. The de la Madrid government rejected Cortez's story out of hand. "I don't see what the great scandal is here," Felipe Flores, spokesman for García Ramírez, said, according to *The Washington Post*. "The state police in Jalisco have explained that he was detained for questioning and then let go and that was that."[1] According to the Associated Press, Jalisco Governor Enrique Alvarez del Castillo told the Mexican government newspaper *El Nacional* that the allegations of torture were "absolutely false. It was only a small incident."[2]

And Jalisco Attorney General Jaime Alberto Ramírez Gil insisted that Cortez was not "tortured" but simply "detained."³

When Lawn saw the Mexican government's denials, he could not keep silent any longer. Late on the afternoon of Friday, August 15, he called a press conference and said what was on his mind. "It is reprehensible to me and to any law-enforcement officer in the world that this conduct could be condoned in the law-enforcement community," he began. "The nature of the questioning would indicate to me that there were corrupt individuals in the Jalisco state police trying to determine the nature of DEA's investigative activity in Mexico, in Guadalajara. . . . It is a tragedy that any country in the world would have to term them police officers."

Asked if he agreed with Meese that the incident could be characterized as "mistreatment," Lawn said tightly, "The special agent was stripped, bound, beaten, and prodded with a cattle prod. I think it would be up to you to determine what adjective you want to use as to the type of interrogation it was."

Neither Meese's solicitous statements nor Lawn's condemnation seemed to make any difference. The Mexican government continued to deny that Cortez had been tortured. In an interview with the *Dallas Times Herald,* de la Madrid himself dismissed the incident as "exaggerated." On Monday, August 18, the State Department lodged a sharply worded protest with Mexico's Foreign Ministry.⁴ For some reason, that produced results, of a sort. The next night, according to news reports, Mexican authorities announced that they had detained eleven Jalisco state police officers for abuse of authority.⁵

There was less to the Mexican government's concession than met the eye. DEA agents in Guadalajara found out that the policemen were not being held in jail. They had returned to their jobs. Officials in the Mexican Attorney General's Office told U.S. embassy officials that since a Mexican doctor judged that Cortez's wounds would heal within fifteen days, the policemen's assault was deemed a misdemeanor punishable by three days to four months in jail—*if* they were prosecuted.

As the weeks passed, neither Attorney General García Ramírez nor his deputies took the logical first step toward prosecution of the policemen: they did not ask Cortez to sign a complaint or other formal statement describing what had happened to him. There was no political capital in it. When the Cortez story broke, Mexican politicians and columnists unleashed a torrent of anti-American rhetoric. A cartoon in the newspaper *Excelsior* showed two skunks, labeled "drug traffickers" and "DEA," scurrying past three disgusted Mexicans. The chairman of the Mexican Senate Foreign Relations Commission announced an investigation into the status of DEA agents in Mexico. On August 27, Mexico's Foreign Ministry issued a diplomatic protest of its own, warning that DEA agents in Mexico were carrying out unauthorized activities and were "causing tensions between the two governments, [and] also creating situations that damage the image of Mexico in the U.S. and other countries."

In the face of the Mexican government's intransigence, it was official Washington that blinked. Few members of Congress really wanted to drag down the Mexican economy, because they feared the repercussions on the Southwestern economy and American banks. Congressional leaders drafted a resolution criticizing the government of Mexico for its "inadequate response" in the Cortez and Camarena cases, but this was a purely symbolic, nonbinding resolution, which called on the president to "consider" such measures as voting against IMF and World Bank loans for Mexico, issuing a travel advisory, and denying Mexico favorable tariff treatment. Reagan ignored it and so did the lending institutions. The IMF and World Bank made commitments to contribute to the emergency loan package de la Madrid needed. By March 1987, the Mexican government had reached an agreement with the commercial banks. In the end, the bailout package would total nearly $14 billion, even more than de la Madrid had sought when he lunched with Reagan on August 13.

Meese did not make an issue of the Cortez case, at least not in public. When six weeks had passed and no prosecutions had occurred, Larry Smith summoned Steve Trott to the House Foreign Affairs Committee to explain what the National Drug Policy Board was doing to see that Cortez's assailants were brought to justice. As head of the drug board's "coordinating group" of subcabinet-level officials, Trott functioned as chief operating officer to Meese's chairman of the board.[6]

"The Cortez case produced considerable concern, outrage, and disgust, and there were questions as to how to handle that," Trott testified. "We convened a meeting of the coordinating group, that was a matter that was on the agenda, various suggestions came out, we utilized the [crisis management] process to task that, to scope it out. At the next meeting of the coordinating group, then, the suggestions that had been made were discussed and we decided as a group what ought to be done and what ought not to be done. This is an example of how the coordinating group and the board work together to tackle each one of these problems. But the coordinating board, as effective as it has been—"

"Do you want to tell me," Smith said impatiently, "what conclusion you came to with reference to Cortez after you scoped all this out?"

"I think we came to the conclusion," said Trott, "that for the time being there has been sufficient activity on the part of the government of Mexico to identify and prosecute the persons involved so that we are willing to wait before anything particular is done in response."

"How long did it take to come to that conclusion?" Smith said, rolling his eyes heavenward.

"I think it was about seven days," Trott replied briskly.

Smith inquired what the drug board intended to use in the way of leverage to secure the cooperation of Mexico and other drug-producing countries.

"Our strategy is to use more carrots than sticks to work with people," Trott replied. ". . . Number one, the executive branch of the [U.S.] government dealing with foreign countries as equals, partners in these programs, can't wear two hats. We can't be both the social worker and the cop or prison guard. We can be aggressive, tough as hell . . . [but] we are more comfortable with wearing the other hat, trying to get things done. If somebody is going to be using the stick, it won't be us."

Smith gave Trott a look of cold appraisal. "That is all right. We will play the bad guy. . . . We will wield the stick. I don't want their love, just their cooperation."

"When I turn around and look at Mexico," Smith added, "I see a man named Félix Gallardo who runs a whole section of the country and they won't arrest him. And the Camarena matter dragging on for two years now, and it occurs to a lot of us that we keep hearing about all the things they are doing. Nobody wants to take them on for the things they are *not* doing. . . . Mr. Cortez has not made any statement. You know very well they must request his statement. . . . The complaining witness, the torturee, has not even been asked for a statement."

"I talked to Mr. Ortega Padilla . . . about that last week," Trott insisted. "They assured me it won't be necessary for him to go to Mexico or Jalisco. It can be done before a competent judicial authority in the United States. There are no lengths to which we will not go to make sure anything they need for that prosecution will be provided to them without any delay at all."

"There may be no lengths to which they will not go to delay this ultimate decision," Smith replied, glowering. ". . . The perception is that things will just drag on there for years, waiting for evidence to wither, for people to die, be kidnapped, be lost, murdered, as in the Camarena case has happened periodically."

What was actually going on within the upper echelons of the Reagan administration would become a matter of considerable dispute.

Willy von Raab's version of events contrasted sharply with Trott's testimony. The Customs commissioner complained that Trott, Assistant Secretary of State Ann Wrobleski, and even Lawn were entirely too calm about what had happened to Victor Cortez. Von Raab recalled sitting at meetings hour after hour, listening to his fellow officials use euphemisms and talk around the problem. At one meeting, von Raab said, he blew up: "I've heard words here like 'bad timing,' 'mistreated,' 'unfortunate.' This is *outrageous*. The response should be that it is *scandalous,* not *bad timing* but *outrage*." As von Raab paused for breath, one of his few allies, Mike Lane, the Treasury Department representative, broke the ice. "I'd like the record to show," Lane said with a grin, "that the *Treasury* Department is outraged."

Von Raab called the board's crisis-management procedure "the black hole" because nothing he proposed ever emerged from the crisis subcommittee. Immediately after the assault on Cortez, he tried to persuade the board to allow him to take dramatic action. He called the idea Operation Jalisco: until the policemen who beat up Cortez were in jail, Customs agents would selectively inspect all cars and trucks with Jalisco plates that appeared at the border crossings. The FAA would cancel landing rights for all airplanes flying out of Guadalajara International Airport.

The crisis subcommittee was chaired by Wrobleski, who had taken charge of the State Bureau of International Narcotics matter a few days after the Cortez incident. She rejected von Raab's plan out of hand because Lawn said it might provoke retaliation against DEA agents in Guadalajara.

The official minutes of the National Drug Policy Board for September 1986 did not mention von Raab's Operation Jalisco proposal at all. Asked to explain the lapse, Customs officials said they were told that the drug board staff was under orders to keep the minutes bland and not to detail interagency controversies.[7]

On January 20, 1987, the National Drug Policy Board published its first "National and International Drug Law Enforcement Strategy." The report was the handiwork of Meese, Trott, and the State Department. Although it was advertised as the consensus of the administration, Lawn and von Raab said they were not shown the final draft before publication and did not agree with many of the statements it contained. Both men were angered by the section on Mexico because it did not mention that corrupt officials were involved in the Camarena murder and Cortez case but rather focused on how those episodes had inconvenienced the Mexican government:

> The publicity surrounding the 1985 death of DEA agent Camarena and the 1986 torture of a second DEA officer has placed PRI politicians in the difficult position of explaining to the Mexican public, which is acutely sensitive to sovereignty issues, why foreign law-enforcement officials are operating in their country. Notwithstanding this austere economic environment and the difficult political climate, the budget of the Attorney General's Office . . . has been augmented and cooperation by Mexican officials is steadily increasing in this area. In short, cooperation with the United States on the narcotic issue entails significant domestic, political costs for the Mexican administration.

The report noted that corruption was a "significant contributing factor" to large-scale trafficking in Mexico but described this and other sources of tension between the police forces of the two nations elliptically. "These productive meetings [between U.S. and Mexican officials] have recognized the unique relationship between the United States and Mexico and have resulted in calls for a strengthened commitment to confront the problem together," the report said. "Both nations acknowledge that the situation requires thoughtful, creative, and most importantly, forceful solutions on both sides of the border."

In early February, Senator Joseph Biden of Delaware, chairman of the Senate Judiciary Committee, summoned Lawn to explain the report's upbeat claims. "To say that is an exaggeration or wishful thinking," Biden snapped, "would be to understate how inaccurate, in this senator's view, that strategy is. . . . There is, to the best of my knowledge, very little cooperative atmosphere. . . . They are flatout not moving with any dispatch to deal with any of these real problems."

Lawn tried to be a good soldier but acknowledged to Biden that "progress has been slow." After the hearing, Lawn was reproached by Trott for not being more positive. "I was asked the question, and I'm not going to lie to them,"

Lawn told an associate. "I said it was better than it was in 1985, but hell, in 1985 it was a zero, and now it's a little better, but it's not outstanding."

To the chagrin of many DEA agents, Lawn would not join von Raab in attacking Mexico openly. As disappointed as he was with the stalemate over the Camarena and Cortez cases, it was not his style to seek a public confrontation. "We can do one of two things," he said. "We can get out. Or we can deal with it."

In private, the DEA administrator was no more sanguine than von Raab that the Mexican government would bring Cortez's assailants to justice. In October 1987, Lawn went to Mexico City and, with Morris Busby, the chargé d'affaires from the American embassy, attempted to corner Ortega Padilla on the issue of the promised prosecutions. As Lawn recalled the conversation, the Mexican official said there would be a delay of some weeks; the judge in Guadalajara considered the case a "no-win" proposition, and so he had bucked it to Mexico City. Ortega Padilla was trying to buck it back.

"We have a complainant, and you haven't taken his complaint," Lawn snapped. "It shouldn't take you several weeks to interview the victim. What you're saying is, you have no interest in what the victim has to say." Busby added that the State Department was in the process of preparing its annual report to the Congress on human rights violations. Failure to take Cortez's complaint would be noted, unless something happened fast, and Mexico's image in the international community would suffer.

In mid-December 1986, Cortez received the Mexican government's request for his deposition. Even then, the Mexican government made no move to jail the accused Jalisco policemen. Ortega Padilla told Lawn that it was Cortez who should be disciplined, for possession of illegal weapons, and he suggested that Cortez might be charged with a crime if he returned to Mexico.

In September 1987, after repeated calls and cables from Lawn and a number of U.S. congressmen, the Federales arrested five of the eleven Jalisco state policemen implicated in the case. Two other police officials were listed as fugitives, but DEA officials concluded that charges had been dropped against four higher officials.[8] Even after the arrests, some Mexican officials contended the whole case had been trumped up; diplomats at the Mexican embassy in Washington said that they believed Cortez had gotten into a fist-fight with the Jalisco cops and had made up the torture story to cover himself.

The ultimate outcome of the Cortez affair was that DEA's position in Mexico grew even more precarious. Lawn often wondered whether it was worth it. If corrupt cops could take DEA agents any time they felt like it and torture them for the names of other agents and their sources, what were American agents but bait? On the other hand, what was Cortez doing out there, behaving as if he were under cover, with a known trafficker, with illegal guns in a car, with none of his partners watching him? What the Jalisco cops had done was despicable, but the DEA did not come out of this one looking good. The Cortez case showed Lawn that nobody at DEA had learned much of anything. He had lost Kiki, and he had nearly lost Vic. Once again, an agent had been out there all alone, and no one had been watching his back. In the end, it was DEA that became engaged in painful self-examination, not the Jalisco state police.

"I know you're upset with my not being vociferous in crying foul with the government of Mexico," Lawn told his senior staff soon after the incident, "but let's go through what happened. Suppose you walk out of DEA headquarters and you see two people apparently malingering. You say, Let me see your registration. One opens the glove compartment and a clip falls out. You ask for their identification. They don't have it. You open the trunk and you find two automatic weapons. And one of the guys says, I've got two friends in the bar across the street who can identify me. What would you do? You'd take him to jail until you found out who he was."

Granted, Lawn said, what happened after Cortez was arrested was unforgivable, but the arrest was legal. Cortez *had* been in an unacceptably vulnerable position. It seldom seemed to occur to street agents that they were mortal. They talked about their jobs with dark sarcasm, but when the telephone rang and someone said a load was coming, they hit the street. The frustrations that would have discouraged most people only made them angry, and anger made them work harder. What had happened to Camarena, and now Cortez, was driving the entire agency to levels of activity that were dangerously intense.

Lawn called the senior managers in the Mexico office to Washington and announced that the post-Camarena rule about going around in pairs was going to be taken seriously from now on, and there were going to be more rules. No dashing out in the middle of the night alone, and no bravado. The agent in charge had to know where every man was at every moment, and why. All the agents had to remember that they were abroad to gather intelligence, not to make nickel buys and set up busts for the Federales. Lawn wanted the men to stop judging themselves in terms of pounds of dope seized and numbers of collars. Look at Peru, he said. Two thousand people had been arrested in a little more than a year, and it had made no difference at all. Intelligence work was sufficiently hazardous without tempting fate by making high-visibility street cases. "They're going to bitch about it, but that's the way it goes," Lawn said. "They can blame me."

Still, Lawn worried about the next time. He was sure that there would be a next time. The pattern of events that had occurred before the shooting of Roger Knapp's car was repeating itself. DEA and Customs offices throughout Mexico and along the border were targeting the Guadalajara trafficking networks more closely than ever before, which meant that the rings would lose more shipments in the coming months. It was clear from the questions the cops had asked Cortez that the traffickers were putting pressure on their allies in the police to plug the leaks and stop the seizures. That much pressure was bound to provoke retaliation. Sooner or later, no matter how many precautions the agents took, something else bad was going to happen.

In every nation in the grip of the drug trade, including the United States, that was the paradox. Push the traffickers and they kill you. Don't push them and they grow so powerful and fearless that they kill you.

22

"Why Are We Bleeding Alone?"

Just before dawn on February 4, 1987, thirty-six Colombian policemen surrounded a mountain chalet in Guarne, a village about eleven miles east of Medellín. They had a tip that a bunch of suspicious characters had been partying inside. They watched the house until dawn, when a handsome young man emerged and showed the face that had dominated the front pages of Bogotá's newspapers for five years. Cornered, the man behaved stupidly. He ran straight into the arms of William Lemus Lemus, police chief of the nearby town of Ríonegro.

"The Virgin has smiled on us," Lemus Lemus told his comrades. "We have captured Carlos Lehder."

President Virgilio Barco Vargas knew that no Colombian jail would hold a man with Lehder's fantastic resources and did not want the trafficker in his custody one minute longer than necessary. As the Colombian Air Force helicopter bearing Lehder bumped south across the mountains toward Bogotá, American diplomats and Colombian officials processed the paperwork for his extradition. By nightfall, Lehder was in a DEA plane on his way to Tampa, Florida.

The capture of Carlos Lehder was a sensational moment in the Colombian government's war against the cocaine traffickers, but it was mostly luck. William Lemus Lemus, the man who found Lehder, was not even a member of the elite Colombian National Police but a newly appointed provincial police official. He had heard that the famous Carlos Lehder was in the area visiting his friend Pablo Escobar and then had learned of the party at a rented chalet in the pine forest near Ríonegro.

Nobody pretended that Lehder's capture would make a

dent in the amount of cocaine landing in the United States. "We cannot say that we have enacted a crippling blow to the cocaine cartel in Colombia by this arrest," Jack Lawn told the reporters who crowded into DEA's small press conference room. "If we want to talk about slowing down the flow of cocaine into the United States, we should think more in terms of demand reduction. The demand is still there, and if the cartel in Colombia is shut down, other cartels in other source countries will merely pick up the customers."

To American officials, the significance of the affair was that, when put to the test, Barco did not flinch. He dumped Lehder like the vicious bully he was, billions or no billions. It was the Colombian president's first step down a road from which there was no return. Barco would have to shatter the cartel's power or it would destroy him and every other official who stood for order.

To many Colombians, Barco's commitment seemed foolhardy and futile. American politicians talked, but it was Colombian leaders who were risking their lives to fight the traffickers, and many had died. Medellín Mayor William Jaramillo Gómez told Alan Riding of *The New York Times,* "When I speak out, I feel moral and intellectual support but I hear silence because there is fear."[1]

There was also resentment. The old elite of cattle ranchers and coffee planters was torn between rage at the traffickers and rancor at the Reagan administration. Why didn't the Reagan administration crack down on the traffic in refining chemicals, most of which came from U.S. manufacturers? And why wasn't Reagan doing more to curb the United States's voracious demand for drugs? Many Colombians suspected that Reagan's 1986 anti-drug crusade was a cynical election-year ploy, and they were sure of it in early 1987, when Reagan's post-election budget proposal contained sharp reductions for the anti-drug program. Lawn found it very hard to argue when Barco complained to him, "We're paying a terrible price, and *your* country is not serious about the problem."

In December 1986, Samuel Buitrago Hurtado, a prominent judge who was head of the Colombian government's

Council of State, proposed to undermine the economic power of the cocaine Mafia by legalizing drugs. "I think we're being 'useful fools' in this conflict by paying an immense social cost without obtaining any benefit in return," Buitrago said, according to news accounts.[2] Colombian officials wondered, as well, why the traffickers were not shooting at more judges and police commanders in Mexico, Panama, the Bahamas, and Latin nations where drug transactions took place. How many senior officials of those nations had chosen silver instead of lead?

"Some responsible people and groups are beginning to ask why Colombia is taking such risks," said Fernando Cepeda Ulloa, Colombia's interior minister. "Why aren't other countries acting with similar heroism? Why are we bleeding alone?"[3]

For the cocaine Mafia, death was a banal thing, a business decision, as rational and inevitable as the purchase of an airplane. The predictability of the cartel's assassination contracts made them all the more dreadful.

On July 23, 1985, Superior Court Judge Tulio Manuel Castro Gil, who had charged Pablo Escobar as the "intellectual author" of the 1984 assassination of Justice Minister Rodrigo Lara Bonilla, was assassinated in Bogotá. President Betancur sent General Víctor Delgado Mallarino, the head of the Colombian National Police, to be ambassador in Rumania. Colonel Jaime Ramírez Gómez, the fierce leader of the National Police force's elite Special Anti-Narcotics Unit (SANU), learned that the Medellín traffickers had taken out an assassination contract on his life. He was pulled out of narcotics work in December 1985 and sent to school to prepare for a general's commission. With the departure of Delgado and Ramírez, the Colombian National Police lost its most aggressive and skillful leaders.

The Colombian police had had some notable successes fighting the marijuana traffickers. In 1984, President Betancur authorized aerial spraying with the herbicide glyphosate, a relatively noncontroversial chemical—even the National Organization for the Reform of Marijuana Laws acknowledged that glyphosate was a "much safer substance" than paraquat, which had been used in Mexico—and SANU troops destroyed much of the marijuana growing in the "traditional" fields near the north coast. The resilient marijuana traffickers moved south and west and continued to dispatch ships loaded with tons of Colombian gold, but they could not make up for the entire north coast crop and lost some of their market to the Mexican traffickers. Colombia replaced Mexico in the U.S. State Department's litany as possessing the "model" eradication program for the rest of the world.

The cocaine traffickers were harder to find and nearly impossible to stop. SANU teams were bloodied badly when they attacked heavily fortified cocaine laboratories in the Llanos region and were literally driven from the field.

In the transition between President Betancur and his successor, Virgilio Barco Vargas, who took office on August 7, 1986, the cocaine lords stepped up their campaign of terror against judges, police officials, and reformers.

On July 31, 1986, Supreme Court Justice Hernando Baquero Borda, who had negotiated the extradition treaty with the United States, was assassinated. On August 13, a young customs court judge in Cartagena released Medellín cartel leader Jorge Ochoa. A few weeks before, a Spanish court had sent Ochoa back to Colombia, rejecting a U.S. request for his extradition in favor of a Colombian claim on an old charge involving the smuggling of 128 fighting bulls from Spain to his father's ranch. When the smuggling case came up, Cartagena Customs Judge Fabiano Pastrana ordered Ochoa to pay an $11,500 fine and to appear once a week before court officials. Not surprisingly, Jorge Ochoa vanished. "I cannot say for sure, but it certainly appears that money or death threats were involved," said Fernando Uribe Restrepo, the new president of the Supreme Court.[4]

Barco, a Liberal party leader and former ambassador to London, had all but ignored the drug issue in his presidential campaign, which had stressed economic and social-justice issues. In his first months in office, he displayed no particular interest in the organized-crime problem. Barco's financial advisers alarmed U.S. officials by proposing to extend a general tax amnesty to all those who had sent their wealth out of the country. Barco's aides explained the idea as a way of raising revenues in general, but DEA officials interpreted it as a nod to the traffickers. However, the escape of Jorge Ochoa, a world-famous cartel leader, was a humiliation Barco could not ignore. He fired Judge Pastrana and ordered a massive search, which resulted in the detention of more than twelve thousand people.[5] None was an important trafficker. Most detainees were quickly released for lack of evidence.

The cartel renewed its attacks on reformers. On September 1, Carlos Arturo Luna Rojas, security chief of Avianca airlines, was assassinated after he discovered four hundred forty pounds of cocaine stashed inside a Boeing 747 cargo plane about to leave for Miami. On September 7, Raúl Echaverría Barrientos, managing editor of *El Occidente,* a newspaper in Cali, was ambushed and shot to death. Superior Court Justice Gustavo Zuluaga Serna of Medellín was killed on October 30. He was the fifteenth Colombian judge killed in two years.

In November 1986, the traffickers wreaked their vengeance upon Colonel Jaime Ramírez Gómez. According to DEA officials in Bogotá, one day Ramírez received a call from someone claiming to represent the Medellín cartel; the caller claimed that the contract on Ramírez's life had been lifted. Ramírez took his family to the country for a long weekend in his jeep instead of the armored car the DEA had given him.

As DEA agents reconstructed what happened, on the way back to Bogotá on Monday, November 17, Elena Ramírez saw her husband's head slump to one side. She told him to stop joking and nudged him, but he fell over. She grabbed the steering wheel, and as the jeep careered into a ditch, three men jumped out of a car, leveled their automatic weapons, and opened fire. Twenty or more rounds slammed into Jaime Ramírez's body. A ricochet crashed into Elena's knee. Another pierced the elder son's hips. Another shattered the younger boy's wrist. When the noise stopped, one of the men walked around to where Elena lay, yanked her up, and aimed his gun at her face. "Please don't kill me," she pleaded. The man dropped her, pumped four more rounds into her husband's body, and drove away.

This was clearly more than an assassination. It was a warning. The forty-seven-year-old soldier had been his own man, incorruptible, relentless, obsessed with duty, and, if not fearless, then resigned to living dangerously. It was Ramírez who had destroyed the giant laboratory complex at Tranquilandia in March 1984, Ramírez who had raided the traffickers' ranches after the assassination of Justice Minister Rodrigo Lara Bonilla. "Jaime was responsible for all the good that Colombia did in 1984 and 1985," said his friend George Frangullie, the DEA attaché in Bogotá at the time. "It started with him, and it ended when he left. If the reward for doing a good job is assassination, and the shooting of your family, what does the next man have to look forward to?"

President Barco attended the funeral, but the attempt at intimidation evidently worked: SANU commanders did not retaliate or even investigate the death of their fallen comrade. According to news reports, in phone calls to Colombian news organizations a group calling itself the Hernán Botero Command claimed responsibility for the murder, repeating the slogan of the Medellín cartel: "We would rather end up in a tomb in Colombia than in a prison cell in the United States." The Hernán Botero Command seemed to be a *nom de guerre* chosen by the traffickers; Botero, a hotelier from Medellín, was in the first group of defendants sent to the United States after the Betancur administration began to enforce the extradition treaty.

A short time after the murder of Ramírez, the Colombian Supreme Court ruled that the law implementing the 1979 extradition treaty with the United States was invalid because the new president had not signed it.

Hoping to nudge Barco into action, Jack Lawn urged White House aides to have Reagan send a note to the Colombian president praising Jaime Ramírez's heroism. He had no luck. The White House's enthusiasm for the anti-drug crusade dissipated once the fall elections had passed. No one there seemed bothered about a dead police colonel in another country.

———

The American law-enforcement community sent its own message to Medellín. The day after Ramírez was killed, U.S. Attorney Leon Kellner of Miami had unsealed a thirty-three-page federal indictment charging Jorge Ochoa and his two brothers, Fabio and Juan David, Pablo Escobar, Carlos Lehder, Gonzalo Rodríguez Gacha, Federico Vaughan, the Nicaraguan previously indicted with the cartel leaders for smuggling cocaine through Nicaragua, and three other men with racketeering in violation of the federal Racketeering Influenced and Corrupt Organizations Act, conspiracy to smuggle at least sixty tons of cocaine into the United States, and other crimes. The indictment represented the most comprehensive set of charges the United States had ever filed against the leaders of the Medellín cartel. Many of the counts were based on the evidence gathered by Barry Seal, the pilot-turned-informant who had penetrated the cartel for the DEA in 1984 and 1985. Some of the racketeering counts were based on the assassination of Seal ten months before, which the grand jury charged was ordered by Escobar and Ochoa. The indictment traced the activities of the Medellín cartel from coca paste purchases in Bolivia and Peru, to clandestine laboratories in Colombia, Nicaragua, and Panama, to transshipment points in Mexico, the Bahamas, and Turks and Caicos, to money laundering in Panama.

Using the richly detailed U.S. court documents as a foundation, the Bogotá newspaper *El Espectador* began publishing a series about the cartel. *El Espectador* editor Guillermo Cano Isaza, a sixty-one-year-old patrician reformer, reproached his countrymen for their passivity in the face of the threat from Medellín. "It is as if the public were itself drugged, unable to see that the power of narcotics traffickers is growing in a colossal way," Cano wrote.

Cano took Barco to task for failing to sign the extradition law. On December 14, three days after the second newspaper article, Barco signed the legislation. Three days after that, Guillermo Cano was dead. He was driving away from *El Espectador*'s office at about seven-thirty on the evening of December 17, when a man walked over to his car and opened fire with a submachine gun.

It was Guillermo Cano's death more than anything else that aroused the Bogotá leadership. After his funeral, four thousand journalists and press workers staged a silent march through the middle of the city. For twenty-four hours the nation's presses were stilled. Finally Barco acted, declaring a state of siege that gave the military broad arrest and search powers and ordered security forces into the trafficking towns. In the next month, nearly two thousand people were arrested, but as in the previous roundup, none were better than "mules." "Much noise, few bosses," scoffed *Semana,* the Bogotá newsmagazine. Harassment, not law enforcement, said DEA agents.

After the New Year, Supreme Court President Fernando Uribe Restrepo, weary of the repeated threats to his life and the lives of his children, resigned and moved to Ecuador. His successor, Nemesio Camacho Rodríguez, resigned a few days later. The U.S. embassy was closed for several days because of bomb threats.

On January 13, 1987, Enrique Parejo González, Betancur's second minister of justice, stepped from his home in Budapest into a blizzard. According to news accounts, a stranger slid alongside him and asked, in Spanish, "Are you Señor Parejo?" Parejo said that he was, and the man opened fire. Three bullets struck Parejo's head and two pierced his arms. Miraculously, he survived.

Parejo, fifty-six, had been sent to Hungary as ambassador from Colombia in order to save his life. He took the place of Rodrigo Lara Bonilla, assassinated April 30, 1984, and became known as an unshakable advocate of extradition. He had personally signed extradition orders for the first ten Colombian traffickers sent to the United States. In May 1986, an organization claiming to represent sixty-five narcotics traffickers, some in jail awaiting extradition, others in hiding, had sent the Colombian press an open letter offering to pay off Colombia's $13.5 billion external debt in exchange for immunity. They promised to dismantle their labs and repatriate their vast holdings. Parejo had scoffed at the proposal, calling it "absurd" and "illegal." When Parejo was in Bogotá, strangers would tell visitors to his house to tell the minister that he was a dead man. He had received cassettes of his telephone conversations in the mail, the cartel's way of demonstrating that its assassins had him under constant electronic surveillance.

Still, no one had imagined that a bunch of semiliterate Latin American hoodlums could reach into an Eastern European police state half a world away. If there was any doubt about the cartel's claim to being most dangerous organized-crime cabal in the world, it was dispelled that white morning in Budapest. "It is obvious now that no one is safe anywhere in the world against the vengeance of the Mafia," said Colombian Attorney General Carlos Mauro Hoyos Jiménez.

The Hernán Botero Command claimed responsibility for the shooting; according to news reports, callers to the Colombian press accused Parejo of "the crime of treason."

DEA agents in Europe went to Budapest to work with the Hungarian police on solving the shooting. They found a hotel room where the alleged gunman might have stayed. He was Italian, not Colombian. DEA agents in Rome prevailed on the Italian police to look into the matter. According to DEA officials in Washington, the trail led to two men and a woman. Carlos Alberto Chiciarelli and Norma Susanna Lazatti were Italian citizens of Argentine extraction. The other man, Moreno Stortini, was an Italian. Most surprising, both men worked for the Italian Treasury Department. All three people were arrested, DEA said, but it would take months to sort out whether the Colombians had arranged an Argentine-Italian hit squad in Budapest. Whatever the truth of the matter, it was clear that as the cartel expanded its cocaine-distribution network into Europe, few places on earth would be safe.

After the attack on Parejo the Barco government began to move more forcefully. Police commanders for the city of Medellín and the state of Antioquia were replaced with others more "efficient."[6] It was soon after these changes that Carlos Lehder was captured, although the Colombian National Police could claim no credit. That triumph belonged to Ríonegro chief Lemus Lemus, an honest small-town cop.

The Colombian Supreme Court was no longer willing to

bear the brunt of the cartel's fury over the extradition treaty. The "old" court had been steadfast in its support of extradition, but the November 1985 deaths of eleven of twenty-four Supreme Court justices in the cross-fire between the M-19 guerrillas and the Colombian Army seemed to have broken the spirit of the survivors and those who replaced the slain jurists. On February 18, 1987, the "new" court announced that it would no longer rule on the extradition of Colombian citizens to the United States. "The Supreme Court is afraid," said Monsignor Darío Castrillón, secretary-general of the Latin American Bishops Conference. "Drug-trafficking violence has sown terror where there should have been heroism."[7] Barco extradited two more traffickers after that ruling because their cases had already been through the legal process. But on June 25 the court struck down the law that ratified the extradition treaty and ended extraditions for the foreseeable future. The way that vote unfolded demonstrated graphically the extent to which the courts had been intimidated. Initially, the justices had tied twelve to twelve. To resolve the tie, an outside jurist had been brought in. Three judges refused the assignment. The fourth candidate tried to decline the job but senior court officers insisted that he vote. He sided with the treaty's opponents.

After that, the cartel leaders' legal problems dissolved. According to Caracol radio, Barco's justice minister, José Manuel Arias Carrizosa, canceled the warrants for the arrest of Pablo Escobar which had been based on the U.S. extradition request. In late July, *The New York Times* reported, a court in Cali acquitted Gilberto Rodríguez Orejuela, the cartel leader who had been arrested in Spain in 1984 with Jorge Ochoa; the presiding judge refused to accept evidence offered by the U.S. Justice Department.[8] After the Colombian case fell apart, a federal grand jury in New Orleans indicted Gilberto Rodríguez and his brother Miguel Angel Rodríguez for drug trafficking.

On December 5, 1987, EFE, the Spanish-language wire service, reported that Judge Andrés Montañez of Bogotá dismissed charges against kingpins Pablo Escobar and Gonzalo Rodríguez Gacha, and a lesser-known trafficker, Everisto Porras, for the murder of *El Espectador* newspaper editor Cano because the investigation had not uncovered sufficient evidence of their participation in the crime.

To reduce internal rivalries, the Colombian National Police drug-enforcement bureaucracy had been reorganized into an expanded Directorate of Anti-Narcotics (DAN) under Brigadier General Miguel Gómez Padilla, a seasoned commander of intelligence and integrity. In June 1987, according to U.S. State Department officials, Gómez Padilla launched a drive in the south that netted more than a thousand "mom-and-pop" operations that converted coca paste to cocaine base. Because the large cocaine hydrochloride laboratories were guarded by cadres of well-armed men, he was unable to make a dent in the supply of finished cocaine. The U.S. State Department spent $2 million armoring a C-47 transport plane so that General Gómez Padilla could move his men into the jungle, but this was a small gesture when compared with the amount of money the traffickers were spending on armaments.

Drug traffickers thrived during periods of anarchy, so the year 1987 seemed very nearly ideal from their point of view. By late summer, the Barco government was distracted by internal strife—Justice Minister Arias Carrizosa resigned in September 1987 after coming under attack from leftist politicians; according to Caracol radio, Arias said he was forced out of government by those who did not share his position on law and order—and by the "dirty war" between left and right. Police in the provinces huddled in bunkers to fend off guerrilla attacks. Right-wing death squads slaughtered professors, community leaders, and human-rights activists. Nearly five hundred members of the Patriotic Union, a legal offshoot of the FARC, were assassinated in 1986 and 1987.

Guerrillas and traffickers seemed to be working together from time to time to thwart government attempts to establish control in the provinces. In June 1987, FARC troops pushed the Colombian Army out of the southern province of Caquetá by ambushing an Army convoy, killing twenty-seven soldiers and wounding forty-two others in the worst defeat the Army had suffered in fifteen years. Also that month, nine Venezuelan National Guardsmen were killed when they went into the mountains along the Colombian-Venezuelan border to destroy a coca plantation. Venezuelan officials blamed an arm of the National Liberation Army (ELN), a guerrilla group founded by Colombian followers of Fidel Castro. The charge seemed confirmed when the ELN took credit for a September attack on Venezuelan guardsmen on the frontier: the group's communiqué called the attack a reprisal "for the injustices perpetrated by the Venezuelan National Guard against Colombian smugglers."

There were also signs that the traffickers were aligning themselves with the violent right wing. In November 1987, Barco's second justice minister, Enrique Low Murtra, announced that accused cocaine kingpin Gonzalo Rodríguez Gacha had paid a henchman 30 million pesos, the equivalent of about $120,000, to assassinate Marxist labor lawyer Jaime Pardo Leal, the leader of the leftist Patriotic Union party.[9] Pardo's death in Bogotá on October 11, which had caused a twenty-four-hour general strike and two days of riots, had been blamed on rightists, but Low Murtra said that Rodríguez Gacha had masterminded the crime because of a territorial dispute with the FARC guerrillas, with whom Pardo Leal was associated.

The cartel leaders took advantage of the political turmoil to dispatch ever-larger loads of cocaine, arrogantly defying American authorities to find them. As the U.S. Customs Service and Coast Guard, flush with funds from the 1986 omnibus drug bill, stepped up radar surveillance of the South Florida shoreline, the traffickers simply packed the contraband in shipping containers and sent it to the States via merchant marine. They expanded their use of Honduras and Panama as transshipment points, probably to thwart U.S. surveillance of shipments direct from Colombia.

In October 1986, Customs inspectors in West Palm Beach happened upon 6,900 pounds of cocaine hidden in two containers. The seizure, which had set a new U.S. record, had been taken for a fluke, but as time passed, a pattern began to form. In July 1987, Customs inspectors in Miami found another 5,320 pounds of cocaine in containers of Honduran bananas. That seizure led Customs to 57 other containers, most of which had been cleaned out by the time Customs agents traced them. Then, on November 19, 1987, acting on a DEA tip, Customs agents in Miami set a new U.S. record, seizing more than 8,000 pounds of cocaine, hidden in two shipping containers. The cocaine was ingeniously stashed inside hollowed-out mahogany boards manufactured in Honduras.

The prospect of thwarting rings who could acquire and dispatch whole shipping containers full of cocaine was a nightmare for Customs Service officials, who could inspect no more than a tiny percentage of the seven million containers that landed in the United States every year. Willy von Raab created a computerized profiling system to focus on containers that had taken suspicious routes or were documented in unusual ways, but this was, at best, a sophisticated way of guessing.

If Customs could inspect every container that landed from South America by sea, which it could not, the traffickers could still move cocaine overland through Mexico. To inspect every truck that crossed the land border would hold up shipments of Mexican fruits and vegetables until they rotted. It would amount to a new Operation Intercept, and the White House had made it clear that nothing like that would happen again.

As von Raab well knew, interdiction was only harassment, a way of raising the economic stakes of the traffickers. "Winning" or even staying even was quite another matter. In 1987, Customs, DEA, and the local agencies with whom they worked would seize about thirty-five tons of cocaine, a figure that could not have been imagined ten years or even three years before. Yet that amounted to perhaps a tenth, maybe less, of Latin America's cocaine-producing capacity, which was estimated in 1987 at about three hundred tons per year. If by some miracle U.S. authorities seized half that amount, the coca growers could plant more. The growing potential of the Andes was virtually limitless. State Department officials still believed in eradication, but no chemical had been found that could be sprayed from the air to kill coca without poisoning the environment.

Steven Bauer as DEA agent Enrique "Kiki" Camarena.

Guadalajara agents Kiki Camarena and Tony Riva (Miguel Ferrer) work the streets.

Camarena as he accompanies Federales on a drug raid prompted by intelligence he had gathered.

Rafael Caro Quintero (Benicio del Toro), the hotheaded young leader of the Guadalajara drug cartel.

DEA agents Harley Steinmetz (Craig T. Nelson), Kiki Camarena, and Ray Carson (Treat Williams).

Agents Steinmetz, Camarena, Matson (J. Kenneth Campbell), and Riva (in foreground) as they are about to move in on a Caro Quintero marijuana plantation.

Camarena and Steinmetz reflect on a major victory before putting the torches to a massive marijuana plantation.

Agents Steinmetz, Matson, Riva, and Camarena survey their impressive drug seizure.

The abduction of Kiki Camarena.

Camarena's widow, Mika (Elizabeth Pena), comforts her children (played by Walter Alamo and Kenny Morrison) at a memorial service for her husband. Her plea, "Don't let my husband become a number," launched the investigation.

DEA agent Steinmetz leads the search for those responsible for the murder of his comrade.

Ray Carson heads the task force pursuing Kiki's killers—all of them. It's the toughest job of his life.

Caro Quintero could buy anything or anybody—except Kiki Camarena, who was literally costing him billions.

Venegas, September 7, 1982. Kiki Camarena stands in the 220-acre marijuana plantation he discovered growing in the central Mexican desert. His persistence, which forced Mexican authorities to raid the plantation, netted four to five tons of high grade sinsemilla, set new records in Mexico, and cost the Guadalajara Cartel $8 billion in lost sales. (Photograph of Kiki Camarena by his friend and boss Jaime Kuykendall)

On November 8, Bogotá's *El Tiempo* ran a somber editorial, entitled "Losing Ground," which declared:

> We have lowered our guard. Valuable ground has been lost in the relentless war against drug trafficking, and we have begun turning in our weapons. This new attitude has led to a dangerous atmosphere of tolerance and permissiveness. The Mafia chieftains move around freely in broad daylight throughout Colombian cities. If we look closely, we will see how they have steadily returned to their privileged positions, reappeared at their businesses, and are using their money and the law to undermine the weak morale of the government organizations. . . . The country's legal structure is not enough to counter such a powerful empire, which can buy off anyone. . . . Our fragile judicial system has allowed drug-trafficking organizations to consolidate themselves very well. The extradition treaty—the only instrument the chieftains fear—has failed; a minister, judges, and journalists have been murdered; the justice sector is terrorized; the authorities have been infiltrated; and the country remains indifferent. Thus, the drug traffickers are guaranteed a sanctuary without risks.

Just when things looked bleakest, the Colombian police pulled off another stunning coup. Again, it was an accident. On November 21, 1987, the Colombian highway police arrested Jorge Ochoa at a routine roadblock near Palmira, about three hundred sixty miles south of Bogotá. Ochoa was driving a $100,000 Porsche registered to a Honduran military attaché stationed in Bogotá, Colonel William Said Speer. According to Colombian news reports, the patrolmen refused Ochoa's offers of hundreds of thousands of dollars and turned him over to the Colombian Army, which imprisoned him at an Army base.

Ochoa's family was not about to let him go without a struggle. The day after Ochoa's arrest, thugs opened fire on the house of Juan Gómez Martínez, a Conservative party candidate for mayor of Medellín and a son of the manager of the Medellín newspaper *El Colombiano*. Gómez and his family escaped injury and afterward received a letter from "the Extraditables," a *nom de guerre* of the Medellín cartel, which declared that he was to be taken hostage to deliver a message to the government. According to news accounts, the message, which was distributed to other Colombian news media, warned that if Ochoa should be extradited, "we will declare total and absolute war against the country's political leaders. We will execute [Colombia's] principal political party chieftains out of hand."

American officials immediately renewed their requests for Ochoa's extradition. Barco assured them he would try to find a way to send Ochoa north, perhaps by using treaties between the United States and Colombia that predated the 1979 treaty the Supreme Court had ruled unconstitutional. In the meantime, a judge ordered Ochoa to serve twenty months in prison for violating his parole on the old bull-smuggling conviction. DEA placed a plane on standby in case a deportation order came through.

On December 30, in the midst of negotiations between U.S. and Colombian lawyers, Ochoa walked out of La Picota prison in Bogotá, boarded a private plane, and flew away. The circumstances of Ochoa's release were murky. According to the Bogotá daily El Tiempo, Justice Minister Low Murtra said in an interview that Ochoa's lawyer had presented prison officials with a writ signed by Bogotá Judge Andrés Montañez, the same judge who had vacated charges against Pablo Escobar.[10]

The next morning's headlines said it all: "The Mafia Once Again Mocks Colombia," chided El Tiempo. "What Shame, Mr. President," scolded El Espectador.

U.S. Attorney General Ed Meese called Ochoa's release "a shocking blow to international law enforcement." "They bought him out," charged Richard Gregorie, the chief assistant U.S. attorney in Miami.

"I'm shocked at the cowardice that the government of Colombia has shown in dealing with the Ochoa matter," Jack Lawn said. "All of those good Colombian citizens who have spoken out at great personal risk, even death, must feel a sense of shame far greater than the anger and disappointment I feel. Law enforcement throughout the world must hang its head because of this shame."

Deputy Secretary of State John Whitehead summoned Colombian Ambassador Victor Mosquera Chaux to the

State Department and, according to State officials, lectured him on the damage done to U.S.–Colombian relations. Whitehead authorized Phyllis Oakley, spokesperson for the State Department, to deliver what was probably the harshest verbal attack on a "friendly" drug-producing country to have issued from State in modern times. "We are disgusted by the fact that this major Colombian narcotics trafficker is now free," Oakley said. "The government of Colombia had a clear responsibility to make certain this dangerous criminal was not released. . . . The interests of both our countries have been damaged and our common struggle against the traffickers has been made more difficult."

In a New Year's speech to the nation, Barco said that Judge Montañez had acted in "open defiance of clear instructions from superiors."[11] Later, in a live broadcast, Justice Minister Low Murtra said the judge "flagrantly ignored the fact" that Ochoa's bail had been revoked and the prison warden released Ochoa "despite orders from the director of prisons."[12] Low Murtra himself was criticized by the Bogotá newspapers for failing to assure that Ochoa was held under tight security.[13]

On Barco's orders, Attorney General Carlos Mauro Hoyos Jiménez launched investigations of all the officials involved in the case, including Low Murtra, Prisons Director Guillermo Ferro, Assistant Prisons Director Benjamín Bustos, and La Picota jail director Alvaro Camacho.[14] Warrants were issued for the entire leadership of the Medellín cartel: Jorge, Fabio, and Juan David Ochoa, Pablo Escobar, and Gonzalo Rodríguez Gacha.

Most of Ronald Reagan's advisers were not inclined to go beyond hard words. The consensus within the administration was that President Barco was sincerely wounded by Ochoa's release and was doing everything he could to prosecute those responsible. "If you move to punish the Colombian government," Assistant Secretary of State Ann Wrobleski asked rhetorically, "aren't you falling into the trap that the *narcos* want you to fall into, which is punishing your allies?"

There were some dissenters. "We find it very curious the lack of any real follow-up," Assistant U.S. Attorney Ana

Barnett of the U.S. Attorney's Office in Miami said caustically. "The people who have the tools are in Washington. As the Department of State always tells us, we don't understand how to do things diplomatically, but if we're doing anything, it's so subtle, nobody knows about it."

Willy von Raab ordered Customs inspectors at all ports to "blitz" cargo from Colombia. Passengers on flights from Colombia were segregated and subjected to extra scrutiny.

Some American politicians urged the administration to take sterner measures. "When you have a government held hostage, you don't hold up the shrimp," scoffed Congressman Charles Rangel. But the Customs blitz provoked a backlash in Colombians, who were tired of bearing the brunt of the drug war. A Colombian government communiqué denied that anyone had ever promised the U.S. that Ochoa would be kept in jail.[15] In a live broadcast on January 13, Barco called U.S. criticisms a "huge injustice." He said Americans did not recognize "the number of Colombians who have been extradited or the fact that one Colombian justice minister has been murdered . . . the various near-fatal attacks on other justice ministers, the horrible attack on the Colombian Supreme Court of Justice, the systematic murder of judges and magistrates who have fulfilled their duties bravely, although their courage and duties as servants of justice will never be sufficiently recognized, and the risks and sacrifices of many newsmen and political leaders."

Despite the growing anti-American sentiment among his constituents, Barco recognized that he had no choice but to keep up the pressure on the drug traffickers. "Those who use vile threats, treacherous attacks, murders, kidnappings, and even bribery and flattery to destabilize the state will not prevail," he said. "We will give exemplary punishment to those who betray their duties."[16]

These were brave words, but the traffickers did not seem to be bothered, at least not by the law. On the day that Barco spoke, the Bogotá government found out that Pablo Escobar's idea of life on the lam was a posh residence in one of Medellín's nicer suburbs. Early on the morning of January 13, a car bomb ripped open the front of a Medellín luxury apartment building. According to news dispatches, neighbors said the building belonged to Pablo Escobar, who fled with his wife and children in Mercedes limousines. Medellín mayor Jaramillo said the place was filled with works of art, fifteen motorcycles, twenty-one cars, and a communications center.[17] Two vigilante groups who called themselves "War Against the Mafia" and "Death to the *Narcos*" called radio stations to claim credit.

On January 22, the group that called itself the Extraditables announced it had kidnapped Andrés Pastrana, a journalist who had produced a 1987 television series, *The Punishment of the Gods*, about drug trafficking in Colombia. Pastrana, a candidate for mayor of Medellín and the son of former Colombian President Misael Pastrana Borrero, was found unharmed three days later. Pastrana told reporters that his captors said that they had abducted him in order to protest Barco's commitment to extradition.[18]

On the same day that Pastrana was released, Attorney General Hoyos, who was investigating the release of Jorge Ochoa, was kidnapped as he was being driven to the Medellín airport. According to news reports, at least six men in three jeeps and a car blocked Hoyos's Mercedes, sprayed it with submachine-gun fire, and killed two bodyguards. Hoyos's body was found on a roadside about nine hours later; Hoyos had been blindfolded, handcuffed, tortured, and shot many times.

"Treacherous murder and kidnappings," Barco declared in a television broadcast, "are the recourse of those who want to subdue the nation and submerge it in pessimism and uncertainty. I want to say to all the criminals who want to frighten and subdue Colombia that terrorism and organized crime cannot intimidate us. We will not yield to vile blackmail and infamous threats."[19] Two days later, the Colombian president announced the creation of four thousand new police and judicial positions. But Barco did not attend the funeral of the attorney general, provoking widespread indignation.[20]

Barco's top advisers openly vented their hostility toward the United States for failing to reduce the demand for drugs. "We're being left to fight this war alone," said Francisco

Bernal, the head of the attorney general's Narcotics Bureau. "We're supplying the dead, the country is being destabilized, and what help are we getting?"[21] Alfredo Gutiérrez Márquez, who replaced Hoyos as attorney general of Colombia, suggested Colombia might have to legalize drugs and negotiate with the cartel. "Our fight has been totally useless," Gutiérrez Márquez said. "We've had a row of corpses in Colombia, and yet the cocaine laboratories are still working, and the Medellín cartel members are still free. . . . It's time we stopped playing the fool." Although he stressed that he personally did not favor legalization, Gutiérrez's remarks, made in an interview with *El Tiempo,* shocked American officials and some Colombian leaders as well. "It is terrible that a person in his position will say these kinds of things publicly," said Enrique Santos, the managing editor of *El Tiempo*. "It's even more horrible if you think that he makes these statements only two months after his predecessor was killed by the Mafia." Low Murtra told *The Miami Herald,* "There have been some difficulties, anguish, and problems, but we're committed to continuing our fight."[22]

Gutiérrez Márquez resigned on March 28, 1988, according to news reports from Bogotá, after it was disclosed that his brother had bought a ranch adjoining Pablo Escobar's Hacienda Nápoles estate from the Escobar family.

There was little more the United States could do to change the situation in Colombia. Jack Lawn doubted that persuasion, pressure, or massive aid programs would cause Colombia or any other Latin nation to accomplish what the United States had not. Lawn advocated tougher law enforcement within the United States. Ultimately, though, he believed that the only solution to the American drug problem was a dramatic change in attitude on the part of the American people. He compared the straits of drug agents to that of the frontline troops during the Vietnam war. "There was no commitment in our Congress," he said. "There was no commitment in the media. There was no commitment in the cities and towns. The best-trained, best-equipped Army in the world lost to an army of peasants without ever losing a major battle."

DEA was winning its share of battles. On May 19, 1988, a jury in Jacksonville, Florida, convicted Carlos Lehder of smuggling three tons of cocaine into the United States.

"This has got to shake them a little bit," U.S. Attorney Robert Merkle of Tampa said of the cartel leaders. "They know we're coming after them." But, like Lawn, Merkle knew that such courtroom victories would not change reality. "Carlos Lehder can stack cocaine on the shores of the United States until it blots out the sun, but it can't hurt us," Merkle said. "He can't make us take drugs if we don't want them."

23

Lies, Delusions, and Wishful Thinking

It took a leap of faith for Kiki Camarena to become a narcotics agent. Growing up poor in a California border town, he knew, better than most, the odds stacked against him. He had seen the misery that led people to take drugs and the desperation that caused them to smuggle. He knew about cops who took bribes, politicians who made promises they had no intention of fulfilling, and judges who jailed poor kids and scolded rich ones. Camarena must have believed that one man could make a difference.

Later he despaired. Nothing in his life had prepared him to deal with the corruption he saw in Mexico or the cynicism and apathy he perceived in his own system. What would it take, he wondered, to make things change? Did somebody have to die?

Kiki Camarena had proved that one man mattered, but at a terrible price. Months after his friend Kiki's death, Shaggy Wallace said bleakly, "What happened to Kiki is a tragedy. But more has happened since Kiki died than when he was alive."

Camarena would have taken grim satisfaction in the uproar caused by his death. The directors of the Mexican Federal Judicial Police and the Federal Security Directorate (DFS) had been replaced. Seven hundred of their subordinates had been dismissed. Rafael Caro Quintero and Ernesto Fonseca were in prison. In August 1987, MFJP *comandante* Guillermo González Calderoni dared to arrest two other legendary drug lords, sixty-year-old Jaime Herrera Nevares, the head of the Durango heroin dynasty, and his son, Jaime

Herrera Herrera. The Mexican Attorney General's Office had acquired new aircraft, hired new pilots, and stepped up the eradication effort. The Mexican Army had launched an assault on trafficking strongholds, called Operation Mars.

The Institutional Revolutionary party (PRI) was even making a stab at cleaning up Sinaloa. In 1986, the party's candidate for governor was Francisco Labastida Ochoa, a Mexico City technocrat who had served as President de la Madrid's energy minister. Shortly after he took office in January 1987, according to news reports, Labastida fired thirteen hundred state police officers and ordered about a hundred officers prosecuted. President Reagan paid tribute to Labastida's housecleaning by staging his February 13, 1988, "summit" with President de la Madrid in Mazatlán, Sinaloa's picturesque beach resort.

Yet, as Camarena would have been the first to point out, all these "reforms" were mostly paint and plaster. In 1988, Mexico retained its unwelcome status as Americans' number-one source of heroin and marijuana and staging area for at least a third of the cocaine entering the U.S. market. Mexico's eradication program had improved, but not enough to keep pace with production.

Lawmen on both sides of the border were setting new records for cocaine seizures, but these were less a measure of success than a sign that Colombian organizations, operating independently or with Mexican associates, were moving in to exploit the empty reaches of the frontier. In March 1988, Willy von Raab estimated that the U.S. Customs air wing was intercepting only 5 percent of the small planes that buzzed across the badlands, compared with about half the smuggling planes that flew into the Southeast. Although the Congress had appropriated money for more radar surveillance in the Southwest, it was doubtful that a radar system could be designed to spot aircraft zigzagging through the border mountain passes. Von Raab continued to press for access to Mexican airspace for radar surveillance and hot pursuit, but Mexican officials would have none of the idea. It was ironic that American, Colombian, and Mexican outlaws, the meanest, crudest members of their societies, could overcome nationalism in the name of greed, while educated, high-minded citizens could not achieve harmony in the pursuit of good.

The Mexican underworld remained dominated by two founders of the Guadalajara cartel: Miguel Angel Félix Gallardo and Manuel Salcido Uzeta (Cochi Loco). Félix Gallardo had not been impeded in the least by DEA's all-points search for him. DEA informants claimed that he shuttled between Europe, where he was reportedly establishing new cocaine routes, and his old haunts in Guadalajara and Culiacán. He was said to be in contact with Pablo Escobar of Medellín and was probably still doing business with his former partner, Juan Ramón Matta Ballesteros, who was living in high style in Tegucigalpa, Honduras—which had suddenly became a major transit point for cocaine. Cochi Loco was seen in and around Mazatlán, where he held sway by terrorizing the local populace. Nine days after the Reagan–de la Madrid summit, according to U.S. and Mexican press reports, three masked men assassinated Mazatlán journalist Manuel Burgueno Orduno, who had criticized the government for failing to curb violence in Sinaloa. On March 16, Lorenzo Groztiza Castro, chief of the Mazatlán municipal police, was critically wounded by seventeen rounds of AK-47 fire. Both attacks were believed to have been ordered by Cochi Loco.

That Caro Quintero and Fonseca were in prison brought no credit to the Mexican Federal Judicial Police, since Caro Quintero had been taken by Costa Rican commandos and Fonseca by municipal police and the Army. Three years after their capture, neither man had been convicted of any crime. DEA officials believed they were running their organizations from their cells in the Reclusorio del Norte, the federal penitentiary in Mexico City, without interference from prison authorities. In early 1987, two DEA agents convinced the warden to give them a tour of the traffickers' living quarters. As they described the scene in a cable to DEA headquarters, the cell block resembled a fraternity house, comfortably furnished with stereos, televisions, a kitchen, a cook, and a dining room, access to a phone, and the right to "conjugal visits" from various women. Fonseca sauntered by, dressed like David Niven, in pajamas and a silk dressing gown, and offered the agents refreshments. Caro Quintero, who lacked Fonseca's sense of humor, shrieked, "You're from DEA!" and snarled that he would sodomize the agents with sticks if they did not get out of his turf. The agents reported that Caro Quintero seemed very much in charge of the situation, even the lineup.

DEA and Customs agents believed that the number of trafficking rings based in Mexico had actually proliferated since the 1985 crackdown began. When Kiki Camarena arrived in Guadalajara, there might have been twenty or thirty significant Mexican rings; four years later, DEA agents were able to chart several hundred smuggling organizations, both Mexican and Colombian, capable of smuggling tons of cocaine and tens of tons of marijuana per month.

In late January and early February 1988, DEA agents in Arizona alerted the MFJP to a huge illicit arsenal that was being stockpiled in warehouses in Sonora and Durango. The Federales seized a weapons cache of a magnitude unheard of in Mexico: 360 Chinese-made and semiautomatic AK-47-type rifles, more than 145,000 rounds of ammunition, nearly 100 bayonets, infrared rifle night sights, 7 light airplanes, a number of vehicles, and 11 tons of marijuana. According to news reports, six of those arrested were Colombians linked to Gonzalo Rodríguez Gacha, a close friend of Pablo Escobar and a particularly violent leader of the Medellín cartel; he was known as El Mexicano, possibly because of his affinity for Mexico, possibly because of his foul language. Two other men arrested at the warehouses, Mexican authorities said, were MFJP agents.[1] Soon after those raids, DEA agents in Mazatlán got word from DEA-Bogotá that Rodríguez Gacha had arranged to store forty-two tons of Colombian marijuana in Sinaloa for transshipment to the West Coast of the United States. When a team of Federales attempted to raid Rodríguez Gacha's warehouse near Culiacán, they were greeted with a fusillade of automatic weapons fire that critically injured four men.

Mexican officials were clearly unsettled by the Colombian incursions, coming as they did shortly after the assassination of Colombian Attorney General Carlos Mauro Hoyos Jiménez. Deputy Attorney General Ortega Padilla warned, "If we don't pay enough attention, the traffickers could become a national security problem."

Ortega Padilla contended that the MFJP had dismantled more than twenty major rings. At the Mazatlán summit, de la Madrid had declared, with evident exasperation, "It is unlikely that any other country has allocated, in percentage terms, the amount of budgetary, technical, and human resources that the office of the [Mexican] attorney general and the armed forces have devoted to this task." Still, the MFJP owed many of its biggest scores—the detection of the Colombian arms and drugs caches, the arrests of the Herreras and several other midlevel traffickers, and several major cocaine seizures—to intelligence provided by the DEA.

In the final analysis, the de la Madrid administration never summoned the will to attack corruption in a systematic way. Some officeholders had been dismissed or allowed to retire, but the system had not changed. Significant elements of the police and military remained dependent upon illegal sources of income. De la Madrid circulated a new code of ethics, but the mechanisms for reform adopted in other nations—commissions of inquiry, special prosecutors—were absent in Mexico. The U.S. State Department "international narcotics control strategy" for 1988 noted that reform measures undertaken by de la Madrid "have probably curbed some abuses but there is no indication that the level of narcotics-related corruption has diminished, either in absolute terms or in its impact on programs." Mexican federal judges, cabinet and subcabinet-level officials, governors, senior police commanders, and influential politicians accused of accepting bribes or torturing prisoners were not prosecuted or investigated, as far as U.S. officials could tell. The DFS had undergone a change of name and more than four hundred officers had been fired, but it remained to be seen whether the security police apparatus had truly changed. Von Raab heard a report that two hundred Mexican customs officers were to be relieved and told his border officers to try to confirm it. "We watched the border very carefully," the customs commissioner told a Congressional panel. "We didn't see a single personnel change what-soever."[2]

Because of what the Camarena case had revealed about the reliance of major traffickers upon protectors within the government, DEA and Customs investigators changed strategies; instead of tracking loads of drugs, they focused on officials who they believed would lead them to the top of the smuggling rings. The findings sickened veteran investigators. DEA agents said they documented incidents, down to names, dates, and methods, in which certain police commanders and state officials had ordered the torture and dismemberment of rivals and suspected informers. The agents said that police officers had yanked off their victims' fingers, one by one, had nearly drowned victims by holding their heads in filthy toilet bowls, had injected chili-oil-laced mineral water up their noses. A number of victims were found with dozens of ice-pick holes in their bodies, evidence of the torture called bone-tickling. Sometimes, body parts had been sawed off. "Corruption has penetrated all levels of the Mexican government," said a senior DEA official. "It's lateral, it's horizontal, and it's total."

Whenever American officials complained about particular officeholders whom they suspected of corruption, senior officials in Mexico City dismissed the allegations as lacking in substance, politically motivated, and an intrusion into Mexican internal affairs.

In the summer of 1987, a DEA agent in San Diego heard from an informant that Caro Quintero's henchmen had bought a couple of abandoned houses across from the prison and were digging a tunnel into the Reclusorio del Norte. Agents in Mexico slipped into the houses and found what looked like a deep mine, its mouth a four-by-four-foot square with neat corners. They found out that the shaft had been designed by a mining engineer, and featured air blowers, lights, and reinforcing lumber. The tunnel descended forty feet, ran more than eight hundred feet laterally, and would ascend near Caro Quintero's cell block. The boldness of the digging, which went on for more than a year, convinced DEA agents in Mexico that some prison officials were in on the scheme.

When workers were two weeks from breaking into the prison yard, Lawn decided to wrap it up. On September 29, a team of DEA agents went into the house and took videotapes of the shaft. The next day, Lawn told Mexican Deputy Attorney General Ortega Padilla about the tunnel. The Mexican official, in Washington for a meeting, said that Lawn was mistaken, that there was no tunnel, that he had heard the story, had already checked it out and found that it was a rumor.

"Would you like me to give you the street address?" Lawn said coldly. Two nights later, the Federales "found" the tunnel.

There were many other reports of plots to bribe, dig, or shoot Caro Quintero out of prison. Most of these stories were uncheckable, but DEA agents took one account very seriously.

On May 26, 1987, DEA and Customs agents secured court orders to seize the San Diego holdings of Francisco Alatorre Urtusuatequi, a Mexico City lawyer who represented Rafael Caro Quintero, Ernesto Fonseca, a number of other accused drug traffickers, and some Jalisco state policemen arrested in the Camarena case. DEA agent David Gauthier filed an affidavit in federal court which said that an informant codenamed S-4 had told Shaggy Wallace that Supreme Court Justice Luis Fernández Doblado and several Mexico City justices "have received monetary payoffs to clear Fonseca and Caro of kidnap/murder charges relative to the S/A Camarena investigation in Mexico." According to the affidavit, this informant and others claimed that Alatorre made these payments on Caro Quintero's behalf from slush funds maintained in several San Diego banks. Customs agent Joe Martinez found bank accounts belonging to Alatorre that contained more than $2 million in cash and certificates of deposit. Agents who executed seizure warrants for Alatorre's holdings in San Diego discovered a bonus: in Alatorre's safe-deposit box in the Bank of America, there was a Colt .45 semiautomatic pistol with a fourteen-karat-gold handle studded with a thousand diamonds, some of which spelled out Rafael Caro Quintero's trademark, R-1. The gun was similar to the one found in Caro Quintero's possession in Costa Rica. According to DEA agents, next to the gun was found $300,000 in cash and a ledger which contained a reference to a payment for a hotel bill in San Diego for Supreme Court Justice Fernández Doblado. The agents believed the notation in the ledger corroborated a tip from S-4 about a meeting in Tijuana on that date between Fernández Doblado and Alatorre.

The Gauthier affidavit, the first U.S. government document to disclose DEA's findings in the Camarena investigation, concluded that Caro Quintero "amassed a number of contacts in the Mexican government whom he bribed in order to safely conduct his drug-trafficking activities in Mexico." Gauthier appended a list of "Mexican government agencies that had a number of their members under Caro Quintero's control." These included the MFJP, the DFS, the office of the Mexican attorney general, the Interior Ministry, state police agencies, Mexican Customs, and the Mexican military.

DEA officials did not alert reporters to the existence of the affidavit, but reporter J. Stryker Meyer of *The San Diego Union* found the document filed away in an obscurely titled case file and broke the story. Mexican officials lodged a furious round of protests. "This is like the pot calling the kettle black," de la Madrid said. "The damaging problem of drug trafficking originates, is nurtured by, and benefits the great industrialized markets, mainly that of the United States."[3] De la Madrid's spokesman, Manuel Alonso, said that Attorney General Sergio García Ramírez and Foreign Secretary Bernardo Sepúlveda were "very, very angry."[4] The Mexican Supreme Court gave Fernández Doblado a vote of confidence. Alatorre denied bribing anyone but boasted that he had won the acquittal of more than twenty Camarena case suspects and would see Caro Quintero freed as well.[5]

At Camarena's memorial Mass, Kiki's mother Dora had turned to Shaggy Wallace and said, "Why did it have to be like *this?*" Yet it was because Kiki died the way he did that he touched so many strangers. When an agent was gunned down on the street, no one but his widow and his partners remembered. But Camarena was betrayed by fellow law-enforcement officers, and betrayal arouses emotions stronger than grief, more complex than pain. This was an aspect of human behavior that agents learned to respect. Jaime Kuykendall would not allow agents who had worked undercover to be present when the time came to make arrests. A man who might have gone to jail peaceably would become uncontrollably violent at the sight of a "friend" who had manipulated and humiliated him.

Perhaps this was the reason that people who had never heard of Kiki Camarena, would not miss him, and might not have liked him were touched by his death. The episode made Americans face the lies, delusions, and wishful thinking that had characterized two decades of war on drugs. From Richard Nixon to Ronald Reagan, American presidents had made speeches, launched task forces, appointed commissions, convened conferences, signed treaties, and dispensed reports. Yet in 1988, dead bodies littered the landscape and the drug warlords were stronger than ever.

The ugly secrets that boiled up to the surface after Camarena's death were quite as unsettling for American policymakers as for Mexican leaders. They raised profound and disturbing questions about the value of pursuing a policy that relied on untrustworthy allies.

Since the 1920s, it had been an article of faith within the American government that the best place to attack the drug problem was outside U.S. borders. "Going to the source" was advertised as a clean, rational, "cost-effective" alternative to rigorous border controls, which disrupted commerce, massive arrests of drug users, which was considered unenlightened, or wholesale arrests of drug dealers, which were expensive. "Source control" or, even more euphemistically, "international cooperation" promised not to inflict pain upon vocal American constituencies, but the theory could not bear close examination. Was it realistic to expect that foreign leaders would gratefully repay Uncle Sam's largesse, usually a few million dollars a year, by dispatching armies of *braceros* into the wilderness to hack and spray the only source of income for hundreds of thousands of peasants? How could the most backward nations on earth be expected to produce results that eluded the American police and military? Cementing international alliances was difficult enough in the early 1960s, when America's problem was a heroin problem. Agents of the old Federal Bureau of Narcotics spent years futilely pleading for help from French and Swiss authorities who shared their values but disliked their presumption. In the 1970s and 1980s, European police forces were competent and dedicated partners, but the reality of most American agents' lives was seldom heroin and Europe. It was cocaine and marijuana and the Third World, with all its inefficiency, poverty, and moral ambiguity. The battle was a guerrilla war in countries that were outright dictatorships or fragile democracies but which, in either case, harbored deep-seated fears of North American interventionism. At best, the United States's allies were badly outmatched. At worst, DEA and Customs agents and officers of the other frontline agencies—the CIA, the State Department's Office of International Narcotics Matters, and the Agency for International Development—had to pin their hopes upon officials who took bribes, tortured prisoners, terrorized innocent people, or used information gained from contacts with the United States to extort criminal organizations.

The shortcomings of the American government's international drug policies had been masked by political expediency and excessive secrecy. From protecting sources and methods, it was a short leap to camouflaging the duplicity of sources and the failure of methods. Secrecy was easy and popular. It served the interests of policymakers at State, Treasury, Defense, and the White House who wanted to improve the United States's position in noncommunist Third World nations. And it insulated operational-level State and DEA officers from having to justify the existence of their bureaucratic fiefdoms.

When meeting with reporters and Congressional delegations, State Department officials responsible for narcotics aid were vague and cheerful, like Dickens's Mr. Micawber, always saying that something would soon turn up—if Congress kept the money coming. Congress was generally compliant. With a few notable exceptions, legislators preferred junkets to exotic climes to plodding through ledgers. From 1977 to 1986, not one Congressional committee asked the General Accounting Office, the legislative branch's auditing arm, to report on U.S. spending for the Mexican eradication program, the most expensive of the United States's international narcotics aid projects.

DEA agents posted abroad, including Kiki Camarena, obeyed the agency's dictum, Shut up and operate, any way you can. It was their job to say "Can do," and they did, or at least they tried. Few agents stationed in countries known for brutal police tactics had any illusions about the kind of people they were dealing with. They knew what their host police forces did to prisoners and were under orders not to be there when it happened, but they did not walk away from any nation on ideological or moral grounds.

In 1987 and 1988, many politicians attacked DEA for maintaining a close relationship with General Manuel Antonio Noriega, the military leader of Panama. The reality was that Noriega was merely the latest of a series of reprehensible characters who used and were used by the U.S. government precisely because they were not squeamish about the dark side of the drug war. Noriega, no stickler for legal process, summarily deported a number of accused drug traffickers to the United States, seized huge shipments of ether, despite the fact that ether possession was not against Panamanian law, allowed DEA agents to operate undercover in Panama, permitted U.S. authorities to board thousands of Panamanian-flag vessels, and passed along some useful tips. Possibly, DEA agents acknowledged, some of Noriega's actions were motivated by the desire to hurt traffickers who were competing with those he protected, but very few of DEA's sources of information were priests and social workers.

In the early 1970s, the United States's best friend in Latin America was General Augusto Pinochet, the Chilean dictator. At the time, a number of European-born traffickers were shipping French Connection heroin and Latin cocaine through Chile. Soon after Pinochet's forces ousted and killed Marxist President Salvador Allende in September 1973, DEA agent George Frangullie warned Pinochet that the communists might use drug money to unseat *him*; he advised Pinochet to treat the traffickers as a national security threat and deport them without going through extradition proceedings. Pinochet bought the idea. The Chilean police rounded up twenty-one men indicted in New York for drug trafficking, marched them onto aircraft chartered by DEA, and sent them on their way. The defendants argued that they were kidnapped and had been given no due process at all; the courts upheld the legality of Frangullie's methods. The only time there was any controversy in the United States was when the Chileans picked up the wrong Choy. A federal warrant in New York had been issued for one Chino Choy, so the Chileans picked up some hapless Chinese fellow who was indeed known as Chino Choy, Chino being a common nickname for any man of Chinese extraction. Choy did not speak English and the public defender didn't speak Chinese, so Choy spent some months in a cell in New York City before someone figured out he was not the Choy in the indictment. Chile would not allow Choy to return because he had a record of drug trafficking and petty offenses. DEA wanted to set him free in New York, but the Immigration and Naturalization Service threatened to arrest him as an illegal alien, so he had to stay in jail. After the judge in the case blew his stack, American diplomats persuaded Chile to take Choy back. The U.S. government awarded Choy $500,000 in damages, which the Chilean government seized in fines.

For good or ill, after the Camarena kidnapping the U.S. government found it virtually impossible to keep secrets. Other voices raised the questions Camarena had asked, not only about the extent of official complicity in drug trafficking in Mexico but about high-level corruption—and what the U.S. government had known about that corruption—in other "friendly" Third World governments such as Panama, Colombia, and the Bahamas.

One lesson to be learned, said Congressman Larry Smith, was "You can't have a mixed message, tell people just say no to drugs at home and then on the diplomatic front turn a blind eye to corruption." That was a principle no one could dispute, but how could it be translated into a policy that achieved the goal of reducing the availability of drugs?

Smith and other legislators wrote a clause into the 1986 omnibus drug bill that tied U.S. aid, loans, and trade preferences to cooperation on the drug issue. It required the president to certify that recipients of aid were "fully cooperative" on drug control. A "decertified" nation would lose half its U.S. economic and military assistance and risked the loss of favorable tariff treatment on imports to the United States. A separate clause aimed at Mexico, which did not accept direct foreign aid from the U.S., would require U.S. representatives to multilateral development banks to vote against loans for decertified nations. A majority of the Congress could override the president's decision.

The State Department had no intention of using the certification process against friendly governments. "We've cut off aid to Bolivia twice in the last decade," said Ann Wrobleski, assistant secretary of state for international narcotics matters. "During that time, the amount of acreage in Bolivia dedicated to coca increased substantially. Did we do the right thing? Yes, we did. Did it have an impact on the drug problem? It probably made it worse."

Other State Department officials, who were charged with pursuing the administration's geopolitical objectives, attempted to use the certification process to tar hostile governments. The administration's first certification list, sent to Congress in March 1987, decertified just three nations: Syria and Iran, which Secretary of State George Shultz had labeled sponsors of terrorism, and Soviet-occupied Afghanistan.

State Department political officers wanted to include Cuba and Nicaragua on the blacklist as well, but DEA and CIA officials objected on grounds that this was a purely dogmatic judgment unsupported by facts. When Wrobleski brought the issue up at an interagency meeting in early 1987, Jack Lawn said with a grin, "Ann, the problem is not our enemies. It's our *friends*." She laughed and crossed out Cuba and Nicaragua.

Wrobleski took Lawn's remark about "friends" seriously

and pondered giving black marks to Mexico, Panama, and the Bahamas, as Congressional conservatives urged. A thirty-four-year-old former Senate staffer and architect of Nancy Reagan's "Just Say No" program, Wrobleski was not a creature of the cloistered world of the diplomatic corps. She understood Congressional frustrations with the State Department's predilection for secrecy and clientism and, though she lacked the clout to change institutional habits, she told her own staff to write candid reports that conveyed bad news as well as good.

When it came to action, however, Wrobleski followed the line set by her predecessors. "The American response is to take control, *do* something, shut down the border, cut off money," she said. "Well, Uncle Sam can pound the table, but governments act in their own self-interest."

Though there was some pressure from Capitol Hill to decertify the Bahamas, the executive branch agencies were united on the question. Bahamian Prime Minister Lynden Pindling, attempting to counter corruption charges against himself and his aides, had given Customs and DEA planes access to Bahamian airspace, had permitted a Customs radar balloon to be deployed on Grand Bahama Island, and had committed Bahamian police to participate in a joint U.S.– Bahamian interdiction project called OPBAT, for Operation Bahamas, and Turks and Caicos. Even von Raab supported certification of the Bahamian government.

The question of Mexico, on the other hand, was excruciating for Wrobleski. She did not know whether the reason was corruption or inefficiency, but it was clear to her in early 1987 that the eradication program was in terrible shape. When she took over as head of the State narcotics bureau in the fall of 1986, Wrobleski pronounced State's program in Mexico "a shambles" and assigned James Gormley, one of her best people, to fix it. Gormley had not worked in Mexico before, but he and his team were soon as frustrated as seasoned border rats. In a memo in October 1986, Marvin Foster, a contract pilot hired by Gormley to introduce a more efficient spray aircraft called the Turbothrush, accused personnel in the Mexican Attorney General's Office of making a "concentrated effort . . . to thwart the goals of INM by dispatching, not dispatching, authorizing, not authorizing, assisting, not assisting whatever was appropriate at the time to cause a slowdown and/or confusion."[6] The Turbothrush program failed. A study published by the U.S. General Accounting Office in 1988 corroborated Foster's impressions: in 1986, GAO investigators found, actual flight hours for the eighty helicopters and planes in Mexico's eradication fleet averaged just forty-six hours a month. The GAO estimated that the fleet's forty-three Bell 206 helicopters devoted just a fifth of their actual flight time to spraying—or about nine hours a month. According to the GAO, U.S. embassy records showed that between June 1986 and January 1987, the Mexican eradication program sprayed fourteen hundred acres of opium poppies and twenty-seven hundred acres of marijuana in Sinaloa but only two and a half acres of opium poppies and thirty-seven acres of marijuana in neighboring Durango. In mid-1987, the Mexican government bought fourteen more helicopters with its own funds. State aviation advisors objected, futilely, that they did not have enough power for operations in the high Sierras. Further, the Mexican government could not find enough trained pilots to fly them.[7]

DEA agents assigned to Operation Vanguard, the eradication-verification project, told Gormley that they believed the figures the Attorney General's Office produced were deceptive. According to a diplomatic cable written by Gormley's staff, the agents suspected that Mexican pilots were deliberately keeping them from seeing areas where the big traffickers based their marijuana and opium farms. Because the Mexican government used fixed-wing aircraft, not helicopters, for verification, the DEA agents said they could not land to determine whether a field had been harvested before it was sprayed.[8] The 1988 GAO report concurred; it said that "U.S. officials had seen some opium poppy and marijuana fields marked with flags, and they believed those fields were somehow off-limits to the spray program."

Despite these problems, the administration certified Mexico as "fully cooperative." Ed Meese and Steve Trott were strongly in Mexico's corner. Justifying the certification of Mexico, Trott told the Senate Foreign Relations Committee that DEA "continues to operate efficiently in Mexico, notwithstanding some of the terrible problems that we have had involving our agents. . . . The president and the high-level officials that we work with in the Attorney General's Office down there—we have complete confidence in them."[9]

Trott's statement contrasted sharply with the information reaching Wrobleski and also with an internal debate then raging within DEA. In early 1987, some officials at DEA headquarters were urging Lawn to reduce the DEA presence in Mexico because cooperation was so poor. According to several DEA headquarters officials, the DEA-Mexico contingent was the least productive of any overseas office by every measure the agency used: arrests, seizures, and production of intelligence about major trafficking organizations. Those officials who supported a reduction in force contended that the large DEA presence served the Reagan administration's diplomatic ends, not real law-enforcement needs.

Lawn rejected the advice. He said that something was better than nothing. Also, he worried that another public fracas between Washington and Mexico City would make life more difficult for the agents in Mexico. For that reason, he agreed with Meese's desire to give Mexico a full certification.

Another source of pressure on Mexico's behalf was the U.S. ambassador to Mexico, Charles J. Pilliod. Pilliod, the retired president and chairman of Goodyear Tire and Rubber Company, put the restoration of normal economic and trade relations at the top of the bilateral agenda and strongly objected to the idea of linking trade and loans to drug control. Pilliod urged his staffers to write more "objective" cables about Mexico, believing, said an embassy spokesman, that John Gavin had fostered "a very negative attitude" toward Mexico within the embassy.

The lone holdout was Willy von Raab of Customs, who argued that the only thing that seemed to motivate the Mexican government to action was public censure. However, his superiors at Treasury opposed any action that would undermine confidence in Mexico's economic reform program.

As it turned out, Congress had more bark than bite. A resolution to decertify Mexico offered by Senators Jesse Helms and John Kerry, a liberal Democratic senator from Massachusetts, failed by eleven votes. Larry Smith did not bother to take the matter to the House floor.

When the certification issue arose in early 1988, Lawn was fed up with diplomacy and ready to join von Raab, who was arguing passionately, and publicly, that the situation in Mexico was worse than ever. Wrobleski told Lawn the White House and Shultz would never agree, not on the heels of the promises made at the Reagan–de la Madrid summit. Lawn and Wrobleski proposed a compromise: a "national security" certification which would express dissatisfaction without exacerbating Mexico's debt crisis or undercutting the eradication program.

Ed Meese overruled them all. "The bottom line is a change in Americans' behavior," he said. When a reporter asked Meese to cite the worst example he knew of drug abuse by a government official, the attorney general replied gallantly, "As bad as I can find is at home. An assistant U.S. attorney swiping cocaine from the evidence room to feed his habit." Meese professed complete trust in his Mexican counterpart. In January 1988, he had alerted Attorney General García Ramírez that DEA and Customs undercover agents were meeting with some men who claimed to be Mexican police and military officials and who offered to arrange surreptitious landings for smugglers' aircraft for a fee of $1 million per ton of cocaine. According to a Justice Department spokesman, Meese called García Ramírez two to three hours before the undercover agents arrested the men. Mexican officials were delighted; they said Meese's call enabled them to put out a quick denial that the suspects were government officials. The undercover agents and their supervisors were horrified when they learned, weeks later, what Meese had done. "One phone call is all it takes," said a senior Customs official.[10]

Wrobleski yielded to Meese on the certification question, knowing that Reagan would take the attorney general's side in an appeal. She insisted that the White House accompany the certification message with a caveat, a sort of unofficial dissent, noting the State Department's view that "Mexico's effort has not kept pace with the increased flow of drugs and is below the level of efficiency and effect of which it is capable."

How could the administration claim Mexico was "cooperating fully" if it could do more? The statement made no sense, and Wrobleski knew it. She also knew it was a red flag to Congress, which would react out of pride if nothing else. Senator Pete Wilson, a California Republican, understood the challenge implicit in the message and introduced a resolution of disapproval. "Diplomatic niceties be damned, let's say it's not good enough, because it's not," he said. "To simply look the other way and vote for a pro forma certification would be a mockery, not only of the requirements of U.S. law but of the sacrifices by both Mexican and American drug agents, and we shouldn't ask the families of those agents to send them off in what we describe as a war on drugs if in fact we're not going to commit the resources both material and legal that are necessary to win that war."

To the surprise of nearly everyone, including Wilson, the Senate voted to reject the certification of Mexico by 63 to 27. Even some liberal Democrats such as Barbara Mikulski of Maryland and Howard Metzenbaum joined Wilson in voting to censure Mexico.

The Mexican government sent hordes of officials to Washington to lobby the House and the press. "A lot of Mexican policemen and Mexican soldiers have died in a more heroic manner than Camarena," argued Deputy Attorney General José Mariá Ortega Padilla. "We are fighting the traffickers, not because Helms or von Raab say a lot of lies, but because we're struggling to preserve the peace and stability of the Mexican people. We don't say police organizations in the United States are corrupt or inefficient, but the most important traffickers in the world operate in the United States, and they are bringing in tons of drugs."

The Congressional border caucus strongly opposed the decertification because Southwestern commercial interests would be hurt if the action led to trade sanctions and the denial of loans to Mexico. Speaker of the House Jim Wright, a Texan, saw to it that decertification resolutions aimed at Mexico and the Bahamas never got to the House floor.

The question of Panama ended much differently, but the result had less to do with drug enforcement than with hemispheric politics.

For years, the American government's approach to the problem of corruption in Panama was to ignore it in public and equivocate in private. Soon after General Manuel Antonio Noriega became commander in chief of the Panamanian Defense Forces, he was widely accused of rigging the May 1984 presidential election, the first since the 1968 military coup, to favor his candidate, Nicolás Ardito Barletta. Noriega did not deny the charge, but the Reagan administration, anxious to bless the most superficial forms of "democracy" in Latin America, decided to keep quiet and make the best of the situation.

On September 14, 1985, the body of Dr. Hugo Spadafora, a prominent Panamanian opposition leader who had charged Noriega with collaborating with drug traffickers, was found in Costa Rica, near the Panamanian border. Spadafora had been tortured, castrated, and slowly decapitated. Costa Rican authorities found witnesses who charged that Spadafora had been taken from a bus by members of the Panamanian Defense Forces. Under pressure from Spadafora's family and the opposition, Ardito Barletta authorized an independent investigation of the crime. Noriega promptly forced Ardito Barletta to resign and replaced him with Eric Arturo Delvalle.

The Reagan administration's reaction to Ardito Barletta's ouster was mild: it withheld $5 million in aid, refused to participate in a joint military exercise with the PDF, and canceled a U.S. Air Force Thunderbirds show. Years later, when reporters and legislators were asking hard questions about the American government's relationship with Noriega, some officials would contend that then Ambassador Edward Everett Briggs and other senior policy hands had argued, unsuccessfully, for harsh economic sanctions. Whatever internal debates occurred at the time remained secret until it was politically acceptable for American diplomats to say that they had been against Noriega all along.

A number of reports reached Washington in 1984, 1985, and 1986 that Noriega was extorting drug and arms traffickers, but DEA and State Department officials said the charges were no better than hearsay and speculation. If the intelligence agencies had harder information, they said they never saw it.

In 1988, Assistant Secretary of State Elliott Abrams would insist that the administration had not ignored allegations of Noriega's excesses: testifying before the House Select Committee on Narcotics Abuse and Control in March 1988, Abrams said that Admiral John Poindexter, then President Reagan's national security adviser, had gone to Panama in December 1985 "to tell Noriega that we could not tolerate what we believed to be the growing, increasing pattern of PDF corruption, and it had to change."

Abrams acknowledged, however, that other senior American officials had given Noriega mixed messages or none at all. A month before Poindexter went to Panama, State Department officials had arranged for Noriega to be invited to Washington, where he would receive a stern lecture on the dire political ramifications of corruption from CIA director William Casey. Abrams would later say that he felt that Casey, at seventy-two an imposing figure and implacable cold warrior whom Noriega knew to be Ronald Reagan's intimate friend, was the best person to intimidate Noriega into cleaning up his act. Casey did not play. He had a friendly chat with Noriega and handed him over to a subordinate, who treated the little general to a pleasant lunch. As those in Abrams's camp told the story, Noriega returned to Panama full of warm feelings about his relationship with the CIA. Abrams and his associates said they arranged Poindexter's mission precisely because of Casey's failure or refusal to deliver a get-tough message.

Whatever was happening behind closed doors, the administration's public posture would not have given Noriega cause for concern. Testifying at a hearing chaired by Senator Jesse Helms in March 1986, Abrams had asserted that the administration was "aware of and deeply concerned by . . . persistent rumors" of corruption, but he did not indicate that these "rumors" centered on Noriega. Abrams went to some lengths to praise Panama's human rights record. "Panama is one of the most open societies in the hemisphere, with pluralistic social and economic institutions, a free enterprise economy," he had said. "There is general freedom to express political dissent and the legal rights of individuals are generally respected."[11]

On June 12, 1986, *The New York Times* published a story by investigative reporter Seymour Hersh which said that U.S. intelligence agencies had evidence that Noriega was "extensively involved" in drug trafficking, money laundering, selling arms to the M-19 and other left-wing guerrillas, and trading U.S. intelligence sources and methods to Cuba. Hersh reported that the Defense Intelligence Agency had information linking Noriega to the Spadafora murder.

"We do not consider this kind of public speculation something that would be helpful for us to engage in, considering our broad interests in Panama," James Michel, Abrams's deputy assistant secretary, told the House Select Committee on Narcotics Abuse and Control. DEA officials in Panama and Washington went to Capitol Hill to vouch for the general's helpfulness.

In October 1986, State Department officials asked Willy von Raab to meet with a delegation of Panamanian officials and to give them some gift-wrapped parcels. Von Raab did not know that the parcels were plaques expressing the U.S. government's appreciation for the Panamanian government's assistance on drug investigations. The Panamanian press splashed the "awards ceremony" all over the front pages. "I was snookered," von Raab raged. He gave a statement to *La Prensa*, an opposition paper, which said: "This depiction is totally erroneous and without merit. . . . The commissioner *did not* praise the Panamanians for their efforts. In fact . . . there are serious problems with drug smuggling in Panama." Panama's government threatened to declare the Customs attaché persona non grata, to which von Raab responded that getting kicked out of Panama would be no great loss.

Curiously, Vice President George Bush would later insist that he was entirely unaware of the controversy over Noriega. During his 1988 presidential campaign, Bush told reporters he did not know that Noriega was supposedly involved in drug trafficking until February 4, 1988, the day the general was indicted. Was it possible that Bush, chairman of the South Florida drug task force, had been kept in the dark about the Poindexter mission and the concerns that prompted it? If Bush had been engaged and alert as director of the CIA in the mid-1970s, why didn't he know that questions had been raised about Noriega's complicity in the drug trade as early as 1972? As head of Panamanian military intelligence, Noriega had been one of the CIA's most important sources of information about Cuban commercial and political activities in Central America and the Caribbean. Bush's position on the Noriega affair mirrored his posture in the Iran-Contra affair, in which he claimed to have been unaware of crucial aspects of arms-for-hostages deals. After his initial denials were assailed as incredible, Bush "clarified" his stance, claiming he had had general knowledge of the allegations against Noriega but had been unaware of specifics.

In March 1987, the administration certified to Congress that Panama had been "fully cooperative" on drug issues. Associate Attorney General Steve Trott explained to the Senate Foreign Relations Committee that Panamanian cooperation in expelling drug traffickers to the United States had been "superb."[12] Jack Lawn cringed at Trott's penchant for superlatives, but he said that as long as Noriega was willing to help DEA fulfill its mission, he did not care about the general's motives, his politics, or his past. In December 1986, the Panamanian legislature had approved a law that would give American lawmen access to bank accounts used by suspected drug-money launderers. Lawn was not sure how much information DEA would get, but he *was* sure that if State decertified Panama, DEA would get nothing. Like many DEA agents and CIA officers stationed abroad, Lawn accepted the idea that defeating the traffickers was worth many a pact with the devil.

"At some point, you become *owned* by the devil," retorted von Raab. "That's a very difficult problem for any

public official, the degree to which he allows himself to be
compromised or suckered in by a bad man. I don't think
you should ever do it. You have to keep your principles
about these things, and if it hurts the short-term mission of
your organization, so be it. The high road may take longer
but it's a lot cleaner."

For once, Wrobleski thought the Customs commissioner
had a point. "We seem to get seduced by these personal relationships and it's not helpful," she said. But she went along
with the consensus at State, Justice, and DEA and recommended that Panama be certified as "fully cooperative."

General Noriega's courtship of Cuba and his dictatorial
ways had managed to offend both the right and the left. The
Senate rejected the Panama certification by one vote, but
the action was merely symbolic; no economic sanctions were
attached, and the House did not act.

Within a year, the administration had reversed its position and put Panama at the top of the decertification list,
mainly because Noriega's status had changed from asset to
liability. "We don't know anything today about Tony Noriega that we didn't know a year ago," one senior State
Department official acknowledged. "What's changed is politics and Panama, not Tony Noriega."

At the time the 1988 certification list was being drafted,
the State Department was using every diplomatic and economic weapon at its command in a vain effort to force General Noriega out of office. The architect of the policy was
Elliott Abrams. Abrams justified his actions by saying that
Noriega's brand of corruption and repression would wreck
the Panamanian economy and destabilize the small but strategically crucial nation. When Abrams decided Noriega had
to go, discretion went out the window.

This turn of events began with a bizarre outburst by
Noriega's former second-in-command, Colonel Roberto
Díaz Herrera, a cousin of the late General Omar Torrijos.
Díaz Herrera reacted to being sacked by Noriega by un-
leashing a torrent of accusations at his former boss. He
charged that Noriega had conspired with the CIA to bomb
Torrijos's plane, had ordered the Spadafora murder, had
stolen the 1984 election, had collaborated with drug traf-

fickers, and had perpetrated various other dirty deeds. Díaz Herrera's accusations ranged from the plausible to the fantastic, but his words struck a nerve among Panamanians, who poured into the streets by the thousands. Noriega had Díaz Herrera arrested, dispatched troops to suppress the demonstrations, suspended the Constitution, closed opposition media, forced opposition leaders into exile, and harassed or expelled foreign reporters.

When Panamanians took to the streets, it seemed to Abrams and his aides that the opportunity was ripe to persuade younger, cleaner officers of the PDF to throw Noriega out. CIA director William Webster and Pentagon officials objected, protesting that those who might take power were no better than the general. Their protests fell on deaf ears. The administration cut off aid to Panama, and Abrams began a noisy campaign to force Noriega into exile.

Fortuitously, at about the same time, a few drug traffickers under arrest in Florida were trying to bargain their way out of trouble by claiming that they had direct knowledge that Noriega had accepted bribes. Their charges had sparked a DEA investigation in Miami and an FBI-Customs investigation in Tampa. Many of the charges seemed less than credible to the agents, but they had to be pursued or the investigative agencies would be accused of covering up for Noriega. At a July 16, 1987, meeting at the Justice Department, Trott told the U.S. attorneys in Florida and the investigative agencies to pull together everything they could find on Noriega and try to settle the question of his complicity one way or the other.

Abrams kibitzed enthusiastically as the investigations proceeded. Around February 1, 1988, U.S. Attorney Leon Kellner of Miami and U.S. Attorney Robert Merkle of Tampa alerted Washington they had enough to justify formal charges against Noriega for drug trafficking, racketeering, and conspiracy with, among others, Medellín cartel leader Pablo Escobar. The cases were not airtight, but Justice officials in Washington approved the indictments, mainly because a new witness had come forward—José Blandón, Noriega's former political intelligence adviser, who had recently joined the Panamanian opposition. Blan-

dón corroborated statements by the smugglers that Noriega
had sold protection to the Medellín cartel.

After the indictments were handed down, more riots and
strikes broke out in Panama City. When Noriega *still* refused
to step down, and dumped President Delvalle for trying to
fire him, the Reagan administration finished what he had
started and wrecked the Panamanian economy. That proved
to be surprisingly simple: the White House supported a court
action that froze $50 million in Panamanian government
funds held in U.S. banks. The dollar shortage reduced Panamanian government employees and pensioners to destitu-
tion, disrupted commerce, and set off more strikes and riots.

As he watched television footage of PDF troops beating
demonstrators and reporters, Jack Lawn's temper rose. People were being killed, children were hungry, property was
being destroyed, and to what end? Lawn did not believe
the U.S. government should be in the business of destabilizing other governments and did not think the Abrams faction was motivated by concern about drug trafficking. Lawn
had authorized the DEA investigation of Noriega because
the allegations were serious, not because he wanted to hand
the State Department a bargaining chip. The State Department, he thought, never kicked a guy when he was up.

The irony of the situation was not lost on those members
of Congress who had been around for a few years. "We
have ignored everybody's drug-trafficking activity as long as
they would support our foreign-policy objective, which is to
fight communism," said Congressman Charles Rangel.
"Now, all of a sudden, they pull this goddamn indictment
out of the sky and use the indictment as a vehicle to tell the
guy to leave the country. We should have better intelligence
than that lousy indictment, which we know can't be pursued
to a trial. That indictment is a political statement. I know
Noriega is perceived to be a bum. To hear people talk
around Washington, he is up to his eyeballs in corruption.
But you don't *think* someone is a drug trafficker. Once you
decide you're dealing with a bum, do all constitutional rights
go out the window? Are we indicting people for political
purposes? I just don't see how we can get away with this
kind of stuff."

Noriega's grip on his office remained unshaken. The racketeering indictment had created a sense of solidarity within the PDF. Noriega had become a hero throughout Latin America for standing up to Uncle Sam's hamhanded intervention.

In early May, Secretary of State George Shultz sent an envoy to Panama City with an offer that smacked of desperation: the indictments would be quashed if Noriega would leave office. Noriega stalled, the plan leaked, and a political firestorm ensued, handing the Democrats a ready-made campaign issue. "I don't think you drop indictments against drug pushers and people who are suspected of murder," Democratic presidential front-runner Michael Dukakis declared. "You cannot put charges on him one day and decide the next by voodoo or astrology that he is not guilty," scoffed presidential contender Jesse Jackson. In a *New York Times*–CBS poll taken in mid-May, Dukakis surged ten points ahead of Vice President George Bush, in part because people felt the Democrats were better than the Republicans at handling the drug issue. Fifty-five percent of those polled said that the Reagan administration was not doing a good job dealing with drugs.

"What you have here," said Republican Senator Alfonse D'Amato of New York, "is an administration that has set its hair on fire and is trying to put it out with a hammer."

Elliott Abrams, the point man of State's oust-Noriega policy, was baffled: he put the word out to the press that he had known very little about the criminal investigations, and anyway, he thought everyone had agreed that the indictments could be dismissed if the need arose. Merkle, Kellner, Lawn, and von Raab, who learned about the secret negotiations from the newspapers, protested bitterly they had agreed to nothing of the sort. "We do not negotiate with narcoterrorists, whether these people are living in huts or whether these people are occupying positions of power in foreign governments," Merkle declared defiantly, announcing he would resign rather than go into court to move to drop the indictment. Kellner had submitted his resignation already and said that he also would refuse to go into court; Meese would have to find somebody else to do the dirty work. At one point, according to DEA officials, Abrams asked Jack Lawn to suspend DEA's continuing probe into corruption within the PDF because the inquiry might upset the negotiations; Lawn refused, slammed down the telephone, and let fly with a litany of invective. CIA director Webster let it be known that he had had no part in charting the administration's course of action, which he considered disastrous. Even George Bush broke with the White House, declaring that he would not "bargain with drug dealers whether they're on U.S. or foreign soil."

Shultz and Abrams stuck by their plan and were backed by Lieutenant General Colin Powell, the president's national security adviser, Attorney General Meese, and Reagan himself. Better to rid Panama of Noriega, they said, than to preserve a criminal case that was never likely to go to trial. In fact, the U.S. terms had been watered down and did not demand Noriega's permanent exile. Had he accepted, he could have remained a political force in Panama.

Even this face-saving solution proved beyond the United States's grasp. Noriega amused himself by toying with Shultz's negotiator, Michael G. Kozak. Several times during the month of May, State Department and White House officials put the word out to reporters to stand by, because a deal was imminent. Each time, they were wrong. On May 25, as Ronald Reagan departed for his historic summit in Moscow with Soviet leader Mikhail Gorbachev, Shultz stayed behind, expecting to announce a resolution of the Noriega talks and to leave Washington on a triumphal note. Late that afternoon, Kozak sent word that Noriega's intermediaries made the deal, but the general did not. Noriega had told Kozak bluntly that he did not intend to budge.

Looking tired and dejected, Shultz faced a crowd of reporters and conceded failure. "No further negotiations are contemplated," he said. "No offers remain on the table." The indictments stayed in force.

The moment of triumph was Noriega's. He rode through the streets, waved to the crowds, and enjoyed a hearty laugh at Ronald Reagan's expense.

24
The Search for Justice

"**W**hen is it going to be over?" Mika Camarena said. "It just keeps coming back. It's all so much politics." Sometimes she imagined how angry Kiki would be at what she had gone through. She tried not to think about it. "These men, these politicians, have taken Kiki from me, and I don't want to let them hurt me anymore," she said.

Three years had passed since Mika had last seen Kiki alive, and his murder had not been solved. American agents were not much closer to the truth, the whole truth, than they had been in February 1985. They did not know who had killed Kiki Camarena, who had ordered him killed, or why.

The best evidence the U.S. government had were the tapes of Camarena's interrogation. DEA agents in Mexico thought they recognized the voices of Rafael Caro Quintero and Sergio Espino Verdín, the former *comandante* of the federal Bureau of Political and Social Investigations. Both men were in prison in Mexico, charged with murder, along with Caro Quintero's partner, Ernesto Fonseca. Yet the tapes themselves did not tell the whole story. There were more than a dozen voices on them. Mexican authorities had more than sixty people in custody, but were they the same people who could be heard on the tape? No one knew; Mexican authorities had not permitted U.S. voice-analysis experts to conduct tests on the defendants in Mexican prisons.

The tapes did not shed light on the identity of those who had actually killed the agent. Nor was there a single witness in the United States or Mexico who would testify that he had seen the death blow struck.

For Mika Camarena, as for Kiki's friends and for all the American lawmen who had been touched by the agent's life and death, not knowing the truth was even worse than seeing the guilty go unpunished. If you thought a man was guilty, you could lay a trap or he might have bad luck and end up dead or in jail for some other crime.

But without access to the most basic kinds of evidence, the search for justice was frustrated. The legal system churned noisily down one track and up another like an old freight train, but where was it heading? There were a number of compelling theories, but that was all they were. DEA agents had a lot of ideas, a few facts, and piles of garbage. Little bags of soil, a few hairs, flakes of dried blood, bad photographs, smudged fingerprints, scraps of cloth, descriptions—black hair, brown eyes, medium height—which might be anyone's.

Since the fall of 1986, Justice Department prosecutors had sent letters rogatory—formal demands for evidence—to the Mexican Attorney General's Office, yet the information they sought had not been produced. In mid-1988 the prosecutors were still waiting for more than seventy categories of evidence listed in written requests, "officios," which DEA had delivered to the Mexican Attorney General's Office. Assistant U.S. Attorney Jimmy Gurule of Los Angeles called the Mexican response "dismal." Mexican officials replied that all written requests for evidence had been answered but many had been denied because they were the subjects of Mexican judicial proceedings. After the U.S. Senate voted to decertify Mexico for noncooperation on drug issues, Mexican Deputy Attorney General José María Ortega Padilla offered to share some additional evidence, but DEA agents in Operation Leyenda said that the new material did not advance the case in any way. For instance, the Mexican official forwarded fingerprints of Rafael Caro Quintero, which had been in DEA's possession since his arrest in Costa Rica in 1985. Another "new" item was the Mexican autopsy report of Camarena and Zavala, which duplicated the report of the American pathologist. Mexican officials would not give what the Americans needed: live witnesses, including the suspects in jail and police officers who had been posted in Guadalajara when Camarena was there.

Mexican officials insisted that there was no deeper mystery to the case. "This one guy killed him, and we put that guy in jail," said José Antonio González Fernández, the law adviser at the Mexican embassy in Washington. He was referring to Rafael Caro Quintero.

If the traffickers had not been convicted, he said, that was only because of the length and complexity of the charges leveled against them. "You have to be reasonable," González said. "You have to trust the justice of Mexico."

The Mexican government's theory of the case was that Caro Quintero ordered Camarena kidnapped, with the complicity of Ernesto Fonseca, Espino, and some Jalisco state policemen, in a vendetta motivated by the destruction of the cartel's Zacatecas and Chihuahua marijuana plantations.

Mika Camarena did not believe the plot stopped with the traffickers, Espino, and Jalisco police officers. She thought Mexican federal officials or people of greater political influence with the federal government were somehow involved in her husband's death. She had to admit that the theory had flaws. If Kiki's kidnapping had been authorized by people of some sophistication, why had the planners failed to calculate the political impact? And why was the execution so amateurish? "If it had been professionally done, we wouldn't have found him," she said. "Why the tapes? Why was that evidence found? Why let *any* of the evidence be found? It's very puzzling."

On the other hand, what else could explain why the truth had not come out? Why else had evidence been withheld or destroyed? Probably, she thought, the motive was to kidnap Kiki and torture him for information, as Victor Cortez had been tortured, and then to let him go. Perhaps things got out of hand. Kiki had died; those involved in the conspiracy had panicked and been unable to clean up the loose ends before DEA and other Mexican investigators moved into the case.

Antonio Vargas,* the Mexican businessman who at Kiki's urging had befriended the traffickers, could not conceive of Caro Quintero and Fonseca's orchestrating the elaborate series of events that led up to the kidnapping and that continued to obscure the truth for three years afterward. "Rafa and Don Neto have no imagination," Vargas said. "They were working under the orders of officials. They don't have the brains."

Jack Lawn, Willy von Raab, and nearly every American agent who had studied the Camarena case agreed with Mika and Antonio: they believed that other, more influential people were involved, at least in the subsequent obstruction of the investigation. It was not wise to underestimate the traffickers, who were immensely resourceful and who hired skilled specialists to handle certain tasks such as protection payoffs, investments, and aircraft and weapons acquisition. It was possible that the cartel leaders, using their own *pistoleros* or low-level policemen who contracted out as hired guns, could have engineered the kidnapping and interrogation of Camarena and Alfredo Zavala, and, as well, the kidnapping and interrogation of informant Anthony Brito.

But there were other, unexplained events in which Mexican federal authorities were directly involved. For instance, the DEA agents said the "confessions" of the sixty or so men arrested in Mexico contained a number of important internal inconsistencies and in some aspects conflicted with other evidence.

"The confessions only paraphrased what the Mexican authorities thought we knew about the investigation," said Bill Coonce, the first Leyenda leader. "They had no resemblance to the actual evidence that we had. That's why we caught them in so many lies."

The first U.S. indictment in the Camarena murder was unsealed on January 6, 1988. Five men had been indicted for the agent's murder: reputed kingpins Rafael Caro Quintero and Ernesto Fonseca Carrillo, their alleged associate

---

* The name Antonio Vargas is a pseudonym.

René Martín Verdugo Urquídez, former Mexican secret police *comandante* Sergio Espino Verdín, and former Jalisco state policeman Raúl López Alvarez. Four others—former MFJP *comandante* Armando Pavón Reyes and alleged Caro Quintero associates Albino Bazán Padilla, Jesús Félix Gutiérrez, and Inés Calderón Quintero—were charged with being accessories after the fact for helping Caro Quintero escape from Guadalajara.

"In what we do for a living, we depend on the integrity of our law-enforcement counterparts," Jack Lawn told reporters pointedly. "In the case of Kiki Camarena, that mutual trust failed. It is very important to note that of nine individuals in this indictment, three are former police officers in Mexico."

Of the nine men charged in the Camarena case, three were in custody in the United States: René Verdugo was awaiting trial on marijuana-trafficking charges and, according to DEA and Justice officials, had maintained a stony silence on the Camarena case. Jesús Félix Gutiérrez, a.k.a. Cachas, had pleaded guilty to a trafficking charge and had been sentenced to fifteen years in prison, but had declined to testify in the Camarena case in exchange for a reduced sentence. The third, Raúl López Alvarez, had been arrested in Los Angeles on October 26, 1987, for conspiring to murder a U.S. Customs agent. Bazán and Calderón were fugitives; in March 1988, Calderón would be reported dead, killed in a shoot-out in Sinaloa. Pavón Reyes was a fugitive when the indictment was returned but was arrested on March 22, 1988, and returned to prison in Guadalajara to complete his sentence for attempted bribery. Caro Quintero, Fonseca, and Espino remained in prison in Mexico City. American congressmen talked loosely of extradition, but this was posturing.

The indictment was meant as a symbol, to mark not the end of the case but its beginning—a sign of the U.S. government's determination to keep the investigation alive. It signaled, said U.S. Attorney Robert C. Bonner of Los Angeles, that "the government of the United States will not let the murder of one of its own by a terrorist narcotics organization go unavenged."

The document offered a thin and unsatisfying account of the murder.[1] The prosecutors were confident that it told the truth, but if the whole truth had been known, they believed, they could have charged literally dozens of other people. The physical evidence they had, such as the tapes and hair and fiber analysis, were useful but could be criticized as circumstantial. The government had some cooperating witnesses, but none was an insider who could tell the story from beginning to end. Jaime Kuykendall, for one, thought the DEA had bought too much of the Mexican government's theory already. If the American government believed that Caro Quintero and Fonseca committed the crime, he said, theories and circumstantial evidence were not enough. The prosecution had to prove beyond a reasonable doubt that those men committed the crime. And that was a risky proposition, given all that the U.S. government did *not* know about Camarena's movements after two o'clock on February 7, 1985. The traffickers were the usual suspects. And perhaps they had played leading roles in Camarena's death. But was it their idea? And did Kiki really die at Caro Quintero's house? Or someplace else? According to an FBI agent's affidavit filed in federal court in Los Angeles, hairs from Camarena's head had been found at Caro Quintero's house on Calle Lope de Vega. The affidavit said that fibers found on a sample of Camarena's burial sheet matched a carpet at the house on Lope de Vega. But hairs and fibers "traveled." They could end up someplace else because they stuck to someone's garment. Fibers could be planted.

Only one federal official, Pavón Reyes, had been convicted of any crime in connection with the Camarena case. Under pressure from the U.S. government Pavón Reyes was arrested April 15, 1985. According to Mexican officials, on August 12, 1986, he was convicted of intending to accept 60 million pesos from Caro Quintero for allowing the trafficker to fly out of the Guadalajara airport on February 9, 1985, two days after Camarena disappeared. Mexican officials said they could not confirm that Pavón Reyes actually took the money, as DEA attaché Ed Heath's informant claimed. Pavón Reyes was sentenced to four years in jail but was released on bail on May 29, 1987. After officials at the U.S. embassy complained, the Mexican attorney general had him rearrested. Pavon Reyes would be released for good in November 1988.

It was not simply the alleged bribe that troubled DEA agents. What about the toll records that indicated that Pavón Reyes made a telephone call to a private line in the MFJP director's office, at the precise hour when his men were blocking Caro Quintero's departure? It was after that call that Pavón Reyes cleared Caro Quintero's departure—but what did it mean? The call might be irrelevant, or it might be of great consequence, but without the ability to trace the call and question the recipient, who could say?

Other questions concerned the discovery of the bodies. What motivated MFJP officers to go to the Bravo ranch and kill five members of the Bravo family? Comandante Alfonso Velázquez Hernández had been charged with homicide and abuse of authority for killing the Bravos, but DEA agents could not explain why he and his men had gone to the ranch in the first place. The rationale was that Velázquez was responding to the anonymous note that Pavón Reyes had shown to Kuykendall and Ayala. But who wrote the note? Why had the Mexican Attorney General's Office declined to submit the note to FBI laboratory analysis? Mexican authorities had given DEA a photostatic copy, but that could not be tested for prints and other markers. Also, the note appeared to have been altered. Kuykendall and Ayala recalled that the note was cleanly written, with no strike-overs. According to agents in Operation Leyenda, the photostatic copy showed that the old date had been struck through and changed to match the date of the postmark on the envelope in which the note allegedly arrived.

Why did the Federales refuse to let DEA agents search the ranch until three days after the shoot-out between the Federales and the Bravos? Why did the Federales delay for more than twelve hours before informing DEA that the bodies might have been located? Why did the Federales move the bodies from the spot where they had been found to a hospital before alerting DEA? What happened to the bags and sheets in which the Federales said the bodies were wrapped?

The FBI laboratory analysis suggested strongly that the bodies of Camarena and Zavala were originally buried in the Bosques de Primavera in Guadalajara, in the same grave with the corpses of two American tourists, John Walker and Alberto Radelat. Why were the bodies of the agent and the pilot exhumed and dumped in Michoacán? The Leyenda team conjectured that someone did not want all four bodies discovered in a mass grave because it would look as if Americans and anyone associated with them were being systematically hunted down and murdered. Worse yet, if the press started writing about anti-American death squads that involved corrupt policemen, the Mexican tourist industry would be devastated. The Reagan administration might enact harsher economic sanctions. Someone had decided that the Camarena case had to be closed, fast, and the only way to do that was to deliver the bodies and some suspects— namely, the Bravo family. Who made that decision? The traffickers? Elements of the police? Or someone interested in protecting Mexican political or commercial interests?

There were many other gaps in the DEA agents' knowledge. Why had the Federales shot and killed Javier Barba Hernández, the Guadalajara lawyer and reputed executioner for the cartel? The confession of cartel henchman "El Samy" Ramírez said that Barba had accompanied Fonseca to the house where Camarena was being held. For that reason, Barba had been near the top of the list of suspects DEA gave the Mexican Attorney General's Office. Why couldn't he have been taken alive? Why had Mexican authorities declined DEA's request for his hair and fingerprints?

"The traffickers and the government were behind it, but I just don't think they've got the right people," said Jaime Kuykendall. "The reason they've been killing people like Barba is because they've got to get rid of people who know what happened. I don't know who did it. And I hope to hell I'm wrong."

The origin of the interrogation tapes remained shrouded in mystery. Who made them? If it was true that they had been found when Ernesto Fonseca and his gang were arrested in Guadalajara, why hadn't Fonseca or his men destroyed them during the shoot-out? Why would Fonseca travel around Mexico with the single most incriminating bit of evidence in the case? He was uneducated, but he had not survived longer than most traffickers by being stupid.

Which government agencies had handled the tapes? Were the gaps in the Camarena tapes caused by someone who had turned the recorder on and off, or by a voice-activated recorder, or had the tapes been edited? Were tapes being withheld? If the transcript DEA had obtained through intelligence sources was genuine, at least one tape had been suppressed, the tape in which Camarena was asked what he knew about the defense minister, General José Arévalo Gardoqui, and former MFJP Comandante Miguel Aldana Ibarra. Why were the two cassettes bearing Camarena's voice found with a cassette recording of the interrogation of FBI informant Anthony Brito? Brito had been abducted a month after Camarena disappeared, and probably from Juárez, just after he met with FBI and DEA agents in El Paso. On that tape, the interrogator had asked Brito what he knew about the then–DFS *comandante* in Juárez, Rafael Aguilar. What was the connection? And what was the reason for the fourth cassette, the recording of DEA/Guadalajara radio signals on the morning of the shoot-out at the Bravo ranch?

What steps had the Mexican government taken to question officials who had been accused of complicity in the drug trade by Caro Quintero and other defendants in custody? Ed Heath, who had sat in on some of the early interrogations, said that when a trafficker began talking about influential persons, MFJP interrogators left those names out of their reports. Ambassador John Gavin complained that when he brought names of those and other high officials to the attention of President de la Madrid or his ministers, he was told that nothing could be done unless he provided his sources and hard evidence.

American investigators pursuing the Camarena homicide would have liked to interview people who had held senior positions in the Mexican government when the Guadalajara cartel was on the rise. Former DFS chief Antonio Zorrilla, whose signature had allegedly been found on DFS credentials in Caro Quintero's possession. Former MFJP Comandante Miguel Aldana Ibarra, who had been head of the federal narcotics enforcement program until a few weeks before Camarena disappeared. Former MFJP chief Manuel Ibarra Herrera, who had delayed the raid on the apartment of Juan Matta Ballesteros, the partner of Miguel Angel Félix Gallardo. There were numerous other men who had held positions of responsibility in the MFJP, DFS, Attorney General's Office, and state governments who might be able to shed some light on how Caro Quintero had arranged protection for his marijuana operations. For instance, who warned Caro Quintero's henchmen that the Chihuahua raid was about to be launched? That question remained unresolved, as did the evident compromising of earlier raids instigated by Camarena and other DEA agents in Mexico. The cocaine-trafficking operations of the Miguel Angel Félix Gallardo organization raised separate questions about protection of the *Padrino*'s network of airplanes, landing fields, and laboratories.

The capture of Raúl López Alvarez had created a brief flurry of hope among the investigators that a cooperative eyewitness had finally materialized. According to Mexican officials, López Alvarez, a former Jalisco state policeman, had been jailed in Mexico on charges relating to the Camarena case but had been released. After that, López Alvarez arrived in Los Angeles and, according to the Justice Department, began negotiating a cocaine deal with an undercover DEA agent named Abel Reynoso. López Alvarez allegedly claimed he was a member of the Fonseca–Caro Quintero drug organization and offered to torture and kill anyone the undercover agent named, at a cost of $10,000 for a civilian and $25,000 for a police officer. A federal grand jury in Los Angeles indicted López Alvarez on charges of conspiring to kidnap, torture, and murder a fictitious Customs agent whom DEA agent Reynoso had proposed as a victim. In videotapes shown at the trial, López Alvarez boasted to undercover agents that he had been present when Camarena was tortured.[2] López Alvarez and three other men were convicted of the attempted-murder conspiracy charges on February 26, 1988.[3]

López Alvarez did not prove to be a willing witness in the Camarena case. Once he was arrested, he retracted his claims of having participated in the Camarena torture and said that he was only repeating what he had heard from another Jalisco police officer, Gerardo Torres Lepe, who had "confessed" in Mexico to being involved in the Camarena kidnapping. Some of the DEA agents who dealt with López Alvarez believed that he knew details of Camarena's murder and Caro Quintero's escape that could not have been passed along by Torres Lepe. But other agents were skeptical: why would a man who had helped commit the most notorious crime in Mexico show up in Los Angeles, where the case was being investigated, and offer to commit a similar crime?

In early April 1988, the odds of a breakthrough were improved when two senior Guadalajara cartel members were taken into custody in the United States. On April 1, DEA agents arrested José Contreras Subias, a close associate of Rafael Caro Quintero, in Salt Lake City.

On April 5 an even more audacious plan succeeded. Howard Safir, chief of operations for the U.S. Marshals Service, persuaded Honduran police to arrest Juan Ramón Matta Ballesteros, the partner of Miguel Angel Félix Gallardo, who was living in Tegucigalpa. Despite Honduran laws against extradition of that nation's own citizens, the Honduran police forced Matta Ballesteros aboard an airplane bound for the Dominican Republic. By prior arrangement with Safir, Dominican authorities ordered Matta Ballesteros expelled for entering their country illegally and forced him onto a flight bound for Puerto Rico. When the plane entered Puerto Rican territory, U.S. marshals aboard the same flight arrested him. By early the next morning, Matta Ballesteros was at the U.S. maximum security penitentiary in Marion, Illinois, facing trial on four separate indictments in the United States.

Matta Ballesteros did not open his mouth all the way from Puerto Rico to Marion, and it was far from certain that he or Contreras Subias would ever agree to cooperate in the Camarena murder investigation. DEA agents had ample reason to believe that, if they chose, both men could shed a good deal of light on corruption within the Mexican government. Costa Rican police had arrested Contreras Subias along with Rafael Caro Quintero in April 1985, but he had escaped from the Tijuana jail the following November with the alleged complicity of several Tijuana law-enforcement officials. Matta Ballesteros had fled Mexico City on February 16, 1985, after then–MFJP director Ibarra Herrera's stalling made possible his escape.

DEA agents blamed the gaps in their knowledge on the de la Madrid administration for stonewalling and the Reagan administration for shrinking from the task of demanding answers.

"It really lets you know about how the system will eat you up," Bill Coonce reflected. "Big government will prevent you from doing a job when other interests are at stake. The life of an agent is secondary to other issues. No one will say so. You get a lot of lip service, but things just get undone and you don't get backed. You're told you're supported, but after a few months of not being able to get a straight answer from anyone, you look back and you realize you've been had."

Lawn was somewhat more optimistic. As the original Leyenda team rotated out of headquarters—Coonce to head the DEA office in Detroit, Matty Maher to take the deputy's job in Denver, Carlo Boccia to the job of DEA attaché in Paris—Lawn gave the Leyenda assignment to Jack Taylor, fresh from the San Diego field office, and tried to make sure that there was always a complement of investigators in the field working on the Camarena case. One of these days, he figured, somebody might turn up who would tell the truth, or a piece of it, and perhaps that would cause other pieces to fit into place.

In public, Lawn had a set phrase: "I believe that ultimately justice will be done in Mexico." He said that because he thought it would help the agents in Mexico, but he did not sound very convincing. He knew that many of the people in the field disagreed strenuously. Hardly any of the men based in Mexico were re-upping. The extreme danger was a consideration, especially for those with families, but in most cases, the agents were simply burning out on embassy politics, DEA politics, Mexican politics, the constant fear for the safety of informants and the dispiriting business of coaxing their MFJP contacts to do something without tipping less trustworthy MFJP officials to their intentions. One of the few DEA men who seemed to want to stay in Mexico was Ed Heath. He got on well with Ambassador Charles Pilliod, who praised Heath to Lawn as a "team player." Not many other agents earned such plaudits from the American envoy, who devoted much of his time to putting out political fires that DEA agents lit.

Lawn often talked to Mika Camarena about progress in the case. She was grateful for his attention and for the quiet concern he showed for her, for her sons, and for the agents in Mexico. Some of her anger toward DEA had faded. She could not understand why the American government, at the highest levels, was not tougher on the Mexican government, but she had confidence that the prosecutors and agents were doing their best. "My faith has grown, and with that my patience," she said. "I won't let go of it. I paid a good price for it." It was hard getting the truth in little pieces. She hoped to know it all someday, even though it would hurt.

"Kiki knows now, better than all of us, that justice will be made by one person," she said. "God will make it."

"It's like Veet-nam," said Ken Miley. "It's the war we're not supposed to win."

"The war on drugs," Jaime Kuykendall said, "began on February 7, 1985. Nobody did anything until Kiki Camarena was gone, and a lot of people just wouldn't let him disappear into the mist."

Spring was relentless on the Rio Grande. The summer sun burned the oxygen out of the air, blistered the bare feet of the children, and turned green things yellow. The tedium of pursuing an unending stream of smugglers was getting to them both.

Kuykendall had a good bunch of young agents in Laredo, but there was nobody like Kiki. Every few months he slipped down to Guadalajara to nose around, but it wasn't the same without Kiki and Roger Knapp and Pete Hernandez and the rest of the crew. He wondered if the riddle would ever be solved.

"The problem is," he said, "when you have a puzzle that depends on the pieces fitting progressively, and there are pieces missing, the rest of the puzzle cannot possibly be there."

Sound advice, but he didn't heed it and kept hoping for a lucky break. He worried about the future of the case, so many agents transferring in and out of Operation Leyenda, going on to other, more promising assignments. He listened to the tapes of his friend's death, though it pained him to do so, and kept track of every detail. "A man's life *has* to mean something," he said. "Too many people in government get caught up in other things, all those other issues. I may have done some things wrong, but I *care*." He figured that if hope did not keep him going, fury would. He concentrated on staying angry.

One day, he found out that his son, James, who was twenty-two, had applied to become a DEA agent. James was a police officer, solid, dependable, strong, and smart. And hardheaded, Kuykendall said, just like his old man. He did not know why his son had chosen this kind of life. The young man knew the odds. No one who had grown up listening to the stories of border rats could have many illusions. But Kuykendall was proud of his son for believing that a man could make a difference.

Epilogue

The prosecutor drew a long breath and turned his owl's face to the jury. The past eight weeks had been Jimmy Gurule's severest test: circumstantial evidence, sleazy witnesses, expensive defense lawyers. Worst, the defense team had a point. They said their clients were small fish who drifted into the government net. The big fish, the men who orchestrated the Camarena murder, were safely down in Mexico.

There was nothing to do but admit it. "The government does not maintain," Gurule told the jury as he summed up his case, "that every individual who had anything to do with the kidnapping and murder of special agent Enrique Camarena and Alfredo Zavala is in the courtroom today. Clearly, there are other individuals who were responsible and culpable as well. Justice in this case can only be done when every individual who had anything to do with the kidnapping and murder of Special Agent Camarena is convicted and brought to justice and prosecuted to the full extent of the law."

No, there might never be justice for all. Even so, Gurule implored the jury not to absolve Raúl Lopez Alvarez, the Jalisco State policeman, who had grinned into the hidden camera as he told how Kiki Camarena's flesh had been scorched and ripped. Nor René Martín Verdugo Urquídez, who had admitted being at Rafael Caro Quintero's side, arranging a drug shipment, while Camarena's life drained away. Nor Jesús Félix Gutiérrez, the Los Angeles pot millionaire, who bought the villa in Costa Rica where Caro Quintero hid out during the manhunt.

"We come to you for justice because *you* are justice,"

Gurule said. "Enrique Camarena from his grave cries out for justice. He will not rest in peace until justice is done."

The jury's deliberations were short, the verdict unequivocal: all guilty, on all counts. The sentences were extraordinary. On October 26, 1988, U.S. District Judge Edward J. Rafeedie ordered Raúl Lopez Alvarez to serve two hundred fifty years plus life in prison. For René Verdugo Urquídez, Rafeedie decreed two hundred forty years plus life in prison, with no possibility of parole for sixty years. Jesús Félix Gutiérrez drew ten years, the maximum for an accessory to murder, to be served after his fifteen-year term for drug trafficking.

Gurule was only sorry there was no death penalty for federal crimes. He was haunted by the image of Dora Camarena, Kiki's mother, her head held high, and those deep, watchful eyes, so much like her son's. Before the sentencing hearing, he had asked her, was there anything more he could do? Yes, there was one thing, she said. Find out the moment when Kiki had died, so that every year, at that hour, she might light a candle and say a prayer.

Gurule's eyes had teared up behind his spectacles. It was such a small thing to ask, and he could not give it. None of the defendants had cracked. Not even René Verdugo, the pretty boy with the sexy wife and the pleasure palace in Baja. René would be ninety-eight years old before he had a chance at freedom, yet he was silent. Why *wouldn't* he bargain? If he was a scapegoat, as his lawyers claimed, whom was he a scapegoat for? He would not, or dared not, say.

The prosecutor and the small band of DEA agents working on the case had a few beers to celebrate and moved on. Operation Leyenda, Phase Two, had begun. Its mission was breathtakingly ambitious: to make cases against all the others who should have been in the courtroom. The list of targets included at least three former governors, several generals, and some cabinet and subcabinet level officials of the Lopez Portillo and de la Madrid administrations. A few of these people were resurfacing in the Salinas administration which took power in December 1988.

But who would deliver up such powerful figures? Not the

current crop of informants. Most of them would not go before the grand jury, much less testify in court. In 1987 and 1988, at least nine DEA informants had been summarily executed by traffickers in Mexico.

In the cases of the most important officials on the target list, the Leyenda team did not have informants with first-hand knowledge—much less pictures or tape recordings—that would support indictments. High-ranking officials who had brokered protection arrangements dealt exclusively with the bosses: Rafael Caro Quintero, Ernesto Fonseca, Miguel Angel Félix Gallardo, and Juan Matta Ballesteros.

Some in DEA hoped that Rafael Caro Quintero might make a surreptitious deal with the United States, once he understood that he was being hung out to dry in Mexico. He and his lawyers had managed to stall the Mexican judicial process for four and a half years, but finally, on September 22, 1988, Caro Quintero was convicted and sentenced to thirty-four years in prison for crimes growing out of the 1984 Chihuahua case, including drug trafficking, criminal association, kidnapping peasants and weapons smuggling. Ernesto Fonseca had been sentenced to eleven years in the same case.

The Institutional Ruling Party was clearly trying to defuse the corruption issue, which had dominated the fiercely contested July 6 presidential election. By official pronouncement, the winner was PRI candidate Carlos Salinas de Gortari, but many Mexicans believed the PRI had stolen the election from Cuauhtémoc Cárdenas, the former governor of Michoacán, behind whom the populist-reformist movement coalesced. In the tumultuous political climate of the presidential transition, the PRI could not hand the Cárdenas movement more ammunition by letting Rafael, that visible symbol of corruption, off the hook.

Whenever they met with American diplomats and members of Congress, Mexican officials pledged that Caro Quintero would spend the rest of his life in prison for the murder of Kiki Camarena and Alfredo Zavala Rafael must have known of these promises: DEA informants in the Mexico City prison said that with every passing day, he seemed more anxious and out of control. Yet, he did not try to leverage his way out by threatening to expose coconspirators in the government.

If Rafael did not talk, there was a chance that Juan Matta Ballesteros would. It was a long shot but at least Matta was in the United States and about to go on trial in Los Angeles for cocaine trafficking. The degree of his involvement in the Camarena murder was unclear, but there was one striking piece of evidence against him: his hair matched a hair found at the house at the Lope de Vega.

The biggest prize of all would be Miguel Angel Félix Gallardo. By all accounts, the *padrino* was very much a part of the social scene in Culiacán, where he entertained and was entertained by political and police leaders. He continued to run his thriving cocaine business from Guadalajara. *Proceso* magazine would write of him, "The most wanted man in the world: for eighteen years, he never hid."[1]

In early October 1988, DEA agents in Mazatlán saw a chance to get Félix Gallardo and his fellow drug lord, Manuel Salcido, Cochi Loco. A DEA informant had arranged a meeting with the traffickers. When it happened, General Roberto Badillo, commander of the military garrison in Mazatlán, would move in. The DEA agents went to Badillo because he had a vendetta against Cochi Loco, who had tried to assassinate his closest friend.

The traffickers smelled a rat and insisted on moving the meeting to Guadalajara, where they said they had "better protection." Badillo sent eighty of his men to Guadalajara. With the help of the informant, the soldiers detained Felix Gallardo's uncle and forced him to disclose Felix Gallardo's location.

Just as Badillo's men were about to stage the raid, General Vinicio Santoyo Feria, the military zone commander for Jalisco state, showed up and protested that Badillo's troops had violated his turf. According to the DEA agents on the scene, Santoyo announced *he* would lead the raid—with his men, not Badillo's, and without DEA observers.

The American agents slept in the U.S. consulate, waiting for word from General Santoyo. Early the next morning, when there was no news, they drove around the city looking at Félix Gallardo's haunts. They saw no bullet holes or other signs of confrontation. At a local trailer park, they found Félix Gallardo's recreational vehicle, a luxury model with a satellite dish. Next to it was a 1957 black-and-white Chevrolet Bel Air in mint condition. That fit: Félix Gallardo collected vintage cars.

Later that morning, two of the agents went to the military garrison, just in time to see General Santoyo drive through the gate—in the same gleaming 1957 Chevy that had been spotted at the trailer park. According to one agent, when the DEA agents asked what had happened, the general said, "Nothing. You sent me on a wild goose chase."

The episode did not end there. Alan Bachelier, the resident agent in charge of the DEA office in Guadalajara, had left his tennis bag in a Mexican Army car which had been commandeered by General Santoyo and his aides when they set off on the raid. Bachelier recovered the bag the next day. His money was in his wallet, but pictures of his wife Nancy and their four children were missing.

On November 10, Nancy Bachelier and a woman friend were walking through a park in Guadalajara when they encountered two men. The women sensed they were being followed and left the park. The two men approached them on the sidewalk, one waving as if he knew them. The women dashed to their car. Looking at mug shots, Nancy Bachelier identified the man who had waved. He looked very much like Miguel Angel Félix Gallardo. The family was pulled out of Guadalajara.

All this was hushed up by the U.S. embassy and the State Department. Once more, political considerations were paramount. DEA officials in Washington were admonished to keep silent, for fear of embarrassing the Mexican government. When a reporter heard about the raid anyway and made inquiries, U.S. Ambassador Charles Pilliod issued a terse response which essentially exonerated the Mexican government: "Unfortunately, just as in previous operations in Mazatlán, the traffickers did not appear. While this was disappointing to all involved, it was not unusual. We, along

with the Mexican authorities, have been after Felix Gallardo
for some years. He is aware of this—and has continually
managed to avoid apprehension."

In fact, the DEA field report of the incident charged that
the Army had compromised the raid and that corruption
continued to be endemic in Guadalajara. The U.S. embassy
did not disseminate the report through normal diplomatic
cable channels, not even in classified form. According to
the agent who wrote the report, his five-page account was
suppressed within the embassy for several weeks and was
circulated only after sections dealing with corruption were
deleted.

The contretemps caused DEA activities in Mexico to
come to a dead stop for the remaining weeks of the de la
Madrid administration. Officials of the attorney general's
office and the MFJP were infuriated that the DEA agents
had sought help from General Badillo instead of the MFJP.
That implied DEA did not trust the Federales—a suggestion
which the American agents did not deny. Army officials
were offended at DEA's complaints, as well. DEA agents
in Guadalajara sensed that they were being shadowed by
Army operatives.

When the Salinas government took power on December
1, the status of DEA in Mexico was extremely tenuous. In
his inaugural address, the forty-year-old Harvard-educated
technocrat, said all the right things, pledging to "pursue
with redoubled energy those who promote trafficking, wherever they may be." Salinas appointed a respected professional prosecutor, Javier Coello Trejo, to direct anti-drug
operations from a new post in the federal attorney general's
office.

But there was also plenty of bad news. Former Federal
Security Directorate Chief Miguel Nazar Haro, indicted in
San Diego in 1982 for running a stolen car ring, been named
by Salinas's aides to command the intelligence division of
the Mexico City police department. (Nazar Haro resigned
in early 1989, after U.S. congressmen and diplomats protested to Salinas.)

Manuel Bartlett Díaz was Salinas's minister of education.

As de la Madrid's interior minister, Bartlett was responsible for the DFS at the time when the DFS became deeply involved in drug trafficking. Bartlett himself was never accused publicly of involvement, but it was on his watch that corruption permeated the interior ministry. The new interior minister, Fernando Gutiérrez Barrios, who had been a senior official of the DFS and the interior ministry from the early 1950s until 1970—the period when the security police were accused of torturing and murdering political dissidents.

Salinas's attorney general was none other than Enrique Alvarez del Castillo, governor of Jalisco from 1982 to 1988, when the Guadalajara drug cartel blossomed into a superpower of the international underworld. When the Federales arrested a number of Jalisco state police officers for kidnapping Kiki Camarena and Alfredo Zavala and perpetrating the Bravo Ranch massacre, Alvarez del Castillo ignored the scandal. When DEA agent Victor Cortez was tortured by Jalisco state police officers, the governor denied that any wrongdoing had occurred. *Proceso* magazine chided Alvarez del Castillo for "manifesting indifference" earlier in 1988, when two Jalisco prison officials were assassinated by traffickers. According to *Proceso*, the governor remarked, "We are very far from resembling Colombia, because in that country the drug trade has penetrated the political system. And fortunately, our system, say what you may, is clean of that evil."[2]

Despite these troublesome signs, and despite Mexico's miserable drug enforcement record over the past year, on March 1, 1989, President Bush sent a message to Congress certifying that Mexico had "cooperated fully" on drug control. The decision was driven by Secretary of State James Baker. It had little to do with the facts and very much to do with Baker's determination to help Salinas stabilize Mexico's desperate economic situation.

Jack Lawn was not consulted about the president's drug message, but he did not object. Attorney General Dick Thornburgh meant to take a much firmer stance with Mexico than had Ed Meese. Thornburgh understood Lawn's frustrations with U.S. policy toward Mexico. He was not the sort to be seduced by toasts and promises. And he was no diplomat. Thornburgh was not averse to compromise, but he drove a hard bargain, a prosecutor's bargain. Meese, endlessly conciliatory, had sought friendship. Thornburgh, short-tempered and acid-tongued, demanded respect. He delayed meeting with Attorney General Alvarez del Castillo until mid-April when, he said pointedly, he hoped to see some tangible progress on the drug front.

A week before his session with Thornburgh, Alvarez del Castillo produced results of a stunning kind: Miguel Angel Félix Gallardo, clapped in irons, was paraded before the press.

As Alvarez del Castillo told the story, at about ten-thirty on Saturday morning, April 8, a team of MFJP agents burst into a house in Guadalajara's fashionable Jardines del Bosque district. Félix Gallardo was in his pajamas, at breakfast with his wife and two small children. No shots were fired. The Federales had observed that the *pistoleros* went out for breakfast between nine and eleven every morning, so they simply waited for an opening.

The raid was sanctioned by Deputy Attorney General Javier Coello Trejo and carried out by MFJP comandante Guillermo González Calderoni, head of a special team of Federales based in Mexico City. In early 1989, González Calderoni installed taps on Félix Gallardo's telephones. At the same time Coello Trejo asked Jack Lawn to assign Tony Ayala, former DEA agent in charge in Guadalajara, to the project. Through Ayalla, Gonzalez Calderoni gained access to DEA intelligence on the godfather's movements. Coello Trejo, and Lawn prevented leaks by keeping the project secret from most officials of the Mexican attorney general's office and the MFJP, and, as well, from U.S. Ambassador Pilliod and DEA attaché Ed Heath.

Trotted out to meet the press, Félix Gallardo looked like a sick man. Alvarez del Castillo explained that he had been using a lot of cocaine and had ulcers: when the Federales moved in, the forty-three-year-old billionaire had been holding an intravenous bottle filled with glucose and water. The godfather's ulcers probably stung when he heard that the Federales were preparing to seize $900 million worth of his properties, including twenty-five houses, seven ranches, some hotels, and numerous bank accounts.

The capture of Félix Gallardo was a great political coup for Carlos Salinas—a fact which led critics to suggest that the timing of the arrest was not accidental. The capture of DEA's most wanted man assured the success of the "law enforcement summit" between Thornburgh and Alvarez del Castillo. It headed off a Senate Foreign Relations Committee vote on a resolution by Senator Jesse Helms to reject the Bush administration's certification of Mexico. It earned a letter of commendation from sixty-seven members of Congress. Most important, from Mexico's point of view, Salinas enjoyed a week of tough-guy headlines, just as he was negotiating with the international lending institutions for better terms for Mexico's debt repayments.

In truth, there was less to the godfather's downfall than met the eye. The system was still very much in place. There were the usual arrests of provincial cops. The day Félix Gallardo was captured, a second team of Federales went into Sinaloa and detained Culiacán City Police Chief Robespierre Lizarraga Coronel, state police chief Arturo Moreno Espiñosa, three federal highway police commanders and Gregorio Enrique Corza Marín, the federal attorney general's representative in the state. Alvarez del Castillo told reporters that Félix Gallardo had admitted paying them off.

"Lamentably, there are officers who err and betray our confidence," the Mexican attorney general said. "The orders we have from President Salinas are to press on, regardless of where this leads."

Perhaps, but most Mexicans and Americans who knew about the drug situation in Mexico believed that Félix Gallardo could incriminate a good cross section of Mexico's power elite. As the weeks passed, there were no signs that the Félix Gallardo case was leading to a break in the Camarena case, nor to a Watergate-style investigation of ties between the ruling party and the trafficking organizations. In an interrogation session which DEA agents were permitted to observe, Félix Gallardo denied that he had had anything to do with the death of Camarena. Why had a

picture of Camarena been found at his house? He did not
know. DEA must have planted it. Who ordered Kiki Camarena killed, and why? He did not know. Like all the
others in custody, he did not know. Consequently, the Mexican attorney general's office declined to charge Félix Gallardo in the Camarena case.

For the DEA, it was disappointing, but not surprising,
when the godfather's interrogators failed to come up with
fresh leads in the Camarena case. Dale Stinson, who had
been the Leyenda case agent in the DEA Mexico City office,
remembered what an interior ministry official had said
shortly after Camarena's body was found: the Mexican government could never afford to unravel the mystery, so inex-
tricably intertwined were the interests of the traffickers and
elements of the government controlled by entrenched and
corrupt power brokers. "For you, this is a drug investigation," the man had explained. "For us, it is a matter of
national security."

Still, Camarena's friends did not abandon hope that the
truth would come out some day. President Salinas seemed
intent on wresting power away from the corrupt old guard
of the Institutional Revolutionary Party and displayed a
remarkable degree of political courage in prosecuting officials who had been considered untouchable. On June 13,
Salinas astonished the cynics by ordering the arrest of José
Antonio Zorrilla Pérez, the former director of the Federal
Security Directorate (DFS). Zorrilla was Mr. National Security during the de la Madrid years. Most Mexicans believed that Zorrilla knew more about the ruling party's dirty
linen than nearly any other man in Mexico.

Captured after two hundred policemen surrounded his
hideout near Mexico City, Zorrilla was charged with being
the "intellectual author" of the assassination of Manuel
Buendia, a prominent Mexican journalist who had been
gunned down on May 4, 1984. Buendia's colleagues had
long contended that the murder was the work of a police
death squad because Buendia died while investigating drug-
related corruption within the DFS. Within minutes of the

shooting in Mexico City's Zona Rosa, DFS agents cleaned out Buendia's files, and Zorrilla himself took charge of the murder case, which remained unsolved until Salinas acted.

After Zorrilla's arrest, Mexican journalists quoting government sources reported that the investigation had determined that the former DFS chief had doled out DFS credentials to Caro Quintero, Fonseca, Félix Gallardo, and other drug traffickers. This report confirmed assertions by DEA attaché Ed Heath that Zorrilla had personally signed Caro Quintero's DFS credentials.

Meanwhile, Zorrilla had been listed as a prime target of the Leyenda Phase Two. The grand jury in Los Angeles and the DEA Leyenda team were trying to verify or discount an informant's claim that Sergio Espino Verdín, the former interior ministry comandante who had interrogated Camarena, had reported directly to Zorrilla. Even more intriguing was a detailed account by an informant about a "round table" meeting among senior Mexican police officials shortly after the kidnappings of Camarena and Zavala. As the story went, when the U.S. government put the heat on Mexico to find Camarena, seven DFS and MFJP comandantes held a strategy session at a Guadalajara hotel. It was at this meeting, the informant said, that key decisions were made that shaped the subsequent cover-up. The police officials agreed to frame the Bravo family by dumping the bodies on their ranch. The informant said that the meeting was presided over by a senior DFS comandante who had handed out twenty million pesos apiece to the other officers for "expenses." There was no claim Zorrilla was present at the "round table," but the American investigators found it hard to believe that if these events had taken place, he would not have been informed. Still another informant professed to have direct knowledge that Zorrilla had been alerted in advance to the traffickers' plan to kidnap Camarena.

Buendia had been asking many of the same questions that Camarena had asked. Buendia died soon after an interior ministry official slipped him a secret dossier allegedly detailing Zorrilla's ties to the Guadalajara cartel. Buendia's source was assassinated nine months later. Zorrilla was accused of both murders. Statements released by Zorrilla's prosecutors confirmed many of the theories held by Camarena and his partners. One prosecution witness, a former DFS captain, said that Zorrilla used to go horseback riding with Rafael Caro Quintero. The confession of a Zorrilla codefendant, former DFS zone commander Rafael Chao López, said that Chao delivered ten million pesos a month to Zorrilla on behalf of the traffickers, in a scheme orchestrated by Miguel Aldana Ibarra, then the MFJP's top drug investigator. This account, which Aldana denied, dovetailed precisely with the story Camarena had been pursuing at the time of his death: that Aldana had been the cartel's "mole" in the Mexico City police bureaucracy.

The Buendia revelations stirred a political fire storm among Mexico's intelligentsia and opposition parties. "Can it be believed that [former Interior Minister] Manuel Bartlett didn't know that [Zorrilla] was selling credentials to the narcos?" demanded Congressman Gerardo Medina Valdés, a member of the National Action Party. "José Antonio Zorrilla, distinguished PRI candidate for Congress, was he the hand or the brains? Who was behind [him]?" Noted author, Jorge G. Casteñeda, wrote in *Proceso*, "Is it realistic to accept the story that Manuel Bartlett and Miguel de la Madrid knew nothing? It is extraordinarily difficult to believe that in three and a half years since [Buendia's death], neither the interior minister nor the president of the republic found out that their old friend was one of the principle suspects in the assassination. In any case, there are few Mexicans who believe that today, and that is perhaps the worst dilemma for the current government." While it was unlikely that Salinas would allow the investigation to go to de la Madrid, clearly he could not contain the political damage by stopping at Zorrilla. There were hints that Salinas meant to sacrifice Bartlett—his former rival for the presidency, now minister of education—and possibly General Juan Arévalo Gardoqui, de la Madrid's defense minister. If Salinas dared, the Buendia affair would become Mexico's Watergate. And there was a chance, just a chance, that someone might reveal what the del la Madrid government had really known about the life and death of Kiki Camarena.

On a dusty Texas road near the Mexican border stands a modest brick building called the El Paso Intelligence Center. Though few members of the public know about EPIC, it is a vital nerve center where intelligence about drug smuggling is collected and disseminated to law enforcement officers throughout the world. On the fourth anniversary of Kiki Camarena's death, the building was dedicated to his memory. On the plaque that bears Camarena's name, there is an inscription, from a poem by Nathalia Crane called "The Colors," which speaks to every many and woman who passes by.

> You cannot choose your battlefield.
> The gods do that for you.
> But you can plant a standard
> where a standard never flew.

Notes

Chapter 1: "The *Comandante* Wants to See You"

1. The description of the scene at the airport, including all references to Comandante Armando Pavón Reyes and other Mexican police officials, are taken from the affidavit of special agent Salvador Leyva, filed Oct. 22, 1987, in *U.S.* v. *Rafael Caro Quintero et al.*, in the U.S. District Court for the Central District of California.

Chapter 2: Silver or Lead

1. "Colombian Cocaine: Troubles for Export," by Cecilia Rodríguez, West Coast correspondent for *El Tiempo*, in *Los Angeles Times*, Apr. 12, 1987; "Breaking Cocaine's Biological Hold," *NIDA Notes*, National Institute on Drug Abuse, Rockville, Md., June 1987.

2. David A. Stockman, *The Triumph of Politics* (New York: Harper & Row, 1986), p. 140.

3. Dr. Agnew's catarrh powder was one-third pure cocaine. A 1905 advertisement for Coca-Cola boasted that the tonic "relieves mental and physical exhaustion and is the favorite drink for ladies when thirsty—weary—despondent." A cocaine wine called Vin Mariani was endorsed by President William McKinley, Thomas Edison, and Pope Leo XIII.

4. David F. Musto, *The American Disease* (New Haven and London, 1973).

5. Ibid.

6. A report of the House Ways and Means Committee, issued in support of the Marijuana Tax Act, asserted:

> Under the influence of this drug, the will is destroyed and all power of directing and controlling thought is lost. Inhibitions were released. As a result of these effects, it appeared from testimony produced at the hearings that many violent crimes have been and were being committed by persons under the influence of this drug. Not only is marihuana used by the hardened criminals to steel them to commit violent crimes, but it is also being placed in the hands of high-school children in the form of marihuana cigarettes by unscrupulous peddlers. Cases were cited at the hearings of school children who have been driven to crime and insanity through the

use of this drug. Its continued use results many times in impotency and insanity. [Quoted in *Marihuana, A Signal of Misunderstanding*, the Official Report of the National Commission on Marihuana and Drug Abuse (New York: New American Library, 1972), p. 131.]

7. The official U.S. government estimate for 1985 said that Americans consumed 72.3 tons of cocaine and 4,694 tons of marijuana. However, many experts believed that these figures underestimated U.S. consumption. The government did not attempt to estimate heroin consumption, which was thought to be roughly 6 tons a year. *The NNICC Report 1985–1986*, report of the National Narcotics Intelligence Consumers Committee, June 1987.

8. Until the late 1960s, many states, as well as the federal government, classified marijuana as a "narcotic," along with heroin, and had criminal codes with mandatory minimum sentences for those convicted of possessing any illegal drug, whether heroin or marijuana. In the federal statutes, the minimums were two years in prison for a first offense involving possession and five years' imprisonment for a first offense involving sale.

9. In 1965, according to the National Commission on Marihuana and Drug Abuse report, 523 people were arrested by federal agents for marijuana-related offenses; 90 percent were convicted and 52 percent were sent to jail, spending an average of 58 months behind bars. In 1971, of 3,323 people arrested on pot charges, just 60 percent were convicted and 28.5 percent incarcerated. The average length of sentence for those sent to jail was down to 39.9 months.

10. The National Commission on Marihuana and Drug Abuse, chaired by Raymond P. Shafer, a former Republican governor of Pennsylvania, declared that marijuana use should be considered a "victimless crime" and recommended legalizing the "private" possession of marijuana for personal use. Nixon repudiated the commission's findings, but some states decriminalized marijuana possession.

11. In early 1972, the Nixon White House had created the Office of Drug Abuse Law Enforcement (ODALE), which borrowed BNDD, Customs, IRS, and Treasury firearms agents for local task forces aimed at street heroin pushers. Later that year, the Office of National Narcotics Intelligence (ONNI) was created to serve a White House enamored of spies.

Nixon's expanding enforcement bureaucracy was widely viewed with suspicion. In April 1973, a scandal erupted. BNDD agents working with an ODALE strike force in St. Louis staged ill-planned raids and hit two innocent households in the working-class community of Collinsville, Illinois. The homeowners claimed they were abused and terrorized. Though many of those assertions were later proved to be false, the Collinsville debacle wrecked the Nixon anti-drug campaign. *The New York Times* editorialized that the incident showed the "extent to which goodness and decency have been despoiled in this country through the perversion of justice that poses as law and order." The agents and eight local officers were indicted for civil-rights violations. They were later cleared of wrongdoing.

12. The Domestic Council Drug Abuse Task Force report said: "Cocaine, as currently used, does not result in serious social consequences, such as crime, hospital emergency room admissions or death. . . . Marijuana is the least serious [drug of abuse]. . . . The task force recommends that priority in federal efforts in both supply and demand reduction be directed toward those drugs which inherently pose a greater risk to the individual and society—heroin, amphetamines (particularly when used intravenously), and mixed barbiturates—and toward compulsive users of any kinds." At that time, cocaine use was still infrequent; a National Institute on Drug Abuse survey in 1974 showed that 3.6 percent of teenagers between twelve and seventeen and 12.7 percent of young adults between eighteen and twenty-five had used cocaine at least once.

13. A *Washington Post* editorial called the task force's recommendations "a half step." A full step, the *Post* said, would be to support making possession of marijuana legal, or at worst a civil offense. "The president in effect gave his sanction to the idea of government's ignoring the law. That is not a good answer. About half a million Americans, mostly young people, are arrested for possession each year, almost all in local jurisdictions. Instead of telling law enforcers to ignore a law, the president would better serve the country by supporting changes in the law. . . . While we think 'decriminalization' is really a code word for a condition just short of legalization, we nonetheless think it is a choice far preferable to ignoring disagreeable laws." *Washington Post*, Jan. 2, 1976.

14. Patrick Anderson, *High in America* (New York: Viking, 1981). See also *New York Times*, Jan. 19, 1977.

15. "The Great Cocaine Myth," by Peter G. Bourne, M.D., *Drugs and Drug Abuse Education Newsletter*, August 1974.

Chapter 3: The Marijuana Border

1. Cocaine hydrochloride, a powerful stimulant and local anesthetic, was extracted from the Andean coca plant in the late 1800s and was widely manufactured in France for medicinal purposes until 1931. A great deal of the cocaine made by legitimate firms filtered into the international black market: in the 1920s, a Mexican importer acquired 1,000 half-kilo vials of cocaine from a Paris manufacturer. By 1931, according to John Cusack, a former DEA official and staff director of the House Select Committee on Narcotics, 750 of those bottles had entered the illegal market in the United States.

2. Timothy Leary, the guru of LSD, was arrested in Laredo in 1966 for trying to smuggle several ounces of marijuana through the checkpoint in his daughter's clothes. The Customs inspector at the bridge thought Leary looked strange, so he searched the car and the daughter. Leary was sentenced to five to thirty years and fined $40,000. His

conviction was overturned by the Supreme Court in 1969 on grounds that the old Marijuana Tax Act under which he was charged violated a defendant's privilege against self-incrimination. The Tax Act made it a crime to possess marijuana without paying a $100-per-ounce tax. Susan Leary, who was eighteen at the time of the seizure, was given probation.

3. Pancho Villa, the outlaw who roamed the northern Mexican border fifty years before, was a hero in all the border towns. Mexican children grew up hearing the story of Villa's successful "invasion" of the United States in 1916. In that year, Villa, who was roaming the border like a feudal warlord, raided Columbus, New Mexico, and killed sixteen American citizens. General John J. "Black Jack" Pershing and a 10,000-man expeditionary force of the U.S. Cavalry spent eleven months scouring northern Mexico in a futile effort to find and punish Villa.

4. In a hearing on July 27, 1976, Egil Krogh, a Nixon assistant who had chaired the White House domestic affairs group on law enforcement and narcotics control, described the decision-making process to the Senate Permanent Investigations Subcommittee:

> The campaign in 1968, from Mr. Nixon's view, focused on the need for much more effective law enforcement. The problem of drugs, and particularly heroin, was seen as a main contributor to the crime problem. In 1969, we received some fairly clear evidence of this linkage between the use of heroin and crime. The president had vigorously campaigned on the specific need to reduce the high level of street crime in the District of Columbia. . . . [The study of D.C. jail inmates] provided firsthand evidence of the link between drugs and crime and, accordingly, it is easier to understand why such emphasis was placed on the need to curb the smuggling and illicit distribution of narcotics.

5. Speech, July 14, 1969: "Street robberies, prostitution, even the enticing of others into addiction to drugs—an addict will reduce himself to any offense, any degradation in order to acquire the drugs he craves. However far the addict himself may fall, his offenses against himself and society do not compare with the inhumanity of those who make a living exploiting the weakness and desperation of their fellow men."

6. Speech, Sept. 18, 1972.

> Three years ago, the global heroin plague was raging almost completely out of control all over the world; time was running out for an entire generation of our children, the potential drug victims of the next few years. But then we launched our crusade to save our children, and now we can see that crusade . . . beginning to roll up some victories in country after country. . . . We are living in an age, as we all know, in the era of diplomacy, when there are times that a great nation must engage in what is called a limited war. I have rejected that principle in declaring total war against dangerous drugs. The men and women who operate the global heroin trade

are a menace not to Americans alone but to all mankind. These people are literally the slave traders of our time. They are traffickers in living death. They must be hunted to the end of the earth. . . . Our goal is the unconditional surrender of the merchants of death who traffic in heroin. Our goal is the total banishment of drug abuse from the American life. Our children's lives are what we are fighting for. Our children's future is the reason we must succeed.

Chapter 4: New Treasures of the Sierra Madre

1. Speech, Sept. 10, 1973.

2. U.S. government analysts had anticipated that the next wave would come from Southeast Asia. The Asian refiners had built up their capacity as thousands of servicemen got hooked on Golden Triangle heroin in the fleshpots of Saigon and Bangkok. But the distributors, who used the soldiers to transport the product, had not built a free-standing pipeline to the West. The Golden Triangle trade collapsed after American troops pulled out of South Vietnam.

3. DEA cable, "The Socioeconomic Impact of Drug Trafficking on the State of Durango," August 1987, from DEA-Mexico.

4. Sicilia Falcón was suspected of compromising a senior DEA official. Joe Baca, the former assistant regional director in charge of the DEA-New Orleans office, was terminated in 1976 after a DEA investigative report turned up in Sicilia Falcón's hands. Scientific tests by DEA traced that copy of the report to the New Orleans regional office. William R. Coonce, then an inspector for DEA, investigated Baca and wrote in his internal report that he had found in telephone records, credit-card charges, and travel vouchers "communications between Baca and associates of Sicilia Falcón at times coincidental to significant smuggling activities being perpetrated by principals in Sicilia's organization. These records also indicate telephone traffic from Joe Baca's residence to the residences of Sicilia Falcón and [Sicilia associate Carlos] Kyriakides-Villaseñor." Baca told DEA inspectors that most of his telephone calls to Mexico were to an MFJP agent and an ex-agent. He denied communicating with traffickers and said he had no "official interest" in the Sicilia Falcón investigation. According to the Coonce report, DEA administrator Peter Bensinger terminated Baca for failing to answer questions pertaining to his official duties and for filing false travel vouchers. Prosecutors in San Diego declined to file charges against the DEA official for lack of sufficient jurisdiction. Source: Report of investigation, Joseph J. Baca, former assistant regional director, New Orleans Regional Office, by William R. Coonce, inspector, Los Angeles, Sept. 17, 1976.

5. Anthony Marro, *Newsweek* correspondent, notes, Feb. 2, 1976.

6. In late 1975, Senate president pro-tem Mike Mansfield drafted an amendment that would have far-reaching implications for DEA operations abroad. The Mansfield amendment, approved by the Con-

gress in June 1976, said: "Notwithstanding any other provision of law, no officer or employee may engage or participate in any direct police action in any foreign country with respect to narcotics control efforts."

On its face, this language seemed to do nothing more than emphasize the obvious: DEA agents could not arrest people in a foreign country, anyway. The provision did not prohibit the DEA or any other agency from passing on intelligence, hiring informants, or acting as advisers. But DEA agents stationed abroad felt shackled. Agency guidelines decreed that an agent could not be on the scene of an arrest; nor could he use force, except to preserve his own life or the lives of others. In practical terms, this meant that the Americans should hang back until the host police had the situation under control. DEA agents stationed in the Third World found this almost impossible to explain to their counterparts.

Travis Kuykendall, who was in Mexico from 1972 to 1978, put it this way: "If you're going to go into a country like Mexico, convince them to go out and eradicate drugs and make arrests, and that country doesn't even recognize the problem, how are you going to tell five Mexican policemen to go out there and arrest that big trafficker, he's got thirty armed guards, and I'm going to stay here in the office, and if you do it, I'll buy you a cup of coffee? It didn't work. The greatest motivator was that *we* were willing to go out and risk our own rear ends for our country. The Mexicans said, You guys are not serious about this. They lost faith in us. They didn't go. They started lying, and they started taking money."

7. "Mexico Net Is Catching Few Top Cops," by Sam Dillon. *Miami Herald*, July 5, 1985.

Chapter 5: Colombian Gold

1. Quoted in testimony by Keith Stroup, national director, the National Organization for the Reform of Marijuana Laws, before the Senate Subcommittee on Foreign Assistance, May 9, 1978.

2. Mexico's share of the U.S. marijuana market dropped to 11 percent, by the federal government's 1979 estimate. That year, Jamaica was said to account for a 7 percent share, and domestic marijuana another 7 percent. The National Narcotics Intelligence Consumers Committee estimated that U.S. consumers bought 10,000 to 13,600 metric tons of marijuana in 1979.

3. In 1978, the Banco de la República, the central bank, reported that Colombian exports had brought $924 million in hard currency into the country the previous year, but only $100 million could be accounted for by legitimate business. Of the rest, perhaps $200 million was attributed to illegal coffee deals, another $200 million to miscellaneous contraband, and $400 million was attributed to the drug trade. Experts estimated that another $600 million generated by drugs was banked in offshore havens. "High Profits," *Time*, Sept. 17, 1979.

4. An editorial in *El Tiempo* said: "To militarize the Guajira is

equal to declaring a state of war with all its risks and dangers. Unhappily the serious situation which results is similar to when a sick person needs an operation to save his life. The sickness [in Mexico and in the Guajira] has similar symptoms, and the remedy, of course, should be equal."

5. The DEA contributed $1.7 million, sent four radar operators to the Guajira, and put together an intelligence package listing suspect boats, airplanes, and people. More DEA agent-advisers were assigned to Colombia, South Florida, and the Bahamas.

6. "The Colombian Connection," *Time*, Jan. 29, 1979.

7. "Colombian Government Ends Unsuccessful Drive to Halt Marijuana Smuggling to U.S.," by Warren Hoge, *New York Times*, Apr. 3, 1980.

8. By 1980, DEA analysts calculated, there were 3,000 top-level traffickers in Colombia and nearly 70,000 other people involved at lower levels of the marijuana and cocaine businesses. In Peru and Bolivia probably several hundred thousand people were engaged in the production of coca paste and base.

9. "Organized Crime and the Use of Violence," hearings, Senate Permanent Investigations Subcommittee, Government Printing Office, Washington, D.C., May 5, 1980, p. 497.

10. The Posse Comitatus statute was passed during Reconstruction to prevent the use of troops to enforce the law in the South.

11. New studies had contradicted the data upon which the Carter administration had relied in assessing paraquat a serious health risk to marijuana smokers. On the basis of further tests, the United Nations laboratory recommended paraquat for spraying opium and marijuana fields. American farmers used paraquat widely as a crop herbicide; ironically, according to a Nov. 18, 1980, article in *The Washington Post*, the state of Oregon, where opposition to anti-marijuana laws was strongest, was using paraquat on weeds that threatened the peppermint crop.

12. Joe Biden's drug czar bill became the centerpiece of an anti-crime legislative package which passed in the closing days of 1982. Objecting to the drug czar concept on bureaucratic and constitutional grounds, Reagan vetoed the entire crime package in January 1983. As Biden and his allies regrouped, the White House proposed a compromise, a National Drug Policy Board, which would be chaired by the attorney general. Biden did not like the idea but did not want to appear unreasonable, so he went along on condition that the Congress get regular progress reports. The rest of the package was resubmitted, expanded, and renamed the Comprehensive Crime Control Act. It would be signed into law in 1984.

13. Mullen wrote:

False credit claimed by NNBIS spokesmen demoralizes the personnel working for a number of federal agencies whose bona fide accomplishments either go unrecognized or are related to unwise overemphasis on NNBIS and the South Florida Task Force interdiction programs. . . . NNBIS has made no material contribution to the administration's interdiction efforts—nor should it. Yet the credits claimed by NNBIS create the impression that NNBIS is operational in virtually all aspects of drug law enforcement. Such impressions, reinforced by unbridled activities of NNBIS regional coordinators as well as Admiral Murphy, are confusing foreign, state, and local law-enforcement officials. . . . Contrary to public statements that NNBIS will not require new resources, that it is a mere coordinating mechanism and not a bureaucratic layer, it is expensive and diverts between 100 and 200 personnel. . . . Combined with the fact that many of its functions are duplicative, NNBIS costs are a real liability. In draining resources from Customs, DEA, FBI, and Coast Guard, many interdiction functions normally carried out by those agencies, such as cargo and border inspections, intelligence collection, and the deployment of fully maintained Coast Guard cutters, are suffering.

14. "Director of Federal Drug Agency Calls Reagan Program 'Liability,' " by Joel Brinkley, *New York Times*, May 13, 1984.

15. Hearing, Senate Committee on Appropriations, May 25, 1984.

16. "Coordination of Federal Drug Interdiction Efforts," General Accounting Office, July 15, 1985.

17. House Subcommittee on Government Operations, Dec. 17, 1987.

18. "Brutal Cocaine Bosses Terrorize Colombia," *Miami Herald*, Feb. 8, 1987.

19. Ibid.

20. "At Its Peak, Drug Cartel Was Untouchable," *Miami Herald*, Feb. 9, 1987.

21. "Cocaine Billionaires," by Alan Riding, *The New York Times Magazine*, Mar. 8, 1987.

22. NBC news, Brian Ross, Mar. 18, 1987.

23. "Scandal in the Bahamas," by Spencer Reiss with Linda R. Prout, *Newsweek*, Feb. 6, 1984.

24. Royal commission of inquiry report, p. 351; NBC news, Brian Ross, Mar. 18, 1987.

25. "Scandal in the Bahamas," by Spencer Reiss with Linda R. Prout, *Newsweek*, Feb. 6, 1984, p. 6.

26. Nottage and another cabinet minister who had been a focus of the commission of inquiry report resigned but were not successfully prosecuted. Pindling stepped up drug enforcement by allowing Bahamian policemen to work in a joint project called OPBAT (Operation Bahamas and Turks and Caicos), in which U.S. Air Force helicopters ferried Bahamian and U.S. lawmen to out islands used by smugglers. He gave Customs pilots the right to fly through Bahamian airspace in pursuit of smuggler planes and allowed the U.S. government to moor a radar balloon on Grand Bahama Island. Still, U.S. officials were not convinced he was doing all he could against corruption. In its "Inter-

national Narcotics Control Strategy Report" for 1987, the State Bureau of International Narcotics Matters criticized the Pindling government for being "slow" to respond to the recommendations of the 1984 commission of inquiry. The report said that "widespread narcotics corruption . . . threatens to undermine the cooperation we now enjoy, as well as the very fabric of Bahamian society."

27. "At Its Peak, Drug Cartel Was Untouchable," *Miami Herald*, Feb. 9, 1987.

28. "America's Habit: Drug Abuse, Drug Trafficking, and Organized Crime," Report of the President's Commission on Organized Crime, Government Printing Office, Washington, D.C., March 1986, p. 102.

Chapter 6: The Guadalajara Cartel

1. In December 1980 the Associated Press moved a dispatch datelined Culiacán that began: "Mexico claims that it has virtually wiped out its once-huge homegrown marijuana and heroin trade with the United States through the use of the latest in electronic surveillance and herbicides."

2. Money handlers for the Mexican drug rings often brought cash through the Tijuana–San Ysidro crossing. Money couriers declared $1 billion yearly at the U.S. Customs checkpoints. Customs agents figured that another billion dollars, at least, was coming through covertly. Just inside the United States in San Ysidro, there were block after block of bank branches and *cambios*, money exchange houses. The San Diego Customs office had a special team of agents who spent full-time working money-laundering investigations. They staked out the *cambios* and jotted down license plates. They ran through computer printouts of customs declarations and currency transaction reports filed by financial institutions, looking for patterns that fit the profile of a drug-money-laundering operation. Late-model sedans that pulled up in the middle of the night often belonged to Mexican police officers and local politicians. The couriers for the drug gangs could be Mexicans or American subcontractors: money laundering had become a profitable cottage industry in San Diego.

3. If Félix Gallardo's bagmen had arrived at the Bank of America with duffel bags full of cash, the bank would have been required by the federal Bank Secrecy Act to file currency transaction reports (CTRs) with the Treasury Department. The law covers deposits and withdrawals of more than $10,000 in cash (and negotiable instruments, such as cashier's checks in bearer form). However, wire transfers from foreign institutions were exempt from the reporting requirements. The bank was not required to file reports on the cashier's checks when the money was withdrawn because they were not drafted in bearer form.

4. Hearings, House Select Committee on Narcotics Abuse and Control, Government Printing Office, Washington, D.C., June 22, 1983.

5. "International Narcotics Control Study Missions to Latin Amer-

ica and Jamaica, Hawaii, Hong Kong, Thailand, Burma, Pakistan, Turkey and Italy," House Select Committee on Narcotics Abuse and Control, Government Printing Office, Washington, D.C., Aug. 2, 1984, p. 2.

6. The undercover meeting between Enrique Camarena and Manuel Chávez is described in an affidavit by DEA agent James Kuykendall which was filed Oct. 9, 1987, in the U.S. District Court for the Central District of California, in *United States of America* v. *Rafael Caro Quintero et al.*

Chapter 7: "War without Quarter"

1. "The Soccer-and-Drugs Scandal," *Newsweek*, Nov. 21, 1983, p. 35.

2. *The New York Times*, quoted in the testimony of Thomas O. Enders, assistant secretary of state for inter-American affairs, in "The Role of Cuba in International Terrorism and Subversion," Subcommittee on Security and Terrorism, Senate Judiciary Committee, Mar. 4, 1982.

3. "Country Reports on Human Rights Practices for 1983," Department of State, Government Printing Office, Washington, D.C., February 1984, p. 508.

4. "America's Habit: Drug Abuse, Drug Trafficking, and Organized Crime," report of the President's Commission on Organized Crime, Government Printing Office, Washington, D.C., March 1986, p. 102.

5. "Developments in Latin American Narcotics Control, November 1985 hearing, House Committee on Foreign Affairs, Government Printing Office, Washington, D.C., Nov. 12, 1985, p. 58.

6. "Drugs and Terrorism," hearing, Senate Subcommittee on Alcoholism and Drug Abuse, Government Printing Office, Washington, D.C., Aug. 2, 1984, p. 18.

7. "Organized Crime and Cocaine Trafficking," hearing, President's Commission on Organized Crime, Government Printing Office, Washington, D.C., November 1984.

8. The embassy cable attributed the statement to a FARC deserter, according to new reports. A later DEA statement attributed the allegation to a pilot who had been kidnapped by FARC forces.

9. "Huge Coke Bust Was Like Invasion," by George Stein, *Miami Herald*, Mar. 22, 1984.

10. "International Narcotics Control Strategy, 1985," report of the State Department Bureau of International Narcotics Control.

11. Seal testified about his activities for the Medellín cartel before the President's Commission on Organized Crime on Oct. 7, 1985.

12. "Crackdown Put Cartel on the Run," *Miami Herald*, Feb. 10, 1987.

13. "Report of the Committees Investigating the Iran-Contra Affair," Government Printing Office, Washington, D.C., November 1987.

14. William O'Boyle testified at a hearing of the Committees Investigating the Iran-Contra Affair on May 21, 1987.

15. Hearing, Senate Subcommittee on Terrorism, Narcotics, and International Communications, Feb. 8, 1988.

16. "Colombians' Bank Seized by Panama," *Miami Herald*, Mar. 13, 1985; "Issues in United States–Panamanian Anti-Narcotics Control," House Foreign Affairs Committee, Government Printing Office, Washington, D.C., June 19, 1986, p. 24.

17. "Colombia's Drug Kings Want a Deal," by David Marcus and Nery Ynclán, *Miami Herald*, July 23, 1984.

18. "Issues in United States–Panamanian Anti-Narcotics Control," House Foreign Affairs Committee, Government Printing Office, Washington, D.C., June 19, 1986, p. 56.

19. "Crackdown Put Cartel on the Run," *Miami Herald*, Feb. 10, 1987.

20. "Scandals Hint at Panama Role in Drug Trade," by Guy Gugliotta, *Miami Herald*, Sept. 3, 1984.

21. Hearing, Feb. 8, 1988, Senate Subcommittee on Terrorism, Narcotics, and International Communications.

22. Ibid.

23. "Crackdown Put Cartel on the Run," *Miami Herald*, Feb. 10, 1987.

24. Marcos Cadavid was convicted of selling and distributing narcotics and sentenced to fifteen years in jail and a fine of $25,000 in Washington, D.C. Hernán Botero Moreno was convicted of conspiracy to defraud the United States. His case is on appeal in Miami, Florida. In 1986, Ricardo Pavón Jatter was convicted of conspiracy to defraud the United States and was sentenced to seven years in prison and ordered to pay a $50,000 fine and one third the cost of prosecution. Said Pavón Jatter was convicted of conspiracy to defraud the United States, sentenced to seven years, and ordered to pay a $50,000 fine.

25. Lehder said: "I believe in Adolf as an admirable warrior. He is the greatest warrior in history. With his army he killed 21 million communists in a frontal assault on a communist nation. He also eradicated the Jews, who tried to kill him. There were never more than one million Jews in Germany. And they died only working in the fields and the factories during the war."

26. According to reports in the Colombian press, in December 1984, M-19 leader Marino Ospina announced that M-19 approved of the drug traffickers' death threats against Betancur and his aides. Ospina said that if he was elected president, he would negotiate with the traffickers to use their money for the nation's benefit.

27. "A Battle with No Holds Barred in a Colombian Court Building," *New York Times*, Nov. 19, 1985; "Colombia's Future: More Violence?," by Alan Riding, *New York Times*, Dec. 12, 1985; Parejo quoted in "Colombia Mourns Dead in Siege," by Martin McReynolds, *Miami Herald*, Nov. 9, 1985.

28. "Colombia Rebel Guns Linked to Sandinistas," Associated Press, in *Miami Herald*, Jan. 5, 1986.

29. Ibid.

30. "Human Rights in Colombia as President Barco Begins," Americas Watch, 36 West 44th Street, New York, NY 10036, September 1986; "El Presidente No Actuó Irregularmente," *El Espectador*, June 17, 1986; "Crackdown Put Cartel on the Run," *Miami Herald*, Feb. 10, 1987.

Chapter 8: "Does Somebody Have to Die?"

1. James D. Rudolph, ed., *Mexico: A Country Study* (Washington, D.C.: U.S. Government Printing Office, 1985), p. 363.

2. Alan Riding, *Distant Neighbors* (New York: Alfred A. Knopf, 1985), p. 103.

3. Thirty-eight people were indicted in two indictments filed in the Operation Cargo case, including twenty-four present or former Mexican officials. Fifteen people pleaded guilty. The rest were listed as fugitives.

The first indictment, dated July 21, 1981, charged twenty-eight men with conspiracy, interstate and foreign transportation of stolen vehicles, and aiding and abetting. Among those indicted were thirteen men identified as having DFS ties: *comandantes* and ex-*comandantes* Estéban Guzmán, Jaime Alcalá, Ramón Peseros, Javier García [Morales], and Guillermo Lira; DFS agents or employees Ricardo Rodríguez, Juventino Prado, Marín Arrambide Davila, Jaime Garza Garza, Raúl Pérez Carmona, Santiago Torres, and Enrique Castillo; and former DFS agent Cipriano Rodríguez. The indictment also charged two men identified as Mexican Customs officials, Francisco Arredondo and (first name unknown) Veytia, and a man identified as an official of the Mexican Registro Federal de Automóviles, Ramón Rangel.

The indictment said that "various agents and employees" of DFS "would place orders for specific makes and models of automobiles with other agents within the force, whose job it was to procure the desired vehicles. Numerous Mexican Dirección Federal de Seguridad agents including *comandantes* and ex-*comandantes* defendants Jaime Alcalá, Ramón Peseros, and Javier García have placed such orders. . . . Various agents of the Mexican Dirección Federal de Seguridad . . . would employ defendant Gilberto Peraza Mayén to steal the desired vehicles from new car sales agencies and service departments in the United States at locations as far north as San Francisco, California, and as far east as San Antonio, Texas. . . . Agents of the [DFS] would normally accompany the stolen vehicles from the United States across the border into Mexico and use their official credentials and contacts so that the transportation of vehicles would be unimpeded. The stolen vehicles would then be transported to various locations in Mexico . . . for sale to various people, including [DFS] agents and officials and other prominently placed individuals, for far below market value. Many of the stolen vehicles would be stored in parking lots controlled by the Mexican Dirección Federal de Seguridad in Mexico City."

The second indictment, filed Apr. 29, 1982, indicted twenty-one people, thirteen fugitives charged in the first indictment and eight additional people, all of whom were identified as present or former Mexican government officials. The most prominent of the new names was Miguel Nazar Haro, former director of the DFS. Other officials charged for the first time were DFS agents Jorge Fernández, Javier Bustos Alcalá, Amado Cruz, (first name unknown) Get; MFJP officers Carlos and Ernesto Otal; Mexican Highway Patrol Comandante Carlos Solís. Charges against Solís were dismissed. Cipriano Rodríguez died.

4. Affidavit of FBI supervisor Thomas J. Summers, Jr., filed in U.S. District Court in San Diego, July 15, 1981.

5. "CIA Intervenes to Block Charges in Car Theft Case," by Jon Standefer, *San Diego Union*, Mar. 26, 1982.

6. "Rafael Aguilar Beats Drug Rap," by Terrence Poppa, *El Paso Herald-Post*, Jan. 29, 1988.

7. The conflict between the DEA and the CIA was unusually sharp in Mexico but was hardly unique. There had been more than thirty years of bad blood between the agencies, going back to the Cold War. Differences in class, education, and upward mobility played their part in breeding a familiar contempt between the bureaucracies, but the fundamental problem was that one man's source was another man's target. Smugglers went places most people could not go and made attractive intelligence assets. At the other end of the social scale were the cabinet ministers, generals, and secret-police commanders with whom intelligence officers formed alliances. In the Third World, it was normal, even expected, that such officials would supplement their meager salaries by selling protection. From La Paz to Peshawar, the agencies were constantly at cross purposes: intelligence officers were paying people that narcotics agents were trying to lock up.

The most aggravated conflicts occurred in Southeast Asia. When communist forces took power in mainland China in 1949, remnants of General Chiang Kai-shek's nationalist forces were pushed into northern Burma and Thailand. Well into the 1980s, the marooned nationalists, known as the Third and Fifth Chinese Irregular Forces, helped the CIA gather intelligence on mainland China. To support themselves, the irregulars began refining opium from the Burma poppy fields. By the 1960s, they dominated the Golden Triangle heroin trade, distributing their product through Chinese associates in Bangkok and Hong Kong.

In the early 1960s, the CIA launched a secret war, hiring Laotian military officers and hill tribesmen to fight the communist Pathet Lao guerrillas. They had no efficient means to run their opium to the low country until Air America, the CIA proprietary, began airlifting military supplies into the mountainous interior. Although Air America's official policy forbade smuggling, there was considerable evidence that some pilots and crews looked the other way.

After the fall of South Vietnam, the CIA and the National Security Agency expanded their facilities in Bangkok and Chiang Mai in northern Thailand to monitor military and political activity in Vietnam, Laos, southern China, and northern Burma. The smugglers were natural allies. DEA agents who served in Southeast Asia in the late 1970s and 1980s said they frequently discovered that they were tracking heroin smugglers who were on the CIA payroll.

8. On July 12, 1984, Kuykendall filed this report:

Guadalajara remains the safe haven for major narcotics traffickers in Mexico. They continue to buy property ranging from empty lots through luxury homes, to hotels and restaurants. Violence within the narcotics-trafficking community has reached alarming proportions and could threaten their protection here from state and federal officials. Marijuana cultivations continue to be reported in all areas under the responsibility of the Guadalajara Resident Office. Opium poppies are reported in large numbers in Zacatecas, Nayarit, and Jalisco. Cocaine trafficking through Guadalajara is on the 1,000-kilo-per-month scale. This is not new, but available information now confirms it.

9. "International Narcotics Control," hearing, House Select Committee on Narcotics Abuse and Control, Government Printing Office, Washington, D.C., June 27, 1984, p. 37.

10. Ibid, p. 6.

11. "In the Drug War, Battles Won and Lost," by Joel Brinkley, *New York Times*, Sept. 13, 1984.

12. "U.S. Narcotics Control Programs Overseas: An Assessment," House Foreign Affairs Committee, Government Printing Office, Washington, D.C., Feb. 22, 1985, p. 38.

13. The announcement of Operation Vanguard should have alerted the Congressional committees and the press that the Mexican program was in trouble. Embassy officials knew this and devoted a good deal of attention to disguising the reasons for the new monitoring project. At one point, embassy officers prepared a list of anticipated questions and suggested answers for Gavin that were a masterpiece of bureaucratic obfuscation. If asked why independent verification was necessary, Gavin should blame "better methods of cultivation and year-round planting and harvesting." Ortega Padilla could be described as a sort of efficiency expert. The candid answer, as a DEA agent who participated in the negotiations put it, would have been: "We're tired of the bullshit. We don't believe the Mexican government is really eradicating the fields." Gavin was not put to the test. Like the Congress, the Mexico City press corps ignored the whole issue.

14. On May 6, 1986, Tomás Valles Corral and Mardoqueo Alfaro

Margariño were indicted by a federal grand jury in Laredo, Texas, for federal currency reporting violations. On Aug. 28, 1985, Alfaro and Valles were indicted by a federal grand jury in Phoenix for conspiring with Miguel Angel Félix Gallardo, Juan Ramón Matta Ballesteros, and sixteen others to traffic in cocaine.

15. "U.S. Narcotics Control Programs Overseas: An Assessment," House Committee on Foreign Affairs, Government Printing Office, Washington, D.C., Feb. 22, 1985, p. 34.

16. *"Drogas y Corrupción: Habla un ex-Jefe de la Judicial Federal,"* by Elisa Robledo, *Contenido*, August 1985, pp. 28–40.

17. "Unsolved Slaying an Issue in Mexico Campaign," by Dan Williams, *Los Angeles Times*, May 21, 1987.

Chapter 9: The Search for Kiki Camarena

1. "U.S. Drug Agent Kidnapped," by Richard J. Meislin, *New York Times*, Feb. 12, 1984.

2. The cable read:
All persons, vehicles, and small aircraft entering the U.S. from Mexico must be given a thorough U.S. Customs and INS inspection. All entering persons must be carefully interviewed and screened to identify and apprehend any of the suspects involved in the kidnapping of DEA agent Camarena. Particularly, DEA request inquiry be made of any persons arriving specifically from Guadalajara, Jalisco, Mexico, and determine if they can provide any information on this investigation.

3. "United States–Mexican Cooperation in Narcotics Control Efforts," House Foreign Affairs Committee, July 17, 1986, p. 30.

Chapter 10: The Bodies at the Bravo Ranch

1. "Body of DEA Agent Is Found in Mexico," by William A. Orme, Jr., *Washington Post*, Mar. 7, 1985.

Chapter 11: Cover-up

1. Neither MFJP director Manuel Ibarra Herrera nor any other member of the Federales was formally charged in the United States or Mexico with charges relating to the escape of Matta. Comandante Armando Pavón Reyes was convicted in Mexico of intending to accept a bribe from Rafael Caro Quintero and was indicted in Los Angeles for conspiring with Caro Quintero to aid his escape after the fact of the murder. As of Apr. 1, 1988, no other member of the Federales had been charged with crimes relating to obstruction of justice in the Camarena case either in Mexico or in the United States.

Ibarra left the MFJP in the summer of 1985 after DEA and Justice Department officials complained to Attorney General Sergio García Ramírez about his handling of the Matta Ballesteros arrest and his general conduct of the search.

On Sept. 10, 1985, Attorney General Sergio García Ramírez announced that MFJP Comandante Alfonso Velázquez Hernández, six MFJP agents, and one Durango state policeman were charged with abuse of qualified homicide and abuse of authority for the manner in which they killed Manuel Bravo Cervantes and his sons Manuel and Hugo Bravo Segura. (No one was charged with a crime in the death of Señora Bravo.) No Federales were charged with framing the Bravo family or attempting to use the Bravo family in an effort to cover up the circumstances of Camarena's murder.

2. "Official Corruption Fuels Growing Mexico Drug Trade," by Juan O. Tamayo, *Miami Herald*, Mar. 24, 1985.

3. "Mexico Holds 6 Policemen in DEA Agent's Death" by William A. Orme, *Washington Post*, Mar. 15, 1985.

4. Statement issued by Gavin's office, Mar. 15, 1985.

5. "Shultz, Mexican Minister Meet," by Joanne Omang, *Washington Post*, Mar. 12, 1985.

6. Between 1975 and 1988, the United States gave $140 million to Mexico for eradication projects, more narcotics aid than to any other nation. The fiscal 1986 State Department budget proposal contained $10.1 million for Mexico, a 13 percent increase over the previous year. The fiscal 1987 budget slated Mexico for $11.3 million, another 12 percent increase. Although many congressmen expressed intense frustration at the way Mexican officials responded to the Camarena kidnapping, no one on Capitol Hill was willing to fight to reduce Mexico's share of the State narcotics aid budget. As a House legislative aide put it, "The perception is that eradication aid benefits us, that it is more important to the United States than to the Mexicans, that we would be shooting ourselves in the foot."

7. "5 Indicted in Killing of Judge; 3-year Inquiry Ends in Texas," by Mack Sisk, Associated Press, in *Philadelphia Inquirer*, Apr. 16, 1982.

8. Harrelson had been released from prison in 1978 after serving time for the 1973 contract murder of a Texas grain dealer. "Convicted Killer, Two Others Guilty in Slaying of Federal Judge in Texas," *Philadelphia Inquirer*, Dec. 15, 1982.

9. "Florida News," by Stephen K. Doig, *Miami Herald*, Feb. 4, 1983.

10. Ibid.

11. "Chagra's Defense: 15 Minutes," UPI, Feb. 3, 1983.

12. The State Department's annual human rights report for 1985, pp. 606–7, noted:

Although torture is prohibited by the Constitution, human rights organizations have charged that the police have tortured both political prisoners and those arrested for common crimes with electric shocks, often applied to the genitals; beatings; deprivation of light, food, and water, exposure to the elements and other means. . . . In the aftermath of the severe earthquakes in Mexico City which occurred in September and destroyed the Federal District Attorney

General's Office building, the local press reported that the bodies
of four Colombian prisoners were found, bearing signs of torture.
The discovery sparked inquiries from the Colombian government,
as well as other governments providing disaster relief. Also found
in the structure was the body of a criminal lawyer, Saul Ocampo,
which, it was reported, showed signs of beating and asphyxiation.
Ocampo had disappeared a week before the earthquake, on September 13. The then attorney general for the Federal District [Vic-
toria Adato de Ibarra] denied before the Justice Commission of the
Federal Chamber of Deputies that the Colombians had been tortured, and she presented forensic statements that injuries and deaths
were caused by the collapse of the building itself, though she admitted the Colombians had been arrested without warrants. On
December 3, the attorney general of the Republic [Sergio García
Ramírez] admitted that police had tortured detainees in Mexico,
although he emphasized that the practice was not "institutional-
ized." Media editorial comment on his statement was critical, ob-
serving that torture had become an established method of police
investigation, based on inefficiency, corruption, and lack of democratic controls on police bodies. On December 26, the Federal
District attorney general [Adato] resigned after being named a Supreme Court justice by President de la Madrid. Her successor stated
. . . that some bad public officials had engaged in torture, and vowed
to eliminate any such practices.

Chapter 12: The Hunt for Caro Quintero
1. Manuel Pérez Toledano, *La Otra Cara de Caro Quintero* (Mexico, D.F.: Publicaciones y Ediciones Oro, S.A., 1985), pp. 9–10.

Chapter 13: Confessions
1. "Accused Drug Trafficker Denies Kidnapping Agent," by William A. Orme, Jr., *Washington Post*, Apr. 10, 1985.
2. Manuel Pérez Toledano, *La Otra Cara de Caro Quintero* (Mexico, D.F.: Publicaciones y Ediciones Oro, S.A., 1985).
3. Ibid.
4. "Mexico Accuses 2 Former Security Chiefs over Amassed
Wealth; 427 Agents Fired," by Juan M. Vasquez, *Los Angeles Times*,
June 7, 1985.
5. Ibid.
6. Affidavit of Special Agent Michael P. Malone, Oct. 13, 1987,
filed in *United States of America* v. *Rafael Caro Quintero, Inés Calderón
Quintero, Armando Pavón Reyes,* no. cr. 87-422, U.S. District Court
for the Central District of California.

Chapter 14: The Secrets of Primavera Park
1. "Disappearances Tied to Drug Case, Families of Missing Men
Told of Beatings," Associated Press, in *Houston Post*, Apr. 14, 1985.

2. "Brutal Slaying of 2 Americans in Mexico Appears Forgotten," by Jerry Seper, *Washington Times*, Aug. 25, 1986.

Chapter 15: The Camarena Tapes

1. On Apr. 17, 1985, by coincidence the day that Jack Lawn confirmed the existence of the Camarena tapes, a *Washington Post* editorial praised the de la Madrid government's commitment to drug enforcement, noting that "however tragic, the first death of a DEA agent took place in a 'war' that has cost the lives of hundreds of Mexican soldiers and police," exhorting the American government to be "more responsive to Mexico's concerns" and "sensitive to the requirement on Mexican politicians not to be seen to be pushed around."

2. Alan Riding, *Distant Neighbors* (New York: Alfred A. Knopf, 1985), p. 326.

3. "Foreign Assistance Legislation for Fiscal Years 1988–1989 (Part I)," hearing, House Committee on Foreign Affairs, Government Printing Office, Washington, D.C., Feb. 16, 19, and 24, 1987, p. 125.

4. Affidavit of Special Agent James Kuykendall, filed in *United States of America* v. *Rafael Caro Quintero et al.*, U.S. District Court for the Central District of California, Oct. 9, 1987.

5. De Herrera testified as a prosecution witness against Lorenzo and César Ontiveros, the brothers of reputed ringleader Gilberto Ontiveros; they were convicted for drug-trafficking offenses in a trial in El Paso in 1987. Gilberto Ontiveros was arrested in 1986, jailed in Mexico on drug-related offenses, and was awaiting sentencing in Mexico in February 1988. De Herrera testified as a prosecution witness and changed his identity by joining the federal witness protection program.

Chapter 16: "We Don't Want a *Solution!*"

1. David Westrate, chief of operations for DEA, testified concerning the destruction of the evidence before the House Foreign Affairs Committee on July 17, 1986, in a hearing called "United States–Mexican Cooperation in Narcotics Control Efforts." Westrate gave the committee a written statement, which said: "We have been told by the Mexican authorities that the body wrappings and clothing were destroyed because of their condition, but we have been provided some samples for technical examination. We still await other forensic exhibits allegedly seized by the Mexican authorities. We have also asked for the court order that the Mexican authorities refer to which ordered the destruction, but as of this date, it has not been provided to us."

2. A few days later the Mexican police suffered a worse setback. On Halloween evening, twenty-two police officers, most of them from the MFJP and the DFS, were tortured and executed by marijuana traffickers in Veracruz. The bodies were found on November 2, which is celebrated in Mexico as "the Day of the Dead." The newspapers called it the worst massacre of police officials in modern times. On top of the Contreras Subias escape, it was doubly humiliating, for the

accounts of the killings raised questions that suggested that the mission was unprofessional at least, corrupt at worst. Army officials responsible for the zone said they found it odd that the MFJP agents did not leave word with the military zone or with Mexico City that they were going on this expedition, which took them miles into the jungle. The MFJP commander did not take a radio with him or arrange for backup assistance before he set out. Two guides who escaped the slaughter said that the policemen were loading the marijuana in their boats when they were surprised by the traffickers, who started shooting at them. Florentino Ventura, who flew to Veracruz to lead the search, told reporters the twenty-two men were killed with small arms and machetes, but witnesses who saw the bodies and their trucks said that they were riddled with automatic machine-gun fire. The situation was murky but the reporters and American agents who looked into it came to suspect that the police had been trying to rip off the traffickers.

3. Verdugo filed a $110 million lawsuit against Attorney General Ed Meese and nearly every senior official in the federal criminal-justice system, claiming he was illegally kidnapped. Although the "black bag deportation," as the technique was called, was politically controversial, case law was against Verdugo. The courts had consistently ruled that the manner in which a fugitive was brought before the bar of justice was irrelevant. Judge Lawrence Irving found that Verdugo's arrest was not illegal and ordered him held without bond.

4. On July 17, 1986, at a hearing of the House Foreign Affairs Committee task force on international narcotics control, DEA operations chief David Westrate was questioned by Congressman Larry Smith, a Democrat from Florida, on the issue of letters rogatory. This exchange took place:

Smith: Has the DEA requested the United States Department of Justice to submit letters rogatory to the Mexican court asking for their assistance in producing this evidence?

Westrate: There is an issue that is being discussed as to how to proceed in certain aspects with certain requests, yes.

Smith: Has the Justice Department so far declined to transmit any such letters?

Westrate: Well, at this point, they have chosen to work together with the Attorney General's Office of Mexico on the issue first. They have selected another course of action, and not declined, but have selected another course of action. This means that we are not utilizing the letter rogatory process at this time but that can always be utilized.

Smith: We are pursuing other avenues?

Westrate: Yes, we are pursuing our needs and our requests through consultation with our Mexican counterparts.

Smith: But isn't it true that DEA has made the request at least three times to the Justice Department and has been refused at least three times to issue these letters?

Westrate: Mr. Chairman, I am not directly in the chain of command in the investigation at this time and am not dealing with the prosecutors directly, so I'm not personally familiar with how many times verbally, versus written or that type of thing. I am certainly familiar with the fact, though, that there is an issue, and a course of action has been selected for the time being, which can be changed later on. . . .

Smith: How long do you think evidence, good physical evidence, can last if, in fact, we have the same kinds of problems attendant to it as we have right now in this case. . . . Can we afford to wait forever, until some people decide they are going to cooperate? Isn't the very existence, the very usefulness, the very nature of some of this physical evidence threatened by this enormously difficult passing of time?

Westrate: . . . In this case, I don't see a problem like that; so, then, the issue is, preservation, and the Mexican government is certainly aware of our interest in these items, and we would certainly expect that they would be preserved.

5. Irving's ruling was based on previous judicial orders which held that "joint ventures" between the United States and foreign officials were subject to U.S. laws. For instance, in 1976 U.S. courts ruled in favor of a group of American dissidents living in West Germany whose telephones were the subject of warrantless taps by U.S. Army officers.

Chapter 17: Conflicts of Interest

1. Francisco Javier Caro Payán was arrested in Montreal, Canada, in June 1987 and extradited to the United States in April 1988. DEA agents said the Royal Canadian Mounted Police believed his ring was the largest supplier of marijuana to the Canadian market. The most serious charge filed against him was a continuing-criminal-enterprise count with a mandatory life sentence. DEA agents traced an estimated $17 million worth of real estate and other assets to him and his associates and filed seizure actions.

2. DEA's analysts could only guess at how much cocaine was moving over the Southwest border, but the frequency and size of seizures indicated a massive new influx of cocaine. Mexican police seizures were running at less than a ton a year, most from amateurs and gringos who tried to carry the stuff through Mexico City International Airport.

In December 1985 a DEA analyst wrote: "Ongoing intelligence operations detail numerous multihundred-kilogram loads of cocaine successfully entering the United States through Mexico with the direct assistance of corrupt Mexican government officials. Unfortunately, and after repeated requests by DEA, no viable system for interchange of information and intelligence exists in Mexico with the MFJP, perhaps for obvious reasons."

3. In September 1985, the Fraternal Order of Border Agents, an organization of active and retired DEA and Customs agents who

worked in Mexico and the Southwest, sent a letter to the House Foreign Affairs Committee which asserted:

Trained Mexican Federal agents, using the latest in radio- and scanner-equipped cars and armed with automatic weapons, have been providing transit security for huge loads of domestically produced marihuana and heroin and in-transit cocaine. Some of these agents and their drug-trafficking associates have purchased and now occupy ranches and riverside houses in Starr and Zapata counties in Texas. These places are used as havens for the drugs being successfully smuggled at night in this area.

. . . In mid-August, a large load of marihuana and cocaine was successfully smuggled below Falcon Dam in Starr county. It was so large that eighteen crossers were employed to unload it from trucks into boats on the Mexican side, cross the Rio Grande, and carry it 500 yards to a house on the U.S. side. Guards, armed with machine guns and wearing .45 caliber automatic pistols (which are lawful in Mexico only to the military and the Federal police), went first to the U.S. side and set up a perimeter defense. They then provided an armed escort to the house where it was stored.

4. The United States paid for maintenance of the eradication aircraft—but it was apparent from the sorry state of the fleet that very little maintenance work had actually been done. After their visit to Mexico in January 1985, Marian Chambers and Richard Peña of the House Foreign Affairs Committee staff wrote that they had found State's Narcotics Assistance Unit in Mexico "in a shambles" with "no adequate records to indicate how funds have been and are being spent, where commodities have gone and whether they are being used properly." One reason was that for nine months in 1984, officials in main State had been unable to recruit a director for the Mexico City unit, whose troubles had become well known within the State bureaucracy.

5. When this writer's account of the stalled eradication program was published in the Dec. 16, 1985, issue of *Newsweek* magazine, Ambassador John Gavin issued a press release denying the story and expressing "satisfaction with the conduct of the government of Mexico's anti-drug efforts." A statement attributed to Meese stressed that "positive results have been achieved and cooperation has been good" and contended that the article "did not represent the views of his department." Elliott Abrams, the assistant secretary of state for inter-American affairs, wrote a letter to the Justice Department asking for a leak investigation. Jack Lawn did not join in the disavowals. He had not been a source for the story, but after it appeared, he told reporters that it was accurate. A few months later, Gavin changed course, confirming major elements of the story and disclosing additional points of conflict.

6. "Impact of Gramm-Rudman on Federal Drug Programs," House Select Committee on Narcotics Abuse and Control, Mar. 18, 1986, p. 6.

7. The article said:

Fed up with Mexico's failure to crack down on narcotics traffic, U.S. Customs Commissioner William von Raab has privately called on the Reagan Administration to declare the entire U.S.–Mexican border a "crisis zone." Following a recent series of violent attacks on Border Patrol agents, von Raab, an outspoken hardliner on law-enforcement issues, has ordered Customs attorneys to review the agency's rules on shooting at suspected drug smugglers. And he is exploring the possibility of banning light planes in certain air corridors favored by drug runners flying out of Mexico. "We're going to take the gloves off," says von Raab. "The introduction of narcotics into the United States is a terrorist act and should be viewed as such." Pointedly declining to attend this week's summit session between top U.S. and Mexican law-enforcement officials to discuss persistent problems related to smuggling, von Raab said, "I believe I can be more productive trying to improve our defenses than going down there to sit and basically talk."

8. Hearing, House Foreign Affairs Committee, "Developments in Mexico and United States–Mexican Relations," Government Printing Office, Oct. 16, 1985.

9. "Mexico Makes a Big Drug Arrest," by James F. Clarity and Milt Freudenheim, *New York Times*, Nov. 2, 1986.

10. Having learned in a closed-door briefing of a Customs informant's allegations of cocaine trafficking against Edmundo de la Madrid, President de la Madrid's cousin, and MFJP chief Florentino Ventura, Senator Frank Murkowski, a Republican from Alaska, asked whether any of the Mexican president's relatives were involved in drug trafficking.

"I would have no comment on that in a public hearing," von Raab said aloud. That was not a denial.

In a matter of days, CBS News and *Newsweek* would identify Edmundo de la Madrid and Florentino Ventura as the subjects of the still-secret Customs investigation. The investigation did not result in the filing of charges against either man. Customs officials said that the exposure of the investigation at the Helms hearing made it impossible for them to pursue their leads effectively.

11. In a May 24, 1986, story headlined "U.S. Reverses Its Criticism of Mexico," Mary Thornton of *The Washington Post* wrote:

In an abrupt reversal of the administration position, Attorney General Edwin Meese III has told the Mexican attorney general that sharp criticism by U.S. officials of public corruption and drug trafficking in Mexico does not reflect the feelings of the Reagan administration.

Mexican Attorney General Sergio García Ramírez told reporters yesterday that Meese called him Thursday and said that the Reagan administration does not concur with the strong criticism of Mexico by officials of the State and Justice departments and the U.S. Customs Service at a May 13 hearing of a Senate Foreign Relations subcommittee.

12. Helms continued to hold hearings in which he lambasted the Mexican government for vote fraud and explored the flaws of Mexico's "socialist" system. Discomfited at the prolonged bout of "Mexico-bashing," State Department officials tried to turn down the heat.

John Gavin, who had returned to private life, had agreed to testify on June 17, but on June 6, Gavin got a call from a State political officer who said that Secretary Shultz thought Gavin should decline. State would tell Helms that Gavin was "unable" to appear. Gavin said he would not appear if Shultz insisted, but he would not lie to Helms. Then he told Helms the whole story. Helms called the State Department and objected.

Shultz relented. Gavin appeared on June 26 and fanned the controversy once more, calling the economic policies of the Mexican government "Marxist or near-Marxist." He defended the governor of Sonora as "an honest public servant" but said intelligence reports showed that several others were "up to their *elbows* in the drug trade."

13. Congressman Larry Smith pressed DEA and State to find a way to keep traffickers and corrupt officials from securing American visas. When committee staffers Chambers and Peña met with Kuykendall and Camarena in January 1985, Kuykendall told them that they had been unable to persuade consular officials to deny visas to Mexicans on DEA's list of narcotics violators. Smith looked into these complaints and added a section to the State Department authorization bill ordering State and DEA to agree on a plan to share information about drug traffickers. The program began to work in 1987.

14. "United States–Mexican Cooperation in Narcotics Control Efforts," House Foreign Affairs Committee, July 17, 1986.

15. "Meese Seeks Press Help in Drug Fight—Assist in Mobilizing Public Opinion, Journalists Urged," by Loretta Tofani, *Washington Post*, Mar. 21, 1985.

Chapter 18: Nightmare in Sinaloa

1. "Suspect in DEA Slaying Said to Live Well in Mexico," by Mary Thornton, *Washington Post*, Feb. 22, 1986. See also, "In the Drug Capital of Mexico, Top Suspect Is the Governor," by William Stockton, *New York Times*, May 22, 1986.

2. Affidavit of Special Agent Douglas W. Kuehl, filed in the U.S. District Court for the Central District of California, Oct. 22, 1987.

3. Report submitted by the U.S. State Department to the House Foreign Affairs Committee. Reprinted in the House Foreign Affairs Committee hearing, "United States–Mexican Cooperation in Narcotics Control Efforts," July 17, 1986.

That hearing record cites a State Department report confirming the arrests of three other suspects wanted in connection with the Camarena murder: former MFJP and DFS *comandante* Rogelio Muñoz Ríos, arrested Mar. 11, 1986, and charged with murder, kidnapping, and drug trafficking; Juan José Esparragoza, "El Azul," arrested Mar. 13 and charged with drug trafficking; and Carlos Delgado Alatorre, reputed drug trafficker and associate of Muñoz, arrested Mar. 11, 1986, and charged with murder, kidnapping, and drug trafficking.

4. "Deaths Mount as Drug War Rages," *Miami Herald,* Feb. 11, 1987. See also, "The Men Who Hold Colombia Hostage," by Alan Riding, *New York Times,* Mar. 8, 1987.

5. Affidavit of Special Agent Douglas W. Kuehl, filed in the U.S. District Court for the Central District of California, Oct. 22, 1987.

Chapter 19: The Andean Coca Wars

1. "Bolivia Envoy Defends Cocaine Lab Raids," by Ronald J. Ostrow, *Los Angeles Times,* July 24, 1986.

2. "Status Report on GAO's Worldwide Review of Narcotics Control Programs," House Foreign Affairs Committee, July 29, 1987, p. 11.

3. On June 27, 1983, a story entitled "Bolivia's Cocaine 'Godfather' Untouched by Crackdown," published in *The Miami Herald,* made the following statements about Roberto Suárez and his alleged ties in the García Meza regime:

> Described as brazen, authoritarian, and self-righteous by his associates, he basks in the reputation he has acquired since he helped finance the July 1980 coup that installed the military government of Gen. Luis García Meza, now in exile in Argentina.
>
> Sources close to Suárez say that he and other big-time operators, fearing that an incoming civilian government would disrupt their operations, provided García Meza and Col. Luis Arce Gómez with several million dollars to finance the coup.
>
> It was the first time in history that an entire government was bought by drug dealers, said a U.S. diplomat in La Paz.
>
> In the aftermath of the 1980 coup, Suárez outmaneuvered rival operators to become kingpin of a vast operation that employed thousands of people. Ranches throughout the Beni and Santa Cruz regions were equipped to handle Colombian planes. Narcotics and interior officials, including Arce, were put on his payroll.

A *Miami Herald* story by James Brooke, published on May 29, 1983, was headlined: "Bolivia's Arce Gómez: A Trail of Dope, Death—'Cocaine Coup' Began Arce Gómez's Reign of Terror." It said, in part:

> On July 17, 1980, Gen. Luis García Meza took control of Bolivia in what was dubbed "the cocaine coup." According to all reports, García Meza's right-hand man, Luis Arce Gómez, quickly moved to grab a big slice of the cocaine action. . . . U.S. Drug Enforcement Agency officials in La Paz have said that Arce Gómez charged Bolivia's top five largest traffickers seventy-five thousand dollars every two weeks in return for freedom to export cocaine. . . . U.S. court documents charge that independent of the drug shakedowns,

Arce Gómez built up his own cocaine-trafficking empire. In a matter of months, Bolivia's interior minister became a millionaire in a country where the annual per capita income is $497. He had a fleet of 11 planes, a mansion in Santa Cruz, a hacienda with a private lighted airstrip in the Beni, another mansion in La Paz, and kept his mistresses in La Paz's best hotel, the Plaza.

4. "The Well-Connected Boys from Bolivia," by Larry Rohter, *Newsweek*, June 8, 1981, p. 10.

5. "Palmy Days Over for a Nazi in Bolivia," by Edward Schumacher, *New York Times*, Oct. 17, 1982.

6. "Bolivia Blooms with Cocaine Kingpin's Cash," by Warren Hoge, *New York Times*, Aug. 15, 1982.

7. "Oversight on Illegal Drug Trafficking from Bolivia and U.S. Application of the Rangel Amendment," House Subcommittee on International Development Institutions and Finance, July 1981, p. 2.

8. Among the traffickers indicted was René Benítez, the man accused of kidnapping DEA agents Kelley McCullough and Charles Martínez in 1982.

9. "Bolivia's Cocaine 'Godfather' Untouched by Crackdown," *Miami Herald*, June 27, 1983. This story reported that Suárez charged that since Roncal took over the ministry 150,000 kilograms of cocaine had been exported from Bolivia. Suárez said this could not have been possible without collaborators in the government. The interior minister took out a newspaper ad to deny his own complicity, but did not dispute Suárez's astounding figures.

10. The Foreign Affairs Committee wrote language into the International Security and Development Act of 1985 that divided Bolivia's fiscal year 1986 economic support and military assistance funding into two parts.

Bolivia could get the first half of the money, about $12 million, when legislation was enacted distinguishing legal coca requirements from illegal coca production. This was done. The second part of the money was tied to an eradication target of 4,000 hectares. That was not done; Bolivia lost $7.5 million in economic support funds.

This bill set tougher targets for fiscal year 1987. Bolivia would have to develop a plan to eliminate illicit narcotics production throughout the country. It would get 50 percent of its aid when half the eradication target was achieved and the other half upon completion of the full eradication target, probably about 15,000 hectares of illegal coca.

On Feb. 25, 1987, U.S. and Bolivian officials signed an agreement on principles of narcotics cooperation. The Reagan administration certified to Congress that Bolivia was making progress in drug-control efforts. The certification was needed by March 1 to prevent automatic suspension of the first half of Washington's economic aid to Bolivia. Seven million dollars was withheld at that time.

11. "Bolivian Barometer: Coca Price Falls," by Bradley Graham, *Washington Post*, July 27, 1986.

12. Interview, July 14, 1986, *Newsweek* magazine, international edition.

13. "Bolivian Runs Risk in Drug Drive," by Bradley Graham, *Washington Post*, July 17, 1986.

14. In April 1986, Roberto Suárez Gómez was once again indicted, this time in Roanoke, Virginia, on charges of conspiracy to import and distribute cocaine and charges of importing and distributing cocaine. An undercover pilot who worked for DEA picked up 700 pounds of cocaine from Suárez in Bolivia, delivered it to DEA agents in Panama, who loaded it in a DEA unmarked plane and flew it to Roanoke, where buyers were waiting. The DEA agents arrested ten people, including Gerardo Caballero, Suárez's son-in-law, who came to the States to collect for the cocaine.

15. U.S. officials estimated that 18,000 unauthorized flights penetrated the U.S. border each year. In August 1986, Pentagon officials calculated that U.S. Air Force AWACS training flights in the Caribbean-Yucatán region over the preceding seven months had produced twenty sightings of suspected smuggler aircraft and twelve actual interceptions and seizures.

Pentagon officials contended that Air Force, Navy, and Marine Corps surveillance planes were on the lookout for smugglers as they soared over the southern coastline. The Pentagon reported that in fiscal 1985 military aircraft flew 3,000 sorties, amounting to nearly 10,400 hours, in support of drug-enforcement agencies. However, such figures as were available suggested that the inauguration of double-duty military training missions did not, as envisioned, contribute substantially to drug seizures. For instance, in fiscal 1985, Pentagon officials said that Air Force AWACS radar-surveillance planes flew 1,308 hours of radar surveillance for the drug-interdiction program. That translated to six AWACS missions a month in the Caribbean-Yucatán area of interest to the Customs Service. "The Role of the U.S. Military in Narcotics Control Overseas," House Foreign Affairs Committee, Aug. 5, 1986, p. 32.

16. "Bolivian Leader Asks 'Global Approach' on Drugs," by Juan de Onís, *Los Angeles Times*, July 25, 1986.

17. "Corruption Hampers Bolivian Anti-Drug Effort, Payoffs Said to Reach Top Levels of Police," by Tyler Bridges, *Washington Post*, Aug. 15, 1987. See also, "Unequal Battle, Bolivia Drug Lords Again Rule Jungle," by William R. Long, *Los Angeles Times*, Mar. 11, 1987.

18. "Future a Black Hole for Bolivian Miners—New Emphasis on Agriculture over Tin," by Tyler Bridges, *Washington Post*, July 5, 1987.

Chapter 20: Drug War Fall

1. "Changing Patterns of Cocaine Use," *Pharm Chem Newsletter*, July–August 1985.

2. "Controlling Drug Abuse and Crime: A Research Update," by Mary G. Graham, National Institute of Justice, March–April 1987.

3. Ibid.

4. An interagency panel called the National Narcotics Intelligence Consumers Committee estimated that Americans consumed 72 metric tons of cocaine in 1985, more than double the 1982 estimate of 31 tons. Some experts believed that estimate was understated and that the true consumption figure was closer to 100 tons.

5. "Drug Abuse and Drug Trafficking Along the Southwest Border (Tucson)," House Select Committee on Narcotics Abuse and Control, Government Printing Office, Jan. 14, 1986, pp. 6–8.

6. See *Congressional Record*, Sept. 17, 1986, S-14007–S-14015.

7. *Congressional Quarterly*, vol. 44, no. 37, Sept. 13, 1986, p. 2125.

8. "Anatomy of an Issue: Drugs, the Evidence, the Reaction," by Peter Kerr, *New York Times*, Nov. 17, 1986.

9. This provision included $138 million for refitting four Navy E-2C Hawkeye surveillance aircraft, two of which would be loaned to Customs and two to the Coast Guard; $99.5 million for acquisition of seven balloon radar platforms to be arrayed along the border from the Florida panhandle to California; $40 million for the procurement of eight Blackhawk helicopters to be loaned to Customs; and $45 million to install 360-degree radar systems on Coast Guard long-range surveillance aircraft.

10. "Impact of Gramm-Rudman on Federal Drug Programs," hearing, House Select Committee on Narcotics Abuse and Control, Washington, D.C., Government Printing Office, Mar. 18, 1986.

Chapter 21: The Torture of Victor Cortez

1. "Mexicans Deny U.S. Agent Tortured," by William A. Orme, Jr., *Washington Post*, Aug. 16, 1986.

2. "Mexico—Drugs," Associated Press, Aug. 20, 1986.

3. "Mexicans Deny U.S. Agent Tortured," by William A. Orme, Jr., *Washington Post*, Aug. 16, 1986.

4. "The mistreatment of an American drug agent has serious implications for U.S.–Mexican cooperation on the narcotics issue," State Department spokesman Charles Redman said. "We expect cooperation from the highest levels of the Mexican government in investigating the Cortez matter."

5. "Eleven Guadalajara Police Detained in DEA Case," *Los Angeles Times*, Aug. 19, 1986. See also, "U.S. Wary on Mexico's Indictments in DEA Case," by Mary Thornton, *Washington Post*, Aug. 28, 1986.

On Aug. 27, 1986, the Mexican Foreign Ministry delivered a protest to the U.S. State Department concerning the possession by Cortez and Garate of illegal weapons and Cortez's failure to carry identification. That document confirmed that eleven men had been charged with "injury and abuse of authority": Salvador Salas Casteñeda; Anselmo Pulido Galván; Antonio Ortiz Bernal; José Magñana Murillo; Fausto Sergio Treviño Galindo; José Gerardo Quirarte Villavicencio; Adrian

Cuevas Camacho; Juvenal Torres González; Aurelio Manuel Castellanos Corona; Enrique García Bernal; and Eduardo Rosas Casillas.

6. The National Drug Policy Board, chaired by the attorney general, was created by a 1984 act of Congress to provide better coordination among the departments and agencies involved in drug enforcement, intelligence, education, treatment, and foreign policy. Associate Attorney General Steve Trott was in charge of the subcabinet-level "coordinating group" that effectively ran the board. There was considerable skepticism on Capitol Hill that the board really accomplished anything.

On June 25, 1987, the House Government Operations Committee published a study entitled "The National Drug Policy Board: A Failure in the War on Drugs." The study, produced by the Subcommittee on Government Information, Justice, and Agriculture, chaired by Democratic Representative Glenn English of Oklahoma, concluded:

> In its two-and-a-half-year existence, the board has been unable to produce any meaningful analysis of resource allocation. It has made no recommendations to the president on budget matters. And there is little evidence that it has actively reviewed agency drug-enforcement expenditures. Despite the attorney general's opinion—and the board's agreement—of its statutory obligations to review budget requests and make recommendations to the president, the board has failed to carry out this duty. The Policy Board has been able to recite a lengthy litany of accomplishments which vaguely resembles the development and implementation of policy as required under the National Narcotics Act of 1984. On close examination, these examples fall short of what Congress intended under the Act. While the Policy Board has taken credit for a wide variety of anti-drug abuse efforts over the last two years, nearly all these efforts would have occurred with or without the board. Administration officials claim that the existence of the board at the very least has helped to facilitate these drug-abuse initiatives by bringing together the disparate elements of the federal government involved in drug law enforcement. While this might be true, it is hardly what Congress had in mind when it created the Policy Board. Policy Board officials have been unable to cite significant policy initiatives which would not have taken place without the board.

Trott told the English subcommittee that the board settled arguments by a process modeled after one developed by the Harvard Negotiations Project that "eliminates winners and losers in policy development and agency disputes and thus allows all participants to embrace the board decisions." In practical terms, the English panel said, no serious disputes were truly resolved by this process. "The intent of the statute creating the Policy Board is not to please agency heads but to wage an effective war against drugs," the subcommittee concluded.

7. The minutes of drug board meetings in late 1986 months contain only passing mentions of the Cortez and Camarena cases. On Septem-

ber 10, according to the minutes, Steve Trott "noted that close working relationships with the Mexican Attorney General's Office had resulted in positive developments related to arrests, asset seizures, and prosecutions. . . . Problems remain with extradition, overflights, and the investigation of the Camarena murder and the Cortez kidnapping and torture. A meeting may be hosted by the Mexicans in Cozumel in October. Mr. Michael Armacost from State, under secretary for political affairs, endorsed the spirit of Mr. Trott's remarks. The chairman [Meese] acknowledged the good cooperation between State and Justice in defining and implementing a sound drug-control policy with Mexico." The minutes of the September 24, November 6, December 12, and December 18 meetings did not mention the Cortez case at all. There was only one further mention of the Camarena case: on September 24, Trott reported that "the situation appears to be stabilizing" and that "Mexico was holding several suspects in the Camarena case and some prosecutions in the United States are a possibility."

8. "We don't really believe that these five to seven policemen took it on their own to beat and torture Cortez, do we?" Congressman Larry Smith asked Dave Westrate at a hearing of the House Foreign Affairs Committee in October 1987. "No, there are some other people around them," Westrate replied, "but I don't think we're going to see much more significant progress there. I'm not even sure it's possible, frankly." "That to me is an indicator of the kind of commitment that Mexico really wants to make," Smith said. "If the federal government of Mexico really wanted to make a commitment to its big neighbors in the north, why is it that they won't . . . investigate who in authority . . . gave the approval. Because it's common knowledge that everybody knew he was a DEA agent. . . . They tortured him because he was and because they thought he had information that they could probably get out of him and sell to other people. . . . Are we just going to tolerate the fact that they'll arrest five policemen, beat cops . . . and that's it? And then these people who authorized this are just going to get away with it?" "No, we're not going to tolerate it," Westrate said. "We pushed it as far as we can in terms of realistic results."

Chapter 22: "Why Are We Bleeding Alone?"

1. "Cocaine Billionaires," by Alan Riding, *New York Times Magazine*, Mar. 8, 1987.

2. Ibid.

3. "Colombia's Drug War Is Out of Control," by William D. Montalbano, *Los Angeles Times*, Feb. 1, 1987.

4. "Colombian Judges Face Threats, Assassination," by Tyler Bridges, *Washington Post*, Nov. 22, 1986.

5. "Drug Lord Got Start in Miami," by Guy Gugliotta and Jeff Leen, *Miami Herald*, Nov. 23, 1987.

6. "Arrest Followed Firing of Top Police Officials," by Andres Oppenheimer, *Miami Herald*, Feb. 6, 1987.

7. "Colombia Drug Laws Annulled; Critic Says Court Is Intimidated," *Miami Herald*, Mar. 7, 1987.

8. "Colombia Effort Against Drugs Hits Dead End," by Alan Riding, *New York Times*, Aug. 16, 1987.

9. Bogotá Inravision Televisión, Nov. 12, 1987.

10. "Colombian, Wanted by U.S., Freed," by Tom Wells, Associated Press, Dec. 31, 1987; in *Washington Post*, Jan. 1, 1988.

11. Bogotá Inravision Televisión, midnight, Jan. 1, 1988.

12. Bogotá Inravision Televisión, Jan. 5, 1988.

13. Caracol, Jan. 4, 1988.

14. Bogotá Inravision Televisión, Jan. 8, 1988.

15. "Colombia Denies Vow to U.S. on Drug Figure," Reuters, Jan. 3, 1988; in *New York Times*, Jan. 4, 1988.

16. Bogotá Inravision Televisión, Jan. 13, 1988.

17. "Car Bomb Kills Two in Medellín," *Miami Herald*, Jan. 14, 1988.

18. Bogotá Inravision Televisión, Jan. 26, 1988.

19. Bogota Television Service, Jan. 25, 1988.

20. "Colombians Grow Weary of Combating Drugs," by Alan Riding, *New York Times*, Feb. 1, 1988.

21. Ibid.

22. "Colombian Drug Fight Called Flop," by Andres Oppenheimer, *Miami Herald*, Feb. 23, 1988; "The Drug Thugs," *Time*, Mar. 7, 1988.

Chapter 23: Lies, Delusions, and Wishful Thinking

1. "Mexico Cracks Major Arms Drug-Trafficking Ring; East Bloc-Manufactured Assault Rifles Were to Be Used by Medellín," by William Branigin, *Washington Post*, Feb. 25, 1988.

2. Hearing, Senate Foreign Relations Committee, Mar. 14, 1988.

3. "Mexico Irritated at U.S. Charge That Judge Took Bribe," by Dan Williams, *Los Angeles Times*, June 4, 1987.

4. "$2 Million Tied to Drug Chief Seized," by J. Stryker Meyer, *San Diego Union*, May 28, 1987.

5. "Mexico Irritated at U.S. Charge That Judge Took Bribe," by Dan Williams, *Los Angeles Times*, June 4, 1987.

6. In an Oct. 6, 1986, memo Foster cast doubt on the claim of the Mexican government that a large part of the attorney general's budget went for drug enforcement. He wrote: "It is evident their channels have somehow sprung large leaks. [Attorney General's Office] support equipment is badly neglected and abused. When asked why, the answer comes through loud and clear, no funds. . . . Pouring in more funds does not seem to correct the situation or plug up the leaks." He concluded: "It is patently clear that the 45-day fall sweep to eradicate opium poppies in Zone 06 [Sinaloa] has been made an unattainable goal due to the actions of MAGO. Whether motivated by personal, patriotic, sovereignty, or constitutional considerations, the end result is the same—*no significant spraying is being realized*. . . . Until the

current political climate changes, we can expect no significant changes or improvements in our abilities to accomplish our mission here in Mexico."

7. There were just forty-two pilots to fly forty-three helicopters, according to GAO, and those pilots were paid $300 to $400 a month, compared with $1,400 available in private industry. GAO investigators said that Mexican Deputy Attorney General Ortega Padilla had rebuffed a U.S. State Department offer to supplement pilot salaries on grounds that "accepting the U.S. offer would lead to conflicting loyalties among the pilots." In mid-1987, the GAO said, the Mexican government gave the pilots a 40 percent pay raise, but inflation was rising so rapidly that the move was not expected to improve the government's ability to attract qualified pilots. "U.S.–Mexico Opium Poppy and Marijuana Aerial Eradication Program," General Accounting Office, January 1988, pp. 3, 30.

8. A cable from the Narcotics Assistance Unit to Wrobleski at main State said:

> It has been known for some time to personnel working closely with the helicopter pilots [who performed the actual spraying missions] that they have made unauthorized landings to secure marijuana plants for their own use or for sale. This personal "ground-truthing" does not seem to extend to the pilots involved in Vanguard. Instead, the program coordinators [on the ground in the Attorney General's Office] have at times prevented DEA agents from viewing areas thought to have larger concentrations of fields or laboratory facilities.

The cable concluded:

> The figures furnished by Vanguard are misleading. Worse, the program may actively divert attention from areas that have higher concentrations of crops than areas being sprayed. . . . The major problem with Vanguard is that using the Cessna 206 [a fixed-wing aircraft] prevents any pre- or post-spray ground-truthing. Such activity is essential to obtain meaningful statistics. . . . The use of fixed-wing aircraft in this job prevents any observer from knowing whether a crop was totally eradicated, whether it was scored prior to spraying, or whether it was mature enough to score after spraying. And, given the genius of the growers in countering our efforts, ground-truthing is necessary to monitor their innovations, such as rinsing the plants of herbicide, a practice [that] is on the rise. The use of this aircraft also affects DEA participation since it reduces the agent to a passive observer. Given the rugged terrain and severe flying conditions encountered in these flights, it is unrealistic to assume that the DEA agent will always be able to accurately monitor the navigator's work in locating the fields or to make detailed enough observations to yield meaningful information. DEA agents' morale is being eroded by their frustration in not being able to land

to ground-truth and by what they see as deliberate attempts to mislead them by those in charge of Vanguard.

9. "Hearing to Receive Testimony on the Fiscal Year 1988 Foreign Assistance Request for the Western Hemisphere," Senate Foreign Relations Subcommittee on Western Hemisphere and Peace Corps Affairs, Mar. 25, 1987.

10. On Jan. 15, 1988, U.S. Attorney Peter Nuñez unsealed an indictment that named two active Mexican Army officers, General Poblana Silva and Lieutenant Colonel Salvador de la Vega, as unindicted co-conspirators in a protection scheme. The indictment charged that Silva and de la Vega agreed with three other Mexicans "to prepare a portion of a highway in the state of Puebla, Mexico, to accommodate the landing and refueling of cocaine-laden aircraft from Bolivia through Mexico into the United States." The grand jury indicted Jorge Carranzas, a retired lieutenant colonel in the Mexican Army, and Pablo Girón and Hector Manuel Brumel Alvarez, who claimed to be members of the security detail of PRI presidential candidate Carlos Salinas de Gortari. Carranzas, Girón, and Brumel were arrested in San Diego on January 14 after allegedly telling undercover agents that they would "provide and coordinate 'official' protection" for a fee of $1 million per ton of cocaine. Mexican government officials denied that the three men had any connection with the government. They supported the story of General Silva, who said that the charges against him were fabricated by his enemies.

11. "Situation in Panama," hearings, Senate Subcommittee on Western Hemisphere Affairs, Government Printing Office, Washington, D.C., Mar. 10 and Apr. 21, 1986.

12. "Hearing to Receive Testimony on the Fiscal Year 1988 Foreign Assistance Request for the Western Hemisphere," Senate Foreign Relations Subcommittee on Western Hemisphere and Peace Corps Affairs, Mar. 25, 1987.

Chapter 24: The Search for Justice

1. Justice Department politics marred the announcement of the indictment. In May 1987, the Los Angeles grand jury had returned an indictment against Caro Quintero, Pavón Reyes, and Inés Calderón Quintero for the murder of Camarena. Bonner kept the indictment sealed in hopes of coming up with evidence to add additional names to the list. Finally, Bonner decided to disclose the Caro Quintero indictment on Oct. 29. Justice Department officials hoped that the disclosure might attract enough publicity to pressure the Mexican government into releasing some evidence sought by the grand jury.

Associate Attorney General Steve Trott delayed the press conference on grounds that bad publicity might derail his negotiations for a new mutual legal assistance treaty with Mexico. Trott contended that the treaty would provide a streamlined way for the U.S. and Mexico to exchange criminal-justice information. Skeptics countered that the reason information was not being exchanged was not process but personalities. Trott persisted, and on Dec. 10, 1987, the treaty was signed. Attorney General Ed Meese hailed the agreement as a signal that "the two countries have taken significant steps to improve cooperative anti-crime programs." However, the treaty would not take effect until it was ratified by legislative bodies in both Mexico and the United States; in the meantime, it could not be used as a vehicle for the exchange of evidence in the Camarena prosecution.

The Justice process was again delayed in December 1987, when a dispute broke out between Bonner and U.S. Attorney Pete Nuñez of San Diego. Nuñez was handling the marijuana-trafficking prosecution of René Verdugo; according to Justice officials, Nuñez objected that the murder indictment of Verdugo in Los Angeles would complicate the San Diego proceedings. Trott and William Weld, the head of the Justice criminal division, overruled Nuñez and gave Bonner permission to add Verdugo to the indictment. Bonner also added Fonseca, López Alvarez, and Bazán to the list. He scheduled the unsealing of the indictment to follow Christmas at the request of Jack Lawn, who wanted the Camarena family to have a relatively peaceful holiday.

2. "Murder Plot Suspects Say Beating Led to Confession," by Kim Murphy, *Los Angeles Times*, Feb. 24, 1988.

3. "Ex-Guadalajara Policemen Also Charged in Camarena Case, 3 Convicted in Death Plot on U.S. Agent," by Kim Murphy, *Los Angeles Times*, Feb. 27, 1988.

Epilogue
1. "Félix Gallardo, 'al hombre más buscado del mundo,' durante 18 años, nunca se ocultó," by Franciso Ortiz Pinchetti, *Proceso*, Apr. 17, 1989.

2. "En el Gabinete, jóvenes y experimentados; la dureza, característica mayoritaria," *Proceso*, Dec. 5, 1988.

Index